OFFICE OF THE PROVOST

Microprocessors and Microcomputers

VICTOR M. ROONEY
University of Dayton

AMIN R. ISMAIL
University of Dayton

MICROPROCESSORS AND MICROCOMPUTERS

Macmillan Publishing Company
New York

Collier Macmillan Publishers
London

Dedication

To our families and the lasting friendship that has grown through the years,

Ada, Greg, Loretta, Naina, Rashid, Riaz, Salma, Sandra

Acknowledgments

We would like to thank Dean Russell Primrose for the use of the School of Engineering's word processor, which made it much easier for us to write and edit the manuscript. Also, Ruth Kelly and Anna Blumenstock deserve our special thanks for their help in the preparation of the manuscript.

Copyright © 1984, Macmillan Publishing Company,
a division of Macmillan, Inc.

Printed in the United States of America

All rights reserved. No part of this book may be
reproduced or transmitted in any form or by any means,
electronic or mechanical, including photocopying,
recording, or any information storage and retrieval
system, without permission in writing from the Publisher.

Macmillan Publishing Company
866 Third Avenue, New York, New York 10022

Collier Macmillan Canada, Inc.

Library of Congress Cataloging in Publication Data

Rooney, Victor M.
  Microprocessors and microcomputers.

  Includes index.
  1. Microprocessors. 2. Microcomputers. I. Ismail,
Amin R. II. Title.
QA76.5.R526   1984   001.64   83-11254
ISBN 0-02-403450-9

Printing: 3 4 5 6 7 8   Year: 6 7 8 9 0 1 2

ISBN 0-02-403450-9

PREFACE

With the rapid advances in microprocessors and related technology it is obvious that we must be in a continual learning process. We believe that in this learning process it is essential for us to understand the concepts rather than only to memorize facts. This philosophy will be followed throughout this book, in the hope that it will build a solid foundation for future learning. This does not mean that memorization will not be required; it will, however, be minimized.

Following the philosophy stated above, each topic covered in this book will begin by establishing its purpose. Once the purpose is understood, its conceptual implementation will be developed through the use of function-block diagrams for hardware-oriented discussions. It is these function blocks that will aid in understanding the specific chips used for actual system implementation. Once the hardware is understood, the software that controls and manipulates the hardware is studied. Emphasis is placed on the use of proper techniques and the application of the appropriate tools in the development of microprocessor software. It is important to note that throughout the text we emphasize the relationships between hardware and software, and their integration into a system.

The ideal approach to studying microprocessors would be first to study a generic standard with the intent of understanding the abstract conceptual principles and then later apply those principles to a specific microprocessor. This approach, although academically sound, is not time efficient since the theoretical concepts and their applications would be treated as two separate subjects displaced in time. Hence the authors have chosen to discuss concepts using specific chips as models. Also, since no generic standard exists for a microprocessor, the authors have chosen a microprocessor whose operation encompasses most of the concepts utilized by other currently available microprocessors. We believe that this "pseudo-standard" microprocessor is the 8080.

By studying the 8080 microprocessor and its support chips, the reader will learn those concepts necessary to understand the detailed workings of microprocessor- and microcomputer-based systems. The advent of LSI and VLSI technology has led to the manufacture of new microprocessors that have several functions integrated on a single chip. The trend in the design of newer microprocessors is to simplify their use and require less understanding by the user. However, the authors believe that by learning microprocessors and their associated systems in detail, one can apply ingenuity to the design and utilization of such systems. An analogy can be seen with the advent of the electronic calculator. One need not understand the mechanics of arithmetic to get answers from an electronic calculator. However, to understand and interpret those answers, one needs an understanding of the solution—which requires that the concepts of arithmetic be understood. It is therefore important that the reader realize that the essence of studying microprocessors lies in the concepts rather than in the specifics. A specific chip may become obsolete, but the concepts remain the same. The thesis of this text is that if the reader learns and understands the concepts presented, regardless of the chip used as the teaching vehicle, he or she will be able to apply these concepts to other chips and hence will be able to self-teach as technology advances. Of course, it is the reader who has the ultimate responsibility for staying technically current.

From the table of contents one can see that the text covers the study of 8-bit microprocessors (8080, 8085, and 6800). Integrating any of these microprocessors into a system requires that the concepts of busses, control signals, memory, and I/O be understood. Thus, with a focus on the 8080 microprocessor, the text covers a system clock, system controller, memory page selector, I/O device selector, isolated and memory-mapped I/O, serial and parallel I/O, and programmable chips, and programming is undertaken in some depth. It is obvious that even a microprocessor system with very sophisticated hardware is not worth much without the appropriate software. An understanding of the proper development tools and techniques is vital to the efficient design of a microprocessor system. Two of the most universally accepted tools, assemblers and compilers, are discussed in detail. In all cases, the emphasis is placed on concepts. In the final chapters we survey the hardware and software operation of two other 8-bit microprocessors, the 8085 and the 6800. The survey concentrates on the similarities and differences (with the 8080) rather than on an indepth study of each microprocessor and illustrates that the same concepts can be applied to almost any commercially available microprocessor.

V. M. R.
A. R. I.

CONTENTS

1 INTRODUCTION TO DIGITAL COMPUTERS — 1

- 1-1 Introduction — 1
- 1-2 Development of a Computer System — 2
- 1-3 Computer Bus Structure — 7
- 1-4 DMA, Interrupt, and Clock — 12
- 1-5 Summary — 15
- Review Questions and Problems — 15

2 INTRODUCTION TO CPU ARCHITECTURE AND AN INSTRUCTION SET — 17

- 2-1 Introduction — 17
- 2-2 CPU Architecture — 18
- 2-3 Control Signals — 34
- 2-4 Creation of a Hypothetical Instruction Set — 37
- 2-5 Chip Pin Configuration — 43
- 2-6 Summary — 44
- Review Questions and Problems — 44

3 THE 8080 MICROPROCESSOR AND ITS ESSENTIAL SUPPORT CHIPS 47

3-1	Introduction	47
3-2	8080 Microprocessor Architecture	48
3-3	8080 Pin Configuration	55
3-4	8228 Controller Architecture and Control Signals	56
3-5	8224 Clock Architecture and Pin Configuration	67
3-6	8080 and Essential Support Chip Interface	70
3-7	Basic Timing of the 8080 Primary Standard System	71
3-8	Summary	73
	Review Questions and Problems	74

4 AN 8080-BASED SYSTEM DESIGN: I/O AND MEMORY INTERFACE 77

4-1	Introduction	77
4-2	Isolated I/O	78
4-3	Memory Addressing	84
4-4	Summary	92
	Review Questions and Problems	93

5 INTRODUCTION TO PROGRAMMING WITH THE 8080 INSTRUCTION SET 95

5-1	Introduction	95
5-2	8080 Instruction Set Coding Scheme	95
5-3	8080 Instruction Set	104
5-4	Introduction to Flowcharts and Programming	136
5-5	Summary	161
	Review Questions and Problems	162

6 ADDITIONAL SYSTEM CAPABILITIES AND ALTERNATIVE ADDRESSING METHODS: INTERRUPTS, DMA, MEMORY-MAPPED I/O, AND LINEAR ADDRESSING 165

6-1	Introduction	165
6-2	Interrupts	165
6-3	Single-Level Interrupts and Polling	167
6-4	Single-Level Interrupts and Vectoring	171
6-5	Multilevel Interrupts and Vectoring	179
6-6	Direct Memory Access	179
6-7	Memory Maps	180
6-8	Memory-Mapped I/O	182
6-9	Linear Addressing I/O	183

6-10	Hex Keypad with Interrupt Capability	184
6-11	Summary	196
	Review Questions and Problems	197

7 PROGRAMMABLE CHIPS: PARALLEL AND SERIAL I/O — 199

7-1	Introduction	199
7-2	Programmable Peripheral Interface (8255)	200
7-3	8255 Operation Modes	203
7-4	Addressing the 8255	214
7-5	8255 Status Word	217
7-6	Summary of the 8255	220
7-7	Serial Data Communications	222
7-8	Serial Data Interface	226
7-9	Serial Data Transmission Format	231
7-10	The 8251 USART	235
7-11	Summary	242
	Review Questions and Problems	242

8 SOFTWARE DEVELOPMENT: TECHNIQUES AND TOOLS — 245

8-1	Introduction	245
8-2	Algorithms and Flowcharts	247
8-3	Structure	250
8-4	Assemblers	254
8-5	Compilers	255
8-6	Linkers and Locators	256
8-7	Interpreters	257
8-8	Simulators and Dynamic Debuggers	258
8-9	Operating Systems	259
8-10	Summary	260
	Review Questions and Problems	260

9 INTRODUCTION TO ASSEMBLY LANGUAGE PROGRAMMING — 261

9-1	Introduction	261
9-2	Operation of the Assembler	263
9-3	Syntax of the Assembly Language	266
9-4	Location Control	267
9-5	Symbols and Constants	268
9-6	Data Storage	272
9-7	Storage Allocation	277
9-8	Object File	279
9-9	Summary	282
	Review Questions and Problems	282

10 RELOCATABLE ASSEMBLY AND UTILITY SUBROUTINES — 285

- 10-1 Introduction — 285
- 10-2 Structured Assembly Language Programs — 287
- 10-3 Subroutine Modules — 288
- 10-4 Utility Subroutines — 292
- 10-5 Main Program — 302
- 10-6 Linkage and Location — 306
- 10-7 Summary — 308
- Review Questions and Problems — 308

11 MACROS AND CONDITIONAL ASSEMBLY — 311

- 11-1 Introduction — 311
- 11-2 Macros — 311
- 11-3 Macros with Parameters — 317
- 11-4 An Application of Macros — 319
- 11-5 Repetitive Macros — 324
- 11-6 Conditional Assembly — 327
- 11-7 Summary — 333
- Review Questions and Problems — 334

12 INTRODUCTION TO THE PL/M-80 COMPILER — 337

- 12-1 Introduction — 337
- 12-2 The General Form of a PL/M Program — 339
- 12-3 Controlling the Flow of a PL/M Program — 344
- 12-4 Address-Type Variables — 348
- 12-5 Manipulation of Tabular Data — 349
- 12-6 Procedures: The PL/M Subroutines — 351
- 12-7 Summary — 355
- Review Questions and Problems — 355

13 ADVANCED PL/M CONCEPTS — 357

- 13-1 Introduction — 357
- 13-2 PL/M Operators and Expressions — 357
- 13-3 Allocation of Declared Variables — 360
- 13-4 Type Conversions — 363
- 13-5 External and Public Labels — 364
- 13-6 Nested IF-THEN Statements — 365
- 13-7 Block Structure and Iterations — 366
- 13-8 Interrupt Procedures — 371

13-9	Built-in Procedures	373
13-10	Built-in Functions	374
13-11	Based Variables	379
13-12	Location References and the Dot Operator	380
13-13	A PL/M Program Example	381
	Review Questions and Problems	390

14 THE 8085 MICROPROCESSOR 393

14-1	Introduction	393
14-2	8085 Architecture	394
14-3	8085 Pin Configuration and Functions	396
14-4	Summary of the 8085	400
14-5	Address Latching	400
14-6	Control Bus for an 8085 Memory-Mapped I/O System	401
14-7	8085 Isolated I/O and Control Bus	405
14-8	8085 Serial Ports SID and SOD	407
14-9	Serial Input Port SID and Instruction RIM	408
14-10	Serial Output Port SOD and Instruction SIM	410
14-11	An 8085 Application	410
14-12	Summary of an 8085-Based System	416
	Review Questions and Problems	417

15 A SURVEY OF THE 6800 MICROPROCESSOR 419

15-1	Introduction	419
15-2	6800 Architecture and Pin Configuration	419
15-3	6800 Interrupt Structure	424
15-4	6800 Microprocessor System	429
15-5	6800 Instruction Set	434
15-6	Summary	446
	Review Questions and Problems	446

APPENDIXES 449

A:	Summary of the 8080/8085 Instruction Set	449
B:	The ASCII Codes	451
C:	Standard Flowchart Symbols	453
D:	Binary–Decimal–Hexadecimal Conversion Tables	455

INDEX 465

CHAPTER 1

Introduction to Digital Computers

1-1

INTRODUCTION

Digital computers play a major role in today's society. For business applications they perform such tasks as keeping track of inventory, payroll, accounts receivable, accounts payable, and word processing. Industrial applications are of the control type; that is, the computer will govern such functions as chemical flow, assembly line operation, machine speed and position, and other such process controls. Medical applications include patient monitoring, body chemical analysis, blood-gas analysis, electrocardiograms—and the list goes on. Both industry and the home can use computers for energy management, security, as an appointments secretary, and for many other duties of a perfunctory nature.

In each of the cases cited above, the computer is given input data, which may be in the form of numbers given by the user or voltages from a machine. From these input data it can perform calculations and make decisions. For the world of commerce, calculations are often the only task required, whereas for industrial applications, such as process control, the computer may first perform calculations, then arrive at a decision based on those calculations, and finally, regulate a machine in accordance with that decision. With this interrelationship of computer, person, and machine in mind, one might begin to form a very general function-block diagram of a computerized system. That is, in addition to the

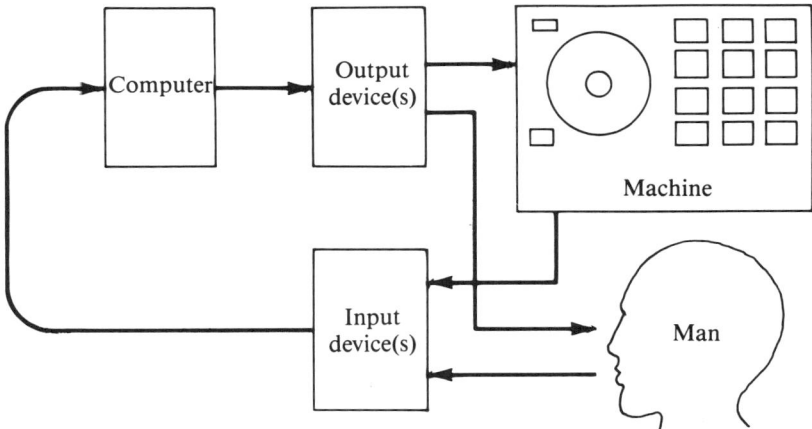

FIGURE 1-1. Computer interfacing with man and machine.

computer, this system must have input and output devices with which the computer can communicate to person and/or machine. This basic concept is illustrated in Figure 1-1.

It is the goal of this text to teach the reader how to design and construct a microprocessor-based computer system. To accomplish this goal the reader must understand and be able to utilize both hardware—the actual electronics of the computer—and software—the intangible instructions that make the electronics work.

This chapter introduces the most fundamental concepts of a digital computer by categorizing computer operations into various functions. These functions will then be pictorially represented by a block and appropriately labeled. To demonstrate the interrelationships between each of these blocks, communicative links will be shown, represented by lines. The result will be a function-block diagram of a computer, illustrating the necessary *building blocks* and their interrelationships. An example of such a diagram is shown in Figure 1-6. The purpose of this approach is to help the reader to visualize the required functions and their communicative links. By understanding these requirements, the study of specific chips toward the goal of utilizing them in a computer design will be a logical process, not a memorized one.

1-2 DEVELOPMENT OF A COMPUTER SYSTEM

As stated previously, when one thinks of a computer it is usually with an association of performing computations and making decisions. These computations and decisions are performed by the *central processing unit* (CPU) of the computer. Hence the "mind" of the computer is the CPU. The CPU has no intelligence except the pseudo-intelligence "given" to it by its user. That is, the CPU is given very explicit instructions by the user as to the operations to

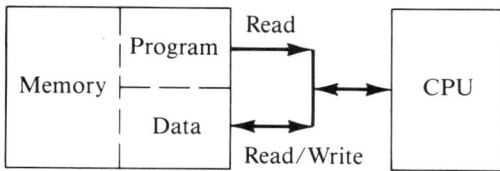

FIGURE 1-2. The CPU and memory.

be performed. This set of instructions is known as a *program*, and the person who writes the program is known as the *programmer*. Just as a person would record, in his or her memory, a set of instructions for doing a task, a computer is designed to do likewise. Thus a CPU will require a *memory* to store its program (the instructions). Memory will not only serve to store the program but will also be used to store data when so instructed. Since memory serves two purposes—to store programs and data—for purpose of concept we shall imagine it as being divided into two parts: *program memory* and *data memory*.

Figure 1-2 is a block diagram of a CPU and its memory. Notice from Figure 1-2 that the CPU only "reads" from program memory (arrow goes to the CPU), whereas it both "reads" and "writes" from data memory; that is, it must store (*write*) and retrieve (*read*) data (indicated by a bidirectional arrow).

It is logical that the CPU will need to communicate with external *input* and *output* devices (I/O peripherals), such as teletypes, keyboards, printers, and displays. Often these I/O devices are not compatible (as to voltage levels, timing, etc.) with the CPU and will require interfacing. Hence an I/O interface block and I/O devices are added, as shown in Figure 1-3. As can be seen from the arrow directions of Figure 1-3, some I/O devices are shown as input devices (0 and N), whereas others are shown as output devices (1).

Notice in Figure 1-3 that all data exchanges between memory and an I/O device must pass through the CPU, which slows the exchange. There are cases of data transfer where time is of paramount importance, and to meet this cri-

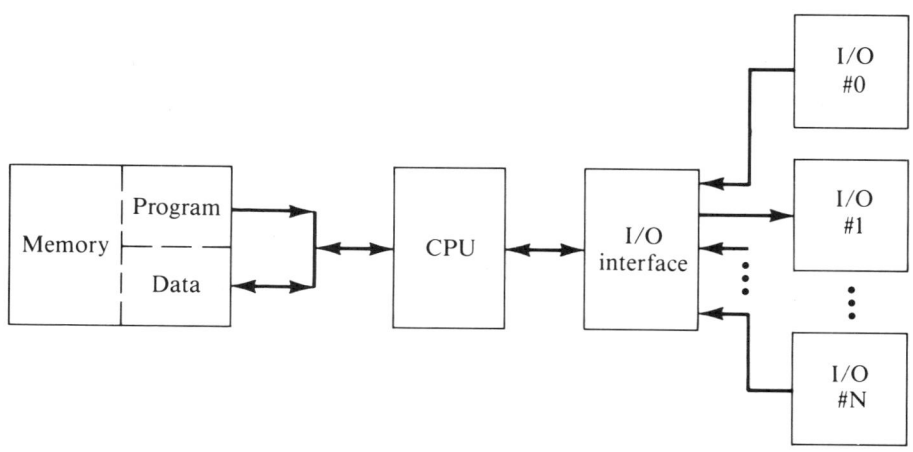

FIGURE 1-3. The CPU, memory, and I/O.

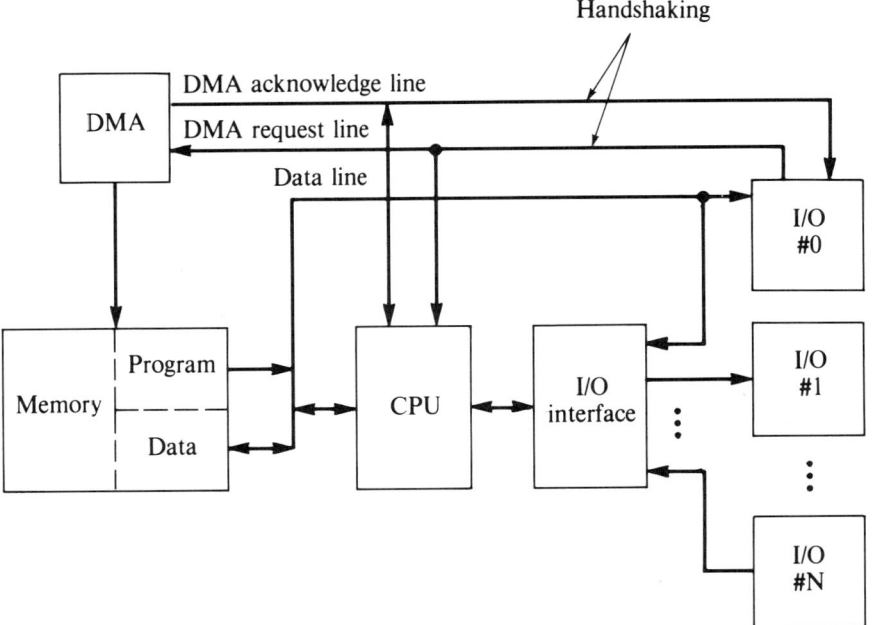

FIGURE 1-4. The CPU, memory, and I/O with DMA capability.

terion, some computer systems allow the memory to be accessed directly by an I/O device. This feature is known as *direct memory access* (DMA). DMA is I/O initiated and is used by I/O devices to access memory directly, thereby circumventing the CPU. DMA is illustrated in Figure 1-4, where I/O device 0 is shown as having direct access to memory via the data line (interfacing may be necessary).

In Figure 1-4, take note of the communication that transpires between I/O device 0, the DMA function block, and the CPU. The requesting I/O device must first request a DMA and does so via the DMA request line. Since the CPU is to be bypassed, it must be notified of the request so that it can isolate itself from the process. When the CPU isolates itself from the system, it will acknowledge its isolation by sending a signal over the DMA acknowledge line. Once I/O device 0 receives an acknowledgment of CPU isolation, it begins to access memory directly by way of the data line. It is important to notice the communication exchange: First the request and then an acknowledgment of the request, which signals the "ok" to proceed. This communication of request and acknowledge is termed *handshaking*. This specific example is DMA handshaking—others will follow. This example shows DMA for the purpose of writing to memory (device 0's arrow direction indicates that it is an input device); however, the same DMA concept is true for read operations. Figure 1-4 shows the DMA function as being separate from the CPU when, in fact, it is often part of it, as will be shown.

The next function block to consider is interrupt request logic. Most computer systems have what is termed *interrupt capability*, which essentially means that an I/O device can interrupt the CPU during an operation. To understand why

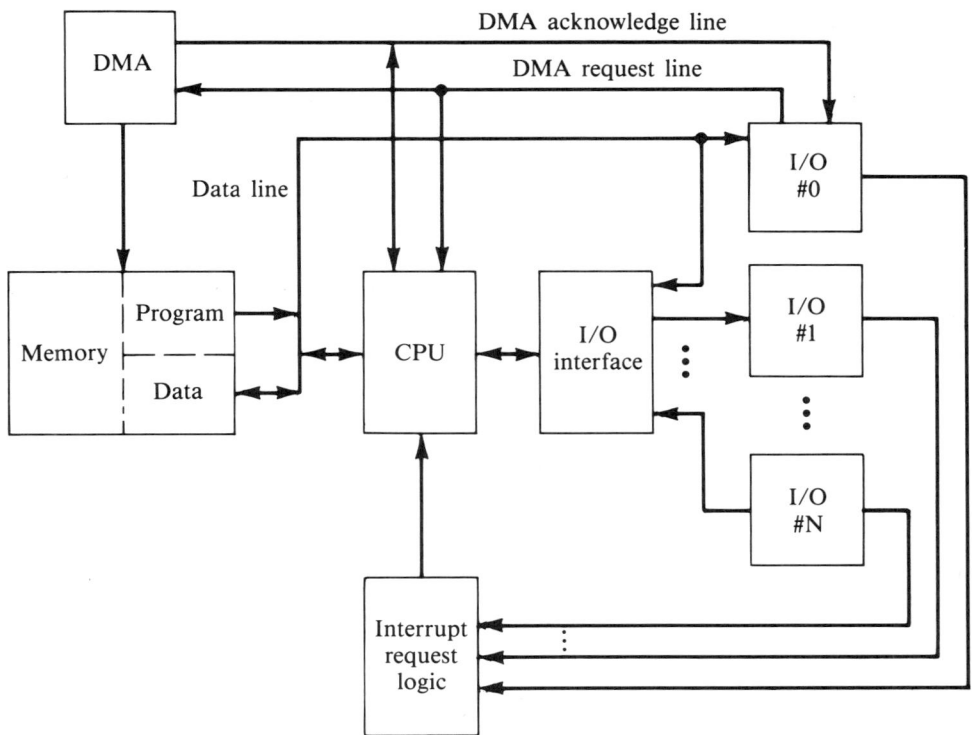

FIGURE 1-5. The CPU, memory, I/O, DMA with interrupt capability.

interrupt capability is desirable, it must be realized that (1) an I/O device needs the attention of the CPU only when an exchange of data is to occur between the CPU and the I/O device, and (2) some I/O devices are much slower in operation than the CPU, causing the CPU to have to wait for the I/O device during data exchanges. Considering these two points, it is more efficient for the CPU to be allowed to perform other tasks and be interrupted by an I/O device only when the I/O device needs the attention of the CPU and is ready for a data exchange to occur. Interrupt capability is illustrated in Figure 1-5. Notice that the actual interrupt request is not made directly to the CPU, but is applied to combinational logic (AND and OR gates, etc., termed *interrupt request logic*), which establishes priority (in cases where there is more than one interrupting device) and performs other "housekeeping" tasks.

There are two remaining blocks to be added to Figure 1-5, the controller and the clock. The *controller* is the "traffic cop"; that is, it correlates the activities of the various function blocks to see that no conflicts exist between them. The *clock* provides the timing of the system. The timing of all activities is referenced to this basic clock. Figure 1-6 repeats Figure 1-5 with these two blocks added.

A synopsis of the microcomputer system of Figure 1-6 is that it has

1. *I/O* (input and output) capability to communicate with the user and machines.

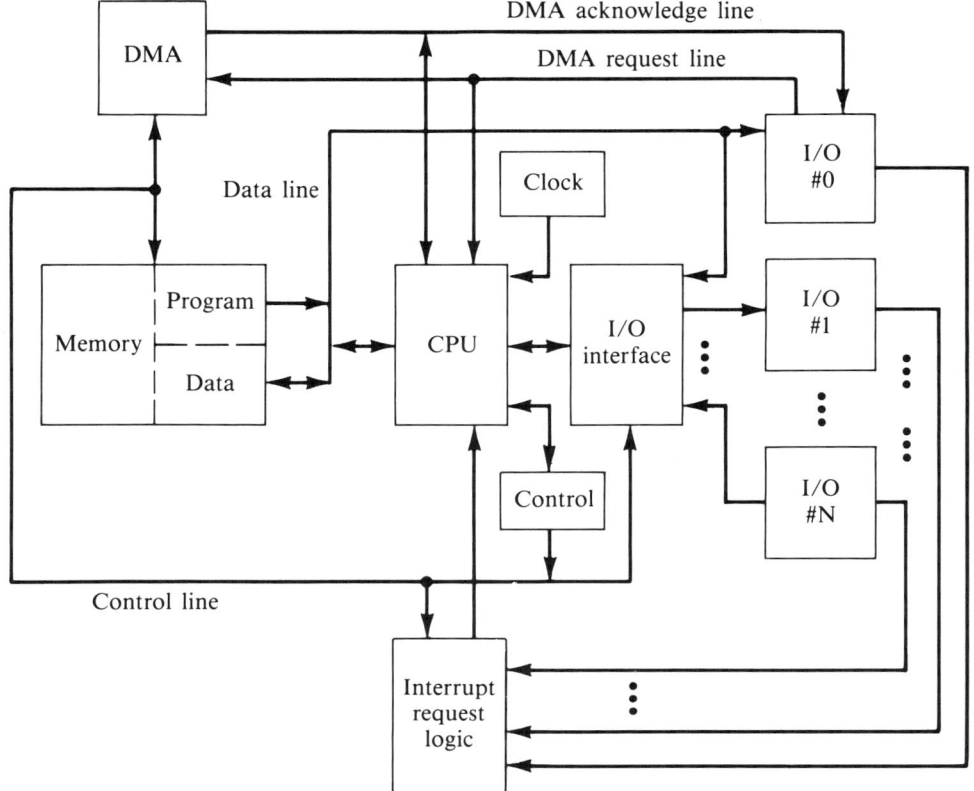

FIGURE 1-6. Microprocessor-based computer (microcomputer).

2. *Interrupt* capability, to make for a more efficient system (i.e., the CPU can be interrupted by I/O devices when needed).
3. *DMA* (direct memory access) capability, which allows an I/O device to have direct access to memory *without* direct involvement of the CPU.

The required function blocks of this system are

1. *CPU* (central processing unit), which is the "brain" of the system.
2. *Memory*, which is used to store programs and data.
3. *Controller*, which is the traffic cop of the system in that it provides nonconflicting uses of communication links among the blocks.
4. *Interrupt request logic*, which receives interrupt requests from I/O devices to interrupt the CPU. This logic may establish priorities of the interrupt request.
5. *I/O interface*, which provides proper voltage levels, timing, and so on, between an I/O device and the computer system.
6. *Clock*, which provides timing of the system. Other blocks will, directly or indirectly, get their timing from this block.

There is a term to describe the conceptual configuration of Figure 1-6 and that term is *architecture*. This descriptive term is used since Figure 1-6 illustrates the function blocks required to *construct* this system. Later references will be made to other architectures, such as CPU architecture and controller architecture. "Architecture" implies simply a function-block diagram showing the combination of function blocks and their system configuration.

1-3 COMPUTER BUS STRUCTURE

Next, it is desired to modify Figure 1-6 slightly to illustrate the system's *bus structure*. It will still be an architectural drawing, but now it will show the buses rather than lines that interconnect the system's function blocks. By way of illustration, consider the simple architectural drawing of Figure 1-7(a). Figure 1-7(b) is considered the same architectural drawing as (a), but now showing the buses that interconnect the blocks rather than the conceptual "lines" of (a). Notice that the bus interconnections of (b) are closer than (a) to being a wiring diagram. The bus representation of Figure 1-7(b) allows a better "picture" of the actual wiring without the necessity of showing a detailed wiring diagram, which for large, complex drawings can become messy. However, when actual connections are to be made, a wiring schematic showing pin connections and other details, such as that of Figure 1-7(c), may become necessary. Also notice from Figure 1-7(c) that the wiring connections of the buses are in parallel.

Figure 1-6 will now be reconfigured and redrawn to show its bus structure. Later, this will aid in understanding the function and requirements of each chip and the pin assignments of those chips. To develop this new drawing, let us begin with Figure 1-2, which shows the CPU communicating with memory. Recall that all program instructions and data are stored in memory. Each program instruction and piece of data is stored at a specific location in memory that is identifiable by a unique number called an *address*. The terminology address is derived from the concept of one's personal mailing address; that is, one's mailing address is used to identify a location (one's residence or business) so that a communication link can be established between sender and receiver for the purpose of exchange of information. By comparison, the CPU and memory must establish similar communication links in order to exchange data. Hence, using the mailing address concept, the term *memory address* is used to describe an identification number of a specific memory location. Later, the term "address" will be expanded to include identification numbers of I/O devices.

Since each location in memory has a unique address, when the CPU wishes to write or read to or from a specific memory location, it must first specify the memory address of that location. It would seem reasonable that since the CPU is to have access to memory locations, it must have a medium over which it can supply the memory addresses. This medium is a bus, and because of its function it is termed the *address bus*. The address bus concept is illustrated in Figure 1-8. Notice that Figure 1-8 still shows memory as being composed of program memory and data memory, both being addressed (in parallel) by the address bus. Also notice that addresses are *unidirectional*—from the CPU, only.

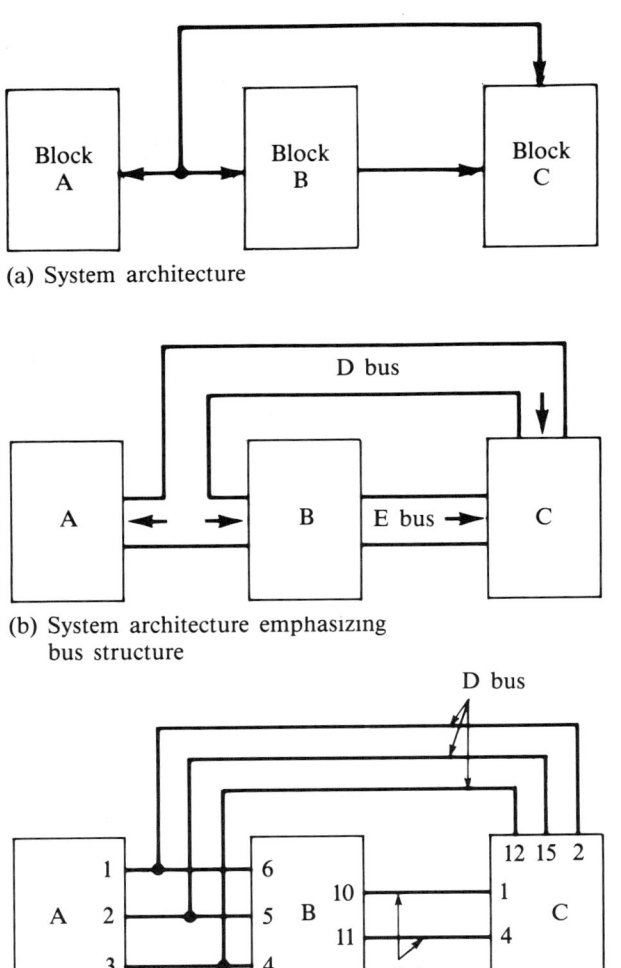

FIGURE 1-7. Various representations of communication paths between function blocks: (a) system architecture, (b) system architecture emphasizing bus structure, (c) system schematic.

Once the CPU addresses a memory location the CPU will either write into that memory location or read from it. Then there must also be a bidirectional bus between memory and the CPU over which these data may flow, where in this case the term "data" is meant in the broadest sense and includes program instructions. This bus will be termed the *data bus* and is represented in Figure 1-9. Hence the communication links of Figure 1-2 are now the address and data buses of Figure 1-9. Again it is noted that bus connections are parallel connections. It is important to realize that only one memory location is putting data on the data bus at any given moment, and that is the location being addressed. If more than one memory location would attempt to put data on the data bus at any given time, no intelligible data would be received by the CPU. When more

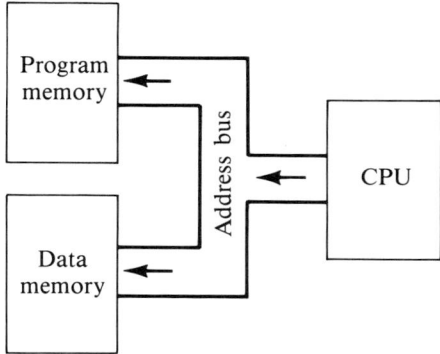

FIGURE 1-8. Address bus.

than one device, memory location, and so on, compete for control of a bus, this bus competition is termed a *bus contention* and *must be avoided*.

Next the I/O configuration of Figure 1-3 will be considered. From Figure 1-3 it is observed that a *bidirectional* path exists between the CPU and I/O—considering the I/O interface to be transparent, where *transparent* means "as though it were not there." After some thought one soon realizes that since the CPU will be reading (inputting data) and writing (outputting data) to the I/O devices, just as it did memory, a bidirectional bus such as the data bus is needed. In fact, the same data bus may be used for I/O data. This is shown in Figure 1-10(a).

There must be a means to select, or address, which I/O device is to communicate with the CPU. To accomplish this selection the CPU will be required first to address (select) the desired I/O, just as it did in selecting a desired

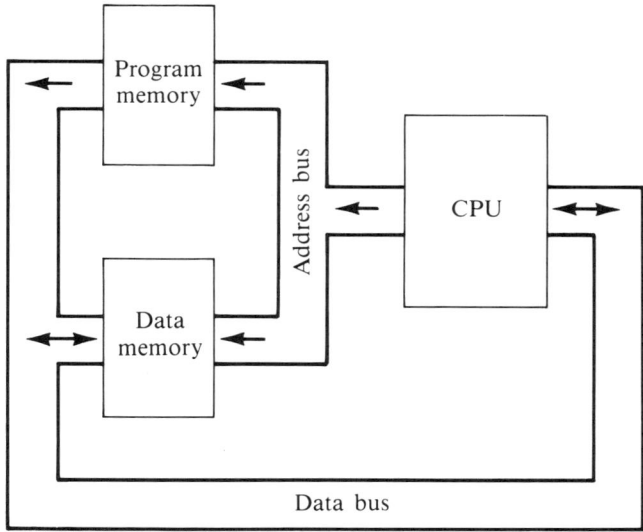

FIGURE 1-9. Address and data bus.

1-3 COMPUTER BUS STRUCTURE

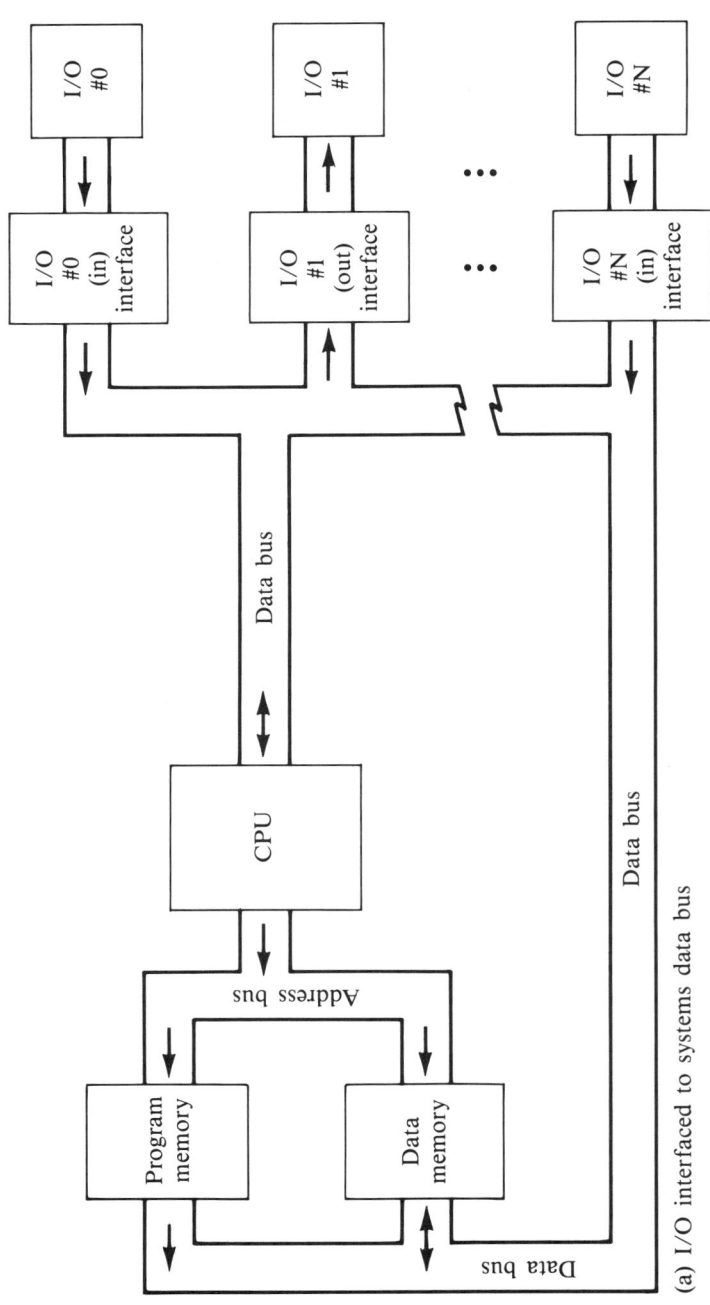

(a) I/O interfaced to systems data bus

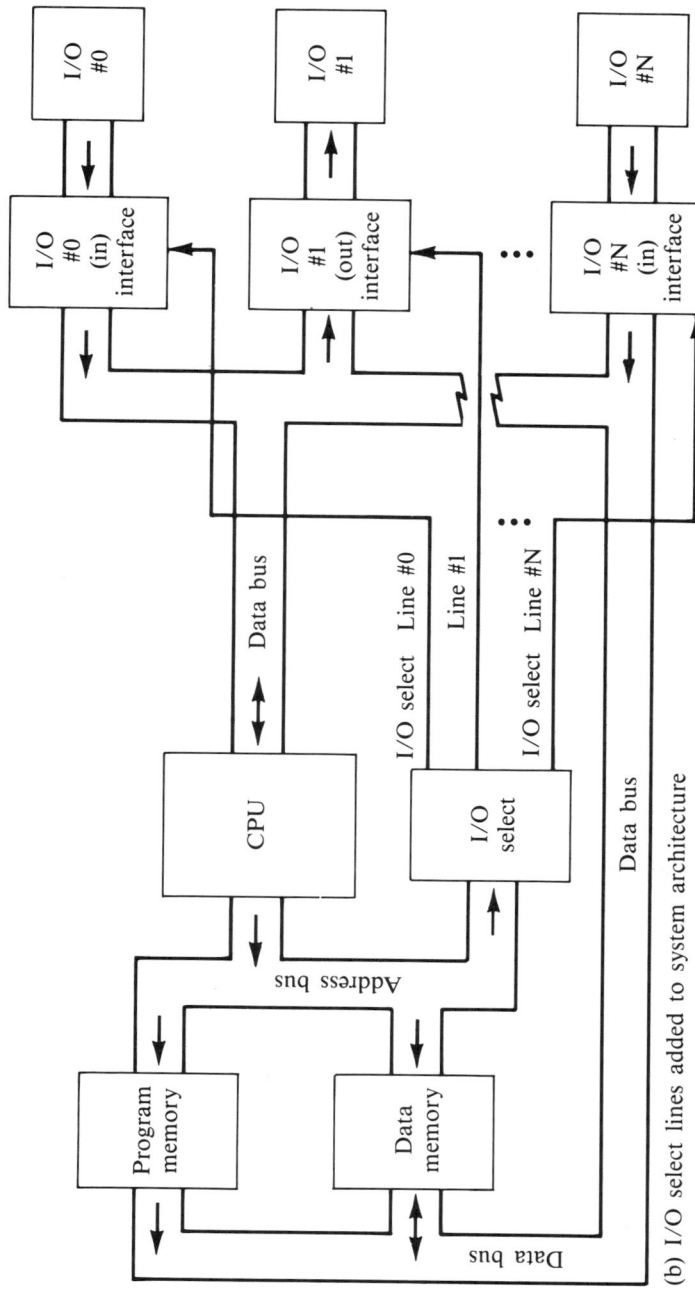

FIGURE 1-10. (a) I/O interfaced to the system data bus; (b) the addition of I/O select lines to the system architecture.

1-3 COMPUTER BUS STRUCTURE

memory location. This I/O address will be output on the address bus by the CPU just as was done for memory, but now the address will select an I/O device rather than a memory location. I/O selection is made via the I/O select lines of Figure 1-10(b), which simply activate the selected I/O device.

There is one remaining bus to consider and that is the *control bus*. The primary function of the control bus is to carry control signals generated by the system controller of Figure 1-6. To understand the function of these control signals, and hence the control bus, recall that the controller is the traffic cop of the system. Buses are often shared by more than one function block, which is known as *multiplexing*, making it necessary to regulate which function block is to control the shared bus; otherwise, bus contention will exist. Thus the controller will regulate which function block has control of the multiplexed bus at any given time. This concept will require that the control bus go to each and every function block that requires the use of a shared bus. As shown in Figure 1-10(b), the data bus is multiplexed, which will require that the following blocks be connected to the control bus: program memory, data memory, I/O interface, and DMA. Controlling the I/O select function block will result in proper control of the I/O interfacing blocks, eliminating the need to connect the interface blocks directly to the control bus. The control bus is illustrated in Figure 1-11.

From Figure 1-11 it is seen that the system illustrated has three buses: an address bus, a data bus, and a control bus; hence this figure represents a *three-bus architecture*.

It should also be noted that there is bidirectional communication between the controller and the CPU, as indicated by the arrow directions. As will be shown later, the controller is really an interpreter for the CPU; that is, the controller will interpret commands from the CPU which instruct it regarding which control signal to generate.

1-4 DMA, INTERRUPT, AND CLOCK

Since the remainder of the functions (DMA, interrupt, and clock) do not necessarily require buses, they will be simply added to Figure 1-11, as shown in Figure 1-12. Also, Figure 1-11 must be modified to allow an I/O device with DMA (0) capability to control the address bus and data bus during DMA operation. This is necessary because the CPU is to be isolated from the process and therefore cannot furnish memory addresses of where the DMA is to occur within memory, nor is it involved in the data flow between the I/O device and memory. Then it becomes the responsibility of the DMA-requesting I/O device to furnish these required memory addresses and take control of the control and data buses. Figure 1-12 illustrates I/O device 0 with DMA capability as having access to the address bus for DMA operations; that is, the address bus is shown directly connected to I/O device 0. It must be emphasized that the I/O device issues memory addresses during DMA operations. As for control of the data bus, assume that somehow the I/O interface will ''connect'' the I/O device to the data bus at the proper time for the DMA, where the proper time will be when

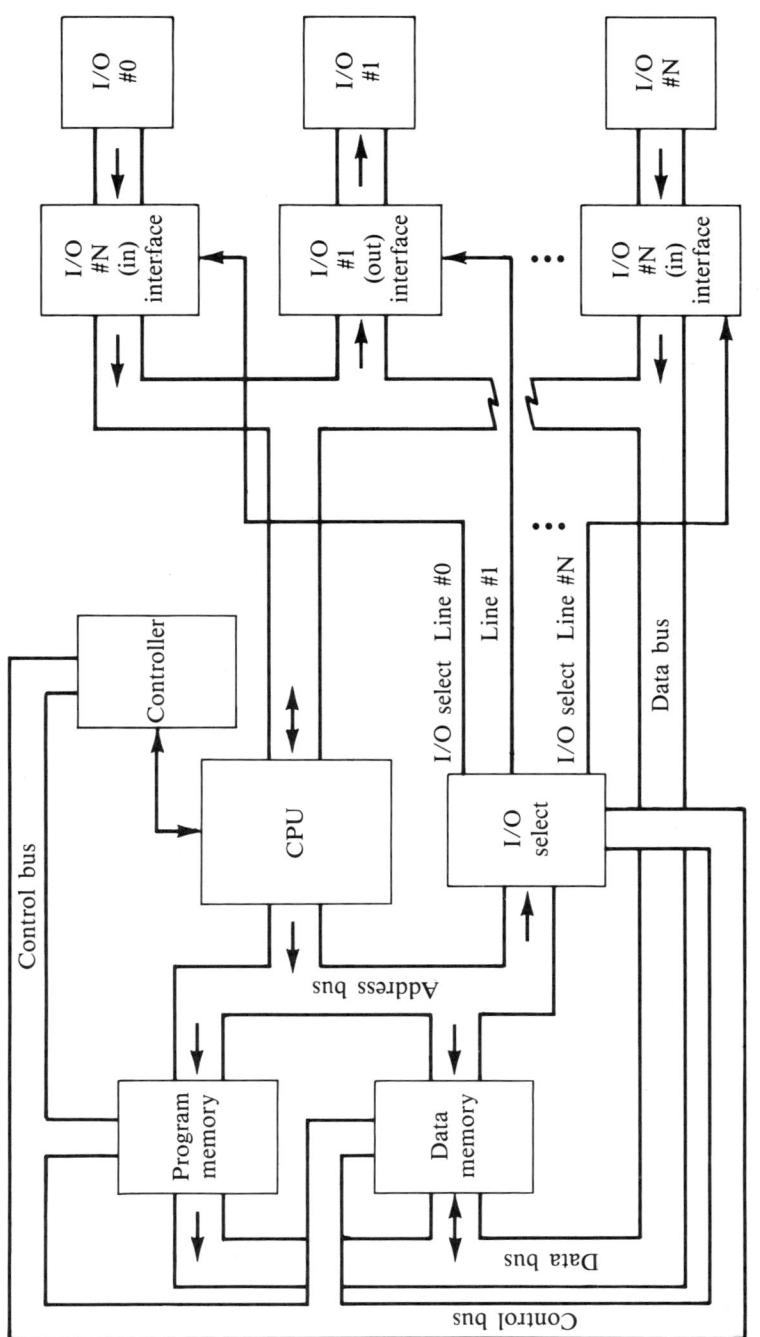

FIGURE 1-11. Control bus added to system architecture.

1-4 DMA, INTERRUPT, AND CLOCK

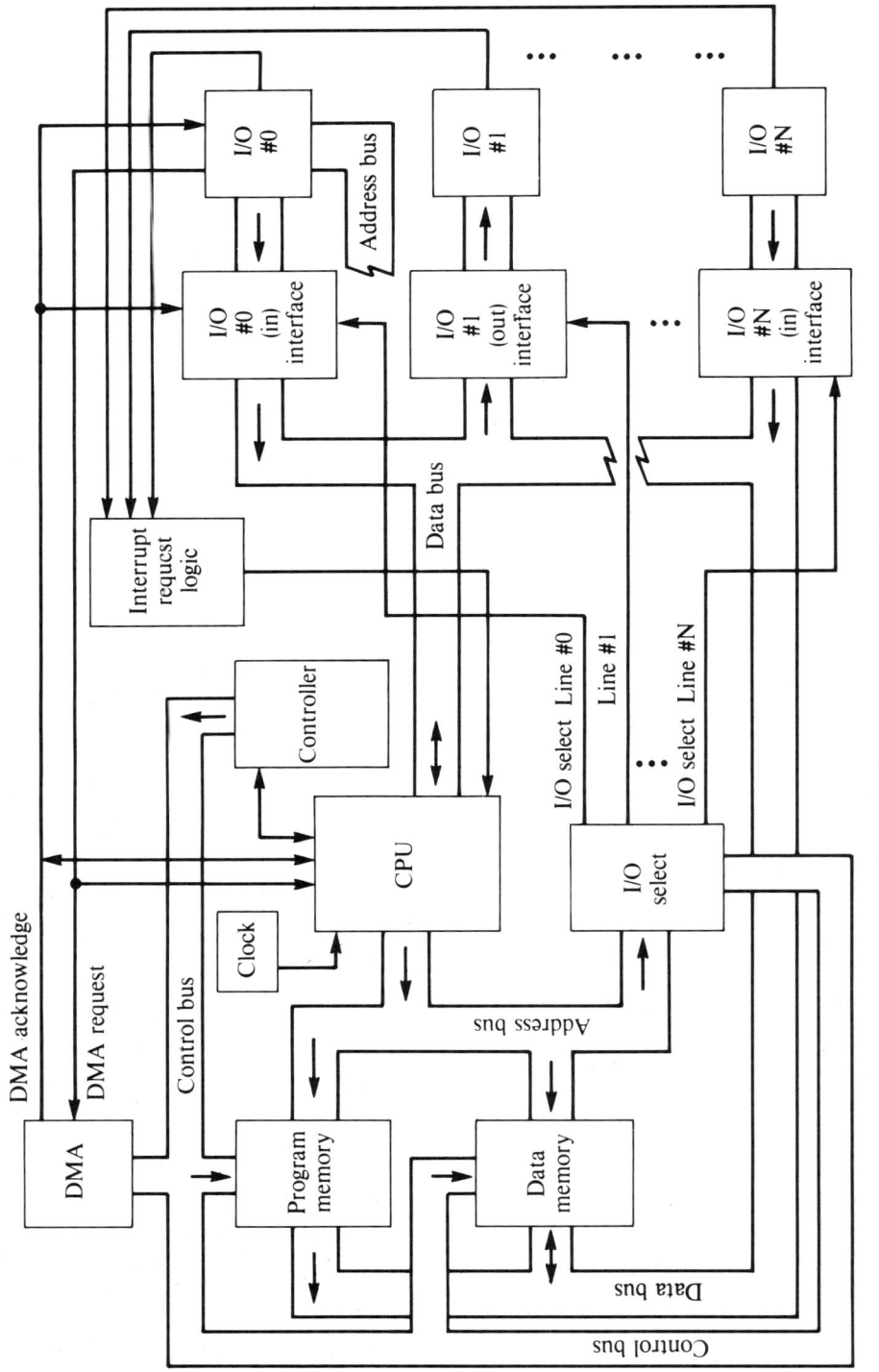

FIGURE 1-12. System architecture with I/O device 0 having DMA capability.

a DMA acknowledge is received. This is indicated by a line from the DMA acknowledge to the I/O interface of device 0. The total computer architecture of Figure 1-6 is illustrated in Figure 1-12, which shows the various buses.

1-5 SUMMARY

Our work in this chapter is summarized in Figure 1-12, which illustrates a system with a three-bus structure. I/O device 0 has the ability to issue a memory address over the address bus during a DMA and controls the control bus for the purpose of directly accessing memory. The data bus is bidirectional and serves as the medium for receiving and transmitting data between the CPU and the other function blocks. These data will often result from an addressed memory location or selected I/O device. The control bus will carry control signals that will regulate the use of a multiplexed bus to eliminate bus contention.

In the next chapter we will study the specific chips that are to perform the functions required of each function block shown in Figure 1-12. It is important that the reader understand the fundamental concepts of this computer architecture.

REVIEW QUESTIONS AND PROBLEMS

1. Even though the CPU provides the computational functions of a computer, why is it not proper to refer to it as a computer?

2. Describe how a computer is instructed to do a task.

3. What two basic purposes are served by memory?

4. What is meant by each of the following statements?
   (a) The CPU is writing to memory or I/O.
   (b) The CPU is reading from memory or I/O.

5. Describe the purpose(s) of each bus.
   (a) Address bus.
   (b) Data bus.
   (c) Control bus.

6. Relative to the CPU, explain what is meant by interrupt and DMA capability. Explain the advantage of each.

7. Why is a controller necessary to a computer system?

8. When using the term "architecture" to describe a system, what is meant?

9. Give a brief discussion of bus contention and why it must be avoided.

10. Relative to Figure 1-12, what is the function of an I/O select line?

11. How are I/O select lines "selected" to become active?

12. Why does Figure 1-12 show I/O device 0 connected to the address bus and the DMA block connected to the control bus?

13. Discuss the meaning of the term "handshaking" and indicate why it is necessary.

14. State the purpose(s) of the I/O interface block of Figure 1-12.

15. What function is served by the clock of Figure 1-12?

CHAPTER 2

Introduction to CPU Architecture and an Instruction Set

2-1 INTRODUCTION

The architecture of a general-purpose microcomputer was developed in Chapter 1 and illustrated in Figure 1-12. From the development of that architecture the reader should have acquired an understanding of function blocks, buses, and their interrelationships. This knowledge will serve as the foundation for this chapter and others.

This chapter focuses on the CPU of Figure 1-12. The approach will be to "reason" an architecture for the CPU using procedures similar to those followed in Chapter 1. Once the CPU architecture has been developed, we will investigate the means by which the CPU can be utilized. That is, we will examine the concept of how the user "instructs" the CPU what to do. This investigation will emphasize concept rather than the specific details of the "instructions" themselves.

The reason for our emphasis on concept at this point is that the reader needs an understanding of how a user can instruct an electronic chip, and of how a chip "understands" those instructions, in order to comprehend the basis of computer operations. In later chapters, when specific CPUs are studied, the emphasis will be on the details, or mechanics, of the instructions.

2-2

CPU ARCHITECTURE

In developing a CPU architecture we must realize that there is no generic standard. In fact, to develop a meaningful CPU architecture, a specific CPU must be used as a model. Then we need to determine which CPU is to serve as our model. Actually, it is a microprocessor that must be chosen as the model for the CPU, for a microprocessor will *always* be required to implement the CPU portion of the system architecture. The microprocessor selected may implement other function blocks as well as the CPU. That is, some microprocessors encompass not only the CPU but the clock and controller as well. Hence by proper selection of the microprocessor, the number of chips required to implement a design may be minimized, or as it is termed, the *chip count* reduced. For our objectives the various reasons for microprocessor selection, based on design implementation criteria, will have little bearing. Rather, the choice will be made on educational objectives. From an educational point of view it is desirable for the chosen microprocessor to

1. Have an architecture general enough that its design philosophies encompass the primary principles of most microprocessors. This will allow readers to extrapolate their knowledge to other microprocessors.
2. Be basic enough that it does not implement more than one function block of Figure 1-12. The reason for this requirement is that as more function blocks are implemented by a single chip, one begins to lose insight into the interworking of the system.
3. Be popular enough that its use in industry will be widely accepted.

A microprocessor that meets these criteria is Intel's 8080. For this reason the CPU developed in this chapter will be modeled on the 8080. Remember, however, that even though our CPU will be modeled on the 8080, many of the same principles will apply to other microprocessors. As specific microprocessors are studied, we will return to this chapter and adapt the concepts learned to the microprocessor being studied.

To begin rationalizing a CPU's essential function blocks, we must realize that the CPU is responsible for all arithmetic and logic operations, such as addition, subtraction, ANDing, and ORing. Since the CPU is responsible for such operations, its architecture must contain a function block indicating this ability. As in combinational logic, such a function block is termed an *arithmetic–logic unit* (ALU). As the ALU performs arithmetic and logic operations, it must have a place within the CPU to store the results. A set of *flip-flops*, which form a *register*, serve this purpose. To identify this register it is imagined that it "accumulates" the results of the ALU; hence it is termed the *accumulator* (A). To illustrate the ALU and accumulator, refer to Figure 2-1, where registers X and Y serve as data input registers.

If the function blocks of Figure 2-1 are to perform an addition, the sum of X and Y will be deposited into A. This operation can be mathematically expressed as

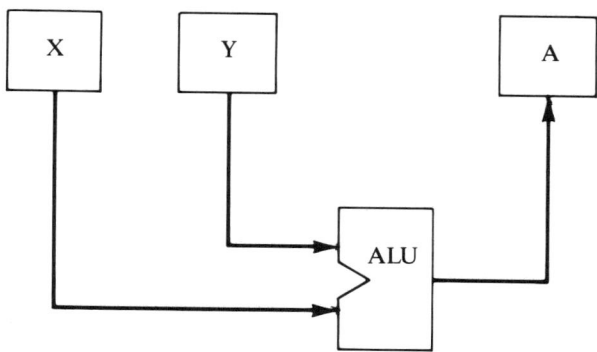

FIGURE 2-1. ALU with inputs X and Y and output A.

$$X +' Y = A \qquad (2\text{-}1)$$

where $+'$ will be used to indicate an arithmetic addition. If a logic AND is to be done, the results of $X \cdot Y$ will be deposited in A, which is expressed mathematically by the Boolean equation

$$X \cdot Y = A \qquad (2\text{-}2)$$

The logic OR of X and Y would be expressed as

$$X + Y = A \qquad (2\text{-}3)$$

Our last example is subtraction, which is expressed as

$$X - Y = A \qquad (2\text{-}4)$$

Also let it be realized that to be compatible, registers X, Y, and A usually have the same number of bits.

In the interest of register economy and efficiency, let registers X and A of Figure 2-1 be combined and identified as A, as shown in Figure 2-2. Figure 2-2 simply illustrates that the result from an ALU operation between A and Y will be stored in A. By way of example, suppose that two numbers are to be added, say 03 and 02. Then numbers 03 and 02 must first be loaded into A and Y. After the addition has taken place, the result, 05, will be output by the ALU and deposited in A. For reasons of register economy the original contents of A are lost, but this is often of no consequence since other means of saving the original contents of A will be provided. Then the ALU operations of Figure 2-1, which are mathematically expressed in Equations (2-1) through (2-4), are now expressed for Figure 2-2 as

$$A +' Y \rightarrow A \qquad (2\text{-}5)$$

$$A \cdot Y \rightarrow A \qquad (2\text{-}6)$$

$$A + Y \rightarrow A \qquad (2\text{-}7)$$

$$A - Y \rightarrow A \qquad (2\text{-}8)$$

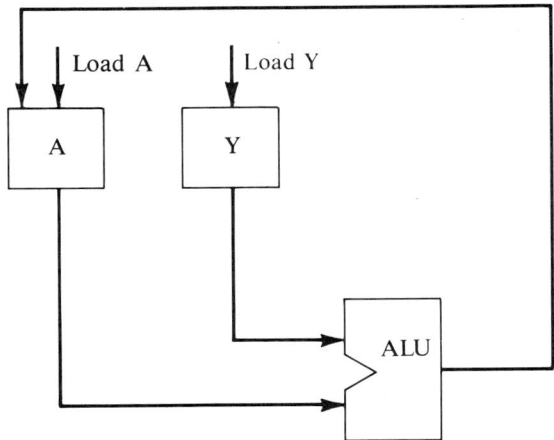

FIGURE 2-2. ALU with inputs A and Y and output A.

"Load A" and "load Y" of Figure 2-2 are the input-data paths used to load registers A and Y with the values on which the ALU operations are to occur. At this time it is not necessary to understand the origin of the data that are being accessed.

It is convenient, but not necessary, to have some memory internal to the CPU in which to store, or accumulate, *partial* results of an ALU operation. An analogy of this *internal memory* is that of many hand-held calculators. By way of example, suppose that a six-step arithmetic operation is to be performed, where the result of the first step (a partial result) must be remembered (temporarily stored) to be used in the sixth step. The internal memory will be used to store the partial result of the first step for use in the sixth step. Figure 2-3 illustrates six internal memory registers that have been added to Figure 2-2.

The term "internal memory" is seldom used to describe these registers. A more common term is *secondary accumulators,* because although the internal memory can be used to accumulate intermediary results, its accumulating responsibilities are *secondary* to register A. Because of this secondary responsibility, any internal memory serving this task is termed a secondary accumulator. Registers used to implement secondary accumulators must be of the same bit size as the ALU output and registers A and Y. The bit size of each register in Figure 2-3 is indicated by the parenthetical number.

Since secondary accumulators are to accumulate ALU partial results, a data path must exist between the register selected to be used for storage and the ALU. This data path is the same as that which goes to register A, since secondary accumulators also accumulate results from the ALU. In addition to incorporating a data path from the ALU to A and the secondary accumulators, a function block that selects the appropriate secondary accumulator register (B, C, D, etc.) to accumulate an ALU partial result must be added to Figure 2-3. Figure 2-4 illustrates these modifications, which are: (1) a common data path from the ALU going to A and the secondary accumulator registers, and (2) the addition of a *register selector,* which is capable of selecting which secondary accumulator register is to be used for ALU output storage.

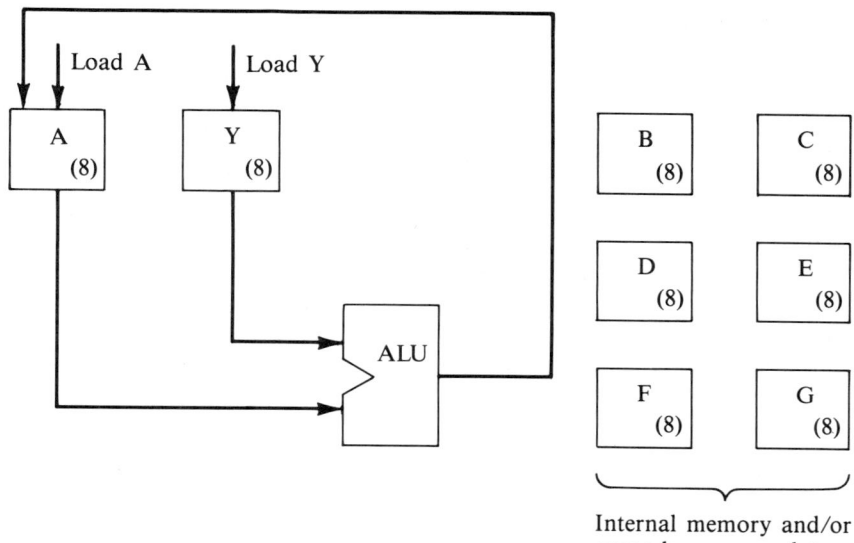

FIGURE 2-3. Development of CPU architecture: ALU with internal memory.

Next let us focus our attention on the inputs load A and load Y of Figure 2-4. Recall that these inputs are the means by which data are loaded into the register indicated. Since registers B, C, D, and so on are used to store partial results from ALU operations (which may be data to be used for other ALU operations), it is necessary to have inputs load A and load Y accessible to secondary accumulator registers. The secondary accumulator register from which A or Y is to receive data will be selected by the register selector, just as the

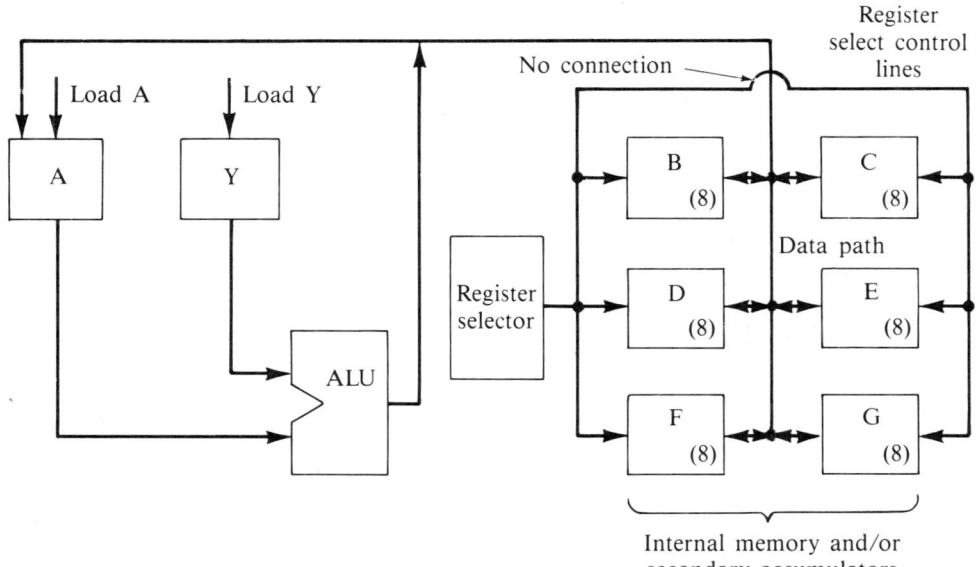

FIGURE 2-4. Development of CPU architecture: Addition of register select.

2-2 CPU ARCHITECTURE **21**

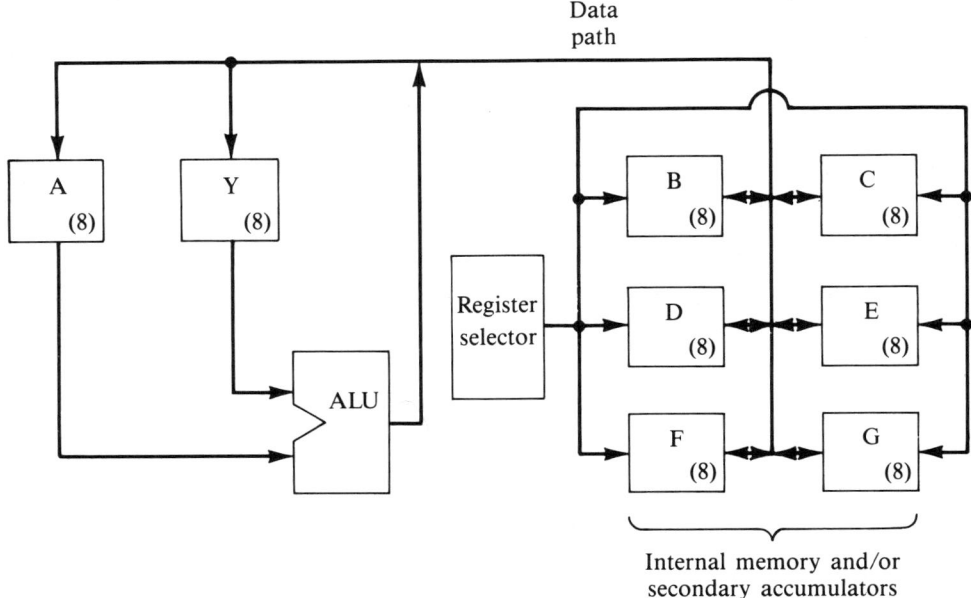

FIGURE 2-5. Development of CPU architecture.

selector determined the destination register for ALU storage. Figure 2-4 will be modified by showing

1. Registers B, C, D, and so on having a common data path between them and registers A and Y. The common data path of Figure 2-4 is bidirectional since the ALU may be storing data (partial results) in the secondary accumulators, or registers A or Y may be retrieving data from a secondary accumulator register.
2. The elimination of the inputs load A and load Y. These inputs can be eliminated since they are common to the data path going to the secondary accumulators.

These modifications are shown in Figure 2-5.

Before continuing to develop CPU architecture, let us take a simple example and make certain that the concepts of Figure 2-5 are well understood.

EXAMPLE 2-1

Suppose that three numbers are to be added, say 1, 2, and 4. Assume that these data points were somehow stored in registers B, C, and D, respectively (we shall see how later).

Solution

Since the architecture of Figure 2-5 shows only two inputs to the ALU, via A and Y, the numbers must be added two at a time. That is, we shall instruct, or program, the CPU to

1. MOVE CONTENTS OF B INTO A; B → A (1 → A)
2. MOVE CONTENTS OF C INTO Y; C → Y (2 → Y)
3. ADD A AND Y [which automatically loads the result into A; see Equation (2-5)]

We realize that after instruction 3 is executed, the arithmetic operation 1 + 2 has been performed (actually, 00000001 + 00000010 since the electronics operates in binary) and the partial result 3 is in accumulator A. It is now necessary that this partial result be added to 4, which is the value stored in register D. Then to complete the required instructions we continue with

4. MOVE CONTENTS OF D INTO Y; D → Y (4 → Y)
5. ADD A AND Y; A +' Y = A (3 + 4 = 7): The answer. ∎

EXAMPLE 2-2

As another example let us suppose that the sum of Example 2-1 is to be used later in other calculations. Hence it must be removed from the "working" accumulator A and stored in a secondary accumulator, such as E. Then to continue our program the next instruction would read: MOVE CONTENTS OF A INTO E. This instruction is added to the other five to complete the program. The six instructions were abbreviated and are as follows:

1. MOVE B INTO A
2. MOVE C INTO Y
3. ADD A AND Y
4. MOVE D INTO Y
5. ADD A AND Y
6. MOVE A INTO E ∎

From these simple examples the reader has not only been shown the workings of the CPU architecture of Figure 2-5, but has also been introduced to the concept of programming the CPU.

To continue our reasoning of CPU architecture, let us ask ourselves two questions:

1. How does the CPU "get" the sequence of instructions that make up the program?
2. Once the CPU receives the instructions, how does it "know" how to interpret and execute them?

For the answer to the first question, review Figure 1-9. Recall that the procedure is for the CPU to address a memory location *containing* the beginning instruction, which in Example 2-2 is MOVE B INTO A. Once addressed, that memory location will "dump" its contents, the instruction, on the data bus, from where it is received by the CPU. Thus the CPU architecture will need two additional function blocks: one to address memory, via the address bus, and another to "receive" the instruction accessed from memory via the data bus. Since both memory addresses and instructions are binary numbers, which are to be temporarily stored, both function blocks are registers. The register used to address memory for instructions is termed the *program counter* (PC), and the register used to receive (latch) instructions from memory via the data bus is called the *instruction register* (IR). These register additions to Figure 2-5 are shown in Figure 2-6. Note that the PC is shown as a 16-bit register, indicating that the CPU can furnish 16-bit addresses. The addressing bit size capability is indicative of its memory capacity, as will be shown later.

The reasoning behind the term "program counter" is worth investigating, for it exemplifies how program instructions are accessed from memory. The PC is used exclusively to address memory for program instructions—never to address memory for data. This explains the "program" portion of "program counter." The "counter" portion of the term is derived from its counter action. That is, after the execution of an instruction the CPU *automatically increments* the PC by one (PC +' 1 → PC), operating as a sequential up-counter. Then if program instructions are stored in sequential order in memory, the PC will properly access each instruction in the order required. As an example, suppose that the program of Example 2-2 was stored in memory in the sequential order shown. The first instruction (MOVE B INTO A) would be accessed from memory by the CPU and executed. After execution of the first instruction the CPU will increment the PC, which is the address of the next instruction. The second instruction is then accessed from memory by the CPU by having the PC supply the address

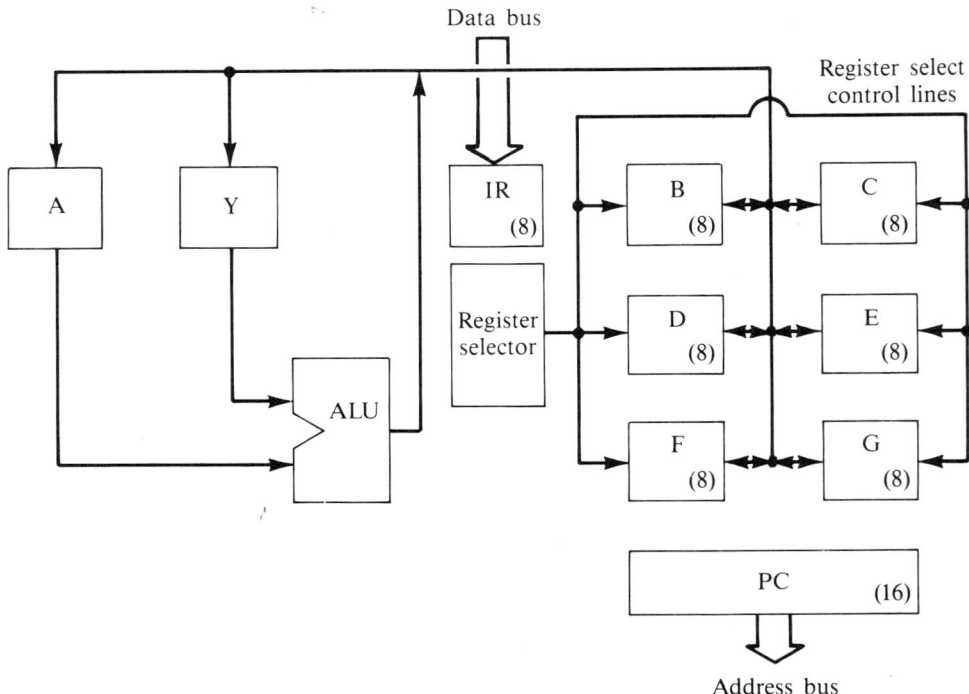

FIGURE 2-6. Development of CPU architecture: The addition of the program counter.

on the address bus. The contents of that addressed memory location (the second instruction) will then be dumped on the data bus, and latched by the IR. The CPU will then execute the second instruction and then increment the PC, which is the address of the third instruction. This cycle continues until the entire program has been executed. *Take note that it is this counter action that lets the CPU know where in memory the next instruction is to be found.*

To answer question 2, "Once the CPU receives the instructions, how does it 'know' how to interpret and execute them?", let us first realize that *all* program instructions are binary codes. That is, the first instruction of Example 2-2, MOVE B INTO A, might be the 8-bit binary code 01000111. MOVE C INTO Y could be represented by 01001110 (notice that all instruction binary codes are of size 8 bits, the same as the IR). In summary, every instruction is represented by a unique binary code. To "interpret" the instruction we can simply "decode" the binary code. As an example, to decode the instruction MOVE B INTO A (01000111), an AND gate could be used. The logic of the AND gate is determined from the Boolean expression of Equation (2-9), which is the application of combinational logic.

$$(\text{MOVE B INTO A}) = \overline{IR_7} \cdot IR_6 \cdot \overline{IR_5} \cdot \overline{IR_4} \cdot \overline{IR_3} \cdot IR_2 \cdot IR_1 \cdot IR_0 \quad (2\text{-}9)$$

where IR_n is used to indicate individual flip-flops which comprise the instruction register. Implementation of Equation (2-9) is illustrated in Figure 2-7.

To continue, suppose that 256 such instructions existed. Then 256 AND gates could be used such that each AND gate would detect an instruction as was done in Figure 2-7 to decode MOVE B INTO A. As we know from combinational logic, these AND gates, used for detection or decoding purposes, are termed *decoders*. Hence we attach to the instruction register a function block that will decode instructions and output appropriate signals. This function block is the IR decoder, shown in Figure 2-8.

To execute the instruction, let us imagine another function block, called the *control unit* (CU). It is the CU that expedites instruction execution within the CPU. As an example, when the instruction 01000111 (MOVE B INTO A) is latched by the IR from the data bus and decoded, there is a unique output signal from the IR decoder. This signal is sent to the CU, which in response enables the register selector such that a direct path will exist between registers B and A. Next, the CU will generate the proper signals so that data transfer between B and A will take place. Finally, the CU will increment the PC so that the next instruction will be fetched from memory. Since the CU must control the activities of *all* other function blocks, control lines must exist from the CU to all other function blocks, as shown in Figure 2-8.

From Figure 2-8 the manner in which the CPU receives instructions from memory via the data bus can be seen; however, the reader should recall from Chapter 1 that in addition to instructions, data is also accessed from memory. When data is accessed from memory by the CPU, the designation register for that data may be any of those shown in Figure 2-8 except IR or PC. Then Figure 2-8 must be modified to allow registers other than just the IR to have access to the data bus. The modification of Figure 2-8, in part, will be an internal bus, termed the *internal data bus,* to which all registers have direct access. The CU

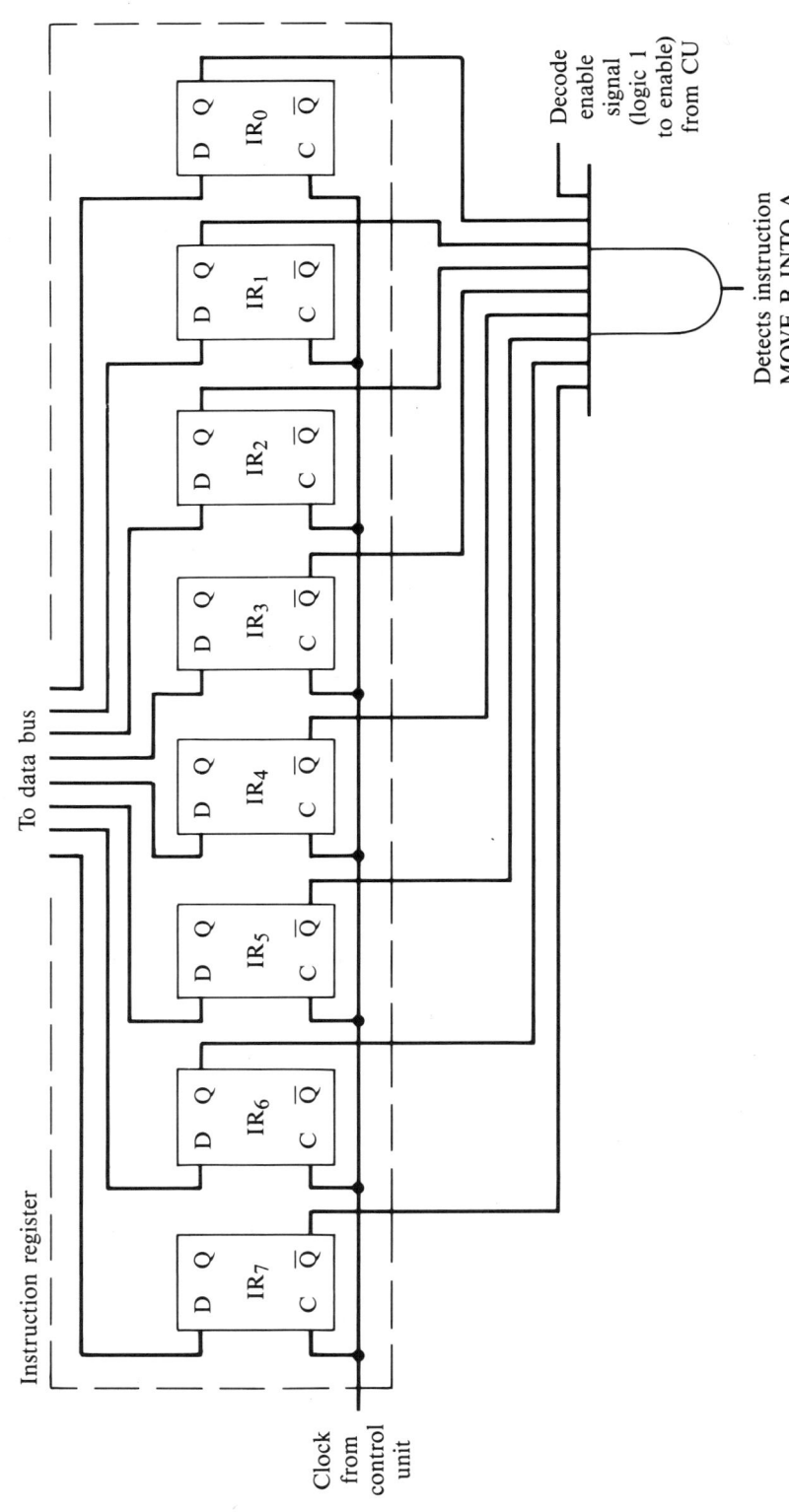

FIGURE 2-7. Decoding the instruction MOVE B INTO A.

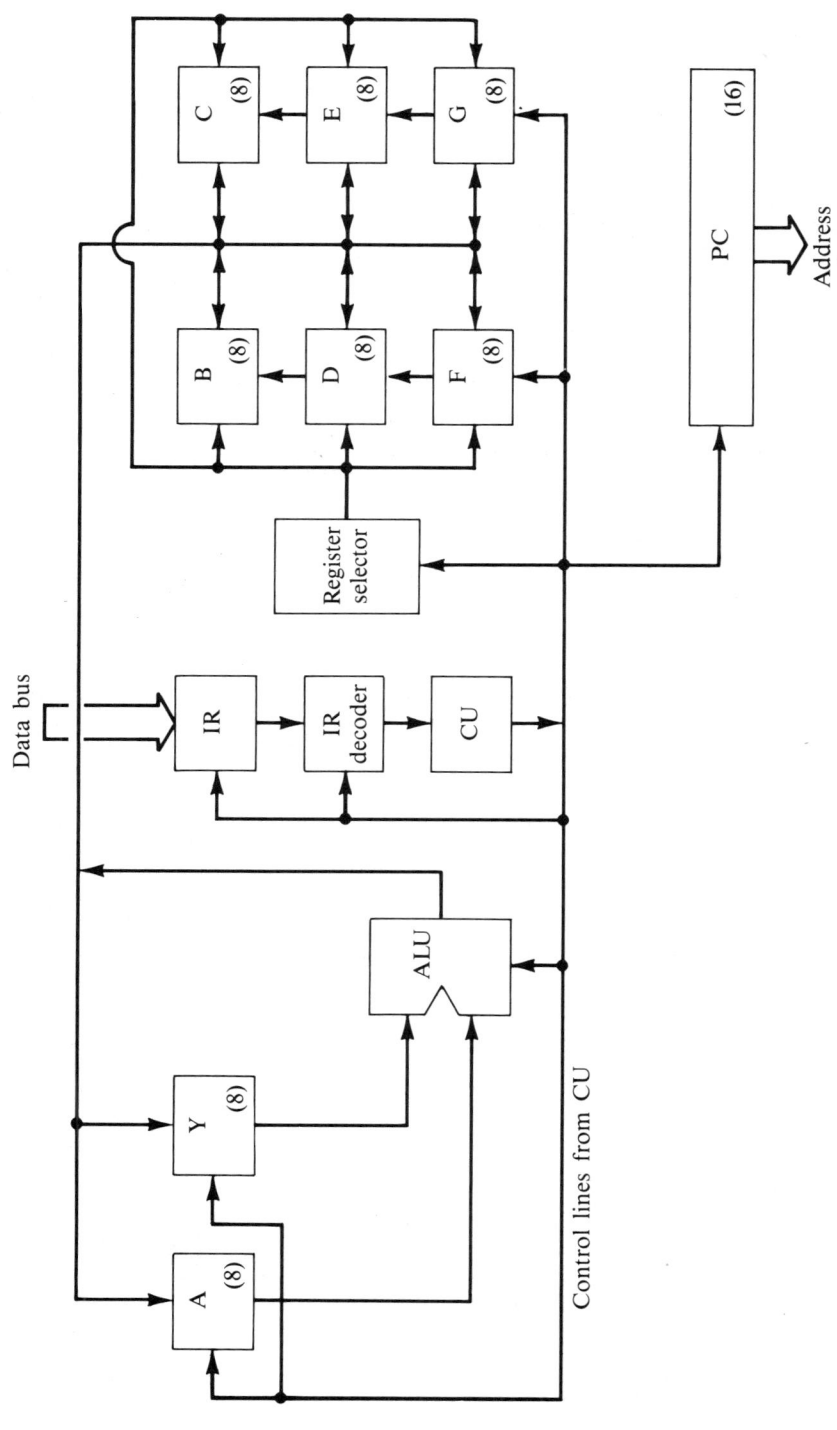

FIGURE 2-8. Development of CPU architecture: The addition of the control unit.

2-2 CPU ARCHITECTURE　　27

will determine and control which register will have access to the internal data bus at any given moment.

Since the CPU's internal data bus is to access the system's data bus, there must be some type of isolation, or buffering, between the two. Therefore, a *data bus buffer* will also be shown in the modification of Figure 2-8. In addition to offering buffering qualities, the data bus buffer will determine data flow direction under the control of the CU. Figure 2-9 illustrates the necessary modifications of Figure 2-8.

Let us make some observations regarding Figure 2-9. First, notice the bus representation of the internal data bus. Second, note that the IR has undirectional access to the internal data bus, complying with the requirement that it receives (instructions) from the data bus. Finally, the bit size of the internal data bus must be the same as the registers it serves, that is, 8 bits.

To add some concreteness to Figure 2-9, let us execute the program of Example 2-1, which is to perform the arithmetic operation $1 +' 2 +' 4$. For ease of reading and to follow convention, hereafter, binary digits (bits) shall be grouped in fours. Recall that the register contents are B = 1 (0000 0001), C = 2 (0000 0010), and D = 4 (0000 0100). Also, recall that all instructions are binary codes that have previously been stored sequentially in memory. Assume that each instruction has the corresponding memory address and binary code shown in Table 2-1, where the beginning addresses of Table 2-1 were assigned arbitrarily.

To begin execution the PC will contain the 16-bit binary address (0000 0000 0001 0000) of the first instruction. Under control of the CU, the PC will output this binary number on the address bus. This address will access memory location 0000 0000 0001 0000 (refer to Figure 2-9). The contents (0100 0111) of this addressed memory location will be dumped on the system's data bus. The CU then sets the data flow direction of the bidirectional data bus buffer to the input mode, which will allow the instruction binary code 0100 0111 to appear on the internal data bus of the CPU. Next, the CU will generate the appropriate signal (clock pulse referred to in Figure 2-7) for the IR to latch that binary code from the internal data bus. The CU "knows" that it has just completed fetching an instruction from memory. The CU also knows that it must execute the fetched instruction. To begin execution the CU must determine which instruction was latched by the IR. It does so by decoding the latched instruction. To decode the instruction, the CU enables the IR decoder of Figure 2-9 (also refer to Figure 2-7). The output signal from the IR decoder enables the proper circuits of the CU to execute the instruction MOVE B INTO A. Execution will require the CU to enable the register selector so that it selects B to have access to the internal data bus. Then the CU will cause B to dump its contents (0000 0001) on the internal data bus and then cause A to latch those data from the internal data bus. Hence the value of A is now 0000 0001. The CU now knows that it has executed the first instruction and will increment the PC by one. The contents of the PC is now 0000 0000 0001 0001, which, as shown in Table 2-1, is the address of the second instruction.

The CPU fetches the second instruction just as it did the first; that is, the contents of the PC (0000 0000 0001 0001) is dumped on the address bus. Thus memory location 0000 0000 0001 0001 is accessed and its contents (0100 0110)

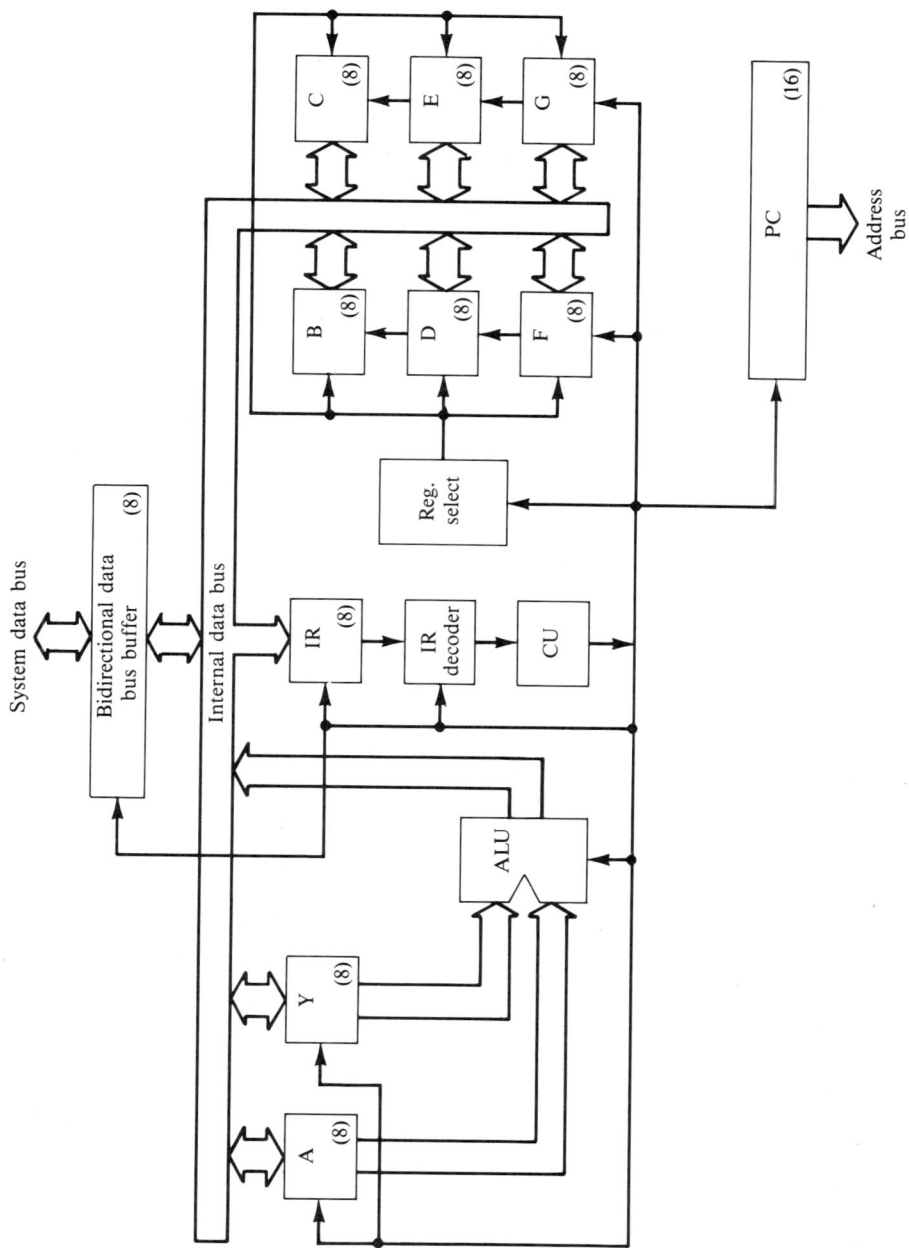

FIGURE 2-9. Development of CPU architecture: The addition of the data bus buffer.

2-2 CPU ARCHITECTURE

TABLE 2-1. Example Program

Memory Address	Instructions	Instruction Binary Code (8-bit)
0000 0000 0001 0000	MOVE B INTO A	0100 0111
0000 0000 0001 0001	MOVE C INTO Y	0100 0110
0000 0000 0001 0010	ADD A TO Y	1011 1110
0000 0000 0001 0011	MOVE D INTO Y	0101 0110
0000 0000 0001 0100	ADD A TO Y	1011 1110
0000 0000 0001 0101	MOVE A INTO E	0111 1011
0000 0000 0001 0110	HALT	0111 0110

is then dumped on the data bus, which is latched by the IR of the CPU. The CU knows that it has completed another instruction-fetch cycle and then decodes the fetched instruction via the IR decoder. The output of the IR decoder signals the CU which instruction is to be executed, which in this case is MOVE C INTO Y. The CU will then select C to have access to the internal data bus, on which C will dump its contents (0000 0010). Register Y will then latch 0000 0010 off the internal data bus, under the control of the CU. The second instruction has been executed and the CU then increments the PC. Now Y = 0000 0010 and A = 0000 0001, resulting from execution of the first and second instructions. Also, since the PC has been incremented, its contents is now 0000 0000 0001 0010.

The instruction fetch cycle is again repeated. That is, the contents of the program counter (0000 0000 0001 0010) is dumped on the address bus. The contents of that memory location (1011 1110) is dumped on the data bus and latched by the IR. The IR decoder decodes which instruction is to be executed and properly signals the CU. Since the instruction is ADD A TO Y, the CU enables registers A and Y to input their contents into the ALU and the ALU to execute an add operation. The ALU then outputs the sum on the internal data bus and the CU generates the proper signal, which causes register A to latch that sum from the internal data bus. Notice that the previous contents of A (0000 0001) has been destroyed since A now contains 0000 0011 (0000 0001 +' 0000 0010 = 0000 0011). The instruction ADD A TO Y has been executed and thus the CU increments the PC by one (PC = 0000 0000 0001 0011).

Again an instruction fetch is executed by the CU and the binary code 0101 0110 is latched by the IR. That instruction is decoded and register D is given access to the internal data bus. D then dumps its contents (0000 0100) on the internal data bus and register Y latches it from that bus, all under the control of the CU. That instruction has been executed and hence the CU increments the PC, which is the address of the next instruction. The next instruction fetch cycle is performed, ADD A TO Y, which is a repeat of third instruction. Since A +' Y → A, the contents of A will be 0000 0111 (0000 0011 +' 0000 0100 = 0000 0111). The PC is incremented by one and thus PC = 0000 0000 0001 0101, which is the address of the sixth instruction of Table 2-1. The instruction-fetch cycle is again performed and the instruction 0111 1011 (MOVE A INTO E) is latched by the IR. After decoding the CU enables the necessary functions for the contents of A to be dumped on the internal data bus and for register E to latch that data from the internal data bus. Hence E latches 0000 0111, which is the resultant sum of 0000 0001 +' 0000 0010 +' 0000 0100. The PC is then incremented and the next instruction is fetched, which halts program execution.

The example program just executed, and its application to the CPU architecture of Figure 2-9, should be well understood. Also be sure to notice the cyclic nature of CPU operations.

At this juncture only a means for addressing program instructions (i.e., via the PC) has been discussed. This implies that any memory location accessed by the PC will have its contents treated as an instruction and therefore will be latched by the IR, which is true as long as an instruction is just 8 bits in size.

Since data are also in memory, how are they accessed? To answer this question, let us reason that since the address bus size is 16 bits, a 16-bit register, similar to the PC, must be used. Yet Figure 2-9 shows no other 16-bit registers. To overcome this problem, *the CU will have the ability to pair 8-bit registers* for the purpose of addressing *data* from memory. That is, using certain program instructions, the CU can pair registers B and C, D and E, or F and G. When paired, these *register pairs* (RPs) form a 16-bit capability that can be used to address memory for data. To the CPU architecture of Figure 2-9 is added a function block that can latch an address from the PC or a register pair, whichever is appropriate, under control of the CU. This modification of Figure 2-9 is shown in Figure 2-10 where the *address latch* performs this function.

The selection of an addressing mode is made by the CU under the dictates of a program instruction. The address latch will latch the contents of the PC or RP as indicated in Figure 2-10, so that it may be held on the system address bus.

Be certain to understand that memory locations addressed by the PC will have their contents latched by the IR (if instructions are limited to 8 bits), whereas if a register pair is used for addressing memory, the contents of that accessed memory location will be latched by register A, Y, B, C, D, E, F, or G. As an example, suppose that it were desired to move the contents of memory location 0000 0100 0000 0000 to register B. If register pair D and E is used for addressing memory, the instruction might appear as MOVE CONTENTS OF (D, E) TO B, where D and E contain the address of the memory location to be accessed. When this instruction is fetched, its decoding will cause the CU to enable the register selector so that the contents of D and E is latched by the *address latch* and then dumped on the address bus. This accessed memory location (0000 0100 0000 0000) will then dump its contents on the system's data bus. Next, the CU will load that data onto the internal data bus via the data bus buffer. The CU will then cause register B to latch that data from the internal data bus. Hence the instruction is executed and the CU will increment the PC.

When registers are used in pairs for the purpose of accessing memory for data, the register pair is referred to as a *data counter* (DC). Registers B, C, D, E, F, and G may be referred to as secondary accumulators when used to temporarily store data, or as data counters when used in pairs to address memory.

As a point of interest, most people prefer not to use the term secondary accumulator but rather *scratch-pad memory* to describe the internal memory of the CPU. The reason for the use of this term is that when registers B, C, D,

2-2 CPU ARCHITECTURE   **31**

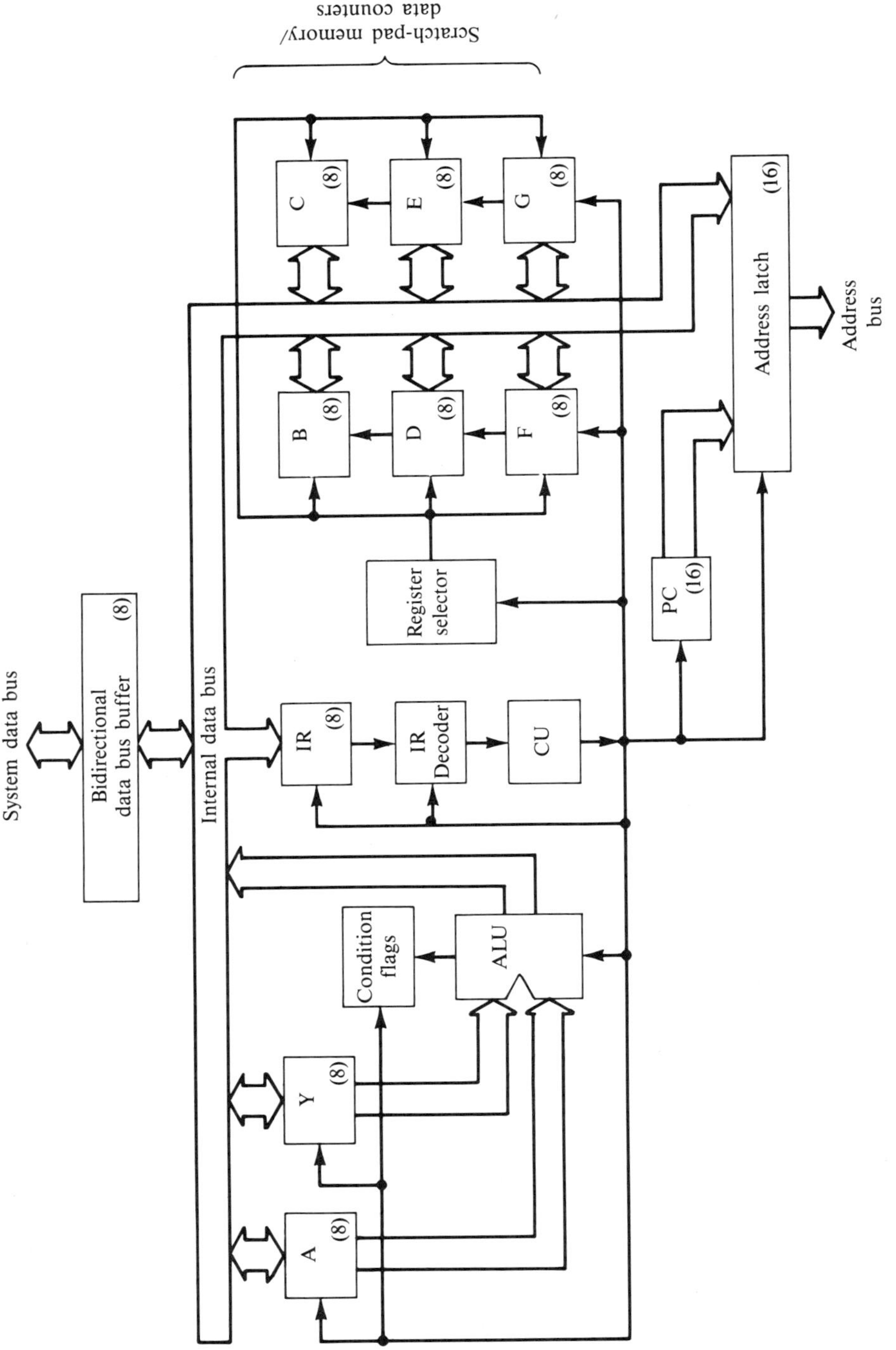

FIGURE 2-10. CPU architecture: The addition of the address latch.

and so on are used to store data temporarily, they are being used as one would use a scratch pad. "Scratch-pad memory" will be the preferred term in this text. Hence, if registers are used for data storage, they will be said to be performing scratch-pad memory functions, and when used as register pairs to address memory, they will be said to be serving as data counters.

The last function block to be added to Figure 2-9 and shown in Figure 2-10 is that of the *condition flags*. Condition flags are flip-flops whose logic state indicates the resultant "condition" of arithmetic and logic operations performed by the ALU. There will be five such flip-flops, termed *flags,* as follows:

1. The sign (positive or negative) of an ALU operation is designated as the *sign flag* (S). If set in the 1 state, the results were positive; if reset, the results were negative.
2. If a carry resulted from an ALU operation, it is indicated by the *carry flag* (C). If a carry is present, the C flag is set; otherwise, it is reset.
3. If the result of an ALU operation is even or odd parity, it is indicated by the state of the *parity flag* (P). Even parity is represented by a set condition.
4. If a carry results between the fourth and fifth bits after an ALU operation, the *auxiliary carry flag* (AC) will be set; otherwise, it will be reset.
5. If the results of an ALU operation are zero, the *zero flag* (Z) will be set; otherwise, it will be reset.

At this point it is not our intention to give any details as to the use of condition flags, but rather to provide some introductory-level concepts. To gain a better understanding of these concepts, let us consider an example.

EXAMPLE 2-3

Suppose that one wishes to search some data in memory, beginning at location 0000 0000 0000 0010 and ending at 0000 0000 0000 0100, for the value 00001111. When that value is found in memory, let it be stored in register E.

Solution

Using register pair B and C as the data counter, the program might appear as follows (refer to Figure 2-10 for the CPU architecture):

1. LOAD 0000 0000 0000 0010 INTO (B, C)
2. LOAD 0000 1111 INTO Y
3. MOVE (B, C) INTO A
4. SUBTRACT Y FROM A
5. IF Z = 1 MOVE (B, C) TO E:
   INCREMENT (B, C) AND CONTINUE
6. MOVE (B, C) INTO A
7. SUBTRACT Y FROM A
8. IF Z = 1 MOVE (B, C) TO E:
   INCREMENT (B, C) AND CONTINUE
9. MOVE (B, C) INTO A
10. SUBTRACT Y FROM A
11. IF Z = 1 MOVE (B, C) TO E OTHERWISE
    STOP

The first instruction initializes RP B, C as the data counter. The second instruction initializes Y with the value sought; that is, Y becomes the reference register. Instruction 3 causes the CPU to access memory location 0000 0000 0000 0010 by dumping the contents of RP B, C (the DC) on the address bus and loading the contents of this accessed memory location into register A. The fourth instrustruction subtracts Y from A and alters the Z flag according to the results, since subtraction is an ALU operation. If the result is zero, the Z flag is set; otherwise, it is reset. Instruction 5 causes the CU to check the Z flag to determine its logic state. It is instruction 5 that allows a *decision* to be made. That is, if $Z = 1$, the contents of A equals the contents of Y ($A = Y$) and the contents of (B, C) should be stored in E. If $Z = 0$, then $A \neq Y$ and the next memory location should be accessed to continue the search. To access the next memory location, RP B, C is incremented by one ($DC +' 1$). As seen, instructions 6 to 11 are repeats of instructions 3 to 5 since the same procedures are to be followed. The reader should note particularly that *the condition flags allowed a decision to be made by the CPU*. ■

Since the introduction of the control unit in Figure 2-8, the reader has been given program examples in which it was stated repeatedly that the CU

1. "Knew" how to execute every instruction once "told" the instruction to be executed via the IR decoder.
2. Expedited instruction execution by controlling the other function blocks.

From this description of the CU responsibilities in the CPU architecture and the program examples given, one begins to feel that the CU is the brain of the CPU. This observation might even be extended to the microcomputer architecture of Figure 1-12. Such observations would be correct. The control unit is a *special-purpose computer* within the CPU. It is *dedicated* to the sole function of executing instructions. As is the case for all computers, it requires a program to instruct it. The program required by the CU instructs it as to the precise procedures to be followed in the execution of instructions, such as the instructions of Examples 2-2 and 2-3. This program is termed the *microprogram* and is manufactured as an intregal part of the CU and is not alterable or accessible to the user. For this reason there is little need to discuss it. There is an exception, for a type of microprocessor termed a *bit-slice microprocessor*. For these microprocessors the user must create the microprogram. Because of their complexity and lack of common usage, we do not discuss them in this book.

2-3 CONTROL SIGNALS

In Chapter 1 it was stated that the controller is the traffic cop of the system shown in Figure 1-12, controlling the operations of all other function blocks via the control bus. It was also stated that the controller was really an interpreter of the CPU. It is the CU which generates the appropriate signals that are input to the controller for "interpretation." The interpretation process done by the controller is actually a decoding process similar to that performed by the IR decoder.

The signals generated by the CU can be classified into one of two categories: timing and CPU operations. Once the controller is given the "present CPU operation to be performed," which is termed the *CPU status,* and the proper timing signal from the CU, it can generate the proper system control signal. This control signal appears on the system's control bus and is used to control the other function blocks accordingly.

The type of timing signals the CU generates are those which indicate that the CPU is

1. *In the input mode*: That is, the CPU is reading data or an instruction from the data bus.
2. *In the output mode*: That is, the CPU is writing data onto the data bus.
3. *Beginning another operation*: The CPU will provide a synchronizing pulse to indicate the start of another operation.

Let us somewhat arbitrarily name the timing signal spoken of in point 1 as the data bus input, or DBIN. Let us name the output mode timing signal the data bus output, or DBOT. The synchronizing is identified as SYNC. These signals are outputs of the CU, as shown in Figure 2-11.

The CPU status signals will indicate such CPU operations as

1. *Memory read.* Data is being accessed from memory.
2. *Memory write.* Data is being stored in memory.
3. *Instruction fetch.* Data is being accessed from memory, where the data constitute an instruction and is to be loaded into the IR of the CPU.
4. *I/O read.* Data is being accessed from an input device (such as a keyboard).
5. *I/O write.* Data is being transmitted from the CPU to an output device (such as a printer).

There may be other CPU operations not shown, but these five are sufficient to demonstrate the concept. The CPU status is a binary code, which can be accomplished by 2 bits. One of these bits is to indicate if the CPU operation involves I/O or memory. Let this bit be an output of the CU and be designated as $IO/\overline{M}$, which is to be interpreted to mean that if the output is a 1, an I/O operation is being performed, and if a 0, a memory operation is occurring. The other bit of the CPU status will be represented by $RD/\overline{W}$, that is, the bit is a 1 for read operations and a 0 for write operations. $IO/\overline{M}$ and $RD/\overline{W}$ are shown as outputs of the CU in Figure 2-11.

As an example of how the timing signals and CPU status are utilized by the controller to generate a control signal, imagine that the CPU is doing an instruction-fetch operation. To do an instruction fetch requires that memory be accessed, or read. This means that the CPU status will be $IO/\overline{M} = 0$ and $RD/\overline{W} = 1$. The proper *timing* is a function of DBIN, which must be present whenever the CPU is to input *any data* (or instruction) from the data bus. Using combinational logic as shown in Figure 2-12, a control signal MEM R is generated that can be used to activate the memory read pin of a memory chip. It

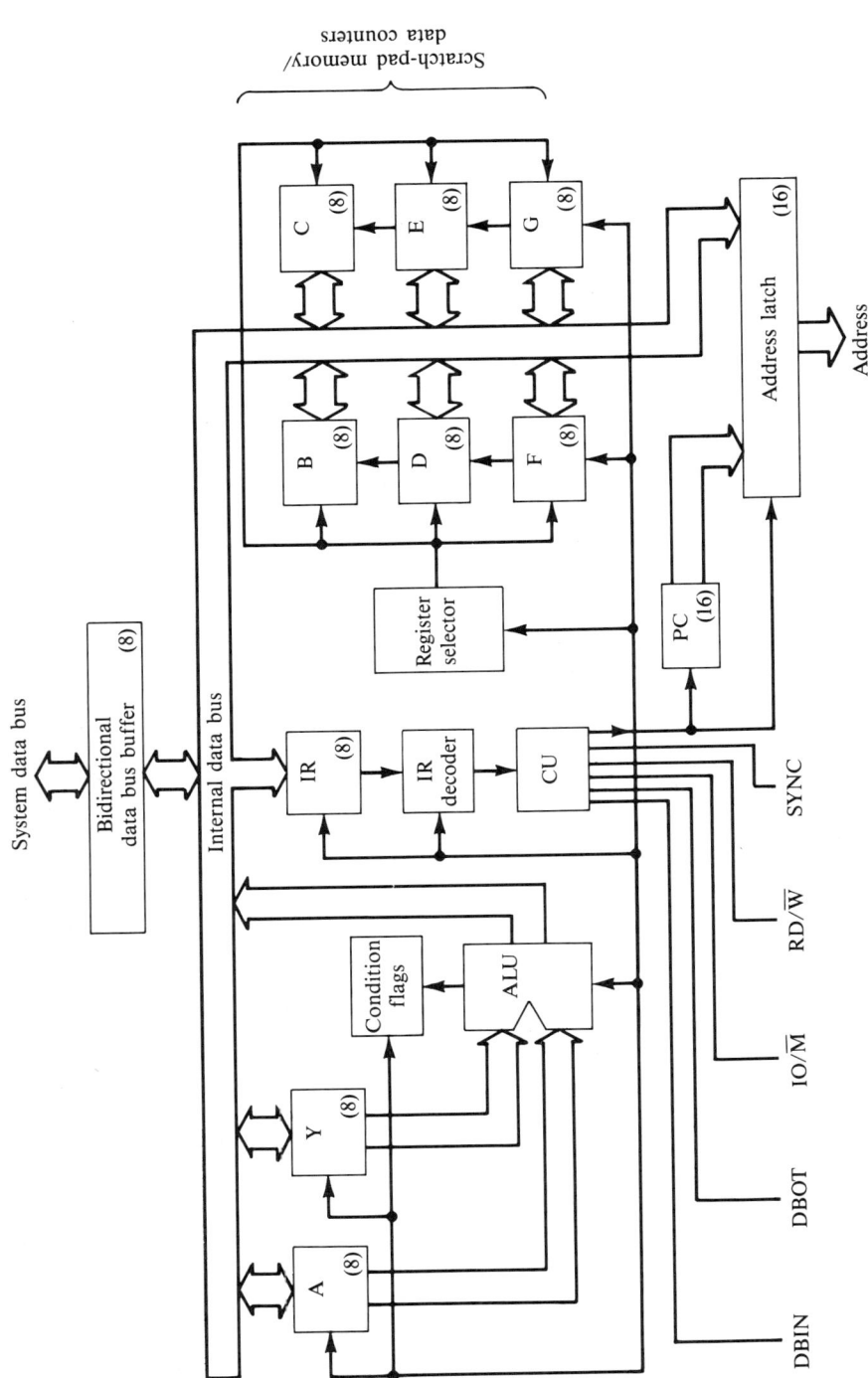

FIGURE 2-11. CPU architecture.

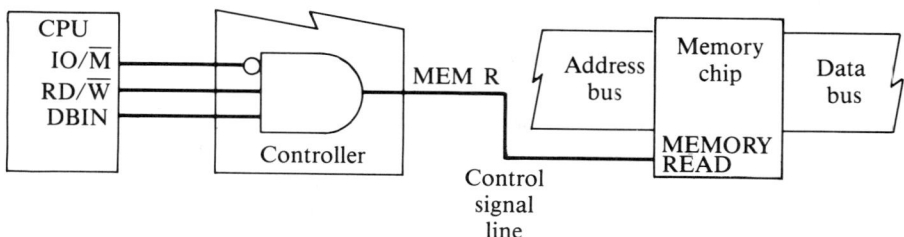

FIGURE 2-12. Controller logic for generating control signal MEM R.

is important that the reader understand the principle used to generate a control signal: The CPU status determined *which control signal* was to be generated, and DBIN determined *when* it was generated.

Other control signals generated by the controller are memory write (MEM W), I/O read (IO/R), and I/O write (IO/W). It is these control signals that form the control bus of Figure 1-12.

2-4 CREATION OF A HYPOTHETICAL INSTRUCTION SET

The CU has a repertoire of instructions that it is capable of executing via its microprogram. This instruction repertoire is referred to as the *instruction set* of the CPU or microprocessor. It is from the instruction set that the user must choose instructions with which to write programs, such as the example program of Table 2-1. To reiterate, the microprogram within the CU instructs the CU on the necessary steps and procedures for execution of these instructions.

To introduce the concepts of an instruction set, let us create a hypothetical instruction set for the CPU architecture of Figure 2-11. We begin with a *truth table* showing all binary combinations that can exist. To determine the number of binary combinations possible, we realize that since the IR is to "receive" the instructions, which are 8 bits in length, 2^8 possible binary combinations exist:

$$\text{number of combinations} = 2^{\text{number of bits}} \qquad (2\text{-}10)$$

Since $2^8 = 256$, there could be 256 unique instructions for this CPU. However, a manufacturer may not choose to utilize all possible binary codes, resulting in an instruction set repertoire of less than 256 instructions. For our hypothetical instruction set, let all binary codes be utilized, which means that our truth table will show all 256 binary codes.

Determining which binary code is to represent which instruction depends on the decoding scheme selected by the designer of the CPU or microprocessor. Suppose that we begin by classifying all CPU operations and then assign a corresponding binary code to each operation. This would allow the CU to determine the operation expected of it from an instruction's binary code via the

IR and IR decoder. To classify CPU operations, suppose that the CPU of Figure 2-11 can perform these basic operations:

1. *Branch control group*: Those instructions that cause program execution to branch or jump from one portion of the program to another.
2. *Data transfer group*: This classification will include those instructions that manipulate data between CPU registers.
3. *Arithmetic and logic (ALU) group*: All arithmetic and logic operations; instructions involving the ALU are included in this classification.
4. *Input/output and CPU management*: This group of instructions will control the exchange of data between the CPU and peripheral devices (input and output devices) as well as the necessary CPU management required for such exchanges.

At this point we shall not concern ourselves with the details of these classifications but rather with the concepts. We have been able to classify all 256 instructions into one of four groups. In order to detect, or decode, one of four classifications, we need 2 bits, as can be derived from Equation (2-10). Let us arbitrarily state that the two most significant bits of our 8-bit instructions will be used to designate the class of operation. Designating these 2 bits as IR_7 and IR_6, the truth table of Table 2-2 could be used.

Next, let us devise a coding scheme for specifying the CPU registers of Figure 2-11. From Figure 2-11 it can be seen that there are eight registers which are programmable, that is, through the instruction set their contents can be programmed by the user (recall MOVE B INTO A, and so on, from Table 2-1). These registers are A, Y, B, C, D, E, F, and G. Since there are eight registers, there must be eight unique codes or binary combinations. This will require 3 bits for decoding purposes, as determined from Equation (2-10). Let us assign the registers to those binary codes shown in Table 2-3.

Let us now consider some binary-coding examples using Tables 2-2 and 2-3.

EXAMPLE 2-4
Construct the binary code which when latched by the IR and decoded by the IR decoder will cause the CU to execute

(a) MOVE B INTO A
(b) MOVE E INTO B
(c) ADD A TO Y

TABLE 2-2. Classification Coding

IR_7	IR_6	Class of Operation
0	0	Branch
0	1	Data transfer
1	0	ALU
1	1	I/O and conditional executions

TABLE 2-3. Register Codes

Binary Code			Register
0	0	0	B
0	0	1	C
0	1	0	D
0	1	1	E
1	0	0	F
1	0	1	G
1	1	0	Y
1	1	1	A

(d) IF Z = 1 MOVE A TO E OTHERWISE INCREMENT (B, C) AND CONTINUE

Solution

There are 8 bits for every instruction which must be accounted for when determining the binary code. Since they are ultimately latched by the IR, let these bits be designated as IR_7 to IR_0.

(a) To do a MOVE B INTO A, which is a data transfer, requires that $IR_7 = 0$ and $IR_6 = 1$, as determined from Table 2-2. From Table 2-3 it is seen that B is specified by the code 000 and A using 111. Assigning IR_5–IR_3 for the source register code and IR_2–IR_0 for the destination register code, then the instruction binary code is as follows:

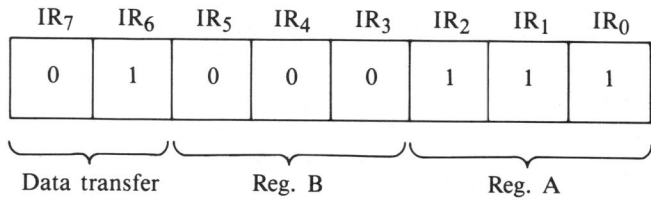

Binary code for instruction MOVE B INTO A.

The binary code 0100 0111 corresponds to the code of Table 2-1 for the instruction MOVE B INTO A.

(b) MOVE E INTO B

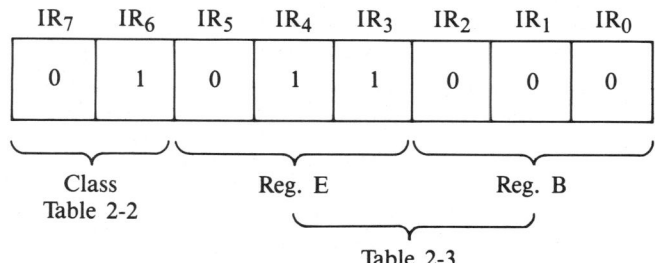

Binary code for instruction MOVE E INTO B.

(c) ADD A TO Y

$$\underbrace{10}_{\text{Table 2-2}} \quad \underbrace{111\ 110 \text{ or } 1011\ 1110}_{\text{Table 2-3}}$$

(d) IF Z = 1 MOVE A TO E OTHERWISE INCREMENT (B, C) AND CONTINUE

In searching Tables 2-2 and 2-3 in an attempt to code this instruction, it becomes obvious that not enough flexibility exists in coding instructions. Thus additional coding must be developed.

The additional coding required results from not presently having a coding scheme for conditional executions, incrementing the data counter, and so on. Let instructions that require combinations of checking condition flags, data transfer, and incrementing the data counter be classified as I/O and conditional executions. From Table 2-2, the two most significant bits for this class of operation will be 1's. Also needed are codes that indicate the condition flag to be checked. Let the binary code be determined by the format of Figure 2-13.

As an example of Figure 2-13, the resultant binary code for coding the instruction of Example 2-4(d) is 11 0 011 00. As determined from Figure 2-13, IR_5 is 0 because the instruction is performing a conditional execution rather than an I/O instruction. IR_4, IR_3, and IR_2 are 011, respectively, since the Z flag is being tested. IR_1 and IR_0 are 00 since register pair B and C is used as the data counter. All that is missing from completing the instruction coding is the MOVE A TO E portion. To accomplish this let us use the coding given in Tables 2-2 and 2-3, which would be 01 111 011. With the addition of this 8-bit code it is obvious that the instruction IF Z = 1 MOVE A TO E OTHERWISE INCREMENT (B, C) AND CONTINUE *cannot* be coded with a single 8-bit code. Instead, this instruction requires two 8-bit codes. Then the total code would be

1100 1100; From Figure 2-13

0111 1011; From Tables 2-2 and 2-3

the two-8-bit binary code for the instruction

IF Z = 1 MOVE A TO E OTHERWISE
INCREMENT (B, C) AND CONTINUE ■

We should understand how a two-8-bit code instruction is executed. First, each 8-bit code will reside in consecutive memory locations. As the program is executed the CU will institute an instruction-fetch cycle and fetch from the first of the two consecutive memory locations the binary code 1100 1100. The IR decoder decodes this instruction and as usual sends the proper signals to the CU. In decoding this binary code the CU will "know" (via its microprogram) that since IR_7 and IR_6 are 1's, the instruction is either I/O or a conditional execution. However, since IR_5 is a 0, the CU knows that a conditional execution is intended. Due to the logic states of IR_2, IR_3, and IR_4, the CU knows that if the flag conditions are met (Z = 1), it must increment the PC and fetch from

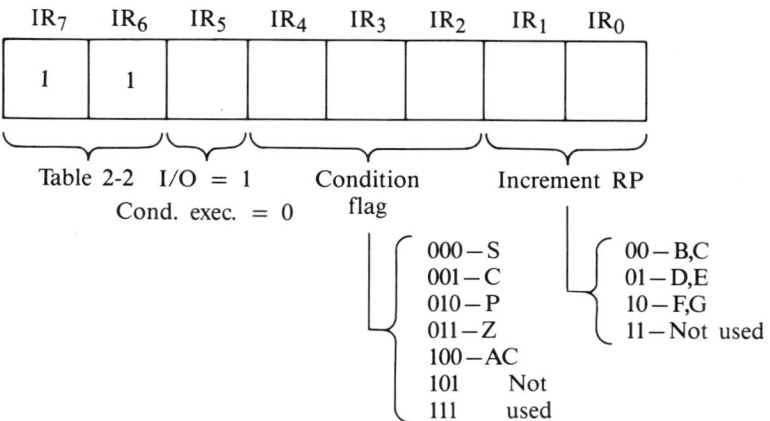

FIGURE 2-13. Binary code format for conditional instruction.

memory a second 8-bit code for the IR (which is MOVE A TO E). However, if $Z = 0$, the CU will increment the DC by one and the PC by two (the next memory location is to be skipped if $Z = 0$).

The importance of those examples given in Example 2-4 is the concept of how instructions are coded by the CPU designer and decoded by the IR decoder for execution by the CU via the microprogram. Also, from Example 2-4(d) we realize that instruction binary codes sometimes require more than a single 8-bit code.

A hypothetical CPU instruction set and its corresponding binary codes might also appear as shown in Table 2-4.

The instruction set of Table 2-4 could have been given just in binary code, but all those 1's and 0's would make it very confusing when being read by the user. Or the instructions could have been written in longer form, such as shown under the "Instruction Operations" column of Table 2-4, but this takes too much space and time when writing programs. What is needed is a time- and space-saving shorthand method of writing an instruction that is not as confusing to *remember* as is binary code. The solution has been the creation of a *symbolic abbreviation* which is indicative of the instruction operation. To accomplish this the computer industry uses memory-aiding symbols called *mnemonics*. Examples of mnemonics are shown in Table 2-4. Notice that mnemonics symbolically represent the operation to be performed. The mnemonic form of the instruction set is used when writing a program.

Be certain to understand that the CPU must have the binary codes in its IR before the CU can execute an instruction, and that mnemonics are only a tool to aid the user in writing and reading program instructions. That is, programs are written in mnemonics so that the user and others reading a program can better interpret how it accomplishes the task. However, before that program is to be executed by the CPU, it must first be *translated* into binary code and stored in memory (review the example program of Table 2-1). Hence it can be said that mnemonics is a *human-oriented language,* whereas binary code is a *machine-oriented language* (microprocessors are often referred to as "ma-

TABLE 2-4. Hypothetical Instruction Set

Binary Code	Instruction Operations	Instruction Mnemonics
00000000	No operation	NOP
00000001	Clear A	CLR A
00000010	Clear Y	CLR Y
00000011	Clear condition flags	CLR F
00000100	Rotate A right one bit	RT A R
00000101	Rotate A left one bit	RT A L
00000110	Rotate carry left	RT C L
⋮	⋮	⋮
01110010	Move B into C	MOV B, C
01110011	Move C into Y	MOV C, Y
01110100	Move B into A	MOV B, A
⋮	⋮	⋮
11111100	Store B in memory	STR B
11111101	Store C in memory	STR C
11111110	Store D in memory	STR D
11111111	Store E in memory	STR E

chines''). In fact, some people use the terms *binary code* and *machine code* synonymously.

In viewing Table 2-4, one is able to get a feeling for each instruction and the CPU operation it determines. However, we also notice that even the "long form" is somewhat lacking in detail. For a detailed explanation of an instruction, the manufacturer of a microprocessor publishes a *programming manual*. This manual will give such details as

1. The mnemonic form of the instruction and a detailed explanation of CPU operations resulting from its execution.
2. The corresponding binary code for each instruction, or the scheme for determining the binary code.
3. The effect on the condition flags, if any, resulting from execution of the instruction.
4. Timing information.

The process of translating an instruction from its mnemonic form to its machine code is termed *assembling*. If the user determines the machine code, as we did in Example 2-4, it is called *hand assembly*. There are computer programs that can assemble programs written in mnemonics. These computer programs are called *assemblers* and will be discussed in great detail in later chapters. Earlier chapters will assemble all instructions in mnemonic form using hand assembly. It is believed that this approach will aid the reader in understanding all the processes involved in microprocessor-based design. It will also develop a deeper appreciation of the assembler.

2-5 CHIP PIN CONFIGURATION

Now that we have "reasoned" a CPU architecture, let us propose a *chip pin* configuration for this microprocessor. From Figure 2-11 we see that the number of pins must correspond to the following:

Address pins	16
Data pins	8
Timing pins	2
CPU status	2
Sync	1
Total	29

Let us add to the number of pins required two more, one for the power supply (some microprocessors require more than one supply) and another for the ground. Using a 32-pin *dual-in-line package* (DIP), the pin configuration might appear as shown in Figure 2-14.

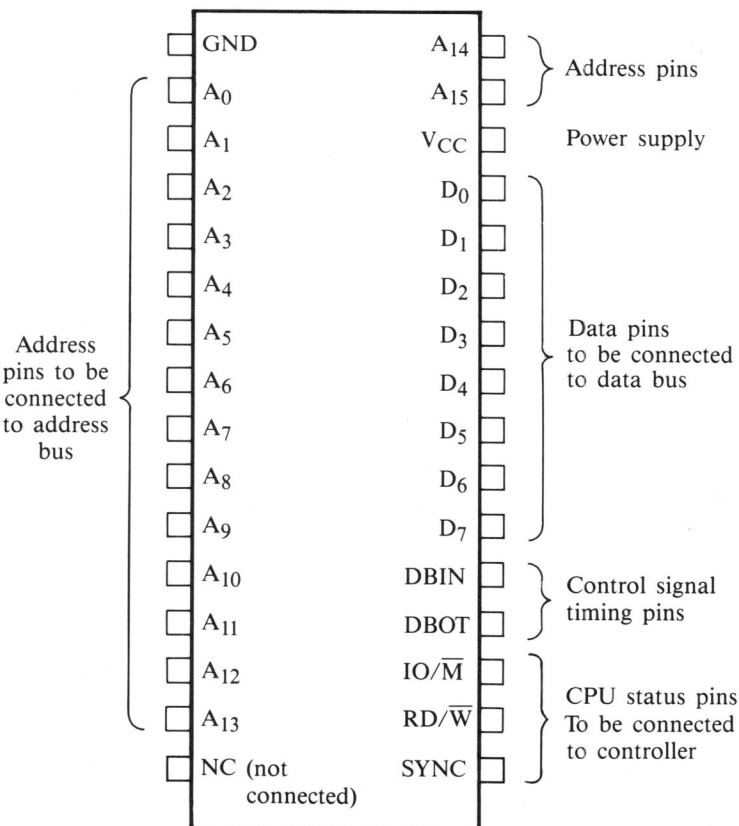

FIGURE 2-14. Pin configuration for microprocessor of Figure 2-11.

2-6

SUMMARY

CPUs are implemented with microprocessors; in fact, the two have become synonymous. The CPU architecture we developed in Figure 2-11 was modeled after Intel's 8080. In developing that architecture we determined that the control unit is the "intelligence" of the microprocessor and is a special-purpose dedicated computer within the microprocessor. The CU implements the execution of program instructions and in doing so controls all other function blocks within the CPU architecture. The CU gets its ability to implement the execution of instructions from its microprogram, which is written by the microprocessor's designers and programmed into the CU during manufacturing. We also determined that the microprocessor has two 16-bit registers with which to supply a 16-bit address necessary for addressing memory. They are the program counter and the data counter. The program counter is used to fetch instructions, and the data counter is used to address data. The data counter is formed from register pairs. When an instruction fetch is being performed, the CU causes the instruction register to latch the instruction machine code from the internal data bus. The instruction is decoded by the IR decoder and executed by the CU. It was observed that very definite cyclic procedures are followed in fetching and executing instructions.

When writing programs the user uses human-oriented codes called mnemonics, which must be assembled into machine code before being executed by the CPU. If assembly is done by the user, it is termed hand assembly. Assembly is often done by a computer program known as an assembler.

Many details have been purposely omitted from this chapter since its purpose was to introduce only the most important concepts. Greater detail will be given when we undertake the study of specific microprocessors.

REVIEW QUESTIONS AND PROBLEMS

1. Describe the distinction between a microprocessor and a microcomputer and state why it is incorrect to refer to a microprocessor as "a computer on a chip."

2. Suppose that you were asked to describe a microprocessor with an architecture as shown in Figure 2-11. How would you describe it in a generalized fashion so that a person knowledgeable as to microprocessors would have a feeling for its capabilities? Keep the description as brief as possible, no more than a paragraph.

3. What function does the ALU serve within the CPU architecture?

4. If a CPU does not have an internal scratch-pad memory, what might be a resulting disadvantage of using that CPU?

5. What function is served by the PC? Describe briefly how the PC implements that function.

6. Why is the address latch necessary in the CPU architecture of Figure 2-11?

7. Relative to CPU architecture, name the various means by which the CPU of Figure 2-11 can address memory and I/O.

8. Suppose that you were shown the pin configuration for a microprocessor, such as that shown in Figure 2-14, and there were 20 address pins and 16 data pins. What conclusions would you arrive at relative to the "horsepower" of this machine (microprocessor)?

9. The CPU architecture of Figure 2-11 shows a function block titled "register selector." Discuss the purpose of such a block.

10. What are condition flags, and how are they utilized by the user when writing programs?

11. Discuss the IR, IR decoder, and CU of Figure 2-11. Your discussion is to be organized so as to point out their interrelationship.

12. Design an IR decoder that will decode two instructions, one having binary code 1110 1100 and the other with the code 1000 0000.

13. Define the term "microprogram" and discuss its relationship to executing program instructions.

14. Discuss each CU output signal of Figure 2-11, that is, DBIN, DBOT, $\overline{IO/M}$, and so on. Orient your discussion toward the system's use of these signals.

15. Design controller logic that will generate control signals $\overline{MEM\ W}$, $\overline{I/O\ W}$, and $\overline{I/O\ R}$, similar to the circuit of Figure 2-12.

16. Define CPU status signals and discuss their purpose.

17. From Tables 2-2 and 2-3, determine the binary codes for the following instructions.
    (a) MOV F, A
    (b) STR F
    (c) ADD E TO C

CHAPTER 3

The 8080 Microprocessor and Its Essential Support Chips

3-1 INTRODUCTION

In Chapter 2 a somewhat general CPU architecture was developed based on the microcomputer architecture of Figure 1-12. It was stated that a microprocessor is used to implement the CPU portion of the system; therefore, it can also be said that Chapter 2 developed a generalized microprocessor architecture. Since no standard generic microprocessor architecture exists, the microprocessor of Chapter 2 was modeled after a specific device, Intel's 8080. In this chapter the 8080 will be studied. As we shall see, the microprocessor architecture of Chapter 2 will be different from that of the 8080, yet very similar.

The reader may have noticed from the table of contents that there is no general treatment for any of the other function blocks of Chapter 1, such as the controller, clock, and so on. The reason for this is that these other function blocks are support function blocks to the CPU. Being support devices, their architecture is tailored to a specific microprocessor. Hence the study of essential support devices will be included in the chapters that study specific microprocessors.

The intent of this chapter is to study the 8080 and its essential support chips, which are the 8228 (controller) and 8224 (clock). In the later part of this chapter these three chips will be configured in a *primary standard system* (Figure 3-15).

However, as we know from Chapter 1, more than the CPU, controller, and clock are required for a complete system. Chapter 4 will introduce memory and I/O and interface them with the essential primary system of this chapter (Figure 3-15), which will result in a simple microprocessor-based system.

3-2
8080 MICROPROCESSOR ARCHITECTURE

The 8080 microprocessor's architecture is shown in Figure 3-1. Comparing Figure 3-1 with Figure 2-11, we see many similarities in architecture. The following are some obvious differences.

1. The scratch-pad memory/data counters of Figure 2-11 are termed simply *register array*. Also, registers F and G of Figure 2-11 are labeled H and L in Figure 3-1.
2. Figure 2-11 has data paths between the internal data bus and registers B, C, D, E, F, and G, whereas Figure 3-1 does not.
3. Figure 3-1 has two temporary registers (W and Z) that Figure 2-11 does not have.
4. Figure 3-1 shows a temporary register instead of register Y.
5. The ALU of Figure 3-1 has a function block labeled *decimal adjust*, whereas Figure 2-11 does not.
6. The control unit of Figure 2-11 is labeled the *timing and control unit* in Figure 3-1. Also the timing and control unit of Figure 3-1 shows additional input and output signals to those of the CU of Figure 2-11.
7. Figure 3-1 has a 16-bit register termed the *stack pointer* (SP), whereas Figure 2-11 does not.

Brief explanations of these differences will now be given. A better understanding of these explanations will be gained later in the chapter when we become more detailed in our studies.

The difference in names noted in item 1 is just that—different names. For difference 2, Figure 3-1 was represented without the detail of Figure 2-11. Figure 3-1 assumes the reader knows that some sort of data path must exist between the registers and the internal data bus. The temporary registers W and Z referred to in item 3 are registers used by the 8080 for CPU internal operations. This simply means that the user cannot directly program data into them as can be done for A, B, C, and so on. That is, W and Z are nonprogrammable, whereas A, B, C, and so on, are programmable. As we trace instruction execution we shall see how the 8080 uses W and Z. The difference referred to in item 4 has to do with the 8080 having one programmable register (A) for ALU operations. The nonprogrammable register (*temporary register*), which serves as a second input to the ALU, is used by the 8080 to expedite ALU-related instructions. Once some example instructions are executed using Figure 3-1, we will see how the 8080 utilizes the temporary register. It should be mentioned here that some microprocessors have two programmable accumulators, as was the case in Figure 2-11. The addition of the decimal adjust function block stated in item 5 is a

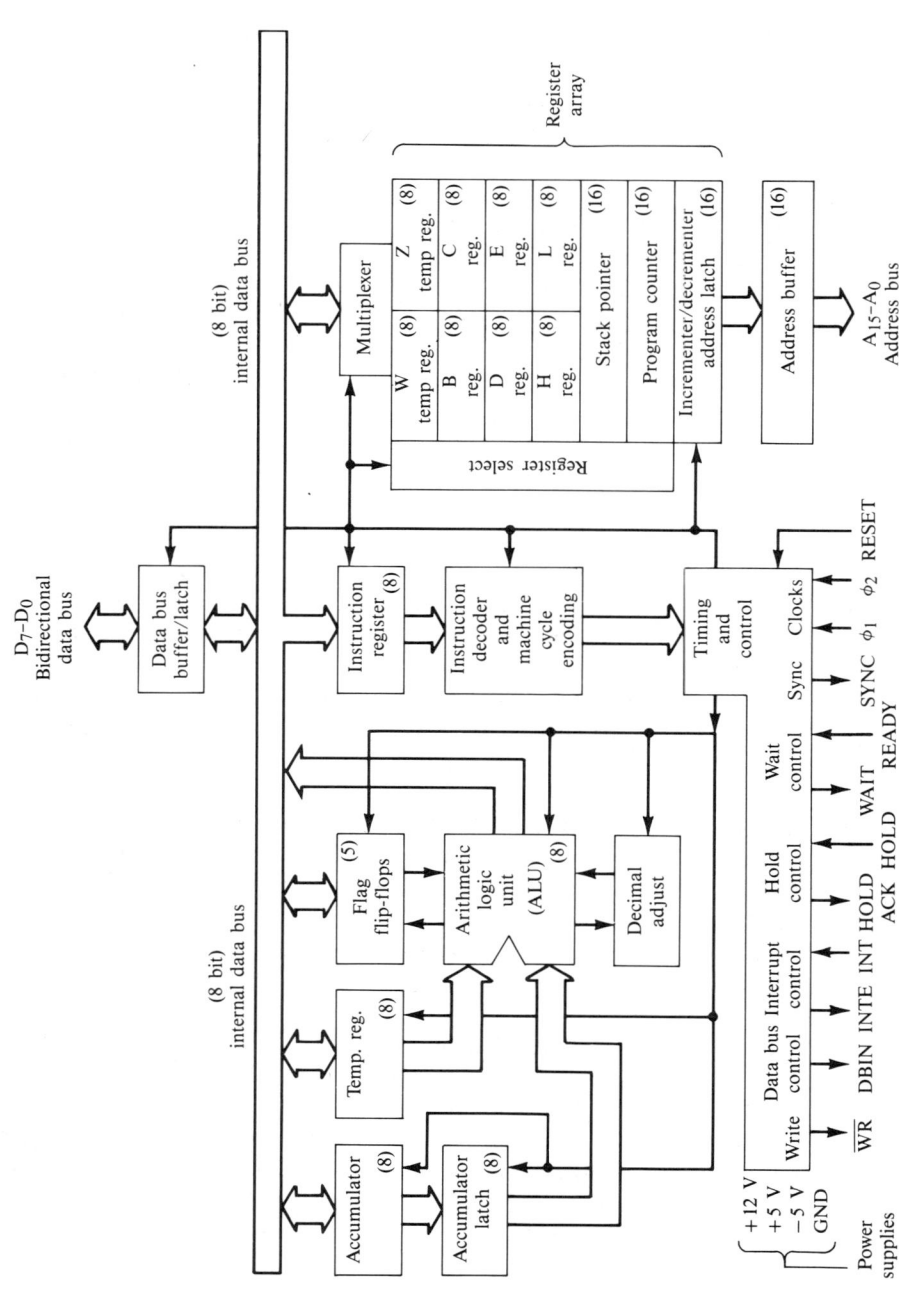

FIGURE 3-1. 8080 architecture. (Courtesy of Intel Corp.)

3-2 8080 MICROPROCESSOR ARCHITECTURE

feature of the 8080 that allows the user to adjust the 8-bit contents of accumulator A to form a 4-bit *binary-coded decimal* (BCD). This is accomplished via the execution of an instruction, DAA. From item 6 we see that Figure 3-1 shows the control unit of Figure 2-11 labeled as the timing and control unit. This is simply a difference in names. For that reason we will continue to refer to that function block as the CU. As for the input and output signals of the 8080's CU, these signals are much like the timing signals (DBIN, DBOT, and SYNC) referred to in Chapter 2. For now, let it suffice to state simply that they perform timing and control functions.

The difference referred to in item 7 is the addition of the stack pointer. First let a definition be given for the stack, and then the stack pointer will be more easily understood. The *stack* is a portion of memory (random access memory, or RAM) *set aside by the user* for the purpose of storing data temporarily. "Data" is meant here in the broadest sense, as any 8-bit binary number. It is the stack that allows a microprocessor to be interrupted by an I/O device and not lose any CPU register data while it is servicing the interrupting device. It does so by storing CPU register contents in the stack when interrupted, thereby freeing CPU registers for "new" data to be processed. Once the microprocessor has completed servicing the interrupting device, it will retrieve the data stored on the stack and return them to the register where they resided before the interrupt. As we shall see, the stack can be used to store other types of data, but regardless, the stack pointer is the addressing register for the stack. (Notice that it is 16 bits in size, as required for addressing memory.) Whenever the stack is to be addressed, the stack pointer will supply the memory address on the system's address bus.

To make certain that the introduction of the SP has not confused the reader, let us quickly review the three different means the microprocessor has to address memory.

1. The PC, which is used to address memory for instructions. Therefore, the contents of any memory location addressed by the PC will be latched by the IR if the instruction fetched is a single 8-bit code.
2. The DC, which is formed by register pairs, is used to address memory for data storage and retrieval. Data accessed by a DC is never latched by the IR, but instead by CPU registers A, B, C, and so on, depending on the specific instruction.
3. Addresses supplied by the SP are always used to store or retrieve data from that area of memory *defined* (by the user) as the stack. Even though both the DC and SP are used to address memory for the purpose of storing or retrieving data, they differ in "mechanics." Data stored on the stack is often data temporarily removed from a register(s) which is to be returned at a later time, such as after the completion of an interrupt. There are instances other than interrupts when the stack is used; however, the mechanics of accessing the stack are the same. Accessing of the stack is always done in a predetermined, organized, cyclic manner, and because of this predetermined cyclic use of the SP, microprocessor designers have been able to make some functions of the SP *automatic*, via the CU's microprogram, whereas the DC's

use is not as predictable and therefore *not automatic*. Using some instructions involving the SP will clarify its purpose and use.

The reason the term "stack" is used to describe this user-defined portion of memory is that the microprocessor stacks the data of registers to be "saved" (stored), much like stacking plates. Using this analogy of stacking plates, we realize that if it is desired to retrieve the first plate stacked, all plates would have to be retrieved in exactly reverse order. This type of stack is known as a *first in, last out* (FILO). There are some stacks which are like having the data stored on a unidirectional lazy susan. This means that the first data loaded into the stack will be the first data retrieved from the stack, or *first in, first out* (FIFO). The 8080 utilizes the FILO stack operation.

Let us return our attention to the timing- and control-related signals of the CU as shown in Figure 3-1. These signals can be categorized into three groups:

1. Timing.
2. Memory and I/O initiated.
3. CPU initialization.

The first group, timing, consists of the signals φ_1, φ_2, SYNC, DBIN, and $\overline{WR}$. These signals will now be discussed.

Timing Signals

φ_1 and φ_2. The φ_1 and φ_2 signals are pulses that are provided by the clock. They are nonoverlapping, that is, out of phase, and provide the primary timing for the microprocessor. All other timing is derived from these signals. Since φ_1 and φ_2 provide the primary timing, they are known as *clock signals*. For this text it is assumed that the clock signals will be generated by a support chip, the 8224, to be examined later.

SYNC. The SYNC pulse is generated by the CU to indicate the *beginning of a CPU operation*. This allows other external devices, which must be synchronized with the CPU, to utilize the SYNC pulse for that purpose.

DBIN. As was the case for the CPU of Chapter 2, DBIN represents the data bus input. Any time the CPU is to input data (data or instructions) from the data bus, DBIN will be active. The CU will activate DBIN over the proper time interval that is required by the microprocessor to latch the data off the data bus. As we shall see, DBIN will be gated with other signals in order to generate control signals for the control bus. These control signals will be used to enable the gating of memory or I/O data onto the data bus during the time interval during which the microprocessor is in the input mode.

$\overline{WR}$. $\overline{WR}$ is active (active low) whenever the microprocessor is outputting data (performing a write operation) on the system data bus for memory or I/O. When $\overline{WR}$ is active, it means that for this time interval the data output by the microprocessor onto the data bus is stable and therefore can be latched by memory or I/O. $\overline{WR}$ will be gated with other signals in order to generate control bus signals that can be used by memory and I/O to latch data from the data bus.

The more important aspects of the discussion on the 8080's timing signals are that the SYNC indicates the beginning of a new CPU operation and that DBIN indicates that the CPU is reading from memory or I/O, while $\overline{WR}$ indicates that a CPU write operation to memory or I/O is being performed.

The second category of CU signals is the memory and I/O initiated group. An examination of these signals will now be undertaken.

Memory and I/O Initiated Signals

HOLD. Whenever this input is activated, the CPU will enter a hold state by relinquishing control, and use, of the address bus, data bus, and control bus. It does so via the CU, causing the tri-state outputs of both the data bus buffer/latch and the address buffer to enter the high-Z state. The control bus is put in the high-Z state via the controller. With the CPU electrically isolated from the address and data buses, an external device may take control of these buses. That is, the external device may store data in memory directly simply by first supplying an address on the address bus and then loading the data to be stored on the data bus. This, of course, is a DMA operation, as discussed in Chapter 1. It is also possible to read data directly from memory using DMA. In either case when a hold is requested, the CPU will complete the execution of the instruction presently in its IR at the time of the request. The CPU then enters the hold state and so indicates with an acknowledgment signal (recall handshaking). The acknowledge signal (HLDA) is used to enable the external device to begin accessing memory for the DMA operation (read or write, whichever is the case).

HLDA. HLDA represents "hold acknowledge." This CU output signal completes the handshake for a hold (DMA) requested by acknowledging that the CPU has entered a hold state. When HLDA becomes active, the requesting I/O device may take control of the control, address, and data buses. Hence HLDA will be used to enable I/O to begin the DMA process. The HLDA output is actually that of a flip-flop which the CU sets and resets accordingly.

READY. When memory or I/O is addressed for a read or write operation, the addressed device *must* be ready for the transaction. Some devices cannot respond in the required time frame of the microprocessor; that is, their *access time* is too long. The 8080 provides the READY input to overcome this problem when relatively slow memory or I/O devices are used. As an example, whenever the 8080 addresses either memory or I/O for a read operation, the CU checks the logic state of the READY input before generating timing signal DBIN (recall that DBIN provides timing for read-type control signals). If the READY input is active (high), the 8080 proceeds with its read operation by generating DBIN; however, if the READY input is low, the 8080 will "wait" until READY is high before continuing. When READY is low, the 8080 will enter and remain in a wait state; that is, the CPU will mark time by "idling." The same can be said for write operations except that $\overline{\text{WR}}$ is the timing signal generated when READY is high. The reason the CPU must idle during wait states is that the CPU cannot complete execution of read or write operations until the slow device is ready to be read or written to, whichever is the case. The addressed slow device must generate the ready signal in accordance with its access time.

WAIT. This output signal is the acknowledgment that the microprocessor is in a wait state. When the 8080 enters a wait state this output becomes active (high). The signal could be used to enable or disable external devices during wait states; this depends on the system requirements. Often this output signal is of little value to the system and as a result is left unconnected.

INT. This is the interrupt request input signal. Whenever an external device (I/O) requests the service of the microprocessor, it may make that request known to the 8080 by driving INT active (high). The 8080 will respond to the request

1. If the interrupt input (INT) has not been disabled by program instruction DI, nor is the CPU in a hold state. The user can disable and enable INT via program instructions DI and EI, respectively.
2. If INT is enabled. In this case the 8080 will respond to the interrupt at the completion of execution of the instruction in the IR at the time of the interrupt request.
3. During a programmed halt if INT is enabled. The user can program the microprocessor to enter an idle state using the HLT (halt) instruction. When this instruction appears in a program, the CPU will idle until an interrupt request is made via the INT input.

Be certain to note that for an interrupt request to be acknowledged by the CPU, the CPU must not be in a hold state (DMA) as well as having INT enabled.

INTE. This output signal is the output of a flip-flop and represents "interrupt enable." Whenever the CPU is disabled from acknowledging an interrupt request, this flip-flop is in the low state. INTE will be reset (low state) by the CU when

1. The CPU accepts an interrupt request. INT is auutomatically disabled when the CPU accepts an interrupt request and therefore the CPU cannot be interrupted again until execution of the EI instruction.
2. INT is disabled via program instruction DI. To set INTE the instruction EI must be given.
3. The CPU is initialized using the reset input signal. This input, which will be discussed shortly, when active (driven high) will cause INT to be disabled and hence INTE to be reset. Thus, after a reset of the CPU, no interrupts will be acknowledged until the EI has been executed.

The remaining one of the three CU control-related signals to be discussed is the CPU initialization group.

CPU Initialization Signals

RESET. When activated this input signal will cause the PC of the CPU to be reset (PC = 0000 0000 0000 0000) by the CU as well as the INTE and HLDA flip-flops. Hence, after the RESET input is activated (driven high), the CPU will go to memory location zero to fetch the next instruction (PC = 0000 0000 0000 0000). Until the user gives the instruction EI following a reset, the CPU *will not acknowledge* (INTE = 0) any interrupt request. Also, since a reset causes the HLDA to be reset (HLDA = 0), this would disable any DMA in progress (see HOLD and HLDA), which would be necessary since the CPU will be entering an instruction-fetch cycle following a reset and therefore must have control of both the address and data buses. A reset does not affect any registers (A, B, C, etc.), condition flags, or the stack pointer.

Other signals observed from Figure 3-1 are the output signals A_0 through A_{15} going to the address bus, and D_0 through D_7, which are the bidirectional signals going to the data bus. Let us begin with A_0–A_{15}.

A_0–A_{15} Address Signals. It is these output signals that the CPU uses to address both memory and I/O. Let us first discuss A_0–A_{15} being used to address memory.

Addressing Memory. Similar to the process described in Chapter 2, when the CPU is reading or writing from or to memory, the CU will first cause the contents of the PC or DC to be latched by the incrementer/decrementer address latch. Then the CU will activate the address buffer (take it out of the high-Z state) so that the latched address will be loaded on the address bus, which will access memory. As we will see later, a control signal will also be generated and used in conjunction with the address on the address bus. Specifically, this control signal will be used to enable the addressed memory chip and therefore provide proper timing. It is generated either from DBIN (read operations) or $\overline{WR}$ (write operations), depending on the CPU operation (CPU status).

Whenever memory is being addressed, all 16 address outputs (A_0–A_{15}) are used. Then from Equation (2-10) up to 65,536 memory locations can be addressed; that is, the 8080 has the capacity (not all have to be used) to address 65,536 memory locations.

Addressing I/O. Addressing I/O occurs *only* as the result of an instruction. There are just two such instructions, IN ADDR and OUT ADDR. Both of these instructions require two 8-bit codes. The first 8 bits comprise the operation (IN or OUT) and the second instruction (ADDR) is an 8-bit address (*port number*) of the I/O device. With an 8-bit port number the IN and OUT instructions can each address 256 I/O devices. To explain how these instructions are executed, we shall begin with the instruction fetch. The CPU first performs an instruction fetch, which means that it first fetches the operation code from memory. Once the operation code (IN or OUT) is latched by the IR, the CU "knows" that it must return to memory to get the *port number of the I/O device*. Hence the CU increments the PC and loads that address on the address bus via the incrementer/decrementer address latch and address buffer of Figure 3-1. Of course, the contents of this addressed memory location is the *port number of the I/O device*. This I/O device address is then loaded onto the system's data bus. The CU latches this data (the address of the I/O device) from the system data bus using the data bus buffer/latch and then loads that 8-bit I/O port number onto the CPU's internal data bus. The CU then selects registers W and Z to latch that I/O port number from the internal data bus. Realize that the *same* 8-bit address now exists in two registers, W and Z. Next, the CU will latch the contents of W and Z into the incrementer/decrementer address latch, from where it is loaded onto the address bus via the address buffer. As a result of the two 8-bit registers (W and Z) being used to copy a single 8-bit I/O address onto the 16-bit address bus, the address bus has a mirrored 8-bit I/O address. That is, A_0–A_7 and A_8–A_{15} are copies of each other (true for I/O addressing *only*).

In summary, address output signals A_0–A_{15} are used to address memory or I/O. When addressing memory, the PC, DC, or SP is used to supply the address, and these are 16-bit addresses. When addressing I/O the CPU uses registers W and Z temporarily to store and supply the 16-bit address to A_0–A_{15}. Under these conditions the 16-bit address furnished is actually an 8-bit address that is duplicated; hence the A_0–A_7 and A_8–A_{15} signals are exact copies.

The bi-directional data signals D_0–D_7 of Figure 3-1 are discussed next.

D_0–D_7 Data Signals. These signals are bidirectional and are responsible for any data communication between the CPU and any external chip, memory, or I/O. In this case "data" is used in the broadest sense and includes instructions. D_0–D_7 signals are received and transmitted over the data bus.

All that remains to be discussed regarding Figure 3-1 are the power supplies indicated in the lower left-hand corner.

Power Supplies

As seen in Figure 3-1, the 8080 requires three power supplies ($+12V$, $+5V$, and $-5V$). These three voltages must meet a 5% tolerance; that is,

$$V_{DD} = +12V \pm 5\%$$

$$V_{CC} = +5V \pm 5\%$$

$$V_{BB} = -5V \pm 5\%$$

Ground is referred to as V_{SS}.

3-3 8080 PIN CONFIGURATION

As seen from Figure 3-2, the 8080 is a 40-pin chip. Comparing Figures 3-1 and 3-2, we see that every input or output signal of Figure 3-1 has a corresponding

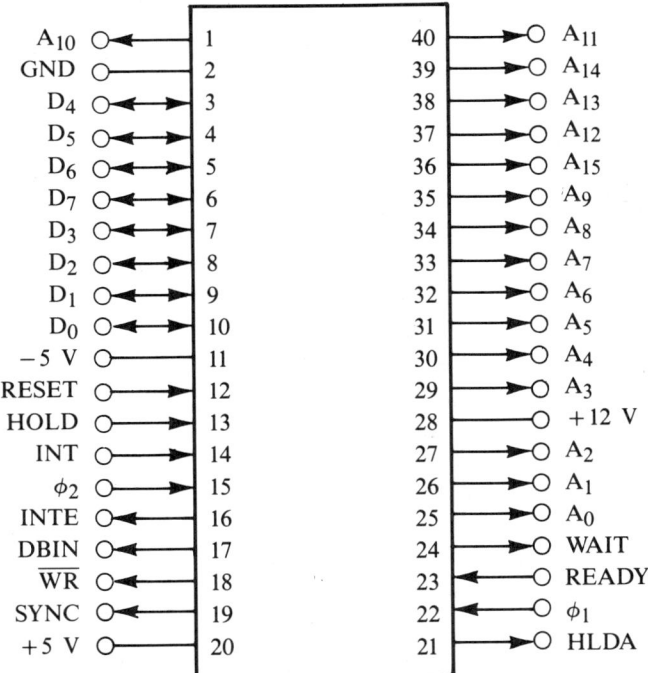

FIGURE 3-2. 8080 pin configuration. (Courtesy of Intel Corp.)

pin shown in Figure 3-2. With the explanations given of the various signals, no discussion need be offered here.

We will now begin to develop the 8080-based primary standard system of Figure 3-15 by examining support chip architectures. The first support chip to be examined is the controller (8228). Next the clock (8224) will be discussed, and then it and the 8228 will be integrated into the 8080 primary standard system. This process of chip examination and their integration with the primary standard system will continue in later chapters until a microcomputer system is developed.

3-4

8228 CONTROLLER ARCHITECTURE AND CONTROL SIGNALS

Recall from Chapter 1 that the controller is the traffic cop of the computer system. From Chapter 2 we also recall that the manner in which the controller is able to control bus traffic is by generating control signals on the control bus. In order to generate these control signals, the CPU provides two types of signals (refer to Figure 2-12). The two types are CPU status and timing (DBIN and $\overline{WR}$), which are generated by the CU of the CPU. Figure 2-11 shows output signals IO/$\overline{M}$ and RD/$\overline{W}$ as being output signals indicative of the CPU status. The 8080 does not have dedicated outputs such as those to indicate the CPU status. Rather, the 8080 conserves the number pins required to indicate CPU status through time sharing. The 8080 CPU status is an 8-bit code which is output on the data bus, via data bus pins D_0–D_7, by the CU during a specific time interval. Then in order for the controller to interpret this code, *it must latch it off the data bus* during the time interval during which it is present. Thus the 8228 will require a latch as part of its architecture.

Once the controller has latched the CPU status from the data bus, it must decode that status in order to "know" what control signal to generate. Just as in the case of the IR decoder, a CPU status decoder will be required. As for all decoders, this will simply require combinational logic (AND and OR gates), which is termed a *gating array*.

Figure 3-3 illustrates both the architecture and pin configuration for the 8228. As shown in Figure 3-3, the 8228 architecture does contain a status latch and a gating array. An additional function block exists and that is the bidirectional bus driver.

To reiterate, the purpose of the status latch of Figure 3-3 is to latch the CPU status's binary code from the data bus. Latching will occur as the result of a strobe pulse labeled "status strobe" ($\overline{STSTB}$), which is generated by the clock. Circuitry to accomplish the status latch function block is similar to that shown in Figure 3-4.

As shown in Figure 3-4, when the 8080 outputs the CPU status 8-bit code onto the data bus, it will be latched by the status latch when the clock-generated pulse $\overline{STSTB}$ (active low) is applied. The strobe pulse $\overline{STSTB}$ must occur synchronously with the 8080's placing of the CPU status code on the data bus. To generate $\overline{STSTB}$, we must recall that the CPU will output its status at the beginning of every new operation. Also, coinciding with the outputting of the CPU status, the CU will output a synchronizing pulse (SYNC) to indicate the start of a new operation by the CPU. Thus a timing diagram of SYNC and CPU status on the data bus relative to the primary timing φ_1 and φ_2 is shown in Figure 3-5.

Notice in Figure 3-5 that φ_1 and SYNC occur coincidentally (dashed time interval) with the CPU status code appearing on the data bus, which indicates that φ_1 and SYNC can be used to generate $\overline{STSTB}$. Just such a circuit which generates $\overline{STSTB}$ is illustrated in Figure 3-6. As we shall see later, the circuit to generate $\overline{STSTB}$ will be an integral part of the clock chip (8224).

Next let us examine the various 8-bit combinations that are used by the CU to indicate the CPU status code. The possible number of combinations that could exist is 256; however, from Figure 3-7 we see that only 10 are necessary. Also notice that the term "status *word*" is used to describe this 8-bit code, where "word" is used to describe the bit size of the microprocessor. As stated earlier, the 8080 is an 8-bit microprocessor; hence it would be correct to describe any group of 8-bit codes on which it is to operate as being a word (relative to the 8080). When discussing 16-bit microprocessors, a word is comprised of 16 bits.

Referring to Figure 3-7, we see that the CPU status word (8-bit code) that will be output by the CU (on pins D_0–D_7 of the CPU) to indicate that the CPU is presently performing an instruction-fetch cycle is $D_0 = 0$, $D_1 = 1$, $D_2 = 0$, $D_3 = 0$, $D_4 = 0$, $D_5 = 1$, $D_6 = 0$, and $D_7 = 1$. The CPU status word indicating an instruction fetch is labeled ①. As another example, status word

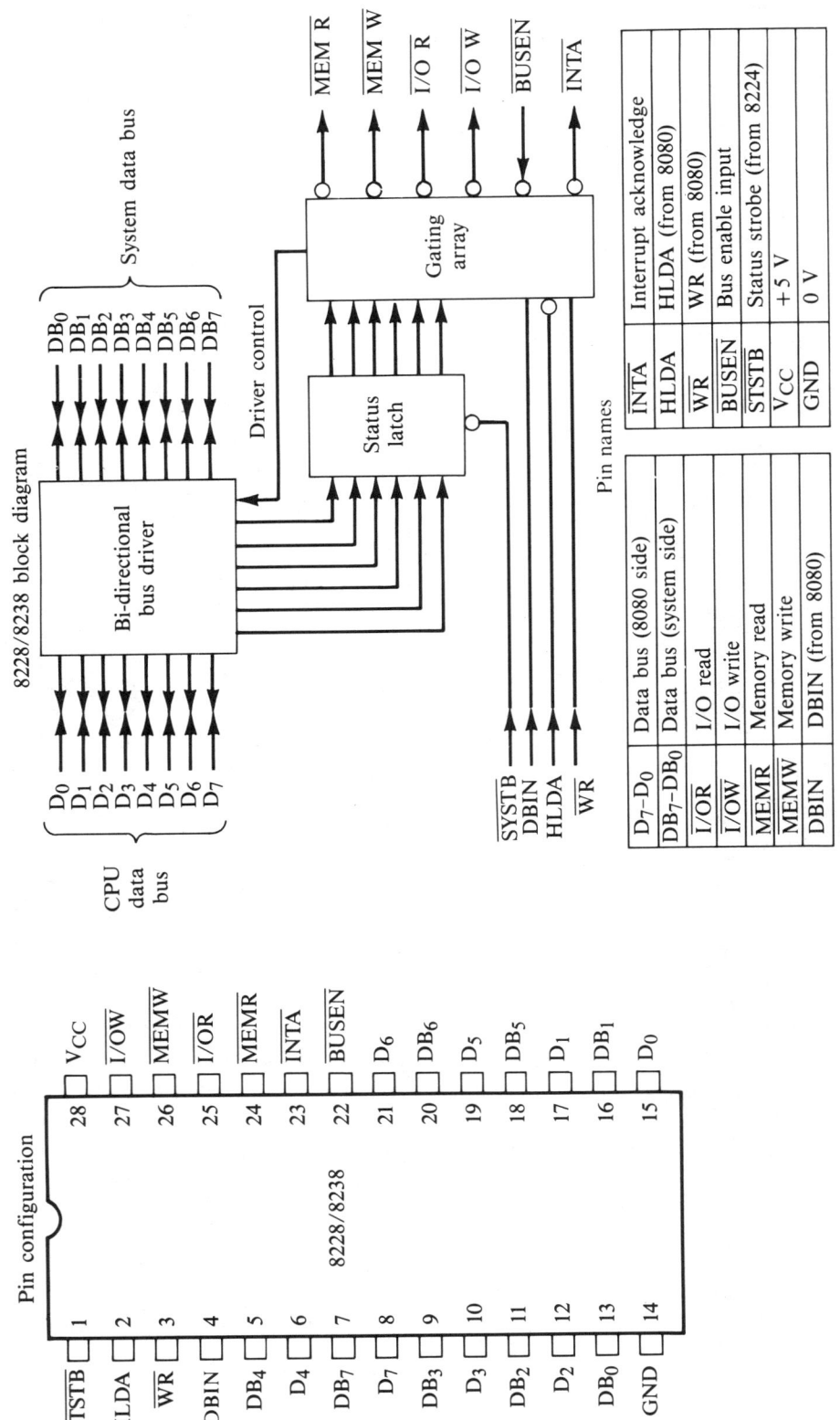

FIGURE 3-3. 8228 architecture and pin configuration. (Courtesy of Intel Corp.)

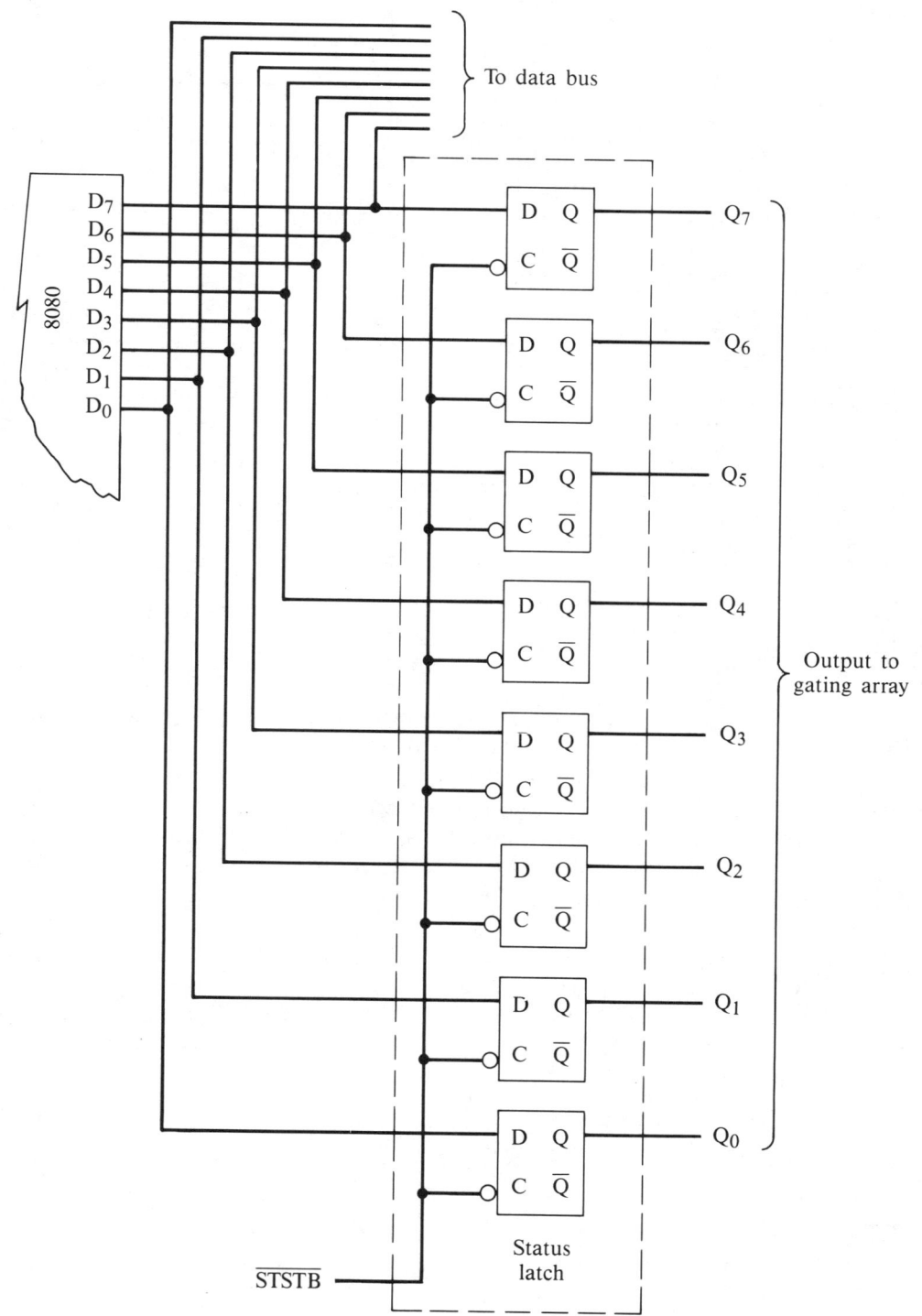

FIGURE 3-4. CPU status word latch.

3-4 8228 CONTROLLER ARCHITECTURE AND CONTROL SIGNALS

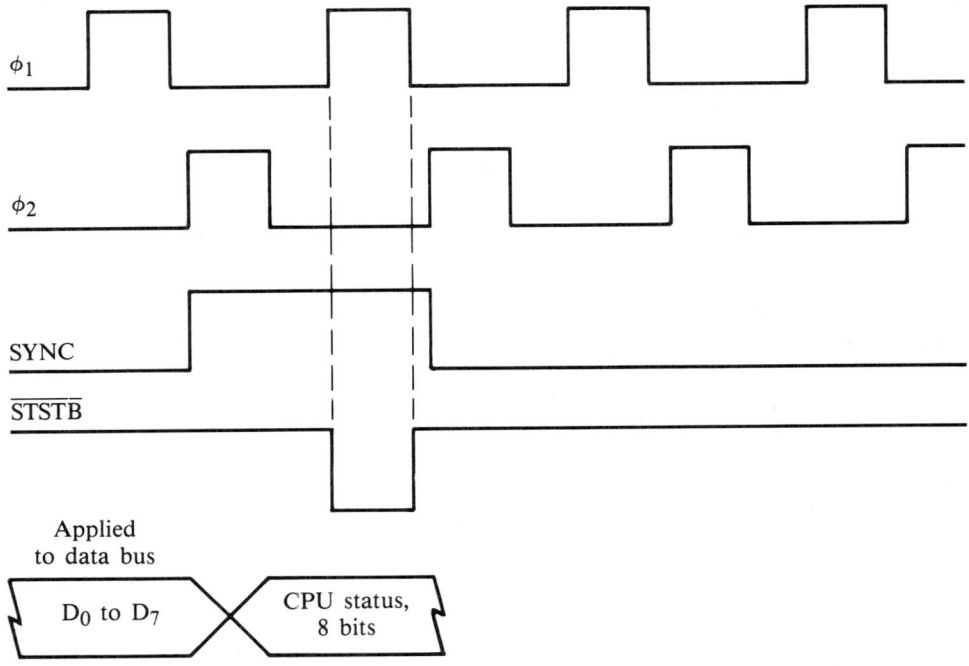

FIGURE 3-5. Timing diagram of strobe-pulse $\overline{STSTB}$.

⑥ indicates an input read, such as the CPU reading from I/O, and for this operation $D_1 = 1$ and $D_6 = 1$, while all others are low.

Recall from previous discussions that these CPU status words are latched by the status latch (Figure 3-3) and then decoded by the gating array, which in turn generates control signals. Figure 3-7 indicates which control signal is generated from each CPU status word. For instance, status word ②, Memory Read, is decoded to generate control signal $\overline{MEMR}$, which in turn is used to enable memory (refer to Figure 2-12) for the read operation.

From Figure 3-7 we notice that data bus pins D_0–D_7 of the 8080 are associated with specific CPU operations. That is, if D_6 is high when the CPU status word is being output on the data bus, this indicates that the CPU is performing an

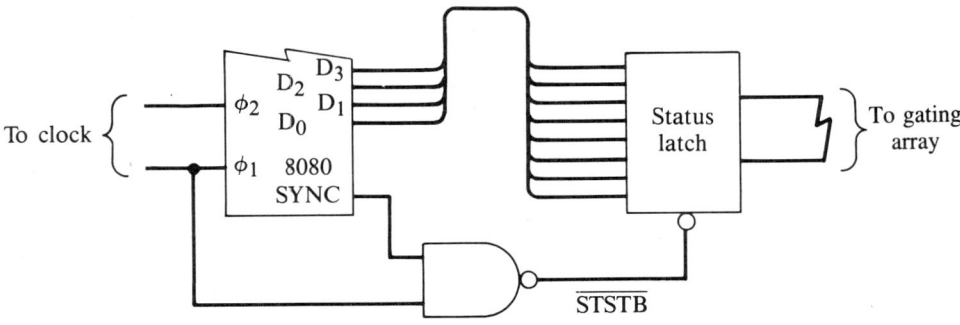

FIGURE 3-6. Logic to generate strobe pulse $\overline{STSTB}$.

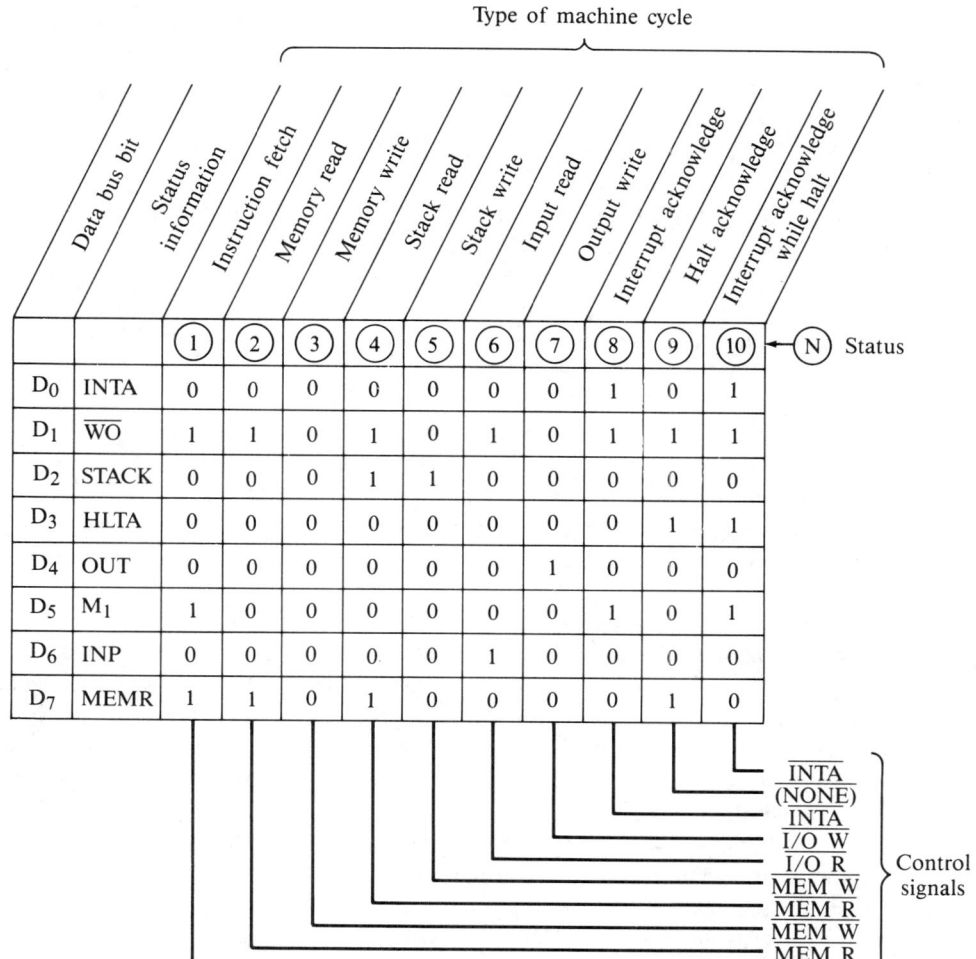

FIGURE 3-7. 8080 CPU status word chart. (Courtesy of Intel Corp.)

input read (status word ⑥). D_2 is high whenever the CPU is doing a stack read (④) or stack write operation. The status information given by D_0–D_7 is indicated by the abbreviations shown in Figure 3-7 in the "Status Information" column. To relate more clearly why specific status word bits are high or low for certain CPU operations requires an explanation of the operations the abbreviations represent.

- *INTA (D_0)*: Represents "interrupt acknowledge." When this bit is high, the status word is indicating that the CPU is acknowledging an interrupt request.
- $\overline{WO}$ *(D_1)*: When D_1 is low, the CPU is performing a write operation to either memory or I/O.
- *STACK (D_2)*: This bit, when high, indicates that a stack read or write operation is being performed.

3-4 8228 CONTROLLER ARCHITECTURE AND CONTROL SIGNALS

- *HLTA (D_3)*: When high for a CPU status word, this bit indicates acknowledgment of a halt.
- *OUT (D_4)*: If this bit is high, it indicates that the CPU is performing a write (outputting) operation to I/O.
- *M_1 (D_5)*: For D_5 to be high for a CPU status word, the CPU is executing an instruction-fetch operation.
- *INP (D_6)*: This bit indicates that the CPU is performing a read (inputting) operation from an input I/O device.
- *MEMR (D_7)*: Signifies that the CPU is reading from memory. The designation MEMR for bit D_7 is not to be confused with control signal $\overline{\text{MEM R}}$. As we shall see, control signal $\overline{\text{MEM R}}$ is generated as a result of MEMR being high.

Now that we understand the meanings of the various bits that made up the CPU status word, let us determine which of those bits are required to generate the control signals of Figures 3-3 and 3-7 ($\overline{\text{INTA}}$, $\overline{\text{I/O W}}$, $\overline{\text{I/O R}}$, $\overline{\text{MEM W}}$, and $\overline{\text{MEM R}}$). Let it be noted that signal $\overline{\text{BUSEN}}$ of Figure 3-3 is not an output signal (note the arrow direction) and therefore is not to be generated by the 8228.

The control signal $\overline{\text{INTA}}$ represents an interrupt acknowledge (active low). We realize that $\overline{\text{INTA}}$ is to be generated as a result of an interrupt request if input INT of the CPU is enabled. Recall our discussion of INT: The CPU could be interrupted during the execution of a program or while it was in the halt state. From Figure 3-7 we see that the CPU status word for an interrupt, which occurs during the execution of a program, is status word ⑧, while ⑩ is the status word resulting from an interrupt request made during a halt state. Now we must compare status words ⑧ and ⑩ and determine the bit or bits that are unique to an interrupt request so that those bit(s) can be used to generate an acknowledgment ($\overline{\text{INTA}}$) of the request. Those bits, which are high for both status words ⑧ and ⑩, are D_0, D_1, and D_5. Searching all status words for the high state of bits D_0, D_1, and D_5, to determine uniqueness, we find that D_0 is unique to an interrupt acknowledge. Of course, this is why Intel labeled pin D_0 "INTA." Then the gating array of Figure 3-3 must decode status words ⑧ and ⑩ and in turn generate control signal $\overline{\text{INTA}}$. To accomplish this, we use flip-flop output Q_0 (Q_0 indicates the logic state of D_0) of Figure 3-4. However, D_0 (INTA) indicates only the event "Interrupt Acknowledge"; it provides no timing. The timing must be provided by one of the CPU's timing signals, which in this case is DBIN. The reason DBIN is active for an interrupt acknowledge is not apparent at this time, but it will be when we study the 8080's instruction set. So for now let us just accept that the CPU's data bus is in the input mode (DBIN active) during an interrupt acknowledge. Since $\overline{\text{INTA}}$ is an active low, a NAND gate will be used to generate $\overline{\text{INTA}}$. That portion of the gating array that could generate $\overline{\text{INTA}}$ is shown in Figure 3-8.

Continuing similar reasoning for the remaining control signals of Figure 3-7 to be generated, we would find:

- $\overline{\text{WO}}$ (D_1): can be used to detect any write operation to be performed by the CPU. This bit will be used to generate memory write ($\overline{\text{MEM W}}$) and I/O

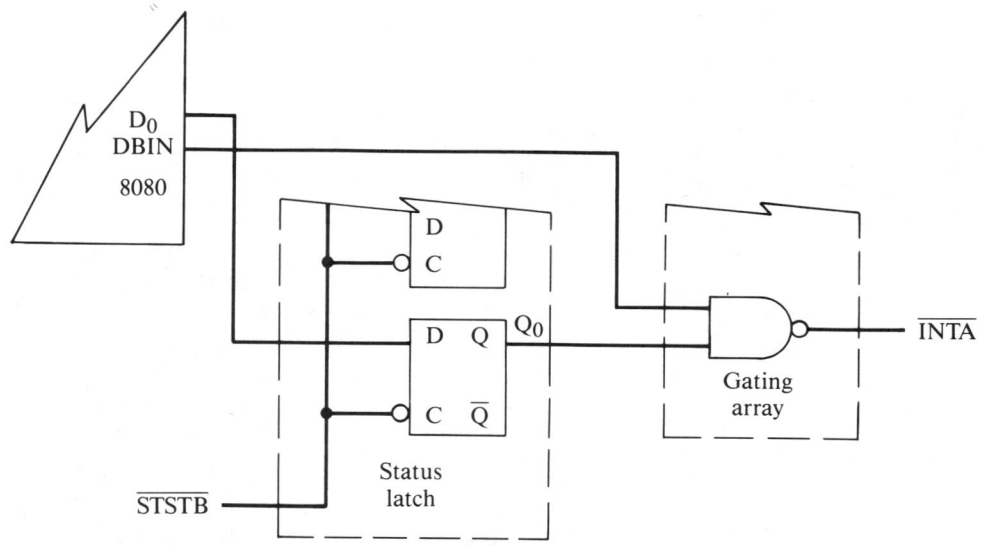

FIGURE 3-8. Logic to generate control signal $\overline{\text{INTA}}$.

write ($\overline{\text{I/O W}}$). The CPU timing signal $\overline{\text{WR}}$ will be used to provide proper timing for these control signals, as shown in Figure 3-9. These two control signals will be used as strobe pulses by memory and I/O to latch data output by the CPU via the data bus.

- *OUT (D_4)*: indicates that the CPU is performing a write operation to I/O rather than to memory. Then bit D_4 can be used to distinguish between write operations to memory or I/O. More specifically, D_4 will be used in the generation of $\overline{\text{I/O W}}$ and inverted to generate $\overline{\text{MEMW}}$, as shown in Figure 3-9.

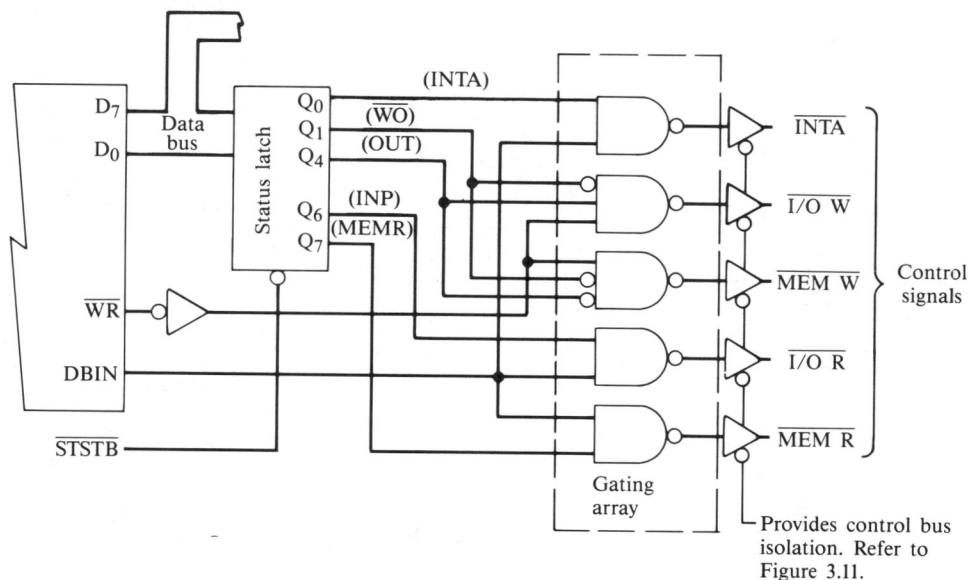

FIGURE 3-9. Logic for generating control signals.

3-4 8228 CONTROLLER ARCHITECTURE AND CONTROL SIGNALS

- *MEMR (D_7)*: will be used to detect memory read operations and when gated with DBIN for timing, will generate $\overline{\text{MEM R}}$. $\overline{\text{MEM R}}$ will be used to gate addressed memory contents on the data bus.
- *INP (D_6)*: is unique to I/O read operations and when gated with DBIN (for timing), the results will produce $\overline{\text{I/O R}}$. $\overline{\text{I/O R}}$ will be used to gate the contents of an addressed I/O input port onto the data bus.

Figure 3-9 illustrates the combinational logic of the gating array which generates the control signals of Figure 3-7. The tri-state buffers of Figure 3-9 are to be discussed later.

Notice that not all status word bits are used. That does not mean that the user cannot use them, but rather, that they are not required to generate the control signals of Figure 3-9. If the user wishes to generate additional control signals, which require that other status word bits be detected, it is the user's option. It should also be mentioned that the control signals of Figure 3-9 could be generated with slightly different status bit utilization than that shown, but these variations are of little concern. Of primary importance are the concepts.

The remaining function block of Figure 3-3 to rationalize is the *bidirectional bus driver*. Conceptually, this function block is not required, but in practice it is often a necessity. Its requirements are due to the current limitation of 8080 data pins D_0–D_7. The current sinking capabilities of these pins is $I_{OL} = 1.7$ mA and the input voltage requirement is $V_{IH} = 3.3$ V minimum. Since even a relatively small 8080-based system often has many chips connected to its data bus (memory and I/O), the current drive capability of the 8080 data pins is exceeded. Also, many of the semiconductor chips might have output voltages (V_{OH}) of 2 to 2.8 V, which will not meet the 3.3-V requirement of the 8080. The solution to this limitation is to buffer pins D_0–D_7. This buffering will have to be bidirectional, since both write and read operations will occur. Also, the buffer must be tri-stated to provide isolation for a DMA. Focusing on a single data pin, say D_n, Figure 3-10 will provide the requirements of a bidirectional data flow and tri-state capability for isolation.

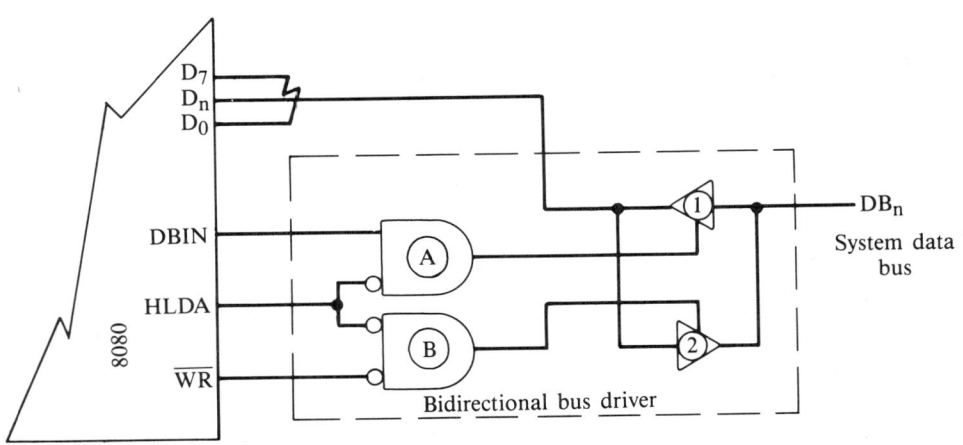

FIGURE 3-10. Line D_n of the bidirectional bus driver.

As an example of how the circuit of Figure 3-10 functions, suppose that the CPU is performing a read operation for either memory or I/O. Under this condition DBIN will be active (high), while $\overline{WR}$ will be inactive (high). Assuming HLDA to be inactive (low), which means that the CPU is not doing a DMA, AND gate A will output a high, while AND gate B will be low. The high from gate A will activate buffer 1 and the low from AND gate B will force buffer 2 into the high-Z state. As a result, the data path direction is from right to left, which is the read direction. For write operations AND gate B will activate driver 2, while driver 1 will be forced in the high-Z state. Notice that if HLDA is high, both buffers 1 and 2 will be forced into the high-Z state, which isolates the 8080 from the system data bus. Of course, HLDA goes active as an acknowledgment of a hold request (DMA), and that requires 8080 isolation.

Adding seven more bidirectional lines to Figure 3-10 would achieve the bidirectional bus driver of Figure 3-3. Before modifying Figure 3-10, notice the driver control line and $\overline{BUSEN}$ signal of Figure 3-3. We will assume that the driver control is similar to the outputs of AND gates A and B. As for $\overline{BUSEN}$ (bus enable), this input signal will force 8080 isolation of the system data bus and control bus when it is inactive (high). To accomplish data bus isolation $\overline{BUSEN}$ must force AND gates A and B low when it is high. Control bus isolation, via $\overline{BUSEN}$, is accomplished by the tri-state buffers of Figure 3-9. Figure 3-11 is Figure 3-10 modified to accommodate seven additional data lines and $\overline{BUSEN}$.

As we can see from Figure 3-11, whenever $\overline{BUSEN}$ is high, AND gates A and B will output low, which in turn will force all buffer/drivers in the high-Z state. Similarly, if HLDA is high, AND gates A and B will output a low, and all buffer/drivers will be forced into the high-Z state. Also, one *can see* that the ORing of HLDA and $\overline{BUSEN}$ will provide control bus isolation via the tri-state buffers of Figure 3-9. At this point one might wonder why data and control bus isolation should occur because of two signals: HLDA and $\overline{BUSEN}$. The reason for HLDA being able to cause data and control bus isolation, via the 8228, and address bus isolation, via the CPU, is due to the necessity of I/O controlling these buses during a DMA, as discussed previously. $\overline{BUSEN}$ allows the CPU to be isolated from the data and control bus while still controlling the address bus. This would enable a designer to use the CPU as an addressing device while some I/O controlled the data and control bus.

Combining the concepts of Figures 3-4, 3-6, 3-9, and 3-11 will enable the reader to view Figure 3-3 with an understanding of how the 8228 accomplishes its functions. To ensure that the reader understands the functions performed, a summary of previous discussions is offered.

The 8228 is the system controller. It is to generate control signals $\overline{I/O\ R}$, $\overline{MEM\ R}$, and so on, and provide CPU isolation from the system data and control bus. Control signals are generated from the CPU status word, which is latched from the CPU data bus by the 8228 and decoded using the gating array. The CPU status word is output by the CPU at the beginning of each CPU operation. CPU isolation from the system data and control bus can be due to either HLDA or $\overline{BUSEN}$ becoming high. When HLDA is active, the CPU is isolated from the address bus as well as the data and control bus. HLDA becomes active as the result of a hold request (DMA) of the CPU, while $\overline{BUSEN}$ can be activated

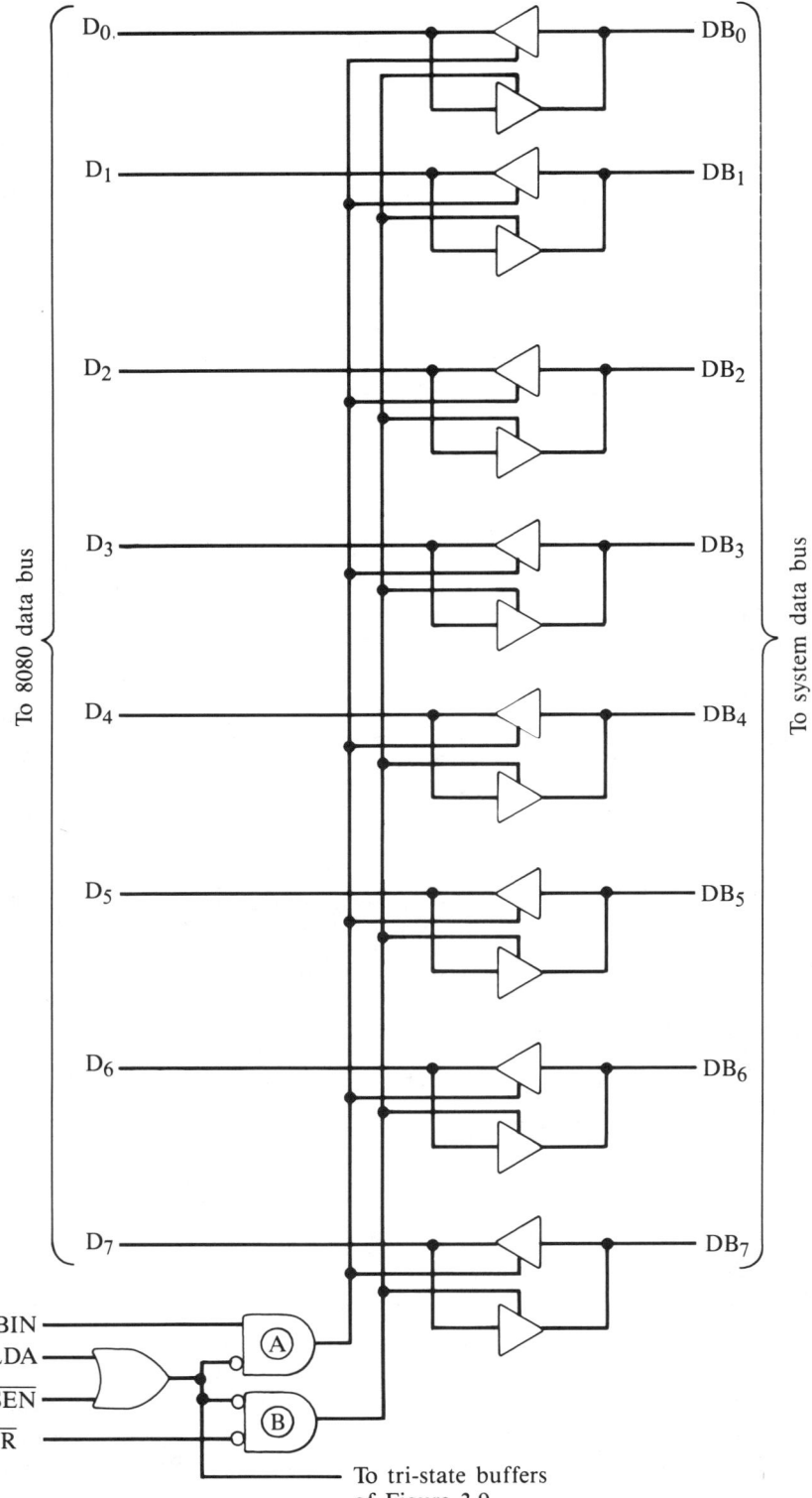

FIGURE 3-11. Bidirectional bus driver of 8228 architecture.

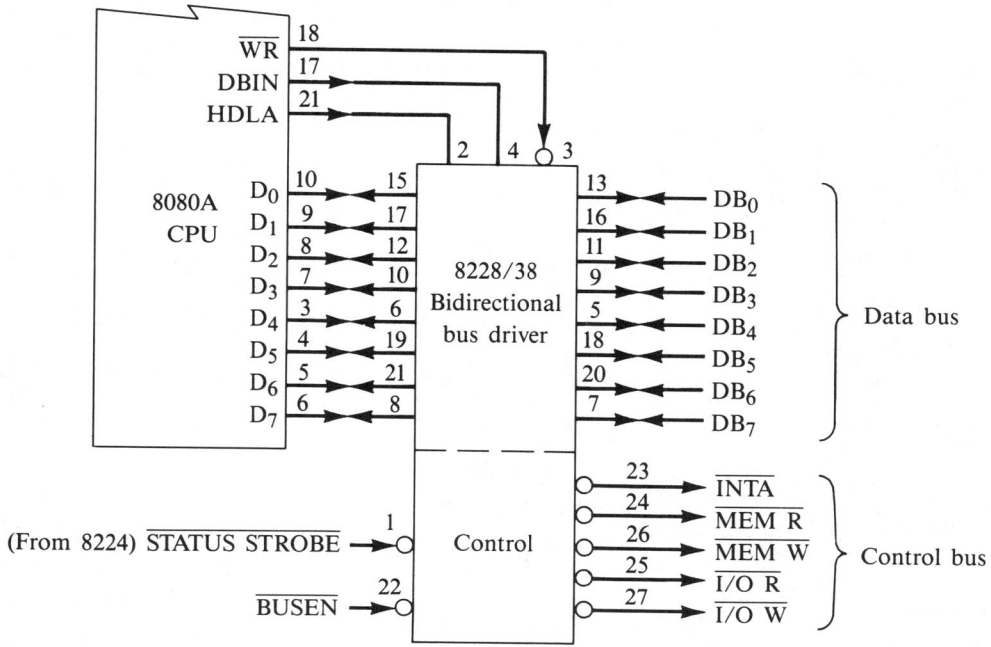

FIGURE 3-12. Wiring diagram of the 8080 and 8228. (Courtesy of Intel Corp.)

any time it is desired to isolate the CPU from the system data and control bus and not isolate it from the address bus. Figure 3-12 is a wiring diagram showing the 8080 and 8228 interfaced with each other. After a discussion of the system's clock (8224), it will be added to Figure 3-12.

3-5

8224 CLOCK ARCHITECTURE AND PIN CONFIGURATION

The next function block of Figure 1-12 to be studied is the clock. To implement the clock, Intel's 8224 will be used. The 8224 architecture and pin configuration are illustrated in Figure 3-13.

The 8224 provides three basic services:

1. Supplies the system's principal timing signals, such as clock pulses (φ_1 and φ_2).
2. Generates a strobe pulse ($\overline{STSTB}$) which is used by the 8228 to latch a status word off the data bus.
3. Synchronizes random (asynchronous) events such as a RESET request or the ready signal from slow memory or I/O.

As seen from Figure 3-13, to generate φ_1 and φ_2 either a crystal (XTAL 1 and 2) or a tank can be used. In either case the frequency from the oscillator block is input to the clock generator, which is a divide-by-9 circuit. This means

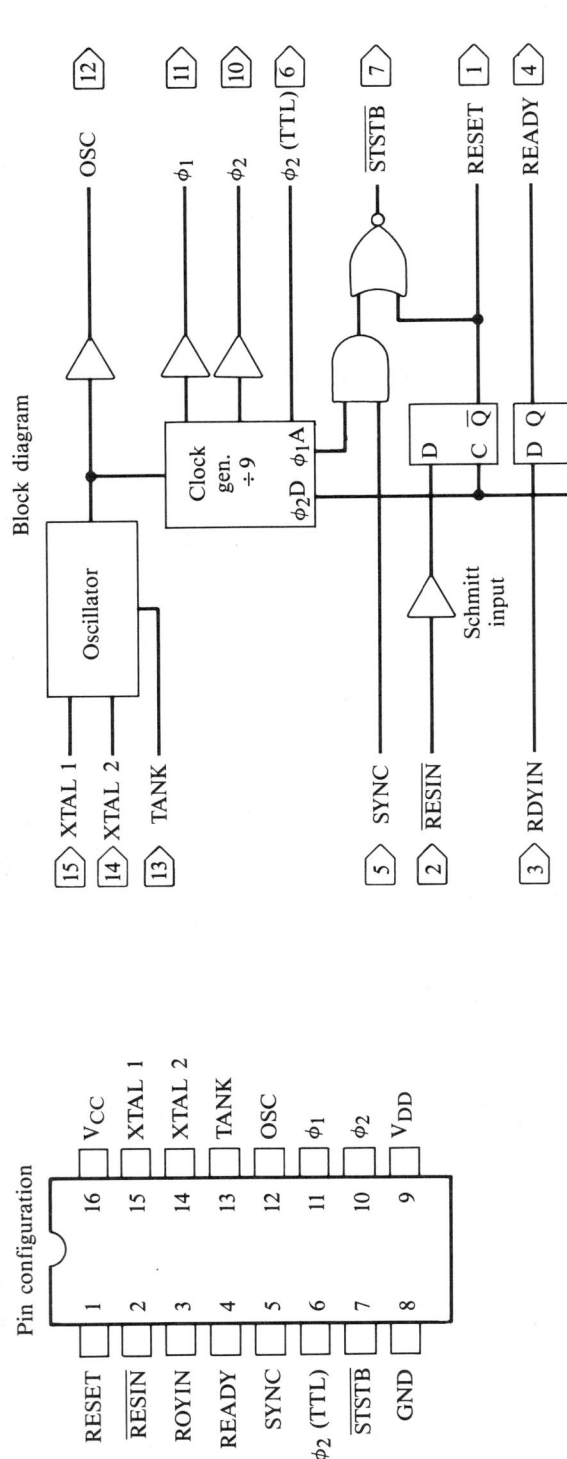

FIGURE 3-13. 8224 architecture and pin configuration. (Courtesy of Intel Corp.)

that an 18-MHz crystal will generate 2-MHz clock pulses φ_1 and φ_2, which for the 8080A is its maximum speed. If the system designer wanted to operate an 8080 at its slowest clock rate of 2 microseconds, which is a pulse repetition rate of 0.5×10^6, a crystal frequency of 4.5 MHz would be used. In addition to φ_1 and φ_2, which are metal-oxide semiconductor (MOS) compatible voltage levels, the clock generator also generates a clock pulse φ_2 (TTL) which is in phase with φ_1 and is TTL compatible. This output could be used as a clock for any TTL logic in the system. Also, a square wave is output on the oscillator. The frequency of this output is the same as that of the crystal. The system designer is free to use this signal in any manner desired. One possible use is as a *baud rate generator* (to be explained later), which is simply a clock for serial I/O devices.

The strobe pulse $\overline{STSTB}$ was utilized in Figure 3-4 and was first generated by the circuitry of Figure 3-6. The timing of $\overline{STSTB}$ is illustrated in Figure 3-5. By comparing the NAND gate of Figure 3-6 to the AND-and-NOR-gate combination of Figure 3-13, we see that they perform essentially the same logic function. That is, the SYNC pulse from 8080 is input to the AND gate of the 8224 and ANDed with φ_1. When both the SYNC pulse and φ_1 are present, the output of the AND gate is high, which in turn is inverted by the NOR gate. This combination results in an active low which corresponds to the $\overline{STSTB}$.

The two asynchronous signals that are synchronized by the 8224 are reset and ready. The input signal $\overline{RESIN}$ (reset input) senses a reset request. From Figure 3-13 we see that this signal is input to a *Schmitt trigger*, which means that the input is voltage-level sensitive. When $\overline{RESIN}$ falls below a threshold voltage of 3.6 V, the Schmitt trigger outputs a low to the D of a D-type flip-flop. On the occurrence of the next clock pulse, φ_2, that flip-flop will be reset. Since the output of that flip-flop is $\overline{Q}$, which is the RESET output, a logic high will result. The reset signal then goes to the 8080. Also notice that a reset also generates a strobe signal $\overline{STSTB}$ via the 8224's NOR gate. The reason $\overline{STSTB}$ must be generated when a reset is performed is that as a consequence of a system reset, the CPU will be forced to perform a *new* operation (an instruction fetch; review our earlier discussion of the 8080 reset input signal) and therefore must output the proper status word on the data bus, which in turn must be latched by the 8228. A suggested circuit to generate $\overline{RESIN}$ is that of Figure 3-14.

Recalling the discussion of the READY input of the 8080, we remember that whenever memory or I/O is addressed by the CPU for a read operation, the CU checks the logic state of the READY input to see if the data from those devices are ready (i.e., the device has the data ready to be gated on the data bus).

If the READY input is high, the CU will activate DBIN and thus the appropriate control signal, $\overline{I/O\ R}$ or $\overline{MEM\ R}$, will be generated, which is used to gate the data onto the data bus (see Figure 2-12). From Figure 3-13 we see that the ready input signal of the 8080 originates from the READY output of the 8224. This output signal is generated as a result of the RDYIN (ready input) being forced high by the addressed slow memory or I/O. Once RDYIN is driven high, that logic state will be latched by the flip-flop shown, which results in the READY output also being high. If the system has no slow memory or I/O, the RDYIN can be tied permanently high (always ready).

3-5 8224 CLOCK ARCHITECTURE AND PIN CONFIGURATION

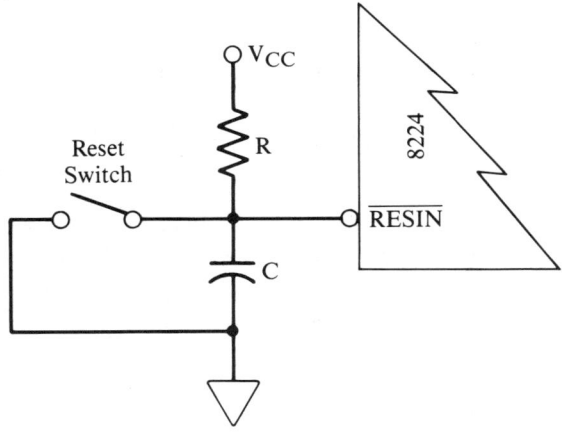

FIGURE 3-14. Reset circuitry.

3-6

8080 AND ESSENTIAL SUPPORT CHIPS INTERFACE

Figure 3-15 shows the 8080, 8228, and 8224 connected in a standard configuration. All 8080-based systems require these chips or chips that perform the same functions. Of course, memory and I/O are essential, but due to the variety of interfaces possible, they are not treated as part of a *standardized* configuration. The reader should study Figure 3-15 and verify each pin connection shown. Pins 13 and 14 of 8080 will be connected to I/O devices with DMA and interrupt capability. Pin 22 of the 8228 would be connected to an I/O device that is to have the capability of isolating the 8080 from the system's data and control bus. Pin 3 of the 8224 is connected to slow I/O or memory and pin 2 is connected to reset circuitry such as that shown in Figure 3-14.

If an 8080-based system did not have slow memory or I/O or DMA or interrupt capability, pins 13 and 14 of the 8080 would be tied to ground to disallow DMA and an interrupt request, while pin 23 of the 8080 or pin 3 of the 8224 would be tied high, which would always activate the READY input. Notice that these inputs cannot be left unassigned (high or low). This is true of all inputs, since open-circuit pins can "float" to an undesired logic level. Also, open-circuit pins are much more susceptible to noise. For instance, if pin 13 were left unconnected and it floated high, the CPU would receive a hold request and hence the system would be in a permanent hold state (DMA).

Before leaving this chapter we should be certain that the interrelations between the 8080, 8228, and 8224 are well understood, especially the generation of control signals. Readers can perform a self-examination by viewing Figure 3-15 and explaining to themselves the "how and why" of each pin connection. That is, the pin connections should be a logical consequence of each reader's understanding of the various chip functions and architectures. To aid in comprehension of Figure 3-15, the next section will examine basic timing requirements of the 8080 Primary Standard System.

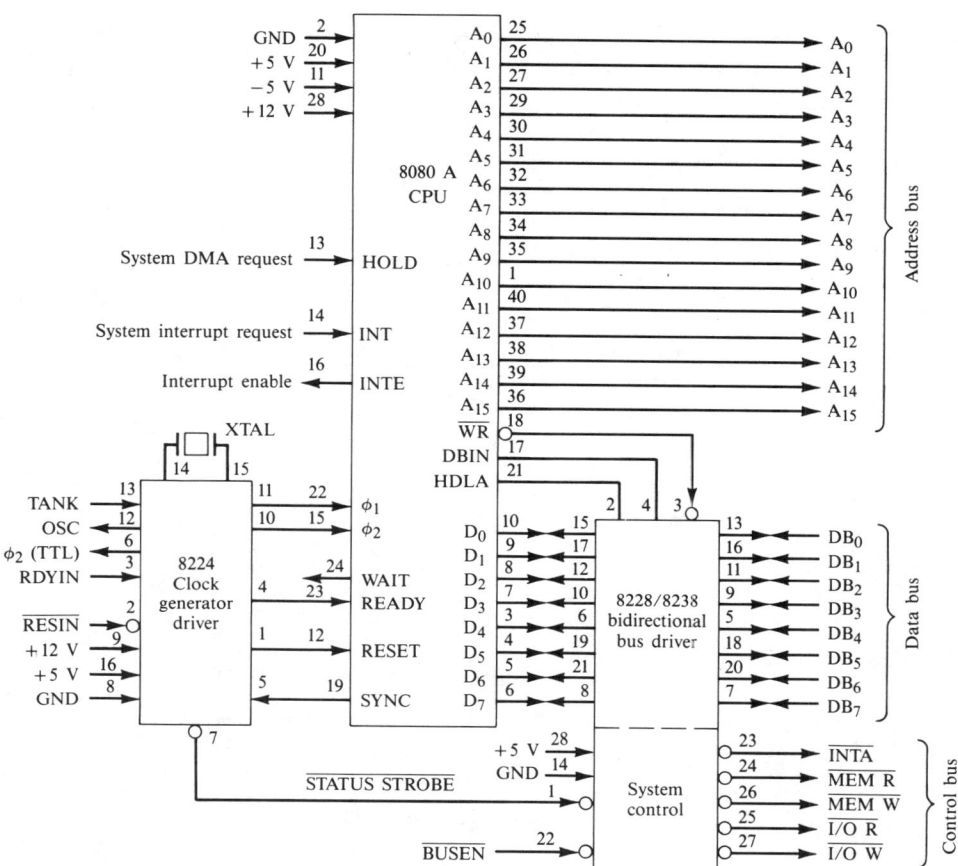

FIGURE 3-15. 8080 primary standard system. (Courtesy of Intel Corp.)

3-7

BASIC TIMING OF THE 8080 PRIMARY STANDARD SYSTEM

Timing for the 8080 is sectioned into *machine cycles* (MCs) as indicated in Figure 3-16. There may be from one to five machine cycles as well as three to five timing states (T_1, T_2, etc.) per machine cycle required to fetch an instruction from memory and then to execute it. The number of machine cycles and timing states required for each instruction is fixed but varies among the different instructions. The number of machine cycles required depends on the number of times the CPU must communicate with external devices (usually chips). For instance, if an instruction is composed of two 8-bit codes, the CPU must communicate with memory (it must read memory) twice in order to fetch that instruction. Thus two machine cycles will be required to fetch that instruction. If an instruction is composed of three 8-bit codes, three machine cycles are required for the CPU to fetch that instruction from memory. In addition to the machine

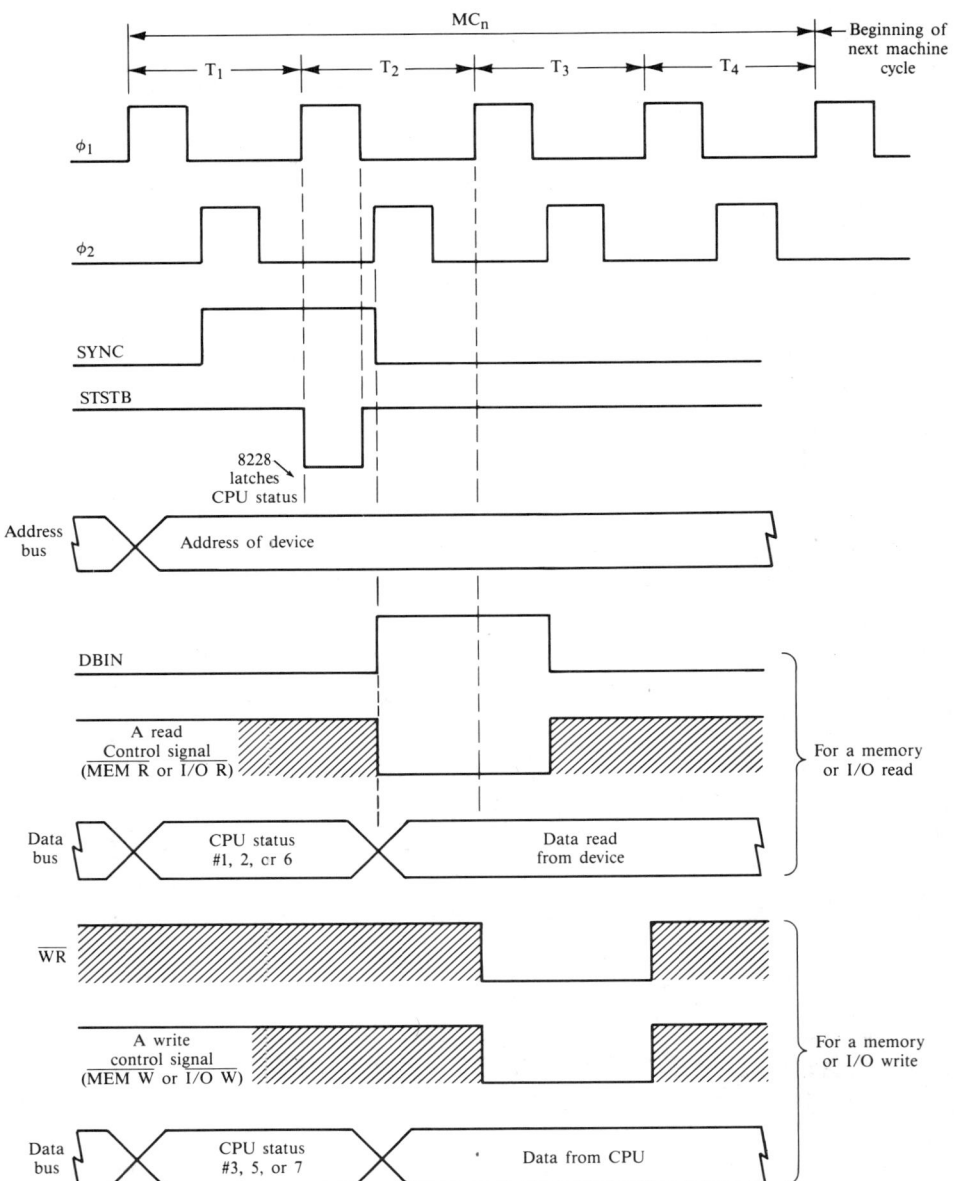

FIGURE 3-16. Control signals for read and write operations.

cycles required to fetch an instruction from memory, there may be additional machine cycles required for the execution of the fetched instruction. That is, suppose that an instruction (composed of two 8-bit codes) were to write the contents of the CPU's accumulator to an I/O device, via the data bus. This write operation is an external communication requiring an additional machine cycle. Then to fetch and execute this instruction, three machine cycles are necessary.

The beginning of each machine cycle is basically determined by the advent of the SYNC pulse being output by the CPU, which is illustrated in Figure 3-16. The reason for SYNC determining the beginning of each machine cycle is easily understood by recalling the description of a machine cycle; that is, a machine cycle is required for each communication external to the CPU. Of course, what is needed electronically to implement this external communication are control signals, and control signal generation begins with the latching of the CPU status word by the 8228, via the $\overline{\text{STSTB}}$ strobe pulse, which the SYNC pulse is ultimately responsible for generating, as depicted in Figures 3-6, 3-13, and 3-16. Figures 3-9 and 3-16 illustrate how the latched CPU status word is decoded for generation of the control signals.

Control signals are used by external devices to either latch data from the data bus, where the data are being sent by the CPU (a write operation), or to gate its data onto the data bus in order that the CPU may receive it from the data bus (a read operation). Then to determine which control signal is to be generated for each machine cycle, one need only determine:

1. Is the external device being communicated with memory or I/O? If the external device is memory, a memory-related control signal is required ($\overline{\text{MEM R}}$ or $\overline{\text{MEM W}}$). If the external device is I/O, an I/O-related control signal is necessary ($\overline{\text{I/O R}}$ or $\overline{\text{I/O W}}$).
2. Is the external communication to be a read or a write operation? If it is a read, then either $\overline{\text{MEM R}}$ or $\overline{\text{I/O R}}$ is required, whereas if it is a write operation, either $\overline{\text{MEM W}}$ or $\overline{\text{I/O W}}$ is necessary.

Refer to Figure 3-16 to confirm the generation of control signals. We can also determine the requirement of the address bus when the appropriate control signal is present (active) on the control bus. Whenever the CPU communicates with an external device (memory or I/O), it identifies that device, with which it wishes to communicate, by furnishing the device's address on the address bus. Hence, when a control signal is active, the CPU must have the address of the external device on the address bus, as indicated by Figure 3-16.

If the reader wishes to apply these principles on a broader scale, refer to Figure 4-8. However, at this point readers should concern themselves only with the control signal generation of Figure 4-8.

3-8

SUMMARY

The 8080 architecture is essentially composed of function blocks that can be categorized into one of five groups: function blocks that (1) receive and implement instructions, (2) perform arithmetic and logic operations on data and indicate the results of the operation, (3) address external memory and I/O, (4) serve as internal memory, and (5) provide control and timing for all operations internal to the CPU as well as external operations that must be synchronized with the CPU, such as read and write operations. Following is a list of each function block according to category:

1. Receive and implement instructions.
   a. Instruction register (IR).
   b. IR decoder.
   c. Control and timing unit (CU).
      (1) The microprogram is an integral part of the CU.
2. Perform arithmetic and logic functions.
   a. ALU.
   b. Condition flags.
   c. Accumulator.
3. Address memory and I/O.
   a. PC.
   b. SP.
   c. Register pairs.
   d. Registers W and Z (I/O).
4. Function as internal memory.
   a. Registers B, C, D, E, H, and L.
5. Provide control and timing.
   a. CU.

The 8228 provides two essential services for an 8080-based system. It provides "driving power" for the 8080 data bus and generates control signals for the system control bus. The data bus driving power is provided by the bidirectional bus driver function block of the 8228 architecture. The system control signals (read and write) are generated by the status latch and gating array function blocks. These system control signals ($\overline{\text{MEM R}}$, $\overline{\text{I/O R}}$, $\overline{\text{MEM W}}$, and $\overline{\text{I/O W}}$) are the result of an appropriate CPU status word being gated with the proper 8080 timing signal (DBIN or $\overline{\text{WR}}$). An appropriate control signal must be generated each time the CPU is to perform an external read or write operation with memory or I/O. Also, the appropriate control signal must be generated when the CPU has output the address of the accessed memory or I/O device on the address bus.

The 8224 not only provides primary timing to the CPU, but also synchronizes asynchronous events, such as ready and reset, with the CPU.

The 8080, 8228, and 8224 comprise the 8080 Primary Standard System and are the minimum components required of an 8080-based microcomputer. Of course, this primary system must still have memory and I/O added, which is the topic of the next chapter.

REVIEW QUESTIONS AND PROBLEMS

1. From the 8080 architecture of Figure 3-1:
   (a) Determine the number of possible instructions, supporting your answer mathematically.
   (b) Calculate the potential memory capacity of an 8080-based system.
   (c) Determine the level of interrupt capability and discuss what this means in possible system efficiency.

(d) Discuss the role of CU output signals $\overline{\text{WR}}$ and DBIN relative to the generation of control signals $\overline{\text{MEM R}}$, $\overline{\text{I/O R}}$, and so on.

2. Discuss the purpose of the CPU status word.

3. Using Figures 3-5, 3-6, and 3-13, describe how the strobe pulse $\overline{\text{STSTB}}$ is generated and used by the 8228.

4. What is a "nonprogrammable register"?

5. Figure 3-1 shows CU control lines going to each and every block, indicating that the CU controls the operation of these function blocks. Discuss why this control is necessary. Be certain to incorporate the role of the microprogram in your discussion. Finally, give an example of when the CU must control the operation of the IR and IR decoder and the register select function block.

6. Define the term "stack" and discuss how it is accessed.

7. What constitutes the data counter of an 8080?

8. Knowing that an 8080 can address 512 input and output devices, discuss I/O addressing, specifying which CPU registers are used.

9. When the PC is used as the addressing mechanism, what do you know about the contents of the memory location(s) being accessed?

10. The CU inputs HOLD and READY are used for what purpose?

11. Discuss the architecture of the 8228 from a very general viewpoint.

12. Discuss the architecture of the 8224 from a very general viewpoint.

13. In a general manner discuss the interrelationship of the 8080, 8224, and 8228, which is shown as a system in Figure 3-15.

14. Suppose that you wanted to generate a control signal which would become active whenever a stack write operation was performed. From the CPU status word chart of Figure 3-7, design the necessary circuit. Use techniques similar to those in Figures 3-8 and 3-9.

15. Describe in detail how the reset circuitry of Figure 3-14 functions.

16. For the instructions described, draw a timing diagram showing the number of machine cycles for fetching and execution. Show φ_1, φ_2, SYNC, $\overline{\text{STSTB}}$, the address bus, DBIN, $\overline{\text{WR}}$, the appropriate control signals, and the data bus. Justify each machine cycle and state the function of the binary code present on the address and data buses, as was done in Figure 3-16.

(a) A two-byte instruction that instructs the CU to add the contents of register D to A, storing the resultant sum in A.
(b) A three-byte instruction that transfers program execution to the memory location given by the last two bytes of the instruction.
(c) A two-byte instruction that compares the second byte of the instruction with the contents of register A and appropriately alters the condition flags.
(d) A three-byte instruction that transfers program execution to the memory location given by the last two bytes of the instruction [just as in part (b)], but also stores the contents of the PC in the stack.

Note: The reader may assume T_4 timing states for each machine cycle.

CHAPTER 4

An 8080-Based System Design: I/O and Memory Interface

4-1

INTRODUCTION

This chapter introduces memory and I/O interfacing with the circuit components of Figure 3-15. The addition of memory and I/O to Figure 3-15 will result in an 8080-based system such as that shown in Figure 4-7. Notice that we are careful not to call the system of Figure 4-7 a microprocessor-based computer (microcomputer) since that terminology implies interfacing with a human user and as a result would require input device 0 to be an input device such as a keyboard and output device 3 to be either a cathode-ray tube (CRT) or a printer. We will choose to leave the I/O devices of Figure 4-7 unspecified, for then Figure 4-7 represents a general microprocessor-based system, which could be a microcomputer, depending on the I/O devices.

Returning to Figure 1-12, we are reminded that both memory and I/O are accessed via the address bus. That is, whenever it is desired to communicate (read or write) with either memory or I/O, the initiator of the communication must supply the address of the specific memory location or I/O device to be accessed over the address bus. We realize from previous discussions that it is the microprocessor that usually initiates access to memory and I/O, but not always, as in the case of a DMA.

This chapter examines one of two methods used to address memory and I/O (the second method is discussed in Chapter 6). The two methods differ in the technique used to partition memory addresses from I/O addresses. The addressing method discussed in this chapter is termed *isolated I/O*. The isolation, or partitioning, of memory and I/O is implemented via software, that is, the program instructions. For isolated I/O systems there are instructions which specifically address memory, and those which specifically address I/O. The second method for addressing memory and I/O, which is discussed in Chapter 6, is termed *memory-mapped I/O*. Program instructions for memory-mapped I/O systems do not distinguish between memory and I/O addresses but rather address both as if they were memory locations. This method relies on the user to "map the memory addresses of the system" and to keep track of those assigned to I/O. As a spin-off of examining memory-mapped I/O systems, we shall also study linear addressing and foldback addressing in Chapter 6.

4-2

ISOLATED I/O

Isolated I/O systems partition memory from I/O, via software, by having instructions that specifically access (address) memory and others that specifically access I/O. When these instructions are decoded by the microprocessor, an appropriate control signal is generated to activate either memory or I/O. That is, to distinguish between memory and I/O addresses, the control signals $\overline{I/O\ R}$, $\overline{I/O\ W}$, $\overline{MEM\ R}$, and $\overline{MEM\ W}$ are generated. As we have already seen in the limited examples of Chapter 3, these control signals are used to enable the device addressed—memory or I/O.

To address memory it will be necessary to select one memory location from a possible 65,536 *if all 16 address lines are used* at a time. To address an I/O device, one of 256 binary codes must be selected if full I/O addressing capacity is utilized. As we have already seen, to detect a binary code implies the use of a decoder. We shall use decoders in conjunction with control signals to select addressed memory locations or I/O devices.

Although various decoders would suffice, we will use Intel's 8205. The truth table, logic symbol, and pin configuration of the 8205 are illustated in Figure 4-1.

As we see from the truth table of Figure 4-1, $\overline{E}_1$, $\overline{E}_2$, and E_3 must have the appropriate logic states ($\overline{E}_1 = 0$, $\overline{E}_2 = 0$, and $E_3 = 1$) before the decoder is enabled. If $\overline{E}_1$, $\overline{E}_2$, and E_3 do not have the proper logic states, the outputs $\overline{O}_0$–$\overline{O}_7$ will be inactive (high). As an example of decoding an address, if the binary code of 011 ($A_0 = H$, $A_1 = H$, and $A_2 = L$) is input on A_0–A_2 and the 8205 is enabled, 011 is decoded, resulting in output O_3 (labeled simply "3" in the truth table) becoming active (low). Be certain to realize that all outputs are active low, which usually is indicated by the NOT symbol ($\overline{O}_0$–$\overline{O}_7$) as shown in the right-hand table of Figure 4-1.

Using an 8205 to implement the I/O selector of Figure 1-12 is shown in Figure 4-2. In this case only three address lines (A_0–A_2) of the address bus are being used, which means that a maximum of eight I/O devices can be selected

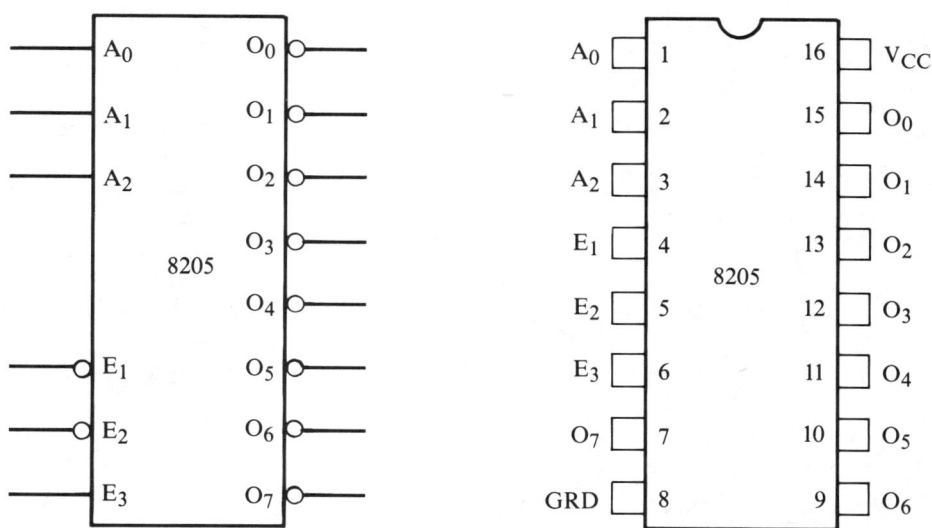

FIGURE 4-1. Intel's 8205 decoder. (Courtesy of Intel Corp.)

($2^3 = 8$). The I/O select lines are identified as $\overline{DV_0}, \overline{DV_1}, \ldots, \overline{DV_7}$. The NOR gate of Figure 4-2 is to account for the other five address lines A_3–A_7 (recall that for I/O addressing, A_0–A_7 and A_8–A_{15} are duplicates). Since the 8205 of Figure 4-2 uses the control signal $\overline{I/O\ R}$ to enable it, this means that all the I/O devices selected by this 8205 are input I/O devices (only I/O read operations are performed).

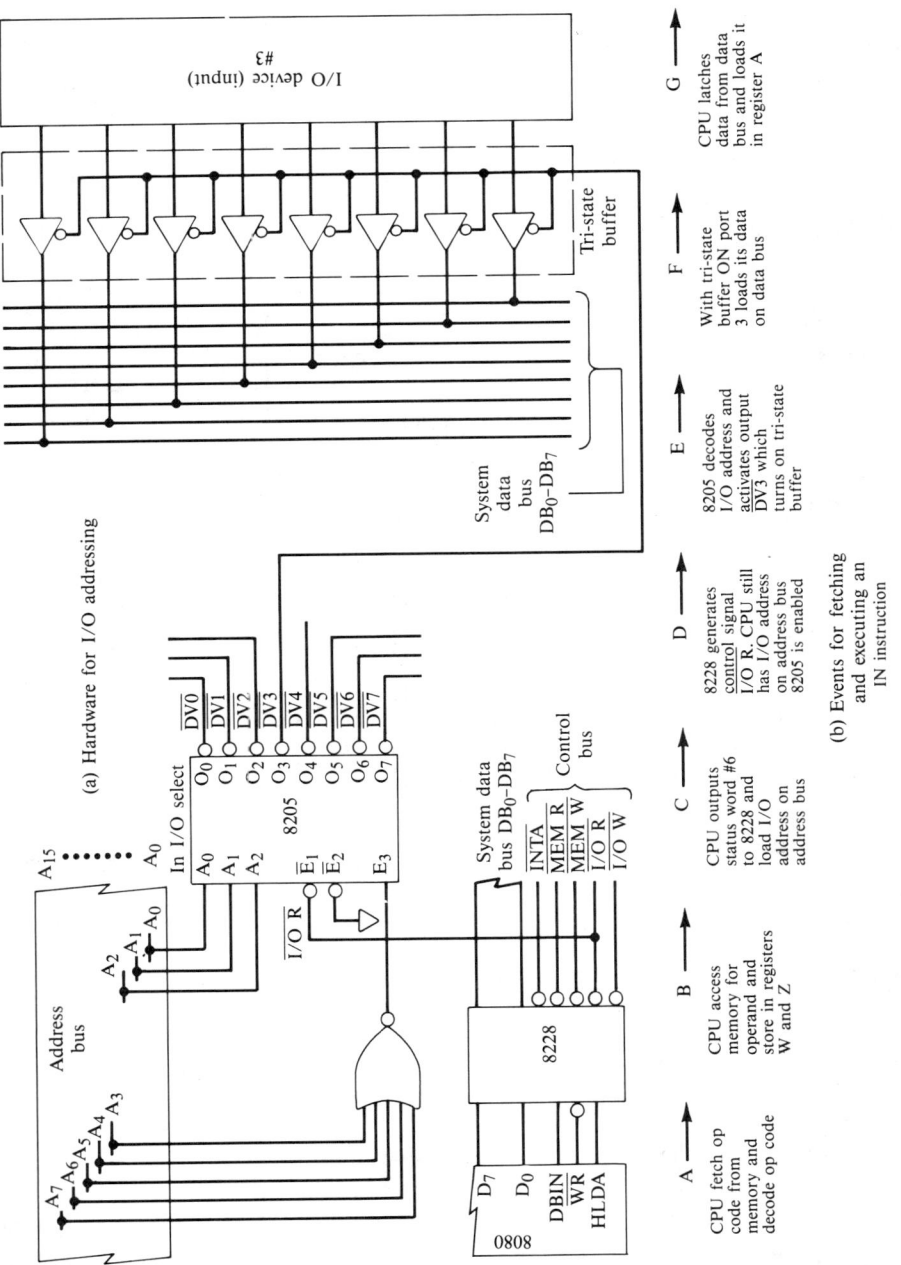

FIGURE 4-2. I/O read addressing.

As a means of providing a fairly comprehensive example of how the hardware of Figure 4-2(a) is controlled by software and also provides I/O isolation, suppose that the instruction IN 0000 0011 is to be executed. Now, the binary code that specifies the operation (IN) is binary code 1101 1011 and the I/O address is 0000 0011, as stated in the instruction. Obviously, the IN instruction is composed of two 8-bit binary codes, one for the operation (called *op code*) and the other for the I/O address, called the *operand*. Then this instruction will occupy two *sequential* memory locations, the first containing the IN op code 1101 1011 and the second the I/O address 0000 0011. For the CPU to perform an instruction fetch for IN 0000 0011, it must first fetch the op code and then the operand. When the op code is fetched and decoded by the IR decoder of the microprocessor, as indicated by event A in the event diagram of Figure 4-2(b), the CU will then know that it is to perform an input read operation. The IN op code will require the CPU to access the next memory location and fetch the I/O port number (input device address). The CPU will fetch the port number from memory and store that 8-bit I/O address in registers W and Z, as indicated in Figure 4-2(b).

At this point the CPU not only knows that it is to perform an input read but now has the address (port number) of the input I/O device as well. The CU of the CPU then outputs CPU status word ⑥ on the data bus D_0–D_7 and at the same time outputs the contents of registers W and Z (0000 0011 and 0000 0011) on the address bus, as indicated by event C of Figure 4-2(b). The 8228 of Figure 4-2(b) latches and decodes status word ⑥ and as a result generates control signal $\overline{I/O\ R}$. Over the same time period that $\overline{I/O\ R}$ is active the CPU is applying the port number on the address bus, as indicated by event D, which will allow the 8205 to decode that I/O address if the 8205 is enabled. With address lines A_3–A_7 low the NOR gate of Figure 4-2 outputs a high, which in conjunction with the low from $\overline{I/O\ R}$, enables the 8205. With the 8205 enabled it then decodes the binary code (011) on address lines A_0–A_2 and activates O_3 ($\overline{DV_3}$ I/O select line), which in turn takes the tri-state buffer of Figure 4-2 out of the high-Z state, as indicated by even E in Figure 4-2(b). This allows input I/O device 3 to load its data onto the data bus. Since the CPU is in the input mode (DBIN is active) when $\overline{I/O\ R}$ is active (recall that DBIN is ANDed with INP of the status word to generate $\overline{I/O\ R}$), the data on the data bus during that time will be input to the CPU, as indicated by events F and G of Figure 4-2(b). The CU will automatically load that data in register A, as we shall see when we study the 8080 instruction set. This completes the execution of the IN instruction and the CU will then increment the PC in preparation for the next 8080 instruction fetch.

The reader should realize that the control signal $\overline{I/O\ R}$ "determined" that the address on the address bus was to be decoded as an I/O device rather than a memory address, and therefore in this case implemented the hardware isolation of memory addresses from I/O.

A concern of Figure 4-2 is that it is limited to eight input devices (DV_0–DV_7). One method, to expand the capacity of the I/O selector, is shown in Figure 4-3.

To understand how the circuit of Figure 4-3 can decode additional I/O addresses, we shall study the truth table of Table 4-1 in conjunction with Figure

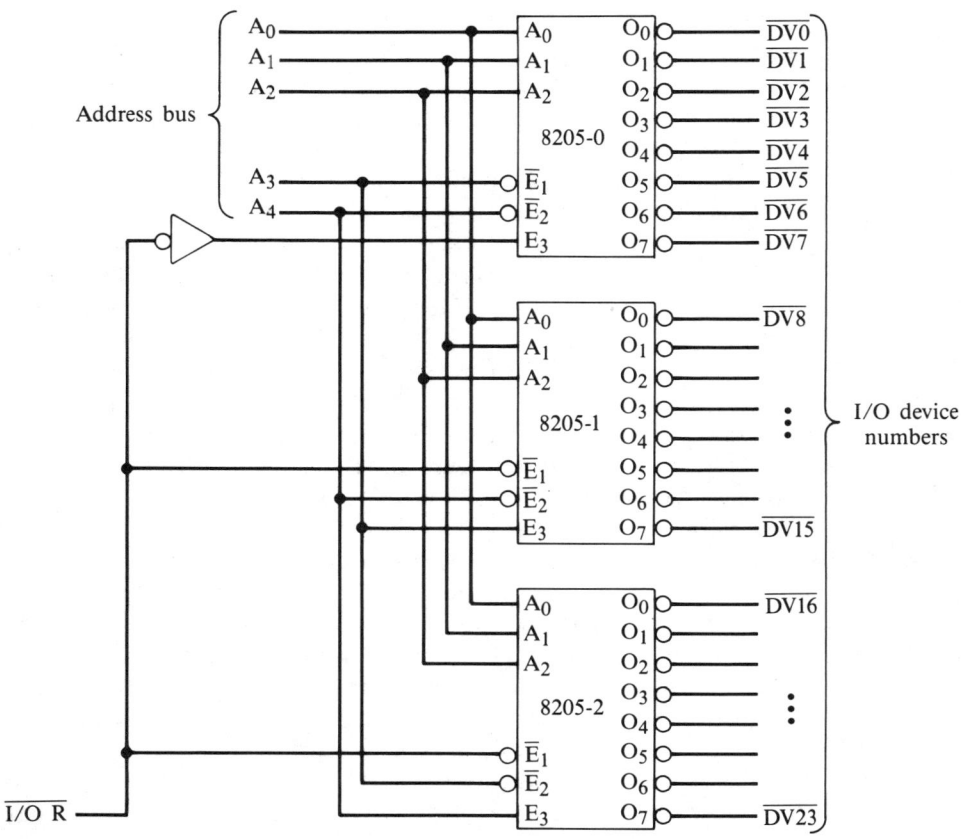

FIGURE 4-3. Expanded I/O selector.

4-3. From Figure 4-3 one realizes that with the three 8205s connected in parallel to address bus lines A_0–A_2, *each 8205 enabled will be selecting an I/O device*. For instance, if $A_0 = A_1 = A_2 = 0$ (low), *and all three 8205s were enabled*, then 8205-0 would select DV_0 by activating its O_0 output (refer to Figure 4-1 and Table 4-1), 8205-1 would select DV_8 by activating its O_0 output, and output O_0 of 8205-2 would become active, thereby selecting I/O device 16. Since only one I/O device can be selected (addressed) at any given time, a scheme is needed that will not only address individual outputs (O_0–O_7) of each decoder but will also individually address (select) each decoder as well. By viewing address lines A_3 and A_4 of Figure 4-3 and relating those address lines to the truth table of Table 4-1, we see that A_3 and A_4 provide the possibilities for just such a decoding scheme. These two address lines will provide the correct logic levels to enable each of the decoders. As an example, when $A_4 = A_3 = 0$, then 8205-0 of Figure 4-3 is enabled since its $\overline{E}_1$, $\overline{E}_2$, and E_3 have the correct logic levels while both 8205-1 and 2 will be disabled (outputs high). Notice from the truth table of Table 4-1 that the I/O addresses begin with binary 00000 and progress sequentially to address 10111, which is a total of 24 addresses.

To perform an I/O write addressing, the concepts of Figures 4-2 and 4-3 apply. The difference is that the $\overline{I/O\ W}$ control signal will be used to enable

TABLE 4-1. Truth Table for Figure 4-3

Decoder Select		Output Select					
		I/O Address					
A_4	A_3	A_2	A_1	A_0	Decoder Enabled	Output Active	I/O Device Selected
0	0	0	0	0	8205-0	O_0	DV_0
0	0	0	0	1		O_1	DV_1
0	0	0	1	0		O_2	DV_2
.	.	.	.	.		.	.
.	.	.	.	.		.	.
0	0	1	1	1		O_7	DV_7
0	1	0	0	0	8205-1	O_0	DV_8
0	1	0	0	1		O_1	DV_9
.	.	.	.	.		.	.
.	.	.	.	.		.	.
0	1	1	1	1		O_7	DV_{15}
1	0	0	0	0	8205-2	O_0	DV_{16}
.	.	.	.	.		.	.
.	.	.	.	.		.	.
1	0	1	1	1		O_7	DV_{23}

the output I/O selector and the addressed output of the output I/O selector will be used to strobe (latch) data *from* the data bus. The latching circuit is composed of flip-flops similar to the latch of Figure 3-4. Circuitry that will perform an I/O write operation is illustrated in Figure 4-4.

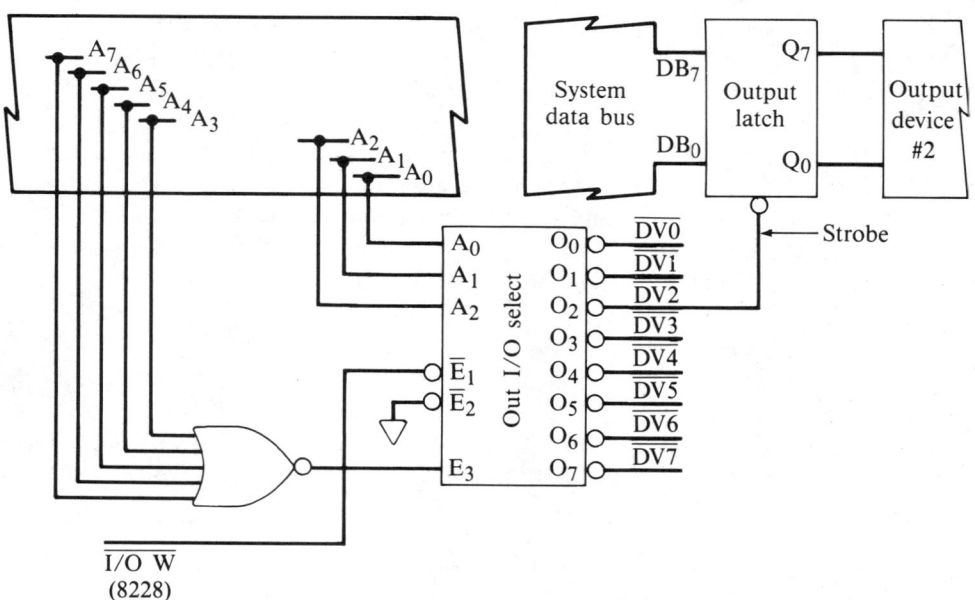

FIGURE 4-4. I/O write addressing.

Since most applications of an 8080 will require both I/O read and write operations, Figures 4-2 and 4-4 will both be present in the same system. I/O capacity expansion of Figures 4-2 and 4-4 would incorporate logic circuits similar to Figure 4-3.

If a system had eight or fewer I/O devices, both input and output combined, then a single I/O selector could be used. For this application $\overline{\text{I/O R}}$ or $\overline{\text{I/O W}}$ must enable $\overline{E}_1$ or $\overline{E}_2$. To enable $\overline{E}_1$ of the 8205 an AND gate with inputs $\overline{\text{I/O R}}$ and $\overline{\text{I/O W}}$ would be used.

4.3 MEMORY ADDRESSING

To decode memory addresses, methods similar to those for decoding I/O addresses will be used except that control signals $\overline{\text{MEM R}}$ and $\overline{\text{MEM W}}$ will be used to provide isolation from I/O addresses. Let us suppose that the memory to be addressed is composed of 2K of *read-only memory* (ROM), which is where the program will reside, and 3K of read/write memory (R/W), commonly known as RAM, which will be used by the microprocessor to store data. [Just as a note, industry often refers to R/W memory as RAM, which is incorrect since RAM (Random Access Memory) refers to the method of addressing and not as to whether the contents of the chip are alterable.] Intel's 2708 will be used to implement ROM and 2114s for RAM. Figure 4-5 shows the necessary data for each of these memory chips.

The 2708 is an EPROM (erasable ROM), which means that it has the ability to have its contents erased by exposure to ultraviolet light and then be reprogrammed by the user. As with the case of any ROM, the microprocessor cannot alter its contents; that is, the CPU can only read a ROM. Erasures and programming are done external to the microprocessor system on a device known as a PROM (programmable ROM) programmer. Pin 18 (program) is used when the chip is being programmed by the user. As a result, pin 18 is tied low when the ROM is in use in the microprocessor system, as shown in Figure 4-6. Pin 20 ($\overline{\text{CS}}$/WE) has a dual purpose. When the chip is being programmed it is forced high [write enable (WE)], but when the chip is in the microprocessor system it serves as the chip select ($\overline{\text{CS}}$) and must be low to enable the chip to be read. Address pins A_0–A_9 will address one of 1024 (2^{10}) memory locations. Addressed memory locations will output their contents at outputs O_1–O_8. The 2708 has tri-state outputs.

From Figure 4-5 one sees for the 2114 that its chip enable ($\overline{\text{CS}}$) is pin 8. In order to write data into the chip, $\overline{\text{WE}}$ must be low and high when performing a read operation. The address pins are A_0–A_9, resulting in a 1K (1024) memory capacity. The data input and output is accomplished with pins I/O_1–I/O_4. I/O_1–I/O_4 are tri-state outputs. Of course, if $\overline{\text{WE}}$ is low, the I/O lines are data input pins and data output pins when $\overline{\text{WE}}$ is high. Since the 8080's word size is 8 bits, 2114s must be used in pairs.

Figure 4-6 shows an addressing scheme to address 2K of ROM and 3K of RAM using 2708s and 2114s. Address lines A_0–A_9 address memory locations *within* each chip. Address lines A_{10}–A_{12} are decoded by the 8205, resulting in its outputs selecting (enabling) individual memory chips, where each chip is referred to as a *page of memory*.

The NOR gate and address lines A_{13}–A_{15} of Figure 4-6 are used to ensure that only addresses beginning at 0000 0000 0000 0000 and ending with 0001 1111 1111 1111 (realize that in every case $A_{13} = A_{14} = A_{15} = 0$) will enable memory. Since the memory page selector of Figure 4-6 is to be enabled any time $\overline{\text{MEM R}}$ or $\overline{\text{MEM W}}$ is active (low), an AND gate, as shown, is used to enable the 8205. Notice from Figure 4-6 that $\overline{\text{MEM W}}$ being input to $\overline{\text{WE}}$ is sufficient to distinguish between read and write operations for the 2114's.

When a memory read is being executed, $\overline{\text{MEM W}}$ will be high, which is the logic level required of $\overline{\text{WE}}$ to perform a read operation. Also, notice that due to 2114s having 4-bit storage, two are required for each address. This is the reason for the page A and B labels. The 2708s do not need to distinguish between read and write operations since a read is all that can be performed; hence the chip select ($\overline{\text{CS}}$) will automatically read the contents of any addressed memory locations.

Figure 4-7 illustrates the concepts and hardware of previous discussions integrated into a simple microprocessor-based system. As shown in Figure 4-7, the system has been modularized into its various parts (Figures 3-15, 4-2, 4-4, and 4-6). Notice that the portion of Figure 4-7 related to Figure 3-15 has been slightly modified. The system of Figure 4-7 does not have DMA or interrupt capability; hence both inputs are made inactive by tying them low. Notice also that $\overline{\text{BUSEN}}$ is permanently activated so that the 8228 does not isolate the 8080 from the system data and control bus. The input I/O circuitry of Figure 4-7 is about the same as Figure 4-2. The output I/O module of Figure 4-4 uses the same NOR gate as the input I/O in order to reduce the chip count.

The reader should review each module of Figure 4-7 until an understanding of the entire system is accomplished. To assist in this review, let us correlate the timing diagram of Figure 4-8 with that of Figure 4-7. The timing diagram of Figure 4-8 is for an instruction fetch and execution of the OUT instruction. The OUT instruction is composed of two 8-bit codes, one 8-bit code for the op code and the other for the port number of the output I/O device. These two 8-bit codes will be stored in memory just as was done for the IN instruction discussed earlier. Let us arbitrarily state that the op code is stored at memory location 0000 0100 0011 0100, which requires that the I/O port number (address) be stored at the next memory location, which is 0000 0100 0011 0101. Execution of an OUT instruction causes the CPU to write the contents of its accumulator (A) to the output port addressed. The mnemonic form of the instruction is OUT 0000 0011 and its machine code is 1101 0011 0000 0011, where 1101 0011 is the op code and 0000 0011 is the I/O port number. To reiterate, the contents of memory location 0000 0100 0011 0100 is 1101 0011 (the op code) and at location 0000 0100 0011 0101 it is 0000 0011 (the I/O device address).

Let us begin the study of Figure 4-8 by first justifying the number of machine cycles (MCs) required and then the control signal generated during each MC. Recall from Chapter 3 that a new machine cycle is defined every time the CPU must communicate, via the data bus, with chips external to itself, and it is because of this external communication that control signals ($\overline{\text{INTA}}$, $\overline{\text{MEM W}}$,

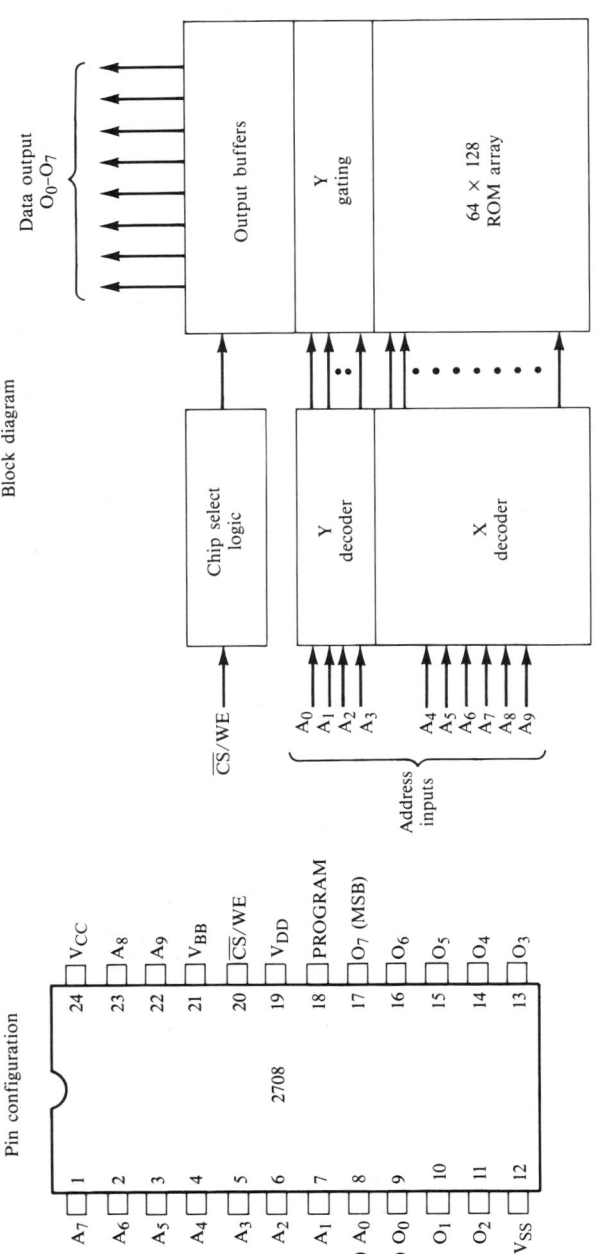

(a) **2708 ROM**

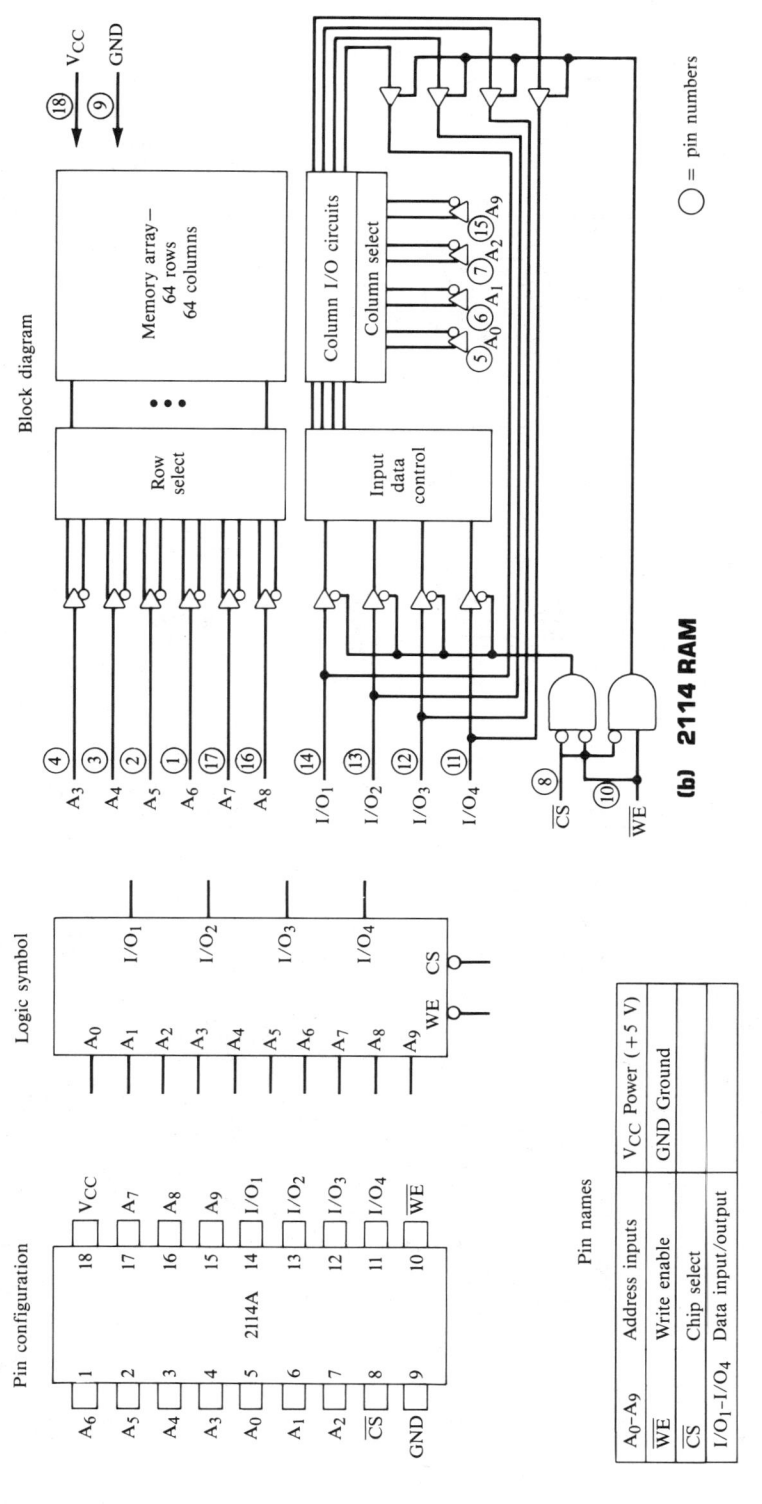

FIGURE 4-5. Memory chips. (a) Intel's 2708 ROM; (b) Intel's 2114 RAM. (Courtesy of Intel Corp.)

4·3 MEMORY ADDRESSING

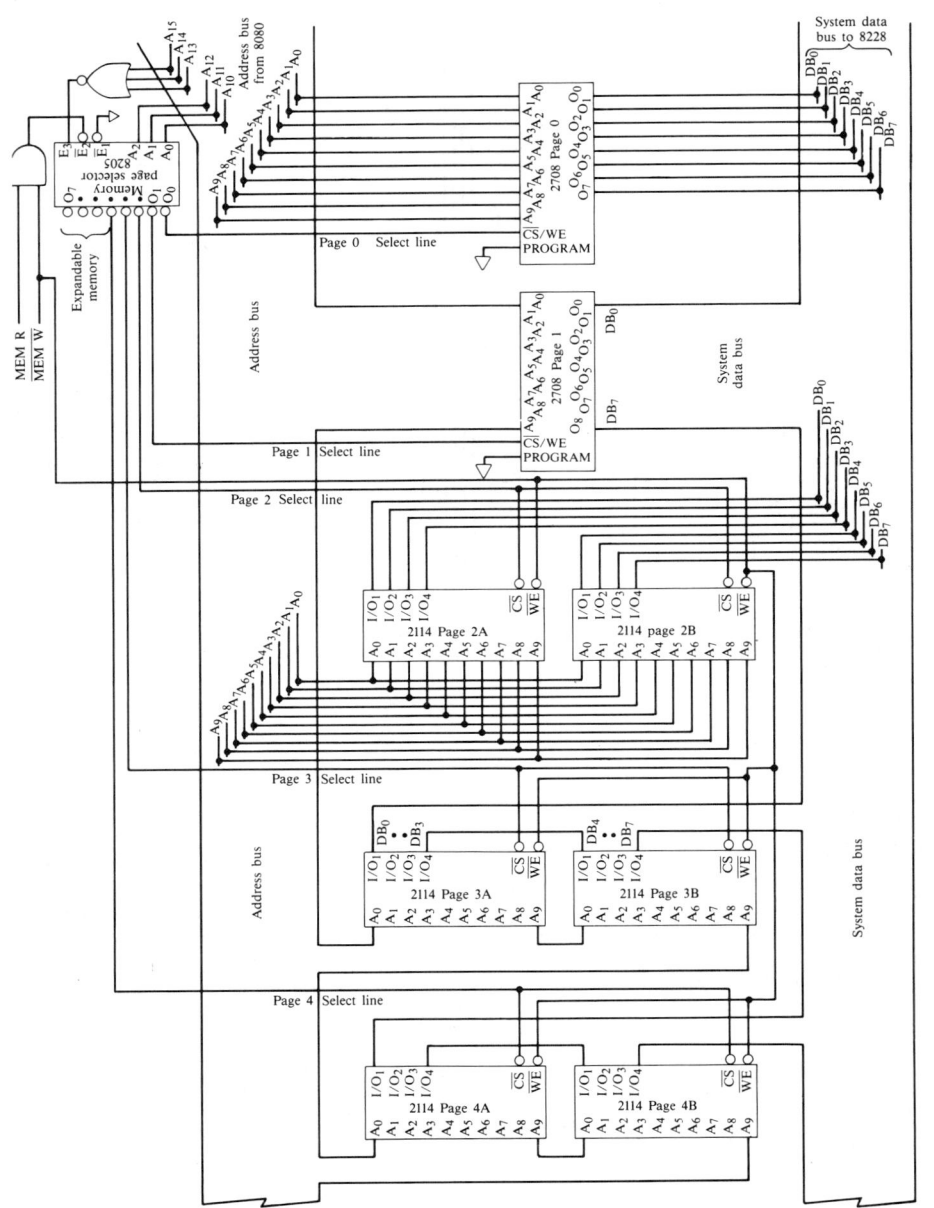

FIGURE 4-6. A memory system.

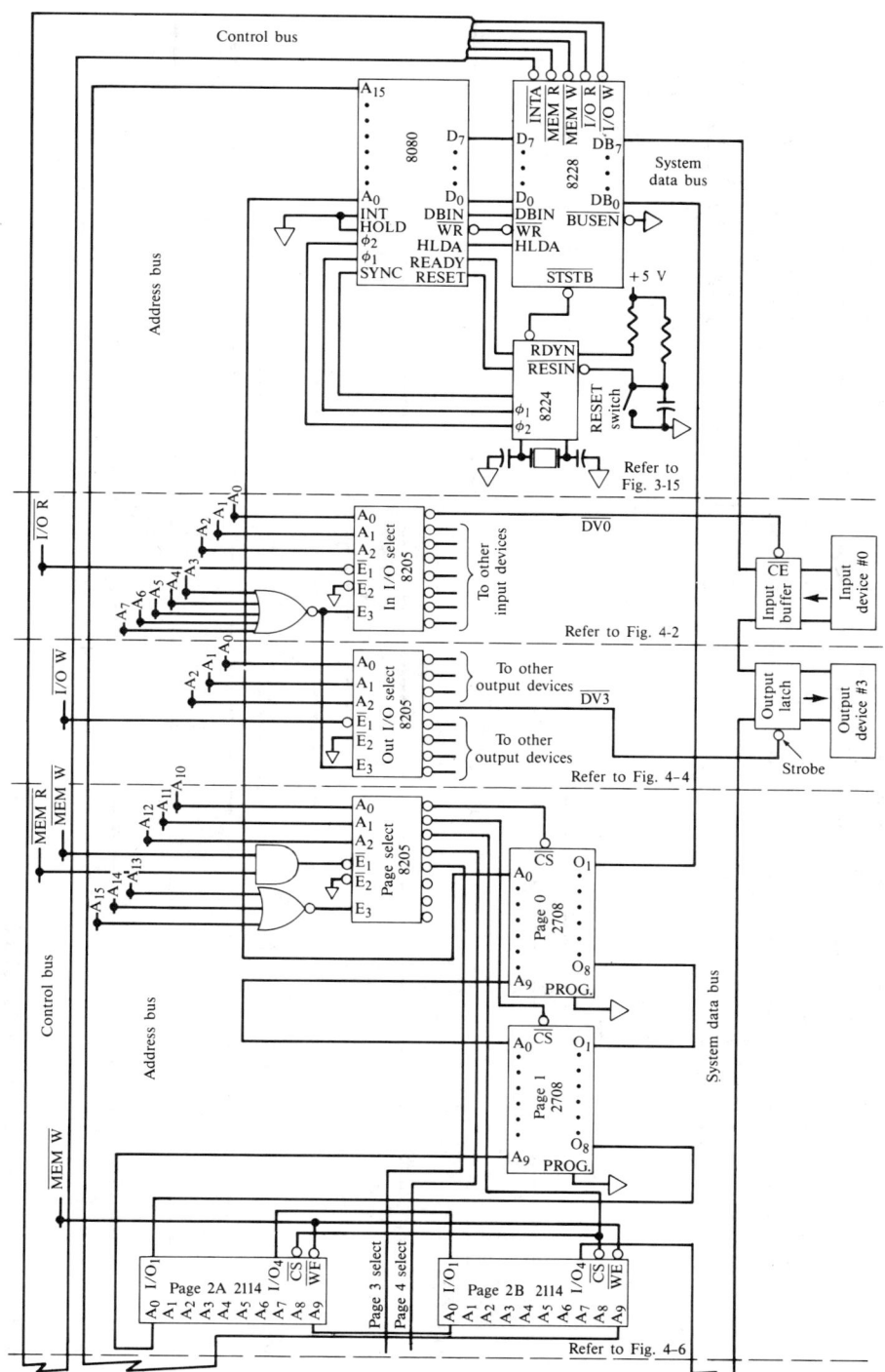

FIGURE 4-7. 8080-based system: no DMA or interrupt capability.

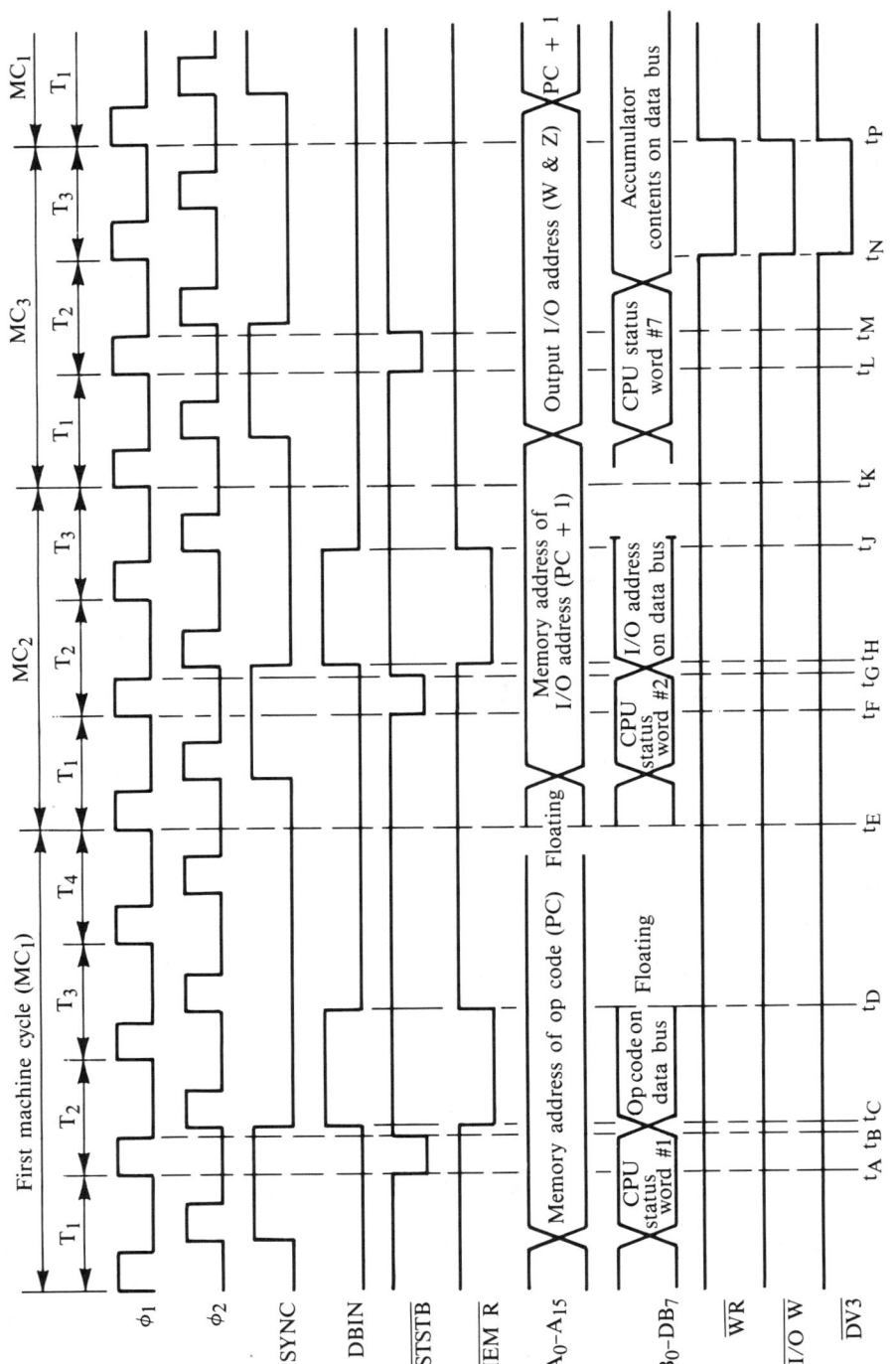

FIGURE 4-8. Timing diagram for the OUT instruction.

$\overline{I/O\ W}$, etc.) are necessary. Once the MCs and control signals are rationalized, the remaining timing functions are a logical consequence.

To rationalize the number of MCs required to execute an instruction, we simply refer to the manufacturer's explanation of that instruction and from that explanation determine the number of times the CPU must perform external communication—knowing there is a one-to-one correspondence between the number of machine cycles required and the number of external communications. As stated previously, the OUT instruction will cause the CPU to write its accumulators' contents to the I/O device addressed. Since this write operation is an external communication, it requires an MC. However, to fetch the instruction from memory, which is external communication, will require two additional MCs, one for each of the two 8-bit codes that make up the instruction. Then to fetch and execute the OUT instruction, a total of three machine cycles are required. The first machine cycle (MC_1) is to fetch the op code from memory. The second machine cycle (MC_2) is to read the port number from memory and MC_3 is required to write the contents of the accumulator to output port 0000 0011. Since the first two machine cycles are to access memory for a read operation, control signal $\overline{MEM\ R}$ must be generated during each of these machine cycles. The third machine cycle is for the CPU to write to the addressed I/O device, thereby requiring control signal $\overline{I/O\ W}$.

In MC_1 during timing state T_1 of Figure 4-8, the CPU outputs the contents of its 16-bit PC on the address bus and also outputs its status word (1) on the data bus. Figure 4-8 shows the address bus A_0–A_{15} as being some binary combination, which for this example is 0000 0100 0011 0100, where the function and logic states are shown in Figure 4-9. During time interval t_A–t_B of Figure 4-8 the 8224 generates $\overline{STSTB}$, which causes the 8228 to latch the CPU status word off the data bus. The 8228 decodes the CPU status word and then generates control signal $\overline{MEM\ R}$, when DBIN is high, as indicated in time interval t_C–t_D. When $\overline{MEM\ R}$ is active, the AND gate connected to $\overline{E_1}$ of the page selector of Figure 4-7 outputs a low and thus enables $\overline{E_1}$. The NOR gate will enable E_3, since address lines A_{15}–A_{13} are all low (see Figure 4-9). Address lines A_{10}–A_{12} will be decoded by the page selector and select page 1. Address lines A_0–A_9 will address memory location 0000110100 within page 1 and that location will output its contents 1101 0011 (op code) on the data bus, as shown in time period t_C–t_D of Figure 4-8. The CPU will fetch that op code into its IR, where it is decoded. The CU of the CPU now knows that it is to execute an OUT instruction, which requires going back to memory for the output port address. The CU then increments the PC by one, which is memory address 0000 0100 0011 0101.

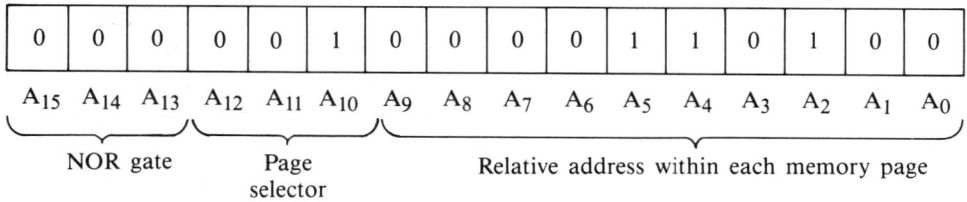

FIGURE 4-9. Memory addressing scheme for Figure 4-7.

The CU of the CPU then causes this address to be output on the address bus at the beginning of MC_2. Also, the CPU outputs the CPU status word 2, which is latched by the 8228 during time interval t_F-t_G. CPU status word 2 will cause control signal $\overline{MEM\ R}$ to be generated by the 8228 during time interval t_H-t_J. Again, when $\overline{MEM\ R}$ is active and a valid memory address is on the address bus, the memory location addressed will output its contents on the data bus, which in this case is port number 0000 0011, as shown during time interval t_H-t_J. During this same time interval DBIN is active; therefore, the CPU inputs this data. The CU of the CPU stores the port number received from the data bus in registers W and Z. The CPU now knows it is to write to output I/O device 0000 0011.

During the last machine cycle (MC_3) the CPU will execute the OUT instruction. This requires that the contents of registers W and Z (0000 0011 and 0000 0011) be output on the address bus by the CU to address the output port and that control signal $\overline{I/O\ W}$ be generated. The CPU status word for an output write (7) will be output on the data bus. $\overline{STSTB}$ is active during time interval t_L-t_M, which causes the CPU status word to be latched by the 8228. The CPU then writes the contents of its accumulator on the data bus. When the data output by the CPU is stable, $\overline{WR}$ becomes active, as indicated during time interval t_N-t_P. When $\overline{WR}$ is active, the 8228 generates the $\overline{I/O\ W}$ control signal, which is used in part to enable ($\overline{E}_1$) the OUT I/O selector. Also enabled is E_3, due to the NOR gate shown in Figure 4-7. With the OUT I/O selector enabled, its address lines A_0-A_2 (011) are decoded, which activates output $\overline{DV}_3$. When $\overline{DV}_3$ is active (time interval t_N-t_P) it will cause the data on the data bus to be latched by output device 3. This completes the execution of the OUT instruction; therefore, the CU increments the PC by one in preparation for the next instruction-fetch cycle, which is a repeat of MC_1. In fact, the timing diagram for all instruction-fetch cycles (MC_1) is the same regardless of the op code being fetched. It should now be clear to the reader that the control signals implement hardware I/O isolation from memory.

The next chapter will be a study of the 8080's instruction set. By utilizing the concepts of Section 3-7 and the development principles used for the timing diagram of Figure 4-8, the reader should be able to construct a timing diagram for any instruction. Keep this in mind as you study Chapter 5.

4-4

SUMMARY

To select either an I/O device or a memory location requires that it be addressed via the address bus. When addressed, the selected I/O device or memory location must have control of the data bus so that the data communication (read or write) may occur with the CPU. Control and timing of the data bus is essential and provided by the control bus via control signals $\overline{I/O\ R}$, $\overline{I/O\ W}$, $\overline{MEM\ R}$, and $\overline{MEM\ W}$. The manner in which these control signals implement control is that they are used to activate, either directly or indirectly, the I/O device or memory chip. We specifically implemented this control by using the appropriate control signal(s) to chip-enable a decoder. During the time interval that the control signal is active, the addressed output of the decoder becomes active and is used as a chip enable signal for read operations or as a strobe pulse for write operations.

A system which has controls signals that differentiate between I/O read and write operations provide for electronic isolation between I/O and memory. This isolation is possible since memory control signals ($\overline{\text{MEM R}}$ and $\overline{\text{MEM W}}$) are used to activate an addressed memory location and I/O control signals ($\overline{\text{I/O R}}$ and $\overline{\text{I/O W}}$) to activate an addressed I/O device. Systems do exist where the controls signals do not differentiate between memory and I/O but only between read and write operations. These systems are referred to as memory-mapped I/O systems and are discussed in Chapter 6.

The generation of a control signal requires that the CPU output the appropriate CPU status word and also provide the proper timing via DBIN and $\overline{\text{WR}}$. The 8228 actually generates the control signal by latching and decoding the CPU status word, where the 8080's timing signals DBIN and $\overline{\text{WR}}$ are utilized to provide proper timing of the decoding.

REVIEW QUESTIONS AND PROBLEMS

1. Explain how the control signals ($\overline{\text{MEM R}}$, $\overline{\text{I/O R}}$, etc.) are used to access an addressed device.

2. For the circuit of Figure 4-2, construct a timing diagram for the IN 03H instruction's fetch and execute cycle. As in Problem 16 of Chapter 3, show φ_1, φ_2, SYNC, $\overline{\text{STSTB}}$, the address bus, DBIN, $\overline{\text{WR}}$, the appropriate control signals, and the data bus. In addition to these signals, add signals E_3 and $\overline{\text{DV}_3}$ of the IN I/O select.

3. Using the timing diagram constructed in Problem 2, provide a narrative explaining how the instruction IN 03H reads the data byte of I/O device 3. That is, explain how the software controls the hardware.

4. Using an 8205, design an I/O address decoder that is capable of decoding 256 addresses. A technique similar to the circuit of Figure 4-3 should be used.

5. Using a single 8205, design a system that will select (address) either input or output ports.

6. For the circuit of Figure 4-4, construct a timing diagram for the fetch-and-execute cycle of the OUT 02H instruction. Show the same signals as Problem 2, except have signal $\overline{\text{DV}_2}$ rather than $\overline{\text{DV}_3}$.

7. Provide a narrative for the timing diagram of Problem 6, explaining how instruction OUT 02H controls the hardware of Figure 4-4 in such manner as to implement the instruction.

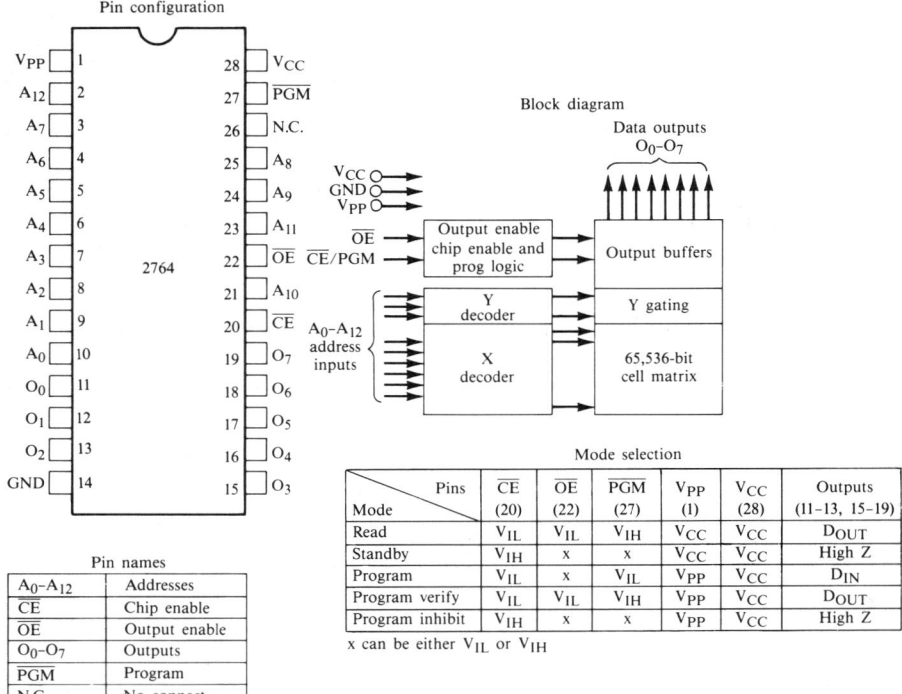

FIGURE 4-10. Intel's 2764 ROM. (Courtesy of Intel Corp.)

8. Add 3K bytes of memory to the memory system of Figure 4-6. This expanded memory is to have 1K of ROM. Use 2708 and 2114 memory chips.

9. Design a memory system that uses similar addressing techniques applied to the system of Figure 4-6 which consist of 16K of ROM and 6K of RAM. Use 2114s and 2764 memory chips. The pin configuration and definition are provided in Figure 4-10 for the 2764.

10. For the latch of output device 3 shown in Figure 4-7, design its internal logic circuitry using the latch of Figure 3-4 as a model.

11. Provide a narrative for Problem 10 explaining how the latch is controlled by the OUT 03H instruction.

12. For the system of Figure 4-7, explain the addressing techniques for both memory and I/O. Be certain to show the details of the address line codes and control signals.

13. Compare your timing diagrams of Problems 2 and 6 with the timing diagram of Figure 4-8 and discuss essential similarities and differences.

CHAPTER 5

Introduction to Programming with the 8080 Instruction Set

5-1

INTRODUCTION

This chapter begins by studying the binary coding concepts of the 8080 instruction set, as was done for the general CPU of Chapter 2. Our purpose will be to gain insight into how 8080 INSTRUCTIONS are decoded and executed by the CPU. Also of importance is for the reader to begin developing a feeling for programming. Later chapters will deal with programming on a much more sophisticated level, but it is this chapter that lays the learning foundation.

As stated in Chapter 4, we will study the control of hardware via software. To detail such a study we will refer to schematics and timing diagrams, such as those shown in Figures 4-7 and 4-8, and correlate the two. This correlation should provide an understanding of how software controls hardware.

5-2

8080 INSTRUCTION SET CODING SCHEME

If you, the reader, were the designer of a microprocessor such as the 8080, an integral part of your design would be the binary codes (op codes) that instruct

CPU operations via the IR, IR decoder, and CU. The collection, or repertoire, of op codes comprises the microprocessor's instruction set. For ease of coding instructions and minimizing decoding requirements in the IR decoder of the CPU, you would like a logical pattern to exist when coding op codes. In developing these binary codes you might begin, as we did in Chapter 2, by categorizing all CPU operations into groups and then assigning binary codes for each group. The 8080 microprocessor manufacturer categorizes CPU operations into four basic groups:

1. Data transfer.
2. Arithmetic and logic.
3. Branch control.
4. I/O and machine control.

For coding purposes these groupings were slightly modified but still held to a group of four. Since basically any 8080 CPU operation is one of four groups, a 2-bit code will suffice for coding purposes. The two most significant bits (MSBs) of the op code are reserved to indicate CPU operation. When these 2 bits are decoded by the IR decoder, the CU knows which of the CPU internal circuits must be enabled to execute this category of instruction. Of course, the microprogram of the CU instructs the CU how to execute the instruction. The coding for CPU operations according to group is approximately as shown in Table 5-1. The op-code bit positions are designated $OP_0, OP_1, \ldots, OP_7$; hence OP_7 and OP_6 are the two MSBs.

From Table 5-1 we see that many operations will involve CPU internal registers A, B, C, and so on. Then in addition to coding CPU operations, a binary coding system is needed to specify those registers involved. Not only will a binary code be required to specify individual registers, but register pairs (RPs) as well (recall a data counter is formed from an RP). Intel's coding schemes for individual registers and register pairs are shown in Tables 5-2 and 5-3.

In Tables 5-2 and 5-3 we see two variations from a strict interpretation of the coding scheme. Table 5-2 contains a nonexistent M register and Table 5-3 contains a stack pointer (SP), which is a single 16-bit register and not a 16-bit register pair. These are just coding variations.

As a note, the symbol M is used in Intel's mnemonics to indicate register pair H and L. Whenever the symbol M is used in an instruction, it refers to a memory location where *the address is the contents of RP H (H and L)*.

As an example of utilizing Tables 5-2 and 5-3 for determining machine code for mnemonic code, let us focus on the group "data transfer between registers"

TABLE 5-1. Coding for CPU Operations

OP_7	OP_6	CPU Operations
0	0	Manipulation of register contents
0	1	Data transfer between registers
1	0	Arithmetic and logic
1	1	Branch control and I/O

TABLE 5-2. Register Coding

Binary Code			Register
0	0	0	B
0	0	1	C
0	1	0	D
0	1	1	E
1	0	0	H
1	0	1	L
1	1	0	M (pseudo-register)
1	1	1	A

TABLE 5-3. RP Coding

Binary Code		Register Pair	
0	0	B	(B and C)
0	1	D	(D and E)
1	0	H	(H and L)
1	1	SP	

of Table 5-1. This group of instructions causes the CU to transfer data from one register to another or transfer data from memory to a register (or vice versa). Intel's mnemonic code is MOV r1,r2 for this group, where MOV is the mnemonic for MOVE and r1,r2 represents the registers involved in the data transfer. Register r1 is the destination register of the data transfer and r2 is the origin register of the data transfer. Specifically, if the contents of register B are to be moved to register A, the mnemonic for that instruction is MOV A,B, where r1 = A and r2 = B. To determine the machine code for MOV A,B, refer to the format of Figure 5-1, which is Intel's coding scheme for the MOV r1,r2 instruction. As shown in Figure 5-1, the binary code for a MOV r1,r2 CPU operation is 01, which agrees with Table 5-1. The destination register, which is A, is to be coded according to Table 5-2 and that code placed in bit positions DDD of Figure 5-1. The source register, which is B, is also to be coded from Table 5-2 and its coding placed in bit positions SSS of Figure 5-1. Then the machine code for MOV A, B is 01111000. Other examples of coding the MOV r1,r2 instruction are shown in Table 5-4.

To continue with the deciphering of Intel's 8080 instruction set binary coding, return to Table 5-1. Now let us consider the coding of arithmetic and logic operations. This group of operations will make use of the CPU's ALU. The CPU architecture of Figure 3-1 shows the ALU with two inputs: register A and the temporary register. Hence all ALU operations must occur between the data of register A and the temporary register. The temporary register will be loaded by the CU with the contents of either a source register (scratch-pad memory) or

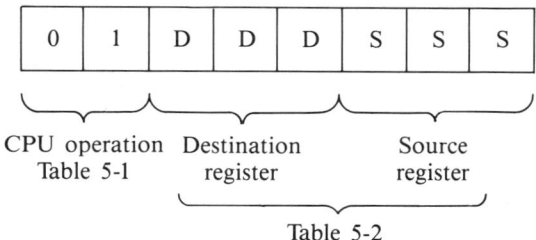

FIGURE 5-1. Machine code format for MOV r1,r2.

5-2 8080 INSTRUCTION CODING SCHEME

TABLE 5-4. Examples of Machine Code for MOV r1,r2

Mnemonic	Machine Code			Comments
MOV C,D	01	001	010	Move data from D to C
MOV D,C	01	010	001	Move data from C to D
MOV M,A	01	110	111	Move data from A to memory location M (RP H furnishes the address)
MOV A,M	01	111	110	Move data from M to A
MOV E,B	01	011	000	Move data from B to E

$$\text{CPU operation} \quad \text{DDD} \quad \text{SSS}$$

external memory, depending on the specific instruction. With some thought it becomes obvious that instructions of the arithmetic and logic groups must have a coding which will determine the ALU operation to be performed (add, subtract, OR, etc.) and also will indicate which register contents are to be loaded into the temporary register. Since all ALU operations involve register A, it need not be specified in the instruction. Table 5-5 gives the coding scheme for arithmetic and logic operations.

The machine code format for arithmetic and logic operations is shown in Figure 5-2. As in Figure 5-1, SSS represents the source register, which is determined from Table 5-2. AAA is the 3-bit code of Table 5-5, representing the arithmeitc or logic operation to be executed.

As an example of coding an arithmetic or logic instruction, consider ADD D. ADD D instructs the CU to add the contents of register D to the accumulator A and the result is to be placed in A (notice that from the mnemonic form, register A is understood). For machine coding we refer to the tables indicated in Figure 5-2, which results in a binary code of 10000010 for the instruction. Examples of other machine codes for various arithmetic or logic instructions are shown in Table 5-6.

The last category of CPU operations that we shall investigate is the coding scheme for the branch control and I/O groups of Table 5-1. In fact, we shall

TABLE 5-5. Binary and Mnemonic Coding ALU Operations

Binary Code	Arithmetic or Logic Operation	Mnemonics	
		Two Letters	Three Letters
0 0 0	Addition	AD	ADD
0 0 1	Add with carry	AC	ADC
0 1 0	Subtraction	SU	SUB
0 1 1	Subtract with borrow	SB	SBB
1 0 0	AND	AN	AND
1 0 1	Exclusive-OR	XR	XRA
1 1 0	OR	OR	ORA
1 1 1	Compare	CP	CMP

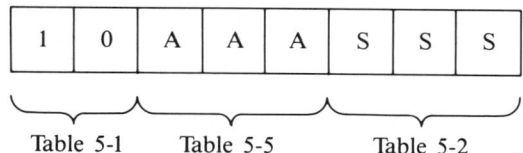

FIGURE 5-2. Machine code format for arithmetic and logic operations.

discuss only conditional branch operations, which should suffice to provide adequate understanding of the coding concepts for this group.

There are three types of branch operations. The branch operations and their binary codes are shown in Table 5-7. At this point the reader need not be concerned with every detail of branch operations, only with the overall concepts. Notice that a jump and a call both allow the CPU to transfer program execution from one memory location to another. However, the call stores the contents of PC + 1 (next memory location), which is the return address, in the stack so that it may be recalled by the CPU when a return instruction is given.

As stated, we are coding conditional branch operations, which essentially means that the CU will check a condition flag for a proper logic state to determine if the branch instruction is to be executed. Then the programmer (you) must be able to determine the machine code, which indicates (1) the branch operation to be executed, (2) the condition flag to be checked, and (3) the logic state required of the condition flag in order that the instruction execution be implemented. The coding requirement of 1 is satisfied by the binary codes of Table 5-7. For the requirements of 2 and 3, see Table 5-8. The machine code format is shown in Figure 5-3.

TABLE 5-6. Examples of Arithmetic and Logic Instructions Machine Codes[a]

Machine Code	Mnemonic	Arithmetic or Logic Operation
10011110	SBB M	The contents of the memory location whose address is contained in H and L are subtracted from the contents of A. The result is placed in A.
10111000	CMP B	The contents of B are compared (subtracted) with the contents of A and the result is indicated by appropriately altering the C and Z flags. The values being compared remain unchanged.
10101001	XRA C	The contents of C are exclusive-ORed with the contents of A. The result is placed in A. Notice that XRA A clears A.

[a]See Tables 5-1, 5-5, and 5-2.

TABLE 5-7. Machine Code for Branch Operations

Machine Code	Branch Operation
000	Return: Used to return the CPU to the execution of an interrupted program.
010	Jump: Used to jump from one memory location to another, with no intention of returning to the memory location where the jump instruction was given.
100	Call: Used to "call up" (jump to) a subroutine (another program) for execution, with the intention of returning after execution of the subroutine. As a result, a call instruction must store (in the stack) the return address.

As an example of machine coding a conditional branch instruction, let us consider the instruction JNZ ADR. The mnemonic JNZ represents "jump on nonzero" and ADR is symbolic of the operand, which is a memory address. When JNZ ADR is executed, the CU will check the logic state of the Z flag. If the Z flag is in a 0 state (see NZ of Table 5-8), program execution will be transferred (jump) to the memory location specified by the 16-bit binary number symbolically represented by ADR. However, if the Z flag is in a 1 state, the CU will not transfer program execution to the memory location specified by ADR but rather continues program execution by fetching the next sequential instruction after JNZ ADR. Determining the machine code, refer first to Figure 5-3 for the format and then Tables 5-8 and 5-7, as specified in Figure 5-3. Hence the mnemonic JNZ will be assembled into machine code 11 000 010. Of course since an address is required, two more 8-bit binary numbers must follow 11 000 010. Then the JNZ instruction will require three 8-bit codes; the first represents the op code (11000010) and two additional codes specify the address. These three 8-bit codes will be stored in successive memory locations.

Other machine codes for various conditional branch instructions are shown in Table 5-9. Refer to Figure 5-3 for the binary formatting. To reiterate, the me-

TABLE 5-8. Machine Code for Condition Flag and Logic State

Machine Code	Condition Flag	Logic State of Flag	Mnemonic Code	Result of the CPU's ALU Operation
000	Zero	0	NZ	Is not zero
001	(Z flag)	1	Z	Is zero
010	Carry	0	NC	There is no carry
011	(C flag)	1	C	There is a carry
100	Parity	0	PO	Has odd parity
101	(P flag)	1	PE	Has even parity
110	Sign	0	P	Is positive
111	(S flag)	1	M	Is negative

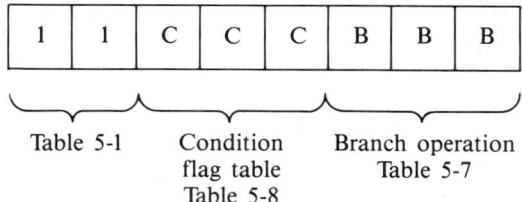

FIGURE 5-3. Machine code format for conditional branch instructions.

chanics of instruction execution are not of primary importance at this time, but rather, the concepts of coding instructions.

This concludes our deciphering of Intel's machine coding of the 8080 instruction set. Even though only a relatively few instructions were coded (there are 245 instructions), it is believed that enough examples were given that the concepts of instruction coding should be well understood. Also from previous discussions the role of the IR and IR decoder should be quite clear. Fortunately, it is not necessary to memorize an instruction coding format, for Intel has already done most of the assembly for the user and provides the machine code in table form. Such a table is shown in Table 5-10 and in Appendix A. For brevity, machine codes are given in their hexadecimal equivalent rather than binary. This presentation will be used primarily throughout the remainder of this book.

Also notice in Table 5-10 that the term *byte* is used in instructions, such as OUT byte (machine code D3) and IN byte (machine code DB). Byte is defined to be any 8-bit binary number. Thus OUT byte is a two-byte instruction; the first byte for the op code and the second byte for the address of the output device. We shall henceforth use "byte" to describe any 8-bit word. That terminology probably arose by imagining that an 8-bit CPU would "bite" (latch)

TABLE 5-9. Examples of Conditional Branch Instruction Machine Codes[a]

Machine Code			Mnemonic	CPU Operation
11	001	010	JZ ADR	Jump to the memory location specified by ADR if $Z = 1$; otherwise, continue program execution.
11	100	010	JPO ADR	Jump to the memory location specified by ADR if $P = 0$; otherwise, continue program execution.
11	001	100	CZ ADR	Jump to the memory location specified by ADR if $Z = 1$, and store (PUSH) the *address* of the next instruction on the stack; otherwise, continue program execution.
11	111	000	RM	If $S = 1$, retrieve (POP) two 8-bit codes from the stack and place them in the PC. Then Return to the address specified by the PC and begin program execution. If $S = 0$, continue program execution.

[a]See Tables 5-1, 5-8, and 5-7.

TABLE 5-10. 8080 Instruction Set

00	NOP			2B	DCX	H		56	MOV	D,M		81	ADD C	AC	XRA H		D7	RST 2	
01	LXI	B,dble		2C	INR	L		57	MOV	D,A		82	ADD D	AD	XRA L		D8	RC	
02	STAX	B		2D	DCR	L		58	MOV	E,B		83	ADD E	AE	XRA M		D9	---	
03	INX	B		2E	MVI	L,byte		59	MOV	E,C		84	ADD H	AF	XRA A		DA	JC	adr
04	INR	B		2F	CMA			5A	MOV	E,D		85	ADD L	B0	ORA B		DB	IN	byte
05	DCR	B		30	---			5B	MOV	E,E		86	ADD M	B1	ORA C		DC	CC	adr
06	MVI	B,byte		31	LXI	SP,dble		5C	MOV	E,H		87	ADD A	B2	ORA D		DD	---	
07	RLC			32	STA	adr		5D	MOV	E,L		88	ADC B	B3	ORA E		DE	SBI	byte
08	---			33	INX	SP		5E	MOV	E,M		89	ADC C	B4	ORA H		DF	RST 3	
09	DAD	B		34	INR	M		5F	MOV	E,A		8A	ADC D	B5	ORA L		E0	RPO	
0A	LDAX	B		35	DCR	M		60	MOV	H,B		8B	ADC E	B6	ORA M		E1	POP H	
0B	DCX	B		36	MVI	M,byte		61	MOV	H,C		8C	ADC H	B7	ORA A		E2	JPO	adr
0C	INR	C		37	STC			62	MOV	H,D		8D	ADC L	B8	CMP B		E3	XTHL	
0D	DCR	C		38	---			63	MOV	H,E		8E	ADC M	B9	CMP C		E4	CPO	adr
0E	MVI	C,byte		39	DAD	SP		64	MOV	H,H		8F	ADC A	BA	CMP D		E5	PUSH H	
0F	RRC			3A	LDA	adr		65	MOV	H,L		90	SUB B	BB	CMP E		E6	ANI	byte
10	---			3B	DCX	SP		66	MOV	H,M		91	SUB C	BC	CMP H		E7	RST 4	
11	LXI	D,dble		3C	INR	A		67	MOV	H,A		92	SUB D	BD	CMP L		E8	RPE	
12	STAX	D		3D	DCR	A		68	MOV	L,B		93	SUB E	BE	CMP M		E9	PCHL	
13	INX	D		3E	MVI	A,byte		69	MOV	L,C		94	SUB H	BF	CMP A		EA	JPE	adr
14	INR	D		3F	CMC			6A	MOV	L,D		95	SUB L	C0	RNZ		EB	XCHG	
15	DCR	D		40	MOV	B,B		6B	MOV	L,E		96	SUB M	C1	POP B		EC	CPE	adr

Hex	Instruction	Operand	Hex	Instruction	Operand	Hex	Instruction	Operand
16	MVI	D,byte	6C	MOV	L,H	ED	---	
17	RAL		6D	MOV	L,L	EE	XRI	byte
18	---		6E	MOV	L,M	EF	RST 5	
19	DAD	D	6F	MOV	L,A	F0	RP	
1A	LDAX	D	70	MOV	M,B	F1	POP PSW	
1B	DCX	D	71	MOV	M,C	F2	JP	adr
1C	INR	E	72	MOV	M,D	F3	DI	
1D	DCR	E	73	MOV	M,E	F4	CP	adr
1E	MVI	E,byte	74	MOV	M,H	F5	PUSH PSW	
1F	RAR		75	MOV	M,L	F6	ORI	byte
20			76	HLT		F7	RST 6	
21	LXI	H,dble	77	MOV	M,A	F8	RM	
22	SHLD	adr	78	MOV	A,B	F9	SPHL	
23	INX	H	79	MOV	A,C	FA	JM	adr
24	INR	H	7A	MOV	A,D	FB	EI	
25	DCR	H	7B	MOV	A,E	FC	CM	adr
26	MVI	H,byte	7C	MOV	A,H	FD	---	
27	DAA		7D	MOV	A,L	FE	CPI	byte
28	---		7E	MOV	A,M	FF	RST 7	
29	DAD	H	7F	MOV	A,A			
2A	LHLD	adr	80	ADD	B			

Hex	Instruction	Operand	Hex	Instruction	Operand
41	MOV	B,C	97	SUB	A
42	MOV	B,D	98	SBB	B
43	MOV	B,E	99	SBB	C
44	MOV	B,H	9A	SBB	D
45	MOV	B,L	9B	SBB	E
46	MOV	B,M	9C	SBB	H
47	MOV	B,A	9D	SBB	L
48	MOV	C,B	9E	SBB	M
49	MOV	C,C	9F	SBB	A
4A	MOV	C,D	A0	ANA	B
4B	MOV	C,E	A1	ANA	C
4C	MOV	C,H	A2	ANA	D
4D	MOV	C,L	A3	ANA	E
4E	MOV	C,M	A4	ANA	H
4F	MOV	C,A	A5	ANA	L
50	MOV	D,B	A6	ANA	M
51	MOV	D,C	A7	ANA	A
52	MOV	D,D	A8	XRA	B
53	MOV	D,E	A9	XRA	C
54	MOV	D,H	AA	XRA	D
55	MOV	D,L	AB	XRA	E

Hex	Instruction	Operand
C2	JNZ	adr
C3	JMP	adr
C4	CNZ	adr
C5	PUSH B	
C6	ADI	byte
C7	RST 0	
C8	RZ	
C9	RET	
CA	JZ	adr
CB	---	
CC	CZ	adr
CD	CALL	adr
CE	ACI	byte
CF	RST 1	
D0	RNC	
D1	POP D	
D2	JNC	ADR
D3	OUT	byte
D4	CNC	adr
D5	PUSH D	
D6	SUI	byte

5-2 8080 INSTRUCTION CODING SCHEME

(Courtesy of Intel Corp.)

data from the data bus 8 bits at a time; hence, relative to the CPU, 8 bits comprise one byte. With this reasoning half of a byte (4 bits) is termed a *nibble*.

In viewing Table 5-10, you will note a number of unfamiliar instructions. The next section gives an explanation of each instruction.

5-3 8080 INSTRUCTION SET

Before writing a program for a microprocessor, the programmer must be aware of the microprocessor's vocabulary; that is, the programmer must know the microprocessor's instruction set. The instruction set of various microprocessors varies from type to type and for that reason the designer/manufacturer of each type must make the instruction set available to the user. The instruction set and an explanation of CPU operations resulting from execution of an instruction are supplied by the manufacturer in a programming manual and/or user's manual. This section includes a reproduction of Intel's instruction set as taken from Intel's *MCS-80 User's Manual*. The author encourages the reader to obtain an Intel manual containing the instruction set—there is no substitute for the real thing.

Do not attempt to memorize the instruction set and explanations; rather, concentrate on understanding the explanation of each instruction. This is the only reasonable approach, since there is just too much to memorize. As one uses the instructions, less and less reference to the manual will be required. This will occur through familiarity and understanding rather than memory. Also, as one learns the instruction set for one type of microprocessor, the foundation is being laid for understanding the basic principles of all microprocessor instruction sets.

To study this section:

1. Confirm the topics and concepts that we have already discussed. This includes:
    a. Instruction categories (data transfer, etc.).
    b. Condition flags and their meaning.
    c. Symbols, abbreviations, and register coding.
    d. Number of machine cycles required and control signals generated.
2. Read the explanation of each instruction and attempt to gain a feeling for CPU operations resulting from execution of that instruction.
3. Study the machine code format of each instruction and attempt to assemble some machine codes for various sample instructions. Verify your assembly of mnemonic code into machine code using Table 5-10. Also confirm the machine code of those examples given in Tables 5-4, 5-5, and 5-9.
4. Study and understand the various addressing modes used in programming the 8080. Some brief explanations and examples of addressing modes will be offered to aid Intel's explanations. For concreteness of addressing modes, read Intel's explanation of each example instruction.
    a. *Direct addressing*. These are three-byte instructions where the first byte is the op code and the remaining two bytes furnish the memory address of the data operation (read or write). Examples are: STA ADR, SHLD ADR, and LDA ADR.

b. *Register addressing*. These are single-byte instructions which involve CPU register content manipulation. The instruction identifies (addresses) the register(s) to be involved in the manipulation. Examples are: DCR B, DAD B, INX D, MOV B, E and ANA D.
c. *Register Indirect Addressing*. This type of instruction requires data from memory. However, being a single-byte instruction, the memory address cannot be coded as part of the instruction. To "extend" the addressing capability of these instructions the instruction specifies a register pair to serve as the DC. Examples are: LDAX B, MOV B, M, ADD M, INR M, and STAX D.
d. *Immediate Addressing*. The data to be manipulated by the instruction is part of that instruction's machine code. As a result this type of instruction is either two or three bytes. The first byte is the op code and the next byte(s) is the data. Examples are: LXI B, 253CH (H identifies 253C as being a hexadecimal value), MVI A, 3DH, and ADI 61H. Notice that the mnemonics identify immediate addressing with the symbol I.

Notice from the instruction set that when an instruction involves a register pair Intel chose to use the symbol X in the mnemonic.

The following is a reproduction of the 8080 instruction set as reprinted from Intel's MCS-80 *User's Manual*.*

A computer, no matter how sophisticated, can only do what it is "told" to do. One "tells" the computer what to do via a series of coded instructions referred to as a Program. The realm of the programmer is referred to as Software, in contrast to the Hardware that comprises the actual computer equipment. A computer's software refers to all of the programs that have been written for that computer.

When a computer is designed, the engineers provide the Central Processing Unit (CPU) with the ability to perform a particular set of operations. The CPU is designed such that a specific operation is performed when the CPU control logic decodes a particular instruction. Consequently, the operations that can be performed by a CPU define the computer's Instruction Set.

Each computer instruction allows the programmer to initiate the performance of a specific operation. All computers implement certain arithmetic operations in their instruction set, such as an instruction to add the contents of two registers. Often logical operations (e.g., OR the contents of two registers) and register operate instructions (e.g., increment a register) are included in the instruction set. A computer's instruction set will also have instructions that move data between registers, between a register and memory, and between a register and an I/O device. Most instruction sets also provide Conditional Instructions. A conditional instruction specifies an operation to be performed only if certain conditions have been met; for example, jump to a particular instruction if the result of the last operation was zero. Conditional instructions provide a program with a decision-making capability.

*Intel Corporation, October 1977, pp. 4-1—4-14. Reprinted by permission.

By logically organizing a sequence of instructions into a coherent program, the programmer can "tell" the computer to perform a very specific and useful function.

The computer, however, can only execute programs whose instructions are in a binary coded form (i.e., a series of 1's and 0's), that is called Machine Code. Because it would be extremely cumbersome to program in machine code, programming languages have been developed. There are programs available which convert the programming language instructions into machine code that can be interpreted by the processor.

One type of programming language is Assembly Language. A unique assembly language mnemonic is assigned to each of the computer's instructions. The programmer can write a program (called the Source Program) using these mnemonics and certain operands; the source program is then converted into machine instructions (called the Object Code). Each assembly language instruction is converted into one machine code instruction (1 or more bytes) by an Assembler program. Assembly languages are usually machine dependent (i.e., they are usually able to run on only one type of computer).

The 8080 Instruction Set

The 8080 instruction set includes five different types of instructions:

- *Data Transfer Group:* move data between registers or between memory and registers.
- *Arithmetic Group:* add, subtract, increment or decrement data in registers or in memory.
- *Logical Group:* AND, OR, EXCLUSIVE-OR, compare, rotate or complement data in registers or in memory.
- *Branch Group:* conditional and unconditional jump instructions, subroutine call instructions and return instructions.
- *Stack, I/O and Machine Control Group:* includes I/O instructions, as well as instructions for maintaining the stack and internal control flags.

Instruction and Data Format. Memory for the 8080 is organized into 8-bit quantities, called Bytes. Each byte has a unique 16-bit binary address corresponding to its sequential position in memory. The 8080 can directly address up to 65,536 bytes of memory, which may consist of both read-only memory (ROM) elements and random-access memory (RAM) elements (read/write memory).

Data in the 8080 is stored in the form of 8-bit binary integers:

Data Word

D_7	D_6	D_5	D_4	D_3	D_2	D_1	D_0
MSB							LSB

When a register or data word contains a binary number, it is necessary to establish the order in which the bits of the number are written. In the Intel 8080, BIT 0 is referred to as the Least Significant Bit (LSB), and BIT 7 (of an 8-bit number) is referred to as the Most Significant Bit (MSB).

The 8080 program instructions may be one, two or three bytes in length. Multiple byte instructions must be stored in successive memory locations; the address of the first byte is always used as the address of the instructions. The exact instruction format will depend on the particular operation to be executed.

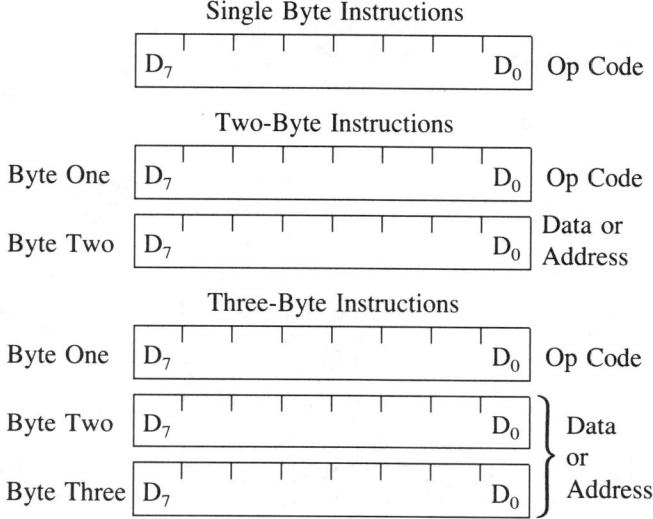

Addressing Modes. Often the data that is to be operated on is stored in memory. When multi-byte numeric data is used, the data, like instructions, is stored in successive memory locations, with the least significant byte first, followed by increasingly significant bytes. The 8080 has four different modes for addressing data stored in memory or in registers:

- *Direct:* Bytes 2 and 3 of the instruction contain the exact memory address of the data item (the low-order bits of the address are in byte 2, the high-order bits in byte 3).
- *Register:* The instruction specifies the register or register-pair in which the data is located.
- *Register indirect:* The instruction specifies a register-pair which contains the memory address where the data is located (the high-order bits of the address are in the first register of the pair, the low-order bits in the second).
- *Immediate:* The instruction contains the data itself. This is either an 8-bit quantity or a 16-bit quantity (least significant byte first, most significant byte second).

Unless directed by an interrupt or branch instruction the execution of instructions proceeds through consecutively increasing memory locations. A branch instruction can specify the address of the next instruction to be executed in one of two ways:

- *Direct:* The branch instruction contains the address of the next instruction to be executed. (Except for the 'RST' instruction byte 2 contains the low-order address and byte 3 the high-order address.)

- *Register indirect:* The branch instruction indicates a register-pair which contains the address of the next instruction to be executed. (The high-order bits of the address are in the first register of the pair, the low-order bits in the second.)

The RST instruction is a special one-byte call instruction (usually used during interrupt sequences). RST includes a three-bit field; program control is transferred to the instruction whose address is eight times the contents of this three-bit field.

Condition Flags. There are five condition flags associated with the execution of instructions on the 8080. They are Zero, Sign, Parity, Carry, and Auxiliary Carry, and are each represented by a 1-bit register in the CPU. A flag is "set" by forcing the bit to 1; "reset" by forcing the bit to 0.

Unless indicated otherwise, when an instruction affects a flag, it affects it in the following manner:

- *Zero:* If the result of an instruction has the value 0, this flag is set; otherwise it is reset.
- *Sign:* If the most significant bit of the result of the operation has the value 1, this flag is set; otherwise it is reset.
- *Parity:* If the modulo 2 sum of the bits of the result of the operation is 0, (i.e., if the result has even parity), this flag is set; otherwise it is reset (i.e., if the result has odd parity).
- *Carry:* If the instruction resulted in a carry (from addition), or a borrow (from subtraction or a comparison) out of the high-order bit, this flag is set; otherwise it is reset.
- *Auxiliary Carry:* If the instruction caused a carry out of bit 3 and into bit 4 of the resulting value, the auxiliary carry is set; otherwise it is reset. This flag is affected by single precision additions, subtractions, increments, decrements, comparisons, and logical operations, but is principally used with additions and increments preceding a DAA (Decimal Adjust Accumulator) instruction.

Symbols and Abbreviations. The following symbols and abbreviations are used in the subsequent description of the 8080 instructions:

Symbols	Meaning
accumulator	Register A
addr	16-bit address quantity
data	8-bit data quantity
data 16	16-bit data quantity
byte 2	The second byte of the instruction
byte 3	The third byte of the instruction
port	8-bit address of an I/O device
r,r1,r2	One of the registers A, B, C, D, E, H, L
DDD,SSS	The bit pattern designating one of the registers A,B,C,D,E,H,L (DDD = destination, SSS = source):

Symbols	Meaning

DDD or SSS	Register Name
111	A
000	B
001	C
010	D
011	E
100	H
101	L

rp — One of the register pairs:
B represents the B,C pair with B as the high-order register and C as the low-order register;
D represents the D,E pair with D as the high-order register and E as the low-order register;
H represents the H,L pair with H as the high-order register and L as the low-order register;
SP represents the 16-bit stack pointer register.

RP — The bit pattern designating one of the register pairs B,D,H,SP:

RP	Register Pair
00	B-C
01	D-E
10	H-L
11	SP

rh — The first (high-order) register of a designated register pair.

rl — The second (low-order) register of a designated register pair.

PC — 16-bit program counter register (PCH and PCL are used to refer to the high-order and low-order 8 bits respectively).

SP — 16-bit stack pointer register (SPH and SPL are used to refer to the high-order and low-order 8 bits respectively).

r_m — Bit m of the register r (bits are number 7 through 0 from left to right).

Z,S,P,CY,AC — The condition flags:
Zero,
Sign,
Parity,
Carry,
and Auxiliary Carry, respectively.

( ) — The contents of the memory location or registers enclosed in the parentheses.

← — "Is transferred to"

Symbols	Meaning
$\wedge$	Logical AND
$\veebar$	Exclusive OR
$\vee$	Inclusive OR
$+$	Addition
$-$	Two's complement subtraction
$*$	Multiplication
$\leftrightarrow$	"Is exchanged with"
$\overline{}$	The one's complement (e.g., $(\overline{A})$)
n	The restart number 0 through 7
NNN	The binary representation 000 through 111 for restart number 0 through 7, respectively.

Description Format. The following pages provide a detailed description of the instruction set of the 8080. Each instruction is described in the following manner:

1. The MAC 80 assembler format, consisting of the instruction mnemonic and operand fields, is printed in BOLDFACE on the left side of the first line.
2. The name of the instruction is enclosed in parentheses on the right side of the first line.
3. The next line(s) contain a symbolic description of the operation of the instruction.
4. This is followed by a narrative description of the operation of the instruction.
5. The following line(s) contain the binary fields and patterns that comprise the machine instruction.
6. The last four lines contain incidental information about the execution of the instruction. The number of machine cycles and states required to execute the instruction are listed first. If the instruction has two possible execution times, as in a Conditional Jump, both times will be listed, separated by a slash. Next, any significant data addressing modes (see Page 4-2) are listed. The last line lists any of the five Flags that are affected by the execution of the instruction.

Data Transfer Group. This group of instructions transfers data to and from registers and memory. Condition flags are not affected by any instruction in this group.

MOV r1,r2   (Move Register)
    (r1) ← (r2)
    The content of register r2 is moved to register r1.

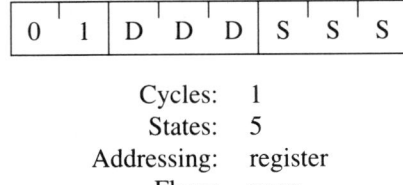

Cycles: 1
States: 5
Addressing: register
Flags: none

MOV r,M   (Move from memory)
(r) ← ((H) (L))
The content of the memory location, whose address is in registers H and L, is moved to register r.

Cycles: 2
States: 7
Addressing: reg. indirect
Flags: none

MOV M,r   (Move to memory)
((H) (L)) ← (r)
The content of register r is moved to the memory location whose address is in registers H and L.

0	1	1	1	0	S	S	S

Cycles: 2
States: 7
Addressing: reg. indirect
Flags: none

MVI r,data (Move Immediate)
(r) ← (byte 2)
The content of byte 2 of the instruction is moved to register r.

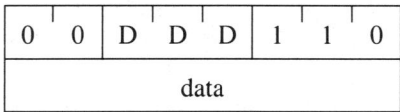

Cycles: 2
States: 7
Addressing: immediate
Flags: none

MVI M,data   (Move to memory immediate)
((H) (L)) ← (byte 2)
The content of byte 2 of the instruction is moved to the memory location whose address is in registers H and L.

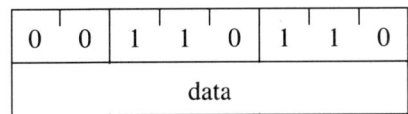

Cycles: 3
States: 10
Addressing: immed./reg. indirect
Flags: none

LXI rp,data 16   (Load register pair immediate)
(rh) ← (byte 3),
(rl) ← (byte 2)
Byte 3 of the instruction is moved into the high-order register (rh) of the register pair rp. Byte 2 of the instruction is moved into the low-order register (rl) of the register pair rp.

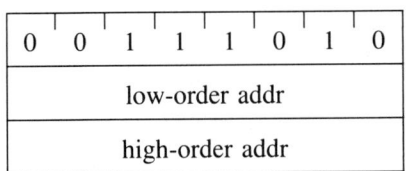

Cycles: 3
States: 10
Addressing: immediate
Flags: none

LDA addr   (Load Accumulator direct)
(A) ← ((byte 3)(byte 2))
The content of the memory location, whose address is specified in byte 2 and byte 3 of the instruction, is moved to register A.

0	0	1	1	1	0	1	0
low-order addr							
high-order addr							

Cycles: 4
States: 13
Addressing: direct
Flags: none

STA addr   (Store Accumulator direct)
((byte 3)(byte 2)) ← (A)
The content of the accumulator is moved to the memory location whose address is specified in byte 2 and byte 3 of the instruction.

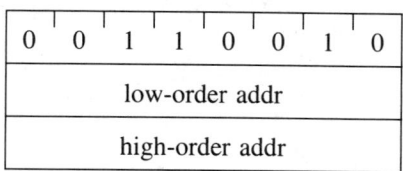

Cycles: 4
States: 13
Addressing: direct
Flags: none

LHLD addr   (Load H and L direct)
(L) ← ((byte 3)(byte 2))
(H) ← ((byte 3)(byte 2) + 1)
The content of the memory location, whose address is specified in byte 2 and byte 3 of the instruction, is moved to register L. The content of the memory location at the succeeding address is moved to register H.

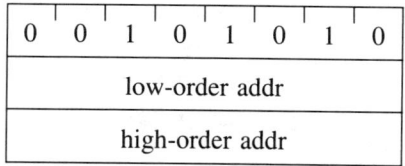

Cycles: 5
States: 16
Addressing: direct
Flags: none

SHLD addr   (Store H and L direct)
((byte 3)(byte 2)) ← (L)
((byte 3)(byte 2) + 1) ← (H)
The content of register L is moved to the memory location whose address is specified in byte 2 and byte 3. The content of register H is moved to the succeeding memory location.

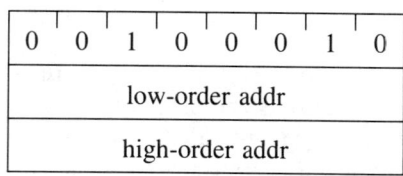

Cycles: 5
States: 16
Addressing: direct
Flags: none

LDAX rp   (Load accumulator indirect)
   (A) ← ((rp))
   The content of the memory location, whose address is in the register pair rp, is moved to register A. Note: only register pairs rp = B (registers B and C) or rp = D (registers D and E) may be specified.

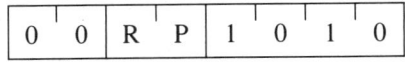

   Cycles: 5
   States: 7
   Addressing: reg. indirect
   Flags: none

STAX rp   (Store accumulator indirect)
   ((rp)) ← (A)
   The content of register A is moved to the memory location whose address is in the register pair rp. Note: only register pairs rp = B (registers B and C) or rp = D (registers D and E) may be specified.

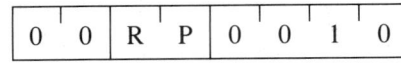

   Cycles: 2
   States: 7
   Addressing: reg. indirect
   Flags: none

XCHG   (Exchange H and L with D and E)
   (H) ↔ (D)
   (L) ↔ (E)
   The contents of registers H and L are exchanged with the contents of registers D and E.

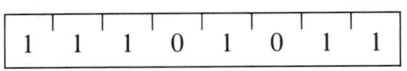

   Cycles: 1
   States: 4
   Addressing: register
   Flags: none

Arithmetic Group. This group of instructions performs arithmetic operations on data in registers and memory.

Unless indicated otherwise, all instructions in this group affect the Zero, Sign, Parity, Carry, and Auxiliary Carry flags according to the standard rules.

All subtraction operations are performed via two's complement arithmetic and set the carry flag to one to indicate a borrow and clear it to indicate no borrow.

ADD r   (Add Register)
(A) ← (A) + (r)
The content of register r is added to the content of the accumulator. The result is placed in the accumulator.

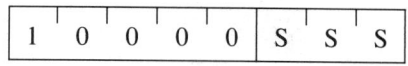

Cycles: 1
States: 4
Addressing: register
Flags: Z,S,P,CY,AC

ADD M   (Add memory)
(A) ← (A) + ((H) (L))
The content of the memory location whose address is contained in the H and L registers is added to the content of the accumulator. The result is placed in the accumulator.

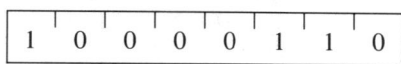

Cycles: 2
States: 7
Addressing: reg. indirect
Flags: Z,S,P,CY,AC

ADI data   (Add immediate)
(A) ← (A) + (byte 2)
The content of the second byte of the instruction is added to the content of the accumulator. The result is placed in the accumulator.

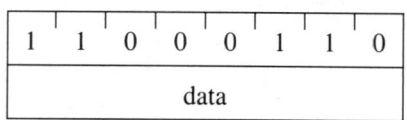

Cycles: 2
States: 7
Addressing: immediate
Flags: Z,S,P,CY,AC

ADC r   (Add Register with carry)
(A) ← (A) + (r) + (CY)
The content of register r and the content of the carry bit are added to the content of the accumulator. The result is placed in the accumulator.

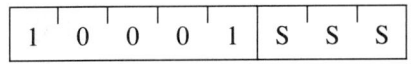

      Cycles: 1
      States: 4
 Addressing: register
       Flags: Z,S,P,CY,AC

ADC M   (Add memory with carry)
(A) ← (A) + ((H) (L)) + (CY)
The content of the memory location whose address is contained in the H and L registers and the content of the CY flag are added to the accumulator. The result is placed in the accumulator.

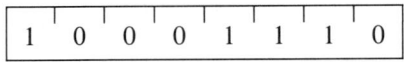

      Cycles: 2
      States: 7
 Addressing: reg. indirect
       Flags: Z,S,P,CY,AC

ACI data   (Add immediate with carry)
(A) ← (A) + (byte 2) + (CY)
The content of the second byte of the instruction and the content of the CY flag are added to the contents of the accumulator. The result is placed in the accumulator.

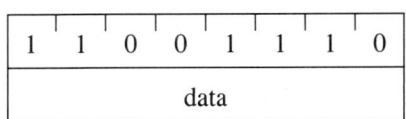

      Cycles: 2
      States: 7
 Addressing: immediate
       Flags: Z,S,P,CY,AC

SUB r   (Subtract Register)
(A) ← (A) − (r)
The content of register r is subtracted from the content of the accumulator. The result is placed in the accumulator.

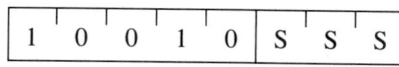

    Cycles: 1
    States: 4
  Addressing: register
    Flags: Z,S,P,CY,AC

SUB M   (Subtract memory)
(A) ← (A) − ((H) (L))
The content of the memory location whose address is contained in the H and L registers is subtracted from the content of the accumulator. The result is placed in the accumulator.

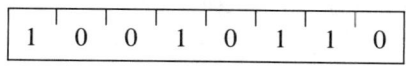

    Cycles: 2
    States: 7
  Addressing: reg. indirect
    Flags: Z,S,P,CY,AC

SUI data   (Subtract immediate)
(A) ← (A) − (byte 2)
The content of the second byte of the instruction is subtracted from the content of the accumulator. The result is placed in the accumulator.

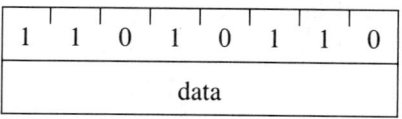

    Cycles: 2
    States: 7
  Addressing: immediate
    Flags: Z,S,P,CY,AC

SBB r   (Subtract Register with borrow)
(A) ← (A) − (r) − (CY)
The content of register r and the content of the CY flag are both subtracted from the accumulator. The result is placed in the accumulator.

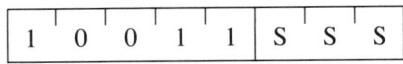

Cycles: 1
States: 4
Addressing: register
Flags: Z,S,P,CY,AC

SBB M   (Subtract memory with borrow)
(A) ← (A) − ((H) (L)) − (CY)
The content of the memory location whose address is contained in the H and L registers and the content of the CY flag are both subtracted from the accumulator. The result is placed in the accumulator.

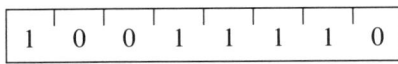

Cycles: 2
States: 7
Addressing: reg. indirect
Flags: Z,S,P,CY,AC

SBI data   (Subtract immediate with borrow)
(A) ← (A) − (byte 2) − (CY)
The contents of the second byte of the instruction and the contents of the CY flag are both subtracted from the accumulator. The result is placed in the accumulator.

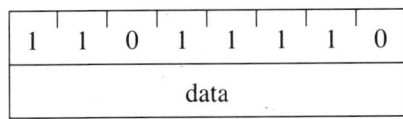

Cycles: 2
States: 7
Addressing: immediate
Flags: Z,S,P,CY,AC

INR r   (Increment Register)

(r) ← (r) + 1

The content of register r is incremented by one. Note: All condition flags except CY are affected.

        Cycles: 1
        States: 5
  Addressing: register
         Flags: Z,S,P,AC

INR M   (Increment memory)

((H) (L)) ← ((H) (L)) + 1

The content of the memory location whose address is contained in the H and L registers is incremented by one. Note: All condition flags except CY are affected.

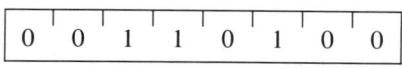

        Cycles: 3
        States: 10
  Addressing: reg. indirect
         Flags: Z,S,P,AC

DCR r   (Decrement Register)

(r) ← (r) − 1

The content of register r is decremented by one. Note: All condition flags except CY are affected.

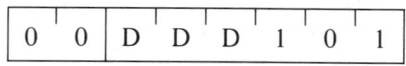

        Cycles: 1
        States: 5
  Addressing: register
         Flags: Z,S,P,AC

DCR M   (Decrement memory)
((H) (L)) ← ((H) (L)) − 1
The content of the memory location whose address is contained in the H and L registers is decremented by one. Note: All condition flags except CY are affected.

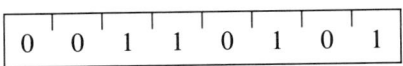

Cycles: 3
States: 10
Addressing: reg. indirect
Flags: Z,S,P,AC

INX rp   (Increment register pair)
(rh) (rl) ← (rh) (rl) + 1
The content of the register pair rp is incremented by one. Note: No condition flags are affected.

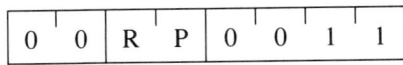

Cycles: 1
States: 5
Addressing: register
Flags: none

DCX rp   (Decrement register pair)
(rh) (rl) ← (rh) (rl) − 1
The content of the register pair rp is decremented by one. Note: No condition flags are affected.

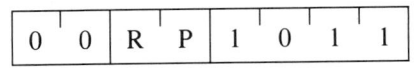

Cycles: 1
States: 5
Addressing: register
Flags: none

DAD rp   (Add register pair to H and L)
(H) (L) ← (H) (L) + (rh) (rl)
The content of the register pair rp is added to the content of the register pair H and L. The result is placed in the register pair H and L. Note: Only the CY flag is affected. It is set if there is a carry out of the double precision add; otherwise it is reset.

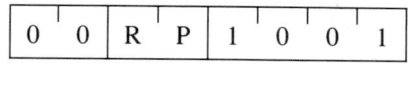

Cycles: 3
States: 10
Addressing: register
Flags: CY

DAA   (Decimal Adjust Accumulator)
The eight-bit number in the accumulator is adjusted to form two four-bit Binary-Coded-Decimal digits by the following process:
1. If the value of the least significant 4 bits of the accumulator is greater than 9 or if the AC flag is set, 6 is added to the accumulator.
2. If the value of the most significant 4 bits of the accumulator is now greater than 9, or if the CY flag is set, 6 is added to the most significant 4 bits of the accumulator.
NOTE: All flags are affected.

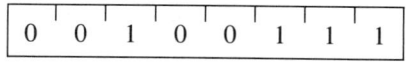

Cycles: 1
States: 4
Flags: Z,S,P,CY,AC

Logical Group.   This group of instructions performs logical (Boolean) operations on data in registers and memory and on condition flags.

Unless indicated otherwise, all instructions in this group affect the Zero, Sign, Parity, Auxiliary Carry, and Carry flags according to the standard rules.

ANA r   (AND Register)
(A) ← (A) ∧ (r)
The content of register r is logically anded with the content of the accumulator. The result is placed in the accumulator. The CY flag is cleared.

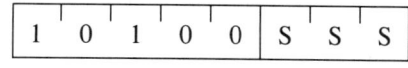

Cycles: 1
States: 4
Addressing: register
Flags: Z,S,P,CY,AC

ANA M   (AND memory)

(A) ← (A) ∧ ((H) (L))

The contents of the memory location whose address is contained in the H and L registers is logically anded with the content of the accumulator. The result is placed in the accumulator. The CY flag is cleared.

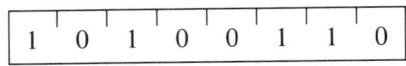

Cycles: 2
States: 7
Addressing: reg. indirect
Flags: Z,S,P,CY,AC

ANI data   (AND immmediate)

(A) ← (A) ∧ (byte 2)

The content of the second byte of the instruction is logically anded with the contents of the accumulator. The result is placed in the accumulator. The CY and AC flags are cleared.

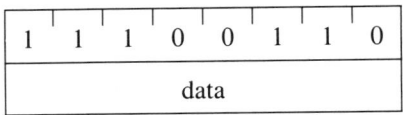

Cycles: 2
States: 7
Addressing: immediate
Flags: Z,S,P,CY,AC

XRA r   (Exclusive OR Register)

(A) ← (A) ⊻ (r)

The content of register r is exclusive-OR'd with the content of the accumulator. The result is placed in the accumulator. The CY and AC flags are cleared.

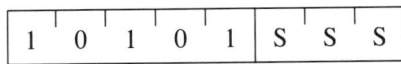

Cycles: 1
States: 4
Addressing: register
Flags: Z,S,P,CY,AC

XRA M   (Exclusive OR Memory)

(A) ← (A) ∀ ((H) (L))

The content of the memory location whose address is contained in the H and L registers is exclusive-OR'd with the content of the accumulator. The result is placed in the accumulator. The CY and AC flags are cleared.

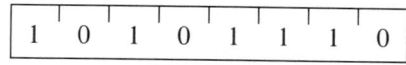

```
Cycles:     2
States:     7
Addressing: reg. indirect
Flags:      Z,S,P,CY,AC
```

XRI data   (Exclusive OR immediate)

(A) ← (A) ∀ (byte 2)

The content of the second byte of the instruction is exclusive-OR'd with the content of the accumulator. The result is placed in the accumulator. The CY and AC flags are cleared.

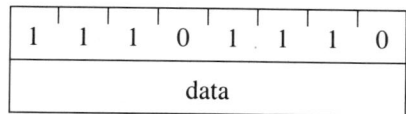

```
Cycles:     2
States:     7
Addressing: immediate
Flags:      Z,S,P,CY,AC
```

ORA r   (OR Register)

(A) ← (A) ∨ (r)

The content of register r is inclusive-OR'd with the content of the accumulator. The result is placed in the accumulator. The CY and AC flags are cleared.

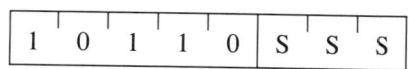

```
Cycles:     1
States:     4
Addressing: register
Flags:      Z,S,P,CY,AC
```

ORA M   (OR memory)
(A) ← (A) ∨ ((H) (L))

The content of the memory location whose address is contained in the H and L registers is inclusive-OR'd with the content of the accumulator. The result is placed in the accumulator. The CY and AC flags are cleared.

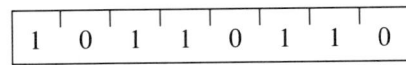

Cycles: 2
States: 7
Addressing: reg. indirect
Flags: Z,S,P,CY,AC

ORI data   (OR Immediate)
(A) ← (A) ∨ (byte 2)

The content of the second byte of the instruction is inclusive-OR'd with the content of the accumulator. The result is placed in the accumulator. The CY and AC flags are cleared.

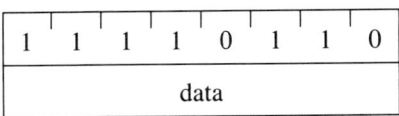

Cycles: 2
States: 7
Addressing: immediate
Flags: Z,S,P,CY,AC

CMP r   (Compare Register)
(A) − (r)

The content of register r is subtracted from the accumulator. The accumulator remains unchanged. The condition flags are set as a result of the subtraction. The Z flag is set to 1 if (A) = (r). The CY flag is set to 1 if (A) < (r).

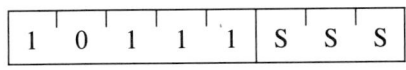

Cycles: 1
States: 4
Addressing: register
Flags: Z,S,P,CY,AC

CMP M   (Compare memory)
(A) − ((H) (L))
The content of the memory location whose address is contained in the H and L registers is subtracted from the accumulator. The accumulator remains unchanged. The condition flags are set as a result of the subtraction. The Z flag is set to 1 if (A) = ((H) (L)). The CY flag is set to 1 if (A) < ((H) (L)).

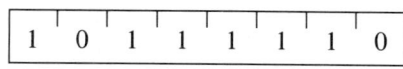

Cycles: 2
States: 7
Addressing: reg. indirect
Flags: Z,S,P,CY,AC

CPI data   (Compare immediate)
(A) − (byte 2)
The content of the second byte of the instruction is subtracted from the accumulator. The condition flags are set by the result of the subtraction. The Z flag is set to 1 if (A) = (byte 2). The CY flag is set to 1 if (A) < (byte 2).

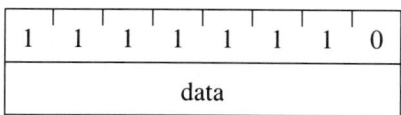

Cycles: 2
States: 7
Addressing: immediate
Flags: Z,S,P,CY,AC

RLC   (Rotate left)
$(A_{n+1}) \leftarrow (A_n); (A_0) \leftarrow (A_7)$
$(CY) \leftarrow (A_7)$
The content of the accumulator is rotated left one position. The low order bit and the CY flag are both set to the value shifted out of the high order bit position. Only the CY flag is affected.

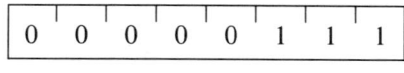

Cycles: 1
States: 4
Flags: CY

RRC   (Rotate right)
$(A_n) \leftarrow (A_{n-1}); (A_7) \leftarrow (A_0)$
$(CY) \leftarrow (A_0)$

The content of the accumulator is rotated right one position. The high order bit and the CY flag are both set to the value shifted out of the low order bit position. Only the CY flag is affected.

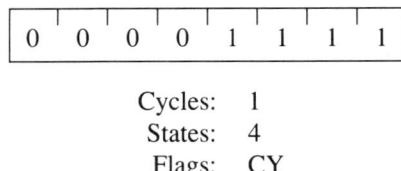

Cycles: 1
States: 4
Flags: CY

RAL   (Rotate left through carry)
$(A_{n+1}) \leftarrow (A_n); (CY) \leftarrow (A_7)$
$(A_0) \leftarrow (CY)$

The content of the accumulator is rotated left one position through the CY flag. The low order bit is set equal to the CY flag and the CY flag is set to the value shifted out of the high order bit. Only the CY flag is affected.

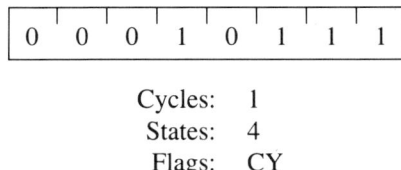

Cycles: 1
States: 4
Flags: CY

RAR   (Rotate right through carry)
$(A_n) \leftarrow (A_{n+1}); (CY) \leftarrow (A_0)$
$(A_7) \leftarrow (CY)$

The content of the accumulator is rotated right one position through the CY flag. The high order bit is set to the CY flag and the CY flag is set to the value shifted out of the low order bit. Only the CY flag is affected.

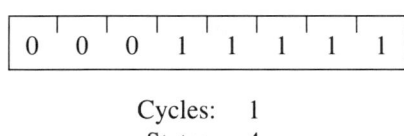

Cycles: 1
States: 4
Flags: CY

CMA   (Complement accumulator)
(A) ← (Ā)
The contents of the accumulator are complemented (zero bits become 1, one bits become 0). No flags are affected.

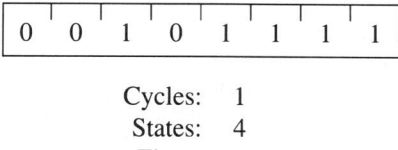

Cycles: 1
States: 4
Flags: none

CMC   (Complement carry)
(CY) ← (CȲ)
The CY flag is complemented. No other flags are affected.

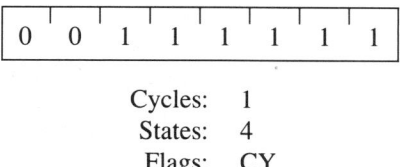

Cycles: 1
States: 4
Flags: CY

STC   (Set carry)
(CY) ← 1
The CY flag is set to 1. No other flags are affected.

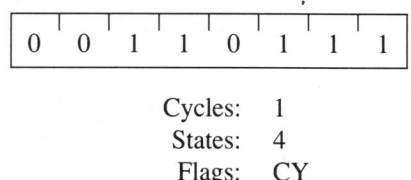

Cycles: 1
States: 4
Flags: CY

Branch Group. This group of instructions alter normal sequential program flow.

Condition flags are not affected by any instruction in this group.

The two types of branch instructions are unconditional and conditional. Unconditional transfers simply perform the specified operation on register PC (the program counter). Conditional transfers examine the status of one of the four processor flags to determine if the specified branch is to be executed. The conditions that may be specified are as follows:

CONDITION	CCC
NZ — not zero (Z = 0)	000
Z — zero (Z = 1)	001
NC — no carry (CY = 0)	010
C — carry (CY = 1)	011
PO — parity odd (P = 0)	100

PE — parity even (P = 1)   101
P — plus (S = 0)   110
M — minus (S = 1)   111

JMP addr   (Jump)
   (PC) ← (byte 3) (byte 2)
   Control is transferred to the instruction whose address is specified in byte 3 and byte 2 of the current instruction.

1	1	0	0	0	0	1	1
low-order addr							
high-order addr							

Cycles: 3
States: 10
Addressing: immediate
Flags: none

Jcondition addr   (Conditional jump)
   If (CCC)
     (PC) ← (byte 3) (byte 2)
   If the specified condition is true, control is transferred to the instruction whose address is specified in byte 3 and byte 2 of the current instruction; otherwise, control continues sequentially.

1	1	C	C	C	0	1	0
low-order addr							
high-order addr							

Cycles: 3
States: 10
Addressing: immediate
Flags: none

CALL addr   (Call)
    ((SP) − 1) ← (PCH)
    ((SP) − 2) ← (PCL)
    (SP) ← (SP) − 2
    (PC) ← (byte 3) (byte 2)

The high-order eight bits of the next instruction address are moved to the memory location whose address is one less than the content of register SP. The low-order eight bits of the next instruction address are moved to the memory location whose address is two less than the content of register SP. The content of register SP is decremented by 2. Control is transferred to the instruction whose address is specified in byte 3 and byte 2 of the current instruction.

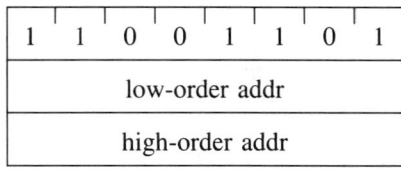

            Cycles: 5
            States: 17
        Addressing: immediate/reg. indirect
            Flags: none

Ccondition addr   (Condition call)
    If (CCC),
        ((SP) − 1) ← (PCH)
        ((SP) − 2) ← (PCL)
        (SP) ← (SP) − 2
        (PC) ← (byte 3) (byte 2)

If the specified condition is true, the actions specified in the CALL instruction (see above) are performed; otherwise, control continues sequentially.

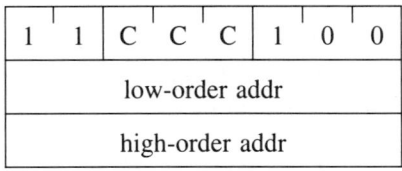

            Cycles: 3/5
            States: 11/17
        Addressing: immediate/reg. indirect
            Flags: none

RET   (Return)
(PCL) ← ((SP));
(PCH) ← ((SP) + 1);
(SP) ← (SP) + 2;
The content of the memory location whose address is specified in register SP is moved to the low-order eight bits of register PC. The content of the memory location whose address is one more than the content of register SP is moved to the high-order eight bits of register PC. The content of register SP is incremented by 2.

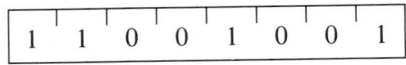

Cycles: 3
States: 10
Addressing: reg. indirect
Flags: none

Rcondition   (Conditional return)
If (CCC),
(PCL) ← ((SP))
(PCH) ← ((SP) + 1)
(SP) ← (SP) + 2
If the specified condition is true, the actions specified in the RET instruction (see above) are performed; otherwise, control continues sequentially.

Cycles: 1/3
States: 5/11
Addressing: reg. indirect
Flags: none

RST n   (Restart)
  ((SP) − 1) ← (PCH)
  ((SP) − 2) ← (PCL)
  (SP) ← (SP) − 2
  (PC) ← 8*(NNN)

The high-order eight bits of the next instruction address are moved to the memory location whose address is one less than the content of register SP. The low-order eight bits of the next instruction address are moved to the memory location whose address is two less than the content of register SP. The content of register SP is decremented by two. Control is transferred to the instruction whose address is eight times the content of NNN.

1	1	N	N	N	1	1	1

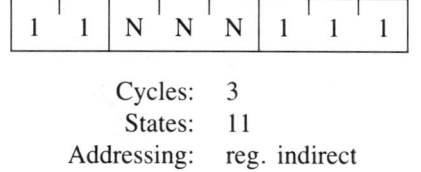

15	14	13	12	11	10	9	8	7	6	5	4	3	2	1	0
0	0	0	0	0	0	0	0	0	0	N	N	N	0	0	0

Program Counter After Restart

PCHL   (Jump H and L indirect — move H and L to PC)
  (PCH) ← (H)
  (PCL) ← (L)

The content of register H is moved to the high-order eight bits of register PC. The content of register L is moved to the low-order eight bits of register PC.

1	1	1	0	1	0	0	1

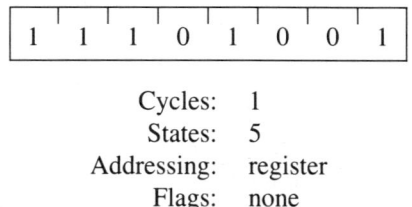

Stack, I/O, and Machine Control Group. This group of instructions performs I/O, manipulates the Stack, and alters internal control flags.

Unless otherwise specified, condition flags are not affected by any instructions in this group.

PUSH rp   (Push)
   ((SP) − 1) ← (rh)
   ((SP) − 2) ← (rl)
   ((SP) ← (SP) − 2

The content of the high-order register of register pair rp is moved to the memory location whose address is one less than the content of register SP. The content of the low-order register of register pair rp is moved to the memory location whose address is two less than the content of register SP. The content of register SP is decremented by 2. Note: Register pair rp = SP may not be specified.

1	1	R	P	0	1	0	1

      Cycles: 3
      States: 11
  Addressing: reg. indirect
       Flags: none

PUSH PSW   (Push processor status word)
   ((SP) − 1) ← (A)
   ((SP) − 2)$_0$ ← (CY), ((SP) − 2)$_1$ ← 1
   ((SP) − 2)$_2$ ← (P), ((SP) − 2)$_3$ ← 0
   ((SP) − 2)$_4$ ← (AC), ((SP) − 2)$_5$ ← 0
   ((SP) − 2)$_6$ ← (Z), ((SP) − 2)$_7$ ← (S)
   (SP) ← (SP) − 2

The content of register A is moved to the memory location whose address is one less than register SP. The contents of the condition flags are assembled into a processor status word and the word is moved to the memory location whose address is two less than the content of register SP. The content of register SP is decremented by two.

1	1	1	1	0	1	0	1

      Cycles: 3
      States: 11
  Addressing: reg. indirect
       Flags: none

FLAG WORD

D_7	D_6	D_5	D_4	D_3	D_2	D_1	D_0
S	Z	0	AC	0	P	1	CY

POP rp   (Pop)
   (rl) ← ((SP))
   (rh) ← ((SP) + 1)
   (SP) ← (SP) + 2
   The content of the memory location, whose address is specified by the content of register SP, is moved to the low-order register of register pair rp. The content of the memory location, whose address is one more than the content of register SP, is moved to the high-order register of register pair rp. The content of register SP is incremented by 2. Note: Register pair rp = SP may not be specified.

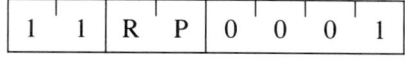

   Cycles: 3
   States: 10
   Addressing: reg. indirect
   Flags: none

POP PSW   (Pop processor status word)
   (CY) ← ((SP))$_0$
   (P) ← ((SP))$_2$
   (AC) ← ((SP))$_4$
   (Z) ← ((SP))$_6$
   (S) ← ((SP))$_7$
   (A) ← ((SP) + 1)
   (SP) ← (SP) + 2
   The content of the memory location whose address is specified by the content of register SP is used to restore the condition flags. The content of the memory location whose address is one more than the content of register SP is moved to register A. The content of register SP is incremented by 2.

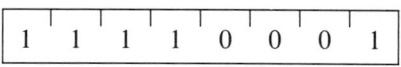

   Cycles: 3
   States: 10
   Addressing: reg. indirect
   Flags: Z,S,P,CY,AC

XTHL   (Exchange stack top with H and L)
   (L) ↔ ((SP))
   (H) ↔ ((SP) + 1)
   The content of the L register is exchanged with the content of the memory location whose address is specified by the content of register SP. The content of the H register is exchanged with the content of the memory location whose address is one more than the content of register SP.

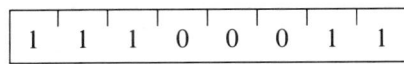

Cycles: 5
States: 18
Addressing: reg. indirect
Flags: none

SPHL (Move HL to SP)
   (SP) ← (H) (L)
   The contents of registers H and L (16 bits) are moved to register SP.

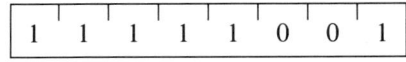

Cycles: 1
States: 5
Addressing: register
Flags: none

IN port   (Input)
   (A) ← (data)
   The data placed on the eight bit bi-directional data bus by the specified port is moved to register A.

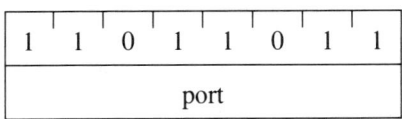

Cycles: 3
States: 10
Addressing: direct
Flags: none

OUT port   (Output)
(data) ← (A)
The content of register A is placed on the eight bit bi-directional data bus for transmission to the specified port.

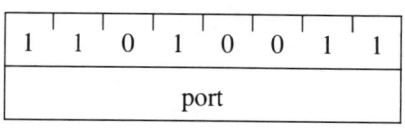

```
            Cycles:  3
            States:  10
        Addressing:  direct
             Flags:  none
```

EI   (Enable interrupts)
The interrupt system is enabled following the execution of the next instruction.

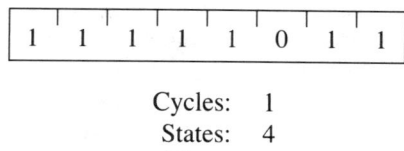

```
Cycles:  1
States:  4
 Flags:  none
```

DI   (Disable interrupts)
The interrupt system is disabled immediately following the execution of the DI instruction.

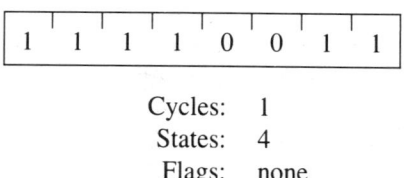

```
Cycles:  1
States:  4
 Flags:  none
```

HLT   (Halt)
The processor is stopped. The registers and flags are unaffected.

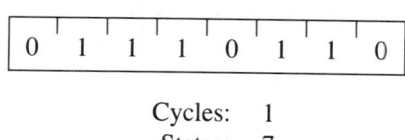

```
Cycles:  1
States:  7
 Flags:  none
```

NOP (No op)

No operation is performed. The registers and flags are unaffected.

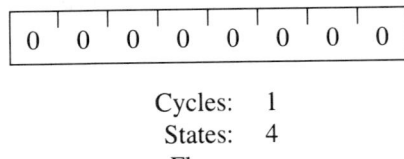

Cycles: 1
States: 4
Flags: none

5-4 INTRODUCTION TO FLOWCHARTS AND PROGRAMMING

This section will serve as an introduction to programming; later chapters will provide depth and sophistication. When a program is to be written, the programmer must choose the language to be used. The choices are: machine language, assembler language, or compiler language. *Machine language* is machine code and the *only* language the microprocessor "understands." However, for human convenience the programmer may use other languages and then *translate* that language into machine code. The act of translating instruction-set mnemonics into machine code is known as *assembly*. When assembly is performed by a computer, the computer program responsible for the translation is known as an *assembler*. Because an assembler "recognizes" instructions (in mnemonic form) from the instruction set and translates (assembles) them into machine code, the instruction set is referred to as an *assembler-level language*. Similarly, there are also programs which translate higher-level languages, such as FORTRAN and PL/1, into machine language. For these higher-level languages the translating program is known as a *compiler*; therefore FORTRAN and PL/1 are known as *compiler-level languages*. Two of the major differences between an assembler language and a compiler language are:

1. Assembler languages are machine oriented; that is, the "words" (instructions) of the language make reference to CPU architecture (e.g., registers), which requires knowledge of the workings of the microprocessor. Compiler languages are task oriented; that is, the "words" of the language (program statements) make reference to the task of the program's objective (add, multiply, print, etc.) and not microprocessor architecture.
2. Compiler languages are more easily read by human beings, since their instructions appear closer to statements in English. It is the closeness to the English language that establishes a programming language level. Compiler languages, being the most like the English language, are the highest-level language; machine language is the least like English and therefore the lowest-level language.

This chapter introduces programming at the assembler level.

Whenever one programs (at all language levels) it is desirable to begin by

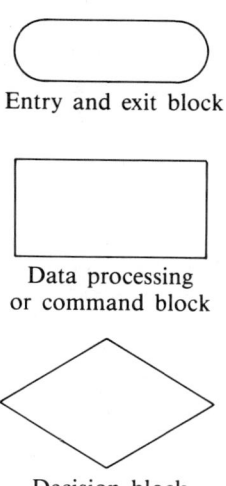

FIGURE 5-4. Symbols used for flowcharts.

modularizing the program's task into steps. Once these steps are determined, they can be presented in graphical fashion (flowchart) and will then provide a "road map" with which the programmer can visualize each step and the role that step plays in accomplishing the task. This allows the programmer to simplify programming by focusing on programming modules rather than attempting to program the entire task. Figure 5-4 illustrates the symbols to be used when determining a flowchart. An example will best illustrate flowchart concepts.

EXAMPLE 5-1
For a microprocessor-based system, such as that shown in Figure 4-7, develop a flowchart for a program that will collect a single byte of data from input port 0 and store that byte at memory location 0800H.

Solution
This programming task can be modularized by dividing the task into two steps:

1. Input the data from input port 0.
2. Store the data at memory location 0800H.

The flowchart for this task is shown in Figure 5-5. ∎

EXAMPLE 5-2
As in Example 5-1, collect data from input port 0. However, now data is to be continuously collected and stored in successive memory locations, beginning with location 0800H, until an end command is given via port 0. The end command is the ASCII (pronounced "ask-key") character E, which is 45H (see Appendix B).

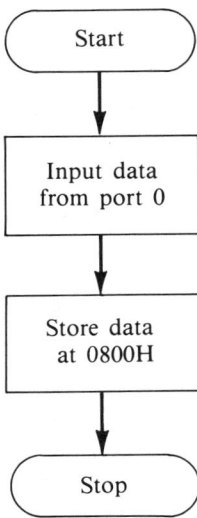

FIGURE 5-5. Flowchart for collecting a single data byte.

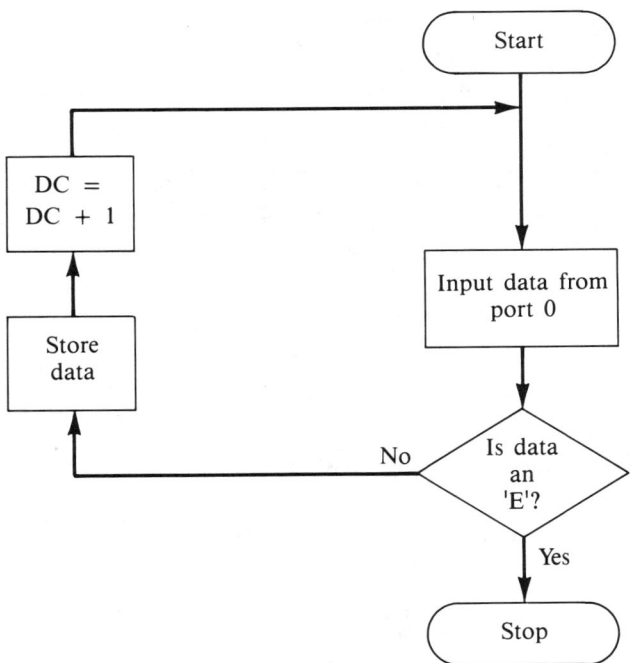

FIGURE 5-6. Flowchart for collecting multiple data bytes.

138   PROGRAMMING WITH THE 8080 INSTRUCTION SET

Solution

The steps involved are:

1. Input data from port 0.
2. Determine if data collected from port 0 is an end command 'E', where ' ' indicates an ASCII character.
3. a. If yes:
      (1) Terminate data collection.
   b. If no:
      (1) Store data at location given by DC.
      (2) Increment DC.
      (3) Return to port 0 for next byte of data.

The flowchart is presented in Figure 5-6. ■

EXAMPLE 5-3

Suppose that a program is required to accomplish the task of Example 5-2 with an additional requirement that a tally be kept of the number of data bytes stored. Store the number that is indicative of the data bytes stored (TALLY) at memory location 0FF0H.

Solution

To accomplish this additional programming task, we must modify steps 3a and 3b. Step 3b will now read:

3. b. If no:
      (1) Store data at location given by DC.
      (2) Increment DC in preparation for storage of next data byte collected from port 0.
      (3) Increment TALLY to account for data byte stored.

Step 3a will be modified to read:

3. a. If yes:
      (1) Store TALLY at location 0FF0H.
      (2) Terminate data collection.

The flowchart for Example 5-3 is Figure 5-7. It is essentially the flowchart of Figure 5-6, but modified to accommodate the modifications of steps 3a and 3b. ■

Now that we have constructed a few simple flowcharts, let us return to those flowcharts as aids to programming. Recall that a flowchart is to serve as a programming "road map."

EXAMPLE 5-4

Utilizing the flowchart of Figure 5-5, write a program that will accomplish the task stated in Example 5-1. It can be assumed that input port 0 has the data byte

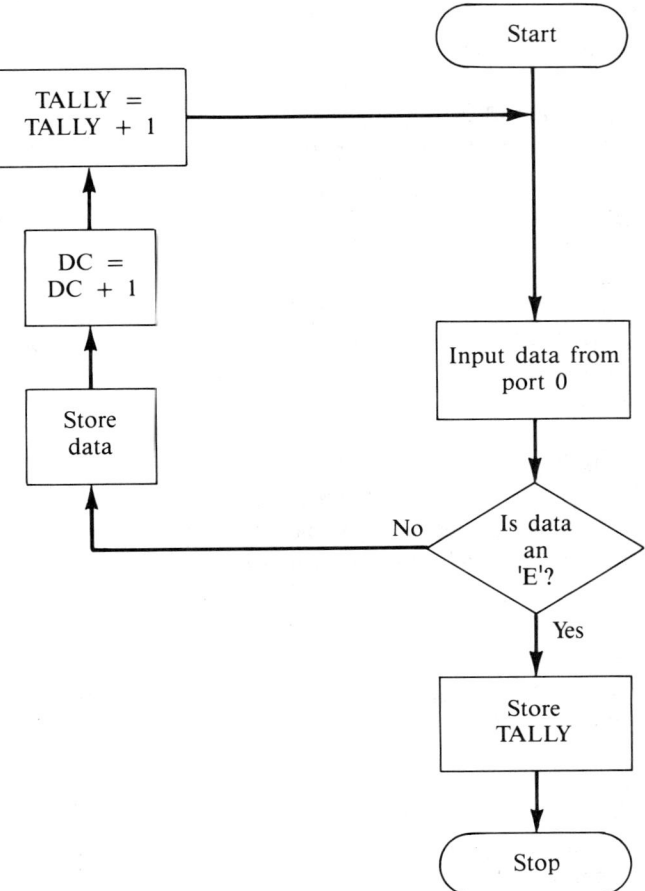

FIGURE 5-7. Flowchart for keeping tally of data bytes collected.

ready. The program is to be stored in ROM at beginning memory location 0100H.

Solution

Since the program we are about to write is to *originate* at memory location 0100H, there must be an instruction *to the assembler* directing it to begin assembly at memory location 0100H. Instructions (directives) to the assembler are known as *directives*. The assembler directive that instructs the assembler as to the beginning address of assembly is the origin (ORG) directive. To direct the assembler to begin assembly at memory location 0100H, the programmer simply writes ORG 0100H at the start of the program. Then for the start block of Figure 5-5, we write

```
          ORG    0100H
```

Notice that ORG looks like an 8080 instruction in form, but since it does not appear in Table 5-10, it is not an 8080 instruction. Directives have meaning only to the assembler (not the microprocessor) and are not assembled. Because directives look like microprocessor instructions but in fact are not, they are also known as *pseudo-ops* (pseudo op codes).

After the start block of Figure 5-5 is the command to "Input data from port 0." Looking through the instruction set as given in Section 5-3, we find that the instruction IN PORT will accomplish the task of that command block. Notice that the byte input from port 0 will reside in the accumulator (A) after the execution of IN 00H. At this point our program appears as

```
ORG   0100H
IN    00H
```

The next command block states that the data byte (in register A) is to be stored at memory location 0800H. From the instruction set we find three instructions that will accomplish the task. These instructions are: MOV M,r, where r is A; STA addr, where addr is 0800H; and STAX rp, where rp would be either B or D. We notice that STAX H is the same instruction as MOV M,A. Of the three, STA 0800H will be best, for the other two require that some register pair be initialized with address 0800H. Hence the program now appears as

```
ORG   0100H
IN    00H
STA   0800H
```

The last command block can be accomplished in two or three ways, but we shall use the most obvious; we shall use HLT. Thus the completed program is

```
ORG   0100H
IN    00H
STA   0800H
HLT
```

For complex programs the programmer wishes to offer as much insight as possible into the purpose of each program instruction. *In addition* to a flowchart, program instructions will be further documented with *comments*. Comments can be written to the right of an instruction, following a semicolon. The assembler is *not* to assemble the semicolon (no such instruction) or anything to the right of the semicolon. Thus to document the program better, let us add comments.

```
ORG   0100H
IN    00H     ; Input data from port 0
STA   0800H   ; Store data at 0800H
HLT           ; Finished
```

A well-documented program is considered to be one having (1) a flowchart and (2) adequate comments. A fully documented program to accomplish the task of Example 5-1 is shown in Figure 5-8. ■

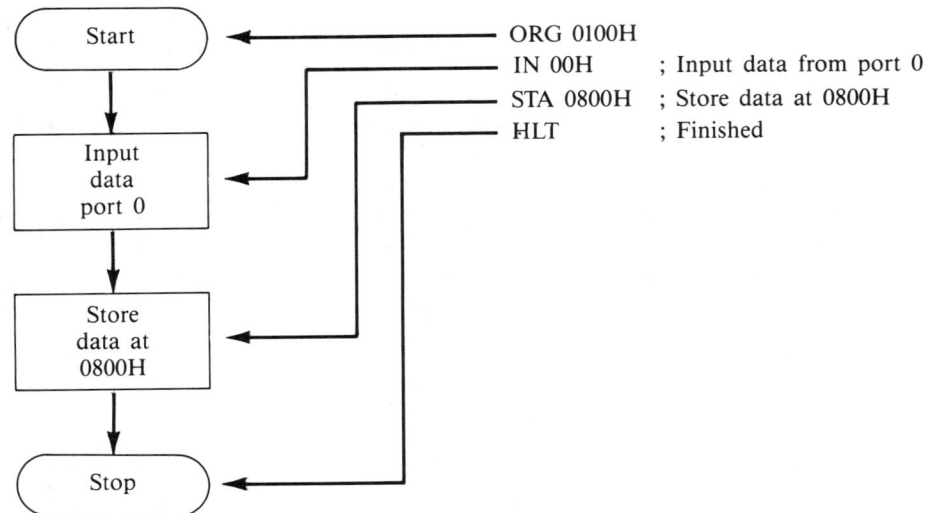

FIGURE 5-8. Program documented with flowchart and comments.

EXAMPLE 5-5
Write a program to accomplish the tasks prescribed in Example 5-2. The flowchart of Figure 5-6 is to be utilized in writing this program and also considered as part of program documentation.

Solution

The command block "Input data from port 0" of Figure 5-6 can be implemented with IN 00H. The decision block of Figure 5-6, "Is data an 'E'?", requires that the data byte received from port 0 be tested to determine if an end command has been given.

Decisions in programming are based on the logic state of a condition flag. To alter the condition-flag logic states appropriately, we will use the instruction CPI 'E'. From Section 5-3 we find that executing CPI 'E' will cause the ASCII value for E (45H) to be subtracted from the contents of A, where A's contents is the data byte from port 0, and the condition flags are appropriately affected by the subtraction.

Of most importance in writing this program is the Z flag, for if the result of the subtraction is zero, meaning that the data byte from port 0 equals 45H, then the Z flag is set; otherwise, the Z flag is reset. Then Z = 1 is the Yes path of the flowchart and Z = 0 is the No path. We shall write this program so as to make "jump" the Yes path and allow the No path to be a consequence of not "jumping." Hence, *if* Z = 1, the program is to jump to an instruction that will stop execution of the program. This calls for a conditional jump instruction. In Section 5-3 under "Branch Group" we find Jcondition addr. The J represents "jump" and "condition" refers to the condition flag/logic state of Table 5-8 (confirm the machine code format of Figure 5-3 with the format given in Section

5-3). The condition flag is Z; hence JZ is the mnemonic for the op code. From Section 5-3 we find that the instruction requires the address (two bytes) to which program execution is to be transferred. Until the program is written and assembled, that address is unknown. For unknown addresses we can use a symbolic address, just as algebraic symbols are used for unknowns in algebra. Let us use FINISHED as the symbolic address, or JZ FINISHED. We must identify the stop command (HLT instruction) of Figure 5-6 with an identifier; that is, we must *label* HLT with the name FINISHED. This is accomplished as FINISHED: HLT. Thus far, our program appears as follows:

```
            ORG 0100H
            IN 00H              ; Input data from port 0
            CPI 'E'             ; Compare data byte with 'E'
            JZ FINISHED         ; Stop if Z = 1 by transferring
              (program still   ; program execution to memory
               to be written   ; location FINISHED: otherwise,
               for No path)    ; continue
FINISHED:   HLT                 ; Stop
```

We must now complete the program by undertaking the No branch of Figure 5-6. Following the No branch we must store the data byte compared with 'E' if $Z \neq 1$. From the instruction set of Section 5-3, we find that STA addr, STAX RP, or MOV M,A would suffice. The best of the three can be determined by realizing that the next command block requires that the memory storage location be incremented by one in preparation for storage of the next data byte. For this reason STA addr is a poor choice since the address of STA addr cannot be incremented. Either STAX rp or MOV M,A is a good choice (STAX H and MOV M,A are the same instruction). Let us use STAX D. To increment the data counter, registers D and E, we may use INX D. Then to "STORE data" and "DC + 1" of Figure 5-6, we add to our program:

```
            STAX D  ; Store data byte
            INX  D  ; DC = DC + 1
```

These additions, as well as others, are shown in Figure 5-9. Notice that RP D must be preloaded with the beginning memory location where the collected data bytes are to be stored (0800H). To initialize RP D we may use LXI rp, data, which for our specific case is LXI D, 0800 H. This instruction will be grouped with Start of Figure 5-6, together with ORG 0100H, as shown in Figure 5-9.

The last function of Figure 5-6 that must be accomplished is that after DC + 1, program execution must jump "back" to "Input data from port 0" in order to input the next data byte. To accomplish this jump we shall use JMP addr. The address that program execution is to jump to is that of IN 00H, which is unknown until after assembly. Hence we shall assign a symbolic address (a *label*) to IN 00H and then refer to that symbolic address. The label assigned is RETURN, as shown in Figure 5-9.

```
                    ORG 0100H
                    LXI D,0800H     ; Initialize RP D
RETURN:             IN 00H          ; Input data
                    CPI 'E'         ; Compare data byte with 'E'
                    JZ FINISHED     ; Stop if Z = 1 by transferring
                                    ; program execution to memory
                                    ; location Finished; otherwise,
                                    ; continue
                    STAX D          ; Store data byte
                    INX D           ; DC = DC + 1
                    JMP RETURN      ; Return for next data byte
FINISHED:           HLT             ; Stop
```

FIGURE 5-9. Example program using labels.

The reader must realize that for complete documentation, Figure 5-6 is to be included with Figure 5-9. ∎

Before undertaking more programming examples, let us return to Figures 5-8 and 5-9 and hand-assemble both programs. To gain the greatest benefits from this exercise, we shall assemble the instructions *just as if* we were an assembler. An assembler assigns memory addresses to assembled instructions via its location counter. The ORG directive sets the location counter to the value specified. Hence ORG 0100H initializes the location counter to a value (address) of 0100H.

All assembled numbers are in hexadecimal, and the H, specifying hexadecimal, will often be omitted.

EXAMPLE 5-6

Hand-assemble the program of Figure 5-8.

Solution

The directive ORG 0100H sets the location counter to 0100H. The assembler (you in this case) next "sees" the IN 00H instruction and assembles that instruction into the machine code DB 00 (refer to Table 5-10). DB is to be stored at the address assigned by the location counter, which is 0100H. The assembler then increments its location counter and assigns the next assembled byte, 00, to memory location 0101H. The assembler then increments its location counter (LC = 0102H) and assembles the next instruction, which is STA 0800H. The assembled op code is 32 and 0800H is assembled into two hexadecimal values: 00 and 08. The low-order byte of the address is assembled first; refer to Section 5-3. Thus STA 0800H is a three-byte instruction with an assembled machine code of 32, 00, and 08. 32 is assigned memory location 0102H by the location counter. 00 is assigned to memory location 0103H and 08 is assigned to memory location 0104 by the location counter. Again the location counter is incremented and the assembled mnemonic code HLT (76) is assigned to memory location 0105H.

The complete assembly of the program of Figure 5-8 is shown in Table 5-11. The assembled program of Table 5-11 would be programmed into a ROM for execution by the CPU. ∎

TABLE 5-11. Assembled Program of Figure 5-8

Instruction	Memory Location Assigned by Location Counter (Hex)	Machine Code of Assembled Instruction (Hex)
IN 00H	0100	DB
	0101	00
STA 0800H	0102	32
	0103	00
	0104	08
HLT	0105	76

EXAMPLE 5-7

Assemble the program of Figure 5-9.

Solution

Notice that before this program can be assembled, addresses must be determined for the labels. Performing as most assemblers, we will need to make two passes of the program in order to complete assembly. The function of each pass is: (1) assign values (memory addresses) to labels, and (2) once values are assigned, assemble the program. To accomplish the purpose of the first pass of the assembler, we shall count the number of bytes of the program and from this information assign values to the labels. Table 5-12 shows the data byte count for the program of Figure 5-9.

From the data byte count of Table 5-12, and knowing that the program is to originate at memory location 0100H, we may determine the memory addresses to be assigned to labels RETURN and FINISHED simply by totaling the data bytes from the origin to the label. From Table 5-12 we find that RETURN is to be assigned the fourth memory location after memory address 0100H, which is 0103H (realize that 0100H is the first address). A convenient equation to use in determining addresses is:

$$\text{memory address} = \text{address of origin} + (\text{data bytes} - 1) \quad (5\text{-}1)$$

TABLE 5-12. First Pass of Assembly

Byte Count	Label	Instruction
3		LXI D,0800H
2	RETURN:	IN 00H
2		CPI 'E'
3		JZ FINISHED
1		STAX D
1		INX D
3		JMP RETURN
1	FINISHED:	HLT

5-4 INTRODUCTION TO FLOWCHARTS AND PROGRAMMING

TABLE 5-13. Symbol Table

Symbol	Memory Address Assigned by the Assembler (Hex)
RETURN	0103
FINISHED	010F

Using Equation (5-1) to determine the address of FINISHED, we have

memory address to be assigned to FINISHED
$$= 0100H + (10H - 1H) = 0100H + FH$$
$$= 010FH$$

Now that addresses have been determined for RETURN and FINISHED, we shall create a table (Table 5-13) which readily gives this information to the programmer. This table is called a *symbol table*.

Now that addresses have been assigned to the labels of Figure 5-9, we may begin assembly. The assembled machine code for the program of Figure 5-9 is shown in Table 5-14. ∎

TABLE 5-14. Assembled Program of Figure 5-9

Program (exclude directives and comments)	Assembled Program	
	Memory Locations Assigned by Location Counter	Machine Code
LXI D,0800H	0100	11
	0101	00
	0102	08
RETURN: IN 00H	0103	DB
	0104	00
CPI 'E'	0105	FE
	0106	45
JZ FINISHED	0107	CA
	0108	0F
	0109	01
STAX D	010A	12
INX D	010B	13
JMP RETURN	010C	C3
	010D	03
	010E	01
FINISHED: HLT	010F	76

A summary of some important points of this example follows:

1. Most assemblers are two-pass assemblers, where the first pass assigns values to labels and the second pass performs the actual assembly.
2. The assembler provides a symbol table for the programmer. This table identifies labels (symbols) and values assigned to them by the assembler's location counter.
3. The assembler will translate mnemonic code into bytes of machine code and assign these bytes to memory locations, as given by the location counter.

Thus the process of assembly includes translation of mnemonics into machine code and the assignment of memory addresses for the assembled mnemonic code. Then the assembled program of Table 5-14 is actually just the two right-hand columns. That is, the computer system that is serving as host to the assembler is storing (probably on disk) the assembled program and assigned addresses of Figure 5-9, which is the two right-hand columns of Table 5-14. The assembled program and assigned addresses are stored in the storage medium (disk) of the host computer, by the assembler, in such a fashion that when a ROM is programmed from this assembled program, it will cause a data byte to be programmed (stored) at its assigned memory location. Then the assembled program of Table 5-14 will be programmed in ROM such that data byte "11" will be stored at ROM address 0100. At ROM address 0101 the data byte "00" will be programmed (burned). This programming of the ROM will continue according to the assembled program of Table 5-14. Once the ROM is programmed, it is removed from the ROM programmer, which is a "box" that programs ROMs, and inserted in the prototype, the microprocessor-based system being designed, at which time the program can be executed by the microprocessor. Of course, the assembled program of Table 5-14 could be "downloaded" (transferred from the host computer to the prototype) to the prototype's RAM and then executed. Either way the assembled bytes of Table 5-14 would be stored at the assigned memory location.

EXAMPLE 5-8

Write a program to accomplish the task of Example 5-3 as documented in the flowchart of Figure 5-7. Just for a change, assemble this program beginning at memory location 0056H. Assemble the program giving the machine code and assigned memory address as well as a symbol table.

Solution
The program is very similar to that of Figure 5-9 except for two additions:

1. Incrementing the TALLY in the No branch of Figure 5-7.
2. Storing of the TALLY value in the Yes branch of Figure 5-7.

To assemble the program of Figure 5-10, we count data bytes on the first pass in order to assign values (addresses) to symbols. This is shown in Table 5-15. Knowing that the assembler was directed to begin assembly at 0056H, the

```
            ORG 0056H

          ; INITIALIZATION OF REGISTERS

            LXI D,0800H      ; Initialize RP D
            LXI H,0FF0H      ; Initialize M to store TALLY
            MVI B,00H        ; Clear TALLY

          ; PROGRAM BEGINS

RETURN:     IN 00H           ; Input data
            CPI 'E'          ; COMPARE data byte with 'E'
            JZ FINISHED      ; STOP if Z = 1
            STAX D           ; Store data byte
            INX D            ; DC = DC + 1
            INR B            ; TALLY = TALLY + 1
            JMP RETURN       ; Return for next data byte
FINISHED:   MOV M,B          ; Store TALLY
            HLT              ; Stop
```

FIGURE 5-10. Program that implements the flowchart of Figure 5-7.

addresses for RETURN and FINISHED can be determined from Equation (5-1).

$$\text{address for label RETURN} = 0056 + (9 - 1) = 5E$$
$$\text{address of label FINISHED} = 0056 + (16 - 1) = 6B$$

Now that the assembler has made its first pass and as a result has assigned values to symbols, that is, it created a symbol table (Table 5-16), it is ready to make its second pass and actually assemble the mnemonics. The assembled program is shown in Table 5-17. As was the case for the assembled program of Table 5-14, the two columns comprising the assembled program of Table

TABLE 5-15. First Pass of Assembler

Byte Count	Label	Instruction
3		LXI D,0800H
3		LXI H,0FF0H
2		MVI B,00H
2	RETURN:	IN 00H
2		CPI 'E'
3		JZ FINISHED
1		STAX D
1		INX D
1		INR B
3		JMP RETURN
1	FINISHED:	MOV M,B
1		HLT

TABLE 5-16. Symbol Table

Symbol	Memory Address Assigned by the Assembler (Hex)
RETURN	005E
FINISHED	006B

5-17 are placed in the memory of the host computer and later programmed in ROM or RAM of the prototype at the memory locations indicated. The host computer will interface with a PROM programmer, which will actually program the assembled program in the PROM. ∎

TABLE 5-17. Assembled Program of Figure 5-10

Program (exclude directives and comments)	Assembled Program	
	Memory Locations Assigned by Location Counter	Machine Code
LXI D,0800H	0056	11
	0057	00
	0058	80
LXI H,0056H	0059	21
	005A	56
	005B	00
MVI B,00H	005C	06
	005D	00
RETURN: IN 00H	005E	DB
	005F	00
CPI 'E'	0060	FE
	0061	45
JZ FINISHED	0062	CA
	0063	6B
	0064	00
STAX D	0065	12
INX D	0066	13
INR B	0067	04
JMP RETURN	0068	C3
	0069	5E
	006A	00
FINISHED: MOV M,B	006B	70
HLT	006C	76

EXAMPLE 5-9

Write a program that will add the contents of memory location 0800H to the data collected from input port 0 of Figure 4-7. The sums are to be stored in memory beginning at memory location 0C00. The program is to be programmed

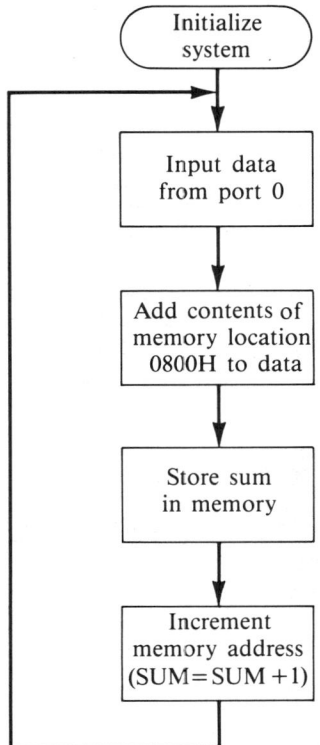

FIGURE 5-11. Flowchart for addition of two data bytes.

in the system's ROM beginning at the first address of page 1. Once the program is written, assemble the program showing a symbol table.

Solution

We begin by developing a flowchart, which is shown in Figure 5-11.

In writing a program from Figure 5-11, let us first program the command block "input data from port 0." The reason for skipping the "Initialization of the system" is that we do not know what is required for initialization and will not know until we have programmed the other command blocks. As we progress in programming the other command blocks, we will keep a record of initialization requirements and when finished we will return to the initialization command block and program it.

```
IN 00H        ; Input data from port 0
ADD M         ; Add data from memory (0800H)
              ; to accumulator (port 0)
```

(We must initialize H and L with 0800H.)

```
STAX B        ; Store sum in memory at
              ; memory location given by RP B
```

(We must initialize RP B with 0C00.)

```
INX B  ; Increment sum storage
       ; location by one
JMP RETURN ; Jump to IN 00H to
           ; collect next data byte
```

(We must add the symbolic address RETURN, which is a label, to IN 00H.) To initialize the system, we must include in the program

```
LXI H,0800H
LXI B,0C00H
```

Also, we must insert the directive ORG 0400H (beginning of page 1) in order to direct the assembler to begin assembly of this program at memory location 0400H. The completed program is shown in Figure 5-12. Notice from the program that we have no way of exiting from this program except by a Reset or, as we shall see, an Interrupt, which is not a good practice. For now we shall not be concerned with this problem.

```
              ORG 0400H

              ; Initialization

         LXI H,0800H    ; Initialize RP H (M)
         LXI B,0C00H    ; Initialize RP B

              ; Program

RETURN:  IN 00H         ; Input data from port 0
         ADD M          ; Add data from memory (0800H)
                        ; to A
         STAX B         ; Store sum in memory location
                        ; given by RP B
         INX B          ; Increment M
         JMP RETURN     ; Jump to RETURN
                        ; to collect next data byte.
```

FIGURE 5-12. Program to implement flowchart of Figure 5-11.

Next we produce the symbol table of Table 5-18 and then assemble the program, as shown in Table 5-19.

TABLE 5-18. Symbol Table for Program of Figure 5-12

Symbol	Memory Address Assigned by the Assembler (Hex)
RETURN	0406

TABLE 5-19. Assembled Program of Figure 5-12

| | Assembled Program | |
Program	Memory Locations Assigned by Location Counter	Machine Code
LXI H,0800H	0400	21
	0401	00
	0402	08
LXI B,0C00H	0403	01
	0404	00
	0405	0C
RETURN: IN 00H	0406	DB
	0407	00
ADD M	0408	86
STAX B	0409	02
INX B	040A	03
JMP RETURN	040B	C3
	040C	06
	040D	04

EXAMPLE 5-10

Write a program that will compare the data bytes from input port 0 of Figure 4-7 and the contents of memory location 0800H until input port 0 inputs the end command 'E', at which time the system will enter an idle state. Data bytes from port 0 that are larger in value than the contents of memory location 0800H are to be stored in memory beginning at memory location 0801H. There are 20H memory locations allocated for storage of these data bytes, and if this storage capacity is exceeded, isolate input port 0 from the system and give an alarm error code by outputting 06H to output port 0, which is a light-emitting diode (LED) display. When the system is in a 06H error alarm state, the system is to be put in an idle condition until the system is reset. For "bookkeeping" purposes, keep a tally of the number of data bytes that are not greater than the contents of memory location 0800H. Load the assembled program in the system ROM beginning on page 1, where page 0 and page 1 are of size 1K (1024) bytes.

Solution

To flowchart this programming task, we shall modularize the requirements. These modules are:

1. Initialize the system.
2. Input data from input port 0 and determine if the data byte is an end command 'E'.
   a. If the data byte is not an 'E', compare it with the contents of memory location 0800H (indicated by [0800H]), where [ ] indicates "contents of . . . ."

(1) If the data byte is greater than [0800H], then store the data byte. Keep a tally of data bytes stored and do not exceed the storage of 20H such data bytes.
  (a) If storage allotment is not exceeded, return to input port 0 for the next data byte.
  (b) If storage of the present data byte equals 20H memory locations used, isolate input port 0 from the system and idle the system. Also, output error code 06H to output port 0.
(2) If the data byte is less than [0800H], ignore the data byte. Keep a tally of the data bytes that are in this category. Return to input port 0 to collect the next data byte.
b. If the data byte is an 'E', store the tally that recorded the number of data bytes that were not greater than [0800H] at memory location 0BFFH and idle the system.

Now that we have modularized the requirements, we can construct flowcharts for each module. These flowcharts will then be combined as a single flowchart, as shown in Figure 5-13. Each dashed rectangle of Figure 5-13 is the modularization of the requirements. The number in the lower right corner identifies a requirement and the command blocks that implement it.

When writing the program from Figure 5-13 we will find that symbolic address (labels) will be needed for jumps, both conditional and unconditional. Knowing that every branch (Yes/No leg) of a decision block implies the possible use of a label, we will assign labels to each conditional branch, as shown in parentheses in Figure 5-13. Figure 5-13 also shows two additional labels in parentheses for the unconditional jumps RETURN and IDLE. To present Figure 5-13 in a more conventional manner, the parenthesized labels and dashed modules have been removed, resulting in Figure 5-14.

A program to accomplish the task of Example 5-10 is shown in Figure 5-15. Even though Figure 5-14 will accompany the program as part of its documentation, Figure 5-13 was the one actually used to aid in writing the program. Notice that to implement the comparison stated by requirement 2.A, which is illustrated graphically in Figure 5-13, a SUB instruction was used rather than CMP. This is due to the C flag indicating quantities equal to or greater than the contents of the accumulator, where we want only the greater-than indication; hence CMP would not work. Also, we see from Figure 5-15 that requirement 2.A.1.b uses output port 01 to isolate input port 0. It does so by addressing output port 01, via the out I/O select 8205 of Figure 5-16, which results in a logic 1 being output by the isolation OR gate. This logic 1 is latched by the flip-flop shown, which holds $\overline{CE}$ of input port 0's buffer high, thereby driving its output into high-Z. The "by pass" OR gate allows the latch or the Isolation OR gate to isolate input port 0, as can be seen from the truth tables for both OR gates provided in Figure 5-16. ■

The math requirements of a task could eliminate MOS-technology microprocessors from some applications. This is especially true where a rather lengthy mathematical program must be executed in a short period of time (a few hundred microseconds) as in a feedback-control application for a high-performance jet fighter aircraft. A means to "speed up" the determination of a mathematical

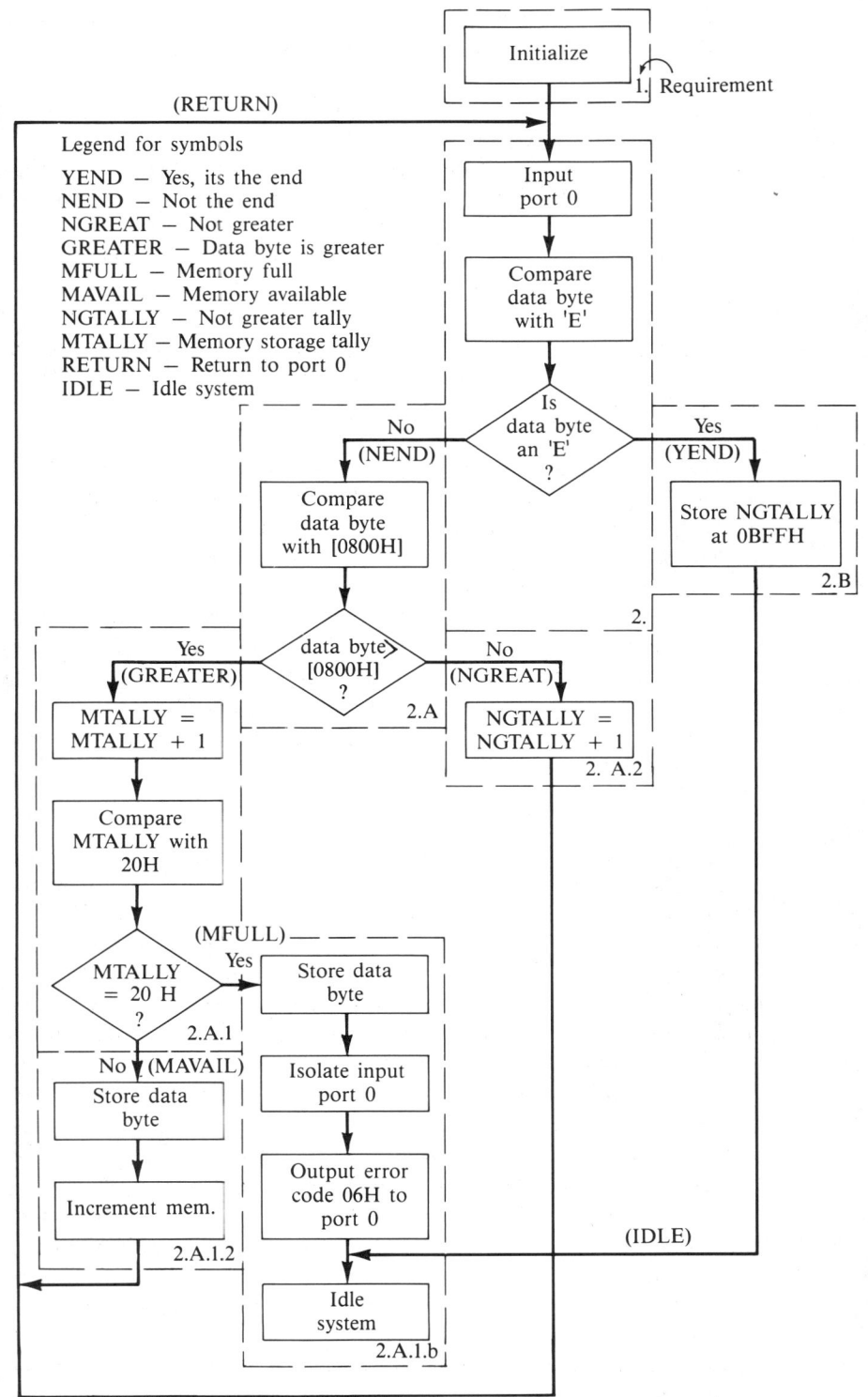

FIGURE 5-13. Flowchart indicating modularization of Example 5-10.

154   PROGRAMMING WITH THE 8080 INSTRUCTION SET

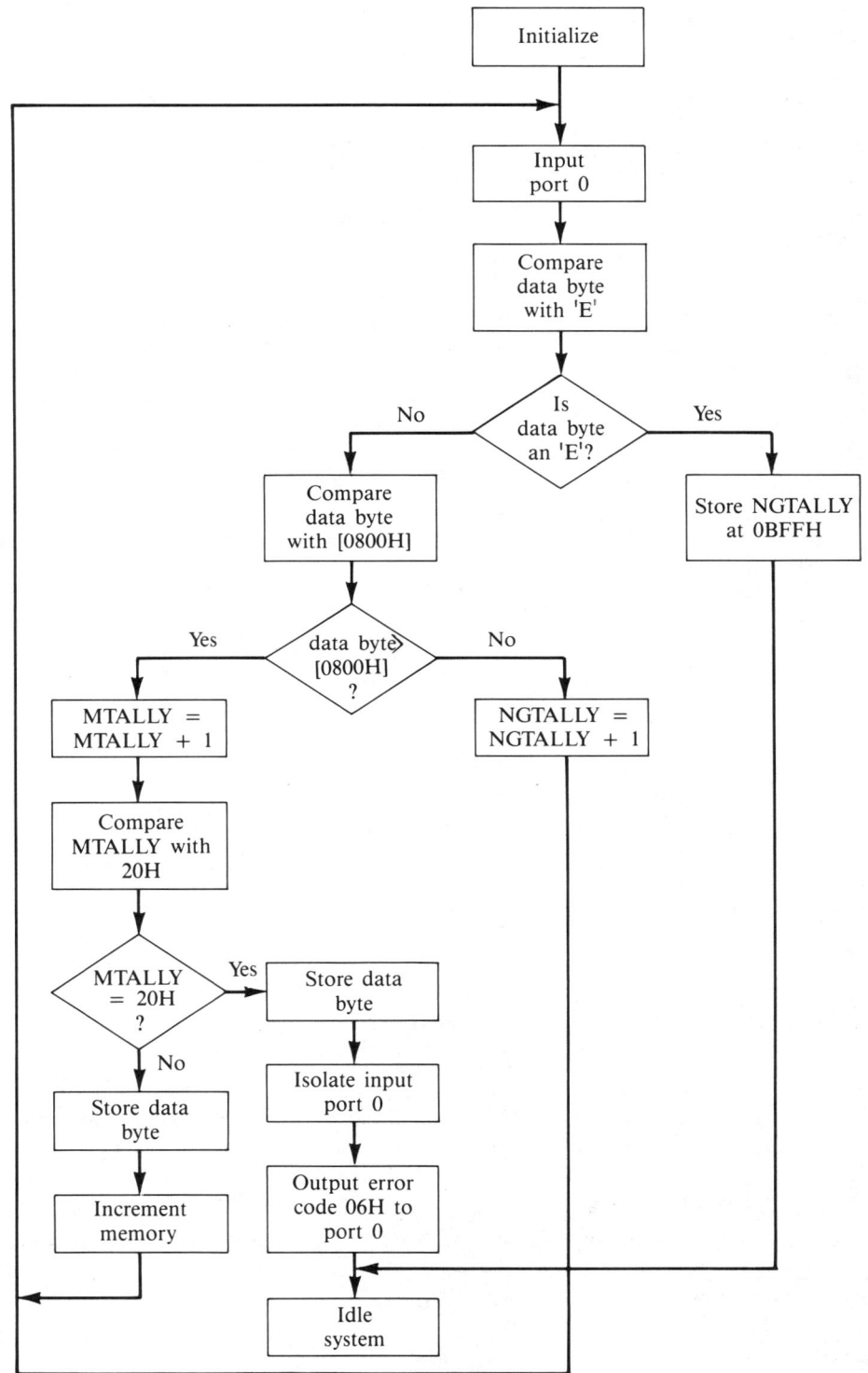

FIGURE 5-14. Flowchart for Example 5-10.

5-4 INTRODUCTION TO FLOWCHARTS AND PROGRAMMING

```
                              ORG 0400H

                          ; INITIALIZE SYSTEM

Requirement        LXI H, 0801H         ; First storage location
number 1. of
Figure 5-12        XRA C                ; Clear C (NGTALLY)
                   XRA D                ; Clear D (MTALLY)

                          ; INITIALIZATION COMPLETE

                   RETURN: IN 00H       ; Input data byte 0
Requirement                CPI 'E'      ; Compare data byte with 'E'
number 2
                           JZ YEND      ; Data byte is 'E' idle system
                           MOV B,A      ; Save data byte in B
Requirement
2.A                        LDA 0800H    ; Get number from 0800H
                           SUB B        ; Determine if data byte is larger
                           JC GREATER   ; Data BYTE is larger
2.A.2                      INR C        ; NGTALLY = NGTALLY + 1
                           JMP RETURN   ; Get next data byte

                   GREATER: INR D       ; MTALLY = MTALLY + 1
                            MOV A,D     ; Move MTALLY into A
2.A.1                       CPI 0020H   ; Compare MTALLY with 0020H
                            JZ MFULL    ; If Z = 1 memory is full
                            MOV A,B     ; Restore A with data byte
2.A.1.a                     MOV M,A     ; Store data byte
                            INX H       ; Increment memory location
                            JMP RETURN  ; Get next data byte

                   YEND:    MOV A,C     ; Move NGTALLY to A
2.B                         STA 0BFFH   ; Store NGTALLY
                            JMP IDLE    ; Idle system

                   MFULL:   MOV A,B     ; Restore A with data byte
                            MOV M,A     ; Store data byte
                            OUT 01H     ; Isolate input port 0
                                        ; just by addressing port 01
2.A.1.b
                            MVI A, 06H  ; Move error code to A
                            OUT 00H     ; Output error code

                   IDLE:    JMP IDLE    ; Idle system
```

FIGURE 5-15. Program implementing flowchart of Figure 5-13 or 5-14.

answer is to use a look-up-table approach rather than actually performing the mathematical calculation. The next example will demonstrate that approach.

EXAMPLE 5-11

Using a look-up table, write a program that will square the integer decimal value input from input port 6. The result is to be output to output port 7. Use 'F' from port 6 to indicate when finished.

Solution

To use a look-up table, an addressing scheme known as *indexing* will be used. In indexing, a register's contents, the index register, serves as a point of ref-

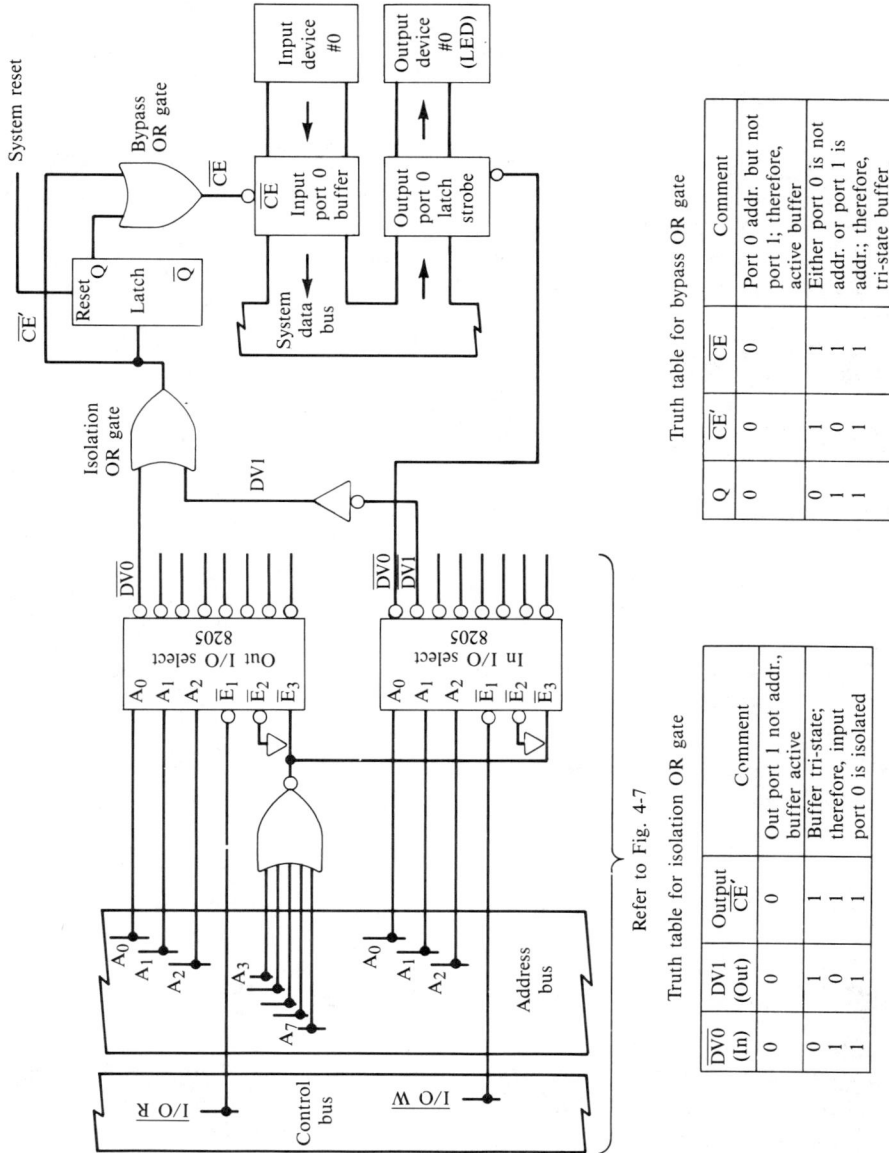

FIGURE 5-16. Hardware to implement the program of Figure 5-15.

5-4 INTRODUCTION TO FLOWCHARTS AND PROGRAMMING

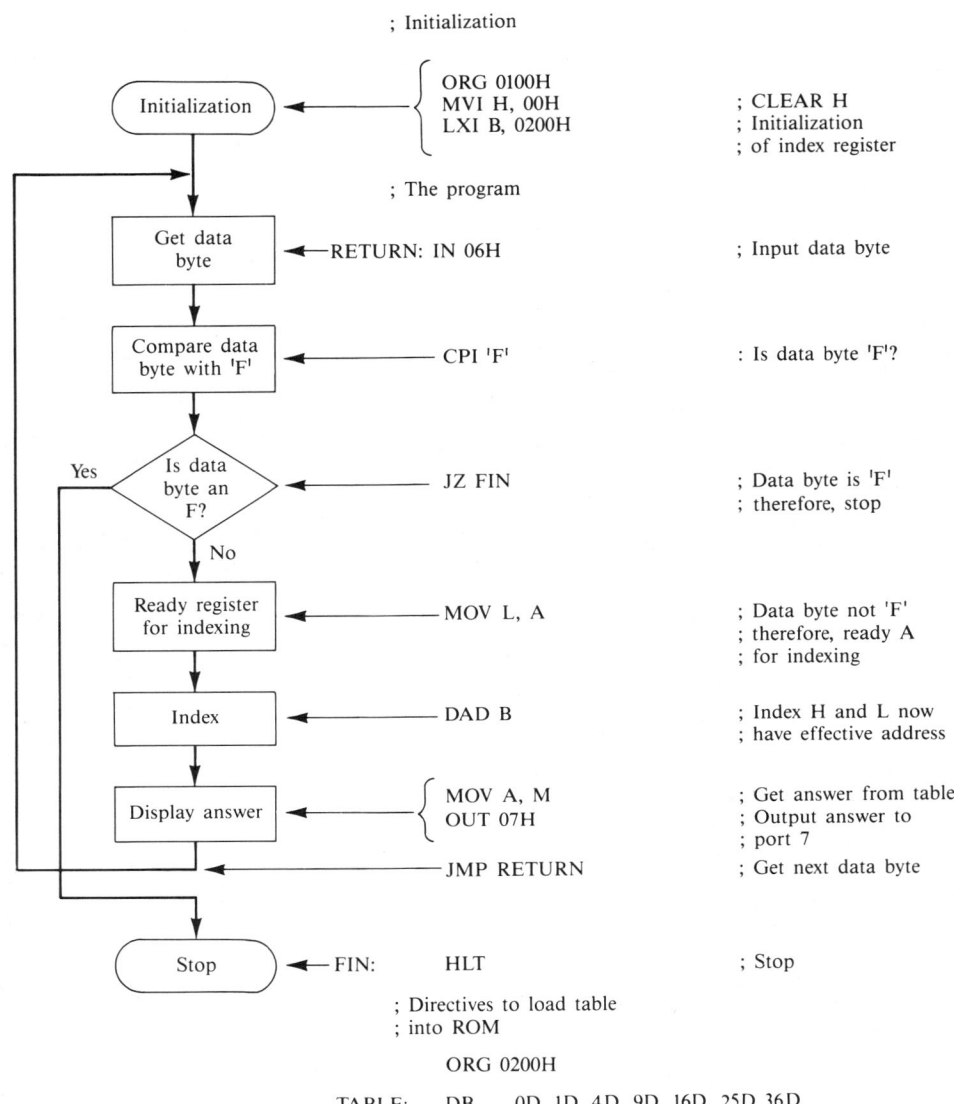

FIGURE 5-17. Flowchart and program using index addressing.

erence for addressing memory. That is, the contents of the index register is added to the contents of another register, and it is the sum which is the *effective* memory address. Specifically, we shall program in a PROM values of 0 to 9 squared, which is the table that will be referenced; then as port 6 inputs decimal values to be squared, these values will be indexed (added to) the index register, which will result in the effective address desired. The contents of this memory location will then be accessed and output to port 7.

Assuming that the system to be programmed is that of Figure 4-7, with the additions of ports 6 and 7, we will somewhat arbitrarily store the program and look-up table in page 0. Let the program be stored in memory beginning at location 0100H and the table beginning with address 0200H. The flowchart and program are shown in Figure 5-17.

The program of Figure 5-17 is straightforward and needs little comment. The comments needed are those concerning the DB directive. DB directs the assembler to store the specified data bytes, that is, the operands, which in this case are 0D, 1D, . . . , 64D, and 81D, in *consecutive* memory locations starting with the current setting of the location counter (D of the operands indicates to the assembler that the quantity is decimal). The location counter would be set to 0200H because of the ORG 0200H directive. ∎

For a final example, conceptual emphasis will be on the role that timing states play in some types of programs. The reader may wish to review Section 3-7.

EXAMPLE 5-12

The circuit of Figure 5-18 is to serve as a *programmable one-shot*. That is, the pulse duration is to be under control of the microprocessor and therefore can be varied according to a parameter (<B2>) of the program.

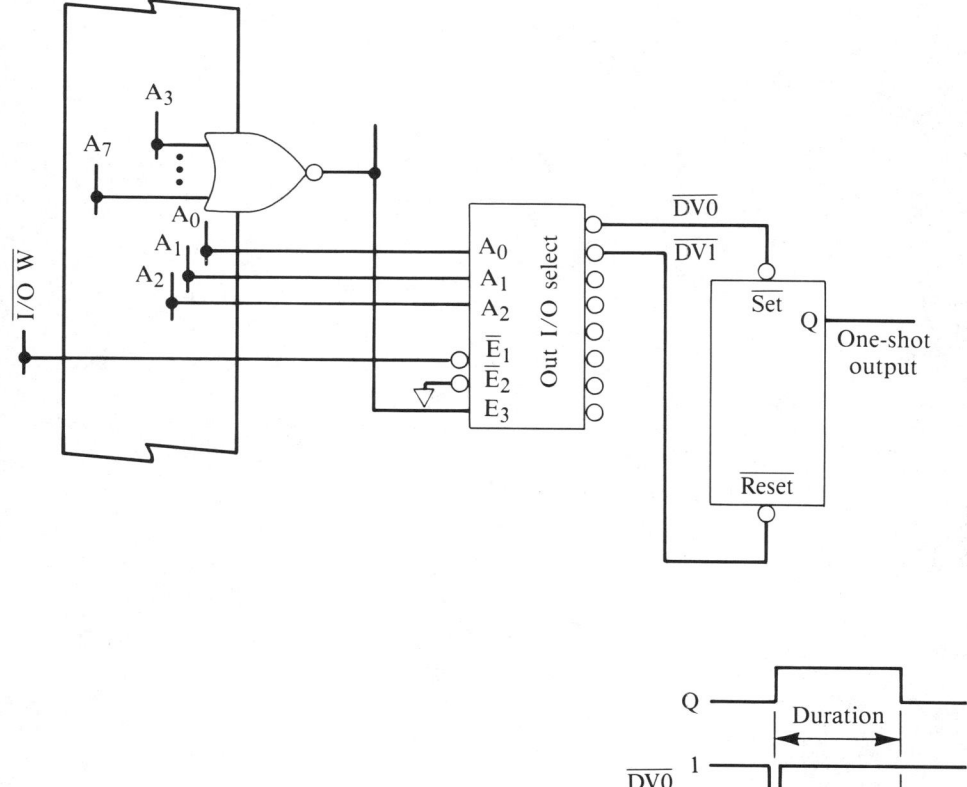

FIGURE 5-18. Programmable one-shot.

Solution

Basically, the flip-flop output Q is set and reset to create the proper pulse duration. $\overline{\text{SET}}$ and $\overline{\text{RESET}}$ of the flip-flop are treated as output ports by the microprocessor: output port 0 for set and port 1 for reset. The flowchart and program are given in Figure 5-19.

The program of Figure 5-19 will require a value <B2>, for it is this value that determines the pulse duration. Therefore, an equation is needed to determine the value of <B2>:

$$\text{pulse duration states} = \text{number loops} \times \text{<B2>} + \text{reset} \quad (5\text{-}2)$$
$$= 15 \times \text{<B2>} + 10$$

$$\text{state period} = \frac{1}{\text{clock frequency}} = \frac{1}{f} \quad (5\text{-}3)$$

$$\text{pulse duration time} = T_D = \text{pulse duration states} \times \text{state period} \quad (5\text{-}4)$$

$$T_D = (15 \times \text{<B2>} + 10)\frac{1}{f} \quad (5\text{-}5)$$

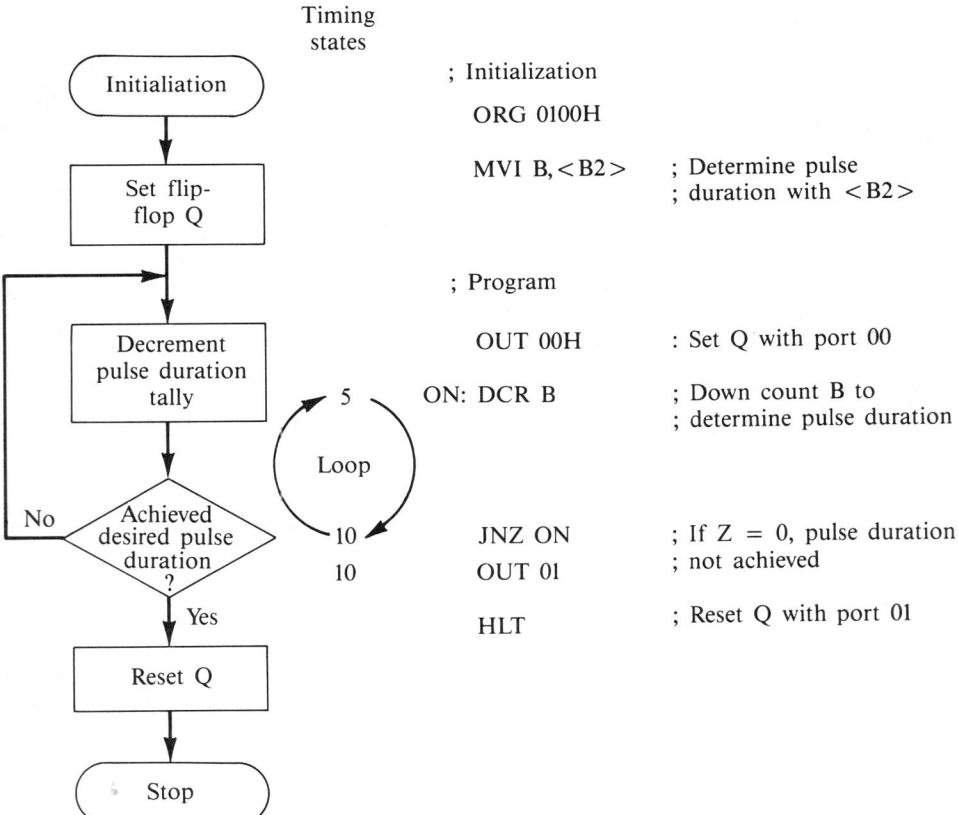

FIGURE 5-19. Flowchart and program for determining pulse duration of programmable one-shot.

Solving for <B2>, we have

$$<B2> = \frac{T_D f - 10}{15} \quad (5\text{-}6)$$

Suppose that a pulse duration of 0.5 millisecond is desired where the frequency is 2 MHz (crystal of 18 MHz). Then from Equation (5-6),

$$<B2> = \frac{(0.5 \times 10^{-3})(2 \times 10^6) - 10}{15}$$

$$= 66 \quad \text{decimal}$$

Since register B must have the hexidecimal equivalant of 66_{10}, then $66_{10} = 42_{16}$; hence <B2> = 42H. Thus for this case, MVI B,<B2> specifically becomes MVI B,42H. ∎

5-5 SUMMARY

As one would expect, all CPU instructions are the result of a logical binary coding scheme. The binary coding scheme of these instructions is such that the binary code is divided into bit combinations which indicate CPU operations (data transfer, etc.) and the CPU register(s) involved. The binary code that represents an instruction is read from memory by the CPU and loaded into its instruction register (IR), where it is then decoded by the CPU's IR decoder. Output signals from the IR decoder are input to the CPU's control unit (CU), which actually executes the instruction. The CU contains a program, which is stored within the CU at the time of manufacture, that instructs the CU on the details for instruction execution. This program is known as the CPU's microprogram.

Each microprocessor has an instruction set from which program instructions must be chosen. When programs are being written, the programmer avoids binary coding (machine code); rather, he uses mnemonic coding. Before a program can be executed by the microprocessor, it must be translated from mnemonic code to machine code. To translate from mnemonic code to machine code, a computer program known as an assembler is used.

To aid in writing programs and for interpretation of those already written, flowcharts are provided. These flowcharts are visual indicators as to how program instructions are used to accomplish a given task. That is, flowcharts provide documentation as to how the programmer modularized a programming task.

It is important to note that all program decision branches are determined by the logic state of a condition flag.

This chapter is intended to introduce programming concepts. From material of this chapter and previous chapters, the reader should

1. Understand basically how machine code controls microprocessor operations via the IR decoder and CU.
2. Understand how the software controls the system hardware electronically via the microprocessor and support chips.
3. Understand the concept of binary and mnemonic coding of instructions.
4. Be able to determine the timing diagram for a program, or at least the essential portions.
5. Be capable of developing a flowchart for a relatively simple task.
6. Be capable of writing programs from flowcharts.
7. Be able to hand-assemble a program.
8. Understand the function of an assembler and basically how it performs that function.

REVIEW QUESTIONS AND PROBLEMS

1. Using Tables 5-1, 5-2, 5-3, 5-5, 5-7, and 5-8, determine the machine code for the instructions given. Confirm your coding with Table 5-10 or Appendix A.
   - (a) MOV A,M
   - (b) ADD E
   - (c) SUB C
   - (d) CMP C
   - (e) ADC H
   - (f) CNZ 1000H

2. Determine which binary codes are not officially part of the 8080 instruction set.

3. With reference to Section 5-3, Intel's instruction explanations state the number of machine cycles (listed as "cycles") required to fetch and execute each instruction. For the instructions given, justify each machine cycle required, and state and justify the control signal generated for each machine cycle.
   - (a) MOV r1,r2
   - (b) LXI rp,data 16
   - (c) STA addr
   - (d) LHLD addr
   - (e) STAX rp
   - (f) ADD r
   - (g) ADD M
   - (h) CALL addr
   - (i) RET
   - (j) RST N

4. Write a program that is properly documented (flowchart and comments) which will input data bytes from input device 0 of Figure 4-7. These data bytes are to be classified into two groups:
   Group A: those less than 010H.
   Group B: those equal to or greater than 010H.
   There is to be a tally for the number of data bytes falling in groups A and B (tally A and tally B). Data collection is to terminate when device 0 inputs an 'E'. Begin your program at 0050H.

5. Suppose that output device 3 is an LED hex display. Modify the program of Problem 4 to include echoing, by device 3, of each input data byte. Assume that the input data bytes are in proper form to be written directly to device 3.

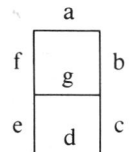

(a) Seven-segment LED display configuration

(b) LED-word format

FIGURE 5-20. Seven-segment LED display and word format.

6. A seven-segment LED display has the format shown in Figure 5-20(a). Using the 8-bit format of Figure 5-20(b) to turn the LED segments of Figure 5-20(a) on and off (a "1" turns a segment on), write a program that will echo hexidecimal values input by device 0 via the seven-segment display represented by device 3 of Figure 4-7. Use a look-up-table approach. Be certain to document your program.

7. Most keyboard inputs use the binary code. Refer to Appendix B for the ASCII code and then write a program that will differentiate between alphabetic characters and decimal numeric values. Echo these ASCII numeric characters to device 5. Begin this program at memory location 0150H.

8. Suppose that device 5 is a seven-segment LED display. Write a program that will convert a decimal ASCII character input by device 0 to an LED seven-segment display character and then echo that character via device 5. This program is to be located at beginning address 0050H. Document this program.

9. Hand-assemble the programs of Problems 4 to 7. On the first pass, create a symbol table.

10. For each instruction of Problem 4, discuss how the instruction controls the hardware of Figure 4-7.

CHAPTER 6

Additional System Capabilities and Alternative Addressing Methods: Interrupts, DMA, Memory-Mapped I/O, and Linear Addressing

6-1
INTRODUCTION

The microprocessor-based system of Figure 4-7 was not given interrupt or DMA capability, as indicated from Figure 4-7, since the input pins INT and HOLD of the 8080 are permanently inactive (both are tied low). This chapter will develop the necessary concepts of hardware and software for the utilization of both of these features. Also, later sections of this chapter will develop a memory-mapped I/O system, as mentioned in Chapter 4, and linear addressing. The last section will use a hex keypad as an example for utilizing interrupts.

6-2
INTERRUPTS

Interrupts allow the CPU to be more productive by permitting an I/O port (most often an input port) to interrupt the CPU only when that port needs servicing by the CPU, therefore freeing the CPU to perform other tasks. An analogy to the interrupt concept is the classroom, where the professor will serve as the CPU and the students as I/O ports. Each student possesses two I/O ports: an input port (speech mechanism for data transmission to the professor) and an output port (listening mechanism for receiving data from the professor).

The classroom scenario for this interrupt analogy will be that the professor will "lecture to the blackboard" (doing a productive task—lecturing and writing on the blackboard) and face the class only when interrupted by an input port (a student requesting service, perhaps to ask a question). The means of requesting an interrupt will be that each student will be given a string, all of which are tied to the professor's left index finger (assuming that the professor is writing with his or her right hand). When any student wishes to request service, he or she simply pulls the string. Once the string has been pulled, the professor acknowledges the request and interrupts the lecture. The professor then turns from the blackboard to face the class. The professor now wishes to service the interrupting student but is unable to do so since the identity of the requesting student is unknown. Thus the professor must *poll* the class to determine who requested the interrupt.

To implement this interrupting scheme, each student is provided with a flag mounted on his or her desk (much like a mailbox flag). They are to raise this flag (to identify themselves) in the up position upon requesting an interrupt; otherwise, it is to be in the down position. To poll the class the professor need only check the state (up or down) of each student's interrupt request flag.

Once the professor has identified the student who requested an interrupt, the professor can then begin servicing by "reading" data from the student's input port (the student will ask the question). Then the professor will "write" the answer to the student's output port (the student will listen to the answer—we hope). This concludes the interrupt, at which time the professor returns to lecturing, continuing at that point of the lecture where interrupted.

From this example several analogies can be drawn, by noting:

1. The professor had just one finger to devote to interrupts, and all student interrupt requests were made via that single finger.
2. Since all interrupt requests were made over a single finger, rather than allocating individual fingers to particular students, the professor had to poll the class to identify the requesting student.
3. The order of events was as follows:
    a. The request was initiated by the student and at the same time the student raised an interrupt request flag.
    b. The professor acknowledged the interrupt request.
    c. The professor polled the class to identify the requesting student by checking the status of all interrupt request flags (up or down).
    d. After student identification and service, the professor returned to the task being performed (lecturing) at the time of the interrupt.

From the first analogy the professor is said to have *single-level interrupt* capability. For a microprocessor this means that all interrupt requests are made via a single input pin of the CPU (INT for the 8080). As in the case of the second analogy, the CPU must poll the I/O ports to identify the requesting port. Polling occurs after the handshake (request and acknowledgment of the request constitute a handshake) and is a software routine that checks the logic state of each port's interrupt request flag, which is simply a flip-flop. This flip-flop is set high by the I/O device at the time the I/O device requests the interrupt. Once the interrupting I/O port is identified, the CPU will service it and then return to the task it was performing before the interrupt. Notice that polling takes *time*.

Now suppose that the professor decides to use all five fingers (thumb included) of his left hand in order better to facilitate interrupts. He could allocate four of his fingers to students to whom he gives the highest priority. Each of these students would attach his or her string to a finger uniquely assigned to him or her, whereas the remainder of the class would still be collectively attached to the index finger. Whenever one of the four high-priority students wishes to request an interrupt, he or she would follow the same procedures as before, that is, pull the string and at the same time set the interrupt request flag high. Now the professor need not poll the class for the requesting student's identity. The student identity is immediately known, since there is a one-to-one correspondence between each of these high-priority students and a specific finger. For this analogy the professor is said to have *multilevel interrupt* capability.

Similar to the classroom analogy above, any microprocessor with more than one interrupt pin has multilevel interrupt capability. Any I/O device that is singularly tied to one of these interrupt pins can be immediately identified by the CPU upon receiving an interrupt request from it. This allows the CPU to go directly to that I/O device and service it without having to poll first. This obviously will save time in processing interrupts. The terminology used to describe the CPU being "pointed" where to go is termed *vectoring*. Hence in this example the CPU was vectored to the I/O device requesting the interrupt (actually, the CPU will be vectored to the service routine of the I/O port).

As a result of a cursory examination of a microprocessor's pin configuration, one may reasonably assume that if multilevel interrupt capability exists, the microprocessor also has vector capability. Vectoring, of course, means a reduction in program length and speed of servicing of those vectored I/O ports, since polling is not required.

In summary, a single-level interrupt capability (one interrupt pin) usually requires polling for I/O interrupt request identification (no vectoring). Multilevel interrupt capability (more than one interrupt pin) usually provides vectoring, thereby reducing or eliminating polling routines. As we shall see, while the 8080 has single-level interrupt capability, it also has some vector capability.

6-3 SINGLE-LEVEL INTERRUPTS AND POLLING

Since for single-level interrupt capability, a single pin (INT) exists for interrupt request, each I/O port with interrupt capability will have its interrupt request flag ORed to the interrupt request pin (INT) of the microprocessor, as illustrated in Figure 6-1.

Knowing that for a single-level interrupt system the interrupt request flags must be polled, a scheme is needed that allows polling via software. What is required is that somehow the logic states of these interrupt request flags be read by the CPU. The circuit of Figure 6-2 will accomplish this task.

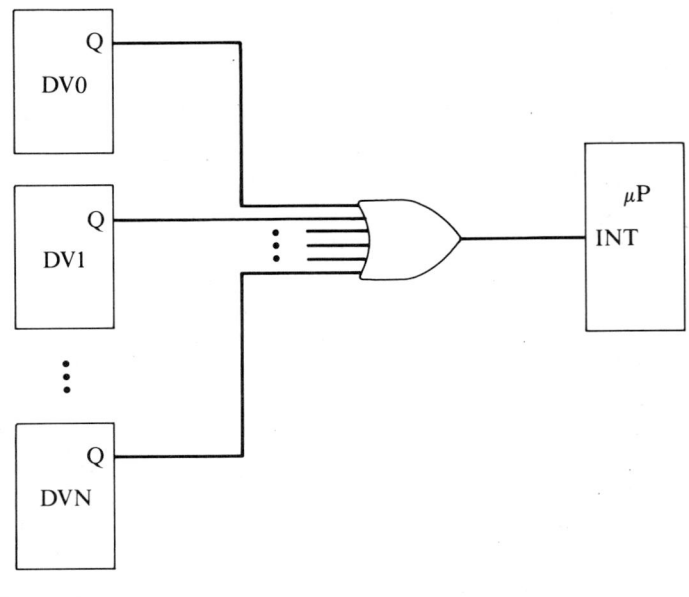

I/O port interrupt
request flags

FIGURE 6-1. Single-level interrupt capability.

Inspecting Figure 6-2, we see that when one or more interrupt request flags are raised, this request(s) will be ORed to the INT pin of the CPU. Also, the output of the interrupt request OR gate will cause the IREQ latch to latch the logic states of these flags; that is, IREQ will latch their status. At the completion of the handshake (interrupt request and acknowledge), the CPU will vector to memory location 0038H. Vectoring to address 0038H is accomplished by tying the 8228's $\overline{\text{INTA}}$ (interrupt acknowledge) pin high via a 1-kΩ resistor, which is shown in Figure 6-2. Tying $\overline{\text{INTA}}$ high causes the CPU to execute an RST 7 instruction upon the acknowledgment of an interrupt request.

As seen from the instruction set of Section 5-3, RST 7 (n = 7) will cause the CPU to vector to memory location 0038H and then save the address of the next memory location (PC + 1), which is the address of the next instruction to have been executed *before* the interrupt, in the stack. Therefore, upon completion of servicing the interrupt, the CPU will "know" where to return in its program execution by retrieving this saved address from the stack. Once the return address is saved on the stack the PC contents are changed to 0038H (NNN = 111), which is the cause for the CPU to vector to 0038H since the PC contents are gated on the address bus in implementing the RST 7 instruction.

At address 0038H will be the beginning of the polling routine. The polling routine flowchart is given in Figure 6-3 and the routine in Figure 6-4. For simplicity the routine of Figure 6-3 assumes that only two I/O ports have interrupt capability, rather than eight.

The program of Figure 6-4 is fairly simple, so only a few comments will be given. Notice from Figure 6-2 that the tri-state buffers are addressed as 09;

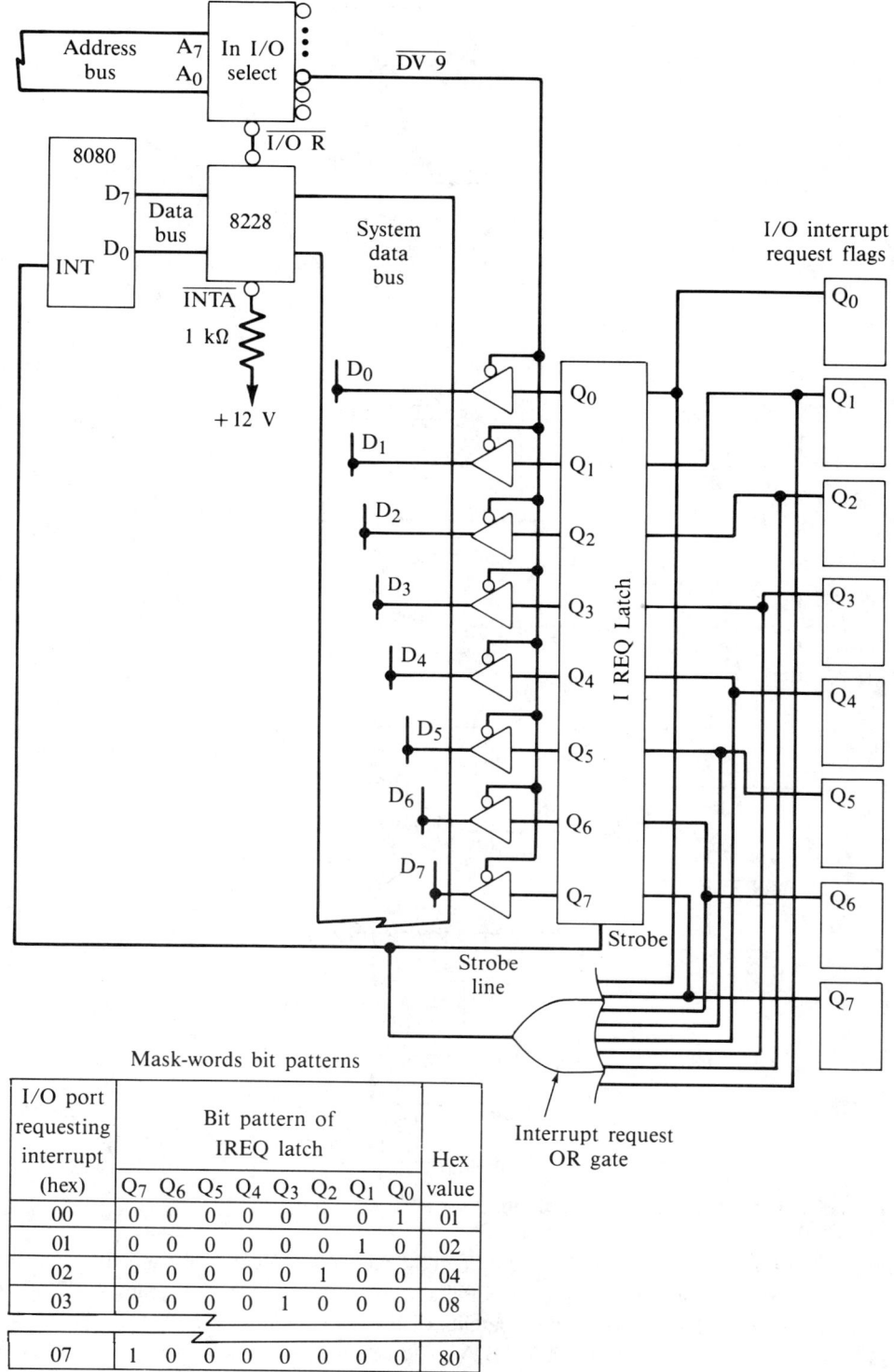

FIGURE 6-2. Logic circuit for polling.

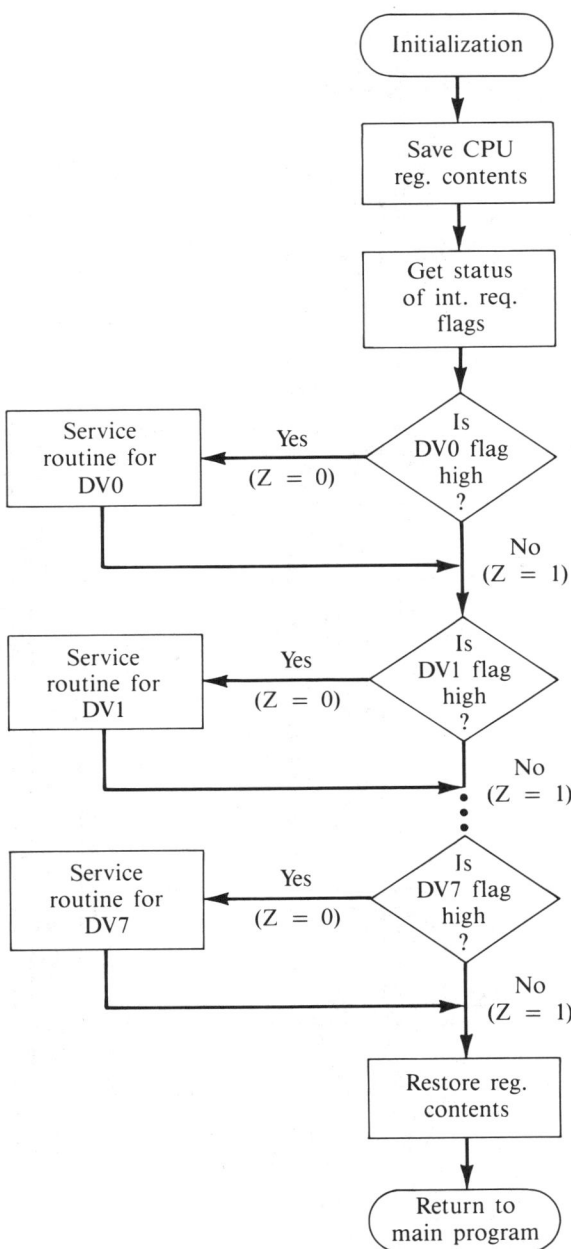

FIGURE 6-3. Flowchart for polling.

hence the instruction IN 09 will load the contents of IREQ, which is the interrupt request flag's status, into the CPU's accumulator. Since a program AND operation is destructive to the contents of the accumulator, a copy must be made, hence the instruction MOV B,A. The second byte of the ANI instructions is referred to as a *mask word*, for it masks out all bits except those of interest. Their values can be reasoned by referring to Figure 6-2 and determining the bit

EXAMPLE 6-1

```
    ORG 0038H

; Initialization

    DI              ; Disable interrupt capability

; Save register contents

    PUSH PSW
    PUSH B
    PUSH D
    PUSH H

; Begin polling

    IN 09H          ; Get Interrupt request status flags
    MOV B,A         ; Copy status in B
    ANI 01H         ; Poll DV0
    CNZ SR0         ; If Z = 0 jump to service routine for DV0
    MOV A,B         ; Copy status in A
    ANI 02H         ; Poll DV1 with mask word 02H
    CNZ SR1         ; If Z = 0 jump to service routine for DV1

; Restore reg. contents

    POP H
    POP D
    POP B
    POP PSW
    EI              ; Enable interrupt capability
    RET             ; Return to main prog.
```

Figure 6-4. Polling routine for the hardware of Figure 6-2.

pattern of IREQ for various interrupt requests. It is seen from the table of Figure 6-2 that if I/O port 00H alone had its interrupt request flag high, the bit pattern of register A would be 01H; similarly, mask word 02H for I/O port 1, 04H for I/O port 02, and so on. Thus, if any I/O port except I/O port 00 requested an interrupt, the instruction ANI 01H would result in A = 0 and the Z flag would be SET (Z = 1). Under this condition, CNZ SR0 would not be executed. However, if I/O port 00H had requested an interrupt; and after the execution of ANI 01H, the accumulator contents would not be zero, resulting in Z = 0. In this case CNZ SR0 would be executed, which would cause the CPU to jump to the address represented by the symbol SR0, which is the beginning address of the service routine for I/O port 0.

6-4

SINGLE-LEVEL INTERRUPTS AND VECTORING

Thus far it has been indicated that if a microprocessor has single-level interrupt capability (single interrupt request pin), polling is a necessary consequence.

Often this is true, but not for the 8080. As will be shown, the 8080 allows both vectoring, as if it had multilevel interrupts, and polling.

The 8080's vectoring capability can be realized by understanding the RST N instruction and the CPU status word for an interrupt acknowledge. Referring to Section 3-4 and comparing the status words for an instruction fetch and interrupt acknowledge, it is noted that the logic states of D_0 (INTA) and D_7 (MEMR) are the only differences. It is obvious why D_0 would differ since it is used to generate the control signal $\overline{\text{INTA}}$ via the 8228's gating array. The logic state of D_7 states that memory is being accessed for an instruction fetch, whereas it is *not* for an interrupt acknowledge. To appreciate the reason for this difference, view D_5 (M1). Bit D_5 is active for both CPU status words, which indicates that the CPU is fetching the *first byte* of an instruction; however, from bit D_7 of the CPU status word for an interrupt acknowledge, it is realized that the CPU is fetching an instruction *but not from memory*. This means that when control signal $\overline{\text{INTA}}$ is active, the CPU will latch a byte from the data bus and treat that byte as an instruction by loading it into the IR. Thus the desired instruction had better be on the data bus *when control signal $\overline{\text{INTA}}$ is active*.

The control signal $\overline{\text{INTA}}$ is used to gate (jam) the desired instruction (RST N) on the data bus at the proper time. As shown for two RST instructions in Figure 6-5, when $\overline{\text{INTA}}$ becomes active, the tri-state logic removes the buffer from its high-Z state, thus gating the binary bit pattern for an RST N onto the data bus. The IR then receives this machine code and the CU will execute it. Figure 6-5(c) gives the corresponding vector address for each RST N.

As stated previously, the 8228 has the feature that when $\overline{\text{INTA}}$ is tied high via a 1-kΩ resistor, as shown in Figure 6-2, the 8228 will automatically jam RST 7 on the data bus when $\overline{\text{INTA}}$ becomes active. This feature saves hardware, of course.

With the circuits of Figure 6-5, only one RST N vector location can be utilized by the system since the control signal $\overline{\text{INTA}}$ is dedicated to jamming a specific RST N instruction (RST 7) on the data bus. If it is desired to utilize more than one RST N, such as when dedicating an RST vector address to a specific I/O service routine, an encoder can be used to supply the bit pattern for bits NNN. This scheme is shown in Figure 6-6(a). Of course, with the scheme of Figure 6-6 only one interrupt request at a time can be received, as indicated from the truth table of the encoder. Then a priority system such as that shown in Figure 6-6(b) is required. Priority is established since if a higher-priority I/O requests an interrupt, the $\overline{Q}$ output of its interrupt request flag will inhibit all lesser-priority AND gates.

An addition to the vectoring circuits of Figures 6-5 and 6-6 is the interrupt request OR gate of Figure 6-2. Also, with priority interrupts, as shown in Figure 6-6(b), there must be a means to "remember" interrupt requests that were ignored by the CPU while it was servicing other I/O devices (remember that all interrupt requests are made via a single interrupt pin). That is, if two or more I/O ports request an interrupt at the same time, or while the CPU is servicing another I/O port, the INT pin will become active (via the OR gate) but will not indicate whether one or more I/O ports are requesting the interrupt. A combination of hardware and software will be used to resolve this problem. Figure

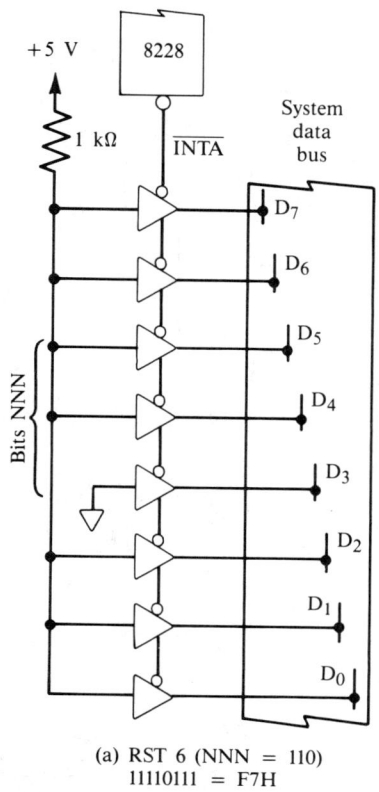
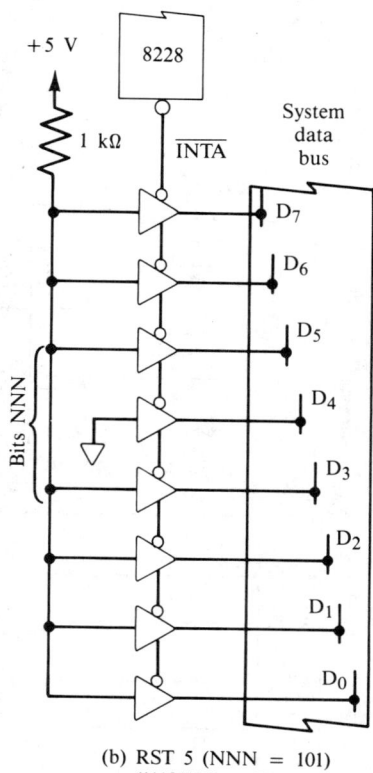

(a) RST 6 (NNN = 110)
11110111 = F7H

(b) RST 5 (NNN = 101)
(11101111) = EFH

Machine code (hex)	Mnemonic code	Vector address
C7	RST 0	0000H
CF	RST 1	0008H
D7	RST 2	0010H
DF	RST 3	0018H
E7	RST 4	0020H
EF	RST 5	0028H
F7	RST 6	0030H
FF	RST 7	0038H

FIGURE 6-5. Gating of RST 6 and RST 7 on the data bus.

6-7 gives the hardware and Figure 6-8 gives the software. For simplicity, three I/O ports are shown, all of which are input ports.

To understand the operations of Figure 6-7, realize that:

1. The interrupt request flags are flip-flops which are set by the requesting input port, via the interrupt request line. These flags are numbered to correspond to the input port for which they serve. Notice that these flip-flops are treated as output ports and can be reset by addressing them as such.
2. AND gates 1 and 2 establish priority and also ensure that only one input to the encoder will be high and that "high" will be determined by the highest priority. These AND gates function similarly to those of Figure 6-6(b).

6-4 SINGLE-LEVEL INTERRUPTS AND VECTORING

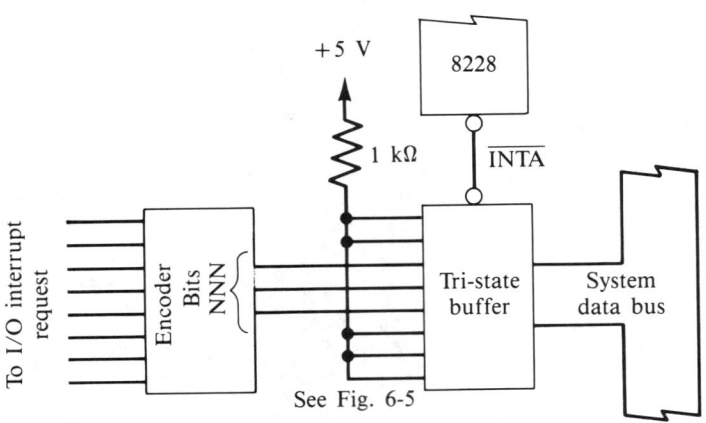

(a) Encoding bits NNN for an RST N instruction

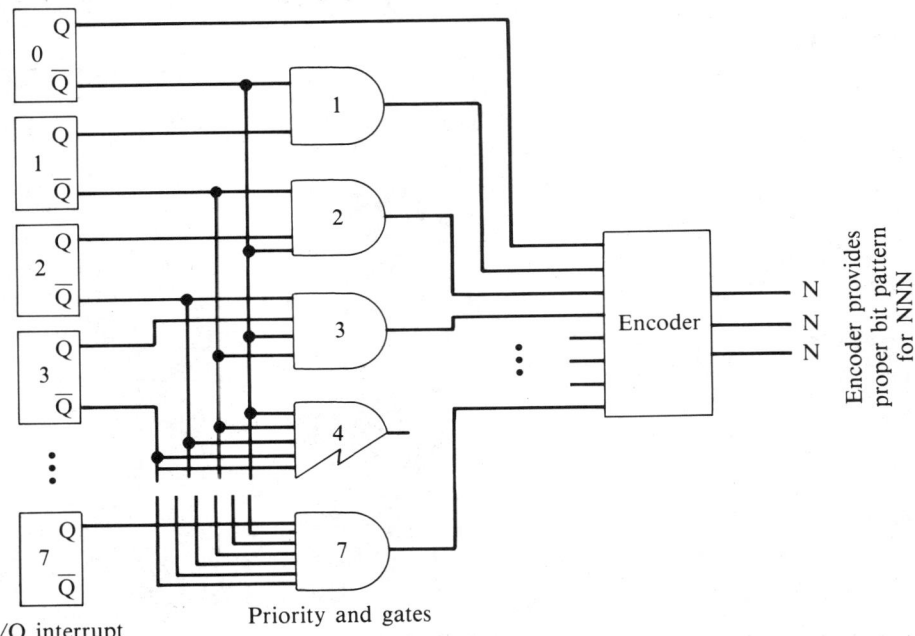

(b) Implementing priority for encoder

Truth table for encoder

Input	Output (NNN)
00000001	000
00000010	001
00000100	010
00001000	011
00010000	100
00100000	101
01000000	110
10000000	111

FIGURE 6-6. The development of vectored interrupts with priority.

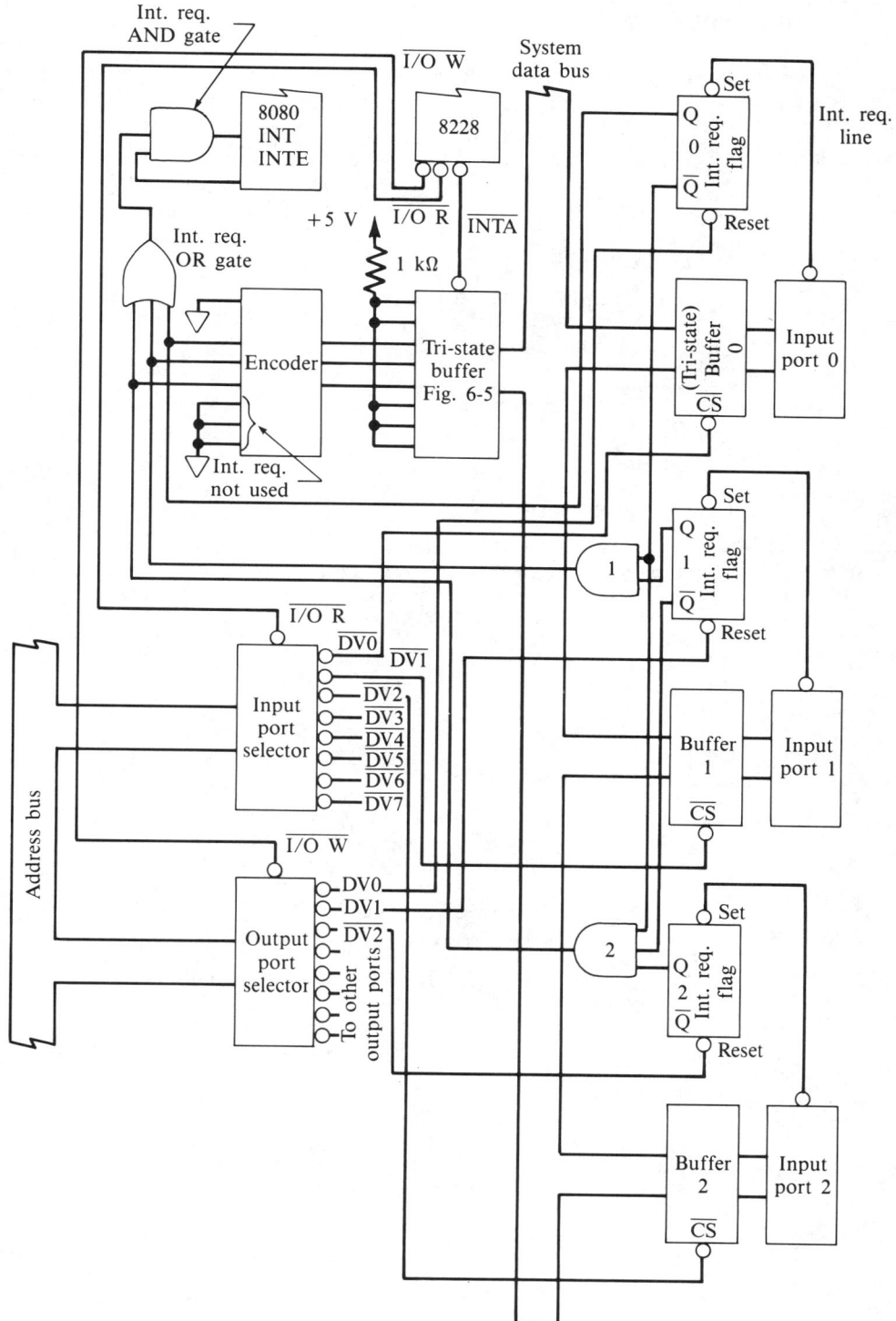

FIGURE 6-7. Logic circuit for priority interrupts with vectoring.

EXAMPLE 6-2

```
; Service routine for input port 0

    ORG 0008H
    JMP 0050H           ; Jump to more memory
    ORG 0050H
    DI                  ; Disable INT and reset INTE
    OUT 00H             ; Reset 0 interrupt request flag

; Initialize CPU

    LXI H,2100H         ; Initialize DC

; Save register contents

    PUSH PSW
    PUSH B
    PUSH D
    PUSH H

; Service input port 0

    IN 00H              ; Get data byte
    MOV M,A             ; Store data byte

; Restore register contents

    POP H
    POP D
    POP B
    POP PSW

; Enable interrupts

    EI                  ; INT enabled and INTE set
    RET                 ; Finished return to
                        ; Main prog.

; Service routine for input port 1

    ORG 0010H
    JMP 0060H           ; Jump to more memory
    ORG 0060H
    DI                  ; Disable INT and reset INTE
    OUT 01H             ; RESET 1 interrupt request flag

; Initialize CPU

    LXI H,2200H         ; Initialize DC

; Save register contents

    PUSH PSW
    PUSH B
    PUSH D
    PUSH H
```

FIGURE 6-8. Service routine for servicing I/O ports of Figure 6-7.

```
; Service input port 1

    IN 01H                  ; Get data byte
    MOV M,A                 ; Store data byte

; Restore register contents

    POP H
    POP D
    POP B
    POP PSW

; Enable interrupts

    EI                      ; INT enabled and INTE set
    RET                     ; Finished return to
                            ; Main prog.

; Service routine for input port 2

    ORG 0018H
    JMP 0070H               ; Jump to more memory
    ORG 0070H
    DI                      ; Disable INT and reset INTE
    OUT 02H                 ; RESET 2 interrupt request flag

; Initialize CPU

    LXI H,2300H             ; DC = 2300H

; Save register contents

    PUSH PSW
    PUSH B
    PUSH D
    PUSH H

; Service input port 02

    IN 02H                  ; Get data byte
    MOV M,A                 ; Store data byte

; Restore register contents

    POP H
    POP D
    POP B
    POP PSW

; Enable interrupts

    EI                      ; INT enabled and INTE set
    RET                     ; Finished return to
                            ; Main prog.
```

FIGURE 6-8. (Continued)

3. The interrupt request AND gate, which is used to input an interrupt request to the 8080, via the INT pin, is enabled or inhibited by INTE. The interrupt request OR gate ORs the interrupt requests of all input ports just as it did in Figures 6-1 and 6-2.

We shall arbitrarily assign input port 0's service routine to begin at memory location 0008H, which requires an RST 1 be jammed on the data bus (see Figure 6-5c) so that the CPU will vector to memory location 0008H as the result of an interrupt acknowledge ($\overline{\text{INTA}}$). The service routine for input port 1 will begin at memory location 0010H, which requires an RST 2. Finally, memory location 0018H will be assigned the service routine for input port 2, which requires RST 3. Note that RST 0 is not used (the low-order pin of the encoder is held low), since this is the same vector address as for a system reset.

For simplicity the service routines of Figure 6-8 assume that input ports 0, 1, and 2 are of the simplest type and require just an IN instruction to acquire their data byte. It also assumed that the data byte is to be stored in memory. To understand the multiple ORG directives for each service routine, the reader must realize that eight storage locations exist between each RST location (RST 1 = 0008H and RST 2 = 0010H), which is insufficient for most service routines. Hence a JMP instruction is used to make more memory locations available for the service routines.

As an example of the priority interrupt system of Figure 6-7, let us suppose that input ports 0 and 2 requested interrupts at the same time. Of course, each of these input ports made the request by setting their respective interrupt request flag in the high state. The $\overline{Q}$ output of the interrupt request flag of input port 0 is in the low state, thereby inhibiting AND gates 1 and 2. The output of these AND gates is zero, resulting in a bit pattern of 00000010 appearing at the encoder's input (notice that the LSB of the encoder is gounded). The output of the encoder is 001, as shown in the truth table of Figure 6-6(c). Since the Q output of flip-flop 0 is in the 1 state, this results in a high output for the interrupt request OR gate. Assuming that the CPU has its interrupt capability enabled, thus enabling the interrupt request AND gate, the interrupt request of input port 0 is applied to input pin INT of the CPU. Before acknowledging the interrupt the CPU completes execution of its present instruction. Upon completion of that instruction, the CPU acknowledges the interrupt request by issuing to the 8228 the proper CPU status word for an interrupt acknowledge. The 8228 decodes that CPU status word and generates the control signal $\overline{\text{INTA}}$. $\overline{\text{INTA}}$ will enable the tri-state buffer of Figure 6-7, thus gating RST 1 on the data bus, which vectors the CPU to memory location 0008H. From the program of Figure 6-8 it is seen that the service routine for input port 0 is at memory location 0008H. Because of a lack of available memory locations, the program jumps to 0050H. The DI instruction of this program is not necessary since the interrupts were automatically disabled by the CPU upon interrupt acknowledge but are included as a safeguard. With the interrupt capability disabled, INTE outputs a logic 0, thereby disabling the interrupt request AND gate. When instruction OUT 00H is executed, the interrupt request flag 0 is reset, which enables AND gate 2. Since the interrupt request flag 2 is also high, AND gate 2 outputs a logic 1. The binary pattern which is now input to the encoder is 00000100, resulting in an output of 010, as seen from Figure 6-6(c). However, since $\overline{\text{INTA}}$ is not active, the tri-state buffer is in the high-Z state. The next two instructions, after the register contents are saved (IN 00H and MOV M,A), actually service input port 0. When EI of that program is executed, it enables the interrupt capability and INTE outputs a high, which enables the interrupt request AND gate, thus requesting another interrupt since the interrupt request OR-gate output is also high. The actual implementation of EI is delayed by the CPU until the execution of the next instruction, which is RET. When RET is executed, the CPU returns to the main program to resume program execution as it was before the interrupt. However, before it can resume program execution, it receives the interrupt request from input port 2. Of course, this was accomplished once EI was actually executed, and INTE enabled the interrupt request AND gate as previously discussed. As before, the interrupt request is acknowledged, $\overline{\text{INTA}}$ becomes low, and RST 3 is jammed on the data bus, causing the CPU to vector to memory location 0018H. The remainder of events is a repeat of those stated for servicing input port 0.

If one does not wish to design a priority interrupt request logic circuit, manufactured circuits may be purchased. The reader is referred to the 8214.

6-5 MULTILEVEL INTERRUPTS AND VECTORING

Some microprocessors have more than one interrupt request pin, such as the 8085, which classifies them as having multilevel interrupt capability. When an interrupt request is made via one of these pins, the CPU will be automatically vectored to a specific memory location. The vectoring is done automatically within the CPU, with no additional hardware required. When the 8085 is studied, the reader will be given specific details.

6-6 DIRECT MEMORY ACCESS

Direct memory access (DMA) operations are quite simple to explain, since the burden of design lies with the I/O port having DMA capability. When an I/O port wishes direct memory access, it simply inputs a high on the HOLD pin of the CPU. When the CPU finishes execution of its present instruction, it enters a state of limbo (the hold state) and does "nothing" but put its address and data pins in the high-Z state. At this time the CPU acknowledges the hold request by outputing a high at its HLDA pin. The HLDA signal is used by the I/O port to enable its circuitry to furnish memory addresses, via the address bus, the proper control signal ($\overline{\text{MEM R}}$ or $\overline{\text{MEM W}}$), via the control bus, and data, via the data bus. To summarize, the *I/O port* must supply memory addresses and provide proper timing. Of course, for multidata bytes the I/O port must increment the memory address, much like a program counter, and then access the next data byte for the read or write operation. To provide timing the I/O port will have to supply the proper $\overline{\text{MEM R}}$ or $\overline{\text{MEM W}}$ control signal, whichever

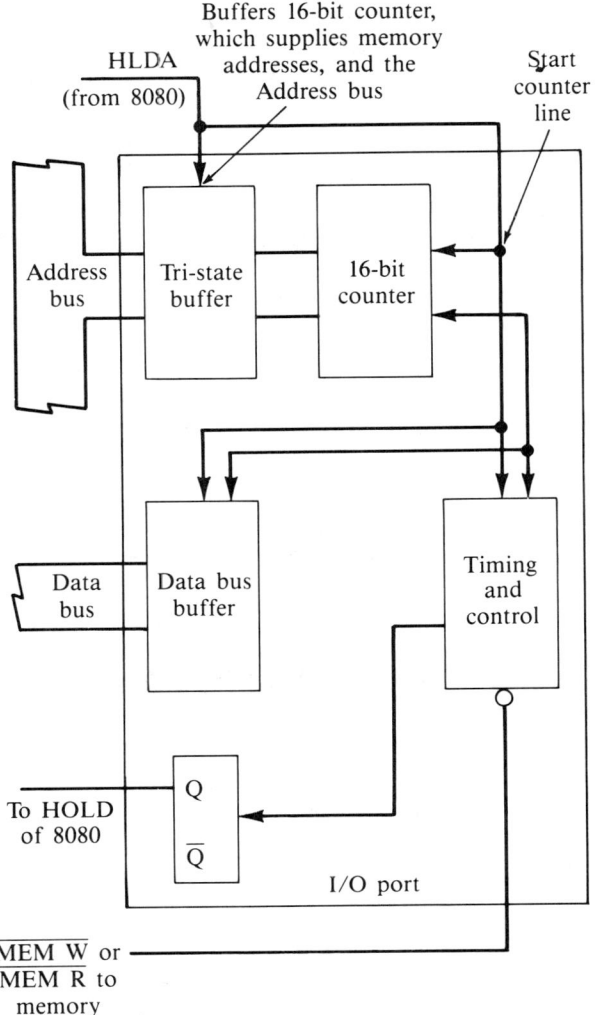

FIGURE 6-9. Architecture of DMA.

is appropriate. By wiring the 8080's HLDA pin to the 8228 HDLA pin, the 8228 will put both its data bus pins and control signal pins in the high-Z state. A simple architectural drawing of the I/O port is shown in Figure 6-9.

6-7

MEMORY MAPS

When programming a microprocessor, the programmer must keep track of memory allocations in order not to overlap those allocations. For instance, for complex programs it is conceivable that the programmer might mistakenly write a program that stores data bytes in memory locations 0100H to 0200H and then, later, forgetting this memory assignment, writes another routine which stores data bytes in memory locations 0150H to 0350H. Obviously, there is an overlap in memory assignment from 0150H to 0200H and the resulting data bytes stored at these locations would depend on which routine was last executed. Data bytes stored at these "shared" memory locations by the first routine would be overwritten by the last routine executed and as a result would be lost.

It would be beneficial for a person programming to have a visual aid that would readily show the memory locations already assigned and the purpose for which they are allocated: in short, a visual aid to assist the programmer in the "bookkeeping" of memory allocations. Such a visual aid is a *memory map*. A memory map is a rectangular representation of a system's memory capacity which is partitioned into subblocks. Each subblock is identified as to its function and memory locations allocated. Figure 6-10 is a hypothetical memory map for a system with 5000H bytes of memory.

The hypothetical memory map of Figure 6-10 shows that as the programmer wrote the routines for this system, he or she *decided* to allocate as follows:

1. The memory location vectored to by a system reset (PC = 0000H) is allocated to the system Monitor program. Since a reset (RST 0 also) has only eight memory locations (RST 1 begins at 0008H) and the monitor program requires more locations, it was necessary to jump to address 0084H to allocate more memory. Just as a note, a monitor program is usually a routine

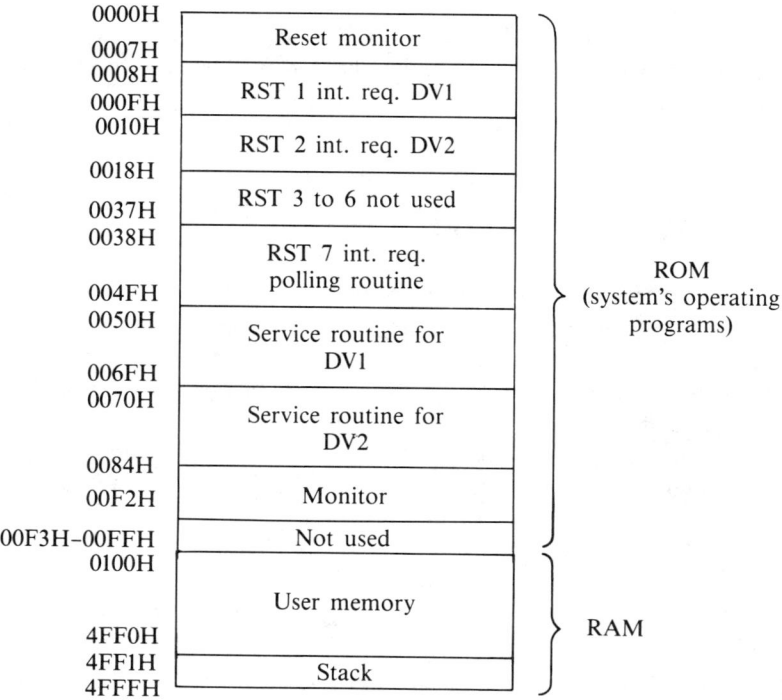

FIGURE 6-10. Hypothetical memory map.

that instructs the CPU how to communicate with the system's principal I/O devices, such as a terminal, CRT, tape reader, disk, or printer.
2. The memory locations vectored to by RST 1 are reserved for the servicing routine of an interrupt request from I/O device 1. Eight memory locations were not sufficient for this service routine, and hence the programmer used locations 0050H to 006FH.
3. Memory locations 0010H to 0018H and also 0070H to 0083H were used for the service routine of I/O device 2.
4. Those memory locations vectored to by RST 3 to RST 6 were *not required* by this system, and even though they could have been used, the programmer decided to reserve their memory spaces for possible further expansion of the present system.
5. Memory locations 00F3H to 0FFH are in excess of ROM locations required. They cannot be eliminated, since the ROM used has 256 (FFH) locations.
6. Locations 0100H to 4F00H are RAM and are to be used by the user for the storage of data and other programs.
7. The stack was defined by the programmer to require FH locations beginning at 4FF1H and ending at 4FFFH.

Realize that ROM contains those bytes that do not change, such as the system's operation programs. RAM stores those bytes which change, such as data and programs not permanent to the system's operation; that is, programs dealing with payroll, BASIC, FORTRAN, games, and so on, are stored in RAM. Those bytes stored in RAM may be loaded into RAM via terminals, floppy disk, tapes, and so on.

Memory maps should be furnished with an operational system, for they will aid the user in using and modifying the system's memory (if modifications are required).

6-8

MEMORY-MAPPED I/O

As stated in Chapter 4, memory-mapped I/O differs from isolated I/O in that a memory-mapped I/O system treats I/O the same as memory relative to the software. Each I/O device is assigned a memory address and therefore becomes part of the system's memory map—hence its name. The advantage of such a system is the increased number of instructions dealing with I/O. Every instruction that refers to a memory location can control I/O, whereas for isolated I/O only two instructions controlled I/O (IN and OUT). Also, the source or desti-

```
LXI H, 0100H    ; Preload M with I/O address
MOV M, B        ; Copy B to I/O
```

FIGURE 6-11. Program to copy a byte of data from register B to an I/O port which is addressed as memory address 0100H.

```
ADD B        ; Adds A and B
STA 0200H    ; Output result to memory location
             ; 0200H (OUTPUT PORT 0200H)
```

FIGURE 6-12. Program demonstrating memory-mapped I/O.

nation of the data is limited with isolated I/O, since for an IN instruction the destination register is always the accumulator, and for the OUT instruction the source register is always the accumulator. However, if for a memory-mapped I/O one wishes to transfer data from register B to an I/O device with address 0100H, the instructions of Figure 6-11 will accomplish the task.

The disadvantage of memory-mapped I/O is that it uses up memory locations for purposes other than the storage of data bytes. However, many microprocessor-based systems do not require as much memory capacity as is available and therefore can spare the allocation of memory addresses for I/O addresses.

As another example of the software for memory-mapped I/O, consider the program of Figure 6-12, which adds the data bytes of registers A and B and outputs the resultant sum to the output port with memory address 0200H. To implement memory-mapped I/O, a technique known as *linear addressing* can be used.

6-9 LINEAR ADDRESSING I/O

Linear addressing is simply another method of implementing addressing. It is the technique of dedicating an address line to the chip enable or strobe pin of a chip for the sole purpose of addressing that chip. Linear addressing simplifies a system's hardware by eliminating the need for a selector (8205). As example, if an I/O device is an output port, the address line dedicated will serve as a strobe line for the output port's latch. If the I/O device is an input port, the address line dedicated to it will serve to activate its tri-state buffer when addressed. These concepts are illustrated in Figure 6-13, where I/O control signals are used for isolated I/O, and memory control signals are used for memory-mapped I/O. Figure 6-13 shows address lines A_3 and A_5 being used in the active high states, but if the logic requires they could provide an active low just as well.

Linear addressing can be used to address memory as well as I/O. Although linear addressing simplifies the hardware, the price paid is less efficient use of available addresses. To illustrate how linear addressing can "eat up" memory space, refer to Table 6-1, which represents addressing for Figure 6-13(b). Realize that the output port of Figure 6-13(b) will be addressed every time A_5 is high. From Table 6-1 it is seen that output port 5 of Figure 6-13(b) is addressed with addresses 0020H–003FH and then again from 0060H to 007FH. This re-addressing of the same memory or I/O device is known as *foldback* and the locations are known as *foldback locations*. Table 6-1 is not completed, so even more memory addresses than indicated are allocated to output port 5.

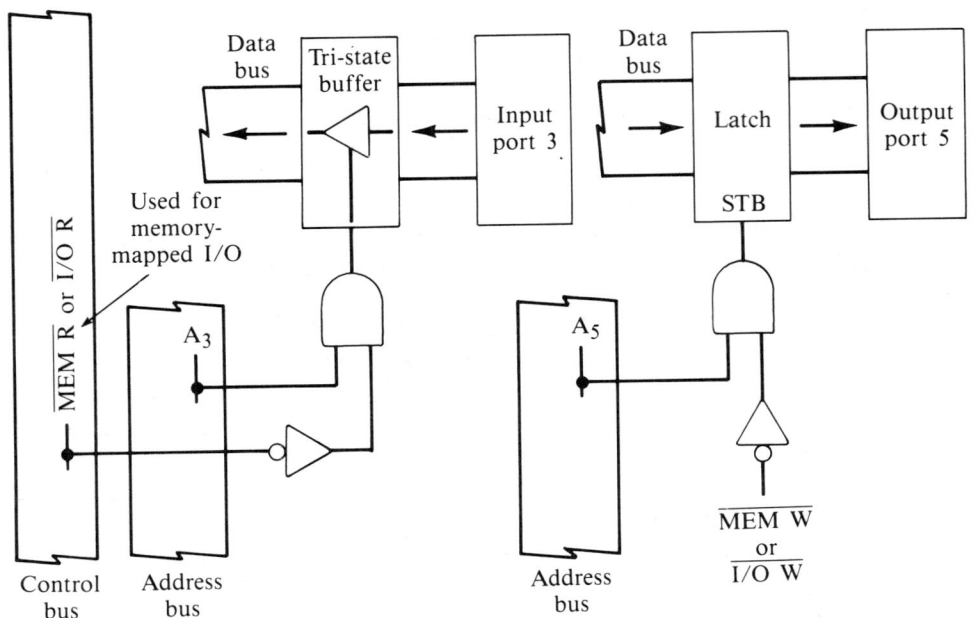

(a) Linear addressing using A_3 for activating tri-state buffer
(b) Linear addressing using A_5 as a strobe line to latch data byte

FIGURE 6-13. Examples of linear addressing.

The number of memory spaces lost to output port 5 could be reduced with added logic, such as shown in Figure 6-14. The NOR gate of Figure 6-14 will output a high only for the address 0020H.

Memory-mapped I/O and linear addressing will be used when studying the 8251. Also, memory-mapped I/O will be used for the 6800 microprocessor, which is discussed in a later chapter.

In summarizing isolated I/O versus memory-mapped I/O, isolated I/O separates (isolates) the addressing of memory and I/O through software and hardware. Software isolation occurs by having separate I/O instructions (IN and OUT). Hardware isolation is a result of separate control signals. The system uses control signals $\overline{\text{MEM R}}$ and $\overline{\text{MEM W}}$ to activate memory (sometimes via a decoder called the page selector) and $\overline{\text{I/O R}}$ and $\overline{\text{I/O W}}$ to activate I/O (sometimes via a decoder called the I/O selector). Memory-mapped I/O systems assign memory addresses to I/O, and only control signals $\overline{\text{MEM W}}$ and $\overline{\text{MEM R}}$ are used to activate I/O. There are no separate I/O instructions.

6-10
HEX KEYPAD WITH INTERRUPT CAPABILITY

Most microcomputer systems need some sort of keyboard input port to serve as the primary communication between the user and the microcomputer. To develop the concept of how a microcomputer might determine which keyboard

TABLE 6-1. Memory-Mapped I/O Addresses for A_5

Address Lines																Memory or I/O Address (Hex)	
A_{15}	A_{14}	A_{13}	A_{12}	A_{11}	A_{10}	A_9	A_8	A_7	A_6	A_5	A_4	A_3	A_2	A_1	A_0		
0	0	0	0	0	0	0	0	0	0	0	0	0	0	0	0	0000	Memory
0	0	0	0	0	0	0	0	0	0	0	0	0	0	0	1	0001	
.	.	.	.	.	.	.	.	.	.	.	.	.	.	.	.	.	
0	0	0	0	0	0	0	0	0	0	0	1	1	1	1	1	001F	
0	0	0	0	0	0	0	0	0	0	1	0	0	0	0	0	0020	Output Port 5
0	0	0	0	0	0	0	0	0	0	1	0	0	0	0	1	0021	
.	.	.	.	.	.	.	.	.	.	.	.	.	.	.	.	.	
0	0	0	0	0	0	0	0	0	0	1	1	1	1	1	1	003F	
0	0	0	0	0	0	0	0	0	1	0	0	0	0	0	0	0040	Memory
.	.	.	.	.	.	.	.	.	.	.	.	.	.	.	.	.	
0	0	0	0	0	0	0	0	0	1	0	1	1	1	1	1	005F	
0	0	0	0	0	0	0	0	0	1	1	0	0	0	0	0	0060	Output Port 5
.	.	.	.	.	.	.	.	.	.	.	.	.	.	.	.	.	
0	0	0	0	0	0	0	0	0	1	1	1	1	1	1	1	007F	
0	0	0	0	0	0	0	0	1	0	0	0	0	0	0	0	0080	Memory
.	.	.	.	.	.	.	.	.	.	.	.	.	.	.	.	.	
0	0	0	0	0	0	0	0	1	0	0	1	1	1	1	1	009F	

AND SO ON AND SO FORTH

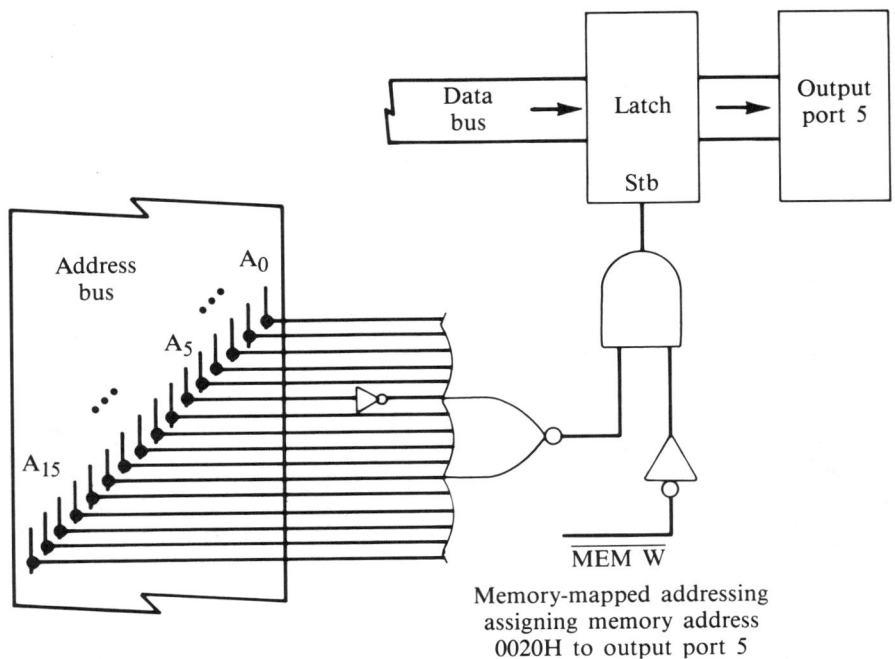

FIGURE 6-14. Memory-mapped addressing assigning memory address 0020H to output port 5.

character was "typed" as a result of a key closure and also how the proper binary code is generated, the *hex keypad* (16 keys representing hex values 0–F) will be studied. Studying a hex keypad rather than a keyboard reduces the number of characters from 127 to just 16; however, even though simplified, the concept is still the same. It should be mentioned that our study will rely on software to identify a key closure and then generate a corresponding binary code. There is hardware available to simplify the task.

We shall use the hex keypad of Figure 6-15, which is a 4 by 4 matrix. Basically, the manner in which the hex keypad of Figure 6-15 works is similar to an *x-y* coordinate system. That is, by knowing the row and column of the depressed key, one can easily identify the key. For instance, if the key closure occurred in row 1 (R_1) and column 2 (C_2), which is noted as (R_1, C_2), key 6 is depressed.

To determine the row and column of a depressed key, a scan of each row will be made. A row scan is made by pulling each row to a low, one at a time, and then checking the resulting logic state of each column. We see from Figure 6-15 that all columns are high, regardless of any row logic state, if no keys are closed. However, if R_1 is forced low with R_0, R_2, and R_3 all high (a row pattern of 1101) and key 6 is depressed, the column output would be $C_3 = 1$, $C_2 = 0$, $C_1 = 1$, and $C_0 = 1$ (1011). By forcing a row pattern of 1101 and receiving a column pattern of 1011, key 6 is identified as the depressed key. Table 6-2 illustrates for each row scan the resulting column pattern for each key closure.

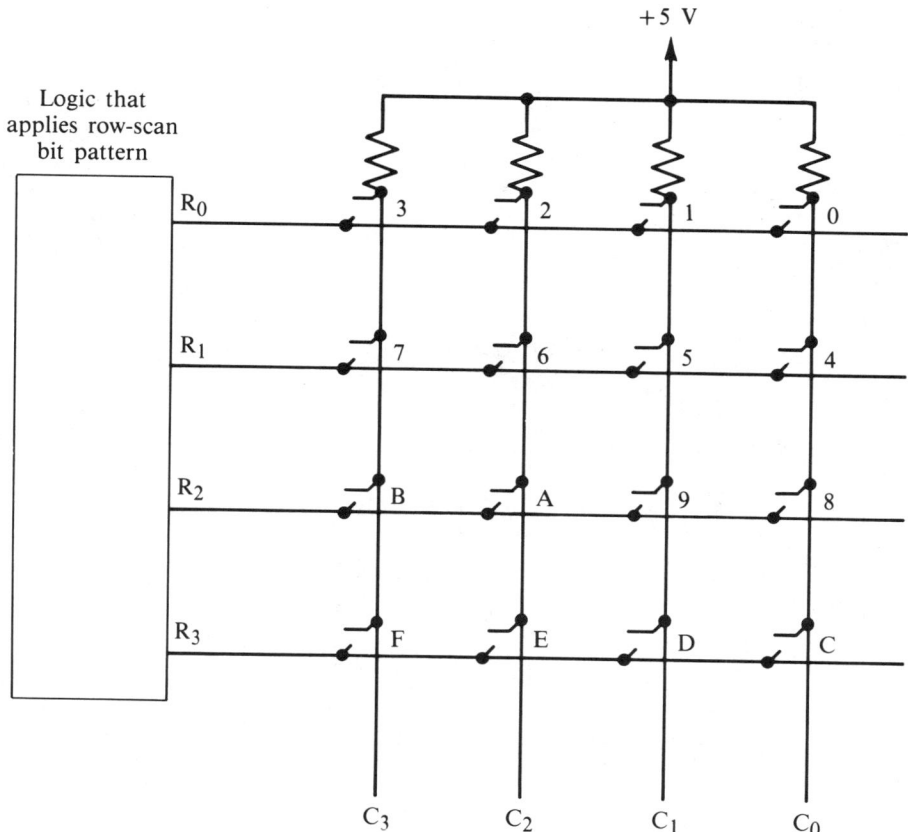

FIGURE 6-15. Hex-keypad circuit.

In examining Table 6-2 one notices that for each row scan there are four possible column patterns, where the four possible column patterns are repeated for each row scan. Thus, if one is told that for a row scan of 1101 (row 1) the column pattern is 0111, then from Table 6-2 one can see that key 7 is closed and that a hex code of 00000111 should be generated. A row scan of 0111 (row 3) and a return column bit pattern of 1110 identifies key C as the depressed key, requiring that a hex bit pattern of 00001100 be generated.

To summarize Table 6-2, the row scan, which is the bit pattern applied, is the x-coordinate and the resulting column bit pattern is the y-coordinate. By knowing the row and column bit pattern, the key closure is identified.

Row-scan bit patterns will be applied to each row via the CPU and the row-scan latch of Figure 6-16. The resulting column bit pattern is latched and loaded into the CPU's accumulator via the column latch of Figure 6-16.

The interrupt request generator buffer and interrupt request NAND gate of Figure 6-16 are the logic required to generate an interrupt request to the 8080 for every key closure. The I/O select (8205), NOR gate 2, and AND gate 1 comprise the logic required to decode addresses for output port 00H (DV_0) and input port 01H (DV_1). The I/O select logic has been discussed previously and will not be repeated here.

6-10 HEX KEYPAD WITH INTERRUPT CAPABILITY

TABLE 6-2. Row-Scan and Column Patterns for Key Closures

Row Scanned	Row Pattern for Each Row Scan				Resulting Column Patterns for Each Key Closure				Key Closure	Eight-Bit Hex Code to Be Generated
	R_3	R_2	R_1	R_0	C_3	C_2	C_1	C_0		
0	1	1	1	0	1	1	1	0	0	0 0 0 0 0 0 0 0
					1	1	0	1	1	0 0 0 0 0 0 0 1
					1	0	1	1	2	0 0 0 0 0 0 1 0
					0	1	1	1	3	0 0 0 0 0 0 1 1
1	1	1	0	1	1	1	1	0	4	0 0 0 0 0 1 0 0
					1	1	0	1	5	0 0 0 0 0 1 0 1
					1	0	1	1	6	0 0 0 0 0 1 1 0
					0	1	1	1	7	0 0 0 0 0 1 1 1
2	1	0	1	1	1	1	1	0	8	0 0 0 0 1 0 0 0
					1	1	0	1	9	0 0 0 0 1 0 0 1
					1	0	1	1	A	0 0 0 0 1 0 1 0
					0	1	1	1	B	0 0 0 0 1 0 1 1
3	0	1	1	1	1	1	1	0	C	0 0 0 0 1 1 0 0
					1	1	0	1	D	0 0 0 0 1 1 0 1
					1	0	1	1	E	0 0 0 0 1 1 1 0
					0	1	1	1	F	0 0 0 0 1 1 1 1
	column closure				3	2	1	0		

x-coordinate (rows 0–3); y-coordinate (column closure)

Let us begin by determining how a key closure requests an interrupt of the CPU. In the examination of Figure 6-16, we see that the interrupt request generator (IRG) buffer is active (assuming that the IRG flip-flop has been set previously, resulting in logic 0's being applied to all rows (since the row-scan latch is inactive, these lows are buffered from the system's data bus). At the same time (without a key closure) each column is high, which is input to the interrupt request NAND gate, resulting in a low output. The logic 0 output of this NAND gate is input to the interrupt request input (INT) of the 8080, thereby not requesting an interrupt, nor does it reset the IRG since its flip-flop, logic state is inverted. When a key is depressed, the corresponding column line will be driven low, thus causing the output of the interrupt request NAND gate to go high, thereby requesting an interrupt of the CPU and also resetting the IRG flip-flop. Resetting the IRG flip-flop puts the interrupt request generator buffer in the high-Z state, which no longer forces all rows low.

Suppose that as a result of this interrupt request RST 5 is jammed on the data bus when $\overline{\text{INTA}}$ goes active. Then the CPU will vector to memory location 0028H (see Figure 6-5). The first instruction of the subroutine for servicing the hex keypad will be at address 0028H (see Figure 6-18). That subroutine will output the bit pattern of Table 6-2 to scan row 0 using the OUT 00H instruction. The bit pattern output on the data bus by instruction OUT 00H will be 1110. The OUT 00H instruction will also cause that bit pattern to be latched in the

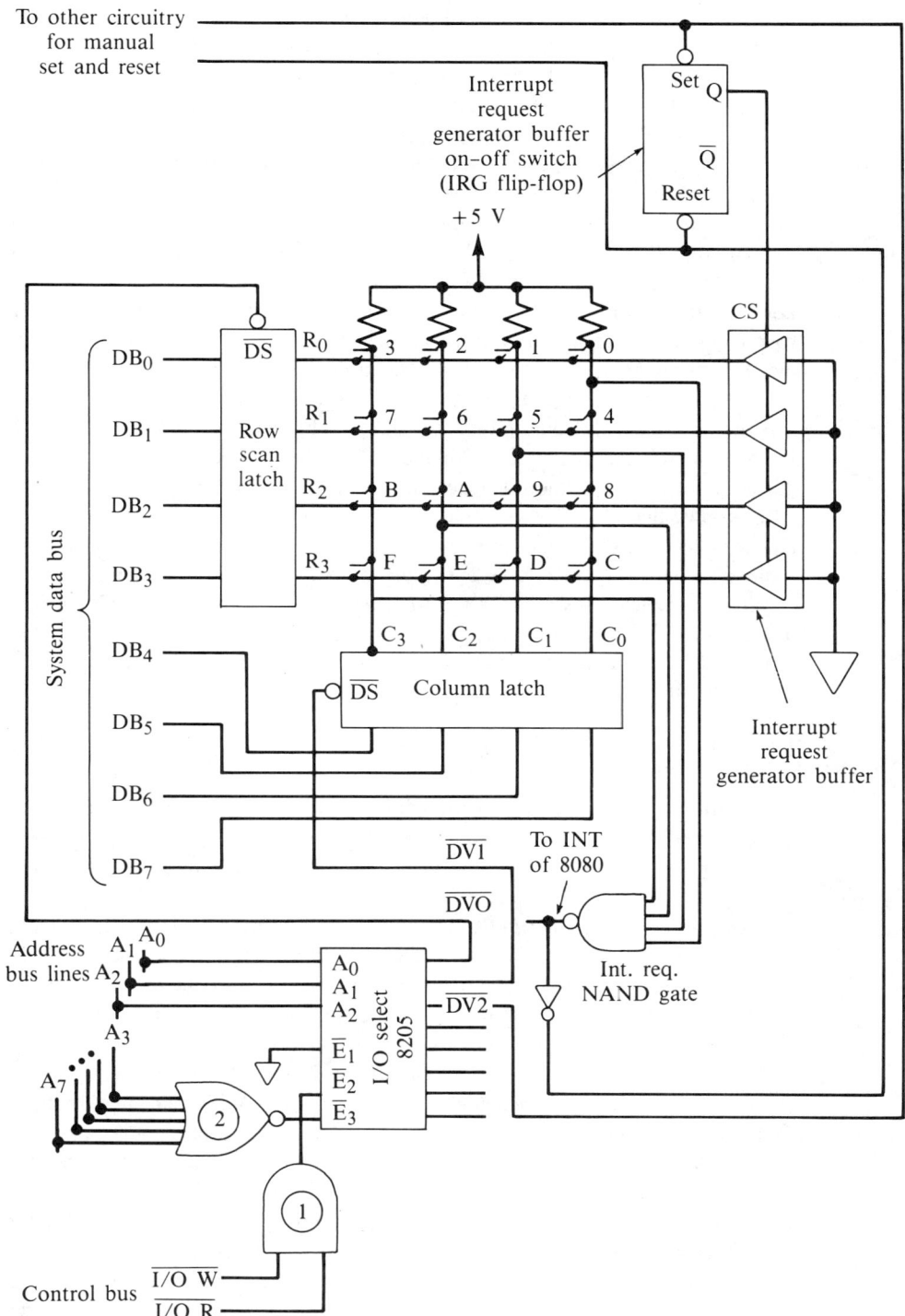

FIGURE 6-16. Hex-keypad scan logic circuit.

6-10 HEX KEYPAD WITH INTERRUPT CAPABILITY

row-scan latch when the I/O select output $\overline{DV_0}$ goes active. Since the rows are all released from being held low by the interrupt request generator buffer (the IRG flip-flop is reset), they may take on the logic states written into the row-scan latch (1110 for row 0). If the key closure is not in row 0 (let us suppose that key 6 is closed), the resulting column logic levels will all be highs. The CPU will latch these highs via the column latch by having an IN 01H instruction following the OUT 00H instruction as seen in Figure 6-18. The IN 01H instruction will activate $\overline{DS}$ of the column latch, which will latch the logic states of the columns and also load these logic states (1111 for this case) into the CPU's accumulator. The CPU can then examine this bit pattern and determine that the key closed is not in that row. The CPU will then output the bit pattern to scan row 1 (1101). Since key 6 is in row 1, which now has a low applied to it, its closure causes column C_2 to be low, resulting in a column bit pattern of 1011 (see Table 6-2). As stated, the IN 01H instruction following the OUT 00H instruction causes the column latch to latch that bit pattern and also to load that bit pattern into the accumulator of the CPU. The CPU can then examine its accumulator and from the bit pattern determine that key 6 is closed. Once the CPU knows that key 6 is depressed, it generates a hex pattern of 0000 0110 and then sets the IRG flip-flop using the OUT 02H instruction ($\overline{DV_2}$ = 0) and returns to the program it was executing before the interrupt. The CPU will continue to execute instructions until the next interrupt request, at which time it will again vector to the keypad service routine at 0028H.

From the explanation above and Figure 6-16, let us generalize and summarize the events in chronological order.

1. All rows are held low via the interrupt request generator buffer, assuming that the IRG flip-flop is set. IRG may be set or reset either manually or by program control. All rows being held low causes an interrupt request to be generated when a key is closed since a key closure will force a column low, which is input to the INT. REQ. NAND gate input, resulting in a high output.
2. The output of the interrupt request NAND gate is applied to the interrupt request (INT) of the 8080 and at the same time inverted and used to drive the interrupt request generator buffer into the high-Z state by resetting the IRG flip-flop. Once the buffer is in the high-Z state, the rows of the hex keypad are available for applying the row-scan bit pattern to each row (see Table 6-2) until the row and column of the depressed key are identified.
3. As was stated in 2, when the interrupt request NAND gate goes high, it forces the interrupt request generator buffer in the high-Z state and also requests an interrupt of the CPU. Upon acknowledgment of the interrupt request ($\overline{INTA}$ goes active), the CPU will be vectored (if the RST jamming circuit of Figure 6-7 is used) to a specified memory address (RST 5—address 0028H was used above). Of course, the polling hardware and software of Figures 6-2 and 6-4 could be used to identify the keypad as the interrupting device. Once the CPU is vectored to the specified RST vector address, the CPU will begin the process of identifying the depressed key. The identifying process will begin by outputting each of four row-scan bit patterns according

to the row-scan patterns shown in Table 6-2. To output the row-scan patterns, the instructions MVI A (row pattern) and output (port number) will be used.
4. When a row-scan bit pattern is output by the CPU, that pattern will be latched by the row-scan latch and also applied to the rows. If the depressed key is in the row that contains the logic 0 of the row-scan bit pattern (again refer to Table 6-2), the column of the depressed key will also be forced low, with the remaining rows being high. The resulting column bit pattern is latched by the column latch when the CPU executes the IN instruction, following the OUT instruction as mentioned in 3. The column latch has a tri-state output, so it not only latches the column bit pattern but also applies that bit pattern to lines DB_4–DB_7 of the system's data bus. Because of the input port instruction, the CPU will latch the column bit pattern into its accumulator. The CPU will then determine if any of these 4 bits is low, and if so which one of the four is low. Once the low column bit is identified for the corresponding low row bit (refer to Table 6-2), the key closure is identified and the CPU can issue (echo) the proper hex code.
5. After the CPU has identified the key closure and issued the proper hex value, the CPU will then set the IRG flip-flop.
6. After setting the IRG flip-flop, the CPU will return to execution of that program before being interrupted by the hex keypad—returning to service another interrupt of the keypad only when interrupted again.

From the six chronological steps above, the flowchart of Figure 6-17 was developed.

A program to implement the flowchart of Figure 6-17 is given in Figure 6-18.

To understand the routine of Figure 6-18, the reader should refer to Table 6-2 for the row-scan bit patterns and resultant column bit patterns for any given key closure. The logic of the routine is indicated in the flowchart of Figure 6-17. Notice from Figure 6-17 that the higher-order column (C_3) is tested first. As we shall see, this manner of column testing was determined from the use of the RAL instruction. It should be mentioned that a more memory-efficient program could be written since much of the routine given in Figure 6-18 lends itself to loops. However, because of the straightforwardness of the program of Figure 6-18, it serves well for understanding concepts.

The program of Figure 6-18 was named KEYPAD so that if the user of the system wishes to access it in any other routine, he or she may do so by a CALL instruction (or conditional jump, jump, etc.). The first instruction DI is redundant but ensures that the interrupts are disabled (INT being acknowledged disables the interrupts). The PUSH instructions save register contents on the stack. The instruction MVI A,0EH loads the row 0 scan bit pattern into the *lower* 4 *bits* of the accumulator. The OUT 00H instruction causes the row-scan latch to latch the bit pattern for row 0 and apply it to the keypad rows. Instruction IN 01H will load the resulting column bit pattern into the accumulator. From Figure 6-16 we see that only the uppermost 4 bits of the accumulator are used to retain the column bit pattern. The ORI 0FH instruction forces the lower 4 bits of the accumulator to all 1's (only the upper 4 bits of A contain column information).

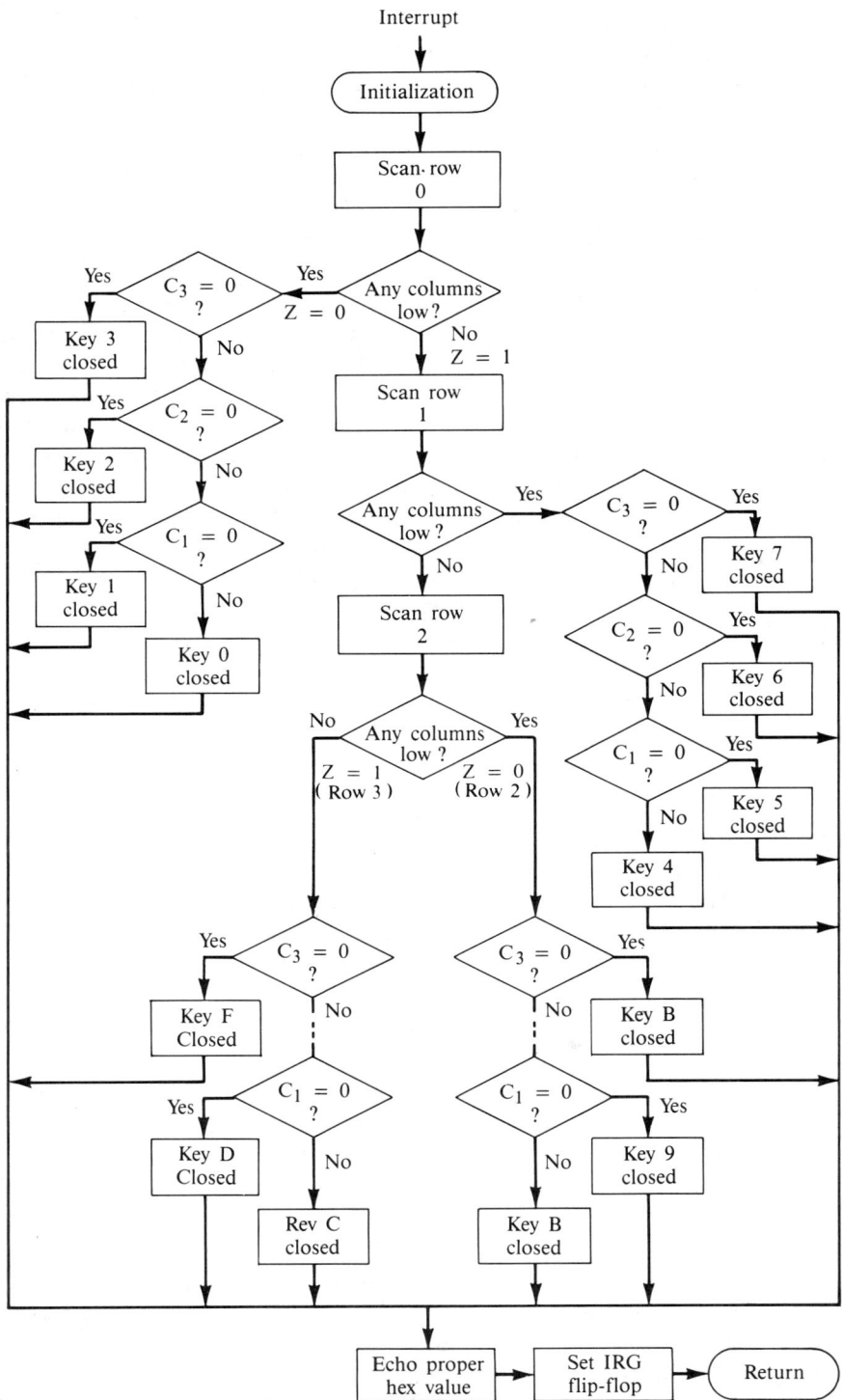

FIGURE 6-17. Flowchart for determining key closure for hardware of Figure 6-16.

```
                ; Initialization—Save register contents

                        ORG 0028H
                KEYPAD: DI              ; Disable interrupts
                        PUSH PSW
                        PUSH B
                        PUSH D
                        PUSH H

        ; Scan row 0

                        MVI A,0EH       ; Load Row 0 bit pattern
                        OUT 00H         ; Scan Row 0
                        IN  01H         ; Read column results

        ; Any columns low?

                        ORI 0FH         ; Force lower nibble high
                        MOV B,A         ; Copy A into B - save A
                        CMA             ; complement A - if any
                                        ; bits are HIGH there is
                                        ; a switch closure in this row.
                        ANI 0FFH        ; Determine if any bits of
                                        ; A are HIGH

        ; If Z = 0 then row 0 has switch closure

                        JNZ ROW0        ; If Z = 0 jump to Row 0 ident.

        ; Scan row 1

                        MVI A,0DH       ; Load Row 1 bit pattern
                        OUT 00H         ; Scan Row 1
                        IN  01H         ; Read column results

        ; Any columns low?

                        ORI 0FH         ; Force lower nibble high
                        MOV B,A         ; Copy A into B - save A
                        CMA             ; complement A
                        ANI 0FFH        ; Determine if any bits of
                                        ; A are high

        ; If Z = 0 then row 1 has switch closure

                        JNZ ROW1        ; If Z = 0 jump to Row 1 ident.

        ; Scan row 2

                        MVI A,0BH       ; Load Row 2 bit pattern
                        OUT 00H         ; Scan Row 2

        ; Any columns low?

                        ORI 0FH         ; Force lower nibble high
                        MOV B,A         ; Copy A into B
                        CMA             ; complement A
                        ANI 0FFH        ; Any bits high?
```

FIGURE 6-18. Hex-keypad echo routine.

```
; If Z = 0 then row 2 has switch closure

        JNZ ROW2    ; If Z = 0 jump to Row 2

; If Z = 1 then row 3 has switch closure
; Test Columns of Row 3

        MOV A,B     ; Restore A
        RAL         ; Rotate $C_3$ to carry
        JNC ID33    ; If C = 0 then $C_3$ has closure
                    ; and key F is depressed
        RAL         ; Rotate $C_2$ to carry
        JNC ID32    ; If C = 0 then $C_2$ has closure
                    ; and key E is depressed
        RAL         ; Rotate $C_1$ to carry
        JNC ID31    ; If C = 0 then $C_1$ has closure
                    ; and key D is depressed
                    ; If C = 1 then $C_0$ has closure
                    ; and key C is depressed
        JMP ID30    ; Echo C

; Test columns of row 0

ROW0:   MOV A,B     ; Restore A
        RAL         ; Rotate $C_3$ to carry
        JNC ID03    ; If C = 0 then $C_3$ has closure
                    ; and key 3 is depressed
        RAL         ; Rotate $C_2$ to carry
        JNC ID02    ; If C = 0 then $C_2$ has closure
                    ; and key 2 is depressed
        RAL         ; Rotate $C_1$ to carry
        JNC ID01    ; If C = 0 then $C_1$ has
                    ; closure and key 1 is
                    ; depressed otherwise key
                    ; 0 is depressed
        JMP ID00    ; ECHO key 0

; Test columns of row 1

ROW1:   MOV A,B     ; Restore A
        RAL         ; Rotate $C_3$ to carry
        JNC ID13    ; If C = 0 then $C_3$ has closure
                    ; and key 7 is depressed
        RAL         ; Rotate $C_2$ to carry
        JNC ID12    ; If C = 0 then key 6 is
                    ; depressed
        RAL         ; Rotate $C_1$ to carry
        JNC ID11    ; If C = 0 then key 5 is
                    ; depressed otherwise key
                    ; 4 is depressed
        JMP ID10    ; Echo key 4

; Test columns of row 2

ROW2:   MOV A,B     ; Restore A
        RAL         ; Rotate $C_3$ to carry
        JNC ID23    ; If C = 0 then echo B
```

```
                RAL             ; Rotate C₂ to carry
                JNC ID22        ; If C = 0 then echo A
                RAL             ; Rotate C₁ to carry
                JNC ID21        ; If C = 0 then echo 9
                                ; otherwise echo 8
                JMP ID20        ; Echo 8

; Column test completed

; Echo to LED proper hex value
ID00:           MVI A,00H       ; Echo 00H
                JMP ECHO        ; Output to LED
ID01:           MVI A,01H       ; Echo 01H
                JMP ECHO        ; Output to LED
ID02:           MVI A,02H
                JMP ECHO
ID03:           MVI A,03H
                JMP ECHO
ID10:           MVI A,04H
                JMP ECHO
ID11:           MVI A,05H
                JMP ECHO
ID12:           MVI A,06H
                JMP ECHO
ID13:           MVI A,07H
                JMP ECHO
ID20:           MVI A,08H
                JMP ECHO
ID21:           MVI A,09H
                JMP ECHO
ID22:           MVI A,0AH
                JMP ECHO
ID23:           MVI A,0BH
                JMP ECHO
ID30:           MVI A,0CH
                JMP ECHO
ID31:           MVI A,0DH
                JMP ECHO
ID32:           MVI A,0EH
                JMP ECHO
ID33:           MVI A,0FH
                JMP ECHO
ECHO:           OUT LED         ; Echo key hex value
                                ; to LED
                OUT 02H         ; Set IRG flip-flop ready
                                ; for another key closure
                                ; interrupt

; Restore CPU registers

                POP H
                POP D
                POP B
                POP PSW
                EI              ; Enable interrupts
                RET             ; Return to main program
```

FIGURE 6-18. (Continued)

6-10 HEX KEYPAD WITH INTERRUPT CAPABILITY

MOV B,A is used to save the resulting bit pattern of the accumulator. The contents of A is copied in B since the CMA instruction is destructive to the contents of A and we will need that data later during the column test. The CMA and ANI instructions are used to determine if any columns of row 0 are low, which indicates a key closure. If any column is low then after execution of CMA, the accumulator bit representing it would be high. If all columns were high (no key closure) then after the execution of CMA the accumulator would be zero. Thus ANI 0FFH being executed after CMA would result in Z = 0 if a column is low (a key closure) and Z = 1 if no columns are low. If Z = 0, then row 0 has a column which is low, meaning that a key is depressed in row 0, and the instruction JNZ R0W0 jumps to the column test routine for row 0, which will determine the specific key depressed. Referring to that routine under: TEST COLUMNS OF ROW 0, we see that the first instruction, MOV A,B, restores the column bit pattern into A (recall that the contents of register A were destroyed with the CMA instruction). The column test routine then rotates the most significant bit (MSB) of the accumulator into the carry and jumps (JNC) when a low is rotated into it. Of course, when a low is rotated into the carry, the key closure is identified and the CPU then jumps (JNC IDRC, where R is the row and C is the column) to the routine that actually echoes the hex value to an LED. The remainder of the program is a repeat. It is recommended that the reader simulate a key closure and then trace through the hardware and software to verify its operation. In studying the flowchart of Figure 6-17, the reader should see the many possibilities of using loops to "save memory space."

6-11

SUMMARY

A microprocessor with interrupt capability can be interrupted from a task by an I/O device, which is an efficient method to service I/O. If a microprocessor has single-level interrupt capability, that is, a single interrupt pin, a software polling routine is *often* required to determine the interrupt-requesting I/O device. A microprocessor with more than one interrupt request pin has multilevel interrupt capability, which allows an I/O device interrupt request to be associated with a specific microprocessor interrupt request pin. This one-to-one correspondence of I/O device interrupt request and microprocessor interrupt request pin eliminates the need for a time-consuming polling routine for I/O device identification. Once the I/O device makes the request for an interrupt, the CPU will vector to the starting address of the service routine of that I/O device.

The 8080 has single-level interrupt capability but can be vectored to any one of eight addresses via jamming a specific RST instruction on the data bus when control signal $\overline{INTA}$ is active. Using an encoder, as illustrated in Figure 6-6 and 6-7, a specific RST instruction can be assigned to a specific I/O device, thus enabling the CPU to vector to a predesignated memory address just as if the CPU had multilevel interrupt capability. Interrupt request priority can also be assigned to I/O devices, as shown in the logic of Figure 6-7.

There are two general techniques for accessing I/O. One technique is named isolated I/O and the other is called memory-mapped I/O. Isolated I/O separates (isolates) I/O from memory by having separate instructions and control signals ($\overline{\text{MEM R}}$, $\overline{\text{I/O R}}$, etc.). Memory-mapped I/O does not distinguish between memory- and I/O-related instructions. For memory-mapped I/O the I/O device is assigned a memory address, just as if it were a memory location, and accessed via a memory reference instruction. The control signals generated are those referencing memory ($\overline{\text{MEM R}}$ and $\overline{\text{MEM W}}$) and are used to gate I/O data onto the data bus or latch data from the data bus, which is the function of control signals $\overline{\text{I/O R}}$ and $\overline{\text{I/O W}}$ in the isolated I/O system. Memory-mapped I/O reduces the number of memory locations available for data storage, but it also expands the number of instructions available for accessing I/O.

Linear addressing is a method of addressing that assigns an address line to a device. When the address line is active it addresses the device.

REVIEW QUESTIONS AND PROBLEMS

1. Explain what is meant by the terms "single-level interrupt" and "multilevel interrupt."

2. Of the two types of interrupts, single level and multilevel, which is more likely to require polling, and why?

3. Relative to servicing an interrupt request, explain the terms "polling" and "vectoring."

4. Suppose that an interrupt request was made via I/O device 4 of the system represented by Figure 6-2. Modify the program of Figure 6-4 so that I/O device 4 is polled.

5. Make a timing diagram for Problem 4 beginning with interrupt request flag 4 being set high and ending with the first poll (instruction ANI 01H of Figure 6-4). To simplify the timing diagram as much as possible, omit showing timing for instruction DI and all the PUSH instructions. Your timing diagram is to show φ_1, φ_2, SYNC, the address bus, the data bus, DBIN, $\overline{\text{STSTB}}$, $\overline{\text{MEM R}}$, $\overline{\text{I/O R}}$, the output of interrupt request flag 0, and the output of the interrupt request OR gate of Figure 6-2. Provide a narrative explaining the relationship between your timing diagram, the program instructions, and the hardware of Figure 6-2.

6. Using tri-state logic as shown in Figure 6-5, design suitable circuits for jamming RST 2 and RST 4.

7. Construct a timing diagram for Figure 6-5(b), showing the events that occur in order that the CPU will be vectored to address 0028H. In your timing diagram, be certain to show the required control signals, address bus, and the data bus—stating the data (address, instruction, etc.) present on each bus.

8. Design a circuit to implement buffer 2 of Figure 6-7.

9. Explain the hardware of Figure 6-7 if input port 2 requested an interrupt. Reference to the program of Figure 6-8 should be made in your explanations.

10. Suppose that the I/O device of Figure 6-9 was an input port with DMA capability. Show it interfaced to the system of Figure 4-7. Provide an explanation of your interfacing.

11. Give an explanation of the term "memory map" and state how it is used by the system designer and user.

12. Design a simple 2K memory system using a 2708 and 2114 that are linearly addressed. Account for each address line and appropriate control signals.

13. The keypad circuit of Figure 6-16 could have the interrupt request generator buffer eliminated by a simple modification of the program shown in Figure 6-18. Make this design modification, explaining the changes.

14. Without detail, explain how the hex-keypad circuit of Figure 6-16 functions.

15. Modify the program of Figure 6-18 so that row-scan bit patterns are generated as a program loop. (*Hint:* Notice that the pattern is OEH, ODH, etc., which is a rotate left.)

16. From the flowchart of Figure 6-17, would you think that a program loop could be written that would test the resultant column bit pattern? Justify your answer.

CHAPTER 7

Programmable Chips: Parallel and Serial I/O

7-1 INTRODUCTION

For greater versatility a manufacturer will often design a chip that is multifunctional, where the function to be used can be selected by the user. This allows the chip to fulfill various design application needs. The mechanism to select which function is to be utilized is varied. However, when function selection is made by applying a binary code to the chip, that is, programming it, the chip is known as a *programmable chip*. An example of such a chip is a *programmable priority interrupt controller*. The versatility of this chip lies in its ability to be programmed to function as a polled interrupt, thereby implementing the logic of Figure 6-2, or programmed to function as the priority vector interrupt logic, such as the circuitry of Figure 6-7. Another example of a programmable chip is a programmable timer, which provides various timing modes and intervals, depending on the programmed binary code applied to the chip for decoding.

The binary code that programs the chip is often referred to as its *control word*. The control word must be latched by an internal register of the programmable chip for decoding purposes. This register will often be referred to as the control register. Once the control word is programmed into the programmable chip (latched by the chip), it is decoded and the chip will then implement the desired function.

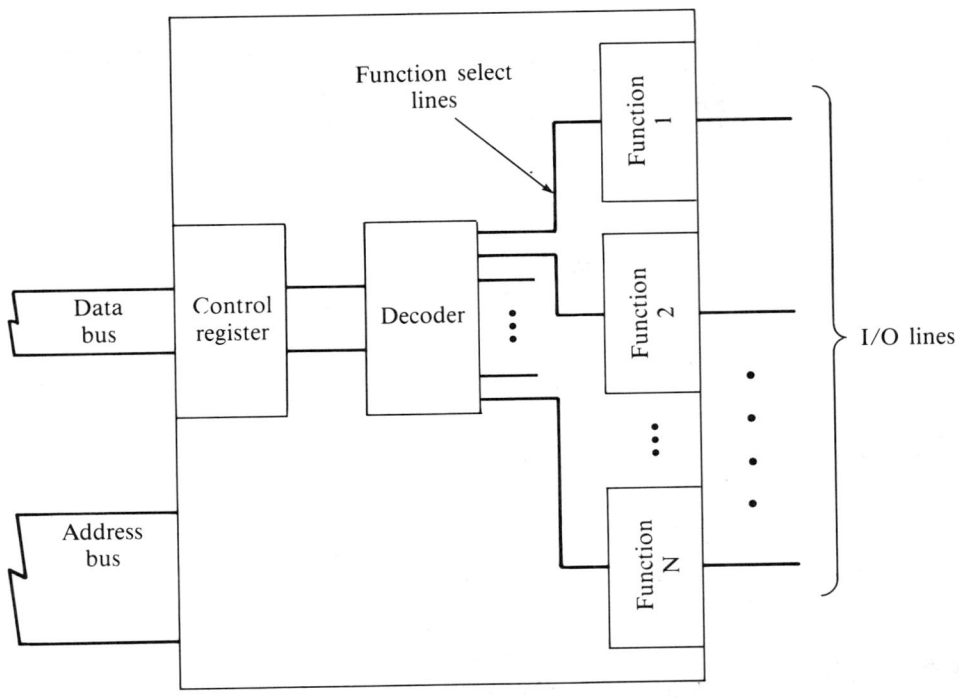

FIGURE 7-1. Conceptual architecture of a programmable chip.

In a microprocessor-based system, programming a programmable chip is done via the CPU; that is, the programmable chip is treated as an output port for the purpose of programming it. Hence the control word is first loaded into the CPU's accumulator and then a write operation is executed to that output port. A generic architectural drawing of a programmable chip is offered in Figure 7-1.

Referring to Figure 7-1, to program the chip it must first be addressed to receive the control word. The OUT instruction is used to address the chip and to write the control word to the chip's control register. The control word is decoded, which activates one of the function select lines. This in turn selects the logic to implement the selected function. There are many specific programmable chips available; however, only the programmable peripheral interface (8255) and the programmable communication interface (8251) will be studied in this book.

7-2 PROGRAMMABLE PERIPHERAL INTERFACE (8255)

This programmable peripheral interface (PPI) has 24 programmable I/O pins. These 24 I/O pins are basically subdivided into three groups, each group consisting of eight pins. The three groupings are labeled as group A, group B, and group C. The 8255 may be programmed such that port A, B, or C can have access to the system's data bus as either input or output ports, as indicated by the simplified architectural drawing of Figure 7-2.

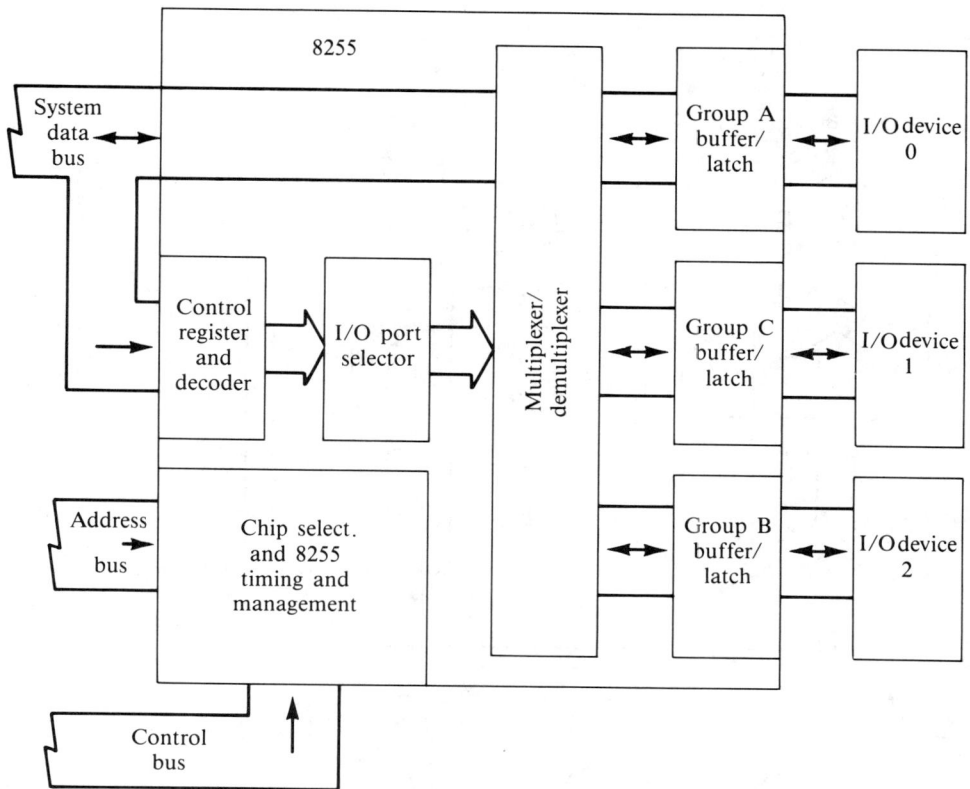

FIGURE 7-2. Simplified architecture of the PPI (8255).

Figure 7-2 illustrates that the 8255 is addressed for use via the address bus. When addressed, the CPU programs the 8255 by writing a control word to the control register via the system data bus. When the control word is decoded, the port selected (A, B, or C) will have access to the system data bus. It is the multiplexer/demultiplexer which implements the accessing of the system data bus by the selected port. The reader should notice that ports A, B, and C are shown as being a buffer/latch. This dual function is required since some ports require latching of the data byte while others require buffering between the 8255 and the port. Also shown as input to the 8255 is the control bus. This is necessary to provide system control and timing to the 8255 for read and write operations ($\overline{I/O\ R}$, $\overline{I/O\ W}$).

From what is known about the 8255 at this point, we can conclude that its programmability resides in the fact that its I/O pins can be programmed to serve as either input or output ports. Although this is true, other function variations are also programmable for this PPI. To investigate all programmable aspects of the 8255, refer to Intel's architectural drawing of the 8255 shown in Figure 7-3.

In viewing Figure 7-3 the reader should notice that group C of Figure 7-3 is actually divided into two 4-bit I/O ports. The upper 4 bits (PC_7–PC_4) are labeled as group A port C upper and the lower 4 bits (PC_3–PC_0) are labeled as group

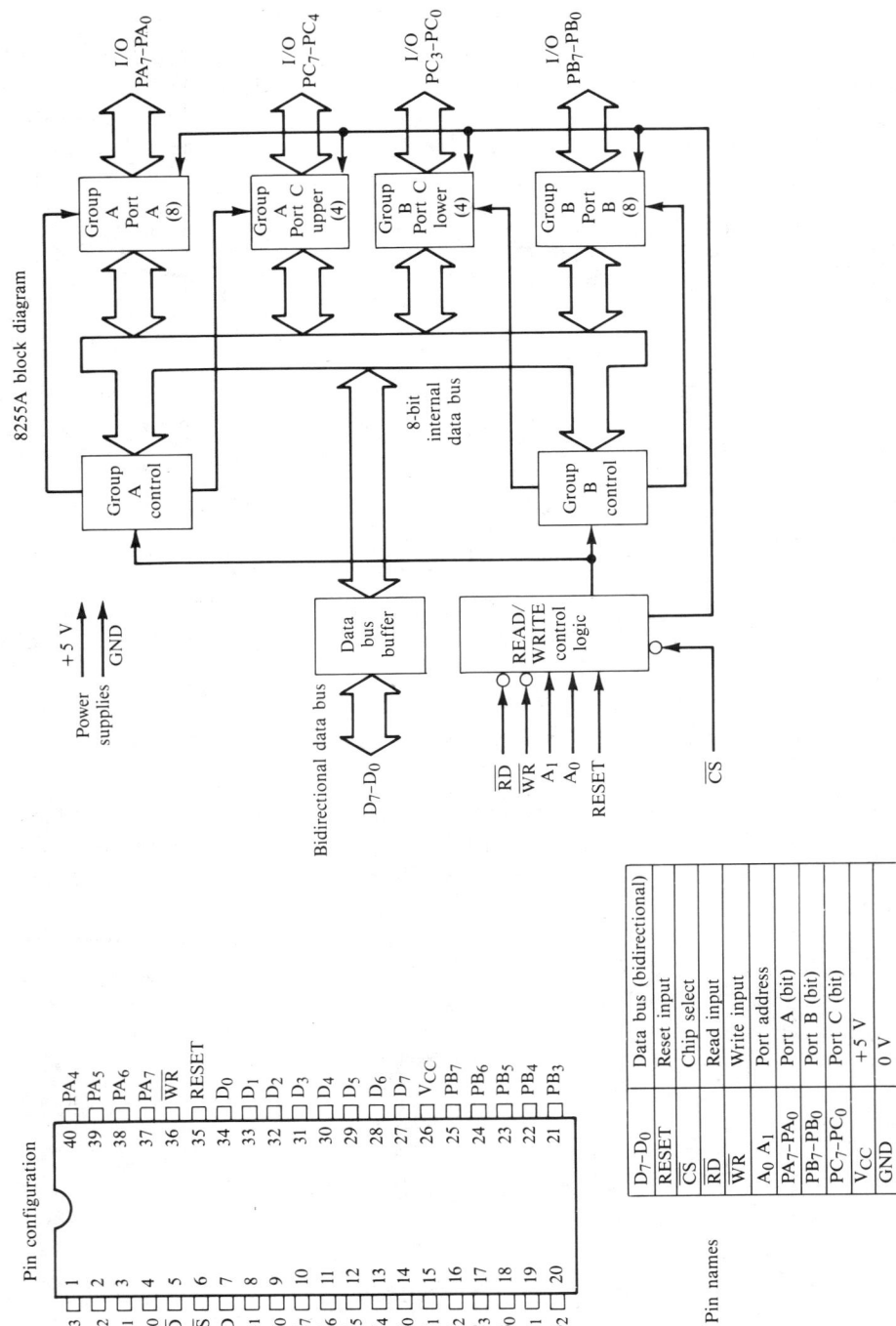

FIGURE 7-3. 8255 architecture. (Courtesy of Intel Corp.)

B port C lower. The reason for this division of port C is versatility. For some applications the user may wish to program group A and B as I/O ports with handshaking (request and acknowledge) capability. Using the 8255 in this mode of operation, port C upper provides the necessary communication to implement handshaking for port A and port C lower provides handshaking for port B. Group C upper and lower can also be programmed to function as an 8-bit port, as indicated in Figure 7-3—it is just a matter of the control word programmed into the 8255.

Since the specific control word programmed to the 8255 determines its functional configuration, or mode of operation, let our detailed investigation of this chip begin there. First we will investigate the bit patterns for various control words and then the means by which they are programmed into the 8255.

7-3

8255 OPERATION MODES

There are three modes of operation, and these are given in Table 7-1.

TABLE 7-1. Modes of I/O Port Operations for 8255

Mode	Comments
0	Basic I/O ports. Output ports are latched, while input ports are not latched. Ports A and B are 8-bit, while port C is divided into two 4-bit ports.
1	I/O ports with handshaking. Ports A and B may be *either* input or output, where both are latched. Port C provides handshaking.
2	Port A becomes a bidirectional port with port C providing handshaking and control signals. Port B may function in mode 0 or 1.

Mode 0

As stated in Table 7-1, when the 8255 is programmed for a mode 0 operation, groups A, B, and C function as I/O ports without handshaking. Each port (A, B, and C) must be programmed to be either an input or output port via the control word. Those ports defined to be output ports will latch the data byte which is being written to the external output device attached to that port, where those ports defined to serve as input ports do not latch the data byte they receive from their external input device.

Port C is unique in that its upper and lower groupings can be programmed separately. That is, the upper 4 bits could be programmed to serve as an input port, while the lower 4 bits are programmed to function as an output port, or vice versa. Or the upper and lower 4 bits can be combined to function as either an 8-bit input or output port.

There are 16 different port configuration combinations that can be programmed from groups A, B, and C for a mode 0 operation. To determine the binary bit pattern of the control word required to program the 8255 for one of

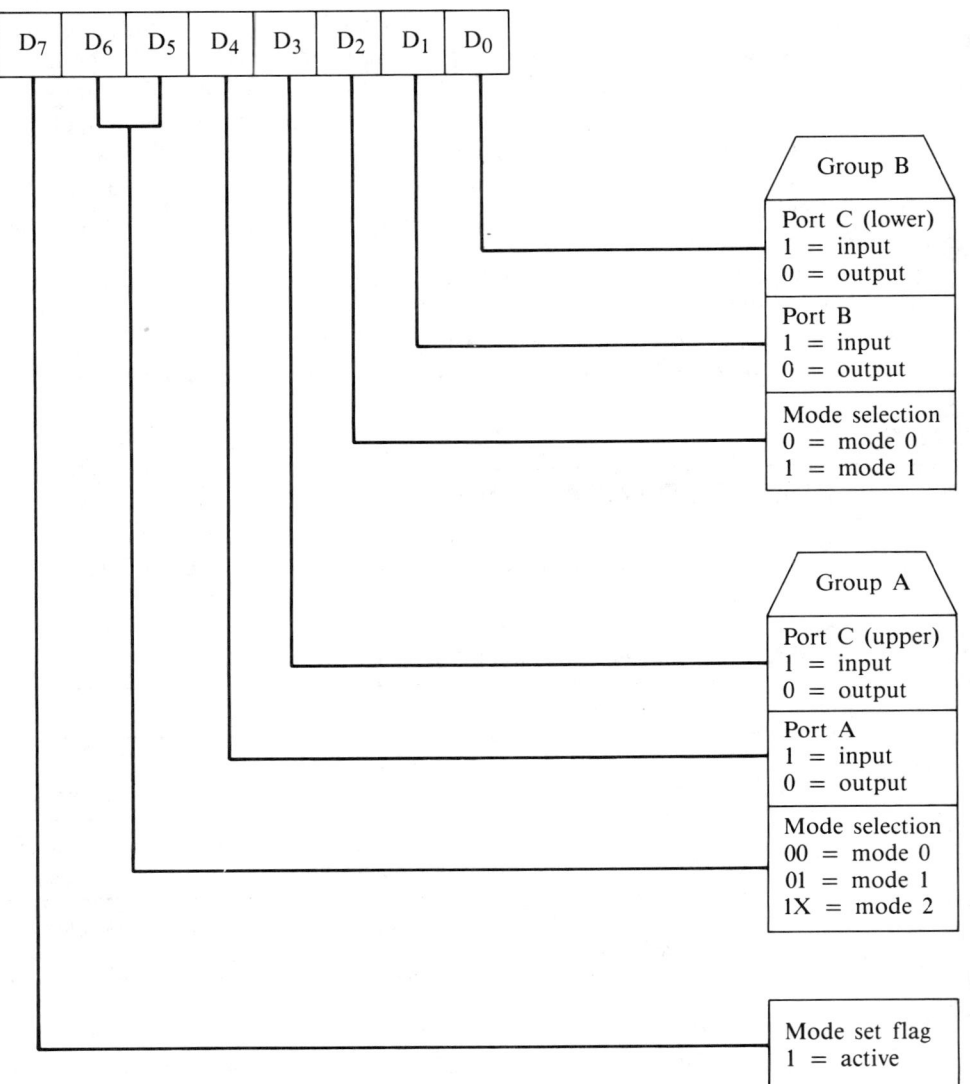

FIGURE 7-4. Control-word format for mode definition. (Courtesy of Intel Corp.)

these mode 0 port configuration combinations, refer to the control-word format of Figure 7-4. From Figure 7-4 it is seen that bits D_5 and D_6 determine the mode of operation for group A (00 for mode 0) and D_2 (0) for group B. D_7 must be high any time the 8255 is being programmed for a mode of operation. Bits D_4, D_3, D_1, and D_0 determine port configuration combinations.

Table 7-2 is essentially a truth table for bits D_4, D_3, D_1, and D_0, showing the 16-port configurations possible. Using Table 7-2 and the control-word format of Figure 7-4, let us determine the required binary bit pattern in order to program the 8255 such that all groups are to serve as output ports. From Table 7-2 we see that this requires bits D_4, D_3, D_1, and D_0 to all be logic 0's. Since this is

TABLE 7-2. Mode 0 Port Definition Chart

D_4	D_3	D_1	D_0	Port A	Group A Port C (upper)	#	Port B	Group B Port C (lower)
0	0	0	0	Output	Output	0	Output	Output
0	0	0	1	Output	Output	1	Output	Input
0	0	1	0	Output	Output	2	Input	Output
0	0	1	1	Output	Output	3	Input	Input
0	1	0	0	Output	Input	4	Output	Output
0	1	0	1	Output	Input	5	Output	Input
0	1	1	0	Output	Input	6	Input	Output
0	1	1	1	Output	Input	7	Input	Input
1	0	0	0	Input	Output	8	Output	Output
1	0	0	1	Input	Output	9	Output	Input
1	0	1	0	Input	Output	10	Input	Output
1	0	1	1	Input	Output	11	Input	Input
1	1	0	0	Input	Input	12	Output	Output
1	1	0	1	Input	Input	13	Output	Input
1	1	1	0	Input	Input	14	Input	Output
1	1	1	1	Input	Input	15	Input	Input

to be a mode 0 operation, bits D_6, D_5, and D_2 are also to be logic 0's, as indicated in Figure 7-4. Also from Figure 7-4, bit D_7 must be a logic 1. This results in the control-word bit pattern, as shown in Figure 7-5. As seen from Figure 7-5(a), the control word is 80H; however, Intel refers to it as control word 0. As another example, let us program the 8255 such that port A is an output port and ports B and C are input ports. This requires the control-word bit pattern of Figure 7-5(b). The hexadecimal value of the required bit pattern is 8BH and Intel refers to it as 7.

Although we have not studied all the details for programming a control word into an 8255, we do have sufficient knowledge to grasp the conceptual essence of the software required. The reader has been told that for programming the 8255, it is treated as an output port, which means that an address is required. Since at this time the details of the required bit pattern of the address are unknown, let us use the symbolic address PPI0 (PPI mode 0). The program to program control word 0 [Figure 7-5(a)] is given in Figure 7-6.

Once we have the details of addressing and have finished studying the other modes of operations, we shall implement some example designs of both hardware and software. Let us move on to another mode of operation.

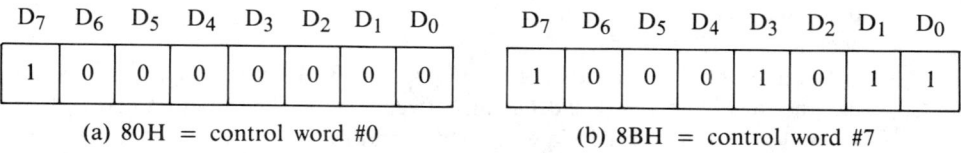

FIGURE 7-5. Example mode control-word patterns.

```
;This program programs control-word 0
;into the 8225
 MVI A,80H      ; Initialize A with control-word
 OUT PPIO       ; The 8255 is programmed
```

FIGURE 7-6. Example of software for programming an 8255.

Mode 1

Referring to Table 7-1, we see that a mode 1 operation is used when I/O ports require handshaking. Under this condition group C, upper and lower, functions as the inputs and outputs to provide handshaking capability. To reiterate an earlier discussion of Figure 7-3, groups A and C upper form one I/O port with handshaking capability, while groups B and C lower form another. The 8225 may be programmed such that groups A and B may be either an input or an output port. As an example, the 8255 architecture for a mode 1 operation with group A functioning as an input port and group B as an output port is illustrated in Figure 7-7(a). Notice that PC_7 and PC_6 are programmed to function as a 2-bit output port. These pins will be discussed in Section 7-5.

Focusing first on input port A of Figure 7-7, we see that bits PC_4 and PC_5 function as the handshaking medium between port A and the I/O device, while PC_3 provides an interrupt request from port A to the 8080 *provided* that flip-flop INTE A is set. If input device 0 is ready to send a byte of data to the CPU, via port A of the 8255, it strobes port A via $\overline{STB}_A$ (strobes PC_4), which causes port A to latch that data byte. Referring to the timing diagram of Figure 7-7(b), we see that once the data byte is latched, the 8255 activates IBF (PC_5), which indicates that port A's input buffer is full. When IBF goes high, and if flip-flop INTE A (interrupt enable for port A) is set, a logic 1 will result at the output of the INT REQ AND gate when $\overline{STB}_A$ goes inactive (high). This high is output at PC_3 ($INTR_A$) and will request an interrupt of the 8080. $INTR_A$ will remain high until port A is read by the CPU. As a result, $INTR_A$ can serve as an interrupt request flag for port A. If polling is used to service I/O, the logic circuit of Figure 6-2 would be used; however, if vectoring is to be used, the logic circuit of Figure 6-7 would be used. A more detailed example of hardware will be given later.

In order for the CPU to read data from input port A, an IN instruction is used. When the IN instruction is executed, control signal $\overline{I/O\ R}$ will be activated, via the 8228. $\overline{I/O\ R}$ will be used (directly or indirectly) to activate $\overline{RD}$ of Figure 7-7. With the proper address on the address bus, as furnished by the operand of the IN instruction, the activation of $\overline{RD}$ will cause the data byte of input port A to be gated onto the system data bus and then latched by the CPU (register A). Since addressing the 8255 will be studied in Section 7-4, for now let us use the symbolic address RPA (read port A). IN RPA will result in the data byte of port A being gated on the system data bus and then latched by the accumulator of the CPU.

Let us now turn our attention to output port B of Figure 7-7 and the timing diagram of Figure 7-8. Handshaking between the 8255 and output port 0, for a mode 1, is accomplished via $\overline{OBF}_B$ (PC_1) and $\overline{ACK}_B$ (PC_2). When the CPU is writing a data byte to an output device (output device 0 in this case), via an

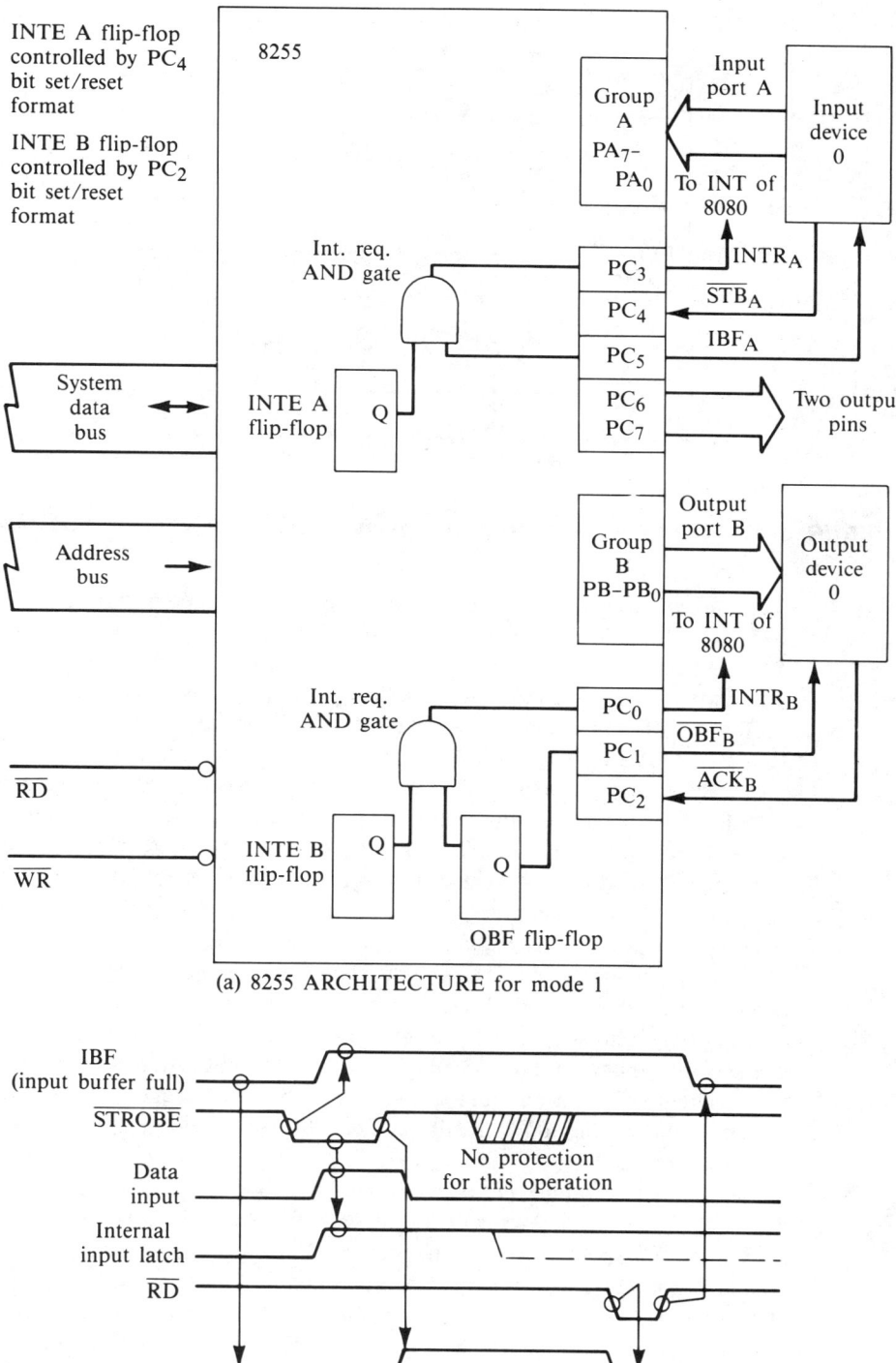

FIGURE 7-7. The 8255 programmed in a mode 1 configuration. (Courtesy of Intel Corp.)

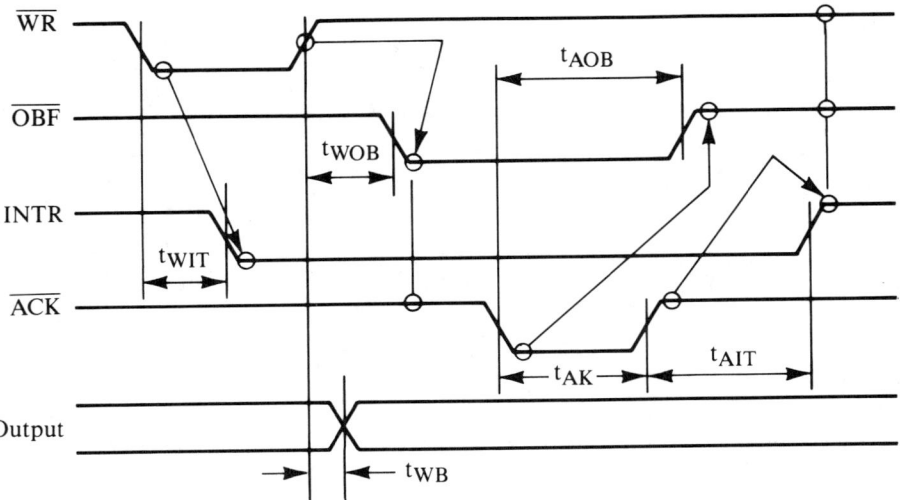

FIGURE 7-8. Timing diagram for mode 1 configuration. (Courtesy of Intel Corp.)

8255, it will use the OUT instruction. The OUT instruction will address the 8255 and also activate its control line $\overline{WR}$ (Write) via the 8228 ($\overline{I/O\ W}$). When $\overline{WR}$ goes active, this will cause port B to latch the data byte off the system data bus. Port B then indicates that it has latched that data byte and that its output buffer is full, that is, it has a data byte for output device 0, by activating $\overline{OBF}_B$ on the rising edge of $\overline{WR}$. $\overline{OBF}_B$ is used by output device 0 to latch the data byte of output port B. When output device 0 has latched the data byte of port B, it acknowledges this action by driving $\overline{ACK}_B$ low. $\overline{ACK}_B$ going low causes $\overline{OBF}_B$ to become inactive (high), which states that port B's output buffer is now empty and therefore can receive another data byte from the CPU. Using interrupts to service output device 0 requires that (in order for the CPU to write another data byte to port B) an interrupt request ($INTR_B$) be generated by port B. $INTR_B$ will interrupt the CPU and request that the next data byte be transmitted. The generation of $INTR_B$ occurs basically when $\overline{ACK}_B$ goes inactive. $\overline{ACK}_B$ going high sets the OBF flip-flop. When the OBF flip-flop and INTE B are set, then output $INTR_B$ goes high, via the INT REQ AND gate for port B, thereby requesting an interrupt of the CPU. To acknowledge and service port B, either the polling logic circuit of Figure 6-2 or the vector circuit of Figure 6-7 could be used.

Next, let us examine the software required to implement the hardware of Figure 7-7. As before, we will use a symbolic address (PPI1) to address the 8255 for the purpose of loading the proper control word into the control register of the 8255. For a mode 1 operation two control words are required, one to determine port configuration (input or output) and the second to set or reset the interrupt enable flip-flops INTE A and INTE B. Figure 7-4 provides the format for the control word, which determines port configuration, and Figure 7-9 determines the logic state of INTE A and B. Both control words are written to the 8255's control register using the same address (PPI1 in this case). The 8255 is able to distinguish between the two by the logic state of bit D_7.

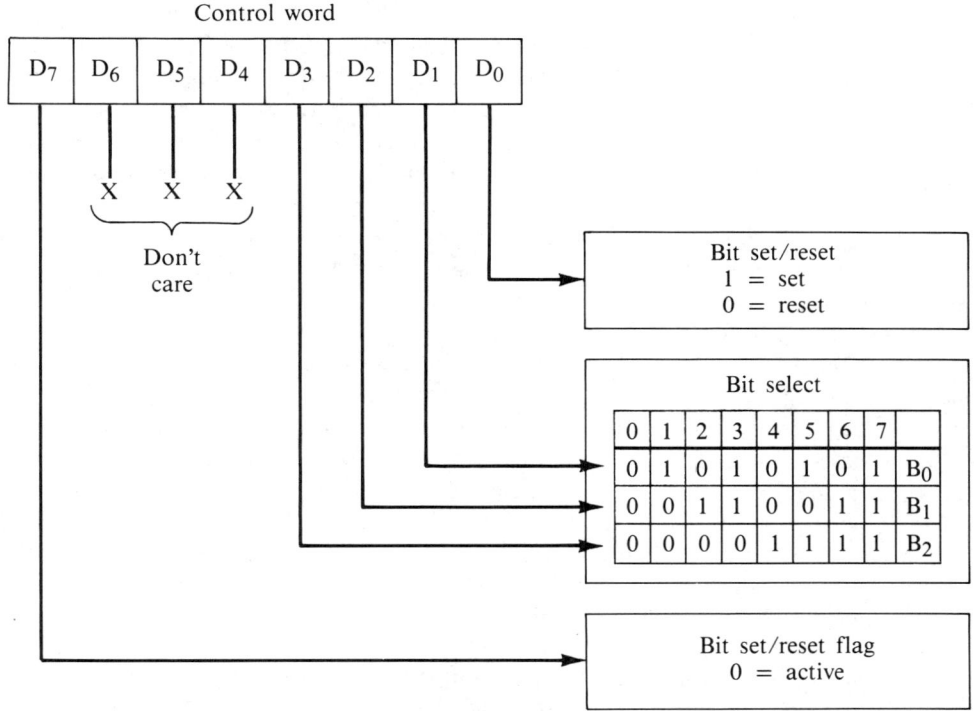

FIGURE 7-9. Bit set/reset control-word format. (Courtesy of Intel Corp.)

The bit pattern for the control word that determines the port configuration of Figure 7-7(a) is as shown in Figure 7-10(a). The control word to set flip-flops INTE A and B is shown in Figure 7-10(b) and (c). Bit D_3 of Figure 7-10(a) defines PC_6 and PC_7 as output pins. D_0 of Figure 7-10(a) has no meaning since all available group C pins associated with group B for a mode 1 operation are

D_7	D_6	D_5	D_4	D_3	D_2	D_1	D_0
1	0	1	1	0	1	0	0

(a) Mode 1 port configuration control word for port A defined as an input port with ports B and C (PC_6 and PC_7) defined as output ports

Control word = B4H

D_7	D_6	D_5	D_4	D_3	D_2	D_1	D_0
0	0	0	0	1	0	0	1

(b) Bit set/reset control word for $INTE_A$ being set

Control word = 09H

D_7	D_6	D_5	D_4	D_3	D_2	D_1	D_0
0	0	0	0	0	1	0	1

(c) Bit set/reset control word for $INTE_B$ being set

Control word = 05H

FIGURE 7-10. Control words for programming an 8255 to function as the configuration shown in Figure 7-7.

7-3 8255 OPERATION MODES

used for handshaking—hence an "X" could be used to represent that we "don't care" which logic state is used. We shall show a 0 for bit D_0. As for the bit pattern of Figure 7-10(b) and (c), we are told (by the manufacturer) that PC_4 and PC_2 in Figure 7-7 set or reset INTE A and B. To set INTE A will require the binary combination as indicated in column 4 (PC_4) of the table given in Figure 7-9, which is $B_2 = 1$, $B_1 = 0$, and $B_0 = 0$. Then as shown in Figure 7-10(b), $D_3 = 1$ (B_3), $D_2 = 0$ (B_1), and $D_1 = 0$ (B_0). To set INTE A, D_0 of Figure 7-10(b) is a 1. Also from Figure 7-9 we see that D_6, D_5, and D_4 are "don't care" logic states—we will use 0's. To set INTE B requires another bit set/reset control word and is shown in Figure 7-10(c).

The program that configures the 8255, as shown in Figure 7-7, is given in Figure 7-11 of Example 7-1.

The program of Figure 7-11 is one that initializes the 8255 (programs it) and therefore would probably be executed on "power-up" of the microprocessor-based system. To actually read a data byte from port A or B will require software in addition to that given in Figure 7-11, mainly the IN instruction. Accessing ports A and B will be the next topic.

To write a program that accesses ports A and B, we must understand the various addresses that apply to an 8255. Since we still have not studied addressing the 8255, let us assign the symbolic address "PORTA" to port A and "PORTB" to port B. As an example program that services ports A and B, let us suppose that input port A is a terminal and output port B is a printer. A data byte input by port A is to be displayed (printed) at port B (displaying input data is known as *echoing*). Also, the input data byte is to be stored in memory at location STORE. The program of Figure 7-12, Example 7-2, will accomplish this task.

In the program of Example 7-2 it is imagined that vectored interrupts are used and port A's service routine is at location 0008H (RST 1) and port B's service routine begins at location 0010H (RST 2). Both service routines are simplified but are sufficient for presenting the concepts of reading and writing to the 8255. It is important to remember that the program of Figure 7-11 must be executed before the program of Figure 7-12, so that the 8255 is properly programmed.

EXAMPLE 7-1

```
; This program will program the 8255
; of Figure 7-7 to perform the functions as shown

        MVI  A,B4H      ; Initialize A with PORT
                        ; Configuration control-word
        OUT  PPI1       ; Program PPI for mode 1
        MVI  A,09H      ; Initialize A with bit Set/Reset
                        ; control-word for INTE A
        OUT  PPI1       ; Set INTE A
        MVI  A,05H      ; Initialize A with bit Set/Reset
                        ; control-word for INTE B
        OUT  PPI1       ; Set INTE B

; The PPI of Figure 7-7 is now programmed
```

FIGURE 7-11. Program to program 8255 as configured in Figure 7-7.

EXAMPLE 7-2

```
; Service routine for port A
    ORG 0008H
    IN  PORTA      ; Get data byte from port A
                   ; This resets IBF to zero
                   ; hence INTR A goes low
    STA STORE      ; Store data byte at location STORE
    RET            ; Return to main program
; End of service routine
; Service routine for port B
    ORG 0010H
    LDA MEM        ; Load A with
                   ; data byte from memory
    OUT PORTB      ; Send data byte to port B
                   ; and active OBF.
    RET            ; Return to main program
; End of service routine
```

FIGURE 7-12. Program for servicing ports A and B of Figure 7-7.

As seen from Figure 7-4, configurations other than that of Figure 7-7 are possible for a mode 1 operation. It is believed that the hardware and software examples of Figures 7-7, 7-11, and 7-12 are sufficient to grasp the concepts of a mode 1 operation for both input and output ports of an 8255. Let us now move on to mode 2.

Mode 2

Mode 2 configures the 8255 as shown in Figure 7-13. Group A functions as a bidirectional I/O port (input and output port) with handshaking. Port B may be programmed to function as either an input or output port in either a mode 0 or mode 1 operation. Both input and output data are latched by port A. There are three bits of group C (PC_2, PC_1, and PC_0) not used for mode 2 handshaking; they can be programmed to be either output or input pins; that is, these three pins can have access to 3 bits of the data bus for CPU read or write operations. However, if port B is programmed to function in a mode 1 operation, PC_2, PC_1, and PC_0 will function either as $\overline{ACK}$, $\overline{OBF}$, INTR (if programmed to an output port) or as $\overline{STB}$, IBF, INTR (for input port) in order to provide handshaking for port B. Port C will be discussed in greater detail in Section 7-5.

As seen from Figure 7-13, handshaking for port A is provided by $\overline{OBF}_A$, $\overline{ACK}_A$, IBF_A, and $\overline{STB}_A$. $\overline{OBF}_A$ and $\overline{ACK}_A$ provide handshaking for port A functioning in write operations (CPU writing to the I/O device) and the pair IBF_A and $\overline{STB}_A$ provide handshaking for read operations. The handshaking of port A is identical to that previously explained for a mode 1 operation, with the exception of the common interrupt request, which is essentially an ORing of mode 1 read- or write-generated interrupts, as previously explained. Then in reality a mode 2 operation, relative to port A, is the combination of both a mode

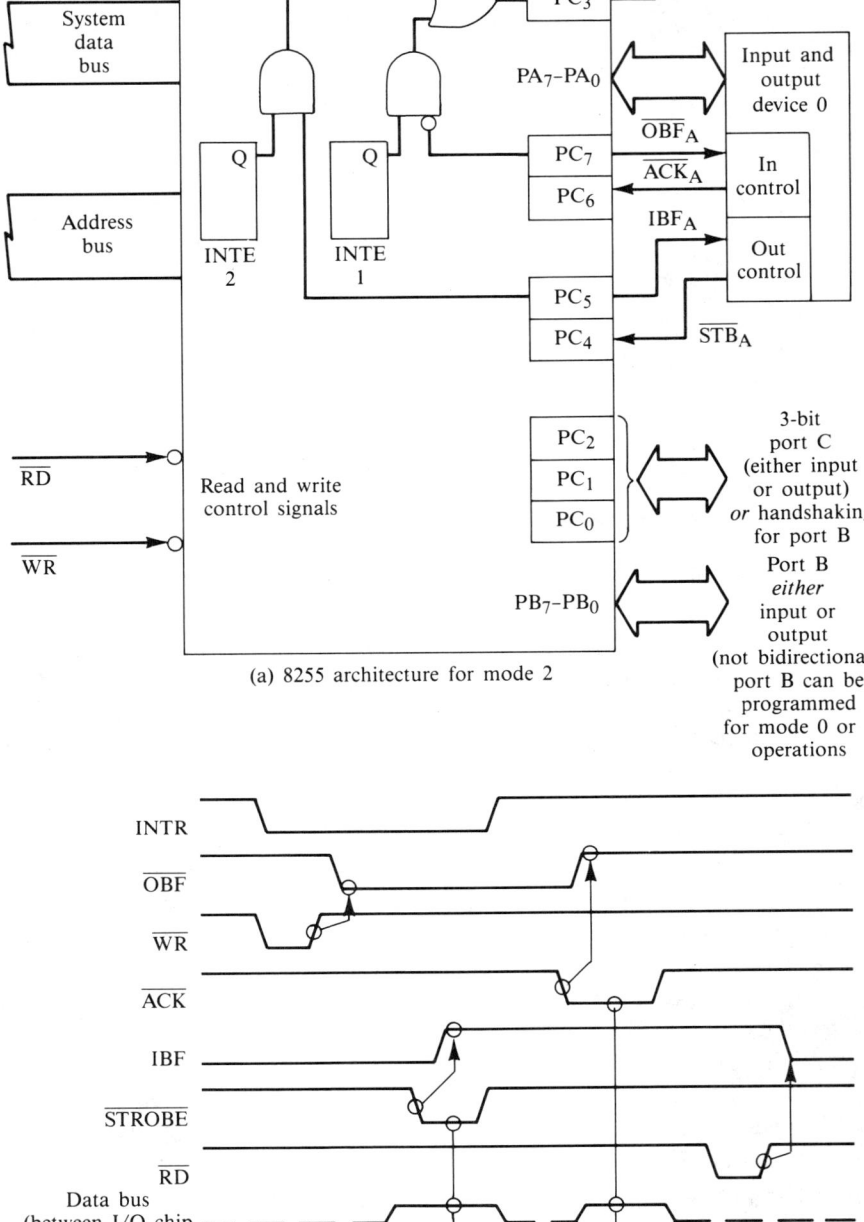

FIGURE 7-13. The 8255 programmed in a mode 2 configuration. (Courtesy of Intel Corp.)

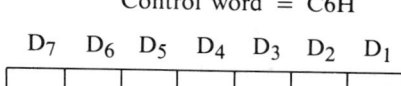

(a) Mode 2 control word for port B input and port C as output

(b) Bit set/reset control word to set $INTE_B$ for input port B

FIGURE 7-14. Control words for mode 2 operation.

1 input and output port with handshaking and the sharing of a common interrupt request.

The mode 2 control word will configure ports A, B, and C. Once configured, the CPU reads (IN) or writes (OUT) to the 8255 via the system data bus with input control signals read ($\overline{RD}$) and write ($\overline{WR}$) providing timing. The control signal $\overline{I/O\ R}$ from the 8228 will activate (directly or indirectly just as any other I/O chip) $\overline{RD}$ and $\overline{I/O\ W}$ will activate $\overline{WR}$, as we shall see in detail when we study addressing of the 8255 in Section 7-4.

The control word for programming the 8255 to operate in mode 2 with port B functioning as a mode 1 input port with handshaking (PC_2, PC_1, and PC_0 provide handshaking) can be determined from Figure 7-4 and is illustrated in Figure 7-14(a). Notice that D_0 of Figure 7-14(a) is a ''don't care'' since PC_2–PC_0 provide handshaking and do not function as I/O pins. The bit set/reset control word for port B (PC_2 as stated in Figure 7-7) is given in Figure 7-14(b). All ''don't cares'' (X's) were arbitrarily assigned as lows.

The program that will program the 8255 for a mode 2 operation with group B configured as a mode 1 input port and group C (PC_2, PC_1, and PC_0) providing handshaking for port B is given in Figure 7-15 of Example 7-3. As before, a symbolic address (PPI2) is used to address the 8255 for the purpose of loading the mode and bit set/reset control words into the 8255 control register.

Once the program of Figure 7-15 is executed, then to write a data byte to port A, the instruction OUT PORTA will suffice, where PORTA is a symbolic address, as used previously. To read a data byte from port A requires the

EXAMPLE 7-3

```
; This program programs an 8255 to
; operate in a mode 2 configuration with
; input port B operating in mode 1

    MVI A,0C6H    ; Initialize A with mode 2 control word
    OUT PPI2      ; Program 8255 for mode 2
    MVI A,05H     ; Initialize A with Set/Reset
                  ; control word for port B
    OUT PPI2      ; Set INTE B

; The 8255 is now programmed
```

FIGURE 7-15. Program to program an 8255 for mode 2.

instruction IN PORTA, where PORTA is again the same symbolic address. To read a data byte from input port B requires the instruction IN PORTB, and instruction OUT PORTC will write to output port C (when available). A more specific and detailed example will be given later.

7-4

ADDRESSING THE 8255

To determine the appropriate address for the 8255, refer to Table 7-3. From Table 7-3 it is seen that A_1 and A_0 address the ports and control register for *all* modes of operation. That is, $A_1 = A_0 = 0$ addresses port A and $A_1 = 0$, $A_0 = 1$ addresses port B for either read or write operations. It is control signals $\overline{RD}$ and $\overline{WR}$ which determine data direction (read or write). As an example of a read operation, from Table 7-3 it is seen that when chip select ($\overline{CS}$) is low, $\overline{RD}$ is low (a read is being performed) and $\overline{WR} = 1$ with address $A_1 = A_0 = 0$, then port A will gate its data byte on the system data bus. In this instance port A would have been previously programmed as an input port. In contrast, for a write operation, when address $A_1 = A_0 = 0$, $\overline{CS} = 0$, and $\overline{WR} = 0$ ($\overline{RD} = 1$), the data byte on the system data bus will be latched by port A. $\overline{WR} = 0$, in conjunction with $A_1 = A_0 = 0$, requires port A to have previously been programmed as an output port. From Table 7-3 we see that to load a control word into the control register requires address $A_1 = A_0 = 1$ as well as control signals $\overline{RD} = 1$, $\overline{WR} = 0$, and $\overline{CS} = 0$.

TABLE 7-3. 8255 Addressing

A_1	A_0	$\overline{RD}$	$\overline{WR}$	$\overline{CS}$	Input Operation (read)
0	0	0	1	0	Port A $\Rightarrow$ data bus
0	1	0	1	0	Port B $\Rightarrow$ data bus
1	0	0	1	0	Port C $\Rightarrow$ data bus
					Output Operation (write)
0	0	1	0	0	Data bus $\Rightarrow$ port A
0	1	1	0	0	Data bus $\Rightarrow$ port B
1	0	1	0	0	Data bus $\Rightarrow$ port C
1	1	1	0	0	Data bus $\Rightarrow$ control
					Disable Function
X	X	X	X	1	Data bus $\Rightarrow$ tri-state
1	1	0	1	0	Illegal condition
X	X	1	1	0	Data bus $\Rightarrow$ tri-state

Courtesy Intel Corp.

EXAMPLE 7-4

As an example of integrating the 8255 into a microprocessor-based system, such a system as Figure 4-7, consider Figure 7-16.

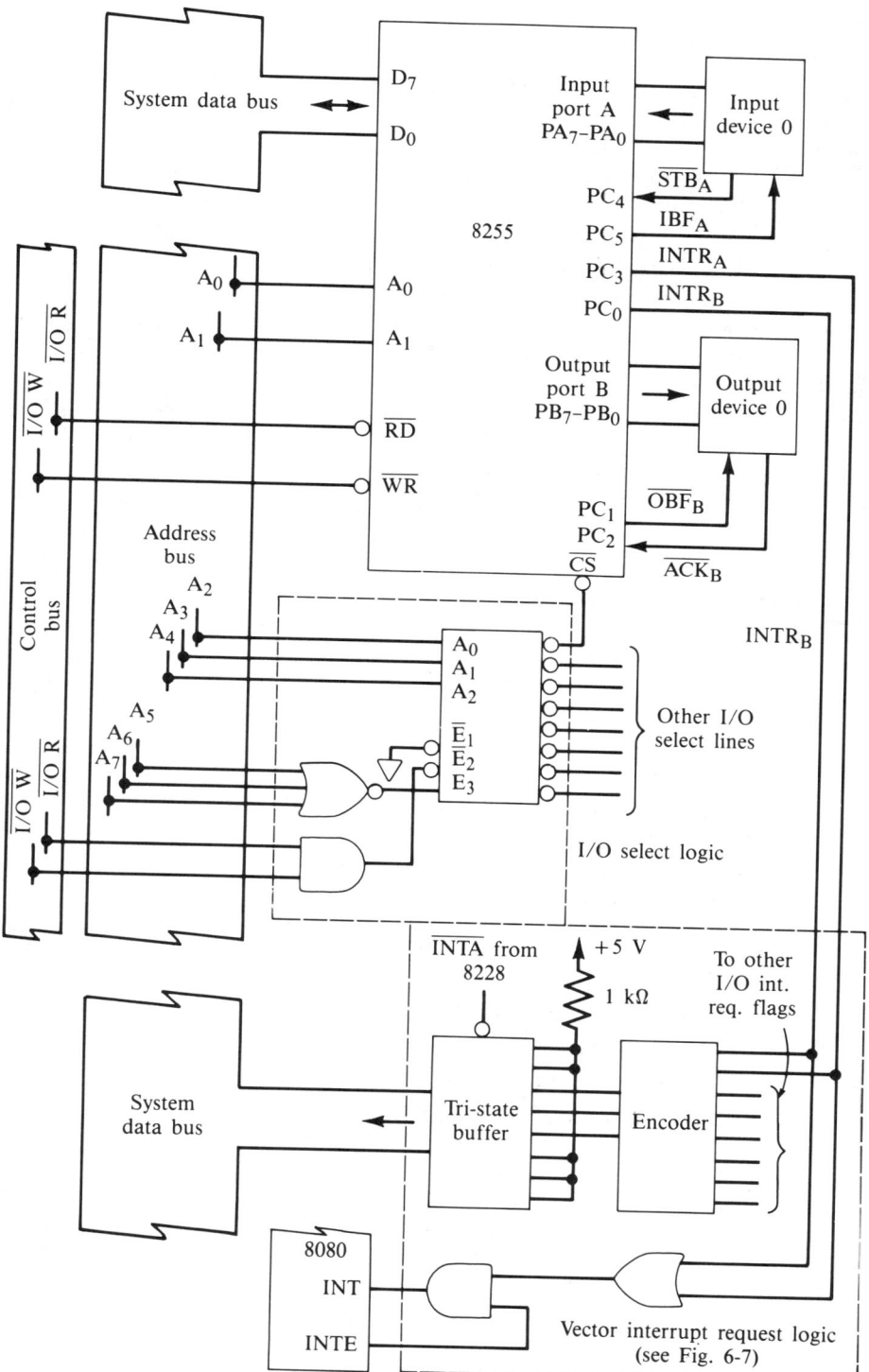

FIGURE 7-16. Hardware for an 8255 programmed to function in a mode 1 configuration.

Solution

As seen in Figure 7-16, addressing of the 8255 is accomplished with A_0 and A_1 lines of the address bus. Address lines A_2–A_7 enable ($\overline{CS}$) the 8255 via the I/O select. The I/O select is an 8205 and operates the same as those discussed in Chapter 4. We see for this example that when address lines $A_2 = A_3 = A_4 = 0$, then select line 0 becomes active and is used to activate $\overline{CS}$ of the 8255. Control signals $\overline{I/O\ R}$ and $\overline{I/O\ W}$ activate $\overline{RD}$ and $\overline{WR}$, respectively.

To address the 8255 of Figure 7-16 requires A_7–A_2 to be as shown in Table 7-4. As stated previously, address lines A_7–A_2 of Figure 7-16 enable the 8255, while address lines A_0–A_1 address the port. The instruction IN or OUT determines whether the addressed port is being read or written to.

Returning to the program of Figure 7-6 and using it to program the mode control word to the 8255 of Figure 7-16, we see from Table 7-4 that the address for PPI0 is 03H. Similarly, the address for PPI1 and PPI2 of Figures 7-11 and 7-15 is also 03H, when applied to the hardware of Figure 7-16, since in each case the control register of the 8255 is being addressed. To reiterate, from Table 7-4 we see that any time port A of Figure 7-16 is addressed, the hexadecimal number 00H is to be used. Similarly, port B's address is 01H and port C is 02H. The data byte direction, data bus to port or port to data bus, is determined by the op code IN or OUT (via $\overline{RD}$ or $\overline{WR}$).

To program the 8255 to function as indicated in Figure 7-16 and also to write service routines for ports A and B, we simply need to determine the proper address values from Table 7-4 and furnish them for the symbolic addresses of Examples 7-1 and 7-2. These modifications are shown in Figure 7-17 of Example 7-5.

As another example of hardware, let us apply an 8255 in a mode 2 operation with port B functioning in a mode 1 configuration (refer to Figure 7-13). The hardware is shown in Figure 7-18, which is the hardware of Figures 7-16 appropriately modified for a mode 2 as stated.

Since the hardware of Figure 7-18 is a combination of circuits discussed previously (Figures 6-7, 7-13, and 7-14), its operation needs little discussion. We see that input/output device 0 is a bidirectional I/O device and therefore is to be connected to port A, which is functioning in a mode 2 operation. The interrupt request from port A ($INTR_A$) generates an RST vectored interrupt. Port B is operating in a mode 1 operation. An interrupt request from port B also

TABLE 7-4. Addresses for 8255 of Figure 7-16

Hex Addr.	8255 Chip Select						Port Addr.		Function Addressed
	A_7	A_6	A_5	A_4	A_3	A_2	A_1	A_0	
00	0	0	0	0	0	0	0	0	Port A
01	0	0	0	0	0	0	0	1	Port B
02	0	0	0	0	0	0	1	0	Port C
03	0	0	0	0	0	0	1	1	Control reg

Refer to Table 7-3

EXAMPLE 7-5

```
; Programming the 8255 to be configured
; as shown in Figure 7-14

    ORG 0100H
    MVI A,0B4H; Initialize A with mode
             ; control-word
    OUT 03H  ; Program PPI for mode 1
    MVI A,09H ; Initialize A with BIT Set/Reset for INTE A
    OUT 03H  ; Set INTE A
    MVI A,05H ; Initialize A with bit Set/Reset for INTE B
    OUT 03H  ; Set INTE B

; Service Routine for input port A

    ORG 0008H
    IN 00H    ; Get data byte from port A
    STA STORE ; Store data byte at location STORE
    RET       ; Return to main program

; Service Routine for output port B

    ORG 0010H
    LDA MEM  ; Load A with data byte stored at memory location MEM
    OUT 01H  ; Output data byte to port B
    RET      ; Return
```

FIGURE 7-17. A routine for programming the 8255 of Figure 7-14.

causes a vectored interrupt. It might be pointed out that the input/output device 0 could be a combined terminal (input) and printer (output).

The software to service the 8255 for a mode 2 operation requires knowledge of the 8255's status word, which is explained in the next section.

7-5

8255 STATUS WORD

The 8255 status word indicates the logic state of INTE, $\overline{OBF}$, IBF, and $INTR_A$ for both ports A and B for modes 1 and 2, as indicated in Figure 7-19. The 8255 status word is obtained by reading port C, which would require IN 02H (see Table 7-4) for the 8255 of Figure 7-16. To understand why port C is used for reading the 8255's status word, refer to the status word format of Figure 7-19 and also port C of Figures 7-7(a), 7-13, and 7-18, taking note of port C's limited number (three or less) of I/O pins. Realize that reading port C (using IN 02H) is going to result in 8 bits from port C being latched by the CPU's accumulator (refer to instruction IN). But since port C has three or fewer I/O (INPUT) pins, the 5 or more bits not used to input data, via port C, must represent something else. The "something else" is the status (the present logic state) of those functions, as indicated in Figure 7-19.

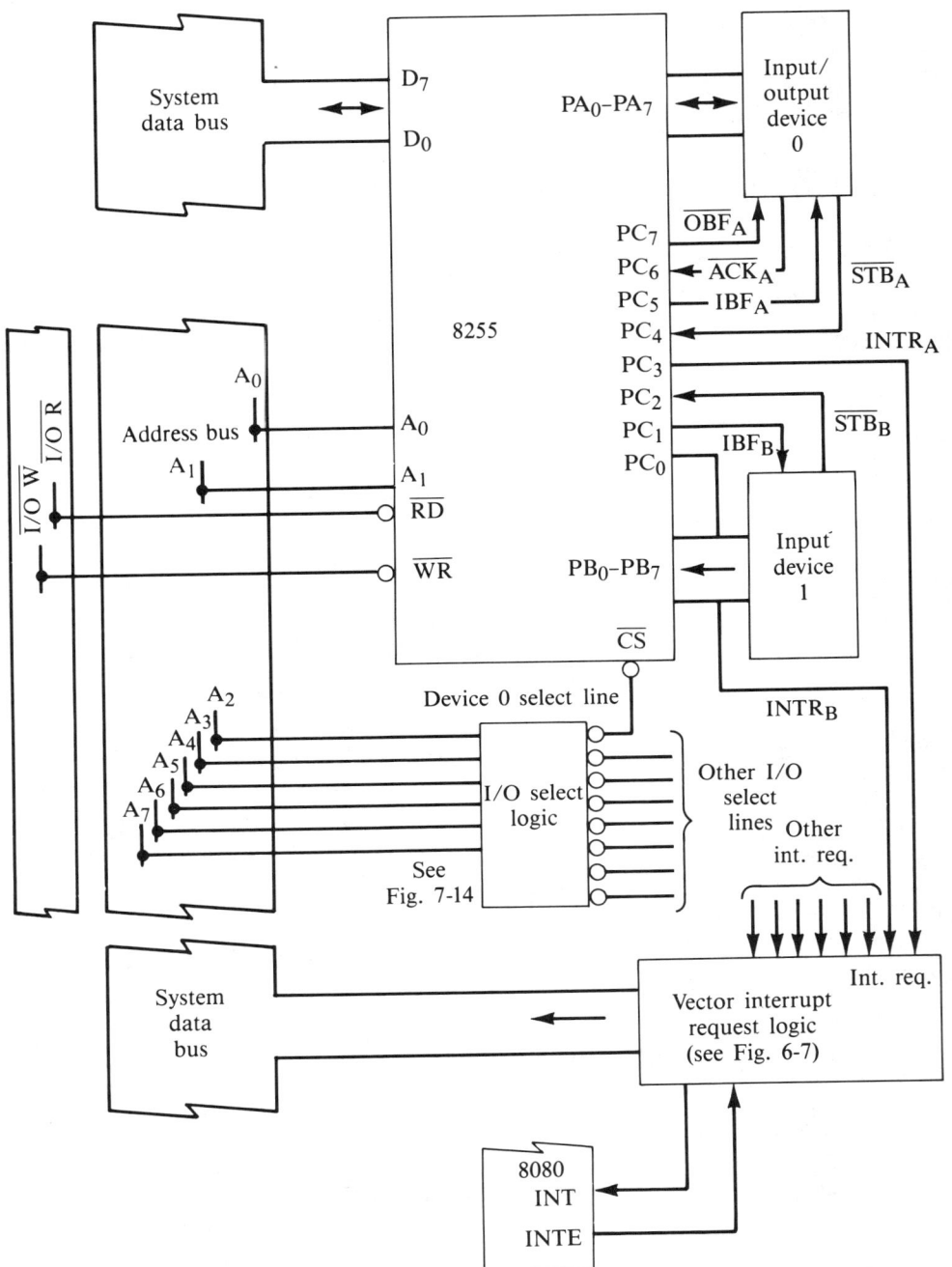

FIGURE 7-18. Hardware for an 8255 programmed to function in a mode 2 configuration.

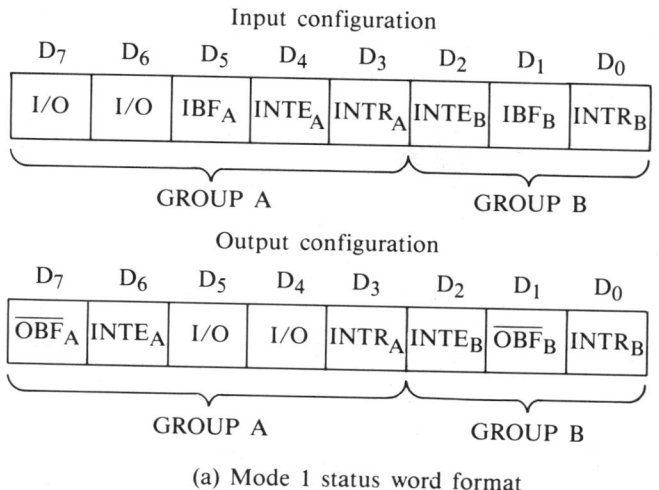

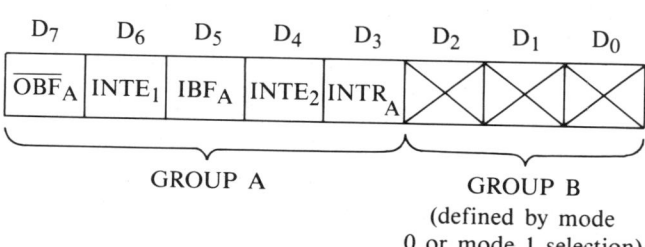

(b) Mode 2 status word format

FIGURE 7-19. 8255 status word format. (Courtesy Intel Corp.)

To utilize an 8255 status word, review Figures 7-13 and 7-18. From Figure 7-18 we realize that if either the input or output of input/output device 0 requested an interrupt, a single interrupt request line ($INTR_A$) would be activated. In order for the CPU to determine which, or both, requested the interrupt, it is required that the CPU poll both ports. It performs the poll by reading the 8255 status word from port C, obtaining the data of Figure 7-19(b), and then specifically determining the logic state of $\overline{OBF}$ and IBF using a *mask word*, as was done in Example 6-1. As seen from the timing diagram of Figure 7-13(b), when the 8255 is writing to I/O device 0, via port A, $\overline{OBF}$ goes low and remains in that logic state until the data byte of port A is latched by I/O device 0 and acknowledgment is given ($\overline{ACK}$ goes low). Also, we notice from Figure 7-13(b) that INTR is high when $\overline{OBF}$ becomes active. Then to determine whether the input or output port requested the interrupt, a software poll of the mode 2 status word of Figure 7-19(b) can be made. Such a routine is given in Example 7-6, with Save Register Contents, and so on, omitted.

EXAMPLE 7-6

```
; This routine reads port C for a
; mode 2 operation and then determines
; whether input or output requested
; an interrupt. Assume that an interrupt
; request from port A of Figure 7-16 resulted
; in the CPU being vectored to 0038H
; (RST 7)

      ORG 0038H
      IN 02H           ; Read port C and obtain the
                       ; mode 2 status word of
                       ; Figure 7-17(b)
      MOV B,A          ; Copy the status word in B
      ANI 80H          ; Poll D_7 for OBF
      CZ SROUT         ; If Z = 1, then OBF_A = 0; jump
                       ; to service routine SR OUT
      MOV A,B          ; Restore status in A
      ANI 20H          ; Poll D_5 for High
      CNZ SRIN         ; If Z = 0, then IBF_A = 1
                       ; and needs service
      RET              ; Return to main program
```

The reader should also be aware that the mode 2 status word of Figure 7-19(b) is needed when polling ports to determine which port requested an interrupt. This would be an application of Example 6-1. That is, two of the interrupt request flag outputs (Q) of Figure 6-2 would be replaced with $INTR_A$ and $INTR_B$ of Figure 7-18. Then when an interrupt request is made, a polling routine similar to that of Figure 6-4 would be executed, which would begin polling, just as in Example 6-1.

7-6

SUMMARY OF THE 8255

The 8255 is a versatile programmable peripheral interface (PPI) chip. It can be programmed for a variety of I/O port configurations. The port configurations possible can be classified into one of three operations, which are:

1. *Mode 0:* This mode of operation provides elementary I/O interfacing requiring no handshaking.
2. *Mode 1:* This mode provides two 8-bit ports for I/O interfacing, requiring handshaking. Either of the two 8-bit ports may be either input or output. Both inputs and outputs are latched.
3. *Mode 2:* This mode of operation provides one 8-bit bidirectional port (port A) and another 8-bit port (port B), which may be programmed to function as either a mode 0 or 1 input or output port.

Table 7-5 is a reprint from Intel summarizing the 8255 port configurations according to mode.

TABLE 7-5. Mode Definition Summary Table

	Mode 0 In	Mode 0 Out	Mode 1 In	Mode 1 Out	Mode 2 Group A Only	
PA_0	IN	OUT	IN	OUT	↔	
PA_1	IN	OUT	IN	OUT	↔	
PA_2	IN	OUT	IN	OUT	↔	
PA_3	IN	OUT	IN	OUT	↔	
PA_4	IN	OUT	IN	OUT	↔	
PA_5	IN	OUT	IN	OUT	↔	
PA_6	IN	OUT	IN	OUT	↔	
PA_7	IN	OUT	IN	OUT	↔	
PB_0	IN	OUT	IN	OUT	—	
PB_1	IN	OUT	IN	OUT	—	
PB_2	IN	OUT	IN	OUT	—	
PB_3	IN	OUT	IN	OUT	—	Mode 0
PB_4	IN	OUT	IN	OUT	—	or Mode 1
PB_5	IN	OUT	IN	OUT	—	Only
PB_6	IN	OUT	IN	OUT	—	
PB_7	IN	OUT	IN	OUT	—	
PC_0	IN	OUT	$INTR_B$	$INTR_B$	I/O	
PC_1	IN	OUT	IBF_B	$\overline{OBF_B}$	I/O	
PC_2	IN	OUT	$\overline{STB_B}$	$\overline{ACK_B}$	I/O	
PC_3	IN	OUT	$INTR_A$	$INTR_A$	$INTR_A$	
PC_4	IN	OUT	$\overline{STB_A}$	I/O	$\overline{STB_A}$	
PC_5	IN	OUT	IBF_A	I/O	IBF_A	
PC_6	IN	OUT	I/O	$\overline{ACK_A}$	$\overline{ACK_A}$	
PC_7	IN	OUT	I/O	$\overline{OBF_A}$	$\overline{OBF_A}$	

Courtesy of Intel Corp.

Port C provides handshaking for ports A and B. Explanations of the handshaking functions provided by port C (for mode 1 or 2 operations, see Table 7-5) are given below.

1. *Handshaking for input port (A or B):* Also refer to the timing diagram of Figure 7-7(b).
   a. $\overline{STB}$. This is an input to the 8255. It provides a strobe by driving $\overline{STB}$ low. This strobe pulse is used by the 8255 to latch the data byte from the peripheral device.
   b. IBF. When an input port of the 8255 has latched a data byte from the inputting peripheral, the 8255 acknowledges receiving the data byte transmission by driving IBF high, which states that that port's input buffer is full.
   c. INTR. When an input buffer is full (IBF = 1) the 8255 requires servicing by the CPU; that is, the CPU must read the port. To get the attention of the CPU, the 8255 generates an interrupt request via INTR. Before INTR can become active, INTE must be set, using the bit set/reset control word of Figure 7-9.

2. *Handshaking for output port (A or B):* In addition to Table 7-5, refer to the timing diagram, Figure 7-8.
   a. $\overline{OBF}$. When the CPU writes to an 8255 output port, the receiving port will latch the data byte and then indicate that its output buffer is full by outputting a low on $\overline{OBF}$.
   b. $\overline{ACK}$. $\overline{OBF}$ going low is used by the peripheral device to latch the data byte from the 8255 output port. When the peripheral device has latched the data byte, it acknowledges the transaction by pulling $\overline{ACK}$ low. When $\overline{ACK}$ goes low, the 8255 is ready to receive another data byte from the CPU and as a result activates INTR.
   c. INTR. INTR is used to interrupt the CPU for the next data byte to be written to the peripheral.

To program the 8255 for any port configuration of Table 7-5 requires that a control word be written to the control register of the 8255. The control word format is given in Figure 7-4. In order to write a control word to the control register of an 8255, the appropriate address must be supplied. From Table 7-4 and specific hardware configuration of the address bus lines A_0–A_7, such as shown in Figure 7-16, the appropriate address can be determined. From Table 7-4 we see that A_0 and A_1 of the 8255 must be high in order to write a control word to the control register. Also from Table 7-4 we see that A_0 and A_1 of the 8255 select the port (A, B, or C) that is being read or written to.

Finally, when the CPU reads port C, it will not only read the I/O pins of port C (if any) but also the status of the 8255. The status word format for the 8255 is shown in Figure 7-19.

A system's wiring of an 8255 for each mode of operation is shown in Figure 7-20. Figure 7-21 shows some 8255 applications as suggested by Intel.

7-7

SERIAL DATA COMMUNICATIONS

In previous sections, applications of the 8255 illustrated the manner in which the chip could be used to allow the CPU to communicate with an external I/O device. That form of data communications is known as *parallel data communications*, since at a given instant, information was transmitted as groups of bits rather than a single bit at a time. For example, in Figure 7-14, input device 0 and output device 0 are connected to the 8255 chip by means of 16 data lines (PA_0–PA_7 for input device 0, and PB_0–PB_7 for output device 0). The 8255 would then receive and transmit data from and to these external I/O devices in the form of bytes (8 bits). In a serial data interface, an external device would be connected to the port by means of a single data line. A byte of data would then be transferred by shifting each bit (of the byte) over the interconnecting line, until all 8 bits were transferred.

The advantages of serial data transfers are obvious. Assuming that the CPU communicates with an external I/O device by using 8 bits of information, a parallel port would require a minimum of eight data lines connected to the external I/O device to accomplish the interface. A serial port, on the other hand,

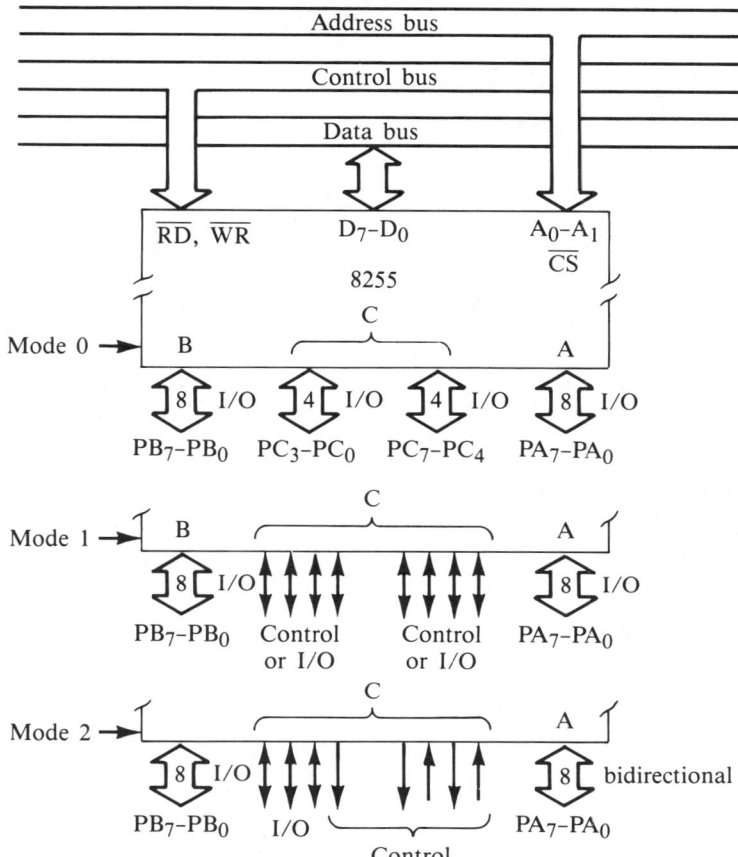

FIGURE 7-20. 8255 bus interfaces for various modes of operation. (Courtesy of Intel Corp.)

would require a minimum of one data line connected to the external I/O device to transmit and receive serial data. Note that both types of ports would have to have an additional line (ground) to provide a common reference for the logic voltages appearing on the data lines.

Eight data lines on a parallel interface or one data line on a serial interface would restrict communications to "one-way traffic" at a given instant. In other words, neither type of I/O port would be able to transmit and receive data to and from the external I/O device at the same time. When data communication is limited to either transmission or reception at any given instant, it is known as half-duplex communication. To overcome this limitation, a parallel port having 16 data lines (eight to receive data, and eight to transmit data) would have the capability to transmit and receive data at the same time. The ability to receive and transmit data at the same time is known as full-duplex communication. Similarly, a serial port having two serial data lines (one to transmit serial data and one to receive serial data) would have the capability to operate in full duplex.

One of the main disadvantages of serial data communications is in the speed with which data is transferred to and from the external I/O device. Since the

7-7 SERIAL DATA COMMUNICATIONS

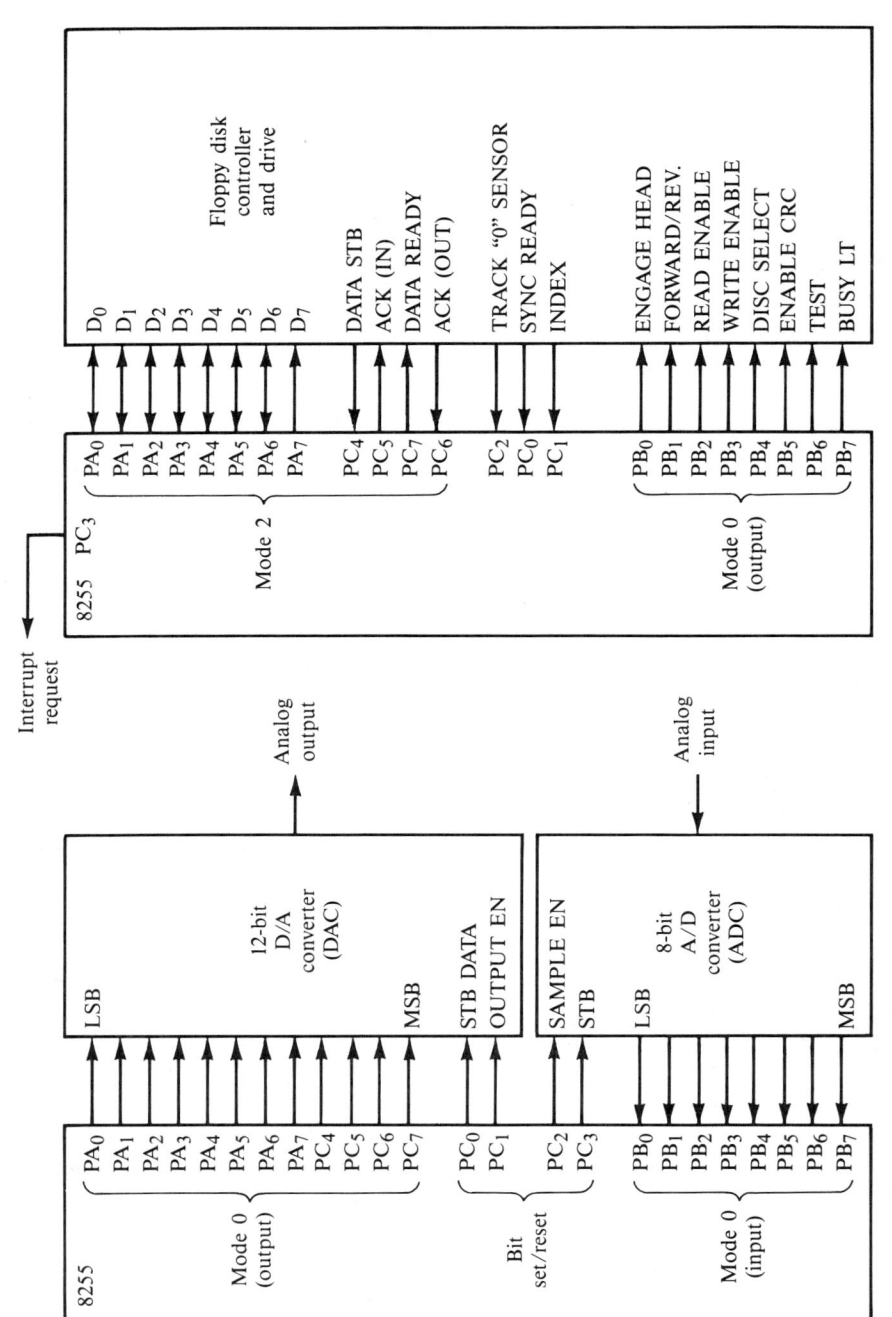

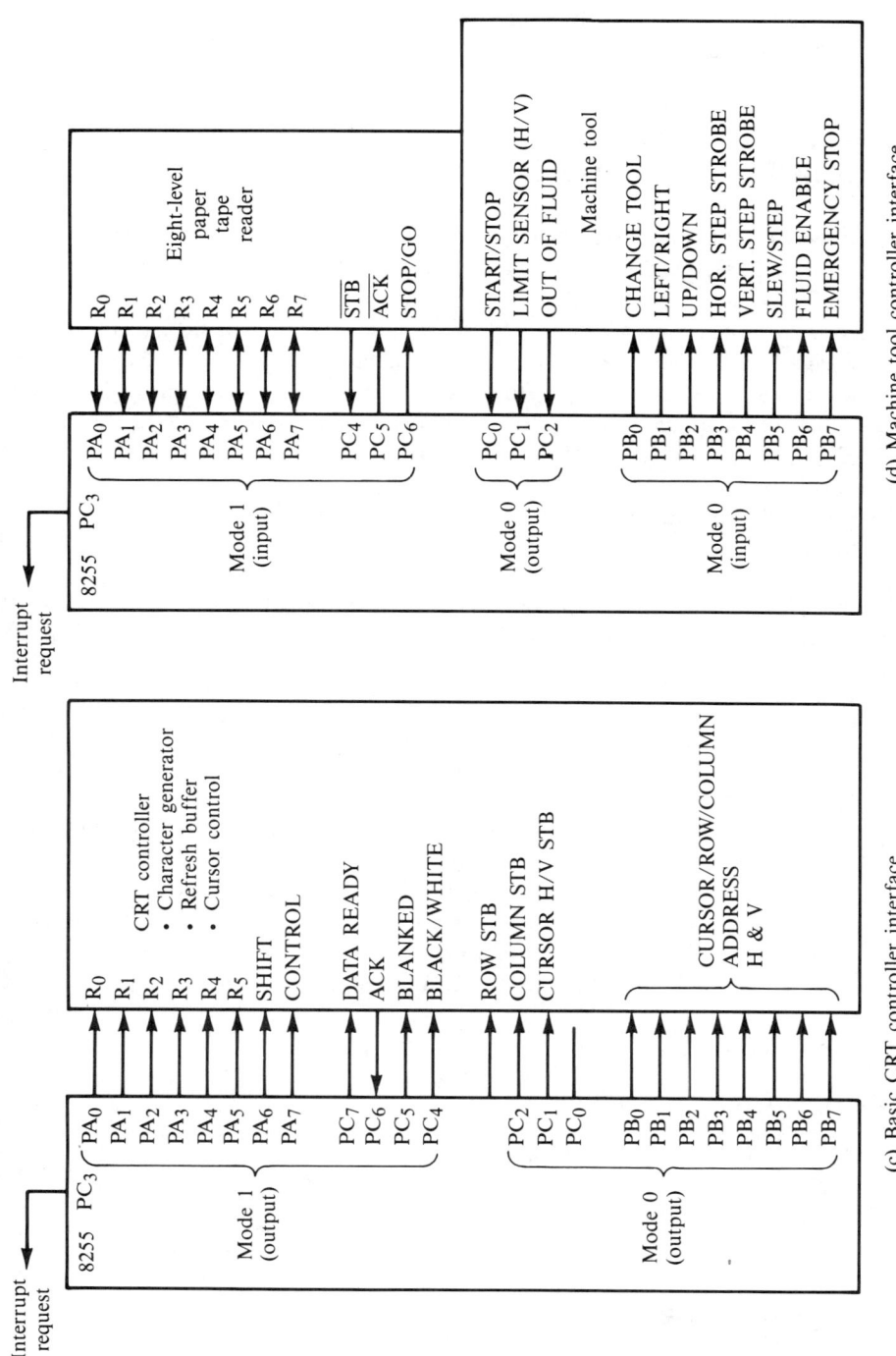

FIGURE 7-21. Some example applications. (Courtesy of Intel Corp.)

7-7 SERIAL DATA COMMUNICATIONS

serial port must shift out parallel data one bit at a time over a single line, and shift in serial data one bit at a time to construct a byte, the time required to do this limits the rate of data transmission. This overhead does not exist in a parallel data communications link.

7-8

SERIAL DATA INTERFACE

In previous sections it was shown that an external I/O device that communicated in parallel data could be connected to the CPU via a parallel I/O port (8255). Similarly, an external I/O device that communicates by using a serial data format can be connected to the CPU via a serial I/O port. Figure 7-22 illustrates a typical full-duplex data link between a serial data port and an external I/O device. In most cases, this external I/O device is a computer terminal (console) with a keyboard and a screen (or printer). The circuit in Figure 7-22 allows the CPU and external I/O device to communicate via a serial I/O port. The serial data link consists of three lines: a *transmit data line* (TxD) to transfer data from the serial port to the I/O device, a *receive data line* (RxD) to transfer data from the I/O device to the serial port, and a *signal ground* (GND) to reference the voltages appearing on the serial data lines. Note that the terms "transmit" and "receive" are relative to the serial port and not to the I/O device.

The interface between the CPU and the serial I/O port consists of a connection to the data bus (D_0–D_7) to enable data transfers to and from the CPU, a read line ($\overline{RD}$) to enable the CPU to read data from the serial port, a write line ($\overline{WR}$) to enable the CPU to write data to the serial port, and a chip select ($\overline{CS}$) line to select the chip for I/O operations when the appropriate I/O address appears on the address bus.

Notice that the circuit in Figure 7-22 uses linear addressing. Recall from Chapter 4 that this addressing technique uses an address line (A_0–A_{15}) to select a device. This simplifies the hardware by eliminating the I/O selector (decoder). However, the disadvantage in this addressing scheme is that the number of addressable I/O devices is limited to eight.

Referring to Figure 7-22, if the CPU executes an "OUT 2" instruction,

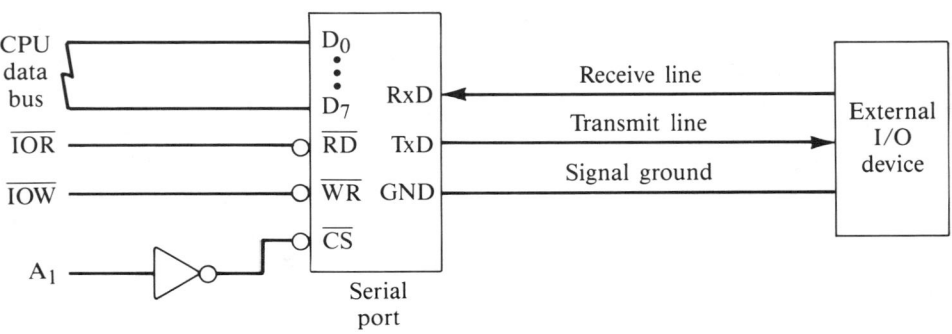

FIGURE 7-22. Basic serial data link.

address line A_1 is set to a logic 1; the logic 1 on address line A_1 is inverted and used to select (via the $\overline{CS}$ line) the serial port for an output operation. The "OUT 2" instruction also activates the 8228's $\overline{I/O\ W}$ control line (connected to $\overline{WR}$ of the serial port) and thus allows the contents of the data bus (contents of register A) to be loaded into the serial port. On receiving the byte of data, the serial port then shifts the data one bit at a time over the TxD line to the external I/O device.

Similarly, if the external I/O device transmitted serial data over the RxD line of the serial port, the serial port would then shift each bit into an internal register and construct an 8-bit data byte. The CPU could then activate its $\overline{I/O\ R}$ ($\overline{RD}$ line of the serial port) and A_1 lines ($\overline{CS}$ of the serial port) by means of an IN 2 instruction to read the data received by the serial port (and stored in an internal register) from the external I/O device.

The serial port thus operates in a manner very similar to a serial-to-parallel, parallel-to-serial shift register. Parallel data from the CPU is shifted out serially over the TxD line to the external I/O device. Serial data from the external I/O device is serially shifted into the serial port and assembled into a parallel byte for input to the CPU.

Notice in the circuit of Figure 7-22 that no provisions have been made for status readback. Since the rate at which serial data is transferred is often much slower than the operating speed of the CPU, the serial port must provide some sort of signal to the CPU, indicating that the serial data transfer has been completed. For example, if the CPU were to transmit a group of data bytes to the serial port, one byte at a time, without checking to see if the previous byte sent was completely shifted out on the TxD line, the serial port would not be able to "keep up" with the CPU, and this could lead to the transmission of erroneous data. Similarly, if the CPU attempted to read data received by the serial port (from the RxD line) without checking to see if the entire data byte was completely shifted in, the CPU could obtain erroneous data. *Status readback* is a process by which the CPU reads *status information* put out by the serial port. From this status information, the CPU determines if the transmitting circuit of the serial port (transmitter) has completely transmitted the previous byte sent, and is ready to accept another byte for transmission. Status information also allows the CPU to determine if the receiving circuit (receiver) of the serial port has received and completely assembled a character from the external I/O device. Many serial ports provide the CPU with other types of status information, as will be seen later in this chapter. To accommodate this status readback facility for the serial data link in Figure 7-22, another line has been added to the serial port—the control/data ($C/\overline{D}$) line, shown in Figure 7-23.

The $C/\overline{D}$ line of the serial port allows the CPU to select between data transfers (previously discussed) or status information. With the $C/\overline{D}$ line set to a logic 0 (data mode), the circuit in Figure 7-23 operates in a manner very similar to the circuit discussed in Figure 7-22; that is, an OUT 2 instruction would cause data from register A to be transmitted over the TxD line and an IN 2 instruction would read data received over the RxD line.

When the $C/\overline{D}$ line is set to a logic 1, the serial port now operates in the control mode, and allows the CPU to read status information. Notice that the $C/\overline{D}$ line of the serial port is tied to address line A_0 of the CPU. Now whenever

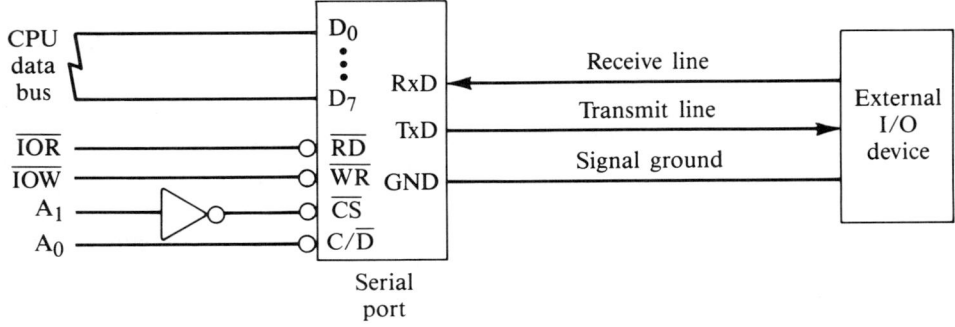

FIGURE 7-23. Serial data link with status readback.

the CPU executes an "IN 3" instruction, address line A_1 is set high and the $\overline{CS}$ line of the serial port is enabled; however, address line A_0 is also set high and the $C/\overline{D}$ line is held at a logic 1 level. (Note that for IN 2 and OUT 2 instructions, address line $A_0 = 0$, and the serial port is in the data mode.) The execution of the IN 3 instruction would now provide the CPU with status information in the form of an 8-bit status word. A typical status word sent to the CPU is shown in Figure 7-24.

Note that the status word shown in Figure 7-24 would appear in the CPU's accumulator as the result of the IN 3 instruction. In the status word of Figure 7-24, bit position 0 represents the least significant bit, and bit position 7 represents the most significant bit. Bit positions 0 and 1 represent the transmitter and receiver status, respectively. If the transmitter is ready to accept another byte for transmission, transmitter ready (TxRDY) will be set to a logic 1 by the serial port; otherwise, it will be reset to a logic 0. Similarly, if the receiver has received a serial data byte over the RxD line (receiver ready, RxRDY), bit position 1 will be set to a logic 1; otherwise, it will be reset to a logic 0. Note that if the RxRDY bit is set, the CPU must read the data received by the serial port. Otherwise, if another character is received over the RxD line, the original character received will be overwritten and hence lost (*overrun error*). At this stage it is assumed that bits 2, 3, 4, 5, 6, and 7 do not provide any status information and will not be used by the CPU.

Transmitting data to the external I/O device via the serial port would then be a two-step process. In order to transmit data to the external I/O device, the CPU would first have to check the T×RDY bit of the status word (transmitter ready status), wait for the transmitter to indicate a ready condition, and then send the data to the serial port for transmission over the TxD line. The software implementation of this process is shown in Figure 7-25. The code shown in Figure 7-25 is called the console output (CONOUT) subroutine, since it is used to transmit a single data byte (character) to the external I/O device (console) via the serial port. The CONOUT subroutine assumes that the character to be transmitted to the console is stored in register C *before* the subroutine is called.

The first instruction in the CONOUT subroutine is an IN 3 instruction that is used to input the serial port's status word into the CPU's accumulator. As mentioned before, bit position 0 of the status word will be set or reset depending

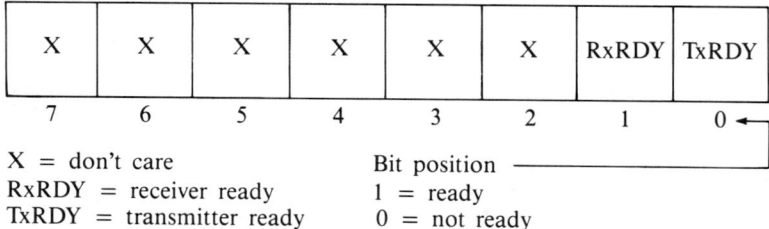

X = don't care
RxRDY = receiver ready
TxRDY = transmitter ready

Bit position
1 = ready
0 = not ready

FIGURE 7-24. Format of serial port status word.

on the state of the serial port's transmitter. The next instruction, ANI 01H, is used to mask out bit position 0 of the status word; this is done by ANDing the contents of the accumulator (status word) with a 01H (00000001 binary). Now if the transmitter is ready (bit position 0 of status word = 1), the result of the ANI instruction will yield a 01H (nonzero) result. If the transmitter is not ready (bit position 0 of status word = 0), the result of the ANI instruction will yield a 00H (zero) result. The third instruction, JZ, is used to check the result of the ANI instruction. If the result is a zero (transmitter not ready), control transfers to the address CONOUT, and the three-instruction sequence is repreated again; this continues until the transmitter is ready. If the result of the ANI instruction is a nonzero (transmitter is ready), control transfers to the next instruction in sequence (MOV A,C), which gets the character to be transmitted into the accumulator. Finally, the OUT 2 instruction sends the character to the serial port for transmission over the TxD line to the console.

Just as transmitting data to the console was a two-step process, receiving data from the console is also a two-step process. The CPU would first have to determine if a character has been received by the serial port from the console; this could be done by checking the state of the RxRDY bit. On detecting a receiver ready condition, the CPU could then input the data received into the accumulator. The implementation of this process is very similar to the CONOUT subroutine and is shown in Figure 7-26. The subroutine shown in Figure 7-26 is called the console input (CONIN) subroutine since its function is to input a character from the console. The character received from the console is returned to the calling program in the accumulator.

The CONIN subroutine works in a manner very similar to the conout subroutine. The first three instructions initiate a loop that causes the CPU to wait until the receiver of the serial port has completely shifted in a character over the RxD line. Notice that the ANI 02H instruction now masks out bit position

```
CONOUT:   IN    03H       ; Get status word
          ANI   01H       ; See if transmitter ready
          JZ    CONOUT    ; Wait till ready
          MOV   A,C       ; Else get data to be transmitted
          OUT   02H       ; Send to serial port
          RET
```

FIGURE 7-25. Console output subroutine.

```
CONIN:  IN   03H      ; Get status word
        ANI  02H      ; See if receiver ready
        JZ   CONIN    ; Wait till ready
        IN   02H      ; Else get char from serial port
        RET
```

FIGURE 7-26. Console input subroutine.

1 (RxRDY) of the status word. Once a receiver ready (RxRDY) condition is detected by the CPU, it executes the IN 02H instruction, which results in the latching of the "received data" into the accumulator.

Notice in the CONIN subroutine of Figure 7-26 that if the console did not transmit a character, the CPU would be in an infinite loop with no means of exit. Thus the only way the CPU could exit the loop created by the first three instructions would be through the detection of a character received by the serial port. In some cases it would be useful to have a subroutine that simply sampled the receiver status and returned a flag that indicated the state of the receiver (ready or not ready). This type of subroutine is known as a console status (CONSTS) subroutine and is shown in Figure 7-27.

The CONSTS subroutine in Figure 7-27 sets the accumulator to 00H if the receiver is not ready (the console has not transmitted a character) and to FFH if the receiver is ready (the console has transmitted a character). The calling program can then check the contents of the accumulator to determine if a character was or was not received by the serial port. This eliminates the possibility of the CPU remaining in a continuous loop in the event that no data was transmitted by the console. Thus if it were required to transmit a character to the console, the following instructions could be used:

(Set register C to the character
to be transmitted to the console)

CALL CONOUT

Similarly, to input a received character:

CALL CONIN

(Register A contains the character
received from the console)

To determine if a character was received from the console:

CALL CONSTS

(Register A contains 00 if no character
received, FF if received

The three subroutines discussed in this section—CONOUT, CONIN, and CONSTS—are known as *utility subroutines* and their applications will be seen in later chapters.

```
CONSTS:  IN   03H      ; Get status word
         ANI  02H      ; See if receiver ready
         RZ            ; Reg A = 00 if not ready
         MVI  A,0FFH   ; Else Reg A = FF if ready
         RET
```

FIGURE 7-27. Console status subroutine.

7-9 SERIAL DATA TRANSMISSION FORMAT

In the preceding section it was seen that the serial port operates in a manner very similar to a shift register. The serial port will usually have two shift registers: one to shift data from the RxD line into the serial port (*receiver shift register*), and one to shift data out of the serial port onto the TxD line (*transmitter shift register*). Both the receiver and transmitter shift registers must therefore have a clock that will cause each bit of a character to be shifted into or out of the serial port at a predetermined transition of the clock pulse. The frequency of the clock will also determine the rate at which serial data is transmitted and received over the TxD and RxD lines of the serial port. Figure 7-28 shows the serial interface of Figure 7-23 with the *transmitter clock* ($\overline{TxC}$) and *receiver clock* ($\overline{RxC}$) added to the serial port.

The transmitter clock ($\overline{TxC}$) shown in Figure 7-28 is used to shift data out of the serial port; each bit is shifted over the TxD line on the *falling edge* of the clock. The frequency of the signal on $\overline{TxC}$ will also determine the rate (speed) at which data is transmitted over the TxD line. Similarly, the receiver clock ($\overline{RxC}$) is used to shift data into the serial port from the RxD line; each bit is sampled on the RxD line on the *rising edge* of the clock. The frequency of the receiver clock will determine the rate at which data is shifted into the serial port. Notice in Figure 7-28 that the $\overline{TxC}$ and $\overline{RxC}$ lines are tied together and connected to a common clock. In most cases the serial port transmits and receives data at the same rate, and hence a common clock is provided for the

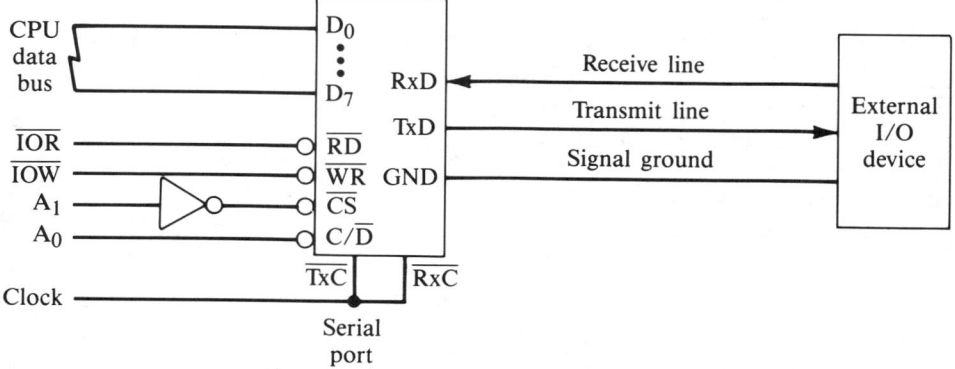

FIGURE 7-28. Serial data link with transmitter and receiver clocks.

transmitter and receiver shift registers. To illustrate the manner in which a serial bit stream is transmitted and received by the serial port, assume that the TxD and RxD lines of the serial port are connected together; now whatever data is transmitted over TxD is also received over RxD. Figure 7-29 shows the transmission of an 8-bit character (10101010) over the TxD line and its reception over the RxD line.

Referring to Figure 7-29, notice that the TxD line is held high until the falling edge of $\overline{TxC}$ causes a transition of the TxD line from a high to a low state. This transition is called the *start bit,* which when detected by the receiver causes the RxD line to be sampled at the rising edge of RxC. As each bit is transmitted over the TxD line on the falling edge of TxC, it is sampled over the RxD line on the rising edge of $\overline{RxC}$. This causes the receiver to sample data at approximately the midpoint of each bit transmitted. When all 8 bits have been transmitted, the TxD line returns to the high state, indicating the end of data transmission (the *stop bit*).

Since data is shifted in and out of the serial port at a particular edge of a clock pulse (rising or falling), the frequency of the clock attached to $\overline{RxC}$ and $\overline{TxC}$ will be equal to the rate at which each bit is shifted in or out of the serial port. This rate of serial data transfer therefore has the units of bits per second and is called the *baud rate*. For example, if the frequency of the clock attached to $\overline{TxC}$ and $\overline{RxC}$ was 9600 Hz, data would be transmitted and received at a rate of 9600 bits per second or 9600 baud.

At this point it is important to note that if the serial port is transmitting data to the external I/O device at a particular baud rate, the external I/O device must receive that data at the same rate to avoid any sampling errors. Similarly, if the external I/O device transmitted data at a particular baud rate, the serial port must receive the data at the same rate. Since data is sampled by the receive line (of both the serial port and the external I/O device) at the midpoint of each bit transmitted, a slight variation (about 2% maximum) between the I/O device's clock and the serial port's clock would not pose a serious problem.

The type of serial data transmission discussed in this section is known as *asynchronous data transmission*, since both the serial port and the external I/O device have separate clocks (synchronized only by the detection of the start and

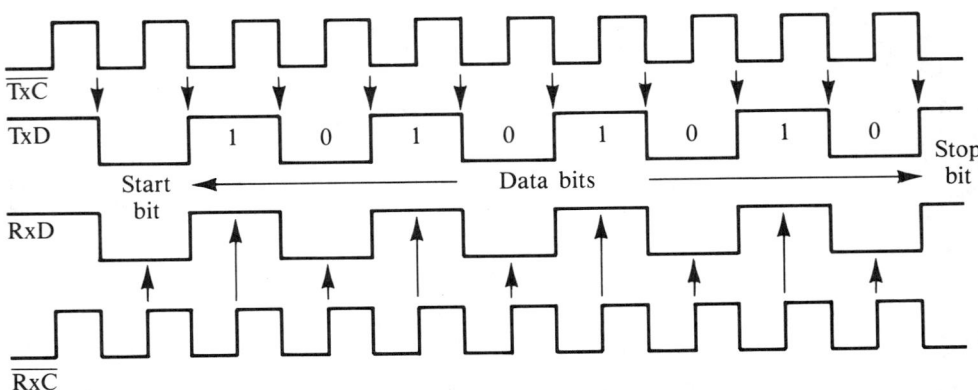

FIGURE 7-29. Transmission and reception of serial data.

stop bits) for transferring data; no synchronizing clock is transmitted with the serial data (as in synchronous data transmission).

Just as the serial port and the external I/O device had to operate at the same baud rate, they must also be conditioned to operate with a certain protocol. A *protocol* is a formal set of conventions governing the format of message exchange between two communicating processes. In this particular case, the protocol identifies the "formalities" of data communications, specifically:

1. Number of data bits transferred.
2. Type of parity used during transmission.
3. Number of stop bits used at the end of transmission.
4. Definition of logic voltage levels.

Most serial ports and external I/O devices have the capability to transmit data in groups of 5, 6, 7, or 8 data bits. The number of data bits transferred would depend on the type of data being transferred. For example, if a serial port and an external I/O device communicated with each other using the ASCII code, the number of data bits transferred would be seven, since ASCII is a 7-bit code. Similarly, communications using the EBCDIC code would require 8 data bits. Again, it is important that both devices communicate in the same code (and consequently with the same number of data bits) to avoid errors.

When data bits are transferred from one serial device to another, it is sometimes useful to have a mechanism to check to see if all data bits have been transmitted properly. Most serial devices use an automatic *parity check* on the data bits being transferred. These serial devices can be programmed to check for even parity, odd parity, or no parity check. For example, assume that two serial devices communicate with each other using the 7-bit ASCII code (refer to Appendix B) with even parity. Now if the ASCII character 'V' (1010110,56H) were to be transmitted by a serial port, it would be shifted over a serial line one bit at a time, starting with the least significant bit. After transmission of the most significant bit, the serial port would transmit one more bit, the *parity bit*. Since the ASCII character 'V' has even parity (i.e., the number of 1 bits is even, 4), the parity bit transmitted will be zero to keep the total number of 1's transmitted to an even number. The device receiving the serial 8-bit character would automatically count the number of 1 bits transmitted. If the number of 1 bits counted was even, the transmission would be considered successful. If during transmission a 1 bit was gained or lost, the count would yield an odd number that would indicate a transmission error (*parity error*). As before, it is important that both serial devices conduct the same parity checks. If the transmitting device transmits data with even parity, the receiving device must check for even parity. Similarly, if odd parity checking is done by the receiving device, the transmitting device must transmit data with odd parity.

As mentioned before, the stop bit indicates the end of data transmission. The stop bit is simply used to "space" out multiple transmissions of data and to allow the receiver to detect the start of the next character transmitted. The number of stop bits transmitted can be 1, $1\frac{1}{2}$, or 2. As will be seen later, the number of stop bits received is not important as long as it is at least one.

Since serial data is often transmitted over fairly long distances, TTL logic

7-9 SERIAL DATA TRANSMISSION FORMAT

levels are very rarely used to represent a logic 1 and a logic 0. This is because of the low-noise-margin characteristic of TTL signals. To overcome this problem and to provide a higher noise immunity during the transfer of serial data, the RS232C logic voltage levels are used to represent bits of information. In the RS232C specification, data signals are considered as *marking* (logic 1) when they are at a negative voltage, and *spacing* (logic 0) when positive. A negative voltage in the range -3.0 to -15 V indicates a mark condition, and a positive voltage in the range $+3.0$ to $+15$ V indicates a space condition. A signal in the range $+3.0$ to -3.0 V is said to be in the *transition region* in which the logic level is undefined. Thus there usually is a hardware interface between two serial communicating devices that converts TTL logic levels to RS232C, and vice versa, in order to maintain standardization between serial communicating devices.

The number of data bits, stop bits, and the type of parity checking done in serial data transmissions set up the protocol of data transfer. Figure 7-30 illustrates the transmission of serial data for the following protocol: 7 data bits, even parity, 2 stop bits. Figure 7-30 shows the ASCII character 'V' transmitted by an external I/O device with the protocol previously specified. The character is received by the serial port by sampling the RxD line at the midpoint of each bit transmitted.

The high-to-low transition of the RxD line triggers the beginning of the start bit and causes the receiver clock to begin sampling data on the RxD line. The receiver checks the validity of the start bit by sampling its value at its midpoint. If it is still zero, it is a valid start bit. Once a valid start bit is detected, the receiver then starts a *bit counter* to count the number of data bits that follow. Each data bit is sampled at its approximate midpoint, and shifted into the receiver. After 8 bits have been shifted in (7 data bits, 1 parity bit) the receiver then checks the parity of the data received. If the parity is even, it assumes that data was transmitted successfully. If the parity is odd, the receiver signals an error condition (to be seen later). After 8 bits have been shifted in, the RxD line stays high for two clock periods (2 stop bits). The receiver samples the RxD line for stop-bit detection. If the line is low, an invalid stop bit is detected, indicating an error in the serial data transmission (a *framing error*). Notice that the receiver will sample the stop bits only once regardless of the number of stop bits transmitted. After the stop bits are detected, the RxD line returns to the high state in preparation for the next data transmission.

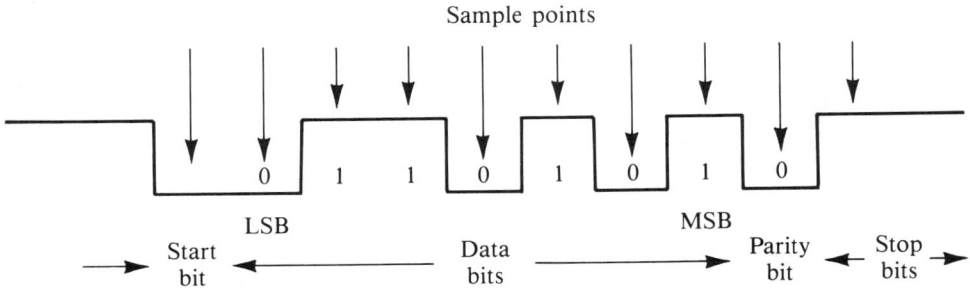

FIGURE 7-30. Transmission of the ASCII character 'V'.

Observe that both serial communicating devices must conform to the same protocol and baud rate. If both devices did not operate at exactly the same baud rate and with the same serial protocol, data transfers would be completely unsynchronized and would consequently lead to transmission errors. Both serial devices, the serial port and the external I/O device, must therefore be set at the same baud rate, and be "programmed" to operate with the same protocol. Setting the same baud rate for both devices can easily be done by providing the same clock frequency at the $\overline{\text{TxC}}$ and $\overline{\text{RxC}}$ inputs of the serial port and the external I/O device. Most external I/O devices such as video terminals and printers have a set of switches to set the baud rate and transmission protocol. The serial port usually can be programmed to operate at a predefined protocol.

Recall from Figure 7-23 that the $C/\overline{D}$ line of the serial port was used to input status information to the CPU. This was done by setting the $C/\overline{D}$ line to a logic high and then executing an IN instruction (so that the $\overline{\text{RD}}$ line would be activated). What if the $C/\overline{D}$ line were set to a logic high and an OUT instruction were executed by the CPU? The OUT instruction (OUT 03H in this case) would cause the $C/\overline{D}$ line to stay high, the $\overline{\text{WR}}$ line and $\overline{\text{CS}}$ line to stay low (activated), and thus cause the contents of the accumulator to be sent to the serial port. Since the $C/\overline{D}$ line is high, the data sent to the serial port would not be transmitted over the TxD line but would be interpreted by the serial port as an instruction. This instruction could now be used by the CPU to dictate the protocol of data transmission to the serial port. This instruction is called the *mode instruction* and will be discussed in the next section.

7-10

THE 8251 USART

The serial port discussed in Sections 7-8 and 7-9 is a commercially available chip known as the 8251 *universal synchronous/asynchronous receiver/transmitter* (USART or UART). The 8251 is capable of both synchronous and asynchronous serial data transmission; however, this section will deal only with the asynchronous operation of the 8251. All the information pertaining to the serial port discussed in previous sections is applicable to the 8251. The 8251 is capable of very sophisticated forms of serial data communications; however, this section will discuss only the elementary concepts needed for a very simple serial interface.

Figure 7-31 shows the pin configuration and architectural block diagram of the 8251 USART. In the figure, notice that two sections of the 8251, the data bus buffer and the read/write control logic section, will provide the interface between the CPU and the 8251. The data bus buffer has eight data lines (D_0–D_7) that connect to the CPU's data bus and contains an 8-bit "holding" register for received data, status information, data to be transmitted, and control information (to be seen later). The read/write control logic section controls the flow of data within the 8251. The reset input to this section is used to reset all the registers and flags within the 8251 and is normally connected to the reset signal of the CPU. The CLK input to this section is used to generate the internal timing of the 8251 and is normally connected to the φ_2 (TTL) clock pulse of the 8224

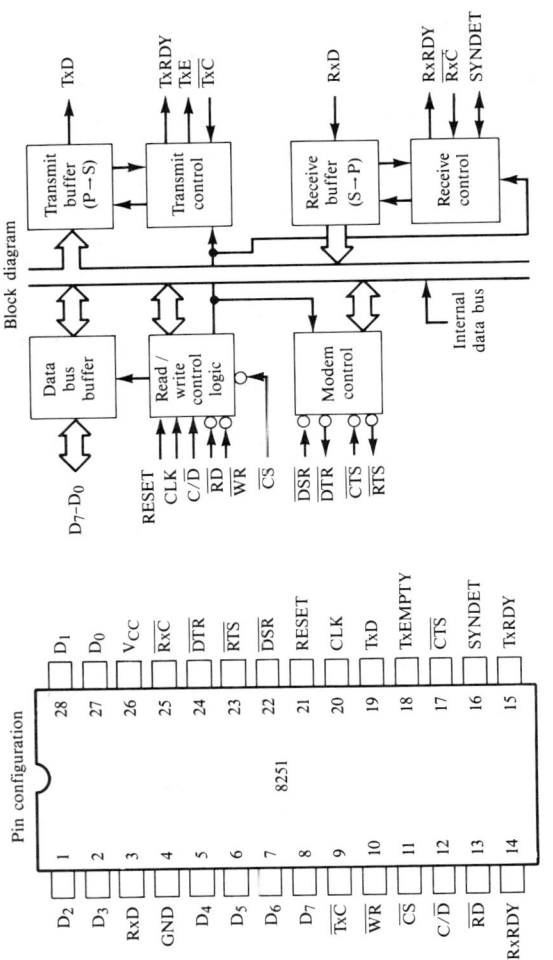

FIGURE 7-31. 8251 pin configuration and block diagram. (Courtesy of Intel Corp.)

236 PROGRAMMABLE CHIPS: PARALLEL AND SERIAL I/O

TABLE 7-6. Basic Operations of the 8251

C/$\overline{\text{D}}$	$\overline{\text{RD}}$	$\overline{\text{WR}}$	$\overline{\text{CS}}$	Function	Operation
0	0	1	0	RxD data loaded on data bus	1
0	1	0	0	Data bus data to TxD line	2
1	0	1	0	Status word loaded on data bus	3
1	1	0	0	Control instruction to 8251	4
X	1	1	0	No operation	
X	X	X	1	No operation	

clock generator. The C/$\overline{\text{D}}$, $\overline{\text{RD}}$, $\overline{\text{WR}}$, and $\overline{\text{CS}}$ inputs to this section provide the same functions as described in Sections 7-8 and 7-9. Table 7-6 illustrates the logic functions of these four inputs, and will be used to describe the internal operation of the 8251. With reference to Table 7-6, notice that the 8251 is capable of four basic read/write operations; these operations are numbered in order after the description of each operation. Each operation of the 8251 will be discussed with reference to the block diagram shown in Figure 7-31.

Operation 1. Assuming that an external I/O device has transmitted serial data over the 8251's RxD line, the serial data is then assembled into a parallel word in the receive buffer. The receive control then causes the RxRDY bit of the status word to be set, and also sets the RxRDY line to a logic 1. If the four control lines shown in Table 7-6 are conditioned for the first operation then, this received data is transferred from the receive buffer to the data bus buffer, and onto the CPU's data bus.

Operation 2. With the four R/W control pins conditioned for operation 2, the contents of the CPU's data bus is loaded into the data bus buffer, and transferred to the transmit buffer. The transmit buffer shifts the data out over the TxD line to the externally connected I/O device. When the entire character has been serially transmitted, the transmit control unit sets the TxRDY bit of the STATUS WORD, and also sets the TxRDY output of the 8251 to a logic 1.

Note that the TxRDY and RxRDY output pins of the 8251 signal the same condition as the TxRDY and RxRDY bits of the status word. The TxRDY and RxRDY output pins are provided for interrupt-driven applications. As discussed before, the $\overline{\text{RxC}}$ and $\overline{\text{TxC}}$ inputs to the receive and transmit control units, respectively, provide the baud rate for serial data transmission.

Operation 3. In this mode of operation, 8251 status information is loaded from the data bus buffer onto the CPU's data bus. As discussed before, the status word is an 8-bit word that supplies the status of the 8251's transmitter and receiver. The 8251 status word also provides other information, as shown in Figure 7-32. Notice in Figure 7-32 that the status word can provide more than receiver and transmitter status. It also provides status on error conditions that may have occurred during the transmission on reception of serial data as well as status information on synchronous transmissions. The status word pro-

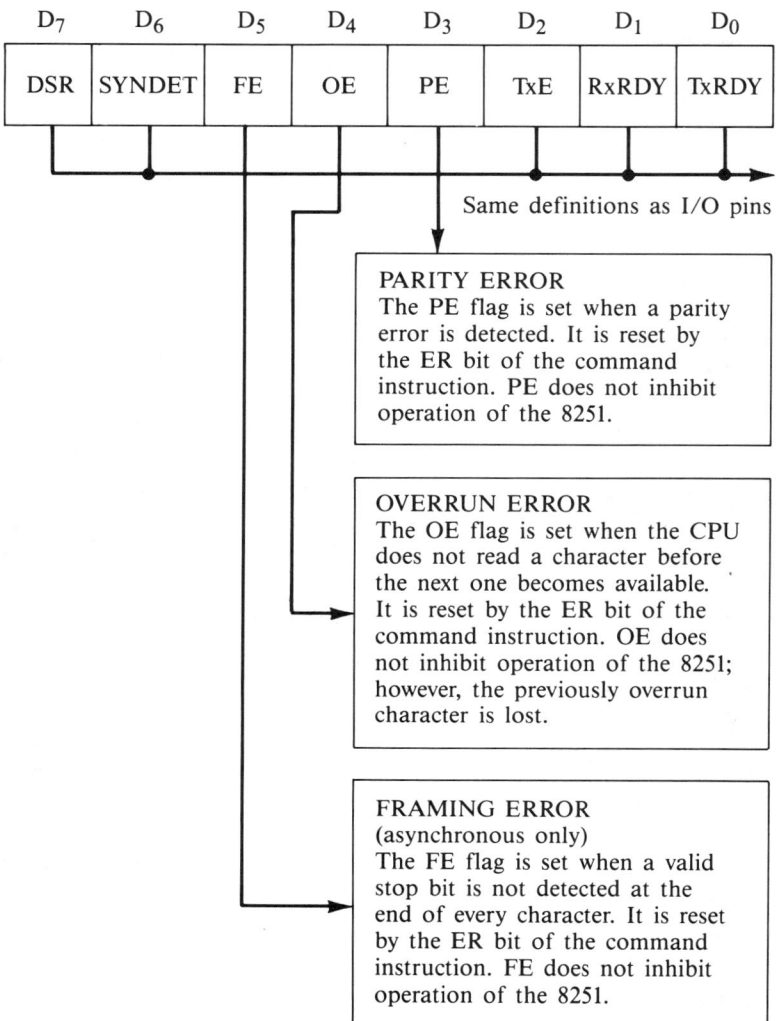

FIGURE 7-32. 8251 status read format. (Courtesy of Intel Corp.)

vided by the 8251 can be used with the CONOUT, CONIN, and CONSTS subroutines (Section 7-8) to check transmitter and receiver status before data is sent or received via the 8251.

Operation 4. In this mode of operation, the 8251 can be programmed to operate at different protocols of serial data transmission. In this mode, the CPU must send two instructions to the 8251, the mode instruction and the command instruction. The format for the mode instruction is shown in Figure 7-33.

The CPU must send the mode instruction to the 8251 whenever the CPU (and consequently the 8251) is reset. The mode instruction specifies which mode of operation the 8251 is to operate at, synchronous or asynchronous, and if asyn-

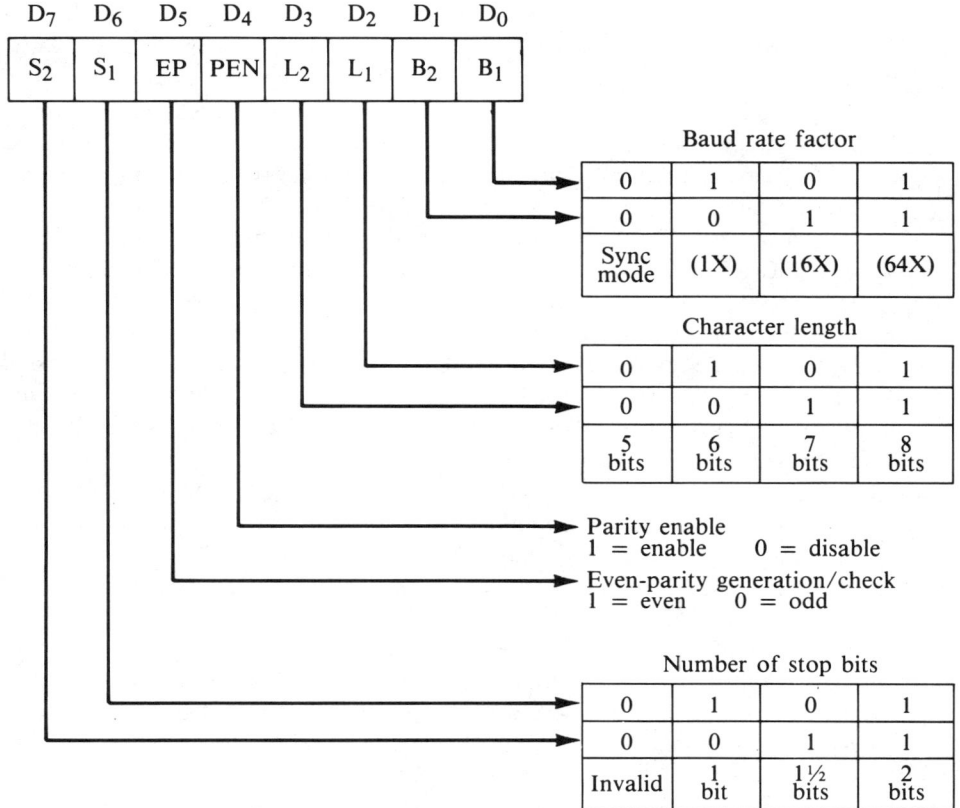

FIGURE 7-33. 8251 asynchronous mode instruction format. (Courtesy of Intel Corp.)

chronous, the format of serial data transmission (protocol). Thus with reference to Figure 7-33, if it were required to program the 8251 as follows:

Asynchronous mode
Seven data bits
Even-parity check
Two stop bits

the mode instruction 11111001 (F9H) would accomplish the task. Once the mode instruction is sent to the 8251 by the CPU via an OUT instruction, the 8251 maintains the same specified protocol until it is reset.

Notice that the first 2 bits of the mode instruction specify a baud-rate factor. This baud-rate factor sets up an internal divider to divide the $\overline{RxC}$ and $\overline{TxC}$ frequencies by the specified factor: $\times 1$, $\times 16$, or $\times 64$. For example, if a baud-rate factor of $\times 1$ was specified, the frequency required at the $\overline{TxC}$ and $\overline{RxC}$ inputs of the 8251 would have to be 9600 Hz for a baud rate of 9600 baud. If a baud-rate factor of × 16 was specified, the frequency at $\overline{\text{TxC}}$ and $\overline{\text{RxC}}$ for 9600-baud operation would have to be 9600 × 16 = 153.6 kHz. Similarly, for a specified baud rate factor of × 64, the frequency at $\overline{\text{TxC}}$ and $\overline{\text{RxC}}$ for 9600-baud operation would have to be 9600 × 64 = 614.4 kHz. The reason for providing this facility in the 8251 is that in many cases the $\overline{\text{TxC}}$ and $\overline{\text{RxC}}$ clock frequencies are obtained from the 8224 oscillator output. Since this frequency has to be divided many times to obtain the desired baud rate, the 8251 has an internal divider that is capable of dividing the input frequency of $\overline{\text{TxC}}$ and $\overline{\text{RxC}}$ by a maximum of 64. This helps eliminate a lot of external circuitry that would otherwise be required.

After the mode instruction is received by the 8251, the CPU can issue another instruction, the *command instruction*. Unlike the mode instruction, the command instruction can be issued to the 8251 any time during its operation. The command instruction provides other facilities for controlling the operation of the 8251 and its format is shown in Figure 7-34.

With reference to Figure 7-34, bit positions 0 (TxEN) and 2 (RxE) enable the transmitter and receiver sections of the 8251, respectively. These bits must be set to a logic 1 in the command instruction if the 8251 is to receive and transmit serial data. Bit position 4 (ER) can be used to reset the error flags of the status word in the event that an error condition occurred during serial data transmission. Bit position 3 (SBRK) is used to interrupt data transmission over the TxD line by forcing it to a logic 0. Finally, bit position 6 (IR) is used to generate an internal reset to the 8251. This allows the 8251 to accept another mode instruction without having to provide a physical hardware reset to the CPU. The other bits in the command instruction are used in the synchronous mode, and for more sophisticated handshaking techniques. Thus the basic command instruction required for normal operation of the 8251 would be 00010101 (15H).

Assuming that the 8251 is connected to the CPU as shown in Figure 7-28, the following sequence of instructions could be used to program the 8251 for subsequent serial data transmissions:

```
MVI   A,0F9H    ; Mode instruction
OUT   03H       ; To 8251 control port
MVI   A,15H     ; Command instruction
OUT   03H       ; To 8251 control port
```

Assuming that the 8251 has been reset (externally or internally), the first two instructions supply the mode instruction to the 8251, and the next two instructions supply the command instruction to the 8251.

Figure 7-35 illustrates the complete interface between the 8251, the CPU, and an external serial I/O device. The circuit in Figure 7-35 is basically an extension of Figure 7-28 and includes the support circuitry for a basic serial interface. Notice in Figure 7-35 that a baud-rate generator has been added to supply the clocks for the $\overline{\text{TxC}}$ and $\overline{\text{RxC}}$ inputs to the 8251. This baud-rate generator can be a simple arrangement of dividers to divide the 8224 clock frequency down to the appropriate value, or it can be a separate square-wave oscillator. Also, the TxD and RxD lines to the 8251 require an interface to

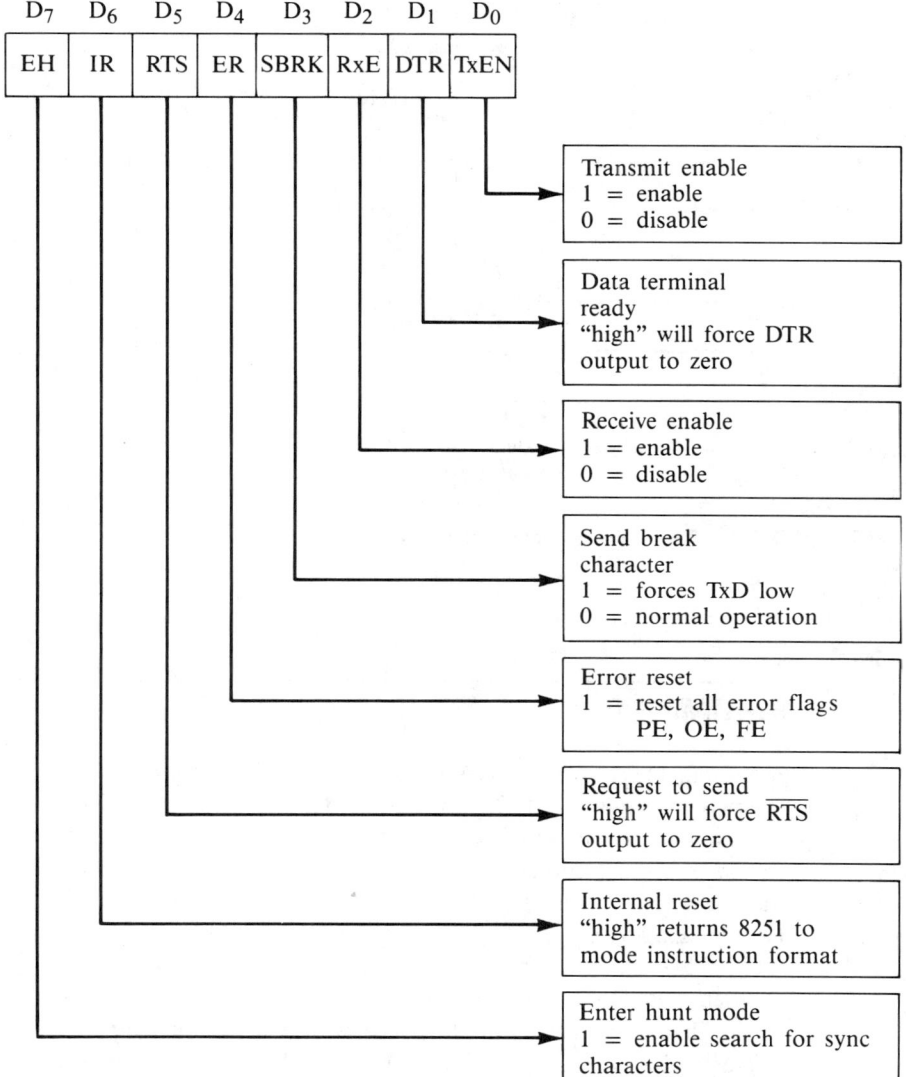

FIGURE 7-34. 8251 command instruction format. (Courtesy of Intel Corp.)

convert the TTL logic levels of the TxD and RxD lines to an RS232C voltage level.

The preceding four sections have discussed a basic serial asynchronous interface between the CPU and an external I/O device via the 8251 serial port. As mentioned before, the 8251 is a device capable of more sophisticated serial data communications in the synchronous mode, and is also capable of being connected to other I/O devices that require extensive handshaking. Even though these topics are beyond the scope of this chapter, a basic understanding of the concepts of serial data communications should allow the reader to experiment with other types of serial data interfaces.

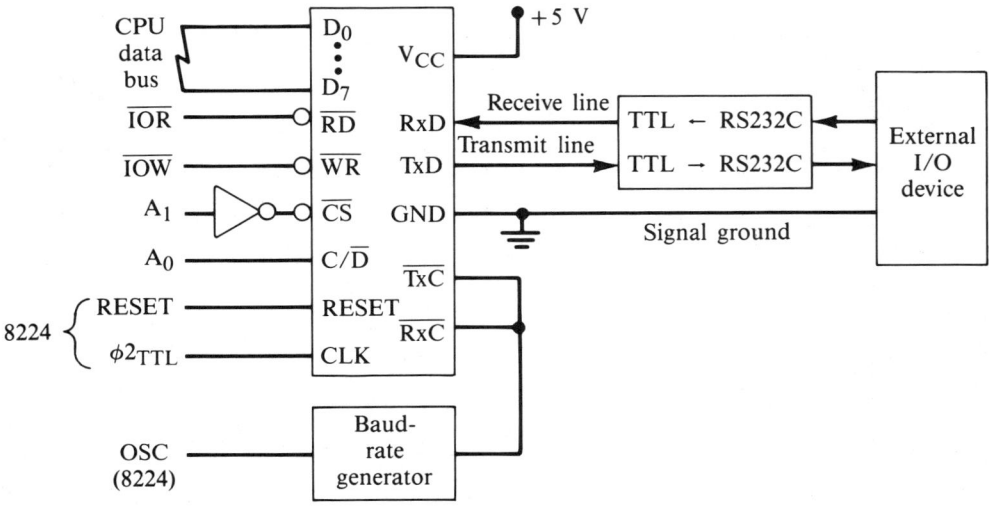

FIGURE 7-35. 8251 serial port interface.

7-11

SUMMARY

Programmable chips have become very common in microprocessor applications. The two programmable I/O chips discussed in this chapter have illustrated some of these applications. The main advantage of having programmable chips in a system is in their ability to free the CPU from conducting trivial tasks. Programmable chips also simplify the software and the hardware interface between the CPU and an external I/O device. These programmable chips are often thought of as being "dedicated processors" designed to perform a particular task without elaborate intervention from the main processor.

This chapter has dealt with the concepts of operation and applications of two programmable I/O chips, the 8251 and the 8255. There does exist a variety of other programmable chips dedicated to perform other functions for disk controlling, arithmetic processing, DMA/interrupt controlling, and so on. The concepts developed in this chapter can be applicable to almost any type of programmable chip.

REVIEW QUESTIONS AND PROBLEMS

1. Using the architecture of Figure 7-1, explain in a general sense how programmable chips function.

2. Give a brief explanation of each pin (or pin grouping) listed in the table of Figure 7-3.

3. Determine the control word for:
   (a) Port A to be mode 0 input port with Port B serving as a mode 1 output port. Port C is to be an input port.
   (b) Port A to operate in a mode 2 fashion with Ports B and C as mode 0 output ports.

4. Explain the various functions of pins PC_7–PC_0 for each mode of operation.

5. In detail explain handshaking relative to an 8255 port. Give specific examples of pins involved for both input and output.

6. Explain the timing diagram of Figure 7-7(b).

7. For a mode 1 operation there are two control words that must be programmed into the 8255. Explain the purpose of each control word.

8. Use an 8255 to replace the row-scan latch and column latch of Figure 6-6. Provide a narrative explaining your design.

9. Modify the program of Figure 6-18 to accommodate the hardware modification of Problem 8.

10. Using an 8255, add three I/O ports to the system of Figure 4-7. Ports A and B are to be output ports, and port C is to function as an input port (mode 0). Write appropriate instructions to program the 8255 and programs to service the ports.

11. Discuss the advantages and disadvantages of serial versus parallel data communications.

12. What is the difference between half-duplex and full-duplex data communications?

13. What is the main reason for having a status readback feature in a serial port? How does the $C/\overline{D}$ line accomplish this?

14. A serial port has the RxRDY bit at position 6 and the TxRDY bit at position 2 (refer to Figure 7-23). A logic 1 indicates a not-ready condition and a logic 0 indicates a ready condition. Develop the CONIN, CONOUT, and CONSTS subroutines for the port. Assume that the data port is 10H and that the status port is 11H.

15. What is the baud rate? What is the purpose of the baud-rate factor provided by the 8251? Why must two serial devices communicate at the same baud rate?

16. What factors set up a serial data protocol? Discuss each factor. Why must two serial devices communicate with the same protocol?

17. Draw a timing diagram of the transmission of the ASCII character 'W', with odd parity and 2 stop bits. Repeat with even parity.

18. Describe the four operations of the 8251 USART.

19. Program the 8251 USART for the following protocol: 7 data bits, odd parity, 1 stop bit, ×1 baud-rate factor.

CHAPTER 8

Software Development: Techniques and Tools

8-1

INTRODUCTION

In almost every application of computers, whether they be micros, minis, or mainframes, the role of software development and related techniques is becoming exceedingly important. The objective of a computer's software is to make the hardware perform specified tasks. These tasks range from simple events such as monitoring lights and switches to more sophisticated tasks such as time sharing and data processing. As the tasks to be performed by the computer increase in complexity, so does the software; this leads to an insatiable demand for software development "tools" that can be used as an aid in program design.

Software development tools cannot be used efficiently without an understanding of the proper techniques. Just as one finds it difficult to tune the engine of an automobile without understanding how the electrical system works, in software development it is difficult to design efficient programs without having a good idea of the various techniques available. By using the proper techniques in designing a computer program, it is often easier to pick the appropriate software development tool that will lead to the generation of memory and speed-efficient program code.

The software development process can be broken down into five steps, from a definition of the problem to the final implementation of the computer program. In many cases these steps can be combined or further broken down to suit the problem at hand. The following steps should, however, serve as a guide to the development of typical application programs.

1. *Problem recognition:* Before a solution can be found to a problem, the programmer must determine if the problem can best be solved by means of a computer program. All problems cannot be solved by a computer, and in many cases a computer "solution" to a problem may even complicate matters further. This phase is thus a screening process that is used to recognize the existence of a problem, define the problem, and then determine if the problem is best solved by a computer.

2. *Determining a method:* Once the problem has been screened and it has been deemed suitable for solution by a computer, the next phase involves a search for the best method of solution (algorithm) to the problem. At this stage, the programmer must examine all the alternatives and select the method that is most efficient and economical. This stage not only involves a selection of the best algorithm to solve the problem but also involves a selection of the best programming language to fit the algorithm.

3. *Implementing the method:* The method of solution to the problem is usually broken down into one or more flowcharts or flow diagrams. These diagrams provide an explicit description of each stage in the implementation of the solution, and take into consideration the logic used in the method of solution. Flowcharts also allow the programmer to structure the solution in a logical manner, thus making it much easier to follow during program development and testing. Thus flowcharts make the solution to the problem more "computer oriented" than "human oriented."

4. *Coding from the flowchart:* The flowchart often provides a clear picture of the solution to the problem from the programming viewpoint. The process of translating a flowchart to a program is therefore much easier than if the program were to be constructed without a flowchart. The coding phase is simply a process where a sequence of instructions to the computer is used to satisfy the logic of the flow diagram. This phase involves the actual implementation of the solution to the problem—the development of the program.

5. *Testing and debugging:* After the program has been completely implemented, it must be checked for correctness. During this phase, existing flaws as well as potential flaws in the program may be revealed. These flaws could exist in the algorithms that make up the program or could be due to logical errors in the flowchart or possibly due to syntax errors made during the program implementation phase. The testing of a program thus involves exercising the program's execution, exposing hidden flaws, and correcting these flaws. The process of finding hidden flaws in a program is known as *debugging* and often a programmer uses various tools to aid in the debugging process.

In the five phases of software development, the programmer must develop the right techniques for efficient program design and must have the right tools available for efficient implementation, testing, and debugging of the program. This chapter is intended to introduce the reader to the various types of software development techniques and tools available for efficient program design. Three of the most important programming techniques described are algorithms, flowcharts, and program structure. These techniques will serve as the foundation in the development of computer programs. Next, the chapter surveys some of the more common tools available for software development, such as assemblers, compilers, interpreters, monitors, simulators, and operating systems. Following chapters will detail the software development tools introduced in this chapter. After going through this chapter, the reader should have a fairly good understanding of the approach to software design, as well as a knowledge of the various options available.

8-2 ALGORITHMS AND FLOWCHARTS

An *algorithm* is a term used to describe a set of procedures by which a given result is obtained; it is therefore a method of solution. A *flowchart* is a graphical representation for the definition, analysis, or solution of a problem, in which symbols are used to represent various operations, such as processing, I/O, decisions, interrupts, and so on. Both algorithms and flowcharts allow programmers to work their way through the solution of a problem in an organized manner and visualize the potential and existing flaws in the solution. Creation of an algorithm and/or flowchart is usually the first step in the development of a computer program.

Consider the task of designing a program to move a block of data from one area of memory to another. The block move would have to be conducted on a byte-to-byte basis; in other words, a byte would have to be moved from the source block to the destination block repeatedly until the entire process was completed. A general-purpose algorithm for this example would be as follows:

Step 1. Get a data byte from the source block.
Step 2. Put the byte into the destination block.
Step 3. See if all bytes have been moved. If so, stop. Otherwise, go to step 1.

A more specific version of the same algorithm would be:

Step 1. Initialize a pointer to the starting address of the source block.
Step 2. Initialize a pointer to the starting address of the destination block.
Step 3. Initialize a count for the number of bytes to be moved.
Step 4. Get a byte from the source block.
Step 5. Put the byte into the destination block.
Step 6. Set the source pointer to the next byte.
Step 7. Set the destination pointer to the next byte.
Step 8. Subtract one from the count (decrement).
Step 9. Check the count. If the count is zero, stop. Otherwise, go to step 4.

Notice that in its first form, the algorithm could be implemented on almost any computer's instruction set. In other words, it was so generalized that it did not give specific details on how the move was to be performed. The second form was much more specific and implied the use of index registers. Thus the second form of the algorithm could be implemented only on a computer that had indexing capabilities. A third and final form of the same algorithm would narrow the solution down to the specific computer being used, as follows:

Step 1. Initialize RP H&L to the starting address of the source block.
Step 2. Initialize RP D&E to the starting address of the destination block.
Step 3. Initialize register B to the number of bytes to be moved.
Step 4. Move the data from the address specified by H&L to register A.
Step 5. Exchange the contents of RP H&L with D&E.
Step 6. Move the data from register A to the address specified by RP H&L.
Step 7. Exchange the contents of RP H&L with D&E.
Step 8. Increment the value of H&L.
Step 7. Increment the value of D&E.
Step 8. Decrement the value of register B.
Step 9. Check register B. If register B is zero, stop. Otherwise, go to step 4.

The final version of the algorithm is now so specific that it can be implemented only on an 8080/8085 (or compatible) microprocessor-based microcomputer. Also notice the relative ease of constructing a program once the algorithm has been written. The program to implement the following algorithm would be as follows:

```
        LXI  H,SOURCE   ; Source address to H&L
        LXI  D,DEST     ; Destination address to D&E
        MVI  B,COUNT    ; Reg B = Count
LOOP:   MOV  A,M        ; Get a source byte
        XCHG            ; Exchange pointers
        MOV  M,A        ; Put byte into destination
        XCHG            ; Exchange pointers
        INX  H          ; Point to next source byte
        INX  D          ; Point to next dest byte
        DCR  B          ; Count down
        JNZ  LOOP       ; Continue if not done
        HLT             ; Else, stop
```

A flowchart is a graphical technique of representing an algorithm. The first method used statements as steps in developing the solution to the problem; the flowchart uses symbols to describe the various steps to the solution. A list of the standard flowchart symbols is presented in Appendix C.

There are basically three types of flowcharts used to represent an algorithm. The first type is called a *general flowchart* (shown in Figure 8-1) and is used to describe the solution in a very general form. The second type is the *algorithmic-level flowchart* (Figure 8-2), which describes the solution in specific steps but is still generalized in terms of the actual instructions to be used. The third type is the *instruction-level flowchart* (Figure 8-3), which expands on each step of the solution process by including specific instructions. Obviously, it is easiest to construct a program from the instruction-level flowchart. At this stage it should be noted that even though the instruction-level flowchart greatly simplifies the implementation of a program, because it is so specific, it can become fairly complex when representing rather large programs. For this reason, instruction-level flowcharts are often eliminated during the development of fairly complex programs.

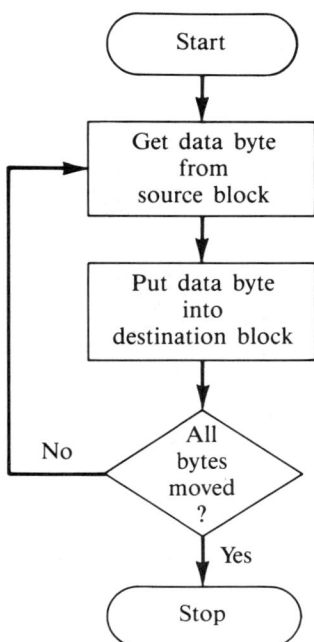

FIGURE 8-1. General flowchart for a block-move algorithm.

Notice that the flowcharts shown in Figures 8-1 through 8-3 correspond closely to the three algorithms described before. The difference lies in the graphic representation of the algorithmic steps and decisions that are apparent in the flowcharts. This graphic representation makes it easier for the programmer to "view" the "flow" of the program.

In developing algorithms before the program is constructed, one can see existing and potential flaws in the solution process since the steps in the algorithms are in plain English rather than in computer instructions. The logical process in developing a method of solution to a particular problem is to start off by a general-purpose algorithm, expand that to individual steps (algorithmic level), include specifics in each step (instructional level), and then write the program. Depending on the experience of the programmer, he or she may wish to skip one or more steps in the process. It should be remembered, however, that algorithms not only aid the programmer in designing a solution to a problem but aid greatly in documentation of the programmer's work. It is much easier for an observing person to read through algorithms before looking at the final program rather than trying to interpret the program directly. Also note that the comments in the final program correspond closely to the algorithms, thereby allowing one to understand easily how the program works.

The preceding example illustrated the use of algorithms for a typical assembly language program. It should be noted, however, that algorithms are not limited in their use for assembly language programs. As will be seen later, algorithms can also be used to develop higher-level programs and in many cases aid the programmer in deciding which programming language to use.

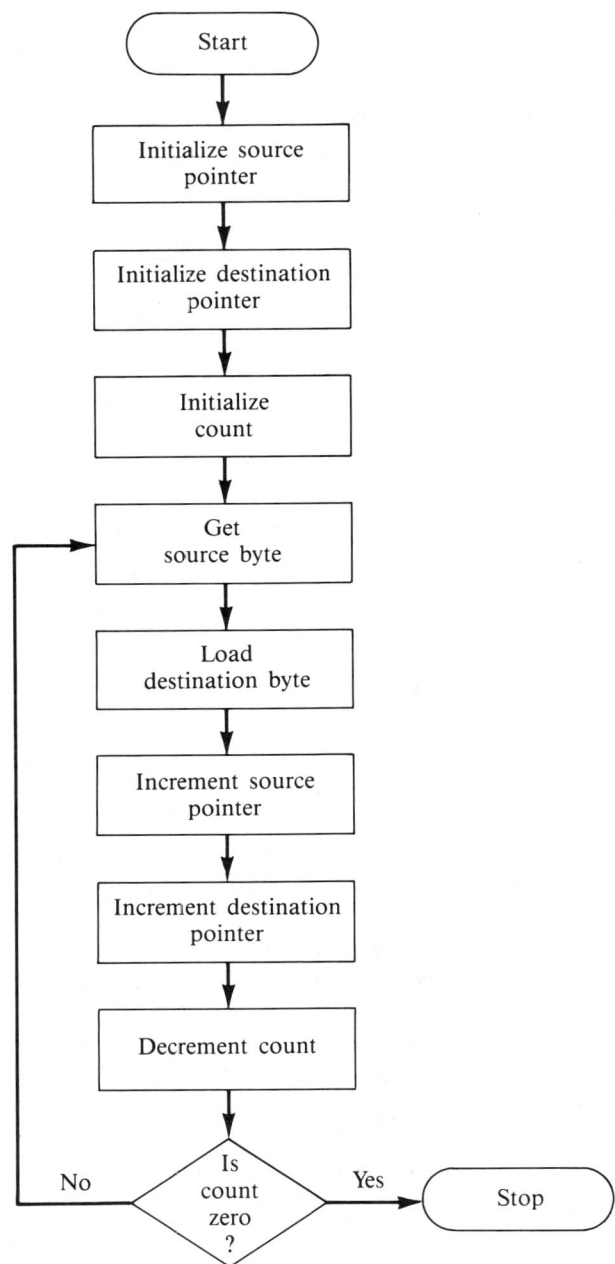

FIGURE 8-2. Algorithmic flowchart for a block-move algorithm.

8-3

STRUCTURE

In the approach to good program design known as *structured programming,* programs are designed hierarchically from the top down; that is, from the main

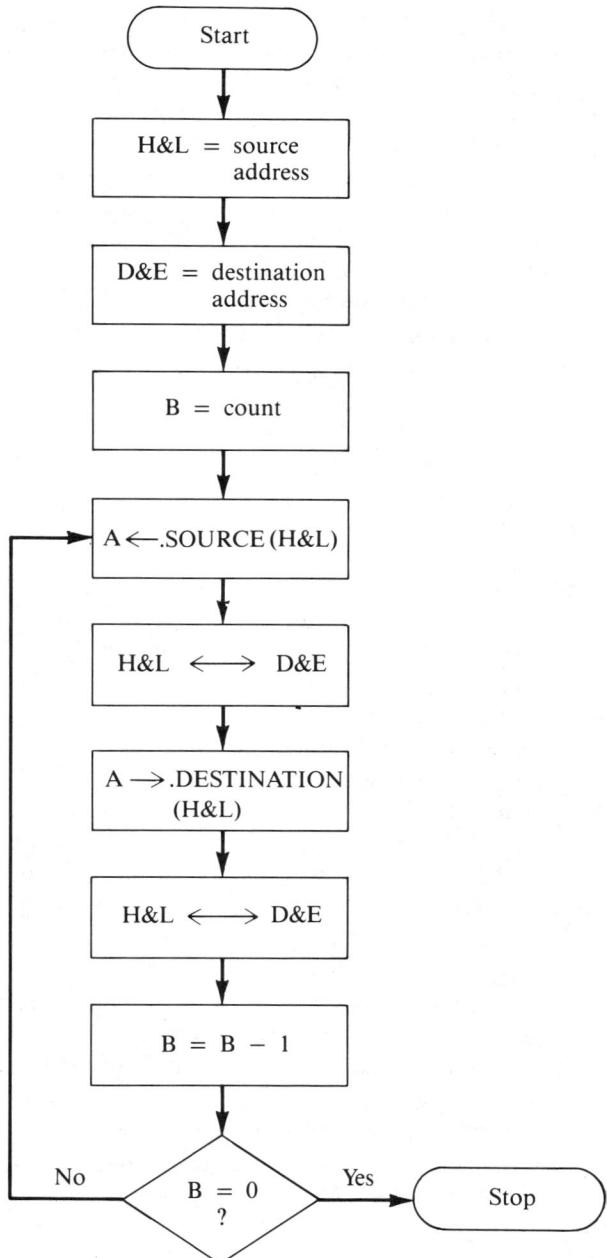

FIGURE 8-3. Instruction-level flowchart for a block-move algorithm.

program to the lowest-level subprograms. When done properly, the resulting algorithm structures are easy to understand, debug, and modify.

When a program is designed in a "top-down" manner, it is developed in a series of successive stages. The first stage, usually called the *main program,* implements the logic of the program at the top (highest) level. In this stage the details of program are usually ignored and only the flow of the program at the highest level is considered. Subsequent stages in the program are used to refine the description of the flow at the main program level by including the actual details. These stages may also reference lower-level stages for further refinement of the details. The hierarchical stages in the program are usually implemented as *subroutines,* each dedicated to performing a single task or series of tasks. The main program would then simply be a series of CALLS to lower-level subprograms.

For example, consider a program that is to read a list of data bytes from an input port, sort the data bytes in a predetermined order, and output the sorted data bytes one at a time to an output port. The main program to implement this specification could simply be a sequence of three CALL instructions:

```
CALL GET
CALL SORT
CALL PUT
```

Notice that the main program calls three lower-level subroutines: GET, SORT, and PUT in the right sequence. Also notice that the details of getting the data (GET), sorting the data (SORT), and outputting the data (PUT) are left out of the main program. The three subroutines would refine the specifications by including the actual code to perform the task.

The GET subroutine would read data from the input port into a sequence of memory locations. The GET subroutine could possibly call another lower-level subroutine to do the actual input from the hardware device. The SORT subroutine would then sort the data in the previously filled memory locations. Finally, the PUT subroutine would be called to output the sorted contents of the memory locations to the output device; as before, the actual output to the hardware device could be done by a calling a lower-level subroutine. The actual implementation of this specification will be presented in a subsequent chapter.

Notice that when a program is structured in a top-down hierarchical design, it is easier to view the flow of the program and easier to debug. Each level in the program can be tested and debugged independently, allowing for quicker diagnostic and development time. The lower-level subroutines can also be used over and over again in other application programs and often become utility subroutines. When an application program is designed using this structure, and the application program uses previously developed and tested utility subprograms, the application program is much easier to debug since problems usually lie at the top level, where the code is in its simplest form. The advantages of designing structured programs will be seen by examples in later chapters.

Another case of a structured program is a *menu-driven application.* For example, consider an application program that constantly monitors the data from a keyboard. Upon receiving the key value, a certain action is performed depending on the key value; the keyboard is then monitored again for another key. The following table illustrates the functions performed, depending on certain key values.

Key	Function
A	Turn on assembly line
B	Turn off assembly line
C	Turn on oven
D	Turn off oven
E	Turn on alarm
F	Turn off alarm
G	Display oven temperature
H	Display parts count

The program is said to be "menu-driven" because, depending on the selection of one key in the list of key values (menu), the program will perform an operation based on that selection. The general flowchart shown in Figure 8-4 represents the solution to the problem.

When actually implementing the algorithm, the program can be structured into one main program that monitors the value obtained from the keyboard and lower-level subroutines that implement the action to be performed when a particular command is received. On completion of each subroutine, control is returned to the main program. In Figure 8-4, the central octagon represents the main program, and each arrow emanating from the octagon represents a subroutine that would implement a certain action, depending on the key value obtained from the keyboard. If, for example, one of the specified functions does not work as intended, the problem is immediately narrowed down to the subroutine that implements that function. This eliminates the possibility of errors existing in other parts of the program.

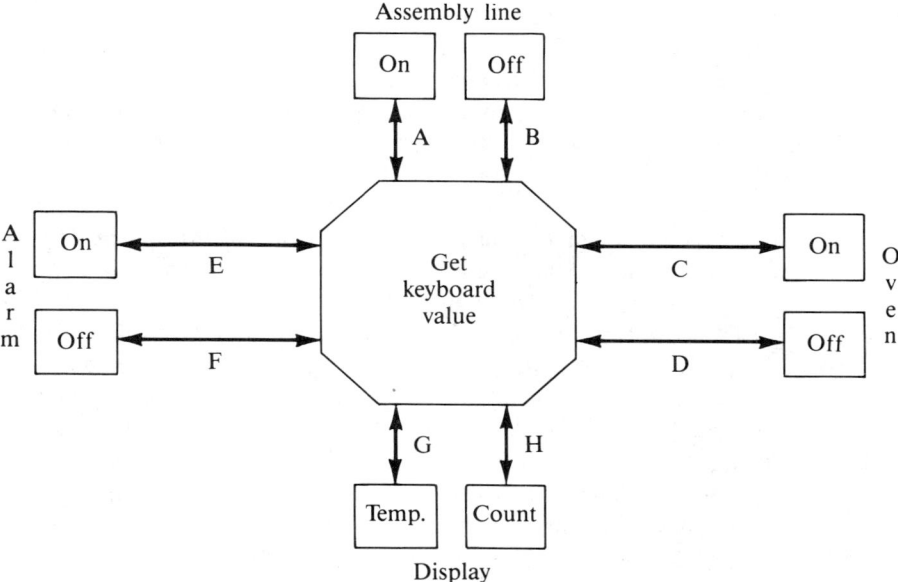

FIGURE 8-4. Menu-driven application program.

8-3 STRUCTURE

Clarity of program structure provides many benefits for the programmer. When the structure of the program reflects the structure of the underlying algorithm, the program immediately becomes easier to write, debug, modify, and understand. Note that a nicely designed algorithm may be completely obscured if the programmer forces it into an unnatural mold.

8-4 ASSEMBLERS

An *assembler* is one of the most powerful tools used in developing microcomputer instruction code. An assembler is a program that translates instruction mnemonics and symbols into machine code for execution by the microcomputer. Note that an assembler is a program and not a piece of hardware.

The input to the assembler could be a sequence of program instructions written in mnemonic form: for example, the block-move program discussed previously. The output of the assembler would be the sequence of bytes in binary machine code (represented in decimal, hexadecimal, or octal), which would represent the operation codes and operands of each instruction in the correct sequence, as well as the address at which each group of bytes resides.

The input to the assembler is referred to as the *source code* and the output of the assembler is referred to as the *object code*. The process by which the source code is translated into object code is called *assembly*. The software development tool that does the assembly is the assembler.

In previous examples, many programs were hand assembled. In other words, the program was written in mnemonics and then the machine code for each mnemonic was derived from a list supplied by the microprocessor manufacturer, and assembled into a sequence of machine instructions for execution by the processor. The obvious reason for using mnemonics in writing a program is that they are much easier to remember (hence the term "mnemonic") than the actual binary or hexadecimal representation of the machine code. For example, the instruction MOV A,M tells the programmer much more than does "01111110" or "7E."

Hand assembly is best suited for application programs that are fairly small and contain few program transfer instructions, such as JMPs and CALLs. However, when the size of the program is relatively large, hand assembly can become rather tedious and time-consuming. Also, if any changes have to be made to the hand-assembled program, all the program transfer instructions would have to be adjusted to reflect those changes. With an assembler, the process is automatic. The disadvantage of hand assembly was observed during the construction of the various example programs illustrated in previous chapters.

When using an assembler, changes to the program are made much more easily. All one has to do is make the appropriate modifications in the source code (the program written in mnemonics) and reassemble the program by using the assembler. More will be said about this in Chapter 9.

Currently, there is a variety of assemblers being supported for microcomputers. The two basic types of assemblers are the resident and cross assemblers. *Resident assemblers* are programs that reside on the microcomputer being used (the "target" microcomputer). In other words, an 8080/8085-based microcomputer system could have a resident assembler that assembled programs for execution by the machine. A *cross assembler,* on the other hand, does not reside on the target microcomputer but on another host computer system. The machine code generated by the cross assembler cannot be executed by the host computer. For example, a large mainframe Univac computer could have an 8080 assembler as part of its library. The assembler would be capable of assembling 8080 programs, but the code generated by the assembler could not be executed by the Univac (remember that each computer has a unique instruction set) since the Univac does not "recognize" 8080 machine code. The Univac could also have a resident assembler that would take programs written in Univac instructions, assemble them, and then submit the code to the computer for execution. Thus the principal difference between resident and cross assemblers is in the execution of the machine code generated.

Two other types of assemblers, absolute assemblers and relocatable assemblers, will be discussed in Chapter 9. In brief, an *absolute assembler* creates an object file that has *absolute* address references; that is, once the object file is created, it is ready to be loaded into the computer for execution at the address at which it was assembled. *Relocatable assemblers,* on the other hand, create object files that have *relative* addresses that are made absolute by a special program called a locator (discussed in a later section). The advantages of using such an assembler will be seen in following sections and chapters. Many of the assemblers discussed in this section have macro capabilities, which greatly aid in program development. *Macros* are relatively small segments of code that superficially allow the programmer to expand the instruction set of the microcomputer. These are called *macro assemblers* and will be discussed in great detail in Chapter 11. Many of the new assemblers currently available integrate absolute and relative assembly and macro capabilities into one package, thus allowing the user enormous flexibility in program design.

8-5 COMPILERS

Compilers are similar to assemblers in the function they perform. Both assemblers and compilers are translators. That is, they accept as input source code in the form of program instructions and translate it into object code in the form a machine can recognize. The object code generated by the compiler and assembler are for all practical purposes identical and indistinguishable. The significant difference between assemblers and compilers lies in the source code.

As mentioned in the preceding section, the source code of an assembler is primarily in the form of mnemonic program instructions. The assembly language programmer would have to be fairly proficient in his or her knowledge of the processor to write such a program. Such a program is usually referred to as a *low-level program,* since the programmer has to construct intricate code to instruct the microprocessor at its lowest level. When programmers write programs in an upper-level language, they usually do not have to know the minute details of the microcomputer's hardware, such as registers, memory map, I/O map, and so on. The program is constructed by using "English-like" instructions called *statements*, which are passed on to the compiler as input. The compiler then translates these statements into machine code.

Assembly-level programs are machine oriented, whereas compiler-level languages are task oriented. Only a person who is experienced with the 8080 microprocessor would have an idea of what the assembly language program does. On the other hand, for the compiler version even a nonprogrammer could get a general idea of the program's function simply by looking at the overall program structure. Thus it can be concluded that compiler-level languages or, more specifically, upper- or higher-level languages are easier to write and easier to understand and therefore easier to debug.

The main disadvantage of using an upper-level language is that the programmer has absolutely no control over the object code generated by the compiler. The code generation phase of the compiler is usually "built in" and cannot be influenced by program statements. This often leads to the generation of bulky code which is very inefficient in terms of memory requirements as well as in terms of execution speed. This fact is understandable considering the tremendous task the compiler has to perform during the recognition phase. More will be said about compiler operation in Chapter 12.

Like assemblers, there are two basic types of compilers: *resident compilers* and *cross compilers*. The differences between the two are very similar to the differences between resident and cross assemblers. With the advent of more sophisticated algorithms and new programming techniques, we now have very efficient compilers called *optimizing compilers* that produce object code comparable to that of an assembly language program. The addition of new upper-level languages has also made it easier to write complex programs and to implement complex algorithms. Some of the newer compilers allow the user to integrate assembly language routines in the main sequence of program statements, thus allowing speed-critical program segments to operate more efficiently. Finally, the use of assembler–compiler–interpreter (to be shown later) combinations in software design has made the task of program development much easier than it had previously been.

8-6 LINKERS AND LOCATORS

As mentioned previously, many resident compilers and assemblers create object code without any absolute addresses. The addresses within the code are all referenced to one memory location (usually zero) and are therefore termed *relative*. Because of this feature, the object code now becomes *relocatable*. In other words, if specific addresses are inserted into the relative object code, it can be moved to any memory location for execution. For absolute object code it is not possible to execute a program at a memory location other than that specified during assembly. To do so would mean reassembling the source code at another specified memory location, and obtaining new object code referenced to the new memory location. This could be quite time consuming!

The function of the *locator* is to accept the relocatable object code as input, insert absolute address references (at a load location specified by the user), and create absolute object code ready for execution. The advantage of using a scheme such as this could be illustrated by an example. A software manufacturer wants to sell an assembly language program to users of different types of computer systems (i.e., the same microprocessors but different memory arrangement schemes). The manufacturer does not want to release the source code for the program since some of the algorithms are considered to be proprietary information. Customizing the object file for each customer's memory map would be an expensive process. The solution to this problem would be to supply the program in relocatable object code, so that each user could use a locator to relocate the program at a desired memory location.

To illustrate the utility of a *linker*, consider the following example. Assume that a programmer finds that an application program design is best accomplished by using a compiled, high-level language. However, certain parts of the design are speed critical and are most efficiently implemented in assembly language. Using a special tool called a linker, the programmer can write his application program both in an upper-level language and in assembly language, obtain relocatable object code from the output of the assembler and compiler, and "link" the modules into one relocatable object code. The locator can then be used to locate the program referenced to a specified memory location.

Linking is also done with code generated by assembly language subprograms or modules. In many instances, a programmer makes use of various utility routines during program development. These utility routines (as the name suggests) are useful algorithms that can be used for a variety of applications. Using the conventional scheme in assembly language programming, whenever a utility is used in an application program, it must be included in the program as part of the source code. Using a relocatable assembler and a linker, the programmer references these utilities as they are needed without being concerned about including them in the source code. A *utility library* containing the utility routines in relocatable form is then constructed. Finally, the linker is used to link the application program to the utility library and include the required utility modules into the final object code. Once the utility library has been constructed, it can be used repeatedly for different application programs.

Thus the primary function of the linker is to combine or link various modules of relocatable object code (usually subroutines) into a single program. Using a scheme such as this, a programmer could use a combination of many types of languages in developing a program. In many cases the linking and locating process is combined. Such a program is called a *linkage editor*.

8-7 INTERPRETERS

Like compilers, *interpreters* are used with upper-level programming languages. The main difference between compilers and interpreters is that in interpreters, no object code is generated. An interpreter is usually coresident with the user's program. Each statement in the user's program is interpreted into machine code and then executed immediately by the computer. This means that the interpreter is part of any program the user writes. In contrast, a program that is compiled can run independently of the compiler; once the object code is created by the compiler, its function is over and it is no longer needed during the execution of the user's program. An interpreter works together with the user's program and provides the necessary translation and execution for the user's program statements. Since the user's program always has to be coresident with the interpreter, the combination requires a lot of memory space and is considerably slower than a compiled program. The primary advantage of using an interpreter is that no compilation is necessary. The program can be written, executed, tested, and debugged "on the spot." A compiled program, on the other hand, would have to be recompiled every time any modifications were made to the source code. Thus the important features to remember about interpreters are: extremely fast development time, very slow execution time, and very large memory requirements.

Often the software development process involves testing and debugging the program using an interpreter. Once the bugs have been removed, the program is compiled into object code. This allows the final program to contain less development overhead, faster execution speed, and lower memory requirements.

8-8 SIMULATORS AND DYNAMIC DEBUGGERS

Often when a programmer develops a program on a computer system other than the computer system for which the program is being developed, he or she faces the problem of testing and debugging the program. In such cases the object code of the program is usually derived from the output of a cross assembler or cross compiler and thus cannot be executed on the host machine. In such cases a development tool called a *simulator* is used.

A simulator simulates the operation of the target computer system by tracing the contents of the microprocessor registers after each instruction is executed. Additional facilities provided by the simulator sometimes include the ability to alter the CPU's registers, interrogation of I/O ports and memory locations, calculation of instruction cycles, breakpoints for stopping the program at critical locations, and simulation of interrupts. Thus using the simulator, the programmer can detect the existing and/or potential flaws in the program before it is actually implemented on the target processor.

The major problem with simulators is that they do not execute a program in "real time." Since the simulator is usually resident on a different computer system, the instruction trace is conducted in conjunction with this computer's characteristics. As a result, precise simulation of interrupts and other speed-critical programs is practically impossible using a simulator. To conduct such testing, a tool is needed that is resident on a computer system with a microprocessor that is the same as the microprocessor on the target computer.

A *dynamic debugger* or dynamic debugging tool (DDT) is similar to a simulator. That is, it provides the programmer with the means to test and diagnose a program before it is actually implemented on the target microprocessor. A dynamic debugger resides on a computer system that contains the same microprocessor as the target system. This allows a real-time trace of each instruction being executed, and therefore a DDT can be used to test programs containing interrupt service routines and speed-critical segments. Program diagnostics is done with the maximum amount of accuracy when using a dynamic debugger since the program is actually being executed by the development microcomputer.

8-9 OPERATING SYSTEMS

An *operating system* is the primary means of accessing the computer's hardware and software resources. As the name suggests, an operating system allows the user to "operate" the computer system. Operating systems are usually a combination of various software modules that provide the user with an extended repertoire of commands and facilities to use the computer system. The facilities provided by an operating system range from the most primitive, such as in a monitor, to the very sophisticated facilities provided by disk operating systems (DOSs).

A *monitor* is an operating system in its most elementary form. The size of the monitor is relatively small (1 to 2 kilobytes), and therefore usually resides in ROM. Monitors are most commonly found on microcomputer development systems and development kits with limited resources. A typical monitor allows the user to load a program into memory (usually RAM), display and modify selected memory locations, display and modify the CPU registers, set program breakpoints, query I/O ports, and execute programs at a specified location. These facilities allow the user to develop relatively simple programs as well as access the (rather limited) resources of the computer.

Some computer systems (particularly the expensive ones) have mass-storage hardware such as disks. This allows for the implementation of very advanced software facilities. In such systems, the main piece of software that controls the entire hardware and software resources of the computer is called the *disk operating system*. The disk operating system is responsible for managing the files stored on disk, bringing various programs from disk into main memory (RAM), executing the programs, and providing the user with a "transparent" interface to the hardware. When the user communicates through a transparent interface such as a disk operating system, he or she usually does not need to know much about the hardware environment. This allows the system to be used by people who are not knowledgeable as to the specifics of the hardware.

There exists a very fine line between the exact definition of a monitor and a disk operating system. Many disk operating systems are called "monitors" and many monitors provide some of the sophisticated facilities of a disk operating system. There are many types of operating systems. Disk operating systems usually provide assemblers, compilers, interpreters, and dynamic debuggers, together with text editors, for the creation and editing of program source code. Monitors are much more limited in the facilities they provide. However, all operating systems enable the user(s) to access the resources of the computer through software. Operating systems are basically divided into two types: single-user and multiuser. As the names suggest, *single-user* operating systems allow only one user to use the processor at a time; *multiuser* operating systems make use of sophisticated hardware and software schemes to provide simultaneous processing of multiple users. Many single- and multiuser operating systems provide *multitasking* facilities, which allow the processor to conduct simultaneous processing of many programs (tasks). Multitasking facilities in an operating system often take maximum advantage of the CPU's processing speed and minimize the amount of "idle time" by having the CPU perform other tasks.

8-10 SUMMARY

This chapter has been an introduction to the programming techniques used in software development. It also introduces the various software development tools available to the user. Since each topic is a course in itself, the next few chapters will be dedicated to an in-depth study of some of the topics covered in this chapter; it is hoped that this will allow the microcomputer programmer to develop a good programming style and allow him or her to make the right decisions when selecting the many software development tools currently available.

REVIEW QUESTIONS AND PROBLEMS

1. Write a block-move program (similar to the one discussed in Section 8-2) to move a block of memory larger than 256 bytes. Start by constructing the general, algorithmic, and instruction flowcharts and then develop the 8080 program.

2. What is the function of an assembler? Can a program be developed without the use of an assembler? Why?

3. What is the difference between resident and cross assemblers?

4. What is the difference between absolute- and relocatable-code-producing assemblers?

5. How does the operation of a compiler differ from the operation of an assembler?

6. Explain the differences between relocatable and absolute object code. Why must relocatable object code be located?

7. Explain some of the advantages of linkage.

8. How does the operation of an interpreter differ from the operation of a compiler?

9. What factors distinguish a simulator from a dynamic debugging tool (DDT)?

10. What is the purpose of having an operating system? Discuss the features of the different types of operating systems available.

CHAPTER 9

Introduction to Assembly Language Programming

9-1

INTRODUCTION

Chapter 8 introduced the reader to a software development tool called the assembler. The chapter also illustrated some of the advantages of using the assembler during the development of machine-language programs for the microprocessor. Some of the major advantages of using an assembler over hand assembling a program are particularly apparent during the development of extremely long programs. The probability of making an error during hand assembly is very high. Modifying a hand-assembled program, such as adding or deleting instructions, can be very time consuming since almost all address references must be checked and modified to reflect any changes. Hand assembly is best suited for application programs that are fairly small and contain few program transfer instructions such as JMPs and CALLs, and other address references.

To illustrate the disadvantage of hand assembling a program, consider the program example in Figure 9-1. The program is a simple 1-second counter that counts sequentially from 00 to FF on a set of seven-segment LED displays. Note that the starting count of the program will depend on the contents of the accumulator before the program is executed. Also notice the address references in lines 3, 6, and 11.

LINE	ADDRESS	CODE	LABEL	MNEMONIC		COMMENTS
1	0000	D305	START:	OUT	05	; OUTPUT TO LED
2	0002	F5		PUSH	PSW	; SAVE COUNT
3	0003	CD0B00		CALL	DELAY	; DELAY 1 SECOND
4	0006	F1		POP	PSW	; RESTORE COUNT
5	0007	3C		INR	A	; COUNT = COUNT + 1
6	0008	C30000		JMP	START	; NEXT COUNT
7	000B	21FF01	DELAY:	LXI	H,01FF	; DELAY COUNT
8	000E	2B	D1:	DCX	H	; COUNT DOWN
9	000F	7C		MOV	A,H	; GET HIGH BYTE
10	0010	B5		ORA	L	; CHECK WITH LOW
11	0011	C20E00		JNZ	D1	; 1 SECOND UP ?
12	0014	C9		RET		; RETURN IF SO

FIGURE 9-1.

In order to modify the program in Figure 9-1 to force the count to start at 00, an instruction must be added to the program to clear the accumulator before its content is sent to the output port. This is done by inserting an XRA A instruction as the first byte of the program. The modified program is shown in Figure 9-2. Note that all the other instructions have been shifted down by one memory location.

In Figure 9-2, notice that one change, the addition of the XRA A instruction, required that three address references in lines 3, 6, and 11 be changed to reflect the new values of the labels START, DELAY, and D1. Visualize the number of modifications that would have to be made to a similar program 10 times longer with many more such address references!

When the programmer uses an assembler, minor and major modifications to a program are much easier to make since all adjustments required are made automatically by the assembler. Since the development of a machine-language program often requires many modifications during testing and debugging, an assembler is a very useful tool to aid the programmer in speeding up software

LINE	ADDRESS	CODE	LABEL	MNEMONIC		COMMENTS
	0000	AF		XRA	A	; CLEAR COUNT
1	0001	D305	START:	OUT	05	; OUTPUT TO LED
2	0003	F5		PUSH	PSW	; SAVE COUNT
3	0004	CD0C00		CALL	DELAY	; DELAY 1 SECOND
4	0007	F1		POP	PSW	; RESTORE COUNT
5	0008	3C		INR	A	; COUNT = COUNT + 1
6	0009	C30100		JMP	START	; NEXT COUNT
7	000C	21FF01	DELAY:	LXI	H,01FF	; DELAY COUNT
8	000F	2B	D1:	DCX	H	; COUNT DOWN
9	0010	7C		MOV	A,H	; GET HIGH BYTE
10	0011	B5		ORA	L	; CHECK WITH LOW
11	0012	C20F00		JNZ	D1	; 1 SECOND UP ?
12	0015	C9		RET		; RETURN IF SO

FIGURE 9-2.

development time, with greater accuracy, lower probability of errors, and consequently lower costs.

Chapter 8 also introduced the reader to two types of techniques used in assembly language software development: absolute and relocatable assembly. This chapter deals with microprocessor software development using an absolute-code-producing assembler. Note that the assembler described in this chapter deals with the operation of a typical 8080/8085 assembler. There does exist a variety of assemblers available for the 8080/8085 microprocessors whose operations and functions may differ slightly from the assembler described in this chapter. The objective of this chapter is therefore not to describe the operation of a specific assembler but to enforce the concepts used in assembly language software development.

9-2 OPERATION OF THE ASSEMBLER

The primary job of the assembler is translation. The assembler is a software development tool that takes a program written in mnemonics (often called the *assembly language program*) and converts it into code suitable for execution by the computer (often called the *machine language program*). This process of translation is called assembly. The assembler itself is a program written specifically to provide this translation. Figure 9-3 illustrates the function of the assembler in a block diagram.

The input to the assembler is the assembly language program called the *source file*. The source file contains the program written in mnemonics in a form specified by the rules of the assembler (as introduced in earlier chapters and to be studied in more depth in a later section). A typical source file for the program example in Figure 9-1 is shown in Figure 9-4.

Note that the program in Figure 9-4 looks very similar (with a few exceptions to be seen later) to the first phase in the hand-assembly process. In other words, the program is written in mnemonic form with symbolic address references

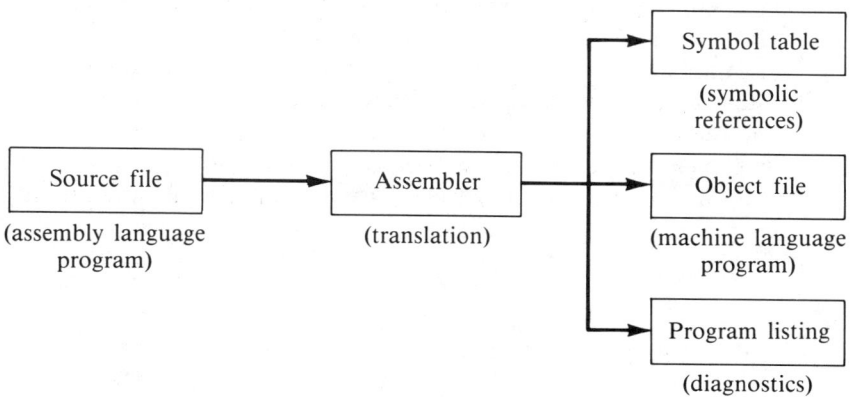

FIGURE 9-3. Operation of the assembler.

```
        ORG   0000H
START:  OUT   05H         ; Output to led
        PUSH  PSW         ; Save count
        CALL  DELAY       ; Delay 1 second
        POP   PSW         ; Restore count
        INR   A           ; Count = count + 1
        JMP   START       ; Next count
DELAY:  LXI   H,01FFH     ; Delay count
D1:     DCX   H           ; Count down
        MOV   A,H         ; Get high byte
        ORA   L           ; Check with low
        JNZ   D1          ; 1 second up?
        RET               ; Return if so
        END
```

FIGURE 9-4. Assembler source file.

before the code is assembled. This program is submitted to the assembler as the source file. The source file can be an area in memory or in most cases a file on disk. Once the source file is written, the programmer's task is complete.

The assembler takes the source file written by the programmer and translates each instruction and symbolic reference to machine code represented in hexadecimal. This machine language program is called the *object file*. For the program in Figure 9-4, the assembler would produce the machine language program shown in Figure 9-5.

The object file in Figure 9-5 is one of the outputs of the assembler after the source file has been translated. Besides containing the machine code for the instructions, the object file also contains other information (to be seen in Section 9-8), such as load addresses and checksums. However, by briefly scanning through the hexadecimal numbers in Figure 9-5, one can see that there is a close correspondence to the code assembled in Figure 9-1.

Most assemblers are *two-pass assemblers*. This means that the assembler goes through the assembly language program (source file) twice before the final machine code (object file) is generated. During the first pass through the source file, the assembler uses a *location counter* (not to be confused with the CPU's program counter) to count the number of bytes for each instruction. As each instruction is encountered, the value of the location counter is increased by one, two, or three, depending on the number of bytes required for the type of instruction scanned. If a symbolic address reference is encountered for a particular instruction, the value of the location counter is assigned to that symbol. When a complete pass is made through all the instructions, the assembler creates a *symbol table* that contains a list of symbols, such as symbolic address references, with their corresponding values.

```
:10000000D305F5CD0B00F13CC3000021FF012B7C93
:05001000B5C20E00C99D
:0000000000
```

FIGURE 9-5. Assembler object file.

```
START   = 0000H
DELAY   = 000BH
D1      = 000EH
```

FIGURE 9-6. Assembler symbol table.

For example, in the source file in Figure 9-4, three symbolic address references—START, DELAY, and D1—exist in the program. The assembler counts each location starting with the first instruction and assigns a numeric address to each symbol. These symbols and their values are stored in a symbol table. For example, the symbol table for the program in Figure 9-4 is shown in Figure 9-6. When the assembler encounters the end of the source file, the first pass is complete and the symbol table either is stored on a file on disk or can be displayed on the computer screen.

The second pass of the assembler is dedicated to producing the machine language program. Each instruction in the program starting with the first is scanned and translated into its corresponding machine code. The technique used by the assembler is very similar to the "look-up-table" approach used in hand assembly. When the assembler encounters an instruction with a symbolic operand, for example CALL DELAY, the value of the symbol DELAY is obtained from the symbol table and assembled with the machine code for the CALL instruction.

As each line in the source file is assembled during the second pass, the assembler lists the address and the machine code produced for the instruction on the line. This results in another output, which provides the programmer with a cross-reference of the mnemonics, the machine code, and the address at which each instruction will be stored in memory (called the load address). This is the *listing file*, and is either stored on disk or displayed on the screen. The listing file for the program example in Figure 9-4 is very similar to the final phase in a hand-assembled program and is shown in Figure 9-7.

Observe that the listing file is an exact duplicate of the source file but contains the machine code in hexadecimal for each instruction on the left-hand side,

```
                        ORG   0000H
0000   D305    START:   OUT   05H      ; Output to led
0002   F5               PUSH  PSW      ; Save count
0003   CD0B00           CALL  DELAY    ; Delay 1 second
0006   F1               POP   PSW      ; Restore count
0007   3C               INR   A        ; Count = count + 1
0008   C30000           JMP   START    ; Next count
000B   21FF01  DELAY:   LXI   H,01FFH  ; Delay count
000E   2B      D1:      DCX   H        ; Count down
000F   7C               MOV   A,H      ; Get high byte
0010   B5               ORA   L        ; Check with low
0011   C20E00           JNZ   D1       ; 1 second up?
0014   C9               RET            ; Return if so
0015                    END
```

FIGURE 9-7. Assembler listing file.

9-2 OPERATION OF THE ASSEMBLER

together with the load addresses. The listing is extremely useful during the testing and debugging of an assembly language program.

9-3 SYNTAX OF THE ASSEMBLY LANGUAGE

Just as every spoken language has syntax rules that specify the arrangement of words in sentences, so does a computer programming language. Assembly language programs must conform to certain syntactical rules before they are submitted to the assembler for translation. These syntactical rules specify the manner in which a "vocabulary" of instruction operation codes and operands is written, the legal use of symbolic references, and the constraints of the language itself. A knowledge of these syntax rules often prevents frustrating errors generated during assembly.

When the programmer prepares an assembly language program for input to the assembler, program instructions are written sequentially and on separate lines; this form of coding was followed in hand assembly (in earlier chapters) and can be seen in the program example in Figure 9-4. During assembly, the assembler scans each line as three separate fields. These fields identify and separate symbolic address references (*labels*), instructions, and comments. For example, in Figure 9-4, the first line in the program can be divided into three fields, as follows:

```
START:   OUT 05H        ; Output to LED
label:   instruction    ; Comment field
```

The *label field* is an optional field and is used to symbolically reference a location in memory. Every line in the program does not have to have a label field, as can be seen in Figure 9-4. Labels are used when the programmer wishes to refer to a particular location in the program, using a symbol rather than a numeric address. The labels used in assembly language programs can be alphanumeric but must start with an alphabetic character and cannot contain any spaces. The ":" (colon) used immediately following the label is not part of the label but is used to separate the label field from the instruction field. Such a symbol that is used to separate two fields is called a *delimiter*.

The *instruction field* contains an executable instruction and must be part of the CPU's instruction set. There is one exception to this, which will be seen in the next section. The instruction field contains the *operation code* and in some cases for multi-byte instructions, the *operand*. The op code and operand are separated from each other by one or more spaces.

The *comment field* is an optional field and is used to document each line in the program. The ";" (semicolon) character serves as a delimiter between the instruction field and the comment field. The assembler simply ignores anything written in the comment field and reproduces it verbatim in the listing file. Even though comments are optional, it is good programming practice to use a lot of comments during the development of assembly language programs since they can be of aid during testing and debugging.

The assembler does allow some flexibility in constructing programs. For example, a label that references an instruction need not be placed on the same line as the instruction itself. Thus

```
START:
        OUT 05H   ; OUTPUT TO LED
```

would have the same meaning to the assembler as would one line containing all three fields.

Comments can also be isolated on single or multiple lines. It may be important to emphasize that whenever the assembler detects a ";" during the assembly process, it ignores everything to the end of the line. The major constraint in the syntax of the assembly language is that fields cannot be broken up into multiple lines.

9-4 LOCATION CONTROL

Before a programmer codes a program for input to an absolute-code-producing assembler, he or she must have an idea of the computer system's memory map. If the system has a RAM and ROM area, the exact boundaries of these areas must be known, so that the assembler can locate the machine language program at the right starting address. This starting address at which the first executable instruction of the program is located is also called the *base address* of the program. The base address of the program is specified in the program itself by means of an *assembler directive* (ORG).

A *directive* is an instruction *to the assembler* that directs the assembly process. These directives are also called *pseudo-operations* since they "look" like CPU instructions in the program but have absolutely no meaning to the CPU. The purpose of these directives is to control the operation of the assembler.

In Figure 9-4, the first line in the program is a directive to the assembler, instructing it to start assembling the program at location 0. This directive is called the *origin* directive and sets the value of the assembler's location counter to a specified value. Notice in Figure 9-7 that the listing file shows the address of the first byte assembled at location 0000. The assembler's location counter is initially always set at zero. The ORG directive is used to change its value. As each byte in the program is assembled, the value of the location counter is incremented sequentially until another ORG directive is encountered or the end of the program is reached.

An assembly language program can have many ORG directives. A typical example is in interrupt-driven programs as shown in Figure 9-8. The program in Figure 9-8 uses ORG directives to instruct the assembler to assemble appropriate jump instructions at the CPU reset location, and the RST 1 and 7 interrupt restart locations. The first ORG directive sets the location counter of the assembler to zero. Note that since the location counter of the assembler is initially set to zero, this directive is optional. The second ORG directive sets the location counter to 0008H and causes the assembler to locate the following three-byte

```
            ORG     0000H
            JMP     MAIN        ; Jump to main program
            ORG     0008H
            JMP     SERV1       ; Service for RST 1
            ORG     0038H
            JMP     SERV7       ; Service for RST 7
            ORG     1000H
MAIN:                           ; Main program starts
            .
            .
            .
SERV1:                          ; Service Routine
            .
            .
            .
```

FIGURE 9-8. Example of a program containing serveral ORG directives.

jump instruction at 0008H. The third ORG directive is similar to the first but locates the following jump instruction at 0038H.

The ORG directives can also be used to separate the assembly language program into *segments*. In software, the area in memory where the program is stored is called the *code segment*. This area can be located in ROM if the application so demands, since it contains the program code itself as well as permanent (nonvariable) data. At this point it should be noted that the programmer must ensure that no temporary data storage is referenced to the code segment if this segment is to be placed in ROM. The area in memory where temporary data and stack data is stored is called the *data segment* (always RAM). The use of the ORG directive together with segment allocation will be seen along with other directives in Section 9-7 and in Chapter 10.

The program in Figure 9-4 contains another directive included as the last line of the program. Although this directive has no relationship to location control, it is worth mentioning at this stage. The END directive signals the assembler to stop assembly. It identifies the logical END of the source file. When the assembler encounters the END directive, it terminates assembly. Anything placed after this directive for all practical purposes does not exist and will be ignored by the assembler. Also, in Figure 9-7 observe the value of the location counter at the end of assembly; its value is one greater than the address of the last byte assembled.

9-5

SYMBOLS AND CONSTANTS

The assembler recognizes five types of numeric *constants* used in operands or address references. These are binary (B), decimal (D), octal (Q), hexadecimal (H), and ASCII constants. When any of the first four types of constants are used in an assembly language program, the programmer must specify a base

(B, D, Q, or H) immediately following the constant. For example, in Figure 9-7, the instruction

$$\text{LXI H,01FFH}$$

caused the assembler to assemble a three-byte instruction as 21FF01. 21 was the op code for the LXI H instruction and 01FFH was a numeric operand specified to be a hexadecimal number. If the following instruction were substituted:

$$\text{LXI H,511D}$$

the assembler would assemble the same code as before since the constant 511 in decimal is 01FF in hexadecimal.

Similarly,

$$\text{LXI H,777Q}$$

and

$$\text{LXI H,0000000111111111B}$$

would be assembled into the same code, since

511 decimal = 01FF hexadecimal = 777 octal = 0000000111111111 binary

If a base is not specified with a constant, the assembler assumes that the constant is a decimal number. For example, the code assembled for the instruction

$$\text{LXI H,777}$$

would be 210903, since 777 is assumed to be a decimal number and evaluates to 0309 hexadecimal. Refer to Appendix D for hexadecimal–decimal conversion tables.

Note that the instruction

$$\text{LXI H,01FF}$$

would cause the assembler to signal an error condition, since 01FF is an invalid decimal number.

Hexadecimal numbers that start with alphabetic characters such as FF03H, F2, and so on, must be preceded by a zero. This is because all labels and symbols start with an alphabetic character and could easily cause the assembler to confuse labels and symbols with hexadecimal constants. Thus the instruction LXI H,F200H would be invalid unless F200H were a label or symbol. However, if the programmer intended to load H&L with the constant F200H, the instruction LXI H, 0F200H would be valid.

9-5 SYMBOLS AND CONSTANTS

ASCII constants are represented by ASCII graphic characters enclosed in single quotes. Any single ASCII graphic character enclosed in single quotes will cause the assembler to assemble its corresponding 7-bit ASCII code. For example, the instruction

$$\text{MVI A, 'E'}$$

would assemble as 3E, the op code for the MVI A instruction and 45, the 7-bit ASCII code of the graphic character 'E' (refer to Appendix B), which becomes the operand of the MVI instruction. Similarly, the instruction

$$\text{LXI H, '12'}$$

would assemble as 213231. The op code for LXI H is 21H, the ASCII code for "2" is 32H, and the ASCII code for "1" is 31H (note that the low-order byte is assembled first).

The assembly language allows identifiers called *symbols* to be used in place of constants anywhere in the program. Symbols are very similar to labels. A *label* identifies a location in memory, whereas a symbol can identify a location in memory and/or a constant. As an example, consider the program example in Figure 9-7 rewritten with symbols and shown in Figure 9-9.

Figure 9-9 introduces another assembler directive, *equate*. The EQU or equate directive is used to assign a constant to a symbol. Like any assignment statement, the constant on the right-hand side of the EQU is assigned to the symbol on the left-hand side. The symbols LED and DCOUNT are assigned the values 05H and 01FFH, respectively, during the first pass of the assembler and the generation of the symbol table. Now during the second pass, whenever the assembler encounters any of the previously equated symbols, it assembles the symbols' assigned value.

The advantages of using symbols in place of constants are obvious in very large programs where a single constant is used over and over again. For example,

```
                        ORG    0000H
0005  =          LED    EQU    05H         ; LED output port
01FF  =          DCOUNT EQU    01FFH       ; 1 second delay count
0000  D305       START: OUT    LED         ; Output to LED
0002  F5                PUSH   PSW         ; Save count
0003  CD0B00            CALL   DELAY       ; Delay 1 second
0006  F1                POP    PSW         ; Restore count
0007  3C                INR    A           ; COUNT = count + 1
0008  C30000            JMP    START       ; Next count
000B  21FF01     DELAY: LXI    H,DCOUNT    ; Delay count
000E  2B         D1:    DCX    H           ; Count down
000F  7C                MOV    A,H         ; Get high byte
0010  B5                ORA    L           ; Check with low
0011  C20E00            JNZ    D1          ; 1 second up?
0014  C9                RET                ; Return if so
                        END
```

FIGURE 9-9.

assume that the program in Figure 9-7 was much larger in size and had many output instructions to port 05H. If for some reasons the port number had to be changed to another value, all the OUT instructions in the program would have to have their operands changed. This could be time consuming, and chances of missing a few changes are very high. However, equating the device number to a symbol as in Figure 9-9 would require that only the equate value be changed. On reassembling the program, the assembler would take care of changing all the OUT instruction operand values from 05H to another value. Symbols are also more descriptive than constants. In Figure 9-9, the instruction OUT LED "tells" a person inspecting the program more about what the output port 05H is than does the instruction OUT 05H.

In assembly language programs, arithmetic expressions can also be used together with or in place of symbols and constants. For example, if the program in Figure 9-9 had the line

```
          DCOUNT    EQU    01FFH+10H
```

the symbol DCOUNT would be assigned the value 020FH. Similarly, the directive

```
          DCOUNT    EQU    256*2-1
```

would direct the assembler to evaluate the expression 256*2-1 = 511 = 01FFH and assign the value to the symbol DCOUNT.

Arithmetic expressions can also be used in operands of instructions. For example, if Figure 9-9 contained the instruction

```
          OUT    LED+3
```

the operand of the OUT instruction would be 05H+3 = 08H. Similarly, the JNZ D1 instruction in Figure 9-9 could be replaced with JNZ DELAY+3, since the label D1 will always evaluate to DELAY+3 (since LXI H is a three-byte instruction). This eliminates having an extra label D1.

Once a symbol has been assigned a value by means of an EQU directive, its value is fixed and cannot be changed through another EQU directive at a later step in the program. However, the assembler recognizes another directive very similar to the EQU directive. The *set directive* (SET) can be used in place of the EQU directive and has exactly the same functions. The difference between the two is that a symbol defined with a SET directive can have its value changed any number of times in the program. Unlike the EQU directive, which operates during the first pass of the assembler, the SET directive operates during the second pass. Each time a SET directive that changes the value of a symbol is detected, the symbol-table entry is adjusted appropriately. SET directives are extremely useful when used with macros (discussed in Chapter 11).

The assembler provides the user with a special reserved symbol, "$." This is a symbol whose value is always equal to the current value of the location counter. Thus if a user-defined symbol is equated to the $, the symbol is assigned the current value of the location counter. For example, in Figure 9-9, if the directive

```
              LAST    EQU    $
```

were inserted just before the END directive, the symbol LAST would be assigned the value 0015H, which would be the current value of the location counter (i.e., the value of the location counter after the RET instruction is assembled). If, for example, the directive

```
              SIZE    EQU    $-DELAY
```

were used in the same place in Figure 9-9, the symbol SIZE would evaluate to 0015H − 000BH = 000AH, the size in bytes of the DELAY subroutine. The $ symbol is extremely useful in string-size calculations, as will be seen in later programs.

Making a decision as to whether to use constants or symbols or both in an assembly language program is left entirely up to the programmer. Although using plenty of symbols always makes good programming practice, there may be some situations where constants seem more appropriate. These situations will become evident in the course of the book and as the reader gains practice in understanding and writing assembly language programs.

9-6 DATA STORAGE

As previously stated, the primary function of the assembler is to translate mnemonic instructions and symbolic references into machine code. Consequently, the machine code assembled is loaded into the computer for execution. In many software applications it is necessary to load different types of data together with the program code into the computer's memory. Examples of such applications are programs that require look-up tables, character string messages, and other forms of data that must be kept permanently (e.g., in ROM) together with the machine instructions. The assembler must therefore provide the programmer with a technique by which these forms of data can be assembled together with the rest of the program. This is done by means of two *data storage directives:* the define byte (DB) and the define word (DW) directives.

For the 8251 microcomputer interface developed in Chapter 7, consider the following application program to print a message (character string) on the screen of the terminal connected to the 8251 USART. To implement this specification, a number of considerations have to be taken into account.

1. The message to be displayed on the screen has to be stored together with the program in ROM so that it is not lost when the system is shut down.
2. Each character in the message must be stored in its 7-bit ASCII code, since the terminal recognizes only this code.

3. The starting address of the first character in the message must be known so that the entire message is printed out.
4. The number of characters in the message must be known so that the program can stop when the entire message has been displayed.

The flowchart to implement this program specification is shown in Figure 9-10. The program to implement the flowchart of Figure 9-10 is shown in Figure 9-11 as the output listing file of the assembler.

With reference to Figure 9-11, observe the use of the DB directive to store the ASCII code for each character in the message immediately following the last instruction in the program. The label MESS is assigned the address of the first character in the message, and the length of the message is calculated by the assembler by subtracting the value of MESS with the current value of its

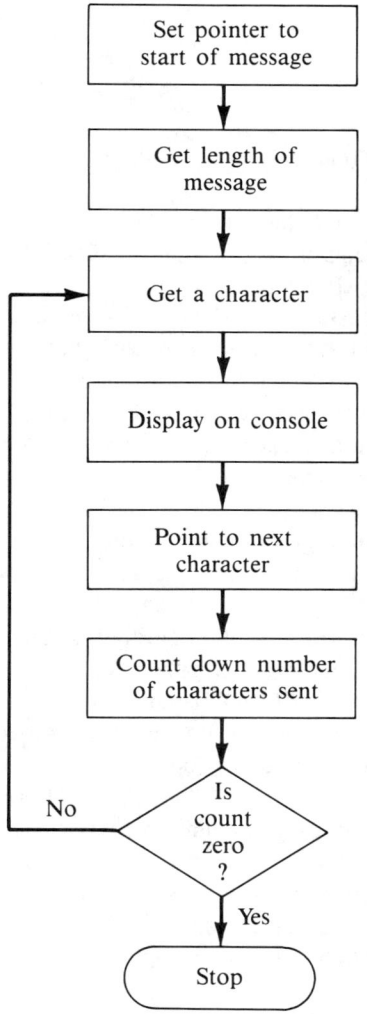

FIGURE 9-10. Flowchart for a message print routine.

9-6 DATA STORAGE

```
0100                          ORG    0100H
                       ; MESSAGE PRINT PROGRAM
0100   210F01                 LXI    H,MESS      ; Pointer to start of message
0103   060D                   MVI    B,LENGTH    ; Length of message
0105   4E           LOOP:     MOV    C,M         ; Get a character
U0106  CD0000                 CALL   CONOUT      ; Display on console
0109   23                     INX    H           ; Point to next character
010A   05                     DCR    B           ; Count down # of chars sent
010B   C20501                 JNZ    LOOP        ; Continue if count not zero
010E   76                     HLT                ; Else stop
                       ; MESSAGE STORAGE
010F   48454C       MESS:     DB     'HELLO TESTING'
0112   4C4F20
0115   544553
0118   54494E
011B   47
000D   =            LENGTH    EQU    $-MESS
011C                          END
```

FIGURE 9-11. Message print program.

location counter (as discussed in Section 9-5). The result is assigned to the symbol LENGTH.

Referring to Figures 9-10 and 9-11 (note how the blocks in the flowchart of Figure 9-10 correspond to the comments in the program in Figure 9-11), the first instruction in the program sets RP H&L to the starting address of the message (MESS). The length of the message (LENGTH) is moved into register B; this will be used as a tally to keep track of how many characters have been displayed. The first character in the message is loaded into register C (preparation for the console output subroutine), and then CONOUT is called to send the character to the terminal. RP H&L is incremented to point to the next character in the message, the number of characters in the message is decremented (counted down to zero), and a test is made to see if the count has reached zero. If not, the next character is loaded into register C and the process is repeated. The loop continues until all the characters in the message have been displayed, at which point the contents of register B is zero. The program then terminates.

Note that the assembler signaled an error condition during assembly by displaying a U on the left-hand side of the line containing the CALL to CONOUT. This error indicates that the address of the CONOUT subroutine is undefined, since the routine itself was not included as part of the program; consequently, the assembler was not able to assemble the address operand of the CALL instruction. To ensure that the program is complete, the CONOUT subroutine (from Chapter 7) must be included in the program either before or after the DB directive.

The use of the DB directives to store data bytes does not have to be limited to ASCII constants or character strings, but can contain any of the other numeric constants or symbols discussed in Section 9-5. For example,

DB 122,56H,326Q,'A','012'

would direct the assembler to assemble the following data:

7A,56,D6,41,30,31,32

at the current value of the location counter.

The DW directive is similar to the DB directive and is used to direct the assembler for data assembly. However, the DW directive is used to store 16-bit data instead of 8-bit data, as did the DB directive. The 16-bit data is stored least significant byte first, and this makes it ideal for the storage of addresses used by an application program.

A common application program used in many types of computer systems is one called a *console command processor* (CCP). The function of the CCP is to get a single character from the console keyboard and interpret the character received as a command. The CCP must detect the command and branch off to a routine to implement the command—the *command implementing routine* (CIR). If an invalid command is entered, the CCP branches off to a routine that prints an error message on the screen. The CCP is thus structured like the "menu-driven" program discussed in Chapter 8.

The flowchart of Figure 9-12 describes the operation of the CCP, and the program shown in Figure 9-13 implements the CCP. Notice that Figure 9-13 contains a look-up table consisting of DB and DW directives. The table basically has four sets of entries, each entry consisting of a DB directive that stores the valid command character, and immediately following, a DW directive that stores the address of transfer, on detection of that command. The program is designed to detect and implement any of the following four commands entered from the keyboard: A, Q, D, or X.

Since each three-byte entry in the table corresponds to one command, that is, one byte for the command character and two bytes for the address of the routine that implements the command, the number of commands is calculated by the assembler by the last EQU directive in Figure 9-13. The number of commands in the table is therefore the number of bytes in the table divided by 3, which in this case is four commands. Obviously, in this example the number 4 could be EQUated to the symbol NCMDS directly without requiring the assembler to do the calculation. But think of a situation where the CCP has to be modified to recognize a few more commands. It would be quite easy to forget to change the NCMDS equate. Using this technique, any addition of table entries (addition of new commands) will automatically adjust the value of NCMDS. Note that additional commands can be added to the CCP's table simply by adding the command character and the address of the command implementing routine for each command.

With reference to Figures 9-12 and 9-13 (again notice the close correspondence between the flowchart and the program), RP H&L is set to point to the start of the command table "TABLE," and register B is loaded with a count of the number of commands. This count will be used to detect when the end of the table is reached. The console input routine (from Chapter 7) is called to get a command character from the terminal keyboard.

On receiving the command character from the console, the character is com-

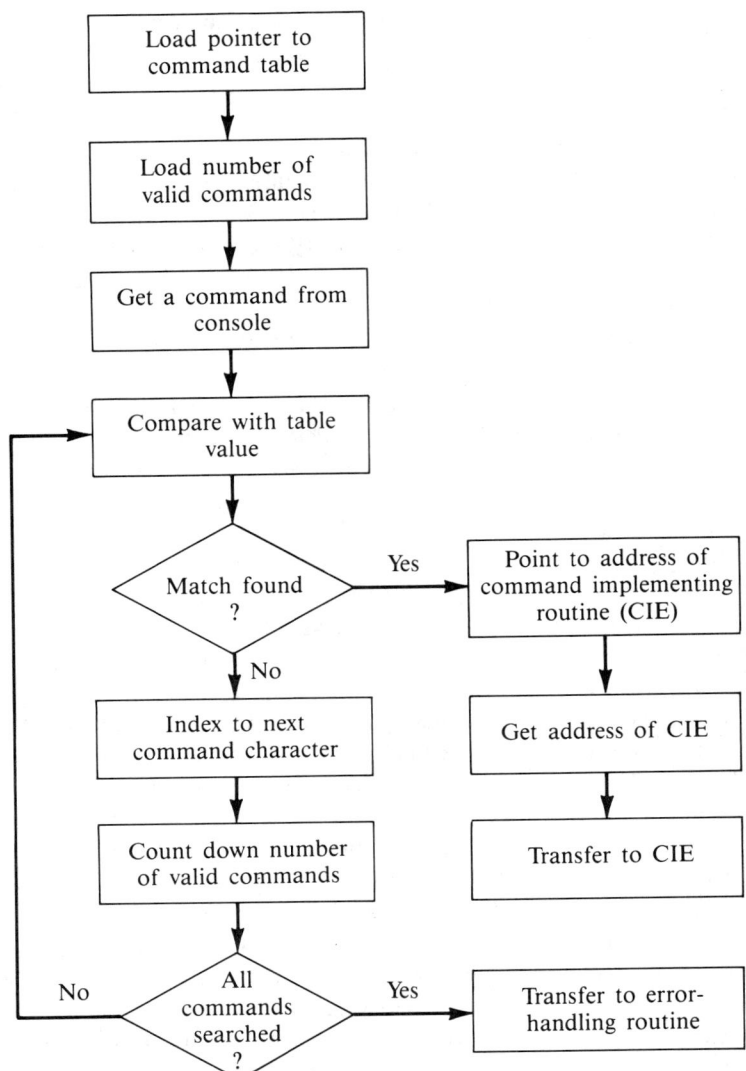

FIGURE 9-12. Flowchart for a console command processor.

pared with the first byte in the table. If a match is not found, RP H&L is incremented three times to index over the address of the previous command implementing routine, and the next command character in the table is compared with the character entered at the console. Each time through, the value of register B is decremented, to keep track of the number of commands searched. When the value of register B reaches zero, all the commands in the table have been searched, no match has been found, and control transfers to an error-handling routine labeled ERROR.

If a match is found during the search, the control transfers to the address "MATCH." Here, RP H&L is indexed to point at the low-order address of the CIR. The low address is loaded into register E and the high address into register

```
        00C8                        ORG    200
                        ; Console command processor
        00C8  21E400    CCP:    LXI    H,TABLE        ; Point to command table
        00CB  0604              MVI    B,NCMDS        ; Number of valid commands
        00CD  CDF000            CALL   CONIN          ; Get command from console
        00D0  BE        SEARCH: CMP    M              ; Compare with table value
        00D1  CADE00            JZ     MATCH          ; Branch if match found
        00D4  23                INX    H              ; Else index to next command
        00D5  23                INX    H              ; Character in the table
        00D6  23                INX    H
        00D7  05                DCR    B              ; Count number of valid commands
        00D8  C2D000            JNZ    SEARCH         ; Search until match found
        00DB  C3F500            JMP    ERROR          ; Error if entire table search
        00DE  23        MATCH:  INX    H              ; Point to cir (low byte)
        00DF  5E                MOV    E,M            ; Low address to register E
        00E0  23                INX    H              ; Point to cir (high byte)
        00E1  56                MOV    D,M            ; High address to register D
        00E2  EB                XCHG                  ; Cir address to H&L
        00E3  E9                PCHL                  ; Execute the cir
                        ; Table of valid commands and their implementing routine addresses
        00E4  41        TABLE:  DB     'A'            ; A command character
        00E5  F100              DW     ACMD           ; A CIR address
        00E7  51                DB     'Q'            ; Q command character
        00E8  F200              DW     QCMD           ; Q CIR address
        00EA  44                DB     'D'            ; D command character
        00EB  F300              DW     DCMD           ; D CIR address
        00ED  58                DB     'X'            ; X command character
        00EE  F400              DW     XCMD           ; X CIR address
        004   =         NCMDS   EQU    ($-TABLE)/3    ; Number of table commands
                        ; The following routine must be added to the program
        00F0  00        CONIN:  NOP
                        ; The following are the CIRs for each of the table commands
                        ; Actual operation of these routines will depend on the application
        00F1  00        ACMD:   NOP
        00F2  00        QCMD:   NOP
        00F3  00        DCMD:   NOP
        00F4  00        XCMD:   NOP
        00F5  00        ERROR:  NOP
        00F6                    END
```

FIGURE 9-13. Console command processor program.

D, so that RP D&E contains the address of the CIR. The contents of RP D&E are then moved to RP H&L. Finally the contents of RP H&L are loaded into the PC and control transfers to the appropriate CIR.

Note that since the CCP is a program that works in conjunction with other programs, the CIRs have not been included with the program in Figure 9-13. The exact code for these routines will depend on the application at hand.

9-7

STORAGE ALLOCATION

In Section 9-4 the reader was introduced to the concept of coding most application programs in the assembly language in two distinct segments: the code segment and the data segment. The *code segment* is the area in memory that will hold the program itself as well as the character-string messages, look-up tables, and other constants. The *data segment* is the area in memory that holds temporary data for the stack, buffers, and other variables. For systems with ROM and RAM hardware, the code and data segments correspond to the ROM and RAM memory, respectively, and therefore it is an absolute necessity to organize the software in a similar manner. For disk-based systems that contain only RAM memory, this organization is desirable but not important.

Section 9-4 also described the use of the ORG directive to set the value of the assembler's location counter to a specified value, thus causing assembly of the program starting at that location in ROM. A second ORG directive could also be used to reset the location counter to an area of RAM so that symbolic references to RAM storage in the program could be assembled by the assembler. Figure 9-14 illustrates a typical program organization for ROM/RAM systems.

The partial program in Figure 9-14 is written for a system that has ROM starting at location 0000H, and 256 bytes of RAM at locations 1000H through 10FFH. Note the organization of the program into the code and data segments to correspond with the hardware memory map. The first instruction in the program is one that sets up the stack pointer. Since the label STACK is in the data segment, and since the stack is usually set to the top of RAM, the ORG RAM+255 directive is used to set the location counter to location 10FFH (top of RAM). The label STACK is set to this value, and during the second pass, assembled as the operand of the LXI SP instruction. This particular example illustrated only one portion of the data segment being used for stack storage allocation. The next example in this section will broaden the use of storage allocation.

Consider a program that reads characters entered from a terminal keyboard and stores the characters obtained in a buffer in the data segment (RAM). The program is to keep on filling the buffer until the buffer is full, at which point the program terminates. The buffer must be capable of holding 80 characters. Assume the same hardware memory map as in the program shown in Figure 9-14. The program to implement this specification is shown in Figure 9-15.

The operation of the program in Figure 9-15 is fairly simple. After the stack pointer is set, RP H&L is set to the start of the buffer area in the data segment, and register B is set to the length of the buffer. The CONIN subroutine (not shown) is called to get a character from the keyboard. The character is stored in memory, H&L set to point at the next buffer location, and the count in register B is decremented. The next character is then read from the keyboard and stored in the buffer. This continues till the count reaches zero, at which point the buffer is full and the program terminates.

```
0000  =           ROM    EQU  0000H         ; Start of ROM area
1000  =           RAM    EQU  1000H         ; Start of RAM area
0000              ORG    ROM                ; Assemble in code segment
0000 31FF10       LXI    SP, STACK          ; Set up stack pointer
   .      .              .                       .
   .      .              <rest of program>
   .      .              .                       .
10FF              ORG    RAM+255            ; Assemble in data segment
10FF  =    STACK  EQU    $                  ; Stack starts here
                  END
```

FIGURE 9-14. Program organized for a ROM/RAM environment.

```
0000 =          ROM     EQU  0000H        ; Start of ROM area
1000 =          RAM     EQU  1000H        ; Start of RAM area
0000                    ORG  ROM          ; Assemble in code segment
0000 31FF10             LXI  SP,STACK     ; Set up stack pointer
0003 21                 LXI  H,BUFFER     ; Pointer to data buffer
0006 0650               MVI  B,LENGTH     ; Length of buffer
0008 CD1200     GET:    CALL CONIN        ; Get a keyboard character
000B 77                 MOV  M,A          ; Store in buffer
000C 23                 INX  H            ; Next buffer location
000D 05                 DCR  B            ; Count down length
000E C20800             JNZ  GET          ; Next if not full
0011 76                 HLT               ; Else stop program
0012            CONIN:                    ; Place CONIN subroutine here
1000                    ORG  RAM          ; Assemble in data segment
1000            BUFFER  DS   80           ; Reserve 80 bytes buffer
0050 =          LENGTH  EQU  $-BUFFER     ; Length of buffer
                        DS   6            ; Reserve 6 bytes for stack
1056 =          STACK   EQU  $            ; Stack starts here
1056                    END
```

FIGURE 9-15. Application of the DS directive for storage reservation.

Notice in Figure 9-15 that a data storage (DS) directive has been used to reserve space for two areas in the data segment: the buffer area and the stack areas. Unlike the DB and DW directives, the DS directive does not instruct the assembler to assemble any code, but merely causes a specified offset to be added to the location counter so as to reserve a portion of memory.

In Figure 9-15, the label BUFFER is assigned the value of 1000H (start of the data segment). Eighty bytes are then reserved for the buffer, from 1000H to 1050H, by using the DS 80 directive. The length of the buffer is then calculated, by subtracting the value of buffer from the current value of the location counter. Then six bytes are reserved for the stack (this is arbitrary) using the DS 6 directive, which causes the location counter to be set at 1056. The label STACK is set to this value. The program thus has six bytes of stack space and 80 bytes of buffer space in the data segment, allowing for very efficient storage allocation.

The DS directive is not limited to use in the data segment, but can also be used in the code segment, to bypass certain areas of the memory map, such as interrupt restart locations, or to leave a blank area in the memory map for memory-mapped I/O systems. Appropriate use of the DS directive can lead to very memory-efficient software design.

9-8 OBJECT FILE

In Section 9-2 the operation of the assembler was described as being the translation of an assembly language program into a machine language program. The machine language program is the actual sequence of machine instructions (and data) that is processed by the CPU. One of the outputs of the assembler is the object file that contains the machine language program.

Figure 9-5 illustrates a typical object file produced by an assembler. This object file is a sequence of hexadecimal digits organized into *records*. As shown in Figure 9-5, a record starts with a ":" (colon) and ends with a *checksum*, which is a two-digit hexadecimal number. The number of records in an object file will depend on the size of the program assembled. Thus in Figure 9-5, the object file has three records ending with checksums 93, 9D, and 00 from first to last record, respectively. The contents of an object file record is mostly the instruction codes and/or data of the assembled program. However, records do contain some additional information. This additional information in the object file is often required since the object file is often passed through a special program called a *loader*. The function of the loader is to read each record, determine where in the computer's memory each instruction is to be loaded, and determine if there are any errors in the object file.

Figure 9-16 shows a dissected view of the first record of the object file in Figure 9-5. Observe that the record is divided into six fields.

Field 1, as mentioned before, is a special character intended to identify the start of an object file record.

Field 5 contains the instructions and/or data (program bytes) in hexadecimal bytes that were translated from the source file. For example, the first two bytes, D305, represent the OUT 05 instruction; the next byte, F5, represents the PUSH PSW instruction; and so on.

Field 2 is a hexadecimal number that identifies the number of program bytes in field 5. In Figure 9-16, the record contains 16 (10 hex) program bytes. The number of program bytes in a record will depend on the type of assembler being used.

Field 3 is a four-digit hexadecimal number that identifies the address at which the first program byte will be loaded into the computer's memory (load address). For example, the first program byte D3 will be loaded at location 0000, 05 at location 0001, F5 at location 0002, . . . , 7C at location 000F. Notice in Figure 9-5 that the load address of the next record is 0010.

Field 4 always contains 00. Its purpose is to separate the preliminary information of fields 1, 2, and 3 from the program bytes in field 5.

Field 6 is two-digit hexadecimal checksum used to detect any errors that may have occurred in fields 2 through 5. This format for each record was developed

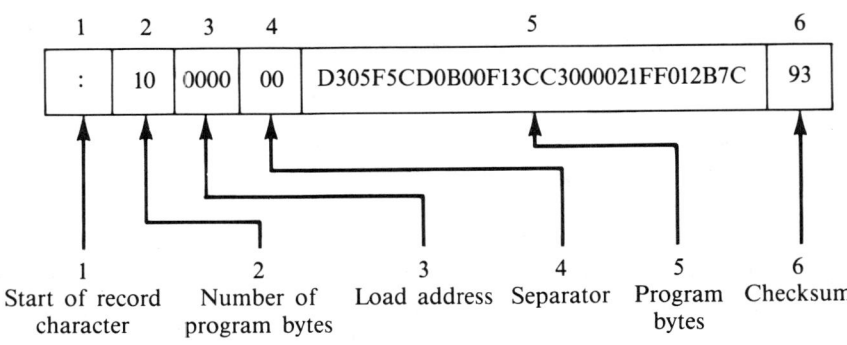

FIGURE 9-16. Object file record format.

during the early years of microprocessor systems. At the time, paper-tape strips were used to store object file information. These paper tapes were prone to many errors when read. As a result, some means of error detection was necessary during the reading of paper tape by the loader. The checksum is calculated by taking the modulo 8 sum of *all* the bytes in the record and then its two's complement. Figure 9-17 shows the calculation of the checksum for the record in Figure 9-16.

In Figure 9-17, by adding all the bytes in fields 2 through 5, the result obtained is 066D. Considering only the least significant 8 bits of this number yields a modulo 8 sum of 6D. The two's complement of 6D is 93, which is the checksum for the record.

As the loader reads in each byte in the record, it also calculates its own checksum based on the preceding algorithm. When all the bytes of the record are read, the loader compares its checksum with the checksum in the record. If they do not match, an error condition was encountered during the read. Chapter 10 deals with the actual implementation of a loader.

At this point it is important to realize that even though the object file contains the machine language program in hexadecimal representation, this is merely a representation of the program in binary form. The CPU "understands" only binary instructions. Hexadecimal representation is used only for convenience

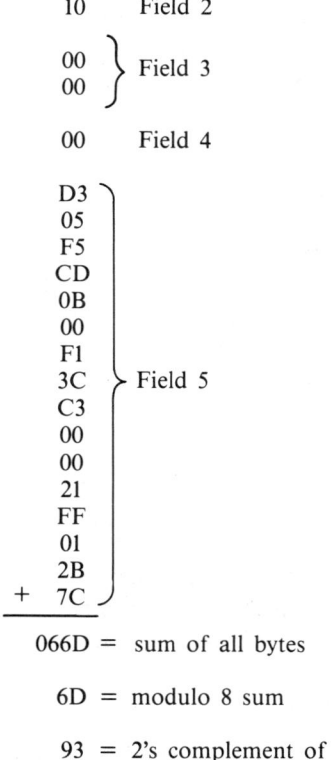

FIGURE 9-17. Checksum calculation.

and for economical purposes, since it greatly reduces the number of digits when printed or displayed. Ultimately, every instruction and data byte is loaded into the computer in binary.

9-9 SUMMARY

The assembler was introduced as a software development tool that could translate an assembly language program into a form suitable for execution by the computer. Besides translating instructions, the assembler could also be used to store data tables and character strings and to reserve specified memory locations for temporary data storage. The user could control the location at which the code and data segments were assembled, so that the software organization corresponds with the hardware environment. The most important feature of the assembler was its ability to allow symbolic references to data and memory locations, thus eliminating a lot of overhead during program development. Finally, the assembler produced the machine language program in the form of an absolute object file; the location at which the machine language program was loaded and eventually executed was fixed after assembly and could not be executed at a different memory address.

In this chapter we discussed the use of an extremely important tool used in developing assembly language programs. The material covered in this chapter serves only as an introduction to assembly language programming, and to introduce the basic directives for controlling assembly. The next two chapters deal with some of the more advanced features of assembly language programming and features of the assembler.

REVIEW QUESTIONS AND PROBLEMS

1. Describe some of the advantages of using an assembler over hand-assembly.

2. Briefly describe the functions of the following:
   (a) Source file.   (b) Symbol table.
   (c) Object file.   (d) Program listing.

3. Describe the operation of a two-pass assembler.

4. The following sequence of hexadecimal bytes (shown as an object file record) represents a machine language program for the 8080. Disassemble (i.e., convert each machine instruction to mnemonics) the program into assembler format.

    :132000000E7B3A502006559180D3303250200DCA0220761A

5. What is an assembler directive? What is the purpose of having an ORG directive to the assembler?

6. Identify the invalid constants in the following list and explain why they are considered invalid.
   - (a) 0F3H
   - (b) '3CH'
   - (c) 3C05
   - (d) 378
   - (e) 'HELLO'
   - (f) 512Q
   - (g) 1010B
   - (h) 1010
   - (i) 823Q
   - (j) 11011021B
   - (k) '13'
   - (l) 753D

7. What is the function of the special reserved symbol "$"?

8. Compare the operation of the two data storage directives DB and DW. How does the DS directive differ from the DB and DW directives?

9. The following program is written in assembler format. Assuming that you are the assembler, fill in the addresses and object code on the left-hand side of the listing.

```
                    ORG   5010H
            PANEL   EQU   35H            ; Display port
____ ____           LXI   SP,STACK       ; Set up stack
                                           pointer
____ ____           LXI   H,TABLE        ; Point to table
____ ____   OVER:   MOV   A,M            ; Get table value
____ ____           CPI   '$'            ; End of table?
____ ____           JZ    QUIT           ; Quit if so
____ ____           OUT   PANEL          ; Else display it
____ ____           INX   H              ; Next table value
____ ____           JMP   OVER           ; Do it again
____ ____   QUIT:   HLT                  ; Quit
____ ____   TABLE:  DB    '9876543210$'
____ ____
____
____ ____           DS    12  ;12 bytes for stack
            STACK   EQU   $
                    END
```

10. The following program contains five syntax errors that will be flagged by the assembler. Identify and explain these errors.

```
                    ORG   1000
            REF     EQU   2000H
                    LXI   H,REF
            START:  MVI   C,F0
                    IN    SWT
                    CMP   'A'
                    JZ    TERM
                    ADD   M
                    INX   H
                    JMP   START
            REF:    DS    12H,'B',5EH,'CCCC'
            TERM:   HLT
                    END
```

CHAPTER 10

Relocatable Assembly and Utility Subroutines

10-1

INTRODUCTION

Relocatable assembly is a process that aids the development of an assembly language program that requires programming in several modular steps. To illustrate the difference between absolute assembly (described in Chapter 9) and relocatable assembly, consider the operation of the assembler in Figure 9-3. The process of assembly involved only one development stage: the assembler translated the source file into the object file. Once assembled, the object file was ready to be loaded into the computer. Relocatable assembly requires an additional step in the software development process, linkage and location. This may seem disadvantageous at first thought, but it does provide a more flexible technique of developing programs, as will be seen in this chapter.

The process of relocatable assembly is shown in Figure 10-1. By comparing the diagram of Figure 10-1 with the function of the absolute assembler (Figure 9-3), one can see that the end result of the assembly is the same—the object file. However, the intermediate steps in the development of the program are quite different.

The input to the assembler consists of one or more source files constructed

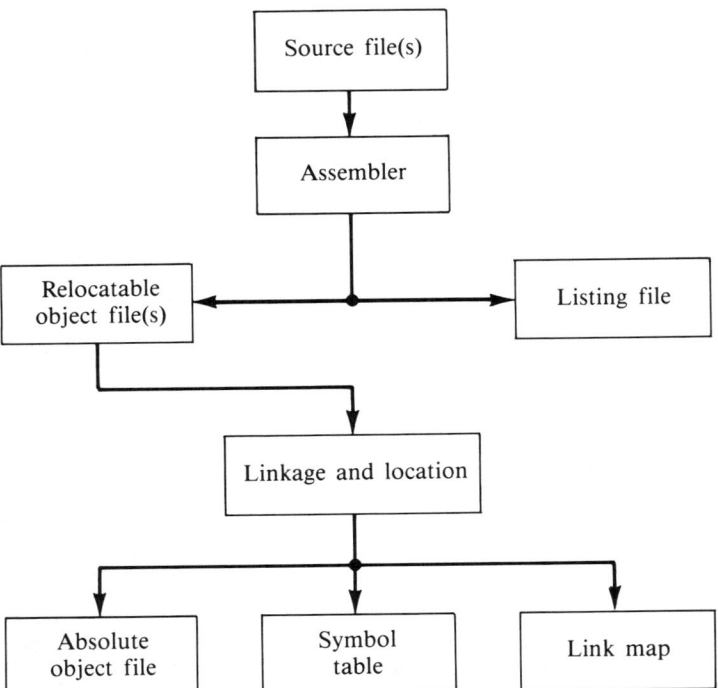

FIGURE 10-1. Process of relocatable assembly.

in a manner very similar to the source files in Chapter 9. The assembler translates these source files into *relocatable object files*. Relocatable object files are similar to absolute object files except that all symbolic address references are variable. For example, any JMP or CALL instructions have operands that reference a location relative to the base of the program rather than an absolute location in memory. Thus, after assembly, these object files can be located anywhere in memory by the linking and locating process.

The relocatable object files (*modules*) are then submitted to a linkage editor, which combines all the object files into a single absolute object file with absolute address references, for loading into the computer. The linkage editor also produces a *link map*, which tells the programmer the absolute addresses of the program modules, and a symbol table, with all the symbols and their absolute values. The process of combining the relocatable object files (modules) into a single module is called *linkage*. The process of adding absolute addresses to the resultant object file so that the machine code is ready for execution at a specified address is called *location*. Linkage and location are usually (but not always) done in a single step in the development stage.

All the directives discussed in Chapter 9 for absolute assembly are applicable to relocatable assembly. There are, however, certain directives used exclusively for relocatable assembly, as will be seen in the following sections.

10-2
STRUCTURED ASSEMBLY LANGUAGE PROGRAMS

A *structured program* is one that is constructed on various levels. A hierarchical tree illustrating these levels of a structured program is shown in Figure 10-2. Notice in the figure that the main program (first level) consists of CALLs to various subroutines (or modules) in the second level, as represented by the arrows. Subroutines in the second level may have calls to a third level, and so on. What this illustrates is a program structure that is divided into separate sections or subprograms. Subprograms at the highest level of the tree are dependent on subprograms at the lower levels, whereas lower-level subprograms are essentially independent of upper-ievel programs. The advantage to such a scheme of program organization is that lower-level subprograms can be tested independently and used when required during the development of the main program. These lower-level subprograms are usually used over and over again in application programs and are hence termed *utility subroutines*.

Consider some of the program examples in Chapter 9. Most of those programs required the use of two subroutines: CONIN (console input) and CONOUT (console output). Now each time a program was written that required one or both of these subroutines, the programmer had to include the source code for the subroutines in the program being written (main program). It would be convenient if these subroutines were written and assembled separately (into relocatable modules) and then included in the final absolute object file during linkage and location. This would preclude the need for including the subroutines at the source level. This is exactly the concept behind relocatable assembly, as shown in Figure 10.3.

The main program is constructed in a organization similar to the hierarchical tree structure shown in Figure 10-2. Since a major portion of the main program will consist of calls to subroutines, the size of the main program will be relatively small at the source level. The programmer does not have to include the source code for the subroutines in the main program. (*Note:* Normally, an absolute assembler would signal an error if a call were made to a subroutine that did not exist in the source file, but a relocatable assembler does not do this.) The

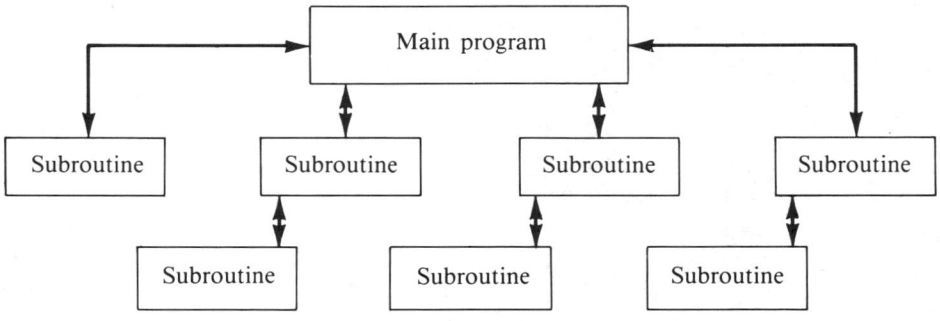

FIGURE 10-2. Hierarchical levels of a structured program.

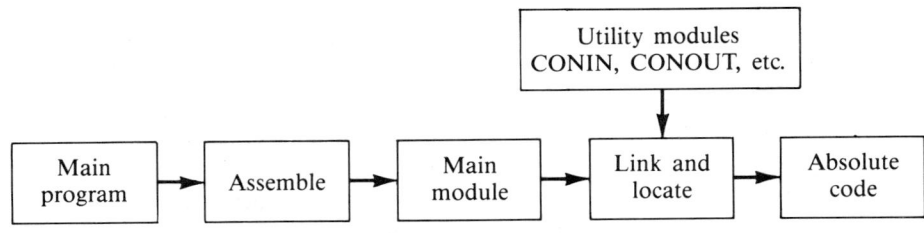

FIGURE 10-3. Development of an assembly language program.

subroutines used in the main program are assembled separately. Finally, the linkage editor is used to combine the main program with its referenced subroutines. The final combined code is then located at a specified location.

The real advantage of this technique of software development is seen during the development of later application programs that require the same modules developed before. Since these modules have been previously developed, all the programmer has to do is construct the main program without being concerned about the subroutines, and the linkage editor takes care of the rest. These utility subroutines (commonly used subroutines) are usually kept in a file (in relocatable form) called a utility library. During the linkage stage, a search is made through the library for modules that are needed in the main program. Only the modules that are referenced in the main program are included in the final object code.

10-3

SUBROUTINE MODULES

There are four basic types of subroutines: subroutines with no parameters, subroutines with input parameters, subroutines with output parameters, and subroutines with both input and output parameters.

A *subroutine with no parameters* is one that is called to perform a task, without sending it any data or receiving any data from it. Such a subroutine could be an interrupt subroutine that is independent of the main program.

A *subroutine with input parameters* in one that must have data passed to it in order to operate properly. A good example of this type of subroutine is the console output subroutine (CONOUT) for the 8251 UART. Before CONOUT was called, register C was loaded with the character that was to be displayed on the terminal. The character in register C was the input parameter to the CONOUT subroutine. If register C were not loaded with the character (data), the subroutine would not work as intended. Note that CONOUT did not return any data to the main program.

A *subroutine with output parameters* always returns data to the main program. An example of such a subroutine is the console input subroutine (CONIN). CONIN was called without sending any data to it (no input parameter) but it returned the ASCII code of the key (in register A) that was entered on the keyboard. The ASCII code returned in register A by the CONIN subroutine was the output parameter of the subroutine. A subroutine with output parameters always returns data to the main program, and in most cases the main program always expects this data to be returned.

A *subroutine with both input and output parameters* accepts input data and returns output data. For example, consider a subroutine to multiply two numbers. Before the subroutine is called, the two numbers to be multiplied will be loaded into appropriate registers. Then the subroutine is called; the subroutine performs the multiplication and returns the product of the two numbers in an appropriate register. The data contained in the two registers before the subroutine was called are the input parameters to the subroutine; the result (the product of the two numbers) returned by the subroutine is the output parameter.

The process of sending and returning parameters to and from a subroutine is known as *parameter passing*. Passing of input and output parameters does not have to be limited to being passed in CPU registers but can be extended to memory locations and status flags as well.

In writing utility subroutines, it is important to document the input and output parameters (if any) of a subroutine. When these subroutines are used in a main program, the user often has to know what these parameters are so that the code in the main program will comply with the subroutine calls. For example, if a main program called CONOUT with the input parameter in register D, the subroutine would be ineffective. The main program must therefore follow the *parameter-passing conventions* of the subroutine. If the subroutine requires that a particular piece of information be passed in a particular register, the main program must conform to the specification; similarly, if a subroutine returns information in a particular register, the main program can expect the data to be there.

Besides documenting parameter passing rules in a subroutine, it is also important to document the registers used (if any) by the subroutine. For example, if a main program is in the process of using a particular register, and a call is made to a utility subroutine that destroys the original contents of the register, the operation of the main program could be affected. In order for the programmer to know what registers are used by the subroutine so that they may be saved (if necessary) before the subroutine is called, documentation of these registers is an important part of writing utility subroutines.

Finally, if a subroutine CALLs another subroutine, it is important to document the subroutine(s) that are called, so that they can be linked into the final object code.

In many cases glancing through an undocumented subroutine will provide the information mentioned above. However, in lengthy and complex subroutines, it is easy to miss vital information about the subroutine.

As an example of subroutine documentation and preparation for relocatable assembly, Figures 10-4 and 10-5 show the CONIN and CONOUT subroutines, respectively. Subroutine documentation is shown as comments before the actual subroutine.

Notice in Figures 10-4 and 10-5 that each subroutine contains header information on the calling name of the subroutine, the inputs (input parameters) to the subroutine, the outputs (output parameters) from the subroutine, the registers destroyed (used up) by the subroutine, any other subroutines called by the subroutine, and a brief description of the subroutine. A programmer who requires

```
;****************************************************************     *
;                                                                      *
; NAME:         CONSOLE INPUT (CONIN)                                  *
; INPUTS:       NONE                                                   *
; OUTPUTS:      REG A = CHARACTER RECEIVED FROM KEYBOARD               *
; DESTROYS'     NOTHING                                                *
; CALLS:        NOTHING                                                *
; DESCRIPTION:  THE CONSOLE INPUT SUBROUTINE WAITS FOR A               *
;               CHARACTER TO BE ENTERED ON THE CONSOLE                 *
;               KEYBOARD AND RETURNS THE ASCII CODE OF THE             *
;               CHARACTER IN REG A.                                    *
;                                                                      *
;****************************************************************     *

                        PUBLIC    CONIN

0002 =          DATA    EQU       02H           ; 8251 data port
0003 =          STATUS  EQU       03H           ; 8251 status port

0000 DB03       CONIN:  IN        STATUS        ; Get UART status
0002 E602               ANI       00000010B     ; See if receiver ready
0004 CA0000'            JZ        CONIN         ; Wait until ready
0007 DB02               IN        DATA          ; Get received character
0009 E67F               ANI       01111111B     ; Strip parity bit
000B C9                 RET

000C                    END
```

FIGURE 10-4. Console input subroutine.

such a subroutine in a main program needs only to glance at the header documentation (without inspecting the actual code) to know what to expect from the subroutine.

There are many variations used by programmers when documenting subroutines with header information. Besides the information shown in Figures 10-4 and 10-5, the programmer may also wish to include his or her name, the date of completion, and the revision number. The date of completion and revision number enable the programmer to keep track of the most current revision, often the one that has been most field proven; programmers can often lose track of which routine was the latest revision.

Some programmers may choose to omit the "destroys" information from the subroutine documentation, by preserving the contents of all CPU registers (on the stack) that are used locally by the subroutine. Just before the subroutine returns to the calling program, the contents of the registers used could then be restored, allowing local register usage to be transparent to the user. This technique relieves the programmer from the burden of saving appropriate registers in the main program before calls are made to the utility subroutines; this is particularly true when a programmer has built a large collection of utility subroutines. Saving the contents of locally used registers does, however, waste a small amount of memory space.

Figures 10-4 and 10-5 also introduce a new directive used in relocatable

```
; ****************************************************************
;                                                                 *
; NAME:          CONSOLE OUTPUT (CONOUT)                          *
; INPUTS:        REG C = CHARACTER TO BE TRANSMITTED              *
; OUTPUTS:       NONE                                             *
; DESTROYS:      REG A                                            *
; CALLS:         NOTHING                                          *
; DESCRIPTION:   THE CONSOLE OUTPUT SUBROUTINE WAITS FOR          *
;                THE UART TRANSMITTER TO BE READY BEFORE          *
;                SENDING THE CHARACTER IN REG C TO THE            *
;                CONSOLE.                                         *
;                                                                 *
; ****************************************************************

                         PUBLIC    CONOUT

0002 =          DATA     EQU       02H          ; 8251 data port
0003 =          STATUS   EQU       03H          ; 8251 status port

0000 DB03       CONOUT:  IN        STATUS       ; Get UART status
0002 E602                ANI       00000001B    ; See if transmitter ready
0004 CA0000'             JZ        CONOUT       ; Wait until ready
0007 79                  MOV       A,C          ; Get character
0008 D302                OUT       DATA         ; Transmit character
000A C9                  RET

000B                     END
```

FIGURE 10-5. Console output subroutine.

assembly, the *public directive* (PUBLIC). The PUBLIC directive instructs the assembler that the following symbol is to be made available for access by other modules (main program or other subroutines). Since the symbol referenced in the PUBLIC directive is the name of the subroutine, the subroutine becomes accessible by other subroutines or main programs. The PUBLIC directive is also used to identify all the modules in a utility subroutine library, consisting of concatenated modules.

Note that the subroutines in Figures 10-4 and 10-5 do not contain ORG directives. This is because the ORG directive implies assembly at an absolute memory location, and since the assembled code for the subroutines will be located elsewhere at link time, the ORG directive is no longer needed. Even though the assembler "seems" to assemble the subroutines at a base address of 0, the actual location of the subroutines will be determined when the subroutine and main program are linked and located. Operands of instructions that have relocatable addresses (which will be changed at link time) are identified by the assembler by the single quote (') shown to the immediate right of the assembled code, such as for the JZ CONOUT instruction in Figure 10-5.

The remainder of this chapter is devoted to developing several utility modules that will be used in a final main program to implement the loader described in Chapter 9.

10-4

UTILITY SUBROUTINES

This section deals with the development of five utility subroutines that will be used with the CONIN and CONOUT subroutines in the construction of an absolute object file loader. The operation of each subroutine will be explained by means of a flowchart, followed by a discussion of the linkage directives.

PRINT Utility

In Figure 9-10, a flowchart for a message print program (Figure 9-11) was developed. The program displayed an ASCII character string on the console. Since this type of program is used fairly often in application programs, it is best to rewrite the program as a utility subroutine. In rewriting the PRINT subroutine, one major change will be made—instead of supplying the subroutine with a count of the number of characters in the string, the string will be terminated with the ASCII nongraphic null character (00H) so that the subroutine can automatically detect the end of the string.

The flowchart for the PRINT utility is shown in Figure 10-6. Assume that a pointer has already been set to the start of the string before the subroutine is called.

Notice that the flowchart in Figure 10-6 is very similar to the flowchart in Figure 9-10. In Figure 9-10 the program determined when the entire string was displayed by decrementing a count that was initially the length of the string. In Figure 10-6 the subroutine does not require a count set to the length of the string. Instead, the requirement of the subroutine is that the string be terminated with an ASCII *null* character. The program gets each character from memory and checks to see if it is a null. If it is, the entire string has been displayed; if

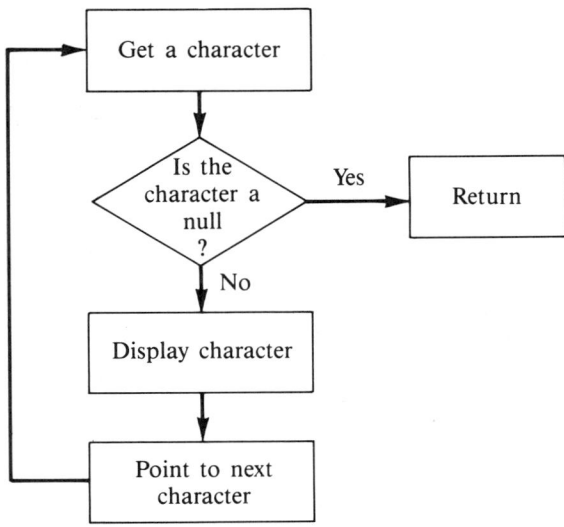

FIGURE 10-6. Flowchart for the PRINT subroutine.

```
;**********************************************************
;
; NAME:         PRINT STRING (PRINT)
; INPUTS:       RP DE = ADDRESS OF STRING TO BE PRINTED
; OUTPUTS:      NONE
; DESTROYS:     REGS A,C,D,E
; CALLS:        CONOUT
; DESCRIPTION:  THE PRINT STRING SUBROUTINE PRINTS THE
;               STRING WITH STARTING ADDRESS SPECIFIED IN
;               RP DE ON THE CONSOLE. THE STRING MUST BE
;               TERMINATED WITH AN ASCII NULL (00).
;
;**********************************************************

                        PUBLIC  PRINT

                        EXTRN   CONOUT

0000 =          NULL    EQU     00H     ; ASCII code for null

0000 1A         PRINT:  LDAX    D       ; Get a character
0001 FE00               CPI     NULL    ; See if end of string
0003 C8                 RZ              ; Return if so
0004 4F                 MOV     C,A     ; Else prepare for CONOUT
0005 CD0000'            CALL    CONOUT  ; Display it
0008 13                 INX     D       ; Point to next character
0009 C30000'            JMP     PRINT   ; Continue until end

000C                    END
```

FIGURE 10-7. PRINT subroutine.

not, the character is displayed, the pointer set to the next character in the string, and the process continued.

Figure 10-7 shows the implementation of the flowchart in Figure 10-6 as a utility subroutine. Before the subroutine in Figure 10-7 is called, RP D&E must be set to the starting address of the string (input parameter). The string can be stored along with the calling program by using a DB directive. The string *must* be terminated by an ASCII NULL character.

Notice in Figure 10-7 that the PRINT subroutine calls CONOUT to display each character in the string. Since CONOUT is another subroutine external to the PRINT subroutine, the EXTRN directive is used, telling the assembler that the absolute address of the CONOUT routine will be determined and filled in at link time. Also notice that before the CONOUT subroutine is called, the character to be displayed is moved to register C (since register C must contain the input parameter) in preparation for CONOUT.

VALDGT Utility

In many application programs it is necessary to accept numeric ASCII graphic characters from the console keyboard for various types of arithmetic and numeric processing. When a numeric ASCII character is entered at the keyboard, it is important to check the validity of the character entered to make sure that the

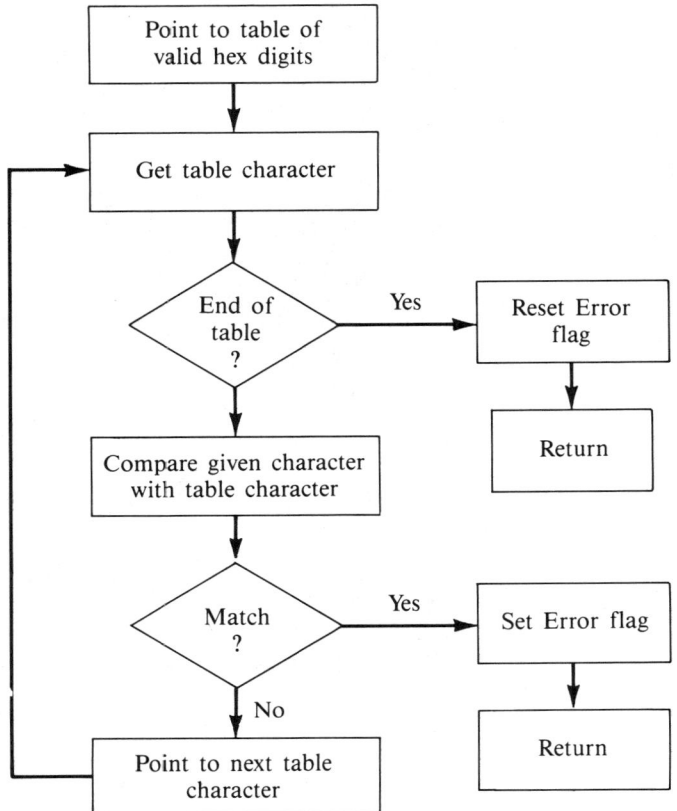

FIGURE 10-8. Flowchart for the VALDGT subroutine.

user did type a numeric key and not any other key. This check ensures that the arithmetic or numeric processing done on the numbers is not erroneous. The VALDGT subroutine checks the validity of hexadecimal numbers (0 through 9, A through F) entered on the keyboard and returns a flag set if the character entered was a valid hex digit, or reset if it was an invalid hex digit. The flowchart to implement the VALDGT subroutine is shown in Figure 10-8.

The flowchart in Figure 10-8 makes use of a look-up table to determine if the given character is a valid ASCII hex digit. The table contains all the valid ASCII hexadecimal digits stored in hexadecimal representation. The program compares each byte in the table with the given character until a match is found; on finding a match, an error flag is set to indicate success. If the search is exhausted and the end of the table is reached (no match has been found), the given character is invalid and the error flag is reset, indicating failure. The program implementation of the flowchart is shown in Figure 10-9.

The subroutine in Figure 10-9 has both input and output parameters. The input parameter is the ASCII digit (in hexadecimal representation) to be checked, and has to be loaded into register C before calling the subroutine. The output parameter is the carry flag, which is set to indicate that the contents of register C is a valid digit, and reset to indicate that the character is an invalid digit. The

```
; *************************************************************  *
;                                                                 *
; NAME:         DETERMINE IF VALID HEX DIGIT (VALDGT)             *
; INPUTS:       REG C = ASCII CHARACTER TO BE CHECKED             *
; OUTPUTS:      CARRY = 1 IF CHAR IS A VALID HEX DIGIT            *
;               CARRY = 0 IF CHAR IS AN INVALID HEX DIGIT         *
; DESTROYS:     H,L,A                                             *
; CALLS:        NOTHING                                           *
; DESCRIPTION:  THE VALDGT SUBROUTINE CHECKS THE ASCII            *
;               CHARACTER IN REGISTER C AND DETERMINES IF         *
;               IT LIES WITHIN THE RANGE '0'-'9', 'A'-'F'         *
;               (30-39, 41-46). IF IT IS WITHIN THIS RANGE,       *
;               THE CARRY FLAG IS SET TRUE INDICATING             *
;               SUCCESS. IF IT IS NOT WITHIN THE RANGE THE        *
;               CARRY FLAG IS SET FALSE INDICATING                *
;               FAILURE.                                          *
;                                                                 *
; *************************************************************  *

                    PUBLIC VALDGT,ERR,OK,HEXTBL

0000 211600'    VALDGT: LXI   H,HEXTBL   ; Point to valid hex table
0003 7E         NXT:    MOV   A,M        ; Get table character
0004 FE24               CPI   '$'        ; End of table?
0006 CA1100'            JZ    ERR        ; No match . . . error
0009 B9                 CMP   C          ; Else compare with given char
000A CA1400'            JZ    OK         ; Match? . . . success
000D 23                 INX   H          ; Point to next table char
000E C30300'            JMP   NXT        ; Loop until end of table
0011 37         ERR:    STC              ; First set carry true
0012 3F                 CMC              ; Now make it false
0013 C9                 RET              ; and return error code C = 0
0014 37         OK:     STC              ; Set carry true
0015 C9                 RET              ; and return success code C = 1

0016 303132    HEXTBL:  DB    '0123456789ABCDEF','$'
0019 333435
001C 363738
001F 394142
0022 434445
0025 4624

0027                    END
```

FIGURE 10-9. VALDGT subroutine.

table of valid digits (HEXTBL) is stored using a DB directive, and is terminated with a "$." The $ will be used in the program to check for an end-of-table condition.

RP H&L is set to the start of the table and the first table character is brought into register A. The table character is checked to see if it is a $. If it is not a $, the table character is compared with the given character in register C. If a match is found, control is transferred to the portion of the program (OK) that sets the carry flag and returns. If no match is found, H&L is set to the next table character and the process is repeated until the table search is exhausted. When the entire table has been searched (a $ is detected), control transfers to ERR, the carry flag is reset, and the subroutine returns.

Note that since VALDGT does not call any other subroutine, no externals have been defined. Besides using the PUBLIC directive to make the VALDGT subroutine accessible, the labels ERR, OK, and HEXTBL have also been made public. This is because these symbolic addresses will be used again by some of the following utility subroutines, and will prevent any duplication of code.

ASCHEX Utility

When numeric digits are entered on the console keyboard, the CONIN subroutine always returns the ASCII representation (in hexadecimal) of the the numeric digit. For example, if the "3" key is depressed, the value returned is 33H, which is the ASCII code for a "3." Similarly, if the hexadecimal digit "B" is depressed on the keyboard, the ASCII code 42H is returned. Since arithmetic and numeric processing require hex key values rather than ASCII codes (i.e., we would like to see a 03H instead of a 33H, and a 0BH instead of a 42H) a utility subroutine to convert the ASCII representation of a hex digit to its hex value is needed. The ASCHEX utility performs this conversion. The flowchart for the ASCHEX subroutine is shown in Figure 10-10.

The flowchart for the ASCHEX subroutine in Figure 10-10 is very similar to the operation of the VALDGT subroutine. The only difference is that a count is maintained to keep track of the position of the character scanned in the table of valid hex digits. When a match is found, the subroutine will return this count as the hexadecimal value of the ASCII character. The manner in which this is done can be seen in the implementation of the ASCHEX subroutine in Figure 10-11.

Notice that the ASCHEX subroutine in Figure 10-11 uses three portions of the VALDGT subroutine. These are HEXTBLE, ERR, and OK, and are declared to be external to the subroutine. Since these three portions already exist in another subroutine, there is no point duplicating the code; the linkage editor will automatically fill in any address references to those labels. The subroutine does error checking on the input parameter in register C, and returns the same codes as in the VALDGT subroutine.

Notice that the position of each character in the HEXTBL (Figure 10-9) corresponds to the hexadecimal value of the character. This can be seen as follows:

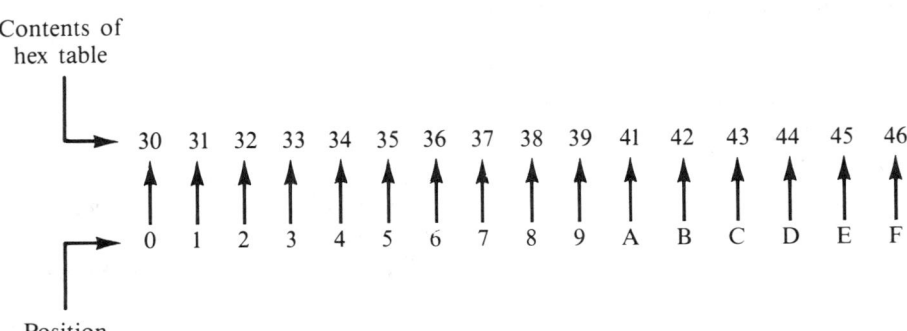

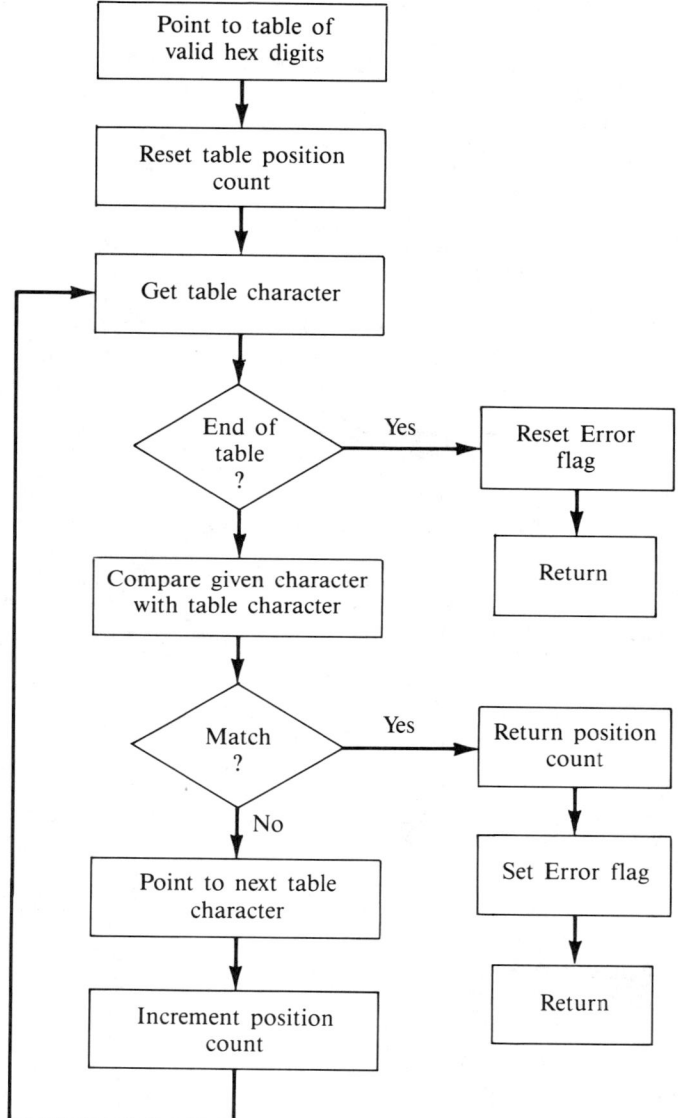

FIGURE 10-10. Flowchart for the ASCHEX subroutine.

Register B is used to keep track of the position of the table value scanned. If a match is found between the table value and the given character, register B contains the hex value of the character. The ASCII representation of the character has thus been converted to its hex value and returned in register A with the carry flag set to indicate success. If no match is found, the subroutine resets the carry flag and returns; the contents of register A is unpredictable. It is thus up to the calling program to check the state of the carry flag before accepting the converted number in register A as valid.

```
;****************************************************************   *
;                                                                    *
; NAME:          ASCII TO HEXADECIMAL CONVERSION (ASCHEX)             *
; INPUTS:        REG C = ASCII CHARACTER TO BE CONVERTED              *
; OUTPUTS:       REG A = CONVERTED HEXADECIMAL NUMBER                 *
;                CARRY = 0 IF INVALID ASCII CHAR                      *
;                CARRY = 1 IF VALID ASCII CHAR                        *
; DESTROYS:      H,L,B                                                *
; CALLS:         ERR,OK,HEXTBL (references)                           *
; DESCRIPTION:   THE ASCHEX SUBROUTINE CONVERTS THE ASCII             *
;                REPRESENTATION OF THE HEXADECIMAL                    *
;                CHARACTER IN REG C INTO ITS HEXADECIMAL              *
;                VALUE. ASCHEX CHECKS THE VALIDITY OF THE             *
;                CHARACTER IN REG C TO DETERMINE IF IT LIES           *
;                IN THE VALID RANGE.                                  *
;                                                                    *
;****************************************************************   *
;
                        PUBLIC  ASCHEX
                        EXTRN   ERR,OK,HEXTBL

0000 210000' ASCHEX: LXI     H,HEXTBL    ; Point to valid hex table
0003 0600            MVI     B,0         ; Table position count
0005 7E      NXT:    MOV     A,M         ; Get table character
0006 FE24            CPI     '$'         ; End of table?
0008 CA0000'         JZ      ERR         ; Error . . . no match
000B B9              CMP     C           ; Compare with given character
000C CA1400'         JZ      NUM         ; Match? . . . found number
00F  23              INX     H           ; Else next table character
0010 04              INR     B           ; Next position
0011 C30500'         JMP     NXT         ; Loop until table end
0014 78      NUM:    MOV     A,B         ; Register B contains number
0015 C30000'         JMP     OK          ; Return success

0018                 END
```

FIGURE 10-11. ASCHEX subroutine.

GET2HX Utility

In application programs that require 8-bit (two hex digits) numeric processing, a subroutine is often required that reads two hex digits from the console keyboard and returns an assembled byte. For example, the subroutine would read two keystrokes, "5," "C," in sequence and return in a register the assembled byte 5CH. Remember that when these two keys are depressed, the ASCII codes 35H and 43H are transmitted from the terminal. It is therefore up to the GET2HX subroutine to read two digits from the keyboard, convert the ASCII codes of the two characters entered into their hexadecimal values, assemble the two hexadecimal values into a byte, and return the result. The GET2HX subroutine must also check the validity of the two digits entered. The flowchart for the GET2HX subroutine is shown in Figure 10-12.

The subroutine to implement the flowchart of Figure 10-12 is shown in Figure 10-13. Observe that the GET2HX subroutine in Figure 10-13 calls CONIN, VALDGT, and ASCHEX. The subroutine also returns the same error code as

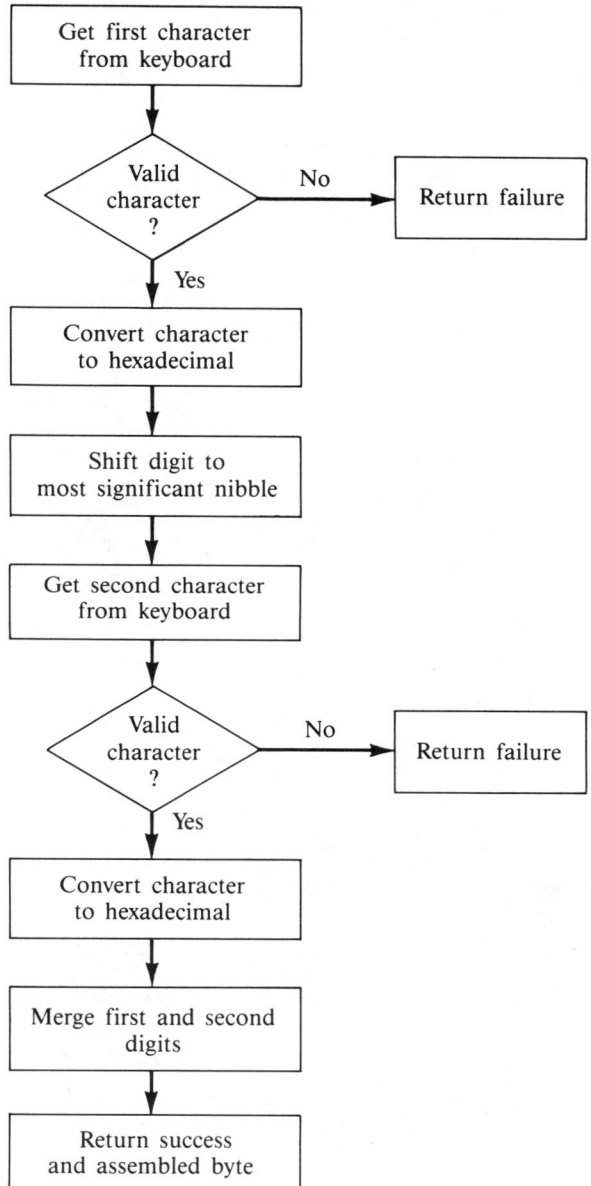

FIGURE 10-12. Flowchart for the GET2HX subroutine.

the previous subroutines in cases where invalid digits are entered on the keyboard.

The subroutine in Figure 10-13 implements the flowchart of Figure 10-12 as follows. The CONIN routine is called to get the first digit entered at the console keyboard. CONIN returns the ASCII value of the character in register A. Next, VALDGT is called with the ASCII character in register C, to check if the entered character is valid. If an invalid digit was entered, VALDGT returns the carry

```
;****************************************************************
;                                                                *
; NAME:          GET 2 HEX DIGITS FROM CONSOLE (GET2HX)          *
; INPUTS:        NONE                                            *
; OUTPUTS:       REG A = ASSEMBLED HEX BYTE                      *
;                CARRY=1 IF VALID BYTE ENTERED                   *
;                CARRY=0 IF INVALID BYTE ENTERED                 *
; DESTROYS:      B,C,H,L,D                                       *
; CALLS:         VALDGT,CONIN,ASCHEX                             *
; DESCRIPTION:   THE GET2HX SUBROUTINE READS TWO HEXA-           *
;                DECIMAL CHARACTERS (REPRESENTED IN ASCII)       *
;                FROM THE CONSOLE, CHECKS THE VALIDITY OF        *
;                EACH, AND ASSEMBLES THEM INTO A HEXA-           *
;                DECIMAL BYTE IN REG A.                          *
;                                                                *
;****************************************************************

                    PUBLIC  GET2HX
                    EXTRN   CONIN,VALDGT,ASCHEX

0000 CD0000'  GET2HX: CALL  CONIN   ; Get a character
0003 4F              MOV    C,A     ;
0004 CD0000'         CALL   VALDGT  ; Check its validity
0007 D0              RNC            ; Error if invalid character
0008 CD0000'         CALL   ASCHEX  ; Convert to hexadecimal
000B 07              RLC            ; Get in M.S. nibble position
000C 07              RLC
000D 07              RLC
000E 07              RLC
000F 57              MOV    D,A     ; Save in register D
0010 CD0000'         CALL   CONIN   ; Get next character
0013 4F              MOV    C,A     ;
0014 CD0000'         CALL   VALDGT  ; Check its validity
0017 D0              RNC            ; Error if invalid character
0018 CD0000'         CALL   ASCHEX  ; Convert to hexadecimal
001B B2              ORA    D       ; Merge two numbers
001C 37              STC            ; Success carry = 1
001D C9              RET            ; Return result

001E                 END
```

FIGURE 10-13. GET2HX subroutine.

flag reset, and the subroutine returns with the carry flag preserved. If the digit entered is valid, ASCHEX is called to convert the ASCII representation of the digit to its corresponding value. The digit value is returned in the least significant nibble of register A; the contents of register A are shifted left four times to get the first digit in the most significant 4-bit position. The first digit is saved in register D. CONIN is then called to get the second digit from the keyboard. The same process is repeated to check the validity of the character and then convert the character to its hexadecimal value. The second digit is now in the least significant 4 bits of register A. The contents of register D (temporary storage of first digit) is ORed with register A to obtain the assembled byte as a result. The subroutine then returns with the carry flag set to indicate success.

Thus if the following keystrokes "A," "5" were entered in sequence on the keyboard, GET2HX returns register A = A5H.

GET4HX Utility

The GET4HX subroutine is very similar to the GET2HX subroutine except that GET4HX waits until four valid digits have been entered on the keyboard and returns the assembled word in a 16-bit register. This type of subroutine is useful for accepting four-digit hex numbers from the keyboard for numeric processing. Since most of the work for the GET4HX subroutine was done in the GET2HX subroutine, implementing GET4HX is fairly simple and is shown in Figure 10-14.

The subroutine in Figure 10-14 first calls GET2HX to input two digits assembled into a byte (most significant) in register A. If any invalid character was entered, the carry flag is reset by GET2HX and the subroutine returns with the value of the flag preserved. The most significant byte is saved in register H. GET2HX is then called again to get the least significant byte. Since GET2HX destroys H&L (recall that register H contains the most significant byte), the contents of H&L is saved on the stack before the second call. On return from

```
;********************************************************************
;                                                                    *
; NAME:         GET 4 HEX DIGITS FROM CONSOLE (GET4HX)                *
; INPUTS:       NONE                                                  *
; OUTPUTS:      RP HL = ASSEMBLED HEX WORD                            *
;               CARRY=1 IF VALID BYTE ENTERED                         *
;               CARRY=0 IF INVALID BYTE ENTERED                       *
; DESTROYS:     B,C,D                                                 *
; CALLS:        GET2HX                                                *
; DESCRIPTION:  THE GET4HX SUBROUTINE READS FOUR HEXA-                *
;               DECIMAL CHARACTERS (REPRESENTED IN ASCII)             *
;               FROM THE CONSOLE, CHECKS THE VALIDITY OF              *
;               EACH, AND ASSEMBLES THEM INTO A HEXA-                 *
;               DECIMAL WORD IN RP HL.                                *
;                                                                    *
;********************************************************************

                        PUBLIC  GET4HX
                        EXTRN   GET2HX,ERR,OK

0000 CD0000'  GET4HX:   CALL    GET2HX      ; Get M.S. byte
0003 D0                 RNC                 ; Error if invalid
0004 67                 MOV     H,A         ; Store in register H
0005 E5                 PUSH    H           ; Save M.S. byte
0006 CD0000'            CALL    GET2HX      ; Get L.S. byte
0009 E1                 POP     H           ; Get M.S. byte
000A D0                 RNC                 ; Error if invalid
000B 6F                 MOV     L,A         ; Save L.S. byte in register L
000C C9                 RET                 ; Success return

000D                    END
```

FIGURE 10-14. GET4HX subroutine.

GET2HX, the value of H&L is restored and the carry flag is tested again to make sure that no invalid digits have been entered for the least significant digits. If the carry flag is set (indicating valid digits), the least significant two digits are moved into register L, so that RP H&L now contains the four-digit assembled word. The subroutine then returns with the carry flag preserved (set). For example, if the keystrokes "1," "B," "D," "5" were entered on the keyboard, GET4HX would return RP H&L = 1BD5H.

10-5

MAIN PROGRAM

Sections 10-3 and 10-4 discussed the operation of seven utility subroutines that were developed as relocatable modules. These utilities will now be used in an application program (main program) structured in a form very similar to the hierarchical tree in Figure 10-2. The application program is a *loader*, which will read individual object file records from an absolute object file (refer to Chapter 9), load the program bytes in each record at their respective load addresses, and determine if the records contain any errors. With the description of the object file format in Chapter 9 and the subroutines in Section 10-4, the reader should have a fairly clear picture of the solution to the specification.

The flowchart in Figure 10-15 describes implementation of the loader. The second record of the object file in Figure 9-5 will be used to illustrate the manner in which each field of the record is detected and interpreted by the loader. These fields are shown on the left-hand side (in parentheses) of each block in the flowchart where data is read in. Note that this program reads each record in the object file from the console keyboard. However, the input device need not be limited to a console keyboard, but can be any serial device attached to the 8251 chip (such as a paper-tape reader, cassette, modem, etc.). The program can easily be modified (by changing CONIN) to read the object file from disk.

The program to implement the flowchart of Figure 10-15 is shown in Figure 10-16. The program illustrated in Figures 10-15 and 10-16 reads in each field of an object file record: the starting character (:), the number of program bytes, the load address, the separators, the program bytes, and the checksum. As each field is read in, the program adds each of the bytes in the field to an 8-bit memory location. Just before the record checksum is read in, the program calculates the modulo 8 checksum of all the fields and compares it to the record checksum. If a match is found, control transfers to the start of the program to read the next record. Each record is read in until the last record in the object file indicates a record count of 00, at which time the program terminates.

The steps in the flowchart and program in Figures 10-15 and 10-16 can be explained as follows. The first part of the main program sets up the stack pointer and clears the memory location that will hold the modulo 8 sum of all the fields in the object file record. Next, the program waits until it receives the ":" character, which indicates the start of a record. On receiving the ":", the program calls GET2HX to input the program byte count from the record. If any invalid character is entered, GET2HX resets the carry flag and the program prints an error message (CERR) and prompts the user to reenter the entire record.

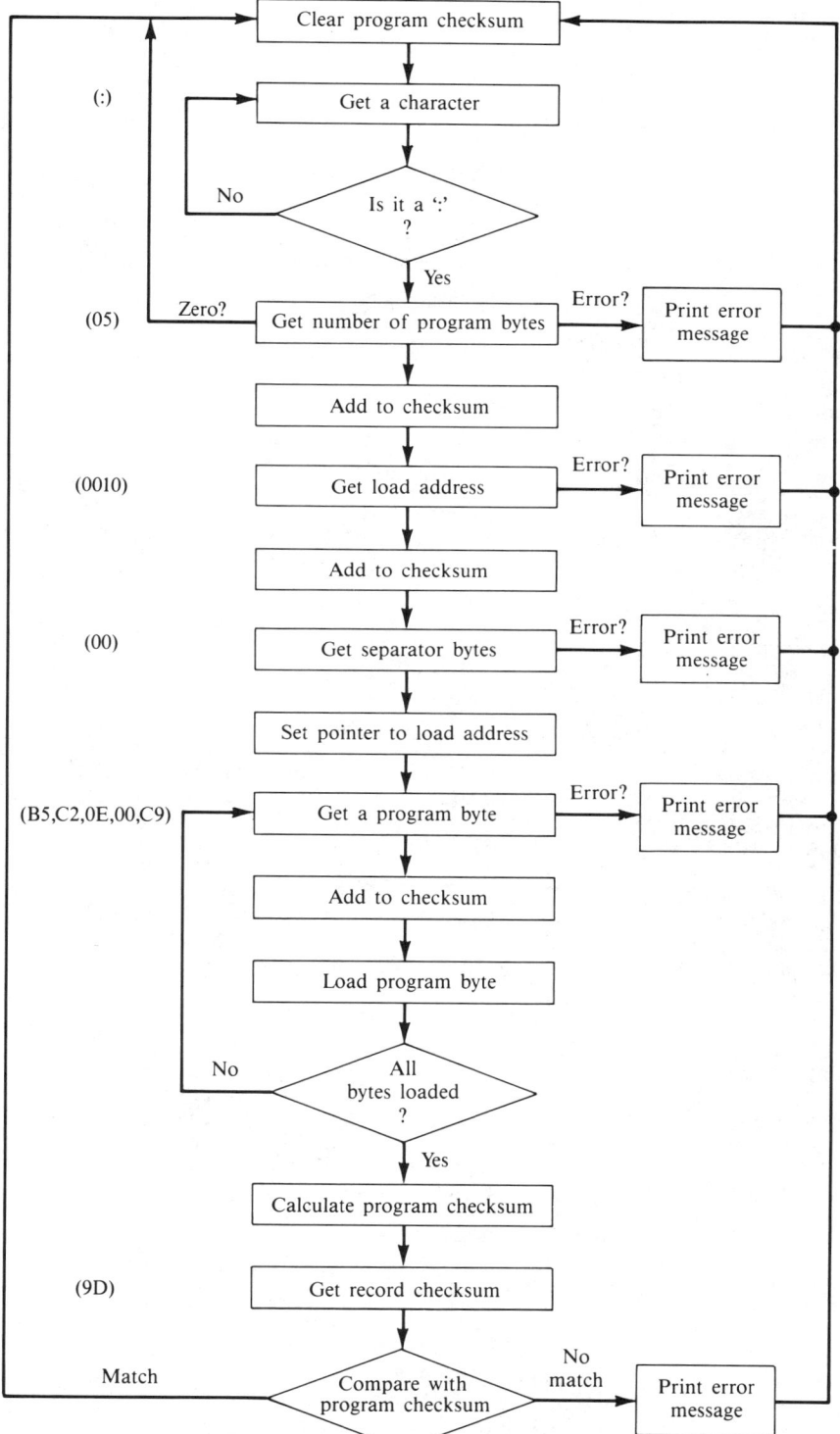

FIGURE 10-15. Flowchart for the loader program.

```
                    ;****************************
                    ;                            *
                    ; ABSOLUTE OBJECT FILE LOADER *
                    ;       MAIN PROGRAM          *
                    ;                            *
                    ;****************************
                    ;
                    ; Assemble in the code segment
                            CSEG
                    ; External utility subroutines
                            EXTRN   GET2HX,GET4HX,PRINT,CONIN
                    ; Nongraphic ASCII characters
0000 =              NULL    EQU     00H             ; Null
000D =              CR      EQU     0DH             ; Carriage return
000A =              LF      EQU     0AH             ; Line feed
                    ; Start of main program
0000 311500'                LXI     SP,STACK        ; Set up stack area in DSEG
0003 3E00           START:  MVI     A,0             ; Set program checksum to zero
0005 320000'                STA     CKSUM
                    ; Wait for ':' to indicate start of record
0008 CD0000'        WAIT:   CALL    CONIN           ; Get a character
000B FE3A                   CPI     ':'             ; Record started?
000D C20800'                JNZ     WAIT            ; Wait until ':' received
                    ; Now get number of program bytes
0010 CD0000'                CALL    GET2HX          ; Get program byte count
0013 D26700'                JNC     CERR            ; Error if invalid
0016 FE00                   CPI     00H             ; Is it zero?
0018 CA6600'                JZ      STOP            ; All records loaded—stop
001B 5F                     MOV     E,A             ; Save count in register E
001C D5                     PUSH    D               ; Save it for now
001D 3A0000'                LDA     CKSUM           ; Get program checksum
0020 83                     ADD     E               ; Add to checksum
0021 320000'                STA     CKSUM           ; Save new checksum
                    ; Get load address
0024 CD0000'                CALL    GET4HX          ; Get the load address
0027 D26700'                JNC     CERR            ; Error if invalid
002A E5                     PUSH    H               ; Save the address
002B 3A0000'                LDA     CKSUM           ; Get the program checksum
002E 84                     ADD     H               ; Add high address
002F 85                     ADD     L               ; Add low address
0030 320000'                STA     CKSUM           ; Save the checksum
                    ; Index over separator zeros
0033 CD0000'                CALL    GET2HX          ; Get separators
0036 D26700'                JNC     CERR            ; Error if invalid
                    ; Get and load the program bytes
0039 E1                     POP     H               ; Restore the load address
003A D1                     POP     D               ; Restore program byte count
003B E5              DBYTES: PUSH   H               ; Save address
```

FIGURE 10-16. Implementation of the loader.

```
003C D5              PUSH    D            ; Save count
003D CD0000'         CALL    GET2HX       ; Get a program byte
0040 D1              POP     D            ; Restore address
0041 E1              POP     H            ; Restore count
0042 D26700'         JNC     CERR         ; Error if invalid
0045 77              MOV     M,A          ; Save the program byte
0046 3A0000'         LDA     CKSUM        ; Get program checksum
0049 86              ADD     M            ; Add to sum
004A 320000'         STA     CKSUM        ; Save checksum
004D 23              INX     H            ; Next load location
004E 1D              DCR     E            ; Count down number of program bytes
004F C23B00'         JNZ     DBYTES       ; Loop until all bytes loaded

             ; Get the record checksum

0052 CD0000'         CALL    GET2HX       ; Get record checksum
0055 D26700'         JNC     CERR         ; Error if invalid character
0058 5F              MOV     E,A          ; Save record checksum

             ; Calculate the program checksum

0059 3A0000'         LDA     CKSUM        ; Get program checksum
005C 2F              CMA                  ; One's complement
005D C601            ADI     1            ; Two's complement

             ; Compare record checksum with program checksum

005F BB              CMP     E            ; Compare the two checksums
0060 C27000'         JNZ     ERROR        ; Error if no match
0063 C30300'         JMP     START        ; Read next record if match

             ; Enter this point when entire object file is loaded

0066 76       STOP:  HLT

             ; Enter this point for invalid character error

0067 117900' CERR:   LXI     D,ICERR      ; Point to error message
006A CD0000'         CALL    PRINT        ; Print the error message
006D C30300'         JMP     START        ; Read record again

             ; Enter this point for checksum error

0070 119F00' ERROR:  LXI     D,CKERR      ; Point to error message
0073 CD0000'         CALL    PRINT        ; Print the error message
0076 C30300'         JMP     START        ; Read record again

             ; Error messages

0079 0D0A494E ICERR: DB      CR,LF,'INVALID CHARACTER-RETYPE',CR,LF,NULL
009F 0D0A4348 CKERR: DB      CR,LF,'CHECKSUM ERROR-RETYPE',CR,LF,NULL

             ; Data segment in RAM

                             DSEG

0000         CKSUM:  DS      1            ; Reserve 1 byte for checksum storage
0001                 DS      20           ; 20 bytes for stack
0015 =       STACK   EQU     $            ; Stack starts here

0015                 END
```

FIGURE 10-16. (Continued)

The program byte count is checked and if zero indicates that all the records in the object file have been read in and the program terminates. If the count is not zero, the count is added to the modulo 8 sum (CKSUM) and saved on the stack for future use.

The subroutine GET4HX is then called to read in the load address of the record. GET4HX returns the carry flag reset if any invalid characters have been entered; control is transferred to CERR and the process in the preceding step is repeated. Each byte of the load address is added to the checksum and then saved on the stack for future use. GET2HX is again called to get the separator field (00) between the load address and the program bytes. Nothing is done with these numbers since they serve only as a separator.

Finally, the program goes through a loop to read and load each program byte in the record. This is done by setting RP H&L to the load address (previously saved) and register E to the count of the number of program bytes (previously saved). As each byte is read in by GET2HX (error checking is done as before) it is stored at the address pointed to by RP H&L; for each byte read in, the count is decremented. This continues until the count is zero, at which time all the program bytes have been read from the record. The loop also adds each byte read to the modulo 8 checksum.

The last step in the program recalls the final modulo 8 sum and by taking its two's complement generates a checksum for all the bytes previously read in. The checksum appended to the end of the object file record is read in (again, by calling GET2HX) and the calculated checksum is compared with the record checksum. If they match, the record has been loaded properly, and control transfers to the start of the program to read the next record. If they do not match, an error exists somewhere in the record that was read in; the program prints an error message, prompting the user to reenter the record and transfers control to the start of the program to read the record again.

Notice in Figure 10-16 that all the subroutines that are used in the program—GET2HX, GET4HX, PRINT, and CONIN—are declared to be external and will be linked into the main program during linkage and location. These subroutines are the first-level subroutines (refer to Figure 10-2). The second-level subroutines, CONOUT, VALDGT, and ASCHEX, will automatically be linked in since they are declared external in the first-level subroutines. Also notice in Figure 10-16 that two new directives used in relocatable assembly have been introduced in the main program: the CSEG (code segment) and the DSEG (data segment) directives. The use of these directives can be related to the discussion of program segments from Chapter 9. The CSEG and DSEG directives will ultimately instruct the linkage editor to locate the following code in the code and data segments of memory, respectively. The manner in which this is done will be seen in the next section.

10-6

LINKAGE AND LOCATION

At this point in the development of the assembly language application program there are seven relocatable utility modules—CONIN, CONOUT, PRINT,

```
GET2HX   111C     GET4HX   113A     PRINT  10D1     CONIN  10BA
CONOUT   10C6     VALDGT   10DD     ERR    10EE     OK     10F1
HEXTBL   10F3     ASCHEX   1104

CODE SIZE         0147  (1000-1146)
DATA SIZE         0015  (5000-5014)
```

FIGURE 10-17. Link map produced by linkage editor.

VALDGT, ASCHEX, GET2HX, and GET4HX—and one main module—LOADER. The next step in the development process is to use the linkage editor to "bind" (link) all these modules into an absolute object code file at specified addresses for the code and data segments.

The linkage editor must be instructed to link all the relocatable utility subroutines to the main program. It must also be instructed to locate the code and data segments at specified addresses. For example, Figure 10-17 shows a link map produced by the linkage editor when instructed to link the previously mentioned untility modules with the main module; the location specified for the code segment is 1000H and the location specified for the data segment is 5000H. (*Note:* Other values could be specified.)

From the link map in Figure 10-17 one can get a picture of how the linkage editor organizes the modules. The interpretation of the link map in Figure 10-17 can be explained as follows. The application program is located in two segments in memory: a code segment of 0147H bytes starting at location 1000H and ending at location 1146H, and a data segment of 0015H bytes starting at location 5000H and ending at 5014H.

The code segment contains all the code assembled for the main program at locations 1000H through 10B9H. The other utility modules are located directly below the main program in the following sequence:

```
1000H-10B9H—main program
10BA-CONIN
10C6-CONOUT
10D1-PRINT
10DD-VALDGT
1104-ASCHEX
111C-GET2HX
113A-GET4HX
```

The data segment simply contains the stack area defined in the main program and the storage location for the checksum (CKSUM). Thus the label CKSUM will have a value of 5000H and the label STACK will have a value of 5015H.

At this point is may be important to point out that the manner in which the linkage editor is commanded to link the modules, and the manner in which the modules are organized, will depend entirely on the type of linkage editor being used. The example given in this section describes the operation of most linkage editors.

10-7

SUMMARY

The purpose of this chapter was to introduce the reader to the concept of relocatable assembly and the techniques used in developing suitable assembly language programs. The construction of structured programs is extremely important for relocatable assembly. Structured programs often lead to the production of more efficient machine code, and also reduce the amount of development time spent on an application program. This is true not only for assembly language programs but also for programs written in higher-level languages (to be seen later). By using many relocatable utility modules, the programmer can eventually build a utility library consisting of well-documented, commonly used subroutintes. When an application program requires one or more of the utility subroutines, all the programmer needs to do is to link the required module into the main program, without spending the time required to develop the subroutines at the source level. Another advantage is that the subroutines are "mature," that is, they have been previously checked and tested, and if the application program does not work as intended, the problem can be narrowed down to the main program. Since the main program is relatively short (a major portion of the main program consists of calls to utility subroutines), debugging the main program is much easier.

This chapter has illustrated one complete example of the development of an assembly language application program using relocatable assembly. However, any well-structured program can fit this scheme.

REVIEW QUESTIONS AND PROBLEMS

1. Compare the process of relocatable assembly with that of absolute assembly.

2. What are the differences between the four basic types of subroutines as far as parameters are concerned?

3. What is the purpose of the PUBLIC and EXTRN directives to the assembler?

4. Modify the utility subroutines developed in this chapter so that each subroutine preserves the contents of the CPU registers (does not destroy any register). Change the LOADER program to access these modified utilities.

5. What is the process of linkage and location? Briefly describe the operation of the linkage editor.

6. What is the purpose of the CSEG and DSEG directives?

7. Develop a utility subroutine, HEXASC, to convert a hexadecimal number in the range 00–0F to its ASCII representation. The input to the subroutine will be register C (hex number in the range 00–0F) and the outputs will be register

A (ASCII representation of the number), CARRY = 0 if the input hex number if invalid, and CARRY = 1 if the conversion was performed correctly. Note that this subroutine will function in a manner opposite to that of the ASCHEX subroutine.

8. Develop a utility subroutine, PUT2HX (function opposite to GET2HX), to display two hex digits in the range 00–FF on the console. The inputs to the subroutine will be register A (hex byte in the range 00–FF). No outputs are required.

9. Develop a utility subroutine, PUT4HX (function opposite to PUT4HX), to display four hex digits in the range 0000–FFFF on the console. The inputs to the subroutine will be RP H&L (hex address in the range 0000–FFFF). No outputs are required.

10. The LOADER program discussed in the chapter read in object file records and stored the data bytes in memory. Write a program called DUMP which will operate in reverse. The DUMP program will display on the console a specified range of memory locations in the form of object file records. Each record should have 10 data bytes together with the remaining five fields.

CHAPTER 11

Macros and Conditional Assembly

11-1

INTRODUCTION

The preceding two chapters dealt with software development using absolute- and relocatable-code-producing assemblers. Both these assemblers usually provide the programmer with additional facilities to aid in software development. Programming with macros provides the programmer with greater flexibility in writing segments of code and also allows the programmer to expand superficially the instruction set of the microprocessor. Another facility provided by most assemblers is conditional assembly. By using certain conditional assembly directives a single "generic" program can be written that includes several possible segments of code, only a few of which are selectively included for assembly. This chapter discusses the applications of macros and conditional assembly during assembly language software development.

11-2

MACROS

Consider a program that is to accept four 4-bit numbers from an input port and assemble the numbers into a 16-bit word. This type of a program is known as *word assembly* and is shown in Figure 11-1.

```
        1000            ORG     1000H

        1000  DB00      IN      0               ; Get first number
        1002  07        RLC                     ; Move to M.S. position
        1003  07        RLC
        1004  07        RLC
        1005  07        RLC
        1006  E6F0      ANI     11110000B       ; Clear L.S. bits
        1008  47        MOV     B,A             ; Save first number
        1009  DB00      IN      0               ; Get second number
        100B  E60F      ANI     00001111B       ; Clear M.S. bits
        100D  B0        ORA     B               ; Merge with first number
        100E  67        MOV     H,A             ; Save first and second numbers
        100F  DB00      IN      0               ; Get third number
        1011  07        RLC                     ; Move to M.S. position
        1012  07        RLC
        1013  07        RLC
        1014  07        RLC
        1015  E6F0      ANI     11110000B       ; Clear L.S. bits
        1017  47        MOV     B,A             ; Save third number
        1018  DB00      IN      0               ; Get fourth number
        101A  E60F      ANI     00001111B       ; Clear M.S. bits
        101C  B0        ORA     B               ; Merge with third number
        101D  6F        MOV     L,A             ; Save third and fourth numbers
        101E  76        HLT                     ; RP H&L contains word

        101F            END
```

FIGURE 11-1. Word assembly program.

The program in Figure 11-1 reads each number from input port 0; the numbers arrive in the least significant 4 bits of the accumulator. Assuming that the 4-bit numbers are brought in most significant digit first, the final four-digit number is assembled in register pair H&L when the program terminates.

The program begins execution by an input from port 0 to bring in the first number. Since the number brought in is positioned in the least significant 4 bits of the accumulator, the four RLC instructions shift the 4 bits into the most significant 4 bits of the accumulator. The contents of the least significant 4 bits of the accumulator is then cleared by ANDing it with 11110000B. The first entered number is then saved in register B. The second 4-bit number is then brought in from port 0 and the most significant 4 bits cleared (in case there exist erroneous bits brought in from the 4-bit port) by ANDing the contents of the accumulator with 11110000B. The contents of register B (first number in the most significant 4 bits) is then "merged" with the contents of the accumulator (second number in the least significant 4 bits), by ORing the two registers. The accumulator now contains the first and second numbers brought in from port 0 as a two-digit byte. This byte is saved in register H.

The process described above is repeated for the third and fourth numbers brought in from port 0. The third and fourth numbers are assembled as a byte and stored in register L. Thus, when the program completes execution, register pair H&L contains the assembled four digits as a single word.

In developing the program shown in Figure 11-1, one can see that it would be nice if the 8080 instruction set included an instruction that would automatically shift 4 bits at a time. In other words, if the 8080 had a single instruction, say SLN (shift left nibble), that would automatically perform four single-bit left shifts and pad the least significant 4 bits of the accumulator with zeros. Since there is no means to expand the processor's instruction set (through hardware), the assembler provides a facility to do this superficially by means of a *macro definition*.

In Figure 11-1, the sequence of four RLC instructions and the ANI 11110000 instruction could be "defined" as a MACRO called SLN:

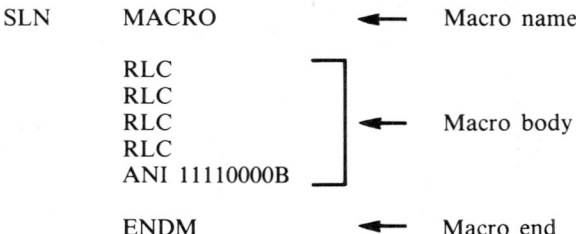

The macro definition shown above consists of three parts. The first line in the definition identifies the name of the macro. In this case the name of the macro is SLN. The *macro name* is defined in the label field of the source file, and the macro directive is used to identify the name. Immediately following the name definition is the *macro body*. The macro body consists of several instructions in sequence. Now whenever the assembler identifies a macro name during the assembly process, the entire body is inserted at that point. This process will be seen in another example. Finally, the ENDM directive identifies the end of the macro definition.

Figure 11-2 shows the source file of the same program in Figure 11-1, with a macro definition for SLN. Notice that the SLN macro is defined before the actual program; this allows the assembler to encounter (and thus remember) the macro definition before the program is assembled. The actual program in Figure 11-2 looks very similar to the program in Figure 11-1, except that it appears smaller in size and includes a new "instruction," SLN.

When the source program of Figure 11-2 is assembled, the assembler "remembers" the macro definition for the macro SLN during its first pass. During the second pass, every time the SLN "instruction" is encountered in the program sequence, a *macro expansion* takes place, as shown in Figure 11-3. A macro expansion is a process by which the assembler inserts the entire macro body of a defined macro every time the name of the macro is encountered during the second pass of assembly. In Figure 11-3, these macro expansions are identified by the assembler with "+" signs between the address and instruction bytes. Notice in Figure 11-3 that two expansions have taken place, one for each SLN instruction encountered. During each expansion the entire macro body has been inserted at the position of the SLN instruction.

If the code generated by the program in Figure 11-1 is compared to the code generated by the program in Figure 11-3, one can see that they are identical. Thus both programs will execute in the same manner. The difference between the two programs lies at the source level. The program portion of Figure 11-3

```
; Macro:          Shift left nibble (SLN)
; Description:    The SLN macro moves the least significant 4
;                 bits of the accumulator into the most
;                 significant 4 bit position. The L.S. 4 bits
;                 are padded with zeros.

SLN     MACRO
        RLC                     ; Shift 4 bits left
        RLC
        RLC
        RLC
        ANI     11110000B       ; Clear L.S. 4 bits
        ENDM

        ORG     1000H

        IN      0               ; Get first number
        SLN                     ; Move to M.S. position
        MOV     B,A             ; Save first number
        IN      0               ; Get second number
        ANI     00001111B       ; Clear M.S. bits
        ORA     B               ; Merge with first number
        MOV     H,A             ; Save first and second numbers
        IN      0               ; Get third number
        SLN                     ; Move to M.S. position
        MOV     B,A             ; Save third number
        IN      0               ; Get fourth number
        ANI     00001111B       ; Clear M.S. bits
        ORA     B               ; Merge with third number
        MOV     L,A             ; Save third and fourth numbers
        HLT                     ; RP H&L contains word

        END
```

FIGURE 11-2. Word assembly with SLN macro.

is much shorter than Figure 11-1. As far as the programmer is concerned, the SLN macro is simply another 8080 instruction and is used as one during program development.

Thus, by using macros at the source level in assembly language programs the programmer can "create" new instructions for the microprocessor. These new instructions do not have any meaning to the microprocessor but are simply a sequence of existing instructions organized to simulate a new instruction. Hence macros can be used to expand superficially the instruction set of the microprocessor. For example, the following macro definition defines a new instruction, SRN, which is similar to the SLN instruction except that it shifts the most significant nibble into the least significant position.

```
; Macro:          Shift right nibble (SRN)
; Description:    The SRN macro moves the most significant 4
;                 bits of the accumulator into the least
;                 significant 4-bit position. The MS 4 bits
;                 are padded with zeros.
```

```
SRN     MACRO
        RRC                     ; Shift 4 bits right
        RRC
        RRC
        RRC
        ANI     00001111B       ; Clear MS 4 bits
        ENDM
```

The existence of a macro name as part of the sequence of instructions in a program is known as a macro call. Macro calls should not be confused with subroutine calls. A *macro call* signals the assembler that a previously defined macro is to be expanded. A *subroutine call* transfers control of the CPU to another portion of the program. Thus, each time a macro is called, the entire code for that macro is inserted at that point, and each time a subroutine is called, control transfers to a common area in memory during execution. The use of macros therefore leads to the generation of code that is very inefficient in memory requirements but very efficient in execution speed.

Another application of macros is in expanding the translation capabilities of the assembler. Most assemblers are designed to assemble instructions of one particular microprocessor. If any instructions that are not part of the microprocessor's instruction set are included in a program for assembly, the assembler signals an error condition.

There are a few implementations of microprocessors that are "upwardly compatible" in software with the 8080. Examples of such microprocessors are the 8085 (discussed in a later chapter) and the Z80. For example, the 8085 microprocessor can execute all the 8080 instructions, but has two additional instructions, RIM and SIM. Since the 8085 is capable of "recognizing" all the 8080 instructions, but not vice versa, the 8085 is said to be upwardly compatible with the 8080.

If it were required to develop a program for the 8085 using an 8080 assembler (one that recognizes the 8080 instruction set only), the programmer could encounter a problem if the RIM and SIM instructions had to be assembled as part of the program. The problem can easily be solved by defining the RIM and SIM instructions of the 8085 as macros.

Recall that during the assembly process, as each instruction is assembled by the assembler, the mnemonics are translated into their corresponding machine code. Thus whenever a RIM or SIM mnemonic is encountered in the program, we would like the appropriate machine codes (20H and 30H, respectively) for each instruction. To do this, two macros are defined for the RIM and SIM instructions as follows:

```
RIM     MACRO
        DB      20H     ; Code for RIM
        ENDM

SIM     MACRO
        DB      30H     ; Code for SIM
        ENDM
```

In both the RIM and SIM macros, the macro body consists of a single DB directive that includes the machine code for the respective instruction. Now assuming that these macros have been defined in the 8085 program, whenever the assembler encounters either the RIM or SIM instruction in the sequence of instructions that make up the program, it substitutes a 20H or 30H at the current value of the location counter. The effect is thus the same as having an 8085 assembler.

```
            ; Macro:        Shift left nibble (SLN)
            ; Description:  The SLN macro moves the least significant 4
            ;               bits of the accumulator into the most
            ;               significant 4-bit position. The L.S. 4 bits
            ;               are padded with zeros.

                SLN MACRO
                    RLC                 ; Shift 4 bits left
                    RLC
                    RLC
                    RLC
                    ANI    11110000B    ; Clear L.S. 4 BITS
                    ENDM

1000                ORG    1000H

1000 DB00           IN     0            ; Get first number
                    SLN                 ; Move to M.S. position
1002+07             RLC                 ; Shift 4 bits left
1003+07             RLC
1004+07             RLC
1005+07             RLC
1006+E6F0           ANI    11110000B    ; Clear L.S. 4 bits
1008  47            MOV    B,A          ; Save first number
1009  DB00          IN     0            ; Get second number
100B  E60F          ANI    00001111B    ; Clear M.S. bits
100D  B0            ORA    B            ; Merge with first number
100E  67            MOV    H,A          ; Save first and second numbers
100F  DB00          IN     0            ; Get third number
                    SLN                 ; Move to M.S. position
1011+07             RLC                 ; Shift 4 bits left
1012+07             RLC
1013+07             RLC
1014+07             RLC
1015+E6F0           ANI    11110000B    ; Clear L.S. 4 bits
1017  47            MOV    B,A          ; Save third number
1018  DB00          IN     0            ; Get fourth number
101A  E60F          ANI    00001111B    ; Clear M.S. bits
101C  B0            ORA    B            ; Merge with third number
101D  6F            MOV    L,A          ; Save third and fourth numbers
101E  76            HLT                 ; RP H&L contains word

101F                END
```

FIGURE 11-3. Macro expansion of word assembly program.

11-3
MACROS WITH PARAMETERS

In Section 11-2 the examples illustrated the use of macros without parameters. Just as one could pass parameters to a subroutine, one can also pass parameters to a macro. For example, the block-move program in Chapter 8 could be converted into a macro with parameters. The parameters passed to the macro would be the source address of the move, the destination address of the move, and the count of the number of bytes to be moved. The manner in which this is done is shown in Figure 11-4.

The macro definition for the block-move program segment in Figure 11-4 is very similar to the definitions discussed for macros without parameters. The definition starts with the macro directive and ends with the ENDM directives. However, notice that the first line in the macro definition (the line containing the macro directive) contains a parameter list consisting of three symbols: SOURCE, DEST, and COUNT. These symbols are called *dummy parameters* and will be used to pass values to the macro body during an expansion. The dummy parameters SOURCE, DEST, and COUNT are also included in the macro body as operands of the LXI H, LXI D, and MVI B instructions, respectively. The name of the macro is MOVE.

Figure 11-5 shows two expansions of the MOVE macro in a skeleton program. Notice that the macro definition appears before the program itself, as was the case in examples discussed previously.

In Figure 11-5, the first macro call, MOVE 1000H,2000H,50H, initiates an expansion of the MOVE macro. The value 1000H (SOURCE) is assigned to the operand of the LXI H instruction, the value 2000H (DEST) is assigned to the operand of the LXI D instruction, and the value 50H (COUNT) is assigned to

```
; Definition for move macro

MOVE      MACRO     SOURCE,DEST,COUNT

          LOCAL     M1

          LXI       H,SOURCE      ; Get source address
          LXI       D,DEST        ; Get destination address
          MVI       B,COUNT       ; Number of bytes to be moved
M1:       MOV       A,M           ; Get source byte
          XCHG                    ; Exchange pointers
          MOV       M,A           ; Put in destination
          XCHG                    ; Restore pointers
          INX       H             ; SOURCE = SOURCE + 1
          INX       D             ; DEST = DEST + 1
          DCR       B             ; Count down bytes moved
          JNZ       M1            ; Continue until done

          ENDM
```

FIGURE 11-4. Macro definition for block move.

```
                MOVE    MACRO   SOURCE,DEST,COUNT
                        LOCAL   M1
                        LXI     H,SOURCE          ; Get source address
                        LXI     D,DEST            ; Get destination address
                        MVI     B,COUNT           ; Number of bytes to be moved
                M1:     MOV     A,M               ; Get source byte
                        XCHG                      ; Exchange pointers
                        MOV     M,A               ; Put in destination
                        XCHG                      ; Restore pointers
                        INX     H                 ; SOURCE = SOURCE + 1
                        INX     D                 ; DEST = DEST + 1
                        DCR     B                 ; Count down bytes moved
                        JNZ     M1                ; Continue until done
                        ENDM

0500                    ORG     0500H             ; Main program
                        .
                        .
                        MOVE    1000H,2000H,50H   ; First call
050F+210010             LXI     H,1000H           ; Get source address
0512+110020             LXI     D,2000H           ; Get destination address
0515+0650               MVI     B,50H             ; Number of bytes to be moved
0517+7E        ??0001:  MOV     A,M               ; Get source byte
0518+EB                 XCHG                      ; Exchange pointers
0519+77                 MOV     M,A               ; Put in destination
051A+EB                 XCHG                      ; Restore pointers
051B+23                 INX     H                 ; SOURCE = SOURCE + 1
051C+13                 INX     D                 ; DEST = DEST + 1
051D+05                 DCR     B                 ; Count down bytes moved
051E+C21705             JNZ     ??0001            ; Continue until done
                        .
                        .
                        MOVE    5000H,1070H,10    ; Second call
0539+210050             LXI     H,5000H           ; Get source address
053C+117010             LXI     D,1070H           ; Get destination address
053F+060A               MVI     B,10              ; Number of bytes to be moved
0541+7E        ??0002:  MOV     A,M               ; Get source byte
0542+EB                 XCHG                      ; Exchange pointers
0543+77                 MOV     M,A               ; Put in destination
0544+EB                 XCHG                      ; Restore pointers
0545+23                 INX     H                 ; SOURCE = SOURCE + 1
0546+13                 INX     D                 ; DEST = DEST + 1
0547+05                 DCR     B                 ; Count down bytes moved
0548+C24105             JNZ     ??0002            ; Continue until done
                        .
                        .
0555                    END
```

FIGURE 11-5. Two expansions of the MOVE macro.

the operand of the MVI B instruction. Notice that the symbols SOURCE, DEST, and COUNT do not appear in the expansion. Similarly, in the second macro expansion, the macro body is exactly the same as before except that the values of SOURCE, DEST, and COUNT are now 5000H, 1070H, and 10, respectively. Thus, each time a macro with parameters is called, the parameter values can be changed as required, allowing for a modified macro expansion each time.

In Figure 11-4 notice that within the macro body, a new directive, the *local directive* (LOCAL), has been used. The LOCAL directive in Figure 11-4 identifies the label M1 as being local (i.e., to exist only in the macro definition) to the MOVE macro and allows its value to change during each expansion, as shown in Figure 11-5.

In Figure 11-5 during the first expansion of the macro, the original label M1 was renamed ??0001 and obtained a value of 0517H during assembly. During the second expansion, the label was referenced as ??0002, and obtained a value of 0541H during assembly. Now if the label M1 were not renamed in each expansion, there would exist a multiple-label definition in the program; in other words, both expansions would contain the label M1, and the assembler would have to keep track of the value of M1 during each expansion. Therefore, the label M1 is defined to be local only to the macro definition and does not exist in the program.

11-4

AN APPLICATION OF MACROS

Consider an application program to control a set of traffic lights at the intersection of two streets: Main Street (north and south), and Third Street (east and west). Two output ports are used to turn the lights on or off as follows:

output port 50H = Main Street (north/south)

output port 60H = Third Street (east/west)

Three bits of each port are used to turn on or off the red, yellow, and green lights:

bit 0 = red

bit 1 = yellow

bit 2 = green

Assuming that a logic 1 turns a light on and a logic 0 turns a light off, the following are some of the instructions that could be used to control the state of the lights at the intersection.

1. Turn on red light for Main Street (yellow and green off).

```
MVI   A,00000001B
OUT   50H
```

2. Turn on green light for Third Street (red and yellow off).

```
MVI   A,00000100B
OUT   60H
```

3. Turn on yellow light for Main Street (green and red off).

```
MVI  A,00000010B
OUT  50H
```

Thus to turn on a specific light (note that only one of the three lights for a particular street is on at a given time), a specific bit pattern is sent to the output port assigned to a particular street. These values are assigned to symbols as follows:

MAIN	= 50H	RED	= 00000001B
THIRD	= 60H	YELLOW	= 00000010B
		GREEN	= 00000100B

The requirements for the software controlling the traffic lights are shown in the flowchart of Figure 11-6.

The program starts by switching the traffic lights on Main Street to green and the Third Street lights to red. A 50-second delay is then initiated. After the delay, Main Street is switched to yellow and after a further 5-second delay, to red, while Third Street is switched to green. Another 20-second delay is initiated. After the delay Third Street is now switched to yellow and after another 5-second delay, the cycle is repeated.

The program to implement the flowchart of Figure 11-6 will be constructed using only macros. In order to do this, three macros will be written as follows:

1. A macro called SWITCH, which will switch the lights on a specified street to a specified color.
2. A macro called WAIT, which will delay the CPU a specified number of seconds.
3. A macro called BEGIN, which will be used to transfer control to the start of the program on completion of a cycle.

Figure 11-7 shows the definition for the three macros SWITCH, WAIT, and BEGIN.

The SWITCH macro simply sets the accumulator to the specified bit pattern (dummy parameter COLOR) and outputs this to the specified port (dummy parameter STREET). Thus the macro call

```
SWITCH   MAIN,RED
```

(assuming that MAIN and RED have been equated to 50H and 00000001B, respectively) will turn the red light on for Main Street by means of the following instructions:

```
MVI  A,01H
OUT  50H
```

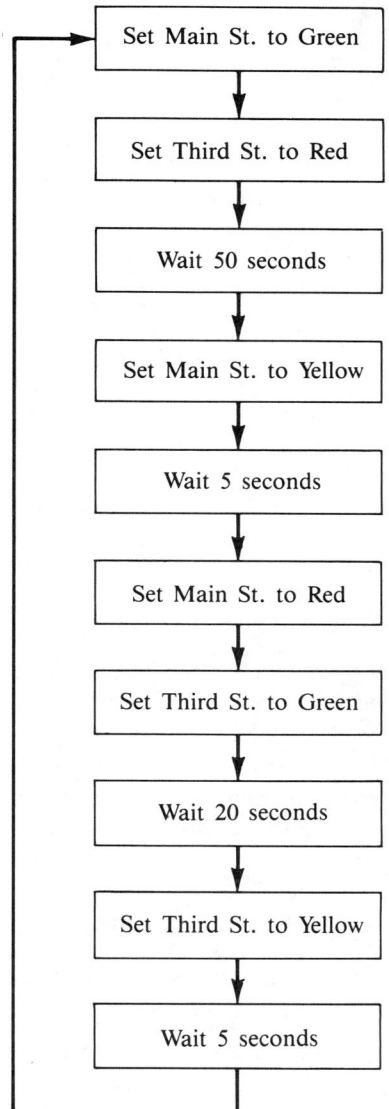

FIGURE 11-6. Flowchart for traffic light controller.

The WAIT macro initiates a calculated delay loop that delays the CPU for a period of time (in seconds) specified by the dummy parameter SECONDS. For example, the macro call

```
               WAIT    6
```

would cause the operand of the MVI D instruction to assemble as 24 and thus delay the CPU approximately 6 seconds.

11-4 AN APPLICATION OF MACROS

```
SWITCH   MACRO   STREET,COLOR
         MVI     A,COLOR           ; Light code
         OUT     STREET            ; Street code
         ENDM

WAIT     MACRO   SECONDS
         LOCAL   W1,W2,W3
         MVI     D,4*SECONDS       ; Basic loop value
W1:      MVI     B,250             ; 250 msec * 4 = 1 sec
W2:      MVI     C,182             ; 182*5.5 μsec = 1 msec
W3:      DCR     C                 ; 1 cy = 0.5 μsec
         JNZ     W3                ; +10 cy = 5.5 μsec
         DCR     B                 ; Count 250, 249, . . .
         JNZ     W2                ; Loop on register B
         DCR     D                 ; Basic loop control
         JNZ     W1                ; Loop on register D
         ENDM

BEGIN    MACRO   WHERE
         JMP     WHERE
         ENDM
```

FIGURE 11-7. Macro definitions for traffic light controller.

The BEGIN macro is used to transfer control of the program to a specified label. The manner in which this is done will be seen in the macro expansion.

The program to implement the flowchart of Figure 11-6 using the macros of Figure 11-7 is shown in Figure 11-8. Notice that a major portion of the program consists of macro calls. In fact, the program in Figure 11-8 barely resembles an

```
MAIN     EQU     50H               ; Output port for Main St.
THIRD    EQU     60H               ; Output port for Third St.
RED      EQU     01H               ; Red-light control
YELLOW   EQU     02H               ; Yellow-light control
GREEN    EQU     04H               ; Green-light control

CYCLE:   SWITCH  MAIN,GREEN        ; Set Main St. Green
         SWITCH  THIRD,RED         ; Set Third St. Red
         WAIT    50                ; Delay 50 seconds

         SWITCH  MAIN,YELLOW       ; Set Main St. Yellow
         WAIT    5                 ; Wait 5 seconds

         SWITCH  MAIN,RED          ; Set Main St. Red
         SWITCH  THIRD,GREEN       ; Set Third St. Green
         WAIT    20                ; Delay 20 seconds

         SWITCH  THIRD,YELLOW      ; Set Third St. Yellow
         WAIT    5                 ; Delay 5 seconds

         BEGIN   CYCLE             ; Start all over again

         END
```

FIGURE 11-8. Traffic light controller program: source file.

8080 assembly language program. Also, by simply scanning through the program one can get a clear picture of the program's operation; this is another advantage of using macros in assembly language programs. Notice how each macro implements the corresponding step in the flowchart of Figure 11-6.

Figure 11-9 shows the macro expansion initiated during the assembly of the program of Figure 11-8. Notice in Figure 11-9 that the MVI D instruction in each expansion of the WAIT macro changes to reflect the amount of time delay. Also notice how the assembler renames the local labels W1, W2, and W3 during each expansion of the WAIT macro. The BEGIN macro at the end of the program simply contains a JMP instruction to the start of the program; this causes the entire monitoring cycle to be repeated over and over again.

```
0050 =              MAIN    EQU     50H
0060 =              THIRD   EQU     60H
0001 =              RED     EQU     01H
0002 =              YELLOW  EQU     02H
0004 =              GREEN   EQU     04H

                    CYCLE:  SWITCH  MAIN,GREEN    ; Set Main St. Green
0000 +3E04                  MVI     A,GREEN       ; Light code
0002 +D350                  OUT     MAIN          ; Street code
                            SWITCH  THIRD,RED     ; Set Third St. Red
0004 +3E01                  MVI     A,RED         ; Light code
0006 +D360                  OUT     THIRD         ; Street code
                            WAIT    50            ; Delay 50 seconds
0008 +16C8                  MVI     D,4*50        ; Basic loop value
000A +06FA          ??0001: MVI     B,250         ; 250 msec * 4 = 1 sec
000C +0EB6          ??0002: MVI     C,182         ; 182 * 5.5 µsec = 1 msec
000E +0D            ??0003: DCR     C             ; 1 cy = 0.5 µsec
000F +C20E00                JNZ     ??0003        ; +10 cy = 5.5 µsec
0012 +05                    DCR     B             ; Count 250, 249, . . .
0013 +C20C00                JNZ     ??0002        ; Loop on register B
0016 +15                    DCR     D             ; Basic loop control
0017 +C20A00                JNZ     ??0001        ; Loop on register D

                            SWITCH  MAIN,YELLOW   ; Set Main St. Yellow
001A +3E02                  MVI     A,YELLOW      ; Light code
001C +D350                  OUT     MAIN          ; Street code
                            WAIT    5             ; Wait 5 seconds
001E +1614                  MVI     D,4*5         ; Basic loop value
0020 +06FA          ??0004: MVI     B,250         ; 250 msec * 4 = 1 sec
0022 +0EB6          ??0005: MVI     C,182         ; 182 * 5.5 µsec = 1 msec
0024 +0D            ??0006: DCR     C             ; 1 cy = 0.5 µsec
0025 +C22400                JNZ     ??0006        ; +10 cy = 5.5 µsec
0028 +05                    DCR     B             ; Count 250, 249, . . .
0029 +C22200                JNZ     ??0005        ; Loop on register B
002C +15                    DCR     D             ; Basic loop control
002D +C22000                JNZ     ??0004        ; Loop on register D

                            SWITCH  MAIN,RED      ; Set Main St. Red
0030 +3E01                  MVI     A,RED         ; Light code
0032 +D350                  OUT     MAIN          ; Street code
```

FIGURE 11-9. Macro expansion of traffic light controller program.

```
                        SWITCH   THIRD,GREEN   ; Set Third St. Green
0034+3E04               MVI      A,GREEN       ; Light code
0036+D360               OUT      THIRD         ; Street code
                        WAIT     20            ; Delay 20 seconds
0038+1650               MVI      D,4*20        ; Basic loop value
003A+06FA     ??0007:   MVI      B,250         ; 250 msec * 4 = 1 sec
003C+0EB6     ??0008:   MVI      C,182         ; 182 * 5.5 μsec = 1 msec
003E+0D       ??0009:   DCR      C             ; 1 cy = 0.5 μsec
003F+C23E00             JNZ      ??0009        ; +10 cy = 5.5 μsec
0042+05                 DCR      B             ; Count 250, 249, . . .
0043+C23C00             JNZ      ??0008        ; Loop on register B
0046+15                 DCR      D             ; Basic loop control
0047+C23A00             JNZ      ??0007        ; Loop on register D

                        SWITCH   THIRD,YELLOW; Set Third St. Yellow
004A+3E02               MVI      A,YELLOW      ; Light code
004C+D360               OUT      THIRD         ; Street code
                        WAIT     5             ; Delay 5 seconds
004E+1614               MVI      D,4*5         ; Basic loop value
0050+06FA     ??0010:   MVI      B,250         ; 250 msec * 4 = 1 sec
0052+0EB6     ??0011:   MVI      C,182         ; 182 * 5.5 μsec = 1 msec
0054+0D       ??0012:   DCR      C             ; 1 cy = 0.5 μsec
0055+C25400             JNZ      ??0012        ; +10 cy = 5.5 μsec
0058+05                 DCR      B             ; Count 250, 249, . . .
0059+C25200             JNZ      ??0011        ; Loop on register B
005C+15                 DCR      D             ; Basic loop control
005D+C25000             JNZ      ??0010        ; Loop on register D

                        BEGIN    CYCLE         ; Start all over again
0060+C30000             JMP      CYCLE

0063                    END
```

FIGURE 11-9. (Continued)

The application program example given in this section also illustrates the use of macros in writing "RAM-less" programs. If the expanded program of Figure 11-9 is examined carefully, it can be seen that there are no references to RAM memory, and no instructions such as CALL, RET, POP, PUSH, and so on, that require the use of a stack. Programs such as these can be implemented entirely in a "RAM-less" microprocessor system (i.e., a system containing only ROM).

11-5

REPETITIVE MACROS

Often, in many assembly language application programs, a sequence of instructions may be repeated many times in the course of the program. A good example of this is in the program shown in Figure 11-1. Notice in Figure 11-1 that the RLC instruction sequence is repeated twice in the program. In developing programs where there exist such repetitive instruction sequences, it would be nice to have some facility that instructs the assembler to assemble a certain instruction (or sequence of instructions) a specified number of times. In other words, instead of the programmer typing in four RLC instructions each time in Figure 11-1, a directive to the assembler could instruct it to assemble the code for the RLC instruction four times. Such a directive is available in most assemblers and is a macro directive known as the *REPT directive*.

Figure 11-10 illustrates the implementation of the program in Figure 11-1 with the REPT directive. Notice in Figure 11-10 that the four RLC instructions have been replaced with a REPT directive instructing the assembler to repeat assembly of the following instruction (between the REPT and ENDM) four times. This is done in both sections in the program where there previously existed four individual RLC instructions (refer to Figure 11-1). The program in Figure 11-10 is the source program before assembly. Figure 11-11 shows the operation of the REPT directive by illustrating the macro expansions after assembly.

In Figure 11-11 notice that for each REPT directive, four RLC instructions were assembled (inserted as in a MACRO). By comparing the programs in Figures 11-1, 11-3, and 11-11, one can see that they are identical in the machine code generated but very different at the source level. The three programs also illustrate different ways of writing the same program, and should help when deciding which of the assembler's facilities to use.

Another application of the REPT macro directive is in the automatic generation of look-up data tables for various application programs. When the REPT directive is used in conjunction with the DB or DW and SET directives, it can be of tremendous aid to the programmer.

```
        ORG     1000H

        IN      0               ; Get first number
        REPT    4               ; Move to M.S. position
        RLC
        ENDM
        ANI     11110000B       ; Clear L.S. bits
        MOV     B,A             ; Save first number
        IN      0               ; Get second number
        ANI     00001111B       ; Clear M.S. bits
        ORA     B               ; Merge with first number
        MOV     H,A             ; Save first and second numbers
        IN      0               ; Get third number
        REPT    4               ; Move to M.S. position
        RLC
        ENDM
        ANI     11110000B       ; Clear L.S. bits
        MOV     B,A             ; Save third number
        IN      0               ; Get fourth number
        ANI     00001111B       ; Clear M.S. bits
        ORA     B               ; Merge with third number
        MOV     L,A             ; Save third and fourth numbers
        HLT                     ; RP H&L contains word

        END
```

FIGURE 11-10. Word assembly program implemented with the REPT macro.

```
           1000              ORG    1000H
           1000   DB00       IN     0              ; Get first number
                             REPT   4              ; Move to M.S. position
                             RLC
                             ENDM
           1002+07           RLC
           1003+07           RLC
           1004+07           RLC
           1005+07           RLC
           1006   E6F0       ANI    11110000B      ; Clear L.S. bits
           1008   47         MOV    B,A            ; Save first number
           1009   DB00       IN     0              ; Get second number
           100B   E60F       ANI    00001111B      ; Clear M.S. bits
           100D   B0         ORA    B              ; Merge with first number
           100E   67         MOV    H,A            ; Save first and second numbers
           100F   DB00       IN     0              ; Get third number
                             REPT   4              ; Move to M.S. position
                             RLC
                             ENDM
           1011+07           RLC
           1012+07           RLC
           1013+07           RLC
           1014+07           RLC
           1015   E6F0       ANI    11110000B      ; Clear L.S. bits
           1017   47         MOV    B,A            ; Save third number
           1018   DB00       IN     0              ; Get fourth number
           101A   E60F       ANI    00001111B      ; Clear M.S. bits
           101C              ORA    B              ; Merge with third number
           101D   6F         MOV    L,A            ; Save third and fourth numbers
           101E   76         HLT                   ; RP H&L contains word

           101F              END
```

FIGURE 11-11. Macro expansion of the REPT macro directive.

For example, assume that an application program requires a look-up table of bytes in the following sequence:

01H, 02H, 04H, 08H, 10H, 20H, 40H, 80H

Instead of defining each byte with a DB directive in the source program, the programmer simply writes the following sequence of code:

```
        NEXT     SET    1              ; First table value

       TABLE:    REPT   8              ; Make eight table entries
                 DB     NEXT           ; Table byte
        NEXT     SET    NEXT*2         ; Next table entry
                 ENDM

                 END
```

```
    0001  #       NEXT      SET      1          ; First table value

                  TABLE:    REPT     8          ; Make 8 table entries
                            DB       NEXT       ; Table byte
                  NEXT      SET      NEXT*2     ; Next table entry
                            ENDM
    0000+01                 DB       NEXT       ; Table byte
    0001+02                 DB       NEXT       ; Table byte
    0002+04                 DB       NEXT       ; Table byte
    0003+08                 DB       NEXT       ; Table byte
    0004+10                 DB       NEXT       ; Table byte
    0005+20                 DB       NEXT       ; Table byte
    0006+40                 DB       NEXT       ; Table byte
    0007+80                 DB       NEXT       ; Table byte

    0008                    END
```

FIGURE 11-12. Automatic generation of data table.

Recall that the SET directive can be used to define the value of a symbol as well as have the value of the symbol changed during assembly. Initially, the value of the symbol NEXT is set to 1. The REPT directive is used to repeat assembly of the following DB directive eight times. The first time the DB directive is assembled, the value of NEXT is 1, and therefore the first byte in the table is assembled as a 01H. The value of NEXT is then set to the old value of NEXT (01) times 2; the new value is now 2. When the DB directive is assembled the second time, a 02H is stored in the table, and the value of NEXT becomes 2 × 2, or 04H. This is then stored as the third table entry, and so on, until eight table entries have been created. The table generated by the assembler is shown in Figure 11-12.

In the expansion shown in Figure 11-12, notice that eight table entries have been created using the DB directive. However, for each entry in the table the value of the symbol NEXT is different (two times greater). This scheme for generating tables with data values following mathematical progressions is very convenient in assembly language programming, especially when the size of such tables is extremely long.

11-6

CONDITIONAL ASSEMBLY

When a programmer develops "universal" assembly language programs (i.e., programs that have to be adapted to a wide variety of systems), these programs must be geared to the hardware environment of the system on which they are being run. For example, the console input subroutine in Figure 10-4 would be compatible only with an 8251 chip. Also, for the subroutine to execute properly, the hardware scheme must be designed such that the data port is addressed as device 02H and the status port as device 03H. If any of these requirements are

```
        FALSE   EQU     0000H           ; False variable
        TRUE    EQU     NOT FALSE       ; True variable

        U8251   EQU     TRUE            ; Set true for 8251 UART
        U1602   EQU     NOT U8251       ; Set false for 1602 UART

                IF      U8251
        DATA    EQU     02H             ; 8251 data port
        STATUS  EQU     03H             ; 8251 status port
        MASK    EQU     00000010B       ; 8251 receiver mask
                ENDIF

                IF      U1602
        DATA    EQU     05H             ; 1602 data port
        STATUS  EQU     06H             ; 1602 status port
        MASK    EQU     00010000B       ; 1602 receiver mask
                ENDIF

        CONIN:  IN      STATUS          ; Get UART status
                ANI     MASK            ; See if receiver ready
                JZ      CONIN           ; Wait until ready
                IN      DATA            ; Get data
                RET
```

FIGURE 11-13. CONIN subroutine written for two UARTs.

not met, the subroutine will not execute properly, and consequently, the program that CALLs the subroutine will not work as intended.

Thus the problem of adapting software to the hardware environment often arises. If a program that is designed for a particular hardware environment is to be executed on another system with a different hardware scheme, the program has to be modified to reflect the characteristics of the new hardware. This can be done by searching through the program for hardware-dependent code, and modifying those segments of code appropriately. To make such modifications to a program easier for the programmer, most assemblers have conditional assembly directives. These directives can be used to define segments of code that can be included or excluded during assembly. The programmer can control the assembly of these segments through a very simple process.

Consider the 8251 console input routine discussed in previous chapters. As mentioned before, the CONIN routine was a hardware-dependent routine, and would work only with the 8251 USART chip. Assuming that the CONIN routine is to be modified for another USART with characteristics that are different from those of the 8251, three modifications would have to be made to the routine: the addresses of the data and status ports, and the receiver mask word. To make these modifications easier it would be convenient to have a directive that would instruct the assembler to assemble CONIN for either the 8251 or some other chip. This can be done in assembly language programming, as shown in Figure 11-13.

In Figure 11-13, two symbols, TRUE and FALSE, are equated as complements of each other. That is, the symbol FALSE is set to zero and the symbol TRUE is set to the complement of FALSE (NOT FALSE) so as to give it the value FFFFH. Similarly, the symbol U8251 is set to the value of the symbol TRUE (FFFFH) and U1602 is set to the complement of U8251 (NOT U8251) to yield a value of 0000H. After the program in Figure 11-13 is assembled, the result of the conditional assembly directives is shown in Figure 11-14.

The program in Figure 11-14 can be assembled as a CONIN routine for either the 8251 USART or the 1602 USART. Notice the differences in the 8251 and 1602 address and mask words. The value of U8251 is set TRUE to direct assembly of the subroutine for the 8251. When the assembler encounters the IF directive, it examines the operand of the directive; if the value of the operand is FFFFH (TRUE), it accepts all code between the IF and ENDIF directives. If the value of the operand is 0000H (FALSE), it ignores everything between the IF and ENDIF directives. In Figure 11-14, since the value of U8251 is TRUE, the DATA, STATUS, and MASK symbols are set to the appropriate values for the 8251. Since U8251 is TRUE in this case, U1602 is automatically equated FALSE, since they complement each other in value. The EQUates for the 1602 are thus ignored. Finally, when the actual code for the subroutine is assembled, the values used for DATA, STATUS, and MASK are specific to the 8251 UART.

Figure 11-15 illustrates the same CONIN subroutine of Figure 11-13 assembled for the 1602 UART (U8251 set FALSE). When the programs of Figures 11-14 and 11-15 are compared, one can see that if the programmer wanted to change the subroutine for either the 1602 or 8251 UARTs, a single byte is all that has to be modified. By adding more conditional blocks, the CONIN subroutine could be modified to include many other types of UARTS and addressing schemes.

```
0000 =            FALSE  EQU   0000H       ; False variable
FFFF =            TRUE   EQU   NOT FALSE   ; True variable

FFFF =            U8251  EQU   TRUE        ; Set true for 8251 UART
0000 =            U1602  EQU   NOT U8251   ; Set false for 1602 UART

                         IF    U8251
0002 =            DATA   EQU   02H         ; 8251 data port
0003 =            STATUS EQU   03H         ; 8251 status port
0002 =            MASK   EQU   00000010B   ; 8251 receiver mask
                         ENDIF

                         IF    U1602
                  DATA   EQU   05H         ; 1602 data port
                  STATUS EQU   06H         ; 1602 status port
                  MASK   EQU   00010000B   ; 1602 receiver mask
                         ENDIF

0000 DB03         CONIN: IN    STATUS      ; Get UART status
0002 E602                ANI   MASK        ; See if receiver ready
0004 CA0000              JZ    CONIN       ; Wait until ready
0007 DB02                IN    DATA        ; Get data
0009 C9                  RET
```

FIGURE 11-14. CONIN subroutine assembled for the 8251 UART.

```
0000 =              FALSE   EQU     0000H       ; False variable
FFFF =              TRUE    EQU     NOT FALSE   ; True variable

0000 =              U8251   EQU     FALSE       ; Set true for 8251 UART
FFFF =              U1602   EQU     NOT U8251   ; Set false for 1602 UART

                            IF      U8251
                    DATA    EQU     02H         ; 8251 data port
                    STATUS  EQU     03H         ; 8251 status port
                    MASK    EQU     00000010B   ; 8251 receiver mask
                            ENDIF

                            IF      U1602
0005 =              DATA    EQU     05H         ; 1602 data port
0006 =              STATUS  EQU     06H         ; 1602 status port
0010 =              MASK    EQU     00010000B   ; 1602 receiver mask
                            ENDIF

0000 DB06           CONIN:  IN      STATUS      ; Get UART status
0002 E610                   ANI     MASK        ; See if receiver ready
0004 CA0000                 JZ      CONIN       ; Wait until ready
0007 DB05                   IN      DATA        ; Get data
0009 C9                     RET
```

FIGURE 11-15. CONIN subroutine assembled for the 1602 UART.

The use of conditional assembly does not have to be limited to the development of universal programs. One of the most useful features of conditional assembly is when it is used together with macros. For example, assume that a programmer desires to create four new instructions for the 8080 by using macro definitions. The mnemonics for these new instructions are as follows:

- COM B   Complement the contents of register B
- COM C   Complement the contents of register C
- COM D   Complement the contents of register D
- COM E   Complement the contents of register E

Instead of writing four separate macros for each instruction (each one containing the appropriate 8080 instructions to implement the macro), the programmer can define a single macro that will conditionally expand a section of code, depending on a macro parameter. This technique is shown in Figure 11-16.

The name of the macro in Figure 11-16 is COM and the macro will be called with a single parameter, which can be B, C, D, or E. One of these symbols will be assigned to the dummy parameter REG. Notice that the first and last instructions in the macro body are a PUSH and POP, respectively; these instructions are used to preserve the contents of the accumulator and will always be the first and last instructions of each macro expansion.

For example, if the macro call COM B is encountered during assembly, a macro expansion is initiated. Since the dummy parameter REG is equal to the symbol B, the instructions within that block are expanded; all other blocks are ignored. Figure 11-17 shows the macro expansions for each macro call.

Notice in Figure 11-17 that each macro call initiates a different set of instructions for assembly. The set of instructions assembled depends on the macro parameter used in the calling macro.

The ELSE directive can also be used with the IF and ENDIF directives to assemble conditionally certain segments of code. For example, Figures 11-18 and 11-19 illustrate the implementation of the console output routine (CONOUT) for the 8251 or 1602 UARTs.

Figure 11-18 shows the CONOUT subroutine assembled for the 8251 (U8251 set TRUE). The use of the ELSE directive in the CONOUT subroutine illustrates an alternative means of developing a universal program. In Figure 11-18, instead of including the mask word as a group condition (as was done for CONIN), the symbol U1602 is tested during the assembly of the subroutine code. In this case, since U1602 evaluated FALSE, the ANI 00100000B instruction was ignored with the ANI 00000001B instruction assembled at the current value of the location counter.

Figure 11-19 illustrates the CONOUT subroutine assembled for the 1602 UART (U8251 set FALSE). Notice in Figure 11-19 that since U8251 is set FALSE, the assembler assembles the instruction immediately following the ELSE directive and ignores the assembly of the preceding instruction.

```
COM     MACRO       REG

        PUSH        PSW             ; Save original contents

        IF          REG=B           ; Complement register B
        MOV         A,B
        CMA
        MOV         B,A
        ENDIF

        IF          REG=C           ; Complement register C
        MOV         A,C
        CMA
        MOV         C,A
        ENDIF

        IF          REG=D           ; Complement register D
        MOV         A,D
        CMA
        MOV         D,A
        ENDIF

        IF          REG=E           ; Complement register E
        MOV         A,E
        CMA
        MOV         E,A
        ENDIF

        POP         PSW

        ENDM
```

FIGURE 11-16. Definition for the 'COM r' macro.

```
                        COM     B
0000+F5                 PUSH    PSW         ; Save original contents
0001+78                 MOV     A,B
0002+2F                 CMA
0003+47                 MOV     B,A
0004+F1                 POP     PSW

                        COM     C
0005+F5                 PUSH    PSW         ; Save original contents
0006+79                 MOV     A,C
0007+2F                 CMA
0008+4F                 MOV     C,A
0009+F1                 POP     PSW

                        COM     D
000A+F5                 PUSH    PSW         ; Save original contents
000B+7A                 MOV     A,D
000C+2F                 CMA
000D+57                 MOV     D,A
000E+F1                 POP     PSW

                        COM     E
000F+F5                 PUSH    PSW         ; Save original contents
0010+7B                 MOV     A,E
0011+2F                 CMA
0012+5F                 MOV     E,A
0013+F1                 POP     PSW
```

FIGURE 11-17. Macro expansions for the **COM r** macros.

```
0000 =          FALSE   EQU     0000H       ; False variable
FFFF =          TRUE    EQU     NOT FALSE   ; True variable

FFFF =          U8251   EQU     TRUE        ; Set true for 8251 UART
0000 =          U1602   EQU     NOT U8251   ; Set false for 1602 UART

                        IF      U8251
0002 =          DATA    EQU     02H         ; 8251 data port
0003 =          STATUS  EQU     03H         ; 8251 status port
                        ENDIF

                        IF      U1602
                DATA    EQU     05H         ; 1602 data port
                STATUS  EQU     06H         ; 1602 status port
                        ENDIF

0000 DB03       CONOUT: IN      STATUS      ; Get UART status
                        IF      U1602
                        ANI     00100000B   ; See if 1602 TX ready
                        ELSE
0002 E601               ANI     00000001B   ; See if 8251 TX ready
                        ENDIF
0004 CA0000             JZ      CONOUT      ; Wait until ready
0007 79                 MOV     A,C         ; Get character
0008 D302               OUT     DATA        ; Transmit character
000A C9                 RET
```

FIGURE 11-18. **CONOUT** subroutine assembled for the 8251 UART.

```
0000  =         FALSE   EQU   0000H           ; False variable
FFFF  =         TRUE    EQU   NOT FALSE       ; True variable

0000  =         U8251   EQU   FALSE           ; Set true for 8251 UART
FFFF  =         U1602   EQU   NOT U8251       ; Set false for 1602 UART

                        IF    U8251
                DATA    EQU   02H             ; 8251 data port
                STATUS  EQU   03H             ; 8251 status port
                        ENDIF

                        IF    U1602
0005  =         DATA    EQU   05H             ; 1602 data port
0006  =         STATUS  EQU   06H             ; 1602 status port
                        ENDIF

0000  DB06      CONOUT: IN    STATUS          ; Get UART status
                        IF    U1602
0002  E620              ANI   00100000B       ; See if 1602 TX ready
                        ELSE
                        ANI   00000001B       ; See if 8251 TX ready
                        ENDIF
0004  CA0000            JZ    CONOUT          ; Wait until ready
0007  79                MOV   A,C             ; Get character
0008  D305              OUT   DATA            ; Transmit character
000A  C9                RET
```

FIGURE 11-19. CONOUT subroutine assembled for the 1602 UART.

To summarize the use of the IF, ELSE, and ENDIF directives, the following points should be noted:

1. When the assembler encounters an IF directive during assembly, it examines the operand of the IF directive. The operand can be a symbol or expression that evaluates to a TRUE (FFFFH) or FALSE (0000H) result.
2. If the operand of the IF directive evaluates TRUE, the assembler assembles all following instructions (or directives) until an ENDIF or ELSE directive is encountered. If an ELSE directive is encountered, all instructions between the ELSE and ENDIF directives are ignored.
3. If the operand of the IF directive evaluates FALSE, the assembler ignores all following instructions (or directives) until an ENDIF or ELSE directive is encountered. If an ELSE directive is encountered, all instructions between the ELSE and ENDIF directives are assembled.

11-7

SUMMARY

The use of macros in assembly language programming often proves to be of tremendous aid to the programmer. There are always advantages and disadvantages of using macros in application programs. A major trade-off lies between execution speed and memory requirements. Since the macro body is expanded "in-line" each time the assembler encounters a macro call, the memory requirements of the final program are very high. Most of the code for macros can be implemented with subroutines. However, the execution time of CALL and RET instructions increases the overall execution time of the program. In this chapter it was also seen that by using macros, the programmer could create "RAM-less" programs; these programs are frequently used in ROM-only systems and therefore cannot have any CALL or RET instructions.

The use of macros also changed the "appearance" of the assembly language program. An assembly language program implemented only with macros was more descriptive at the source level in terms of its operation. Many assemblers provide facilities for storing macros in files called macro libraries. These libraries are used in a manner similar to the subroutine library discussed in Chapter 10. The programmer stores various utility macros in a library and the assembler automatically references the library for the macro definitions. This technique allows the programmer to treat macros as if they were mnemonic instructions.

Perhaps the greatest advantage of using macros in assembly language programming is in creating new instructions for the microprocessor. By using the right sequence of code in macros, the programmer can simulate the instruction set of large computers. Macros can also be used to force the assembler to recognize instructions of upwardly compatible microprocessors. In fact, by creating a library of macros, one could make the assembler recognize and assemble instructions for any microprocessor.

Conditional assembly provided an easy way of changing the operation of a program. It allowed the programmer to create a single "generic" program with a number of alternative program segments, that were included or excluded as part of the final assembled code. Control of conditional segments of a program was done by simply setting a symbol TRUE or FALSE, thus eliminating the need for searching through a program during modification.

The use of conditional assembly directives in macros allowed the programmer to develop a single macro that would change its function depending on the value of an operand (dummy parameter). This application is used extensively in superficially expanding the instruction set of the microprocessor.

Macros and conditional assembly are optional features provided by most 8080 assemblers. All assembly language programs can be developed without such features. The use of macros and conditional assembly in application programs will depend on the type of program being designed. It is up to the programmer to decide when a program can be implemented more efficiently with macros and/or conditional segments or without such code.

REVIEW QUESTIONS AND PROBLEMS

1. How does a macro differ from a subroutine? Give examples.

2. Describe briefly two applications of macros in assembly language programming.

3. By means of an example, describe the manner in which a macro definition is constructed.

4. How are parameters used with macros?

5. What is the purpose of defining a label LOCAL within the macro body?

6. Convert the utility subroutines developed in Chapter 10 to macros.

7. Use the macros developed in Problem 6 to implement the LOADER program of Chapter 10.

8. Compare the loader program of Problem 7 with the LOADER program developed in Chapter 10.

9. Define a macro to generate automatically a data table containing the following 16-bit words:

$$0001H, 0003H, 0009H, 001BH, 0051H, 00F3H,$$
$$02D9H, 088BH, 19A1H, 4CE3H$$

10. What is conditional assembly? How is it used in the development of assembly language programs?

11. Without using an assembler, identify the instructions that will be assembled in the following program segment.

```
YES     EQU     0FFFFH
NO      EQU     NOT YES
STEP    EQU     NO
ALTER   EQU     NOT STEP
NOW     EQU     YES
        LXI     SP,STACK
        IF      STEP
        LXI     H,DATA
        ELSE
        LXI     H,TABLE
        ENDIF
        IF      NOW
        IF      NOT ALTER
        MOV     A,M
        OUT     LED
        ENDIF
        MOV     C,M
        ENDIF
        IF      STEP AND NOW
        INX     H
        DCR     C
        ENDIF
```

12. Repeat Problem 11 by setting the label STEP to YES.

13. Define a new instruction for the 8080 using macros and conditional assembly. The general form of the instruction should be

    BIT   p,r

where p is the position (0 through 7) of a bit to be set in an 8-bit register "r" (A,B,C,D,E,H, or L). For example, if it were desired to set the most significant bit of register C (without affecting any other bits), the instruction BIT 7,C could be used.

CHAPTER 12

Introduction to the PL/M-80 Compiler

12-1

INTRODUCTION

Chapter 8 introduced the reader to two basic techniques used in the development of microcomputer software. The first type dealt with the use of the assembler in developing programs in assembly language. Assembly language programming was studied comprehensively in the preceding three chapters. This chapter introduces the reader to another technique used in the development of microcomputer software. This technique is the use of a *compiler* in the development of programs written in a *higher-level language*.

    The notion of software development with a compiler was discussed briefly in Chapter 8. At this stage it may be appropriate to emphasize the differences between assembly language software and compiler language software, as well as the differences between an assembler and a compiler. A basic knowledge of these differences will serve as an aid in understanding the concept of higher-level languages and their relationship with compilers.

    The building blocks of a higher-level language consist of "English-like" program statements rather than mnemonics. A single statement could be used to perform a number of machine instructions, hence the term "higher-level

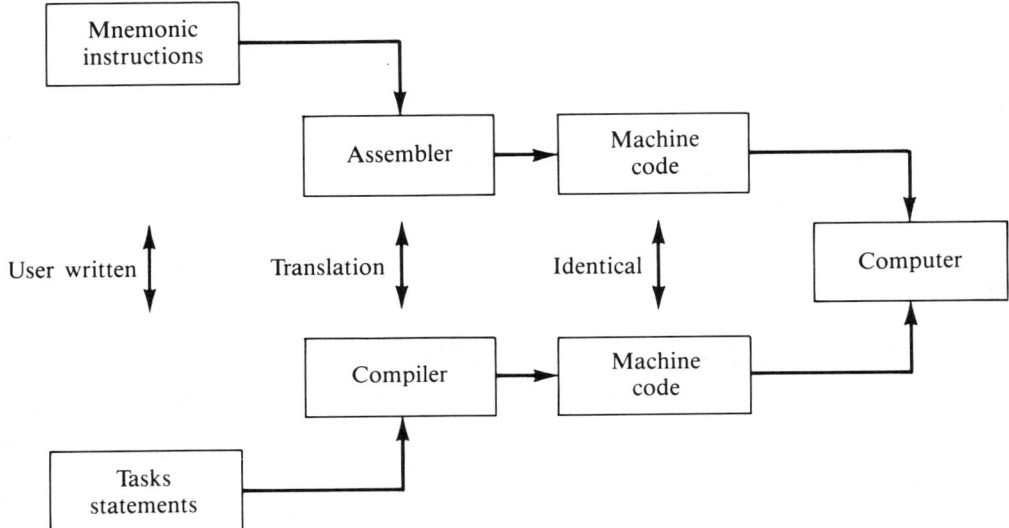

FIGURE 12-1 Software development using assemblers and compilers.

language." In the development of higher-level programs, the user codes the program as a sequence of tasks rather than a sequence of mnemonics. This therefore leads to the concept of a higher-level language being task oriented versus the machine orientation of assembly language. In an assembly language program, the software tool that was used to translate the sequence of mnemonic instructions into machine code was the assembler. Similarly, the software tool used to translate a higher-level lanaguage into a sequence of machine instructions is a compiler. Higher-level languages are therefore also known as compiler-level languages. Figure 12-1 illustrates the software development process using both an assembler and a compiler.

Note in Figure 12-1 that the only difference in the development of a program at the compiler level and at the assembler level is in the manner in which the programs are written. As far as execution of the translated machine code is concerned, the computer cannot distinguish between the code generated by the compiler and that generated by the assembler; for all practical purposes, they are identical.

This chapter introduces the reader to the PL/M-80 compiler and the PL/M-80 programming language. The PL/M compiler and programming language are by no means the best available. When compared to other high-level languages, such as BASIC, FORTRAN, and Pascal, PL/M appears to have significant restrictions and limitations. However, the simplicity of the workings of the compiler and the language itself makes it an excellent tool for the study of a high-level language. The concepts learned in this and the following chapters can be applied to almost any higher-level programming language available today. The material covered in this chapter serves only as introductory material to PL/M programming. Emphasis is placed on the differences that exist between assembly language programming and PL/M programming. Chapter 13 continues the discussion of PL/M with emphasis on the more advanced constructs of the PL/M language and compiler.

12-2 THE GENERAL FORM OF A PL/M PROGRAM

To illustrate the general form of a PL/M program, a simple program specification will be implemented in both assembly language and PL/M.

A microcomputer has three parallel I/O ports. Two of the ports are 8-bit input ports that are connected to sets of eight switches. The third port is an output port connected to a set of seven-segment LED displays. A program is to be written that gets the data bytes from these two switches, computes the sum of the two bytes, and displays the result on the LEDs. Assuming that the port numbers for the switches are 54H and 55H and that the port number for the LED is 60H, the assembly language implementation of this specification is as shown in Figure 12-2.

The assembly language implementation of the program specification is fairly straightforward, as can be seen in Figure 12-2. The PL/M implementation of the program specification is shown in Figure 12-3. Line numbers have been added to the program in order to reference the individual statements for explanation. Note that these numbers are not part of the PL/M program.

Figure 12-3 also illustrates the general flow and characteristics of a PL/M program. The PL/M program in Figure 12-3 contains eleven statements (numbered 2 through 12). A statement is always terminated with a ";" and does not have to be limited to a single line. The 11 statements can be divided into two basic types: nonexecutable statements (numbered 2 through 7) and executable statements (numbered 8 through 12). The *nonexecutable statements* can be thought of as being "directives" to the compiler and are only used at compile time (i.e., while the program is being compiled), whereas the *executable statements* could be considered the actual "tasks" that are translated into machine code by the compiler and executed at run time (while the program is being executed).

```
; Calculate the sum of two bytes

SWITCH1   EQU   54H        ; Port number for switch 1
SWITCH2   EQU   55H        ; Port number for switch 2
LED       EQU   60H        ; Port number for LED

          IN    SWITCH1    ; Get data from switch 1
          MOV   B,A        ; Save it in register B
          IN    SWITCH2    ; Get data from switch 2
          ADD   B          ; Add the two values
          OUT   LED        ; Output result to LED
          HLT

(9 BYTES ASSEMBLED)
```

FIGURE 12-2. Assembly language program to calculate a sum.

```
                                                    Line
/* CALCULATE THE SUM OF TWO BYTES */                  1

DECLARE DATA1 BYTE;                                   2
DECLARE DATA2 BYTE;                                   3
DECLARE SUM BYTE;                                     4
DECLARE SWITCH1 LITERALLY '54H';                      5
DECLARE SWITCH2 LITERALLY '55H';                      6
DECLARE LED LITERALLY '60H';                          7

DATA1 = INPUT (SWITCH1);                              8
DATA2 = INPUT (SWITCH2);                              9
SUM = DATA1 + DATA2;                                 10
OUTPUT(LED) = SUM;                                   11
HALT;                                                12
```

FIGURE 12-3. PL/M program to calculate a sum.

By viewing the general form of the PL/M program, one can see that hardware registers are no longer used to represent the storage of numeric data; instead, unique names called *identifiers* are used to reference a numeric quantity, such as DATA1, DATA2, SUM, SWITCH1, SWITCH2, and LED in Figure 12-3. An identifier is a unique reference to a memory location. With a few exceptions (to be seen in Chapter 13), any reference made to an identifier refers indirectly to the contents of the memory location allocated for the identifier. Similarly, the *value* of an identifier refers to the data stored at the identifier's memory location. If an identifier allows the contents of its memory location to be modified, it is known as a *variable*.

Identifiers and variables are referred to by names that can be up to 31 characters in length and are not restricted to alphabetic characters only. However, the first character in the identifier must be alphabetic. Names chosen by the programmer are also limited by the *reserved words* listed in Table 12-1. Spaces are not permitted; however, the "$" character has the effect of improving

TABLE 12-1. PL/M Reserved Words

ADDRESS	ENABLE	MOD
AND	END	NOT
AT	EOF	OR
BASED	EXTERNAL	PLUS
BY	GO	PROCEDURE
BYTE	GOTO	PUBLIC
CALL	HALT	REENTRANT
CASE	IF	RETURN
DATA	INITIAL	STRUCTURE
DECLARE	INTERRUPT	THEN
DISABLE	LABEL	TO
DO	LITERALLY	WHILE
ELSE	MINUS	XOR

readability in extremely long identifier names. A "$" present in the name is simply ignored by the compiler. Thus DATA$1 is the same as DATA1 during compilation.

Line 1 is a comment string. In PL/M two delimiters are required to enclose a comment string: a left delimiter pair "/*" and a right delimiter pair "*/." The text within the delimiters serves only as documentation and is completely ignored by the compiler. A comment does not have to be limited to a single line but can extend to a paragraph or even a page, as long as the comment starts and ends with the delimiter pairs mentioned above. Comments can be used anywhere in the PL/M program.

Lines 2, 3, and 4 are nonexecutable statements known as *declarations*. Declarations instruct the compiler to allocate a specified amount of storage for a named variable. Thus line 2 causes the compiler to allocate 8 bits (a byte) of storage for the variable DATA1, line 3 causes the allocation of a byte of storage for DATA2, and line 3 directs the compiler to allocate a byte of storage for the variable SUM. Every variable used in a PL/M program must be declared in such a statement before it is used in an executable statement later in the program. Any reference made to the name of the variable indirectly refers (with a few exceptions, to be seen later) to the contents of the memory location allocated for the variable. The variables DATA1, DATA2, and SUM are called *byte-type variables*. The compiler can also be instructed to allocate 16 bits of storage for variables. These variables are called *address-type variables* and will be examined in a later section.

Lines 5, 6, and 7 are also nonexecutable statements and are similar to the declare statements discussed previously. These statements are called *macro declarations* and do not cause the compiler to allocate any storage. Macro declarations, or literal declarations, can be thought of as "equates," similar to the "equates" used in assembly language programming. These declarations are used to assign a constant to a symbol. For example, line 5 instructs the compiler to substitute the constant 54H for the symbol SWITCH1 every time the symbol is encountered in the program during compilation, hence the term *macro declaration* (derived from macro expansions in assembly language). Similarly, the symbols SWITCH2 and LED are defined in lines 6 and 7.

Lines 8 and 9 are executable statements called *assignment statements*. After the program is compiled, and when the program is executed (run time), the variable DATA1 will be assigned the data at input port 54H and the variable DATA2 will be assigned the data at input port 55H. In other words, the byte of storage allocated for DATA1 will contain the data at input port 54H; similarly, the byte of storage allocated for DATA2 will contain the data from input port 55H. An assignment statement takes on a right-to-left orientation; that is, the variable, constant, or expression (to be seen later) on the right-hand side of the "=" is assigned to the variable on the left-hand side. For example, INPUT (SWITCH1) (line 8, Figure 12-3) can be thought of as a variable that holds the value of an input port. This value is then assigned to DATA1. Similarly, in line 9, the data from input port 55H is assigned to the variable DATA2.

Thus an assignment statement can be thought of as one that is used to alter the contents of a memory location allocated for a variable. It is important to note that the "=" symbol does not indicate algebraic equality, but indicates an assignment of data on the right-hand side of the statement to the memory location allocated for a variable on the left-hand side.

Line 10 is also an executable assignment statement, but the right-hand side of the statement contains a construct in PL/M called an *expression*. In this case it is an arithmetic expression. The construct DATA1 + DATA2 indicates the arithmetic sum of the variables DATA1 and DATA2. The result of the arithmetic operation, that is, the sum of DATA1 and DATA2, is then assigned to the variable SUM.

Line 11 is an executable assignment statement that assigns the value of the variable SUM to the output port 60H (LED). The left-hand side of the assignment statement references output port 60H. As before, the construct OUTPUT(LED) could be thought of as a reference to a variable. Chapter 13 deals with a more detailed explanation of this function.

Finally, line 12 is a HALT statement, very similar to the HLT instruction, and is used to suspend execution of the program at run time.

In comparing the programs illustrated in Figures 12-2 and 12-3, it can be observed that both programs perform exactly the same function. However, there is a considerable amount of syntactical difference in the forms in which the two programs are constructed. Note that the PL/M program in Figure 12-3 has no direct reference to registers or memory locations. The only hardware references that are made are to the I/O ports. As will be seen in Chapter 13, it is not an absolute necessity that the programmer be aware of the hardware environment when coding programs in PL/M. However, this is an absolute requirement for assembly language software development.

The tremendous task of compiling each statement in the source program into a sequence of related machine code often leads to the generation of inefficient code, both in speed and in memory requirements. This is particularly true during the translation of very simple tasks, such as in the preceding example. To illustrate the manner in which code is compiled, let us examine the code generated by the compiler for the preceding example.

Like the assembler, the compiler produces a symbol table and the object code as an output. The symbol table for the preceding example program is shown in Figure 12-4.

The symbol table produced by the compiler only provides information on the storage allocation for each variable declared in the program. Note that since the symbols SWITCH1, SWITCH2, and LED were not allocated any storage, they do not appear in the symbol table. Figure 12-4 shows the memory allocation for the three variables declared in the PL/M program of Figure 12-3. Since these are variables, that is, their values can be changed, the compiler always allocates storage for them in the data segment (allocation of variables is discussed in Chapter 13). Note that each variable has been allocated a byte of storage, as specified in the declaration.

Figure 12-5 shows the machine code generated by the PL/M compiler in mnemonic form. Note that the output of the compiler is not mnemonic code but machine code, as illustrated in Figure 12-1, and is similar to the output of the assembler. This machine code has been converted to mnemonic form (for clarity) and shown in Figure 12-5. The PL/M statement corresponding to each set of machine instructions is also shown in commented form.

```
DATA1 = 3FDH
DATA2 = 3FEH
SUM   = 3FFH
```

FIGURE 12-4. Compiler's symbol table.

The equivalent machine code compiled for the assignment statement

```
DATA1 = INPUT (SWITCH1);
```

consisted of three machine instructions: the IN instruction, which gets the data from port 54H; the LXI H instruction, which points to the memory location allocated for DATA1 (03FDH from symbol table); and the MOV M,A instruction, which stores the data from the port into the memory location. Similar code was generated for the DATA2 = INPUT (SWITCH2); statement. Notice that the code generated for the SUM = DATA1 + DATA2; statement simply took the contents of DATA1 and DATA2, added them, and stored the result in the memory location allocated for SUM.

Finally, the OUTPUT (LED) = SUM; statement was compiled into three equivalent machine instructions: the LXI H instruction, which pointed to the memory location allocated to SUM; the MOV A,M instruction, which retrieved

```
; DATA1 = INPUT (SWITCH1);
        IN    54H
        LXI   H,03FDH     ; Location for variable "DATA1"
        MOV   M,A

; DATA2 = INPUT (SWITCH2);
        IN    55H
        LXI   H,03FEH     ; Location for variable "DATA2"
        MOV   M,A

; SUM = DATA1 + DATA2;
        LXI   H,03FDH     ; DATA1
        MOV   A,M
        LXI   H,03FEH     ; DATA2
        ADD   M
        LXI   H,03FFH     ; Sum
        MOV   M,A

; OUTPUT (LED) = SUM;
        LXI   H,03FFH     ; Location for variable "SUM"
        MOV   A,M
        OUT   60H

; HALT;
        HLT

(30 BYTES COMPILED)
```

FIGURE 12-5. Machine code generated for each compiler statement.

the data stored in the memory location; and the OUT 60H instruction, which sent the data to the output port.

Figure 12-5 clearly illustrates some of the redundancies in the code generated by the compiler to perform the simple task of adding two numbers. By comparing the equivalent assembly language program in Figure 12-2 with the compiled code in Figure 12-5, it can be seen that the size of the code generated by the compiler is very large (30 bytes compiled as compared to 9 bytes assembled). Consequently, execution speed of the compiled program would increase.

Because a compiler makes a simple programming task fairly complex, such simple tasks are much easier to perform in assembly language. On the other hand, complex programming is much more easily performed by a compiler level language, as will be shown later in this chapter.

12-3
CONTROLLING THE FLOW OF A PL/M PROGRAM

The program examples in Section 12-2 did not illustrate the advantages of programming in PL/M. In fact, by comparing the programs shown in Figures 12-2 and 12-3, one can see that it would be easier to write such a simple program in assembly language rather than in PL/M. A simple program specification such as that mentioned in Section 12-2 would be more efficient in execution speed and memory requirements if it were implemented in assembly language; this fact is illustrated in more detail in Chapter 13. However, in cases where the complexity of the program specification is increased, coding the program in PL/M is much easier than coding it in assembly language.

Consider a program to monitor the temperature of an oven and maintain this temperature at 90°C. The oven temperature is obtained through an input port connected to an analog-to-digital converter (ADC) and a thermocouple. The program has to make a decision based on the temperature read from the oven. The flowchart for the program is shown in Figure 12-6.

Two bits of an output port are used to control the state of the oven and an alarm. The following summarizes the hardware scheme for the I/O ports:

Input port 12H: ADC/thermocouple (oven temperature)
  0°C converted to 0000 0000
  100°C converted to 0110 0100 (100 decimal = 64 hex)

Output port 78H: oven/alarm control
  Bit 0:   1 = oven on
           0 = oven off
  Bit 1:   1 = alarm on
           0 = alarm off

The program works as follows: The initialization sequence involves turning on the oven and turning off the alarm. The program then inputs the temperature from the ADC and checks to see if the oven is overheating (temperature greater

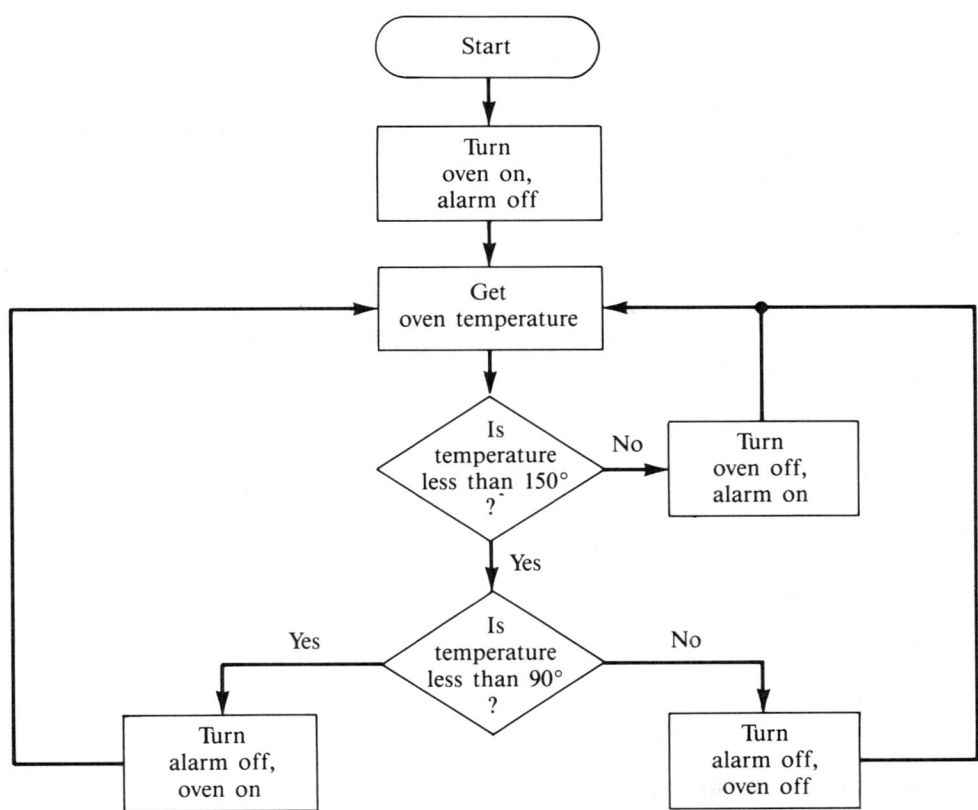

FIGURE 12-6. Flowchart for temperature monitor.

than 150°C). If this happens, the alarm is turned on and the oven is turned off. The temperature is then continuously monitored until it reaches below 150°C. When this happens, the alarm is turned off and a check is made to see if the temperature is less than 90°C. If it is less, the oven is turned on; if it is greater than 90°C, the oven is turned off. The entire sequence is then repeated.

The PL/M program to implement the flowchart in Figure 12-6 is shown in Figure 12-7. Notice how each executable statement in the PL/M program of Figure 12-7 corresponds to each step of the flowchart in Figure 12-6. The descriptive nature of PL/M statements make it very easy to view the general operation of the program.

Lines 1 through 4 define the four combinations of control bits used to control the state of the oven and alarm. The symbols in these statements are equated to numeric data and are called constants. A constant is a symbol whose value is fixed during compilation of the PL/M program and cannot be changed while the program is in execution (similar to the constants used in assembly language programs). For example, the macro declaration in line 1 defines the symbol OVENOFFALARM$OFF (note the use of the "$" to make the symbol name more readable) to have a value of 00000000B. Now during compilation, wherever the compiler encounters the symbol OVENOFFALARM$OFF, it sub-

```
                                                                    Line
/* CONTROL WORDS FOR ALARM AND OVEN */
DECLARE OVEN$OFF$ALARM$OFF LITERALLY ('00000000B');      1
DECLARE OVEN$ON$ALARM$OFF LITERALLY ('00000001B');       2
DECLARE OVEN$OFF$ALARM$ON LITERALLY ('00000010B');       3
DECLARE OVEN$ON$ALARM$ON LITERALLY ('00000011B');        4
/* SYSTEM I/O PORTS */
      DECLARE ADC LITERALLY ('12H');                     5
      DECLARE CONTROL LITERALLY ('78H');                 6
/* VARIABLE TO HOLD OVEN TEMPERATURE */
      DECLARE TEMPERATURE BYTE;                          7
/* MAIN PROGRAM */
/* TURN OFF ALARM AND TURN ON OVEN */
      OUTPUT (CONTROL) = OVEN$ON$ALARM$OFF;              8
/* GET OVEN TEMPERATURE */
MONITOR:                                                 9
      TEMPERATURE = INPUT (ADC);                        10
/* SEE IF OVER HEAT */
      IF TEMPERATURE < 150 THEN GO TO MAINTAIN;         11
      OUTPUT (CONTROL) = OVEN$OFF$ALARM$ON;             12
      GO TO MONITOR;                                    13
/* MAINTAIN TEMPERATURE AT 90 DEGREES */
MAINTAIN:                                               14
  IF TEMPERATURE < 90                                   15
      THEN OUTPUT (CONTROL) = OVEN$ON$ALARM$OFF;        16
      ELSE;                                             17
      OUTPUT (CONTROL) = OVEN$OFF$ALARM$OFF;            18
      GO TO MONITOR;                                    19
```

FIGURE 12-7. PL/M program for temperature monitor.

stitutes the number 00000000B. These symbols thus serve only as documentation, since the symbol OVENOFFALARM$OFF tells the reader much more than the binary number 00000000B. Note that since the value of a symbol defined in a macro declaration is static (i.e., it cannot be changed at run time), it can never appear on the left-hand side of an assignment statement.

Numeric data used in a PL/M program can be specified in any of the four bases—decimal, hexadecimal, octal, or binary—or can be represented as an ASCII character. The same conventions used for assembly language programming are used in PL/M. That is, a base (D, H, Q, B) must be specified immediately following the number; otherwise, the default is decimal. Any character enclosed in single quotes represents its corresponding ASCII code.

Lines 5 and 6 are macro declarations that define the port numbers for the ADC and the oven/alarm control port. Line 7 allocates a byte of storage for the variable TEMPERATURE. This variable will hold the temperature reading from the ADC. Line 8 is used to turn on the oven and turn off the alarm. This is done by assigning the constant OVENONALARM$OFF (00000001B) to the control port.

Line 9 is an identifier called a label. A label is an address reference that is used to control the flow of the PL/M program. Just as labels were used in assembly language to cause a branch instruction (JMP, CALL, etc.) to transfer control to a specified symbolic address, labels are used with transfer statements in PL/M to reference a particular portion of the program. In its simplest form, a label is an identifier that has the value of a location in memory. Labels may be any valid PL/M identifier name and must be followed by the colon ":". The use of labels in conjunction with the flow of the program will be seen shortly.

Line 10 is another assignment statement that assigns the data from the ADC input port to the memory location allocated to the variable TEMPERATURE. Line 11 is a special statement used in PL/M, called an IF-THEN statement. One of the uses of the IF-THEN statement is to conditionally transfer program execution to another point in the PL/M program. Like an assembly language program, PL/M statements are executed in sequence; or to be more precise, the machine instructions compiled for each statement are executed in sequence until a conditional or unconditional (to be seen later) statement is encountered.

The statement in line 11 checks the content of the memory location allocated for the variable TEMPERATURE. If the content of the location is less than 150 (96H), program control transfers to the label MAINTAIN (line 14), and all statements following line 11 up to line 13 are skipped. However, if the value of the variable TEMPERATURE is greater than or equal to 150, program control transfers to line 12. The expression TEMPERATURE < 150 is called a relational expression and the character "<" is called a relational operator, indicating a "less-than" condition. Relational expressions and operators are used to compare various PL/M identifiers and constants and are explained in more detail in Chapter 13.

Line 12 is an assignment statement used to turn off the oven and turn on the alarm. This statement and the following statement are executed only if the temperature is greater than or equal to 150.

Line 13 is an unconditional program transfer statement very similar to the unconditional jump instruction (JMP) in assembly language programming. The GO-TO statement in line 13 forces program execution to resume at the statements following the label MONITOR.

Lines 15 and 16 illustrate another application of the IF-THEN statement. In this case the IF-THEN statement is used as a conditional assignment statement. The value of TEMPERATURE is checked against 90. If the value of TEMPERATURE is less than 90, the statement OUTPUT(CONTROL) = OVENONALARM$OFF; is executed (the oven is turned on and the alarm turned off). Control then transfers to line 19, which is an unconditional GO-TO statement that forces the program to resume at location MONITOR. However, if the value of TEMPERATURE is greater than or equal to 90, the statement in line 18 is executed. This is done by the ELSE statement. The ELSE statement is used explicitly to force execution of the following statement. Note that if the ELSE statement did not exist, line 18 would be executed regardless of whether the temperature was less than, greater than, or equal to 90; the program would therefore not execute as intended.

Line 18 is used to turn off the oven and alarm if the temperature is greater than or equal to 90. Line 19 is then executed and control is transferred to the label MONITOR.

Lines 15 and 16 also illustrate the *free-format* feature of the PL/M programming language. This feature allows the programmer to write multiple statements per line, and to use multiple lines for a single statement. In other words, there is no restriction put on the programmer in formatting statements at preset columns or lines.

12-4

ADDRESS-TYPE VARIABLES

In the PL/M program examples discussed so far, the variables used were all declared as byte-type variables. This limited their values to a maximum of 255, since only one byte of storage was allocated. In cases where a variable is to hold data having a numeric value greater than 255, two bytes of storage must be allocated for the variable. Such a variable is called an *address-type variable*.

An address-type variable is allocated two bytes of contiguous storage by means of a DECLARE statement similar to the statements discussed before. However, instead of specifying BYTE, the specification ADDRESS is used. When such a DECLARE statement is encountered by the compiler, two bytes of contiguous storage are automatically allocated for that variable. The term ADDRESS can sometimes be misleading and is occasionally confused with labels. A variable of the address type has nothing to do with labels; unfortunately, the term ADDRESS is used to indicate that 16 bits have been allocated for the variable. The address-type variable is the largest data type supported by PL/M, and therefore the maximum numeric value an address-type variable can represent is 65535. Signed numbers are not allowed in PL/M.

To illustrate the use of the address-type variable, consider the program example shown in Figure 12-3. The program did not consider the fact that if the sum of DATA1 and DATA2 exceeded 255, the variable SUM would contain an invalid result. To overcome this problem, the variable SUM is declared as an address-type variable, so that numbers greater than 255 could be represented after the result of an arithmetic operation. The resulting program is shown in Figure 12-8. The program in Figure 12-8 does not reference any I/O ports (as did Figure 12-3) but simply calculates the sum of two variables.

With reference to Figure 12-8, line 1 declares the variables DATA1 and DATA2 as byte-type variables. Note that line 1 also illustrates the use of *factored declarations* in PL/M. In other words, variables of similar types can be factored in parentheses and declared in a single DECLARE statement, instead of having a separate declaration for each variable. Line 2 declares the variable SUM to

```
                              Line
DECLARE (DATA1, DATA2) BYTE;   1
DECLARE SUM ADDRESS;           2
DATA1=200;                     3
DATA2=150;                     4
SUM=DATA1+DATA2;               5
HALT;                          6
```

FIGURE 12-8. PL/M program with an ADDRESS type variable.

be of address type and causes the compiler to allocate two bytes of storage for it. Lines 3 and 4 assign the constants 200 and 150 to the variables DATA1 and DATA2, respectively. Line 5 calculates the sum of DATA1 and DATA2 and stores this result (350) in the 16 bits allocated for the variable SUM. If the variable SUM were declared a byte, as in Figure 12-3, the most significant 8 bits of the result of the arithmetic operation would be ignored and the remaining least significant byte would be assigned to the variable SUM. These operations are called *type conversions* and are discussed in Chapter 13.

Declaring a variable to be of byte or address type is left entirely up to the programmer. If it is anticipated that the value of a variable will always be less than 255, it is more efficient to declare it as a byte; otherwise, the variable can be declared an address-type variable.

12-5 MANIPULATION OF TABULAR DATA

Array variables are used in PL/M to reference tables of data. The data could be 8-bit data or 16-bit data, depending on the type of array variable declared. An array variable can be used to reference a group of contiguous memory locations by a unique name. When an array variable is declared, the compiler allocates a certain amount of storage that will depend on the type of the variable as well as the dimension of the array variable. For example, the declaration

```
DECLARE TABLE(10) BYTE;
```

declares an array variable TABLE of byte type having a dimension of 10. The dimension indicates the number of members contained in the array variable TABLE. The compiler will then allocate 10 bytes of storage for the variable TABLE. If the programmer wanted to reference the first byte allocated for TABLE (i.e., the first member of the array), he would do so by referring to it as TABLE(0). Similarly, the third byte allocated for the variable (third member of the array) would be referenced as TABLE(2), and so on. In simple terms, the programmer has allocated space for 10 variables, named TABLE(0), TABLE(1), . . . , TABLE(9). The number within parentheses is called the *subscript* of the array. Thus an array variable must be referenced by its name and by its subscript; its subscript indicates its relative position in memory. Each unique variable that references a part of the array is called an *array member*.

The real advantage of using arrays in PL/M can be seen in the following example. It is required to monitor the temperature of an oven through an ADC. Over a specified time period, 100 samples of the temperature have to be read and stored in contiguous memory locations. To implement this program without an array, 100 variables would have to be declared, and each variable would have to be assigned the value of the temperature, as shown in Figure 12-9. Assume that the temperature is monitored from input port 20H.

To avoid redundancy, all the variables declared and all the assignment statements have not been shown in Figure 12-9. Obviously, the program in Figure

```
DECLARE (TEMP0,TEMP1,TEMP2, . . . . . . . . . TEMP99) BYTE;
TEMP0 = INPUT (20H);
TEMP1 = INPUT (20H);
     .
     .
     .
TEMP99 = INPUT (20H);
HALT;
```

FIGURE 12-9. PL/M program without an array variable.

12-9 would be very tedious to write. A lot of development time could be spared by using an array variable, as shown in the program of Figure 12-10.

With reference to Figure 12-10, line 1 declares the array variable TEMP with dimension 100 and of byte type. This will cause the compiler to allocate 100 bytes of storage for the array TEMP. Each location in the array can be uniquely referenced by the name of the array and by its subscript. The first element of the array is TEMP(0) and the last element is TEMP(99).

Line 2 declares a byte-type variable J. The variable J will be used to reference the location of each of the elements of the array TEMP. Line 3 is an assignment statement that initializes the variable J to zero.

Since the value of J is initially zero, the statement in line 4 assigns the contents of port 20H to the array member TEMP(0). Each time line 4 is executed, the array member being referenced will depend on the value of J. Note that line 4 also contains a label GET that is used to reference the following statement.

Line 5 is an assignment statement that increments the value of J by one. Note that the statement in line 5 would be algebraically incorrect since it implies that the value of J is equal to the value of J + 1. However, as discussed before, in PL/M, this statement takes on an entirely different meaning; the constant "1" is added to the contents of the memory location allocated for the variable J, and the result is stored in the same memory location. This is a very useful means of incrementing a location in memory (i.e., the value of a variable).

Line 6 checks the value of J by means of an IF-THEN statement. If the value of J is less than 100, control transfers to line 4 (by means of the label GET). If the value of J is greater than or equal to 100, control is transferred to line 7, and program execution is terminated.

The program thus repetitively executes lines 4 and 5; each time the variable referenced in line 4 is the next consecutive member in the array TEMP. This is done by incrementing the value of J in line 5. This continues until the last

```
     DECLARE TEMP(100) BYTE;                1
     DECLARE J BYTE;                        2
          J = 0;                            3
GET: TEMP(J) = INPUT (20H);                 4
          J = J + 1;                        5
          IF J < 100 THEN GO TO GET;        6
          HALT;                             7
```

FIGURE 12-10. PL/M program with an array variable.

member of the array has been filled with data from the port, at which time line 6 causes the termination of the program.

Array variables in PL/M are not restricted to being of byte type only. PL/M allows the declaration of address-type arrays. For example,

```
DECLARE TABLE (50) ADDRESS;
```

Declares the array variable TABLE of dimension 50, each element in the array having the address type. The compiler will allocate two bytes for each element of the array, thus allocating a total of 100 bytes for the entire array.

The only restriction put on arrays is that the maximum dimension of an array (byte or address) must be no greater than 255. Arrays must be single-dimensioned only. For example, declaring an array variable TABLE with two dimensions (10,20) would be invalid.

12-6

PROCEDURES: THE PL/M SUBROUTINES

In previous chapters dealing with assembly language development, it was found that subroutines proved to be an extremely useful means of creating a structured program. Subroutines were also useful in cases where the same segment of code had to be executed several times in the course of a program. There were four basic types of subroutines written in assembly language: subroutines with no parameters, such as a DELAY subroutine (no data was passed to the subroutine and no data was returned); subroutines with input parameters, such as CONSOLE OUTPUT, which took a given character as input and did not return any result; subroutines with output parameters, such as CONSOLE INPUT, which did not accept any data as input, but returned a result; and subroutines with input and output parameters, such as a MULTIPLICATION subroutine, which accepts two numbers as input and returns the product of the two numbers as output.

PL/M provides the programmer with the same type of subroutine facilities with parameter passing. The PL/M subroutine is called a *procedure*. As an example, assume that in the course of writing a PL/M program, it is required to find the average of two variables several times in the program. To make the program more efficient, and to prevent redundancy of code, the averaging is best implemented as a procedure. The code shown in Figure 12-11 illustrates the simplest form of a PL/M procedure to average two numbers.

The procedure shown in Figure 12-11 averages the values of two variables X and Y and assigns the result to the variable Z. Assuming that the variables X,

```
                        Line
AVERAGE: PROCEDURE;      1
   Z = (X + Y)/2;        2
END AVERAGE;             3
```

FIGURE 12-11. Simple procedure to average two numbers.

Y, and Z have been declared previously, with reference to Figure 12-11: line 1 is called the *procedure entry point*, and is a nonexecutable statement that defines the following statements to be part of a subroutine called AVERAGE. AVERAGE is the name of the procedure. Similarly, line 3 is a nonexecutable statement that defines the end of the procedure AVERAGE. Thus lines 1 and 3 set up the bounds of the procedure body.

All the statements between lines 1 and 3 are called the *procedure body*. These statements form the actual subroutine. In this case line 2 is the procedure body, which simply calculates the average of the variables X and Y and assigns the result to the variable Z.

Note that in the arithmetic expression $(X + Y)/2$, the "/" symbol is the division operator. The parentheses enclosing the subexpression "$X + Y$" is used to force evaluation of "$X + Y$" first, followed by dividing the result of the evaluation by 2. Chapter 13 details the techniques by which arithmetic expressions are evaluated in PL/M.

Now let us assume that the programmer wanted to calculate the average of two variables, A and B, and to assign the result to the variable C. The following sequence of statements would have to be included in the program:

```
X = A;
Y = B;
CALL AVERAGE;
C = Z;
```

First, the values of the variables A and B would have to be assigned to the variables X and Y, since the AVERAGE procedure calculates the average of X and Y and not A and B.

Next, the AVERAGE procedure is called by means of a CALL statement. The CALL statement refers to the procedure by the name of the procedure used in the procedure entry point.

The AVERAGE procedure calculates the average of X and Y and assigns the result to Z. Since the result of the average of A and B is to be assigned to C, the assignment statement C = Z has to be used.

Now assume that the programmer has to use the AVERAGE procedure again in his or her program to calculate the average of two other variables, D1 and D2, and to assign the result to the variable D3. The following code would accomplish this:

```
X = D1;
Y = D2
CALL AVERAGE;
D3 = Z;
```

This type of parameter passing was used in assembly language programming, where registers were used to pass input and output parameters. However, in a high-level language such as PL/M, this does not prove to be an efficient means of calling procedures, since each time a procedure is called, several assignment statements have to be used to pass parameters.

PL/M allows the user to pass parameters automatically to a procedure by including a parameter list in the entry point of the procedure. The AVERAGE procedure of Figure 12-11 could be implemented as a procedure with parameters as shown in Figure 12-12.

The AVERAGE procedure shown in Figure 12-12 is very similar to that of the preceding example (Figure 12-11), except that the procedure entry point has a parameter list. The parameter list consists of the variables X and Y, enclosed in parentheses and separated by a comma. Variables X and Y are called the *formal parameters* of the procedure average. All formal parameters must be declared within the body of the procedure.

Line 2 declares the formal parameters X and Y as byte-type variables. This causes the locations allocated for these two variables to be local to the procedure AVERAGE. This means that their values can only be accessed inside the body of the procedure AVERAGE. The advantage of this feature will be seen later. Line 3 calculates the average of X and Y as before and assigns the result to the variable Z. Line 4 indicates the end of the procedure average.

The real advantage of using this form of the AVERAGE procedure comes about when the procedure is called. For example, to calculate the average of the variables A and B (assuming that A and B have been assigned values previously) and assign the result to C, the calling sequence for the procedure in Figure 12-12 would now be

```
CALL AVERAGE (A,B);
C = Z;
```

Notice that the two assignment statements before the CALL statement have been eliminated. This is due to the fact that when the AVERAGE procedure is called, the values of the variables A and B are automatically assigned to the variables X and Y, respectively. The average of X and Y is then calculated (actually the average of A and B, since X = A and Y = B) and assigned to the variable Z. The assignment statement C = Z; then assigns the value of Z to the variable C.

Variables A and B are called the *actual parameters* of the procedure AVERAGE. When a procedure containing a parameter list is called, the values of the actual parameters are always assigned to the formal parameters on a one-to-one basis.

Recall that the values of local variables (i.e., variables declared within the body of a procedure) can be accessed only within the body of the procedure, not outside the procedure. If this were not the case, and if X and Y were global variables (variables declared outside the procedure), any change made to X and

```
                                    Line
AVERAGE: PROCEDURE (X,Y);             1
  DECLARE (X,Y) BYTE;                 2
  Z = (X + Y)/2;                      3
END AVERAGE;                          4
```

FIGURE 12-12. Average procedure with a parameter list.

```
                                      Line
AVERAGE: PROCEDURE (X, Y) BYTE;        1
  DECLARE (X,Y,Z) BYTE;                2
  Z = (X + Y)/2;                       3
  RETURN Z;                            4
END AVERAGE;                           5
```

FIGURE 12-13. Average procedure that returns the result.

Y within the body of the procedure would affect the values of X and Y outside the procedure. This could be undesirable at times, especially since the programmer would have to make sure that variables used within the procedure body are not used outside the procedure. However, using the scheme of local and global variables, two variables X and Y could have been declared outside the procedure AVERAGE. These would be considered global variables. When the AVERAGE procedure is executed, any change made to the local variables X and Y would not affect the values of the globally declared X and Y variables.

Another problem exists in the previous AVERAGE procedure. The programmer would have to remember that the AVERAGE procedure always returns the result in the variable Z. Since Z was not declared within the body of the procedure, it is a global variable. As mentioned before, using a global variable within a procedure could cause problems.

A third type of procedure in PL/M automatically returns a value to the calling statement and eliminates the requirement of having an additional assignment statement after the CALL. The previous procedures discussed are known as *untyped procedures*. That is, they did not automatically return a data type—byte or address. Data was always returned through a global variable (Z in this case). A procedure that automatically returns a data type to the calling statement is called a *typed procedure*.

For example, the AVERAGE procedure could be implemented as a typed procedure, as shown in Figure 12-13. The difference between this typed procedure and the procedures previously discussed is that this procedure automatically returns a data type—a byte value in this case. The data type is returned through a special type of CALL statement called a *function call*.

Line 1 is the same as before, but now specifies the type of data returned. This specification is included after the parameter list. In this case, the average of the two numbers is of byte type. If the procedure were returning a 16-bit number to the calling statement, ADDRESS would have been specified.

Line 2 is the same as before and is used to declare the formal parameters X and Y as local variables. Note that the variable Z has also been declared as a local variable. Line 3 calculates the average of X and Y and assigns the result to the variable Z. Line 4 is a special statement always used in typed procedures and is used to return the value of the variable Z to the calling statement. The operation of the return statement in conjunction with the calling statement will be seen as follows. If it were required to calculate the average of two global variables A and B, with the variable C holding the result, the calling statement for the typed procedure would be

```
           C = AVERAGE (A,B);
```

Note that an explicit CALL statement is not used for a typed procedure; instead, an assignment statement is used to call the procedure AVERAGE. The calling statement initiates a call to the AVERAGE procedure, and passes the actual parameters A and B to the procedure. The AVERAGE procedure assigns the values of the actual parameters to the formal parameters X and Y, calculates the average of the two as the local variable Z, and returns the value of the variable Z. When the procedure returns to the calling statement, the value of Z is assigned automatically to the variable on the left-hand side, in this case the variable C.

Note that the RETURN statement in line 4 could have been used with an expression. For example,

```
RETURN (X+Y)/2;
```

would perform the same operation as lines 3 and 4 in Figure 12-13 while eliminating the need for the variable Z. Consequently, the code generated by the compiler would be more efficient.

Calls made to typed procedures are also known as *function calls*, and provide an extremely flexible means of accessing procedures that accept input parameters and produce an output parameter. There is, however, one restriction in a typed procedure—it can return only one result.

12-7

SUMMARY

This chapter serves as a brief introduction to the PL/M programming language and the PL/M compiler. The material covered in this chapter is sufficient to get the reader started on very elementary programs written in PL/M.

Some of the inefficiencies of the compiler were also illustrated in this chapter, particularly in cases where the task was extremely simple. This should help in deciding whether to use a high-level language or assembly language for developing software. In some cases it may be more efficient to write a program in a higher-level language such as PL/M, whereas in other cases a program may be better written in assembly language. Speed and memory requirements are the primary considerations. There are applications where certain parts of a program could be written in a higher-level language, while speed-critical segments could be implemented in assembly language. These and some of the other features of PL/M are discussed in the next chapter.

REVIEW QUESTIONS AND PROBLEMS

1. Compare the features of assembly language programs and compiler level programs in terms of the source code written and the translation.

2. What are nonexecutable program statements? How do they differ from executable program statements?

3. What is the purpose of a PL/M declaration?

4. Identify the invalid assignment statements in the following list (assume that all variables shown have been declared) and explain why they are considered invalid.
   (a) A = A + 5;
   (b) SUM + 3 = DATA3;
   (c) VALUE = 15 + 3 = CHECK;
   (d) SUM = DATA$4 * 3;
   (e) QUIT = START − '*';
   (f) LINK = A + B
   (g) JOE = DATA / 12F3H;

5. What is the difference between macro declarations and the other types of declarations?

6. What is the purpose of having an address-type variable? How does the address-type variable differ from the byte-type variable?

7. Write a complete PL/M program to read 10 data bytes from input port 50H. When all 10 bytes have been read in, display the 10 data bytes at output port 60H in reverse order.

8. Discuss the differences between a typed and an untyped PL/M procedure.

9. Write a typed PL/M procedure called LOWEST that returns the lowest value of two given numbers. For example, if

    ```
    A = 5;
    B = 10;
    C = LOWEST (A,B);
    ```

    the variable C will be set to 5. Note that if the values of A and B are equal, the returned value should be 0.

10. For the following PL/M program segment, determine the value of the variable RESULT after the last statement in the segment is executed.

    ```
    CHAR = 3;
    RESULT = 0;
    IF CHAR < 'A' THEN CHAR = CHAR + 30H;
    IF CHAR > 65 THEN CHAR = CHAR − 30H;
    RESULT = RESULT + CHAR;
    ```

11. Repeat Problem 10 by changing the assignment statement CHAR = 3; to
    (a) CHAR = 41H
    (b) CHAR = 'Z'

CHAPTER 13

Advanced PL/M Concepts

13-1

INTRODUCTION

This chapter expands on the previously learned concepts of the PL/M programming language and illustrates some of the more sophisticated features of the language. The topics of discussion in this chapter include a discussion of the various types of expressions and operators available in PL/M, evaluation of expressions, allocation of declared variables, nesting of IF-THEN statements, use of DO blocks in a PL/M program, interrrupt procedures, built-in procedures and functions available to the programmer, based variables and location references, and procedure parameter-passing conventions.

This chapter concludes by illustrating the development of a structured PL/M program. This program should serve as a guide to the PL/M programmer in the creation of PL/M application programs and in helping to decide if PL/M is the right choice for the application at hand.

13-2

PL/M OPERATORS AND EXPRESSIONS

Chapter 12 introduced the reader to the use of expressions in assignment statements. An expression in PL/M can be of three basic types: arithmetic expres-

TABLE 13-1. PL/M Arithmetic Operators

Precedence	Operator	Function
1	*	Multiplication operator
1	/	Division operator
1	MOD	Modulus operator (remainder of division)
2	+	Addition operator
2	−	Subtraction operator

sions, logical expressions, and relational expressions. It is possible to mix these expressions in an assignment statement. Expressions in PL/M are made up of operands and operators and often resemble a conventional algebraic expression. For example, in the expression

$$A + B - C - 5$$

The operands are the variables A, B, C and the constant 5. The operators are the arithmetic symbols "+" for addition and "−" for subtraction.

There are five *arithmetic operators* in PL/M. These are listed in order of precedence in Table 13-1. The order of precedence is important when the compiler evaluates an expression. The *, /, and MOD operators have the highest precedence (indicated by 1). The + and − operators have the next highest precedence.

These precedence rules can be illustrated as follows. Consider the arithmetic expression

$$A + B * C + D$$

In the preceding expression, since the * operator has the highest precedence, the subexpression B * C is evaluated first and its result is added to A and D.

PL/M allows the use of parentheses to force precedence during evaluation: for example,

$$(A + B) * (C + D)$$

In this example the subexpressions A + B and C + D are evaluated first and then multiplied together. These precedence rules of evaluation are exactly the same for the evaluation of algebraic expressions.

Logical operators in PL/M are used to perform Boolean operations on operands. The four logical operators supported by PL/M are listed in the order of precedence in Table 13-2.

TABLE 13-2. PL/M Logical Operators

Precedence	Operator	Function
4	NOT	Complement operator
5	AND	Logical AND operator
6	OR	Logical OR operator
6	XOR	Logical XOR operator

Precedence rules for the evaluation of Boolean expressions are treated in a manner similar to the evaluation of any expression in Boolean algebra. Note that logical operators have a precedence less than that of arithmetic operators. Thus when arithmetic and logical operators are mixed in an expression, the arithmetic operators are always evaluated first. As before, parentheses can be used to force precedence of evaluation. For example, the expression

$$(2 \text{ AND } 3) * 4 \text{ OR } 3 - 2$$

would be evaluated in precedence as follows. (2 AND 3) evaluates to 2; the expression becomes

$$2 * 4 \text{ OR } 3 - 2$$

2 * 4 evaluates to 8; the expression becomes

$$8 \text{ OR } 3 - 2$$

3 − 2 evaluates to 1; the expression becomes

$$8 \text{ OR } 1$$

8 OR 1 evaluates to 9; the final evaluation is

$$9$$

A PL/M expression must always exist on the right-hand side of an assignment statement since assignment of values is conducted from right to left.

Relational operators are used to compare operands. Table 13-3 lists the relational operators supported by PL/M in order of precedence. Note that the precedence of logical operators is less than the precedence of arithmetic operators but higher than the precedence of logical operators.

Relational operators are always used with two operands. Relational expressions are evaluated to a true or false result only. In other words, if the relational expression evaluates true, the result of the expression is 0FFH (11111111B); if the relational expression evaluates false, the result of the expression is 00H (00000000B). Thus, in all cases, the evaluation of a relational expression yields

TABLE 13-3. PL/M Relational Operators

Precedence	Operator	Function
3	<	Less-than operator
3	>	Greater-than operator
3	<=	Less-than or equal-to operator
3	>=	Greater-than or equal-to operator
3	<>	Not-equal-to operator
3	=	Equality operator

an 8-bit result, indicating a true or false condition. For example, consider the following relational expressions:

$$(5 > 4) \quad \text{result is 0FFH (true)}$$
$$(4 >= 5) \quad \text{result is 00H (false)}$$

Relational operators can be combined meaningfully with logical operators to yield true or false results:

$$\text{NOT } (5 > 4) \quad \text{result is 00H (false)}$$
$$(6 > 5) \text{ OR } (1 > 2) \quad \text{result is 0FFH (true)}$$

Finally, relational and logical operators can be used to test an expression with variables:

$$(X = Y) \text{ OR } (Z < 2)$$

In the example above, the expression evaluates true if the variable X has the same value as the variable Y, or it evaluates true if the variable Z has a value that is less than 2.

In Chapter 12, the use of relational expressions and operators was seen in IF-THEN statements. For example, consider the following PL/M statements:

```
IF A < 2 THEN GO TO L1;
    ELSE;
    GO TO L2;
```

If the relational expression "A < 2" evaluates true, control is transferred to the label L1. If the expression evaluates false, control is transferred to the label L2.

13-3

ALLOCATION OF DECLARED VARIABLES

In Chapter 12 it was observed that every variable used in a PL/M program must be declared in a declaration statement before it can be referenced anywhere in the body of the program. When a variable is declared, the compiler allocates storage for the variable in memory. This allocation is static and is done during the compilation of the user's program. The compiler can never allocate storage dynamically, since once the program has been translated into machine code, all locations of variables are fixed and cannot be changed by the program. Note that dynamic allocation of storage could be potentially dangerous in a program that is restricted to the memory boundaries set up in the hardware.

Global variables can be declared only once in the PL/M program, whereas local variables can be declared many times in the sequence of a PL/M program. Each time a global variable is declared, the compiler allocates a unique location

```
DECLARE (A,B) BYTE;
      .
      .
      .
    PROCESS: PROCEDURE;
      DECLARE (A,B) BYTE;
         .
         .
         .
    END PROCESS;
         .
```

FIGURE 13-1. Local and global variables.

in memory for that variable; the allocated storage is referenced by the name of the declared variable. Thus declaring the same variable again in the program would imply another storage location for the same variable and would lead to ambiguity when referencing the variable. Since local variables cannot be accessed outside the block in which they were declared, the compiler allows a multiple-name definition. The example in Figure 13-1 will help to clarify the allocation of local and global variables.

In Figure 13-1, variables A and B were declared twice in the program. The first declaration outside the procedure PROCESS was a global declaration and caused the compiler to allocate storage for the variables. The second declaration inside the procedure PROCESS was a local declaration and caused the compiler to allocate another two bytes of storage for the variables. However, even though the variables have the same names, their values are maintained in different memory locations. The local variables A and B cannot be accessed outside the procedure PROCESS. However, global variables can be accessed from within a block.

The AT attribute is used to force memory allocation of a variable at compile time. When the compiler encounters a declaration, it statically allocates storage for the variable during compilation. The programmer has no control of the allocation for a simple declaration statement. A declaration with the AT attribute allows the programmer to control the memory allocation for the variable. For example, the declaration

```
DECLARE XYZ BYTE AT (0100H);
```

will force the compiler to allocate storage for the variable XYZ at memory location 0100H. The information within the parentheses could be a constant, or an expression that evaluates to a constant of byte or address type.

The use of the AT attribute in DECLARE statements to force allocation of variables at specified memory locations is very useful for hardware schemes that have memory-mapped I/O. For example, consider an I/O port mapped at location E000H. Now to send and receive data from the I/O port, the declaration

```
DECLARE PORT BYTE AT (0E000H);
```

forces allocation of the BYTE variable PORT at location 0E000H. This means that whenever the variable PORT appears on the left-hand side of an assignment statement, data is stored at location E000H (sent to the port). Similarly, whenever the variable PORT appears on the right-hand side of an assignment statement, data is retrieved from location E000H (received from the port).

In assembly language programming, the user always constructed programs in two distinct segments: the code segment, which contained the program itself, together with other nonvariable data, tables, character strings, and so on, that had to be present in memory at program startup; and a data segment, which was used to store temporary data used during program execution, as well as the stack. The PL/M compiler automatically compiles code into these two segments; the code segment contains the compiled executable program statements, and the data segment contains the stack area as well as the storage for declared variables.

Whenever a variable is declared in a DECLARE statement, the compiler allocates storage for that variable in the data segment. This seems logical since a variable is an identifier that changes in value, and for its value to change, it must be allocated storage in the data segment. When storage is allocated for a variable, the contents of the memory location(s) allocated for the variable is undefined (since the contents of RAM is undefined on system startup). There are two methods used to initialize the value of a variable. The first is to initialize its value at run time by means of an assignment statement. This is the most reliable means of doing so. The second is to let the compiler initialize the value of the variable at the time storage is allocated for it; this compile-time initialization can be done through the DECLARE statement.

Some situations may require that an identifier be allocated storage in the code segment instead of the data segment. This is particularly true for look-up tables in the form of arrays, character strings, ASCII messages, and so on. In other words, these constants should exist in the code segment so that they can be used on system startup. The declare statement does allow the user to force the compiler to allocate storage for identifiers in the code segment, as well as to initialize their values at compile time. Note that identifiers that have been allocated storage in the code segment cannot have their values changed (and therefore cannot be initialized) at run time.

The DECLARE statement provides two forms of initializations: DATA and INITIAL. The DATA initialization initializes the value of the declared identifier in the code segment, and the INITIAL initialization initializes the value of the declared identifier in the data segment. If the program is to be executed on hardware having a ROM/RAM environment, constants such as look-up tables and ASCII character strings could be allocated storage in the code segment (ROM), and variables could be allocated storage in the data segment (RAM). Variables declared with the INITIAL declaration can have their values changed at run time, but constants declared with the DATA initialization cannot be changed at run time.

The following declaration defines storage for a variable FLAG in the data segment and initializes its value to 0FFH.

```
DECLARE FLAG BYTE INITIAL (0FFH);
```

The following declaration defines storage for an array variable TABLE with dimension 5, and initializes each element in the array to 2, 4, 6, 8, and 10, respectively.

```
DECLARE TABLE(5) BYTE INITIAL (2, 4, 6, 8, 10);
```

The following declaration does the same as the preceding example except that the location of the array TABLE will be in the code segment:

```
DECLARE TABLE(5) BYTE DATA (2, 4, 6, 8, 10);
```

It is possible to declare an array variable with fewer initializations than its dimension:

```
DECLARE TABLE(10) BYTE DATA (2, 4, 6, 8, 10);
```

In such a case the first five elements of the array get initialized.

It is not possible to initialize an array with more initializations than the dimension specified. The following declaration would be illegal:

```
DECLARE TABLE(2) BYTE DATA (2, 4, 6, 8, 10);
```

At this point it should be noted that the initializations specified in the declare statement are static and are performed during compilation of the user's program. Variables can have their values dynamically modified (at run time) through assignment statements only if they were initialized with the INITIAL initialization, or if no initialization parameter was specified. Identifiers initialized with the DATA initialization can never appear on the left-hand side of an assignment statement. Also, if the compiled code were being implemented in a ROM/RAM hardware environment, variables initialized with the INITIAL attribute could cause unpredictable results.

13-4
TYPE CONVERSIONS

The PL/M compiler automatically performs type conversions when mismatched variables are used in expressions. For example, consider two variables SUM (address type) and DATA1 (byte type). If the program contains an assignment statement of the form

```
SUM = DATA1;
```

the value of SUM will be assigned the value of DATA1 with 8 high-order zero bits appended to the value of SUM. On the other hand, the assignment statement

```
DATA1 = SUM;
```

will cause the 8 high-order bits of the variable SUM to be dropped and the low-order 8 bits to be assigned to the variable DATA1.

When expressions are used on the right-hand side of an assignment statement, the value of the expression is automatically converted to match the type of the variable on the left-hand side. The same conventions are followed during parameter passing in procedures where there is a mismatch in type between actual and formal parameters.

In summary, type conversions are done from byte to address by appending 8 high-order zero bits to the byte value, from address to byte by dropping the 8 high-order bits of the address value.

13-5
EXTERNAL AND PUBLIC LABELS

As mentioned in Chapter 12, a label is an identifier that identifies a memory location. The appearance of a label in front of an executable statement is an implicit declaration of the label, and therefore in most cases labels need not be declared. However, if reference is made to the address of a module outside the program, explicit declaration of the label is required. This is particularly true for PUBLIC and EXTERNAL labels. A label is declared with the following syntax:

```
DECLARE <identifier> LABEL <attributes>;
```

DECLARE and LABEL are required keywords, <identifier> is the name of the label, and <attributes> can be PUBLIC or EXTERNAL.

The EXTERNAL attribute declares a variable, label, or subroutine to be external to the program. This allows linkage between seperate modules. The EXTERNAL attribute is very similar to the EXTRN directive in assembly language. The following declaration defines the variable COUNT (of byte type) to be an EXTERNAL variable defined in another module.

```
DECLARE COUNT BYTE EXTERNAL;
```

The PUBLIC attribute is similar to the PUBLIC directive in assembly language and allows a variable, label, or subroutine to be made accessible by other modules. For example, the declaration

```
DECLARE COUNT BYTE PUBLIC;
```

declares the variable COUNT to be accessible by other modules. Note that a variable cannot be declared PUBLIC and EXTERNAL in the same program. Also, if a variable is declared EXTERNAL in a program, and is to be linked to another module, it must be declared PUBLIC in the module. These two attributes also allow linkage between modules written in assembly language and PL/M.

The following declaration defines the label RESTART to be external to the user's program.

```
DECLARE RESTART LABEL EXTERNAL;
```

This makes it possible to transfer control to address RESTART, which was defined PUBLIC in another module.

PL/M allows LABEL declarations to be factored, as was the case for variable declarations:

```
DECLARE (ENTRY,EXIT,MAIN,ERR1,ERR2) LABEL PUBLIC;
```

The preceding example declares the labels ENTRY, EXIT, MAIN, ERR1, and ERR2 to be PUBLIC labels whose values can be accessed by other modules. Note that these labels must be explicitly defined in the program before they can be declared PUBLIC.

13-6

NESTED IF-THEN STATEMENTS

IF-THEN statements and ELSE statements can be nested to reasonable limits in PL/M. For example, assume that the programmer wanted to test the value of two variables, DATA1 and DATA2, and, based on the values of these two variables, set the value of the variable FLAG to 0FFH or 00H. The following nested IF-THEN statement serves the purpose:

```
IF DATA1 = 10 THEN
        IF DATA2 = 50 THEN FLAG = 0FFH;
                ELSE; FLAG = 00H;
```

If the value of DATA1 is 10 and if the value of DATA2 is 50, then FLAG is set to 0FFH; otherwise, the value of FLAG is set to zero. What if the value of DATA1 is not equal to 10? Would the value of FLAG be zero? The answer to this is no! The ELSE clause belongs to the inner IF statement. When IF-THEN statements are nested, the outer IF statement cannot have an ELSE clause. This prevents any ambiguity concerning "who the ELSE belongs to." Thus FLAG will be set to zero if the value of DATA2 is not 50, but will remain undefined if the value of DATA1 is not 10. This problem is easily solved by including a logical comparison:

```
IF (DATA1 = 10) AND (DATA2 = 50) THEN FLAG = 0FFH;
                                 ELSE FLAG = 00H;
```

If the expression DATA1 = 10 and the expression DATA2 = 50 evaluate true, FLAG is set to 0FFH. If they evaluate false, FLAG is set to 0.

BLOCK STRUCTURE AND ITERATIONS

PL/M is a programming language designed to provide the user with a structured means of constructing programs. The primary means of approaching a structured program is by using DO statements to enclose blocks of independent yet related code. The simplest form of a DO statement is in enclosing a group of statements to act as one statement. This single DO block can then be used anywhere in a program where a single executable statement is required. For example, a portion of a PL/M program requires that the variable SUM be tested against the constant 20. If the value of SUM is 20, then the variable FLAG must be set to 0FFH, the variable X set to 1, and the variable COUNT must be set to 0. If the value of SUM is something other than 20, FLAG is set to 0, the variable X is set to 5, and COUNT is set to the value of SUM. Using a DO block, this is easily accomplished as follows:

```
IF FLAG = 20 THEN  DO;
                       FLAG = 0FFH;
                       X = 1;                } Block 1
                       COUNT = 0;
                       END;
               ELSE;
                   DO;
                       FLAG = 0;
                       X = 5;                } Block 2
                       COUNT = SUM;
                       END;
```

The DO-END blocks in the preceding example are treated as one statement. If SUM = 20, then block 1 is completely executed, and block 2 is ignored. If SUM <> 20, block 1 is ignored and block 2 is completely executed. In this manner DO-END blocks may be used to "bracket" or enclose a set of statements that is to be treated as a single statement.

In the preceding example of a simple DO-END block, the compiler simply treated the block as one statement and on encountering the block executed the sequence of statements within the block. The block was only executed once, after which control transferred to the next executable statement (or another DO-END block) outside the block.

The DO WHILE statement allows the programmer to cause successive repetition of execution of the block until a certain condition is satisfied. The format of the DO WHILE block is as follows:

```
DO WHILE <expression>;
    <statement 1>;
    <statement 2>
          .
          .
          .
    <statement n>;
END;
```

This construct causes the execution of the statements within the DO-END block to execute repetitively until the <expression> evaluates to a false condition. In other words, program execution remains in a loop while the specified expression is true. Execution of the block is terminated as soon as the expression yields a false result. As an example, consider the following program segment:

```
DO WHILE COUNT < 200;
   SUM = DATA1 + COUNT;
   COUNT = COUNT + 1;
END;
```

The expression to be tested is COUNT < 200. As long as the value of COUNT is less than 200, the following two statements are executed. Each time through the loop the value of COUNT in increased by one until COUNT reaches 200. When this occurs the next executable statement after the DO-END block is executed.

Note that in the DO WHILE block there must be some statement that will ultimately cause the <expression> to yield a false result. If this does not occur, the program will remain in the DO WHILE block indefinitely.

Simple DO-END blocks and DO WHILE blocks may be nested to reasonable levels in the user's program. The restrictions on the number of levels of nesting allowed is a function of the type of PL/M compiler. Figure 13-2 illustrates a PL/M program that makes use of a nested DO WHILE block.

The program in Figure 13-2 represents an implementation of the popular bubble sort algorithm used to sort a 13-element array STRING in increasing order. The program works as follows. A flag called INTERCHANGE initially set to 0FFH is used to keep track of completion of the sorting process. The elements of the array STRING are scanned in pairs, starting from the first

```
/* BUBBLE SORT PROGRAM */

DECLARE INTERCHANGE BYTE INITIAL (0FFH);
DECLARE (TEMP,J) BYTE;
DECLARE STRING (13) BYTE DATA (2,12,76,28,37,1,9,5,74,4,9,1,35);

   DO WHILE INTERCHANGE = 0FFH;
     INTERCHANGE = 0;
     J = 1;

     DO WHILE J < 12;
       IF STRING (J) > STRING (J+1) THEN DO;
                                         TEMP = STRING (J);
                                         STRING(J) = STRING(J+1);
                                         STRING(J+1) = TEMP;
                                         INTERCHANGE = 0FFH;
                                         END;
          J = J + 1;
     END;

   END;
```

FIGURE 13-2. Nested DO blocks: bubble sort program.

element of the array. If the pairs scanned are out of order, an exchange is made between the positions of the two elements, and the interchange flag is set to zero. The next consecutive pairs are then scanned, and are switched if out of order; this continues until the last element in the array has been checked. The entire process is repeated over and over until no more interchanges have occurred. At this point the array STRING has been completely sorted. As the program sorts through the array, the smaller values seem to "bubble" up to the top of the list, hence the term *bubble sort*. A trace of the array STRING is shown in Figure 13-3 for the sorting of four members of the array.

Note the use of indentation in Figure 13-2 when writing nested DO blocks. This is not an absolute requirement in terms of program execution but serves a good practice to make the program more readable. Using indentations for each level of nesting makes clear identification of these different levels, and can be extremely useful when debugging the program.

The third type of DO statement in PL/M is the iterative DO statement. The syntax of the iterative DO statement is as follows:

```
DO <index> = <initial expr> TO <final expr>;
   <statement 1>;
   <statement 2>;
          .
          .
          .
   <statement n>;
END;
```

The DO and TO keywords are required, <index> is a scalar variable (not dimensioned), and <initial expr> and <final expr> are any valid PL/M expressions that evaluate to a constant. The value of <index> is initially set to the value of <initial expr>. The statements within the DO-END block are repeatedly executed until the value of <index> reaches the value of <final expr>. Each time through the block the value of <index> is increased by one. When

```
                  Pass 1
STRING (0)    56  ← 49        49       49
STRING (1)    49  ← 56  ← 12        12
STRING (2)    12        12  ← 56  ← 51
STRING (3)    51        51        51  ← 56

                  Pass 2
STRING (0)    49  ← 12        12       12
STRING (1)    12  ← 49  ← 49       49
STRING (2)    51        51  ← 51  ← 51
STRING (3)    56        56        56  ← 56
```

FIGURE 13-3. Trace of array STRING in bubble sort.

the value of <index> reaches the value of <final expr>, control is transferred to the next executable statement outside the block.

EXAMPLE 13-1: CALCULATION OF N FACTORIAL

The factorial function, whose domain is the natural numbers, is defined as

$$\text{factorial (N)} = \begin{cases} 1, \text{ if } N = 0 \\ N * \text{factorial } (N - 1), \text{ otherwise} \end{cases}$$

Solution

The program in Figure 13-4 makes use of the preceding algorithm and an iterative DO construct to calculate FACTORIAL (N). This particular program uses the factorial of the number 4 as an example.

The first step in the program is to declare all variables that are to be used. The variable N is the number whose factorial is to be calculated. J is an index for the number of iterations performed. FACTORIAL is the variable that will hold the factorial of N. FACTORIAL is declared to be of type address and is initialized to 1 (at compile time).

The next step is to initialize the value of N to 4 (at run time) through an assignment statement. At this point, note that the value of FACTORIAL could also have been initialized with an assignment statement, and the value of N could have been initialized at compile time with a DECLARE statement. The method used to do this would depend entirely on the programmer.

Next, a test is performed to see if the value of N is either 0 or 1. If N is 1 or 0, the answer is immediate and the variable FACTORIAL is set to 1. If N is not 0 or 1, the iterative DO block calculates the factorial of N.

In this case since the value of N is 4, the statements within the DO block will be executed four times (until J reaches a value of 4). Table 13-4 illustrates the values of the variables J and FACTORIAL during each pass. Once the value of J reaches 4, the loop is terminated and the final value of FACTORIAL is 24, which is the correct calculation for 4 factorial. ∎

```
DECLARE (J,N) BYTE;
DECLARE FACTORIAL ADDRESS INITIAL (1);

N = 4; /* THIS IS THE FACTORIAL TO BE CALCULATED */

/* SEE IF N = 0 OR 1. IF SO, FACTORIAL = 1 */
IF (N = 0) OR (N = 1) THEN FACTORIAL = 1;
                     ELSE;
                          DO J = 1 TO N;
                             FACTORIAL = FACTORIAL * J;
                          END;

/* AT THIS POINT THE VARIABLE "FACTORIAL" HOLDS THE
   ANSWER TO THE PROBLEM */
```

FIGURE 13-4. Calculation of N factorial.

TABLE 13-4. Trace of the Variable J in the Factorial Program

J	FACTORIAL = FACTORIAL * J
1	= 1 * 1 = 1
2	= 1 * 2 = 2
3	= 2 * 3 = 6
4	= 6 * 4 = 24

This program could be used to calculate factorials for N = 0 to 8 since 8 factorial is 40320 (within the limits of the address type), while 9 factorial is 362880 (out of the range of the address type).

In an iterative DO block it was found that the value of <index> was incremented by one during each pass through the statements within the block. The number by which the <index> is incremented can be modified by using the BY clause with the iterative DO statement. The syntax of the iterative DO statement with the BY clause is as follows:

```
DO <index> = <initial expr> TO <final expr>
                            BY <step expr>;
```

All parameters in the statement remain the same except that now the programmer can control the number of times <index> is stepped up during each pass through the block. For example, the statement

```
DO J = 1 TO 20 BY 2;
```

would cause the index J to obtain values of 1, 3, 5, 7, 9, 11, 13, 15, 17, and 19 during subsequent passes through the block. Note that the value of J will never reach 20 in this case, but the iteration will be terminated the moment the value of J exceeds 20.

PL/M does not allow the user to specify a downward step by setting <step expr> to a negative number. This is due to the fact that the compiler operates only with unsigned numbers. Thus substituting a number like −2 would be the same as 254.

The last type of DO block supported in PL/M is the DO CASE block. The DO CASE block does not cause execution of *all* the statements within the block but causes *selective execution* of statements within the block. The syntax for the DO CASE statement is

```
DO CASE <expression>;
  <statement 1>;
  <statement 2>;
         .
         .
         .
  <statement n>;
END;
```

The <expression> is any valid PL/M expression that *must* evaluate to a number between 0 and n − 1 (n is the number of statements within the block). If the expression evaluates to 0, <statement 1> is executed; if the expression evaluates to 1, <statement 2> is executed; and so on; if the expression evaluates to n − 1, statement n is executed.

Thus *only one* statement is executed within the block, and this statement is executed only once. The execution of a particular statement will depend on its sequential position in the block and the result of the evaluation of the expression. For example,

```
DO CASE J;
    SUM = J;
    DATA1 = SUM;
    COUNT = 5;
END;
```

would be the same as

```
IF J = 0 THEN SUM = J;
IF J = 1 THEN DATA1 = SUM;
IF J = 2 THEN COUNT = 5;
```

Note that if the value of J is 3 or greater, none of the statements in the block will be executed.

As mentioned before, DO blocks can be nested. If other DO blocks are nested within a DO CASE block, the nested DO blocks are treated as single statements.

13-8
INTERRUPT PROCEDURES

When developing software using high-level languages, the user does not often have control over the compiler's translation. This means that the code generated by the compiler is fairly fixed and does not offer much flexibility; this was not the case in assembly language software development. There are, however, many features built into the PL/M compiler that allow the user to control storage allocation and the generation of code. Some of these features were seen in previous sections of this chapter.

For example, consider the implementation of an interrupt service routine. In assembly language, the service routine would be written as a subroutine that would automatically be called when a hardware interrupt was generated. If the hardware interrupt generated an RST 7 vector, the user would have to make sure that either the service routine was located at location 0038H or provisions were made for a jump vector at location 0038H, leading to the actual service subroutine for the interrupt.

A programmer writing an interrupt service routine in PL/M would immediately think of a procedure, since procedures are the PL/M "subroutines." However, the position of the procedure in the hardware memory map is an important consideration when dealing with interrupts. Normal PL/M procedures are compiled together with the rest of the program into code, without any real restrictions on the location of the code compiled. A logical process in developing a PL/M interrupt procedure would be to write it as one would any procedure, then examine the object code generated by the compiler, determine the starting address of the procedure, and then, perhaps in another assembly language module, place a jump vector to the starting address of the procedure at the desired restart address. It is obvious that this could be a difficult process. For this reason, PL/M has provisions for a special procedure called the *interrupt procedure*.

The interrupt procedure in PL/M is a special procedure that is used to service interrupts. This procedure is written by the user and included as part of the program being developed. However, the compiler automatically takes care of the restart jump vector at a restart location for a specified interrupt level. This allows for entry into the procedure whenever a hardware interrupt is received by the CPU. The syntax of the interrupt procedure entry point is as follows:

```
<name>: PROCEDURE INTERRUPT n;
```

PROCEDURE and INTERRUPT are required keywords, <name> is the name of the procedure, and "n" is a numeric constant having a value of 0 to 7 (inclusive). The constant n corresponds to one of the eight levels of interrupts provided by the 8080 microprocessor. Thus if the value of n is 7, on receiving an RST 7 vector, the CPU starts the execution of the procedure; a jump vector to the procedure is automatically inserted at location 0038H by the compiler. The procedure body can be any sequence of executable statements used to service the interrupt condition. The exit point of the procedure is the same as any other procedure in PL/M.

To illustrate the use of the interrupt procedure consider the following example. A real-time clock attached to the RST 5 interrupt line of the CPU generates an interrupt to the CPU every 10 milliseconds. On receiving the interrupt the CPU is automatically vectored to location 0028H. The user's program is to have an interrupt service routine that adjusts the value of four global variables each time an interrupt occurs. These variables are all of BYTE type and have the following functions:

- TICK   Time intervals of 1/100 second (10 milliseconds)
- SECOND   Time intervals of 1 second
- MINUTE   Time intervals of 1 minute
- HOUR   Time intervals of 1 hour

The service routine works as follows. On entry to the procedure (when an interrupt is received) the value of TICK is incremented, and a check is made to see if the value of TICK has reached 99. If it has, TICK is reset to zero, and SECOND is incremented. A check is made to see if SECOND has reached a value of 59. If so, SECOND is reset to zero and MINUTE is incremented. Finally, if the value of MINUTE has reached 59, MINUTE is reset to zero and HOUR is incremented. The service routine is terminated and control returns to the point of interruption. The interrupt procedure to implement this operation is

```
CLOCK: PROCEDURE INTERRUPT 5;
    TICK = TICK + 1;
    IF TICK = 99 THEN  DO;
                       TICK = 0;
                       SECOND = SECOND + 1;
                       END;
    IF SECOND = 59 THEN DO;
                        SECOND = 0;
                        MINUTE = MINUTE + 1;
                        END;
    IF MINUTE = 59 THEN DO;
                        MINUTE = 0;
                        HOUR = HOUR + 1;
                        END;
END CLOCK;
```

FIGURE 13-5. Interrupt procedure for a real-time clock.

shown in Figure 13-5. Interrupt procedures must be untyped and cannot have any parameters. Interrupt procedures may also be called from within the user's program, as is done with any other PL/M procedure.

13-9

BUILT-IN PROCEDURES

PL/M provides the user with two built-in untyped procedures. These procedures may be called by the programmer and do not have to be included in the PL/M program; the code for these procedures is built into the PL/M compiler. The two built-in procedures in PL/M are the TIME and MOVE procedures.

TIME Procedure

The TIME procedure initiates a CPU time delay for an amount of time specified by the programmer. This procedure is very similar to a DELAY subroutine in assembly language. The format for the TIME procedure is

```
CALL TIME (<expression>);
```

where <expression> is any valid PL/M expression that evaluates to a constant in the range 0 to 255. The TIME procedure causes the CPU to delay execution for a period of time based on a multiple of the evaluated expression or constant. This time delay is based on a 2-MHz CPU speed and is a multiple of 100 microseconds. Thus the statement

```
CALL TIME (255);
```

would delay the CPU for 25.5 milliseconds. This would be the largest delay allowed. To increase the amount of delay, an iterative DO block could be incorporated with the TIME procedure as follows:

```
DO I = 1 TO 40;
    CALL TIME (250);
END;
```

This would delay the CPU 40 × 250 × 100 microseconds, or approximately 1 second.

MOVE Procedure

The built-in procedure MOVE is used to move a block of memory from one area to another. The format for the block-move procedure is

```
CALL MOVE (<count>,<source>,<destination>);
```

where <count> is the number of bytes to be moved, <source> is the starting address of the source block, and <destination> is the starting address of the destination block. All three parameters specified in the MOVE procedure can be expressions or constants, and can be of byte or address types. The following procedure call will move 512 bytes of data from location 1000H to location 5000H:

```
CALL MOVE (512,1000H,5000H);
```

Note that if the source and destination areas overlap, the result may be unpredictable.

13-10

BUILT-IN FUNCTIONS

The built-in procedures mentioned in Section 13-9 were untyped procedures. The procedures performed a certain task but did not return a result. PL/M also provides the user with several built-in typed procedures (*built-in functions*) that operate in a manner similar to that of untyped procedures but return a result. These built-in functions can be summarized as follows.

INPUT Function

Format

```
<variable> = INPUT (n);
```

where <variable> is any valid declared PL/M variable identifier and "n" is an integer CONSTANT in the range 0 to 255. The value of n corresponds to one of the 256 possible input ports of the 8080 microprocessor. The INPUT function assigns the data at input port n to the <variable>.

```
CONSOLE$INPUT: PROCEDURE BYTE;
   DECLARE (STATUS,CHARACTER) BYTE;
   STATUS = 0;
     DO WHILE STATUS = 0;
       STATUS = INPUT (03H) AND 00000010B;
     END;
   CHARACTER = INPUT (02H) AND 01111111B;
   RETURN CHARACTER;
END CONSOLE$INPUT;
```

FIGURE 13-6. 8251 console input procedure.

Example

$$SWITCH = INPUT (20H);$$

The variable SWITCH is set to the value of the data at input port 20H.

Figure 13-6 illustrates an implementation of the 8251 console input procedure using the INPUT function to access the data (02H) and status (03H) ports of the 8251. The CONSOLE$INPUT procedure is a typed procedure that returns the character entered from the console keyboard. No parameters are passed to the procedure. The procedure first sets the status flag to 0 and waits for a receiver status-ready condition at the status port (03H). Once this condition has been satisfied, the DO WHILE loop terminates and the data from the console is received from the data port (02H).

LENGTH Function

Format

$$<variable> = LENGTH (<array\ name>);$$

The LENGTH function is used to determine the size of an array represented as <array name>. The <array name> must be a nonsubscripted reference to a previously declared array.

Example

$$EXTENT = LENGTH (TABLE);$$

Assuming that an array TABLE (25) has been previously declared, the LENGTH function returns a value of 25 to the variable EXTENT.

LAST Function

Format

$$<variable> = LAST (<array\ name>);$$

The LAST function is similar to the LENGTH function in format except that it returns the subscript of the last element in a previously declared array.

Example

```
ABC = LAST (TABLE);
```

Assuming the same array TABLE (25) as in the preceding example, the variable ABC is assigned the value 24, which is the subscript of the last element in the array.

LOW Function

Format

```
<variable> = LOW (<expression>);
```

The LOW function is used to convert an address variable, or an <expression> that evaluates to an address constant, to a byte constant, by assigning the lower 8 bits of the constant to the <variable> on the left-hand side.

Example

```
SMALL = LOW (LARGE);
```

If the value of the variable LARGE was 1234H, the LOW function will assign the value 34H to the variable SMALL.

HIGH Function

Format

```
<variable> = HIGH (<expression>);
```

The HIGH function is used to convert an address variable, or an <expression> that evaluates to an address constant, to a byte constant, by assigning the higher 8 bits of the constant to the <variable> on the left-hand side.

Example

```
SMALL = HIGH (LARGE);
```

If the value of the variable LARGE was 1234H, the HIGH function will assign the value 12H to the variable SMALL.

DEC Function

Format

<variable> = DEC (<expression>);

The DEC function performs a decimal adjust operation (similar to the DAA instruction of the 8080) on the specified <expression> and assigns the adjusted value to <variable>. The <expression> must evaluate to a byte value.

Example

RESULT = DEC (DATA+2);

If the value of DATA is 56H, after the decimal adjust, the variable RESULT is assigned the value 88.

Rotation Functions

Format

<variable> = ROR (<expression>,<count>);
<variable> = ROL (<expression>,<count>);

The ROL and ROR functions perform logical rotate operations on byte-type variables, or <expression>s that evaluate to byte constants. ROL is the rotate-left function, and ROR is the rotate-right function. The bits of the specified constant are rotated left or right a certain number of times based on the value of <count>. For rotate-left operations, the most significant bit position is moved to the least significant bit position, and vice versa for rotate-right operations.

Example

PATTERN = ROR (DATA,3);
PATTERN = ROL (DATA,3);

Assuming that the variable DATA has a value of 10010010B, the ROR function rotates the bits in DATA three times and assigns the variable PATTERN the value of 01010010B. The ROL function assigns the variable PATTERN the value of 10010100B.

Two other functions, SCL and SCR, which have the same format as the rotate functions, can also be used to rotate the bits in a constant, the only difference being that the bits are rotated through the carry flag.

Shift Functions

Format

```
<variable> = SHR (<expression>,<count>);
<variable> = SHL (<expression>,<count>);
```

The SHR and SHL functions perform logical shift operations on byte-type variables, or <expression>s that evaluate to byte constants. SHL is the shift-left function, and SHR is the shift-right function. The bits of the specified constant are shifted left or right a certain number of times, based on the value of <count>. For shift-left operations, the most significant bit is discarded, and the least significant bit position is filled with zeros, and vice versa for shift-right operations.

Example

```
PATTERN = SHR (DATA,3);
PATTERN = SHL (DATA,3);
```

Assuming that the variable DATA has a value of 10010010B, the SHR function shifts the bits in DATA three times and assigns the variable PATTERN the value of 00010010B. The SHL function assigns the variable PATTERN the value of 10010000B.

OUTPUT Array

Even though the OUTPUT "function" is not really a built-in PL/M function, for all practical purposes it can be considered to be one. However, it does work somewhat differently from the other built-in functions discussed in this section.

The predeclared variable OUTPUT is an array variable of byte type containing 256 elements. Each of these elements corresponds to an 8080 output port. If the OUTPUT variable appears on the left-hand side of an assignment statement, the expression, variable, or constant on the right-hand side is sent to the output port corresponding to the subscript of the OUTPUT variable: for example,

```
OUTPUT (26H) = 2 + DATA5;
```

Assuming that the value of DATA5 is 13H, the constant sent to output port 26H is 15H. Note that since the OUTPUT array deals with output ports, the OUTPUT variable can never appear on the right-hand side of an assignment statement.

Figure 13-7 is an implementation of the 8251 console output routine in PL/M

```
CONSOLE$OUTPUT: PROCEDURE (CHARACTER);
    DECLARE (STATUS,CHARACTER) BYTE;
    STATUS = 0;
      DO WHILE STATUS = 0;
        STATUS = INPUT (03H) AND 00000001B;
      END;
    OUTPUT (02H) = CHARACTER;
END CONSOLE$OUTPUT;
```

FIGURE 13-7. 8251 console output procedure.

using the OUTPUT array to access the data port of the 8251. The CONSOLE$OUTPUT procedure is similar to the previously discussed CONSOLE$INPUT procedure (Figure 13-6) except that the parameter passed to the procedure is the character to be sent to the console. No value is returned by CONSOLE$OUTPUT. After the DO WHILE loop completes the transmitter status check at port 03H, the local variable CHARACTER is assigned to the predeclared array identifier OUTPUT (02H), which sends the character to the 8251 data port.

13-11
BASED VARIABLES

The PL/M programming language provides the user with a special type of variable called a *based variable*. A based variable is one whose value is based on the contents of a memory location. With based variables it is possible to change the value of the variable by changing the memory location on which the variable is based. Thus a based variable is always of byte type and always works in conjunction with a variable of address type. For example, the following declaration defines the based variable CONTENT, based on the address variable POINTER.

```
DECLARE POINTER ADDRESS;
DECLARE CONTENT BASED POINTER BYTE;
```

Note that a based variable must have two declarations: one that declares the address variable that the based variable works with, and one that declares the based variable itself. In the example above, the variable CONTENT is declared to be based on the variable POINTER. Assuming that the value of POINTER is 03FFH, the value of CONTENT will then be the contents of memory location 03FFH. Or if the variable CONTENT is assigned the value 23H, this value would be stored at location 03FFH. If the value of POINTER is changed, the variable CONTENT will reference the new value of POINTER. Thus a based variable will change values as a function of the values taken on by its ADDRESS variable. If POINTER were set to another address value, CONTENT would correspondingly change to reference that new value.

An example to illustrate the use of a based variable would be a block-move program similar to the block-move built-in procedure. The program is required to move a 300-byte (COUNT) block of memory from address 2000H (SOURCE) to address 8000H (DESTINATION). The program is illustrated in Figure 13-8.

Two variables are declared for the source block: SOURCE and SDATA. SOURCE is initialized to the address of the source block, while the variable SDATA is based on the value of SOURCE and always is the contents of SOURCE. Similarly, the variable DESTINATION is initialized to the location of the destination block and has the based variable DDATA associated with it. The variable DDATA always refers to the contents of the memory location pointed to by DESTINATION. The variable COUNT is declared as an address and initialized to 300. The DO WHILE initiates a byte-to-byte block move until the

```
DECLARE SOURCE ADDRESS INITIAL (2000H);
DECLARE SDATA BASED SOURCE BYTE;
DECLARE DESTINATION ADDRESS INITIAL (8000H);
DECLARE DDATA BASED DESTINATION BYTE;
DECLARE COUNT ADDRESS INITIAL (300);

DO WHILE COUNT <> 0;
  DDATA = SDATA;
  SOURCE = SOURCE + 1;
  DESTINATION = DESTINATION + 1;
  COUNT = COUNT - 1;
END;
```

FIGURE 13-8. PL/M implementation of a block move.

value of COUNT has reached zero. Within the DO WHILE block, bytes are moved from the source block to the destination block as follows. Initially, the source and destination pointers point to the start of the source and destination blocks, respectively. The value of SDATA is then assigned to DDATA; this causes the contents of the memory location pointed to by SOURCE to be assigned to the memory location pointed to by DESTINATION. The source and destination pointers are then incremented, the value of COUNT is decremented, and the process continues until the value of COUNT reaches zero; at this point all the bytes from the source block have been moved to the destination block.

13-12

LOCATION REFERENCES AND THE DOT OPERATOR

The dot operator is a special character in the PL/M character set that allows the programmer to determine the address of an identifier or constant list at run time. In a PL/M statement, if any identifier of byte or address type is used with a decimal point (dot) to its immediate left, the value of the identifier becomes the address at which the identifier is stored and not the contents of the memory location(s). For example, assume that the compiler allocates space for the byte variable DATA1 at memory location 2100H. If the value of DATA1 is set to a constant, that constant will be stored at memory location 2100H. The assignment statement

```
TEST = DATA1;
```

will then assign the value of DATA1 (contents of location 2100H) to the variable TEST. However, using the dot operator with DATA1, the assignment statement

```
TEST = .DATA1;
```

will assign the value 2100H (memory location of DATA1) to the variable TEST.
In the first case TEST was assigned a byte value; in the second case it was assigned an address value. Thus, the dot operator, when used with any variable,

```
DECLARE STRING ADDRESS;
DECLARE CHARACTER BASED STRING BYTE;

STRING = .('THIS IS A TEST MESSAGE',0);
DO WHILE CHARACTER <> 0;
  CALL CONSOLE$OUTPUT (CHARACTER);
  STRING = STRING + 1;
END;
```

FIGURE 13-9. Application of the dot operator to display an ASCII STRING.

will release the memory location at which the variable is stored. The dot operator is therefore a pointer to the variable used as an operand. Address-type variables require two contiguous storage locations; in cases with address variables, the dot operator releases the first address of storage. The dot operator can also be used with array-type variables; for array-type variables, the address of the first element of the array is released.

The dot operator can also be used with a constant list as follows:

```
STRING = .('THIS IS A CHARACTER STRING')
```

The constant list is stored contiguously in memory one byte per ASCII character, and the address of the first byte in the list is assigned to the variable STRING. Note that the constant list is not limited to ASCII strings but can be a list of valid PL/M constants separated by commas and enclosed in parentheses.

The real capabilities of the dot operator can be seen when it is used in conjunction with based variables. Consider a program to print an ASCII string on the CONSOLE. The program is illustrated in Figure 13-9. The variable CHARACTER is a based variable, based on the address variable STRING. The value of STRING is set to the starting address of the *constant list*. The constant list is an ASCII character string terminated with a zero (ASCII null). The DO WHILE loop sends each character in the string to the console via the CONSOLE$OUTPUT procedure (the value of STRING is incremented each time) until an ASCII null (zero) is detected in the string. Since the variable CHARACTER is based on STRING, the value of CHARACTER is always the contents of the address pointed to by STRING (i.e., an ASCII character).

13-13

A PL/M PROGRAM EXAMPLE

Figure 13-10 is a PL/M program that makes use of some of the concepts derived from this chapter. The program is one that inputs an unsorted character string from the console, uses the bubble sort algorithm to sort the string, and outputs the sorted string to the console. The technique for developing a PL/M program is similar to the technique used in assembly language programming. First, the source file is created using a text editor; next, the source file is submitted to the compiler for compilation (syntax checking, and translation); and finally, the object file generated by the compiler is linked and loaded for execution. Figure

```
8080 PLM1   VER4.1 COMPILATION of SORT.PLM
00001  1
00002  1
00003  1    /**************************************************
00004  1    *            SORTING ROUTINE IN PL/M-80           *
00005  1    *                 PL/M   COMPILER                 *
00006  1    *                  23 FEB   1982                  *
00007  1    **************************************************/
00008  1
00009  1    /* THE FOLLOWING PROGRAM SORTS A CHARACTER STRING IN
00010  1       INCREASING ORDER. THE MAXIMUM STRING LENGTH IS 80
00011  1       CHARACTERS AND IS OBTAINED FROM THE CONSOLE ONE
00012  1       CHARACTER AT A TIME UNTIL THE CARRIAGE RETURN
00013  1       DELIMITER IS ENCOUNTERED.
00014  1    */
00015  1
00016  1    DECLARE STRING(80) BYTE INITIAL (0);
00017  1    DECLARE (J,N) BYTE;
00018  1    DECLARE DPORT LITERALLY '2';
00019  1    DECLARE SPORT LITERALLY '3';
00020  1    DECLARE CR    LITERALLY '0DH';
00021  1
00022  1
00023  1
00024  1    /**************************************************
00025  1    *                                                 *
00026  1    *            CONSOLE INPUT SUBROUTINE             *
00027  1    *                                                 *
00028  1    **************************************************/
00029  1
00030  1    /* THE FOLLOWING SUBROUTINE GETS A CHARACTER FROM
00031  1       THE CONSOLE AND RETURNS THE CHARACTER AS A USER
00032  1       DEFINED FUNCTION CALL (TYPED PROCEDURE). THE
00033  1       ROUTINE PROVIDES FOR A BUILT-IN ECHO FOR FULL
00034  1       DUPLEX.
00035  1    */
00036  1
00037  1    CONSOLE$INPUT: PROCEDURE BYTE;
00038  2       DECLARE (STATUS,CHAR) BYTE;
00039  2       STATUS = 0;
00040  2       DO WHILE STATUS = 0;
00041  2          STATUS = INPUT(SPORT) AND 00000010B;
00042  3       END;
00043  2       CHAR = INPUT(DPORT) AND 01111111B;
00044  2       OUTPUT(DPORT) = CHAR;
00045  2       RETURN CHAR;
00046  2    END CONSOLE$INPUT;
00047  1
00048  1
00049  1
```

FIGURE 13-10. PL/M program compilation: a sort program.

```
00050  1    /************************************************
00051  1    *                                               *
00052  1    *           CONSOLE OUTPUT SUBROUTINE           *
00053  1    *                                               *
00054  1    ************************************************/
00055  1
00056  1    /* THE FOLLOWING ROUTINE OUTPUTS A SINGLE CHARACTER
00057  1       TO THE CONSOLE. THE DATA TO BE TRANSMITTED IS
00058  1       INCLUDED AS A FORMAL PARAMETER TO THE ROUTINE
00059  1       IN A CALL STATEMENT.
00060  1    */
00061  1
00062  1    CONSOLE$OUTPUT:    PROCEDURE (CHAR);
00063  2       DECLARE (STATUS,CHAR) BYTE;
00064  2       STATUS=0;
00065  2          DO WHILE STATUS=0;
00066  2             STATUS = INPUT(SPORT) AND 00000001B;
00067  3          END;
00068  2       OUTPUT(DPORT) = CHAR;
00069  2    END CONSOLE$OUTPUT;
00070  1
00071  1
00072  1
00073  1    /************************************************
00074  1    *                                               *
00075  1    *           READ INPUT DATA INTO ARRAY          *
00076  1    *                                               *
00077  1    ************************************************/
00078  1
00079  1    /* THE FOLLOWING ROUTINE READS THE INPUT DATA ONE
00080  1       CHARACTER AT A TIME FROM THE CONSOLE INTO THE
00081  1       ARRAY STRING. ON EXIT, STRING WILL CONTAIN
00082  1       THE DATA WITH THE LAST ELEMENT BEING A CARRIAGE
00083  1       RETURN. THE VARIABLE N HOLDS THE NUMBER OF
00084  1       DATA ITEMS ENTERED.
00085  1    */
00086  1
00087  1    GET$DATA: PROCEDURE;
00088  2       J=0;
00089  2          DO WHILE STRING(J) <> CR;
00090  2             J=J+1;
00091  3             STRING(J) = CONSOLE$INPUT;
00092  3          END;
00093  2       N=J-1;
00094  2    END GET$DATA;
00095  1
00096  1
00097  1
```

FIGURE 13-10. (Continued)

```
8080 PLM1   VER 4.1 COMPILATION of SORT.PLM
00098  1    /************************************************
00099  1    *                                                *
00100  1    *            WRITE INPUT DATA FROM ARRAY         *
00101  1    *                                                *
00102  1    ************************************************/
00103  1
00104  1    /* THE FOLLOWING ROUTINE WRITES THE DATA FROM THE
00105  1       ARRAY STRING TO THE CONSOLE. THE DATA IS SENT
00106  1       ONE CHARACTER AT A TIME UNTIL THE CARRIAGE RETURN
00107  1       DELIMITER IS ENCOUNTERED. AT THIS POINT THE
00108  1       SUBROUTINE TERMINATES.
00109  1    */
00110  1
00111  1    PUT$DATA: PROCEDURE;
00112  2        J=0;
00113  2        DO WHILE STRING(J) <> CR;
00114  2            J=J+1;
00115  3            CALL CONSOLE$OUTPUT(STRING(J));
00116  3        END;
00117  2    END PUT$DATA;
00118  1
00119  1
00120  1
00121  1    /************************************************
00122  1    *                                                *
00123  1    *              SORT DATA IN THE ARRAY            *
00124  1    *                                                *
00125  1    ************************************************/
00126  1
00127  1    /* THE FOLLOWING ROUTINE USES THE BUBBLE SORT
00128  1       ALGORITHM TO ARRANGE THE ELEMENTS OF THE
00129  1       ARRAY STRING IN INCREASING ORDER. THE ARRAY
00130  1       IS SCANNED FROM TOP TO BOTTOM FOR ANY MISPLACED
00131  1       ELEMENTS UNTIL THERE ARE NONE. EACH TIME AN
00132  1       INTERCHANGE IS CONDUCTED THE INTERCHANGE FLAG
00133  1       IS SET. THE ROUTINE EXITS WHEN THE FLAG IS RESET
00134  1       OR WHEN THERE ARE NO MORE INTERCHANGES. AT THIS
00135  1       POINT THE ARRAY STRING HAS BEEN COMPLETELY
00136  1       SORTED
00137  1    */
00138  1
00139  1    SORT$DATA: PROCEDURE;
00140  2        DECLARE (INTERCHANGE,TEMP) BYTE;
00141  2        INTERCHANGE=1;
00142  2        DO WHILE INTERCHANGE=1;
00143  2            INTERCHANGE=0;
00144  3            DO J = 1 TO (N-1);
00145  3                IF STRING(J) > STRING(J+1) THEN
00146  4                    DO;
00147  4                      TEMP = STRING(J);
00148  5                      STRING(J) = STRING(J+1);
00149  5                      STRING(J+1) = TEMP;
00150  5                      INTERCHANGE = 1;
00151  5                    END;
00152  4            END;
00153  3        END;
00154  2    END SORT$DATA;
```

FIGURE 13-10. (Continued)

```
00155  1
00156  1
00157  1
00158  1    /*****************************************
00159  1    *                                         *
00160  1    *          MAIN PROGRAM SEQUENCE          *
00161  1    *                                         *
00162  1    *****************************************/
00163  1
00164  1    /* THE MAIN PROGRAM CONSISTS OF THREE MAJOR STEPS:
00165  1       THE SUBROUTINE GET$DATA READS THE DATA FROM
00166  1       THE CONSOLE INTO THE ARRAY STRING.
00167  1       THE SUBROUTINE SORT$DATA SORTS THE ELEMENTS
00168  1       OF THE ARRAY STRING.
00169  1       THE SUBROUTINE PUT$DATA DISPLAYS THE SORTED
00179  1       DATA ON THE CONSOLE.
00171  1    */
00172  1
00173  1    CALL GET$DATA;
00174  1    CALL SORT$DATA;
00175  1    CALL PUT$DATA;
00176  1
00177  1
00178  1    EOF;
NO PROGRAM ERRORS
```

FIGURE 13-10. (Continued)

13-10 is the output of the compiler's first pass. Observe that the compiler inserts line numbers for each line in the user's program. This allows the user to cross-reference the compiler's output with the source file. The compiler also includes a numerical nesting level. The nesting level starts at "1," and for the start of every DO block or procedure module in the program the nesting level is incremented by one; the nesting level is then decremented at the end of DO blocks and procedure modules. If the program started off with a nesting level of "1," it must end with the same nesting level; else, a nesting error condition exists. Nesting errors are common in PL/M, for often a programmer forgets to include the termination of a PL/M module. The nesting-level column thus allows the user to scan through the program to check for nesting errors.

The program is structured into six distinct modules: the console input procedure, the console output procedure, the get data procedure, the put data procedure, and the main program itself. The main program consists of three basic steps, and is implemented by making calls to procedures that perform the required steps.

The first procedure, GET$DATA, reads the character string from the console until a carriage return is entered. Each character entered from the console is stored as an element of the array STRING. The carriage return is stored as the last element of the array. The GET$DATA procedure calls the CONSOLE$INPUT procedure to receive each character.

The second procedure, SORT$DATA, performs a bubble sort (similar to the program discussed in Figure 13-2) on the array STRING. All the elements of the array are sorted, with the exception of the carriage return, which is maintained as the last element of the array.

The third procedure, PUT$DATA, outputs the sorted array STRING to the console one element at a time. Each element is sent to the console (via the CONSOLE$OUTPUT procedure) until a carriage return is encountered in the array. At this point the entire sorted string has been displayed and control returns to the main program.

The last statement in the program is the EOF; statement, signaling the compiler that the program has reached its logical end. Note that the program is organized with all the procedures entered first and then the main program. PL/M requires that a procedure be included first in sequence before any calls are made to it.

The first pass of the compiler through the user's program is intended for syntax checking and the generation of a symbol table. If the PL/M compiler is one that generates absolute object code, an *intermediate object code* is also generated during pass 1. Intermediate object code is a temporary object code file without any symbolic references. Syntax checking yields a result of "NO PROGRAM ERRORS" or "X PROGRAM ERRORS," where X is the number of syntax errors detected. The compiler identifies the line at which the error exists by referring to its line number.

The second pass of the compiler takes the intermediate code and symbol table from pass 1 and generates the object code for execution by the computer. The object code can be absolute or relocatable, depending on the type of compiler being used. If the compiler produces relocatable object code, the next step would be to link and locate the code with other modules (if any) to produce absolute object code. If the compiler is an absolute-object-code-producing compiler, the programmer can specify the origins of the code and data segment during the second pass. The commands used to specify these origins will depend on the type and version of the PL/M compiler being used.

Figures 13-11 through 13-13 show the output of a typical PL/M compiler during its second pass. The compiler illustrated in this example is an absolute-object-code-producing compiler; the code segment has been located at an origin of 2000H and the data segment is specified to lie directly below the code segment.

Figure 13-11 is a cross-reference listing of line numbers and the approximate memory locations where the code for a particular line has been compiled. For example, the assignment statement in line 41 has its equivalent machine instructions compiled at memory location 2014H. This allows for the programmer to debug the object code while referencing high-level statements in the PL/M program.

Figure 13-12 illustrates the listing of the symbol table with absolute memory references. The code segment has been located at locations 2000H through 2124H, and the data segment lies directly below, extending to location 21FFH. Note that the memory variable points to the base of the data segment. Also, the temporary variables STRING, J, N, INTERCHANGE, and TEMP are all located in the data segment. However, the procedures CONSOLE$INPUT, CONSOLE$OUTPUT, SORT$DATA, and so on, are stored in the code segment. The variables STATUS and CHAR have been defined twice since they are local

1 = 2003H	38 = 2006H	40 = 200BH
41 = 2014H	42 = 2018H	43 = 201CH
44 = 2020H	45 = 2022H	46 = 2026H
63 = 202AH	65 = 202DH	66 = 2036H
67 = 203AH	68 = 203EH	69 = 2042H
70 = 2043H	89 = 2048H	90 = 2057H
91 = 205CH	92 = 206BH	93 = 2072H
94 = 2077H	95 = 207AH	113 = 207FH
114 = 208EH	115 = 2093H	116 = 209DH
117 = 20A0H	118 = 20A1H	142 = 20A6H
143 = 20AEH	144 = 20B0H	145 = 20BFH
146 = 20D3H	147 = 20D6H	148 = 20E0H
149 = 20F9H	150 = 2106H	151 = 210CH
152 = 210FH	153 = 2116H	154 = 2119H
155 = 211AH	173 = 211DH	174 = 2120H
175 = 2123H		

FIGURE 13-11. Cross-reference listing produced by the compiler.

variables to the console input and output procedures, and even though they have the same name, they have different memory locations. The amount of stack space required by the compiled program is four bytes.

The user also has the option of examining the code generated by the compiler. This option is very useful for determining the boundaries of the code segment. It also provides the programmer with an understanding of how the compiler generates code, and some of the inefficiencies of the code produced by the compiler. Figure 13-13 illustrates a listing of the disassembled absolute object code produced by a typical PL/M compiler for the SORT program. Using the information from the symbol table in Figure 13-12 and the object code from Figure 13-13, the programmer can construct a memory map of the program load locations. This map is illustrated in Figure 13-14.

With reference to Figures 13-12 and 13-13, note that the first instruction is one that sets up the stack pointer. Next a jump is made to the main program at

```
Stack Size = 4 bytes
MEMORY              2200H
STRING              21A8H
J                   21F8H
N                   21F9H
CONSOLEINPUT        2006H
STATUS              21FAH
CHAR                21FBH
CONSOLEOUTPUT       2026H
CHAR                21FCH
STATUS              21FDH
GETDATA             2043H
PUTDATA             207AH
SORTDATA            20A1H
INTERCHANGE         21FEH
TEMP                21FFH
```

FIGURE 13-12. Symbol table generated by the compiler.

13-13 A PL/M PROGRAM EXAMPLE

```
2000H LXI  SP  A6H        21H      JMP         1AH      21H      LXI  H   FAH        21H
2009H MOV  MI  00H        LXI  H   FAH         21H      MOV  AM  SUB  I   00H        JNZ
2012H 1CH      20H        IN       03H         ANA  I   02H      MOV  MA  JMP        0BH
201BH 20H      IN         02H      ANA  I      7FH      INR  L   MOV  MA  OUT        02H
2024H MOV  AM  RET        LXI  H   FCH         21H      MOV  MC  INR  L   MOV  MI    00H
202DH LXI  H   FDH        21H      MOV  AM     SUB  I   00H      JNZ          3EH    20H
2036H IN       03H        ANA  I   01H         MOV  MA  JMP          2DH      20H    DCR  L
203FH MOV  AM  OUT        02H      RET         LXI  H   F8H      21H      MOV  MI    00H
2048H LXI  H   F8H        21H      MOV  CM     MOV  BI  00H      MOV  LI  A8H        DAD  B
2051H MOV  AM  SUB  I     0DH      JZ          72H      20H      LXI  H   F8H        21H
205AH INR  M   MOV  CM    MOV  BI  00H         MOV  LI  A8H      DAD  B   XCHG       LXI  H
2063H A6H      21H        MOV  ME  INR  L      MOV  MD  CALL         06H      20H    LHLD
206CH A6H      21H        MOV  MA  JMP         48H      20H      LXI  H   F8H        21H
2075H MOV  CM  DCR  C     INR  L   MOV  MC     RET      LXI  H   F8H          21H    MOV  MI
207EH 00H      LXI  H     F8H      21H         MOV  CM  MOV  BI  00H      MOV  LI    A8H
2087H DAD  B   MOV  AM    SUB  I   0DH         JZ       A0H      20H      LXI  H     F8H
2090H 21H      INR  M     MOV  CM  MOV  BI     00H      MOV  LI  A8H      DAD  B     MOV  AM
2099H MOV  CA  CALL       26H      20H         JMP      7FH      20H      RET        LXI  H
20A2H FEH      21H        MOV  MI  01H         LXI  H   FEH      21H      MOV  CM    DCR  C
20ABH JNZ      19H        21H      MOV  MI     00H      MOV  LI  F8H      MOV  MI    01H
20B4H LXI  H   F9H        21H      MOV  CM     DCR  C   MOV  AC  DCR  L   SUB  M     JC
20BDH A6H      20H        MOV  CM  MOV  BI     00H      MOV  LI  A8H      DAD  B     MOV  AM
20C6H LXI  H   F8H        21H      MOV  EM     INR  E   MOV  DI  00H      MOV  LI    A8H
20CFH DAD  D   MOV  CA    MOV  AM  SUB  C      JNC      0FH      21H      LXI  H     F8H
20D8H 21H      MOV  CM    MOV  BI  00H         MOV  LI  A8H      DAD  B   MOV  AM    LXI  H
20E1H FFH      21H        MOV  MA  MOV  LI     F8H      MOV  CM  MOV  BI  00H        MOV  LI
20EAH A8H      DAD  B     XCHG     LXI  H      F8H      21H      MOV  CM  INR  C     PUSH D
20F3H MOV  BI  00H        MOV  LI  A8H         DAD  B   MOV  AM  POP  H   MOV  MA    LXI  H
20FCH F8H      21H        MOV  CM  INR  C      MOV  BI  00H      MOV  LI  A8H        DAD  B
2105H XCHG     LXI  H     FFH      21H         MOV  CM  MOV  AC  STAX D   DCR  L     MOV  MI
210EH 01H      LXI  H     F8H      21H         INR  M   JNZ      B4H      20H        JMP
2117H A6H      20H        RET      CALL        43H      20H      CALL     A1H        20H
2120H CALL     7AH        20H      EI          HLT
21A8H 00H
```

FIGURE 13-13. Disassembled object code produced by the compiler.

location 211AH. The main program at location 211AH consists of three instructions, corresponding to the PL/M main program:

```
CALL 2043H    ; Call GET$DATA
CALL 20A1H    ; Call SORT$DATA
CALL 207AH    ; Call PUT$DATA
```

After the three call instructions, the compiler includes the HLT instruction to terminate execution.

Some of the inefficiencies in the code produced by the compiler can be illustrated by examining the CONSOLE$OUTPUT routine after compilation. From the symbol table in Figure 13-12, the subroutine CONSOLE$OUTPUT is located at 2026H. Isolating this segment from Figure 13-13, we have the compiled subroutine in commented mnemonic form shown in Figure 13-15.

When the size of the console output subroutine generated by the PL/M compiler is compared to the subroutine written in assembly language, one can see that the compiler is very inefficient in producing code. This results in very large memory requirements, and consequently in a considerable amount of degradation in execution speed. There thus exists a trade-off: simplified programming using a high-level language at the sacrifice of fast execution and low memory

Code segment

2000H	Initializations
2006H	CONSOLE$INPUT
2026H	CONSOLE$OUTPUT
2043H	GET$DATA
207AH	PUT$DATA
20A1H	SORT$DATA
211AH	Main program

Data segment

21A3H to 21A6H	Stack 4 bytes	
21A8H to 21F7H	String (80) 80 bytes	
21F8H	J	
21F9H	N	
21FAH	STATUS	← Local to CONSOLE$INPUT
21FBH	CHAR	
21FCH	CHAR	← Local to CONSOLE$OUTPUT
21FDH	STATUS	
21EEH	INTERCHANGE	
21FFH	TEMP	
2200H	Memory (base)	

FIGURE 13-14. Memory map of compiled program.

```
2026    LXI   H,21FCH   ; Point to CHAR
        MOV   M,C       ; Get CHAR in register C
        INR   L         ; Point to STATUS
        MVI   M,0       ; Set STATUS to zero
202D    LXI   H,21FDH   ; Point to STATUS
        MOV   A,M       ; Get STATUS in register A
        SUI   0         ; See if transmitter ready
        JNZ   203EH     ; Jump if ready
        IN    03H       ; Get 8251 status
        ANI   01H       ; Mask off transmitter ready bit
        MOV   M,A       ; Store in STATUS
        JMP   202DH     ; Check ready condition
203E    DCR   L         ; Point to CHAR
        MOV   A,M       ; Get CHAR to register A
        OUT   02H       ; and output to data port
        RET
```

FIGURE 13-15. Code generated for the console output routine.

13-13 A PL/M PROGRAM EXAMPLE

requirements. The choice is left entirely to the programmer and the application at hand.

REVIEW QUESTIONS AND PROBLEMS

1. Evaluate the following PL/M arithmetic expressions if SUM = 5, X = 10, and Y = 12. In each case, determine if the expression evaluates to a BYTE- or ADDRESS-type value.
   (a) X + SUM * SUM − Y + SUM
   (b) (X + SUM) * (SUM − Y) + SUM
   (c) X / SUM * SUM + (Y − X)

2. Evaluate the following PL/M logical expressions if A = 50H, B = 27H, C = 36H, and D = F3H.
   (a) A AND B OR B AND C OR NOT D
   (b) A AND (B OR B) AND (C OR NOT D)
   (c) NOT D XOR NOT C AND (B OR A)

3. Evaluate the following PL/M relational expressions if X = 3, Y = 24, and Z = 6.
   (a) (X = 3) AND (Z > 3)
   (b) NOT (X < 7) OR (Y = 23)
   (c) (Y < 3) OR 0FFH OR (Z <> 7)

4. Discuss the differences between a global variable and a local variable in the PL/M programming language.

5. What is the purpose of declaring an identifier "AT" a memory location?

6. What is wrong with the following PL/M program segment?

        DECLARE MESSAGE BYTE DATA ('A');
        OUTPUT (3) = MESSAGE;
        MESSAGE = MESSAGE + 1;

7. If the variables P and Q are declared as being of byte and address type, respectively, and have the values 37 and 513, respectively, determine the values of the variables after each of the following assignments statements is executed.
   (a) P = Q   (b) Q = P

8. For the following values of the variable TEST,
   (a) TEST = 12H   (b) TEST = 20   (c) TEST = 23H
   Determine the value of the variable RESULT after the following statement is executed:

390 ADVANCED PL/M CONCEPTS

```
            IF TEST > 5 THEN
                IF TEST < 30 THEN
                    IF TEST = 18 THEN
                        RESULT = 29;
                    ELSE;
                        RESULT = 19;
```

Note that the initial value (before the statement is executed) of RESULT is 0.

9. Modify the bubble sort program of Figure 13-2 to sort the same data in decreasing order.

10. What is the value of the variable SUM after the following sequence of statements is executed?

```
            SUM = 1;
            DO J = 1 TO 13 BY 3;
                SUM = J + SUM;
            END;
```

11. For the given values of the variables A, what is the value of the variable RESULT (initially 17) after the following sequence of statements is executed?

```
            DO CASE (A-3);
                RESULT = A;
                RESULT = A+A;
                RESULT = A-3;
                RESULT = A+3;
            END;
```

(a) A = 17 (b) A = 3 (c) A = 6 (d) A = 4 (e) A = 1

12. What is the purpose of having an interrupt procedure in the PL/M programming language?

13. Write a PL/M program to read data from input port 1 and store each data byte at consecutive memory locations starting at location 4000H. Stop reading data when a 00H byte is entered. Implement the program with based variables.

14. What is the function of the dot operator? How can it be used in a PL/M program?

15. Convert the utility subroutines developed in Chapter 10 to PL/M procedures.

16. Implement the LOADER program developed in Chapter 10 entirely in PL/M by using the utility procedures written in Problem 15.

17. Compare the PL/M implementation of the LOADER program with the assembly language implementation in terms of speed and memory requirements.

CHAPTER 14

The 8085 Microprocessor

14-1

INTRODUCTION

This text was written with the belief that by studying and understanding a specific microprocessor (in this case the 8080) the essence of all microprocessors would be learned. The same can also be said of microprocessor-based systems; that is, the same concepts exist for all microprocessor-based systems—only the details change. It was with this philosophy that the authors chose a general-purpose microprocessor like the 8080 to teach microprocessors, for in the opinion of the authors, the 8080 came about as close to being a generic standard as presently exists. This does not mean that the 8080 is the most current microprocessor, for it is not, nor is it the best suited for every application. What it does mean is that the 8080 and its support chips encompass most microprocessor architectural concepts. Of course, once these concepts are understood for the 8080, it is relatively simple to apply them to other microprocessors.

This chapter will study the 8085 microprocessor, believing the above to be true. For that reason the approach of study will be to make comparisons and extrapolations of prior understanding of the 8080 and its support chips.

14-2
8085 ARCHITECTURE

Figure 14-1 illustrates the 8085 architecture. Comparing Figure 14-1 with the 8080 architecture of Chapter 3, we see five major differences:

1. Multilevel interrupts as indicated by the interrupt control function block. This is a good indication that the 8085 has vector capability without the need to jam an RST N instruction on the data bus. As a side note, notice that the control signal $\overline{\text{INTA}}$ is generated by the interrupt control function block, which was generated by the 8228 in the 8080 system of Chapter 3.
2. Control signals $\overline{\text{RD}}$ and $\overline{\text{WR}}$ are the outputs of the timing and control function block. The timing and control function block is essentially the same as the CU of the 8080, and hence it will also be referred to as the CU. $\overline{\text{RD}}$ and $\overline{\text{WR}}$ are control signals for read and write operations, just as $\overline{\text{I/O R}}$, $\overline{\text{MEM R}}$, $\overline{\text{I/O W}}$, and $\overline{\text{MEM W}}$ were for an 8080 system. These control signals are generated internal to the 8085. Since all control signals ($\overline{\text{INTA}}$, $\overline{\text{RD}}$, and $\overline{\text{WR}}$) are generated internal to the 8085, *the 8085 does not need a controller (8228) as a support chip.*
3. The CU of the 8085 also indicates that all clock (8224) functions are on-board the 8085. This is indicated by the crystal inputs X_1 and X_2 as well as RESET and READY (internally synchronized) inputs; hence *the 8085 does not require a support clock chip* such as the 8224.
4. Serial I/O control function block. This is the most significant architectural difference between an 8080 system and the 8085 chip. The 8080 could have serial I/O capability only with the addition of an 8251 or similar chip(s) as support, whereas the 8085 has serial I/O capability within itself. This serial I/O capability will result in the 8085 having two more instructions than the 8080—otherwise, the instruction set for the 8085 is the same as the 8080.
5. There are two address buffers. One function block is labeled "ADDRESS BUFFER" and contains eight address lines, A_8–A_{15}. The other function block is also 8 bits (AD_0–AD_7) but is labeled "DATA/ADDRESS BUFFER." The dual name implies dual functions, which is the case. This function block functions as a bidirectional data buffer and address buffer. Hence AD_0–AD_7 are time-shared or multiplexed. When we study a timing diagram of the 8085 we shall see that during T_1 of the first machine cycle, AD_0–AD_7, serve as address lines and as data lines during other portions of the machine cycle.

The rest of the architecture is the same as the 8080. Figure 14-1 does not show as many temporary registers, register select, and control lines coming from the CU as the 8080 architecture does. These items are also present in the 8085, but to simplify the architectural drawing they were not shown.

Even though the instruction set is compatible with the 8080 (except for two additional instructions) and the architecture is quite similar, the pin configuration is very different. Having a different pin configuration means that the hardware connections will be totally different. Next we shall study the 8085 pin configuration and discuss the functions of the pins.

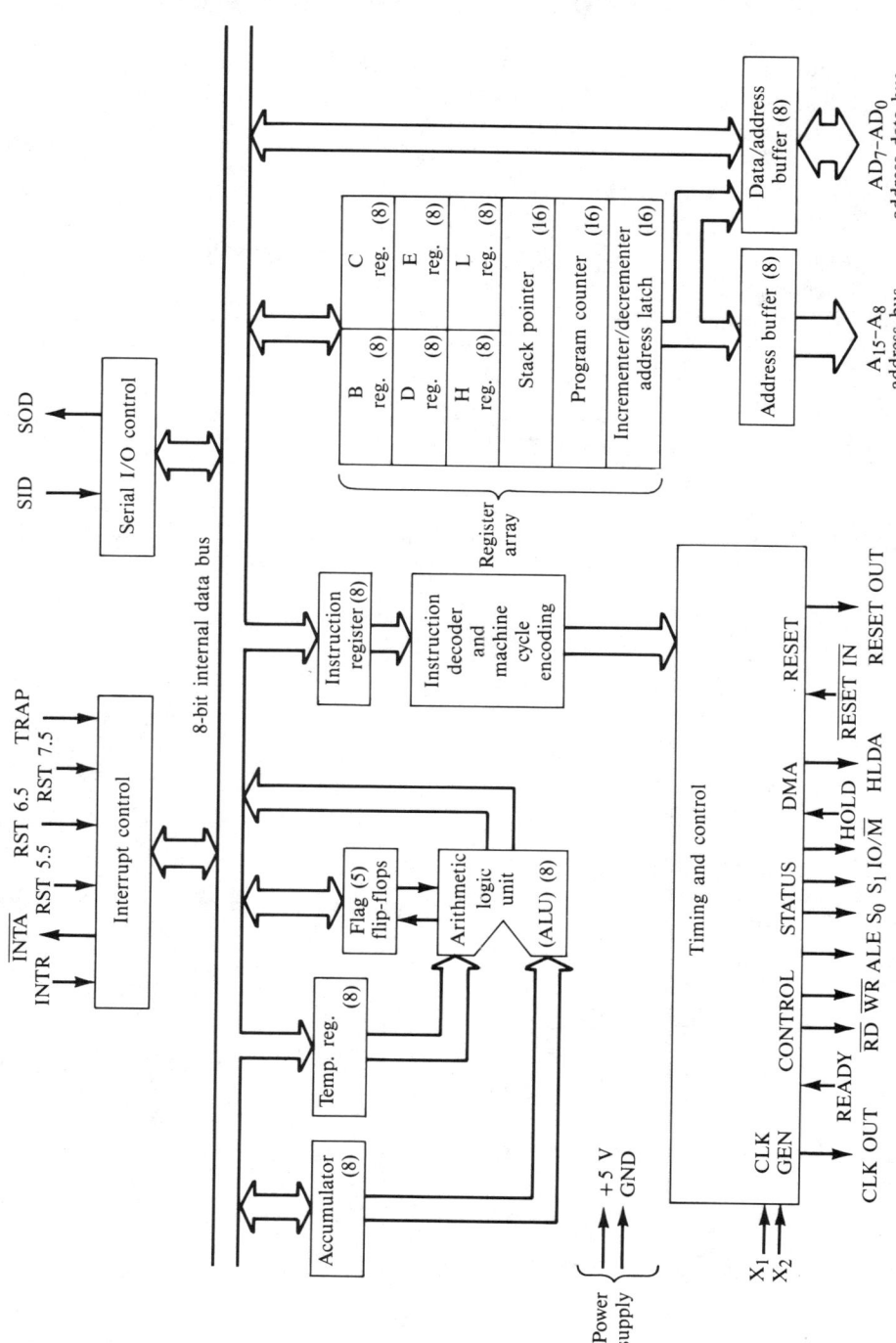

FIGURE 14-1. 8085 CPU architecture. (Courtesy of Intel Corp.)

14-2 8085 ARCHITECTURE

14-3 8085 PIN CONFIGURATION AND FUNCTIONS

Figure 14-2 is the pin configuration for the 8085. Comparing this pin configuration with that of the 8080, we find that the chips are not hardware compatible. The function of each pin is discussed below.

A_8–A_{15}. These address pins are tri-stated outputs and furnish the 8 most significant bits of memory and I/O addresses. As shown in Figure 14-3, the address lines A_8–A_{15} have the high-order address byte present during the entire machine cycle. As is the case of the 8080, when addressing I/O, the upper and lower 8 bits are mirror images of each other. Also as in the case of the 8080,

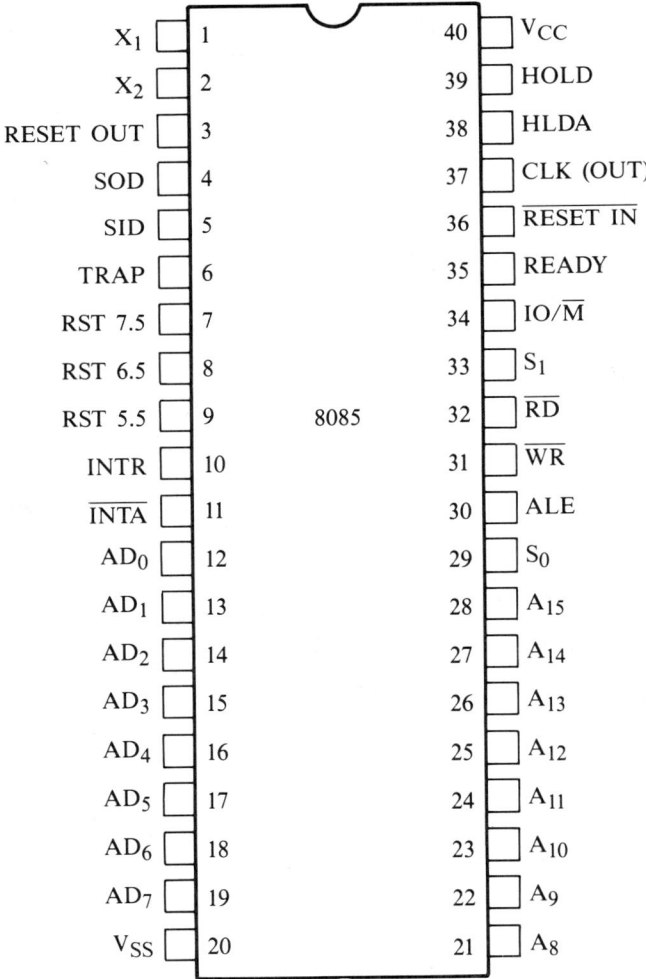

FIGURE 14-2. 8085 pin configuration. (Courtesy of Intel Corp.)

these address bits can be put in the high-Z state during HOLD (DMA) or HALT operations.

AD_0–AD_7. These eight lines function as tri-state multiplexed data/address lines. As previously stated, and as is illustrated in Figure 14-3, AD_0–AD_7 have the lower-order byte of an address at T_1 of each machine cycle.

ALE (Address Latch Enabled). This is a tri-stated output and is used by an external latch to latch the address on lines AD_0–AD_7. It can also be used to latch the CPU status off status lines S_0 and S_1 (to be explained) if desired. It is generated by the CPU during T_1 of each machine cycle, which is when AD_0–AD_7 have the low-order byte of an address present and lines S_0 and S_1 have the data bus status (CPU status), as illustrated in Figure 14-3.

S_0, S_1 (Data Bus Status). These are outputs and indicate the status of the data bus pins (AD_0–AD_7) during each machine cycle. From Table 14-1 we see that S_0 and S_1 also indicate CPU status. The binary code for each data bus activity (status) is shown in Table 14-1.

$\overline{RD}$ (Read). This is a tri-stated output and becomes active whenever the CPU is performing a read operation (memory or I/O). It is similar to $\overline{MEM\ R}$ and $\overline{I/O\ R}$ of an 8080-based system and for that reason it constitutes part of the control bus. When $\overline{RD}$ goes active, the CPU will latch the data byte present on the data bus pins (AD_0–AD_7). This can be seen from the timing diagram of Figure 14-3. $\overline{RD}$ can be put into high-Z during DMAs or HALTs to allow a

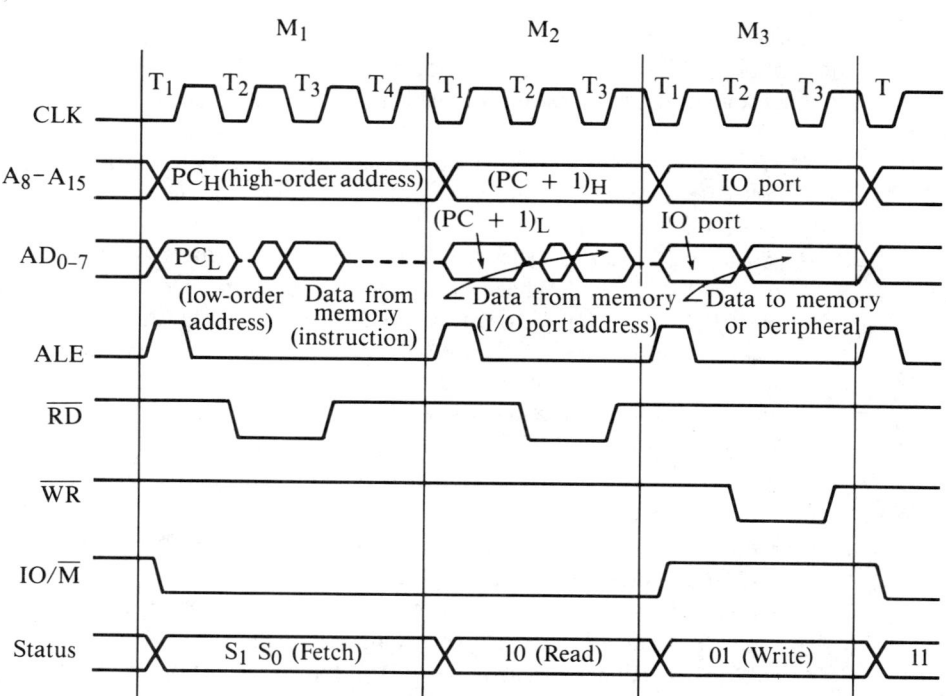

FIGURE 14-3. 8085 basic timing diagram. (Courtesy of Intel Corp.)

TABLE 14-1. Data Bus Status

S_1	S_0	Data Bus Activity
0	0	Halt state
0	1	Write operation
1	0	Read operation
1	1	Instruction fetch

peripheral device to gain control of the system's control bus in order to enable memory for the transfer of blocks of data.

$\overline{WR}$ **(Write).** This tri-stated output also consitutes part of the control bus. It becomes active whenever the CPU is performing a WRITE operation. Therefore, $\overline{WR}$ serves the same purpose as $\overline{I/O\ W}$ and $\overline{MEM\ W}$ of an 8080-based system. As in the case of $\overline{RD}$, it is tri-stated to allow a peripheral device to take control of the control bus during DMAs and HALTs.

IO/$\overline{M}$. The logic state of this output indicates whether I/O or memory is being accessed. If this output is high, I/O is being accessed, and if low, memory is being accessed (see Figure 14-3). IO/$\overline{M}$ combined with $\overline{RD}$ and $\overline{WR}$ can generate control signals $\overline{I/O\ R}$, $\overline{I/O\ W}$, $\overline{MEM\ R}$, and $\overline{MEM\ W}$ for an isolated I/O system. Since IO/$\overline{M}$ is part of the control bus, it is also a tri-stated output.

Interrupts. The 8085 has multilevel interrupts. There are five separate interrupt pins (INTR, RST 5.5, RST 6.5, RST 7.5, and TRAP). All except TRAP are maskable; that is, they can be enabled or disabled via software.

> *INTR:* This interrupt request input is exactly the same as the INT line of the 8080. Therefore, its use could result in software polling or vectoring via an RST instruction.
>
> *RST Interrupt Request:* There are three of these interrupts (RST 5.5, RST 6.5, and RST 7.5). Whenever a request is made via one of these inputs, the CPU will be automatically vectored to a specific location in memory. These locations are four addresses above the locations vectored to using RST 5, RST 6, and RST 7, which is the reason for the ".5" notation. These interrupt requests require no additional hardware, such as is the case when the CPU is vectored to a memory location resulting from RST 0, 1, 2, 3, 4, 5, 6, and 7. RST 5.5, 6.5, and 7.5 are priority interrupts; their priority and vector addresses are as follows:
> - *RST 5.5:* Lowest priority. Vectors to memory location 2CH. It is voltage-level sensitive, requiring a high to be activated.
> - *RST 6.5:* Second lowest priority. Vectors to memory location 34H. It also is voltage-level sensitive, requiring a high.
> - *RST 7.5:* Highest priority. Vectors to memory location 3CH. It is edge sensitive and is activated on the rising edge (0 to 1) of the input signal, which could be a pulse. The rising edge of the interrupt request sets an

internal flip-flop and therefore maintains the request. The flip-flop is automatically reset upon acknowledging the request.

It also can be reset using a reset to the CPU or by the instruction SIM, as we shall see. RST 7.5 is the only interrupt with such an internal flip-flop; the others require the I/O device to maintain the request. Notice that this internal flip-flop serves as an interrupt request flag, discussed in Chapter 6 and illustrated in Figure 6-7.

TRAP: This is a nonmaskable interrupt and has the highest priority of all interrupts. When an interrupt is requested over this input, the CPU will vector to memory location 24H.

$\overline{\text{INTA}}$. This output serves the same function as $\overline{\text{INTA}}$ of an 8080-based system. It is the acknowledgment of an interrupt request, via input INTR, and $\overline{\text{INTA}}$ will be used to jam an RST N instruction on the data bus just as was done with an 8080-based system. $\overline{\text{INTA}}$ will not be affected by the RST 5.5, RST 6.5, RST 7.5, or TRAP interrupts since vectoring is accomplished automatically by the 8085.

HOLD. A high at this input will request a DMA in a manner similar to the 8080. Upon acknowledgment of a HOLD request the CPU will put its address and data/address pins, as well as its control signal pins $\overline{\text{RD}}$, $\overline{\text{WR}}$, IO/$\overline{\text{M}}$, and ALE, in the high-Z state.

HLDA. Acknowledgment of a HOLD request. Its function and use are the same as an 8080 $\overline{\text{HLDA}}$ output.

$\overline{\text{RESET IN}}$. An active low on this input requests the system (including the CPU) to be reset. Upon activating $\overline{\text{RESET IN}}$, the PC (PC = 0000H) as well as the internal flip-flops Interrupt Enable and HLDA will be reset. This input serves the same function as the $\overline{\text{RESIN}}$ input of the 8224 of an 8080 system.

RESET OUT. This output acknowledges that the CPU has been reset. This output can be used to reset the rest of the system. RESET OUT serves the same function as the RESET output of the 8224 in an 8080 system.

READY. A high on this input applied by an addressed I/O or memory indicates that the addressed I/O or memory is ready to receive or transmit data from or to the CPU. This input serves the same function as the READY input of the 8080.

SID (Serial Input Data). This input is a single-bit input port onboard the 8085. The data bit present at this input port when the RIM instruction is executed will result in that data bit being loaded into the most significant bit of the CPU's accumulator.

SOD (Serial Output Data). The most significant bit of the CPU's accumulator will be output via this serial output port when the SIM instruction is executed.

X_1, X_2. These inputs are used to connect a crystal, just as X_1 and X_2 of the 8224 do for an 8080 system. The 8085 can operate between 0.5 and 3 MHz and thus requires a crystal within this range.

CLK. This output can be used as a clock to the system if needed.

V_{CC}. Requires a +5-V power supply.

V_{SS}. Ground.

Notice that the 8085 requires only one power supply rather than three, as is the case for the 8080.

14-4

SUMMARY OF THE 8085

The 8085 has an architecture very similar to the 8080. However, it differs in that it

1. Has the controller (8228) and clock (8224) onboard, thereby reducing the system's chip count.
2. Has multilevel interrupts with four (RST 5.5, RST 6.5, RST 7.5, and TRAP) of the five interrupt request inputs having automatic vectoring. The fifth (INTR) may have vector capability by the addition of hardware, just as in the 8080 system.
3. The 8085 has a serial input and output PORT. The serial input port (SID) may be read using the RIM instruction and the serial output port (SOD) may be written to using the SIM instruction.
4. The control signals are IO/$\overline{M}$, $\overline{RD}$, and $\overline{WR}$.
5. The 8080 instruction set is completely compatible with the 8085. Thus 8085's instruction set is said to be upwardly compatible with the 8080's, since all 8080 instructions can be executed on the 8085. Two additional instructions (RIM and SIM) are found in the 8085 instruction set.
6. The low-order byte of the 8085's address lines (AD_0–AD_7) is multiplexed with the 8085 data lines. Output ALE is active when AD_0–AD_7 are being used by the CPU to output an address and therefore can be used as a strobe to latch the lower byte of an address.
7. The 8085 requires only one 5-V power supply.

14-5

ADDRESS LATCHING

Since the low-order byte of an address is present on address/data lines AD_0–AD_7 for approximately one clock period (see Figure 14-3), it must be latched off AD_0–AD_7 during that period for decoding (I/O selector) purposes. From the timing diagram of Figure 14-3 we see that output ALE (trailing edge) can be used to provide the strobe for latching. Figure 14-4 will implement the required

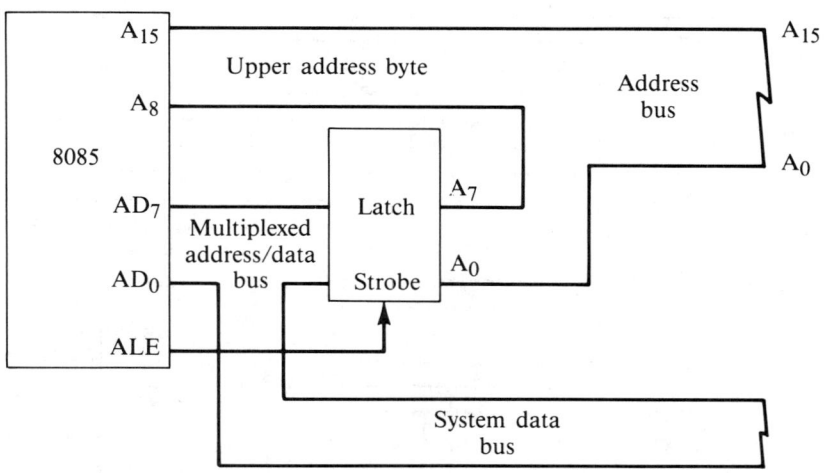

FIGURE 14-4. Latching of address low-order byte.

latching of the low-order byte of the address. Any 8-bit latch that strobes on the trailing edge of the strobe pulse ALE will suffice to implement Figure 14-4.

Specifically, an 8212 could be used as the latch of Figure 14-4, as shown in Figure 14-5(a). As seen from Figure 14-5(a), the 8085 output ALE strobes the 8212, thereby latching the address lower-order byte on the trailing edge of ALE. Latching the address demultiplexes AD_0–AD_7, allowing them to function as data bus pins the remainder of the machine cycle. By studying the data sheet from Intel on the 8212 architecture [Figure 14-5(b)], the reader can verify that for STB to be enabled the mode input MD must be low. When MD = 0, latching will occur on the trailing edge of ALE. Also, the reader can verify that it is necessary that the device select inputs $\overline{DS}_1$ and DS_2 (chip enables) be active ($\overline{DS}_1 = 0$ and $DS_2 = 1$). The CLK input of the 8212 resets all latching flip-flops, and since this feature is not required, CLK is to be wired inactive. [The authors believe that by this point the reader is sophisticated enough to decipher the operation of the 8212 from its architecture, shown in Figure 14-5(b), and to understand the chip from its specification sheet from an Intel data manual.]

From Figure 14-5(a) the reader should also realize that except for the control bus we have a microprocessor system which can replace the 8080 system of Figure 3-15. Let us next develop and discuss control signals which constitute the control bus of an 8085 system using memory-mapped I/O and then for one using isolated I/O.

14-6

CONTROL BUS FOR AN 8085 MEMORY-MAPPED I/O SYSTEM

If an 8085-based system is using memory-mapped I/O, the 8085 output control signal $IO/\overline{M}$ has no meaning. (Recall that for a memory-mapped I/O an I/O

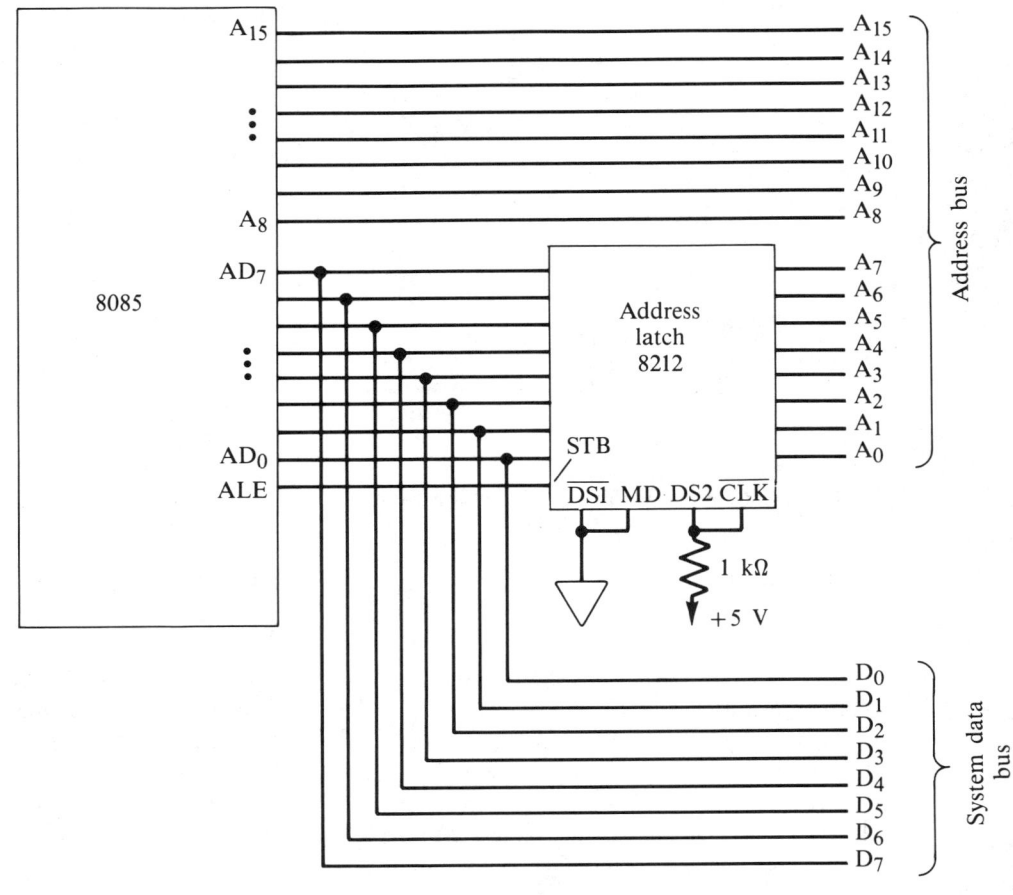

(a) Using an 8212 to latch lower byte of address

FIGURE 14-5(a).

device is addressed as a memory location.) As a result, the only control signals required will be those which distinguish between a read ($\overline{RD}$) or write ($\overline{WR}$) operation. As an example of an 8085-based system using memory-mapped I/O, refer to Figure 14-6. Figure 14-6 is the 8080-based system of Figure 4-7 upgraded to an 8085 [refer to Figure 14-5(a) for the 8085 address/data lines demultiplexer].

Examining the 8085 of Figure 14-6, we see that this system has no interrupt or DMA capability since TRAP, RST 5.5, RST 6.5, RST 7.5, INTR, and HOLD are wired inactive. Also, all I/O and memory are considered sufficiently fast since READY is tied high. From the buses of Figure 14-6 it is seen that demultiplexing of the address/data lines (AD_0–AD_7) is implemented using an 8212 latch, as was done in Figure 14-5(a). Since address lines A_{13} and A_{14} are used to select (chip enable) input port 0 and strobe (latch) output port 0 (after being ANDed with the appropriate control signal), respectively, this system is using

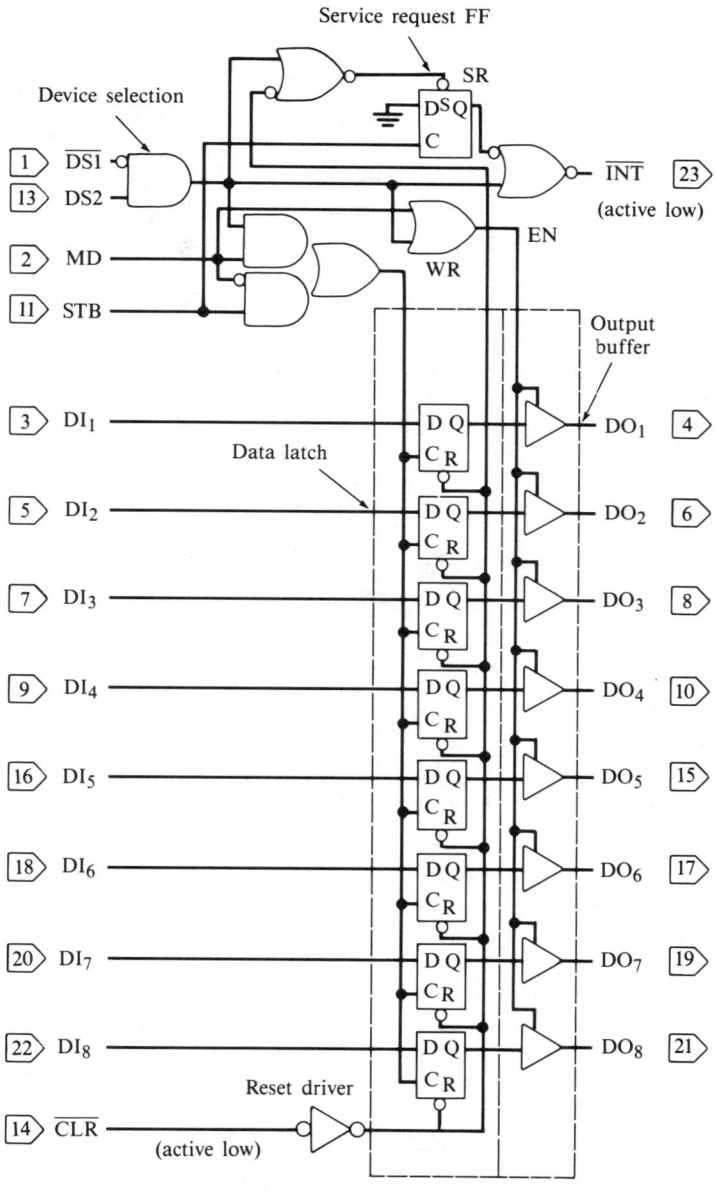

FIGURE 14-5(b). (Courtesy of Intel Corp.)

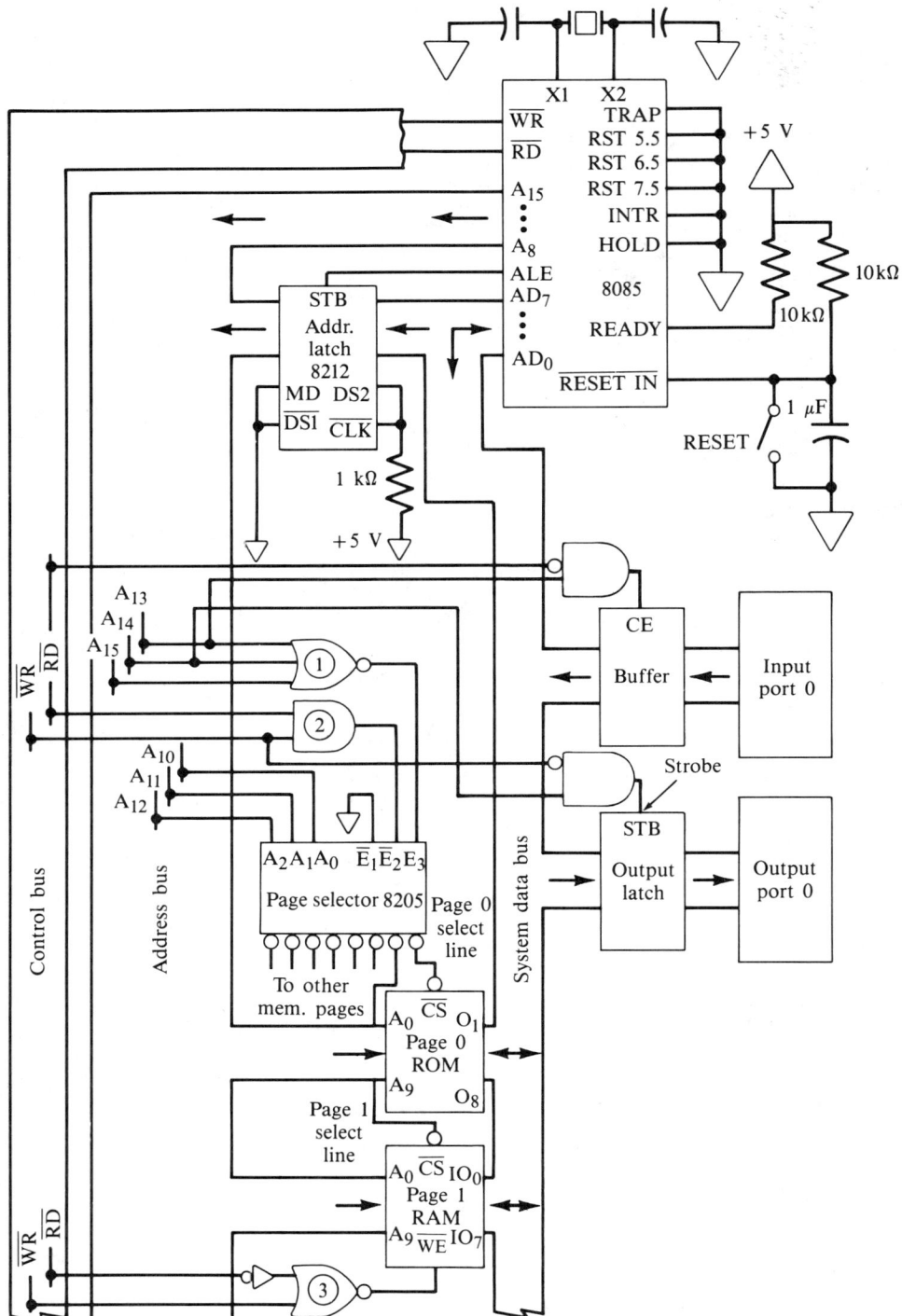

FIGURE 14-6. 8085 memory-mapped I/O.

the technique of linear addressing. Because of the addressing technique, there is no need for an I/O selector. Also, we notice that the control bus is composed of only read ($\overline{RD}$) and write ($\overline{WR}$) control signals. Since this system *does not* distinguish between memory read and write operations, as opposed to I/O read and write operations, we can conclude that the system is a memory-mapped I/O.

The system memory page selector (chip select) is comprised of the 8205 decoder and NOR gate 1 and AND gate 2. NOR gate 1 ensures that address lines A_{13}, A_{14}, and A_{15} must be low before the page selector is enabled ($E_3 = 1$ if A_{13}, A_{14}, and $A_{15} = 0$). This ensures against false addressing, as discussed previously. AND gate 2 will activate $\overline{E_2}$ whenever $\overline{RD}$ or $\overline{WR}$ is low, thus enabling the page selector for both read or write operations. Address lines A_{10}, A_{11}, and A_{12} actually provide the page numbers, as indicated in Table 14-2; OR gate 3 activates $\overline{WE}$ (write enable) when $\overline{WR} = 0$ and activates a read operation ($\overline{WE} = 1$) when $\overline{RD} = 0$.

From Table 14-2 it is seen that when either A_{13} or A_{14} goes high it inhibits the page selector via NOR gate 1 and also enables its respective I/O port. Also from Table 14-2 it is seen that input port 0 "uses up" 8192 addresses as well as output 0. This, of course, represents a foldback of 8191 addresses on the memory map. So many addresses being allocated (any time A_{13} or A_{14} is high) to an I/O port is the greatest disadvantage against linear address if expansion is desired. Of course, linear addressing has simplified the hardware by eliminating the need for an I/O selector.

To reiterate, Figure 14-6 is an example of a memory-mapped I/O system and also foldback addressing. Because it is a memory-mapped I/O system, its control bus requirements are simply composed of read and write control signals $\overline{RD}$ and $\overline{WR}$; that is, there is no need to distinguish between memory and I/O.

The next 8085-based system we wish to consider is one that has I/O isolated.

14-7

8085 ISOLATED I/O AND CONTROL BUS

For an isolated I/O system the control signals must distinguish between memory and I/O for read and write operations. Then the control signals required will be the same as the 8080's, that is, $\overline{MEM\ R}$, $\overline{MEM\ W}$, $\overline{I/O\ R}$, and $\overline{I/O\ W}$. Now these control signals could be designed to be active high, but since many of the uses of 8085 systems are to upgrade 8080 designs, let us make the control signals compatible.

To distinguish between I/O and memory operations, the 8085 output pin $IO/\overline{M}$ is necessary. Hence outputs $\overline{RD}$ and $\overline{WR}$ will distinguish between read and write operations and $IO/\overline{M}$ will be used to differentiate between I/O and memory. Using combinational logic techniques, let us use a truth table to aid in designing the logic for generating control signals $\overline{MEM\ R}$, $\overline{MEM\ W}$, $\overline{I/O\ R}$, and $\overline{I/O\ W}$. From Table 14-3 the reader can verify that the logic of Figure 14-7 will generate the control signals indicated.

TABLE 14-2. Addressing Scheme for Figure 14-6

Page	Hex Address	I/O Select		Page Select Number				Memory Location within Page										Number of Address Locations (decimal)
		A_{15}	A_{14}	A_{13}	A_{12}	A_{11}	A_{10}	A_9	A_8	A_7	A_6	A_5	A_4	A_3	A_2	A_1	A_0	
0	0000	0	0	0	0	0	0	0	0	0	0	0	0	0	0	0	0	1024
	03FF	0	0	0	0	0	0	1	1	1	1	1	1	1	1	1	1	
1	0400	0	0	0	0	0	1	0	0	0	0	0	0	0	0	0	0	1024
	07FF	0	0	0	0	0	1	1	1	1	1	1	1	1	1	1	1	
2	0800	0	0	0	0	1	0	0	0	0	0	0	0	0	0	0	0	1024
	0BFF	0	0	0	0	1	0	1	1	1	1	1	1	1	1	1	1	
. . .	. . .																	. . . .
7	1C00	0	0	0	1	1	0	0	0	0	0	0	0	0	0	0	0	1024
	1FFF	0	0	0	1	1	1	1	1	1	1	1	1	1	1	1	1	
Input port 0	2000	0	0	1	0	0	0	0	0	0	0	0	0	0	0	0	0	8192
	3FFF	0	0	1	1	1	1	1	1	1	1	1	1	1	1	1	1	
Output Port 0	4000	0	1	0	0	0	0	0	0	0	0	0	0	0	0	0	0	8192
	5FFF	0	1	0	1	1	1	1	1	1	1	1	1	1	1	1	1	
Caution		X	1	1	X	X	X	X	X	X	X	X	X	X	X	X	X	

TABLE 14-3. Truth Table for Generating Control Signals

$\overline{RD}$	$\overline{WR}$	$IO/\overline{M}$	Operation Required	Required Control Signal
0	0	0	None; illegal since $\overline{RD} = \overline{WR} = 0$	None
0	0	1		
0	1	0	Read memory	$\overline{MEM\ R}$
0	1	1	Read I/O	$\overline{I/O\ R}$
1	0	0	Write to memory	$\overline{MEM\ W}$
1	0	1	Write to I/O	$\overline{I/O\ W}$
1	1	0	None since $\overline{RD} = \overline{WR} = 1$	None
1	1	1		

Figure 14-8 represents a basic 8085-based system with isolated I/O. As is the case of the system represented in Figure 14-6, this system also does not have interrupt or DMA capability.

To integrate the 8085 of Figure 14-8 into a system with isolated I/O, refer to Figure 4-7. Replace the 8080-based portion of Figure 4-7 (that portion which is Figure 3-15) with that of Figure 14-8. The rest of the system, *including software*, remains unchanged.

14-8

8085 SERIAL PORTS SID AND SOD

As was stated in Section 14-2, the 8085 has two serial ports, which are SID and SOD. As stated in Section 14-3, to read the single bit of data at input SID

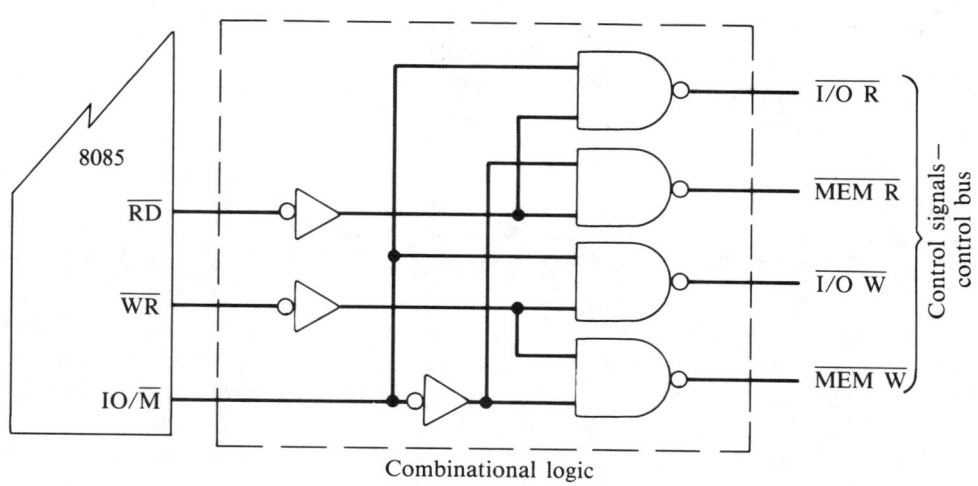

FIGURE 14-7. Combinational logic for generation of isolation I/O control signals.

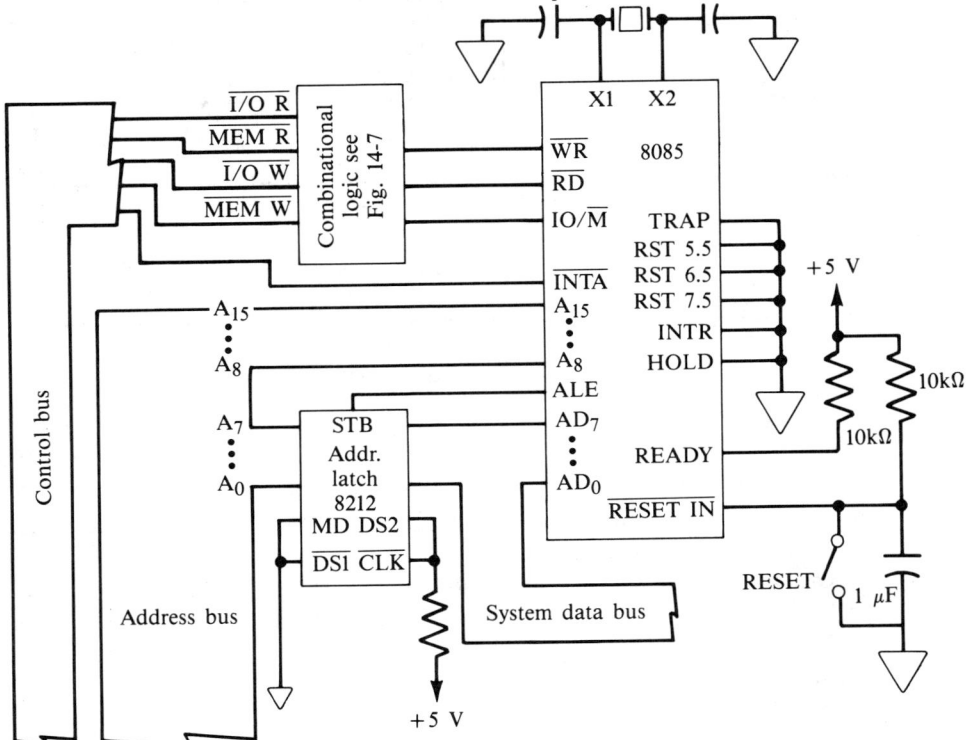

FIGURE 14-8. 8085 isolated I/O system.

requires that the CPU execute the RIM instruction. Execution of RIM will result in the data bit at input SID being loaded into the most significant bit (MSB) of the accumulator (AC_7). To output a single bit of data, the CPU must execute instruction SIM. The execution of SIM results in the CPU outputting the MSB of the accumulator (AC_7) to output SOD.

Each serial I/O port, SID, and SOD will now be discussed, as well as their associative instructions RIM and SIM.

14-9

SERIAL INPUT PORT SID AND INSTRUCTION RIM

Since the 8085 instruction set is upwardly compatible with the 8080's, instruction RIM must be added to those instructions of Section 5-3 to complete the 8085 instruction set. Figure 14-9 is a reproduction of an explanation of instruction RIM as taken from an Intel programming manual for the 8085.

As you know from the beginning explanation, RIM loads into the accumulator (AC_7) the serial data bit as well as 7 other bits of information. An explanation of the other 7 bits will now be offered:

RIM (8085 PROCESSOR ONLY)   READ INTERRUPT MASK

The RIM instruction loads eight bits of data into the accumulator. The resulting bit pattern indicates the current setting of the interrupt mask, the setting of the interrupt flag, pending interrupts, and one bit of serial input data, if any.

                          Opcode   Operand

                          RIM

Operands are not permitted with the RIM instruction.

The RIM instruction loads the accumulator with the following information:

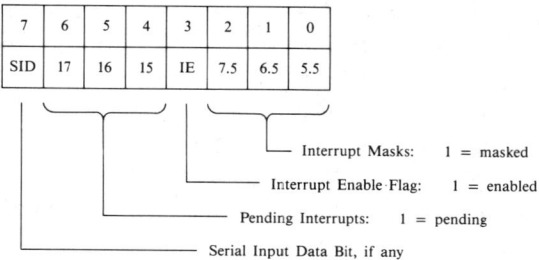

The mask and pending flags refer only to the RST5.5, RST6.5, and RST7.5 hardware interrupts. The IE flag refers to the entire interrupt system. Thus, the IE flag is identical in function and level to the INTE pin on the 8080. A 1 bit in this flag indicates that the entire interrupt system is enabled.

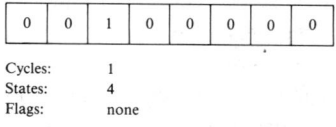

Cycles: 1
States: 4
Flags: none

FIGURE 14-9. The RIM instruction. (Courtesy of Intel Corp.)

Interrupt masks (accumulator bits AC_0, AC_1, and AC_2): These 3 bits give the status of the maskable interrupts RST 5.5, 6.5, and 7.5. For instance, if after the execution of a RIM the accumulator bits are such that $AC_0 = 1$, $AC_1 = 0$, and $AC_2 = 1$, then RST 5.5 and 7.5 have been disabled or masked ($AC_0 = 1$, $AC_2 = 1$) and will not *acknowledge* any interrupt request, but RST 6.5 is enabled and therefore can receive and will acknowledge interrupt request ($AC_1 = 0$). As we shall see, masking the RST interrupt inputs is accomplished by execution of the SIM instruction.

Interrupt enable flag (AC_3): This bit indicates the same information as the output INTE of the 8080. That is, a logic 1 for AC_3 indicates that the entire interrupt system is enabled, whereas a 0 indicates that it is disabled. However, the TRAP interrupt request input is excluded—it cannot be disabled.

Pending interrupts (AC_4, AC_5, and AC_6): These 3 bits indicate whether an interrupt request is being made, via RST 5.5, RST 6.5, or RST 7.5, but for one reason or another is not being acknowledged by the CPU, such as when the interrupts are disabled using instruction DI. When the CPU "has time" to acknowledge the interrupt request, it can check the status of the

RST interrupts, via the RIM instruction, and determine which inputs (RST 5.5, 6.5, or 7.5) are sending an interrupt request.

Serial input data bit (AC$_7$): As stated previously, this is the accumulator bit that receives the serial data bit from input port SID.

14-10
SERIAL OUTPUT PORT SOD AND INSTRUCTION SIM

As was the case with the instruction RIM, the SIM instruction must be added to the 8080 instruction set of Section 5-3 in order to complete the instruction set for the 8085. Figure 14-10 is a reprint from an Intel programming manual.

From reading Intel's explanation of the SIM instruction, we see that in addition to it outputting the logic state of accumulator bit AC$_7$, via SOD, it also enables or disables (masks) the RST interrupt inputs (recall that the RIM instruction allows the status of those interrupts to be determined). Also notice that RST 7.5 has the latching interrupt request feature. Therefore, if an I/O device does not have an interrupt request flag (flip-flop) but instead produces a pulse when needing service from the CPU, that pulse can be used to set the RST 7.5 flip-flop. The RST 7.5 will remain high (making an interrupt request) until the RST 7.5 is "turned off" (reset). Resetting the RST 7.5 flip-flop is accomplished by execution of the SIM instruction, by a system reset, or by acknowledging the request at the time of the request. Be certain to understand that the accumulator must be preloaded with the desired bit pattern (using instruction MVI A—or equivalent) before SIM is executed.

Do not confuse the masking of an interrupt input with its logic state for making a request. Rather, masking simply means that the interrupt input is available for an interrupt request or it has been masked "out" and is not available.

14-11
AN 8085 APPLICATION

Since any application using the 8080 can be easily redesigned using the 8085 (refer to Figure 14-8), then to exemplify its uniqueness we must seek out an application that is unique to the 8085. This will require use of serial I/O and/or use of one or more of the RST interrupt request inputs. Let us suppose that we are using the 8085-based system of Figure 14-11 to collect data from a remote serial input device. The 8085 system is to assemble the serially collected data bits into a byte (using the CPU accumulator). Each byte is to be stored in memory and also printed out (echoed). Also suppose that the input device is relatively slow and therefore it is to interrupt the CPU only when it has a data bit. It is also reasonable to expect the printer to be slow; hence, when the printer's input buffer is empty (IBE = 1, which means that it is ready for another data byte from the CPU), it will request another data byte from the CPU. The request for another data byte will be made via an interrupt request to the CPU via the printer's output IBE. Since IBE will be high until the request is acknowledged, a level-sensitive RST will be used (RST 5.5). The

SIM (8085 PROCESSOR ONLY)　　　　　　　　　　　　　　　　　　　　　　SET INTERRUPT MASK

SIM is a multi-purpose instruction that uses the current contents of the accumulator to perform the following functions: Set the interrupt mask for the 8085's RST5.5, RST6.5, and RST7.5 hardware interrupts; reset RST7.5's edge sensitive input; and output bit 7 of the accumulator to the Serial Output Data latch.

　　　　　　　　　　　　　Opcode　　　　　　　Operand
　　　　　　　　　　　　　　SIM

Operands are not permitted with the SIM instruction. However, you must be certain to load the desired bit configurations into the accumulator before executing the SIM instruction. SIM interprets the bits in the accumulator as follows:

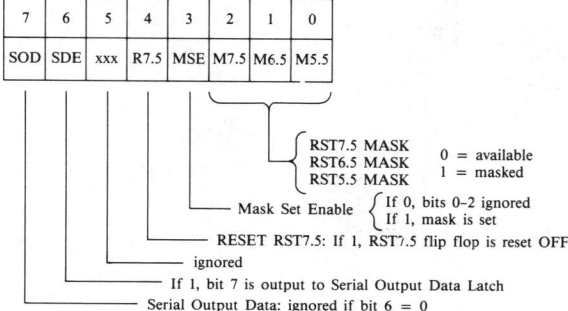

Accumulator bits 3 and 6 function as enable switches. If bit 3 is set ON (set to 1), the set mask function is enabled. Bits 0 through 2 then mask or leave available the corresponding RST interrupt. A 1 bit masks the interrupt making it unavailable; a 0 bit leaves the interrupt available. If bit 3 is set OFF (reset to 0), bits 0 through 2 have no effect. Use this option when you want to send a serial output bit without affecting the interrupt mask.

Notice that the DI (Disable Interrupts) instruction overrides the SIM instruction. Whether masked or not, RST5.5, RST6.5, and RST7.5 are disabled when the DI instruction is in effect. Use the RIM (Read Interrupt Mask) instruction to determine the current settings of the interrupt flag and the interrupt masks.

If bit 6 is set to 1, the serial output data function is enabled. The processor latches accumulator bit 7 into the SOD output where it can be accessed by a peripheral device. If bit 6 is reset to 0, bit 7 is ignored.

A 1 in accumulator bit 4 resets OFF the RST7.5 input flip flop. Unlike RST5.5 and 6.5, RST7.5 is sensed via a processor flip flop that is set when a peripheral device issues a pulse with a rising edge. This edge triggered input supports devices that cannot maintain an interrupt request until serviced. RST7.5 is also useful when a device does not require any explicit hardware service for each interrupt. For example, the program might increment and test an event counter for each interrupt rather than service the device directly.

The RST7.5 flip flop remains set until reset by 1) issuing a RESET to the 8085, 2) recognizing the interrupt, or 3) setting accumulator bit 4 and executing a SIM instruction. The Reset RST7.5 feature of the SIM instruction allows the program to override the interrupt.

The RST7.5 input flip flop is not affected by the setting of the interrupt mask or the DI instruction and therefore can be set at any time. However, the interrupt cannot be serviced when RST7.5 is masked or a DI instruction is in effect.

FIGURE 14-10. The SIM instruction. (Courtesy of Intel Corp.)

request generated by the serial input device will be a pulse, thus requiring RST 7.5 be used, as shown in Figure 14-11. The acknowledgment of the serial input device request will be issued using SOD. The serial input device will use the output of SOD to shift its buffer to the right one bit in preparation for the next data bit transmission.

The program that services the serial input device of Figure 14-11 is given in Figure 14-12. In order to focus on the essentials of this application it is assumed that the reader realizes that PUSH and POP instructions probably (depending on specific system) should be added to the program of Figure 14-12. It is also

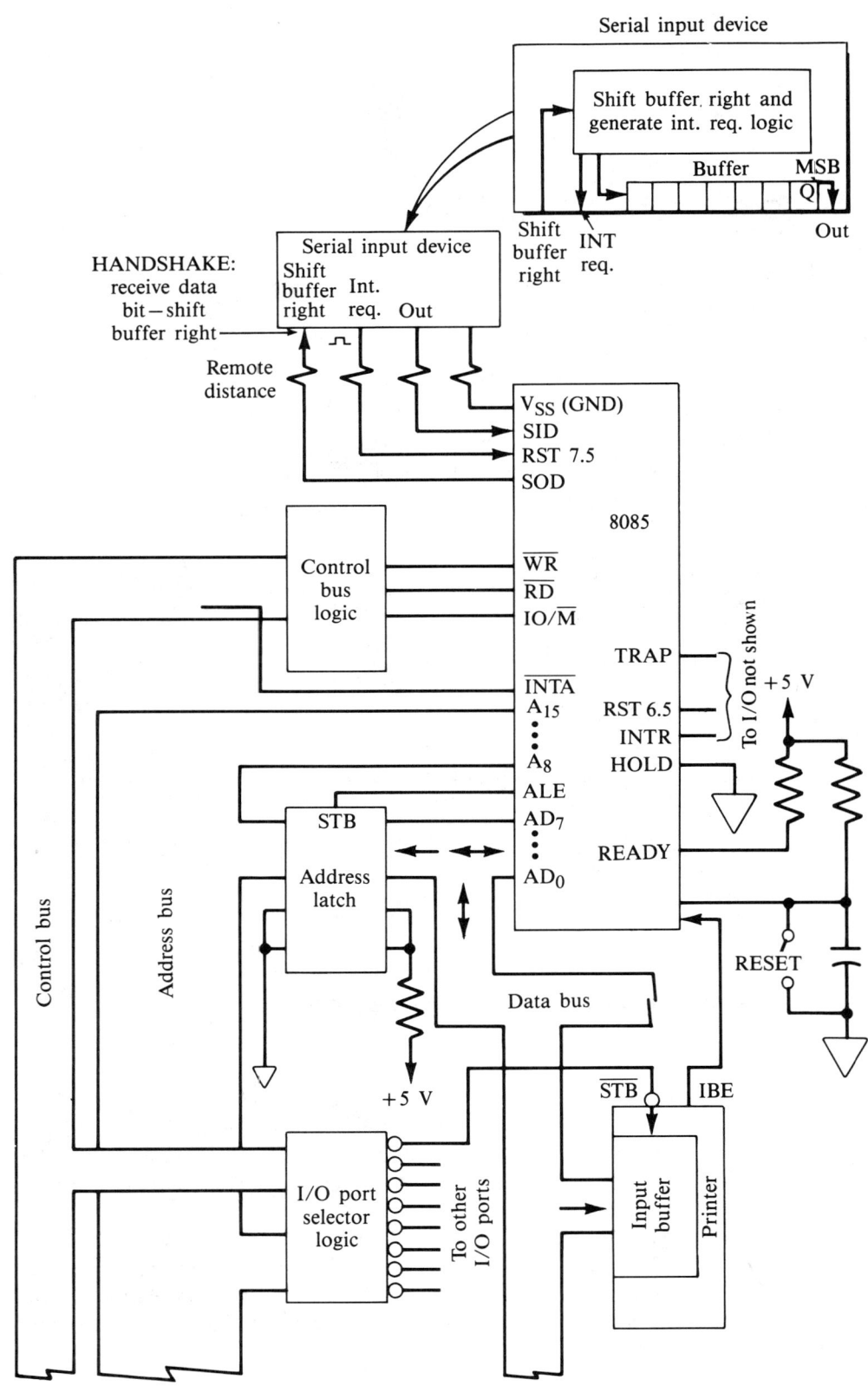

FIGURE 14-11. 8085 serial input port interface.

```
                ; SERVICE ROUTINE FOR SERIAL INPUT PORT
                    PRINT SET 00H
                    ORG 003CH
                ; INITIALIZATION
                        MVI A,1FH       ; Initialize A to
                                        ; reset RST 7.5 and
                                        ; mask RST 5.5 and 6.5;
                                        ; also disable SOD.
                        SIM             ; Reset and mask RST.
                        DI              ; Disable interrupt INTR.
                        MVI C,00H       ; Clear register C.
                        MVI B, 0F8H     ; Initialize TALLY with -8.
                ; READ data BIT
                GBIT:   RIM             ; Get data bit.
                        ANI 80H         ; Mask A except bit AC$_7$.
                        ADD C           ; Add previously collected bits.
                        RLC             ; Rotate accumulator left.
                        MOV C, A        ; Save partially assembled byte.
                ; ACKNOWLEDGE RECEIVING DATA BIT
                        MVI A,0C0H      ; Initialize A to output 1 at SOD.
                        SIM             ; Acknowledge receiving
                                        ; data bit-rotate serial
                                        ; INPUT PORTs BUFFER right.
                        INR B           ; Increment TALLY.
                        JNZ GBIT        ; If Z = 0 get next bit.
                ; Serial data assembled into byte-check printer
                ; to see if it is ready (IBE=1) for data byte. If
                ; ready RST 5.5 will be high.
                WAIT:   RIM             ; Get RST interrupt status.
                        ANI 10H         ; Check printer by checking pending
                                        ; interrupt from RST 5.5.
                        JZ WAIT         ; Wait until printer's
                                        ; input buffer is empty.
                ; Output assembled data byte to printer.
                        MOV A,C         ; Restore A with assembled
                                        ; data byte.
                        OUT PRINT       ; Output assembled data byte
                                        ; to printer.
                        STAX H          ; Store data byte.
                        INX H           ; Increment storage location.
                        EI              ; Enable INTR.
                        RET             ; Return to main program.
```

FIGURE 14-12. Program for serial input port of Figure 14-11.

assumed that another program will be required to provide the current memory address as required for the STAX H instruction.

To explain the program of Figure 14-12, we will refer to the hardware of Figure 14-11. The reader should also follow the flowchart of Figure 14-12. To begin, the serial input device fills its buffer and then generates an interrupt request by activating its interrupt request output, that is, by generating a pulse. This pulse is sensed by RST 7.5 of the 8085, which sets the internal flip-flop of RST 7.5. When the 8085 completes execution of its present instruction, it advances its PC by one and acknowledges the interrupt request. In acknowledging the request, the CPU resets the RST 7.5 flip-flop, automatically pushes

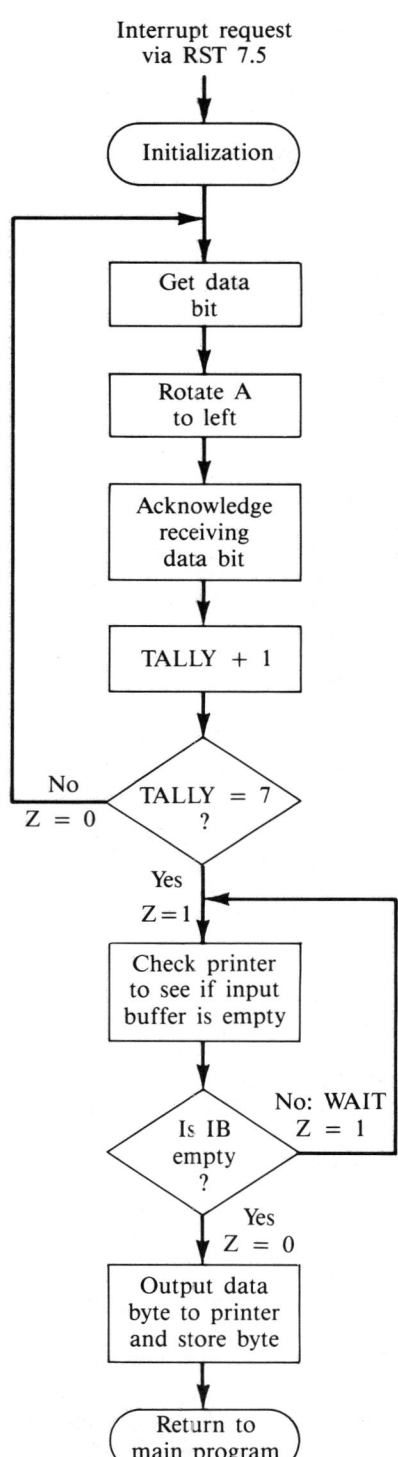

FIGURE 14-12. (Continued).

the contents of the PC on the stack, and then vectors to memory location 003CH. From the program of Figure 14-12 the reader sees that at address 003CH the CPU will fetch instruction MVI A,1FH. This instruction loads register A with the proper byte (1FH) according to the instruction format of SIM, which will mask RST 5.5 and 6.5. This is done so that these interrupt inputs cannot acknowledge any interrupt request (if they are being used). RST 7.5 was also reset, which is redundant but is a measure of certainty. Also, byte 1FH will disable the SOD output, which is necessary since we do not wish to acknowledge a data bit transmission at this time. After the execution of MVI A,1FH the SIM instruction is fetched and executed, which results in RST 7.5 being reset (if not already done), RST 5.5 and RST 6.5 being masked, and output SOD being disabled. The next instruction fetched and executed is DI, which disables the remaining interrupt request input INTR. Instruction MVI C,00H clears register C of any previous data. MVI B,0F8H will initialize the TALLY (register B) with −8 (two's complement). TALLY will be used to keep track of accumulator rotations as serial bits are input to the CPU and rotated in order to form a byte.

After the execution of MVI B,0F8H the CPU is initialized and ready actually to service the interrupt request of the serial input port. For all input ports thus far the IN instruction has been used to read data from those ports. For this application the RIM instruction must be used. The execution of instruction RIM will cause the most significant bit (MSB) of the serial input ports buffer (see upper right corner of Figure 14-11) to be loaded into the most significant bit (MSB) of the CPU's accumulator via input SID. We now have the first bit of a total of eight data bits which are to be read from the serial input port. As stated, the collected serial data bit is in the MSB of the accumulator, but because of the nature of the RIM instruction the other seven bits of the accumulator contain information unrelated to the data byte of the serial input device that is being transmitted serially to the CPU. To "rid" the accumulator of this unrelated information bits AC_6–AC_0 of the accumulator are masked using the instruction ANI 80H. If the reader looks four instructions ahead (MVI A,0C0H) he or she sees that the accumulator must serve other functions, and hence the collected serial data bits will be destroyed.

As each serial data bit is collected, it must be properly positioned and then saved in a register other than A. The register chosen to save the collected data bits (contents of A) is C (see instruction MOV C,A). Thus, after the mask instruction ANI 80H, the contents of C are added to A using instruction ADD C. Of course, ADD C assembles those previously collected serial data bits, which were stored in C, to the most recently collected bit; however, the bit just collected is out of proper bit position. The instruction RLC properly positions the most recently collected data bit. Instruction MOV C,A saves the contents of A in register C, which is the partially assembled data byte. The MVI A,0C0H (the assembler requires that the 0 precede an alphanumeric value—A, B, C, D, E, and F) loads the accumulator with the proper bit pattern in order to output a 1 at output SOD when the SIM instruction is executed, where SOD is used as an acknowledgment. That is, the execution of the SIM instruction following MVI A,0C0H will result in a high being output at SOD, which is input to the serial input port via its shift buffer right input—the output at SOD is an acknowledgment by the CPU that it received the last bit transmitted and is ready for another. The high input at shift buffer right will cause the serial input port to shift the contents of its buffer one bit to the right in preparation for the next serial transmission. After execution of SIM, the CPU then executes INR B, where B is the TALLY that keeps track of the number of shifts (there are to be eight). Next the TALLY must be checked to determine if all data bits have been collected. Then after execution of INR B the JNZ GBIT instruction is fetched. If the Z flag is a zero (meaning that TALLY $\neq$ 0), the CPU will execute the instruction, causing it to jump to address GBIT, which will collect the next data bit. If Z = 1, which means that all 8 serial bits have been collected and assembled into a byte (and JNZ will not be executed), the CPU must store this byte in memory and transmit it to the printer to be printed.

Let us suppose that Z = 0 and loop to address GBIT. Upon jumping to address GBIT, the CPU again fetches and executes instruction RIM. Instruction ANI 80H will mask out nonrelated information in A. ADD C will assemble the previously collected bits with the most recently collected bit. Instruction RLC causes CPU to rotate the accumulator left one bit, which properly positions the most recently collected bit. MOV C,A saves the contents of A in register C just as before. Let us advance to instruction JNZ GBIT and this time assume that Z = 1, which means that the instruction will not be executed and the instruction at address (label) WAIT will be fetched and executed. When the CPU executes this RIM instruction, the accumulator will be loaded with the byte, as indicated by the format of the RIM instruction. This time we are not reading in a serial data bit but rather obtaining the status of *pending* RST interrupts, specifically RST 5.5. For if RST 5.5 has a pending interrupt request (recall a pending interrupt is all that can happen since SIM in the initialization masked RST 5.5), the printer's input buffer is empty (IBE = 1) and the printer is ready to receive the assembled data byte. To check the accumulator for an RST 5.5 pending interrupt, ANI 10H is executed. If after the execution of ANI 10H the Z flag is high (Z = 1) (the result of the AND operation was 00H), RST 5.5 has no pending interrupts and the CPU should wait for the printer to empty its buffer. It waits by staying in a loop, via JZ WAIT, and continuously checks for an RST 5.5 pending interrupt request via the RIM instruction in that loop. When IBE = 1 the execution of RIM and ANI 10H will result in Z = 0, meaning that the printer is ready to receive the data byte. When Z = 0 the CPU will next execute MOV A,C. The MOV A,C instruction is required to restore the assembled data byte in the accumulator (recall that the assembled data byte was stored in C earlier). The data byte is then output on the data bus by the instruction OUT PRINT (OUT 00H), which also causes the printer to latch that byte from the data bus via the I/O port selector logic (just like the 8080) of Figure 14-11.

14-12

SUMMARY OF AN 8085-BASED SYSTEM

An 8085-based system is a three-bus architecture. As with an 8080-based system, the three buses are the address bus, data bus, and control bus. The lower byte of the address lines is multiplexed with the data lines (AD_7–AD_0) requiring a latch for the lower address byte. Output ALE is used as a strobe to latch the lower address byte. The 8085 control bus may be composed of control signals $\overline{RD}$ and $\overline{WR}$ for a memory-mapped I/O system. If the 8085-based system is an isolated I/O system, control signals $\overline{RD}$, $\overline{WR}$, and $IO/\overline{M}$ must be properly gated to generate control bus signals $\overline{I/O\ R}$, $\overline{I/O\ W}$, $\overline{MEM\ R}$, and $\overline{MEM\ W}$. Technically, control signal $\overline{INTA}$ is to be included as a control signal of the control bus for either an I/O isolated or for an I/O memory-mapped system.

The 8085 architecture is very similar to the 8080 architecture except for serial I/O (SID and SOD) and multilevel interrupts (RST 5.5, RST 6.5, RST 7.5, TRAP, and INTR). These architectural additions to the 8080 architecture allow an 8085-based system to have serial I/O and automatic vectored interrupts with priority using interrupts RST 5.5, RST 6.5, RST 7.5, TRAP, and INTR. Due to the serial I/O of SID and SOD, two additional instructions (RIM and SOD) are added to the 8080 instruction set. Since the 8080 instruction set is a subset of the 8085 instruction set, the 8085 instruction set is upwardly compatible with the 8080 instruction set. Because the 8085 is software upwardly compatible, all programs written for an 8080-based system will also work for an 8085-based system.

Since the 8085 has the controller (8228) and clock (8224) on-board, the chip count of an 8085-based system is reduced compared to an 8080-based system. Also, the 8085 requires a single +5-V power supply.

Hopefully, the reader now agrees that by knowing the 8080, he or she also knows the essentials of the 8085, and understanding the 8085 was not a difficult task. It is also believed that a similar ease of transition from 8080 to 6800 will be found. However, it will not be as straightforward a transition since (as you will see) their architecture and instruction set are different.

REVIEW QUESTIONS AND PROBLEMS

1. Compare each pin or pin groupings of the 8085 to similar pins of the 8080, stating their similarities.

2. List advantages of the 8085 over the 8080.

3. List the major differences between 8080 and 8085 architecture.

4. What is meant by "maskable interrupt"?

5. State how 8085 interrupts are masked.

6. Using TTL (low power), design the address latch required by the 8085.

7. Discuss the instructions that access the 8085's serial I/O ports.

8. Suppose that you were designing an 8085-based system which required four vectored interrupts. Since the 8085 has only three (excluding TRAP), you must improvise. Use the input SID to create a pseudo-vectored interrupt. The system is to be such that when an interrupt request is made, via INTR, the CPU will

check SID, which is connected to the interrupt request flag of the fourth I/O device, requiring a vectored interrupt. Show the hardware and software needed to achieve this task.

9. Update the system of Figure 4-7 by replacing the 8080 primary system with an 8085 and its required support chips.

10. Take the 8080-based system of Figure 7-16 and upgrade it to an 8085-based system.

11. Write a program to service the redesigned system of Figure 7-16.

12. Modify the memory system of Figure 4-6 to accommodate an 8085 using linear addressing.

13. From the basic timing diagram of Figure 14-3, construct a timing diagram for the following instructions.
    (a) OUT 02H   **(b)** IN 05H   **(c)** JMP 0100H
    (d) JZ addr   **(e)** CZ addr   **(f)** ADD D
    Show the control signal for an isolated I/O system.

14. Suppose that you wished to use the TRAP interrupt to detect a power failure and to save the CPU register contents in the event of such a failure. In block diagram form, show your design and discuss how it works.

CHAPTER 15

A Survey of the 6800 Microprocessor

15-1

INTRODUCTION

The objective of Chapter 14 was to use the 8085 microprocessor to emphasize the fact that the same concepts exist for all microprocessor-based systems, with differences in the details of operation. A comparative study was conducted between the 8080 and 8085 microprocessors and their associated systems, with emphasis on the similarities and differences between the two microprocessors.

This chapter reinforces the objectives of Chapter 14 by examining the characteristics of a different family of microprocessors, the 6800 family. As will be seen in this chapter, the concepts required to understand the operation of the 6800 remain the same, even though there are major differences between the 8080 family and 6800 family of microprocessors. This chapter will therefore deal with a comparative study of the 6800 microprocessor, using the 8080/8085 microprocessor as the object for comparison.

15-2

6800 ARCHITECTURE AND PIN CONFIGURATION

The architecture of the 6800 microprocessing unit (microprocessor) is shown in Figure 15-1. The architecture of the 6800 has three major differences from the

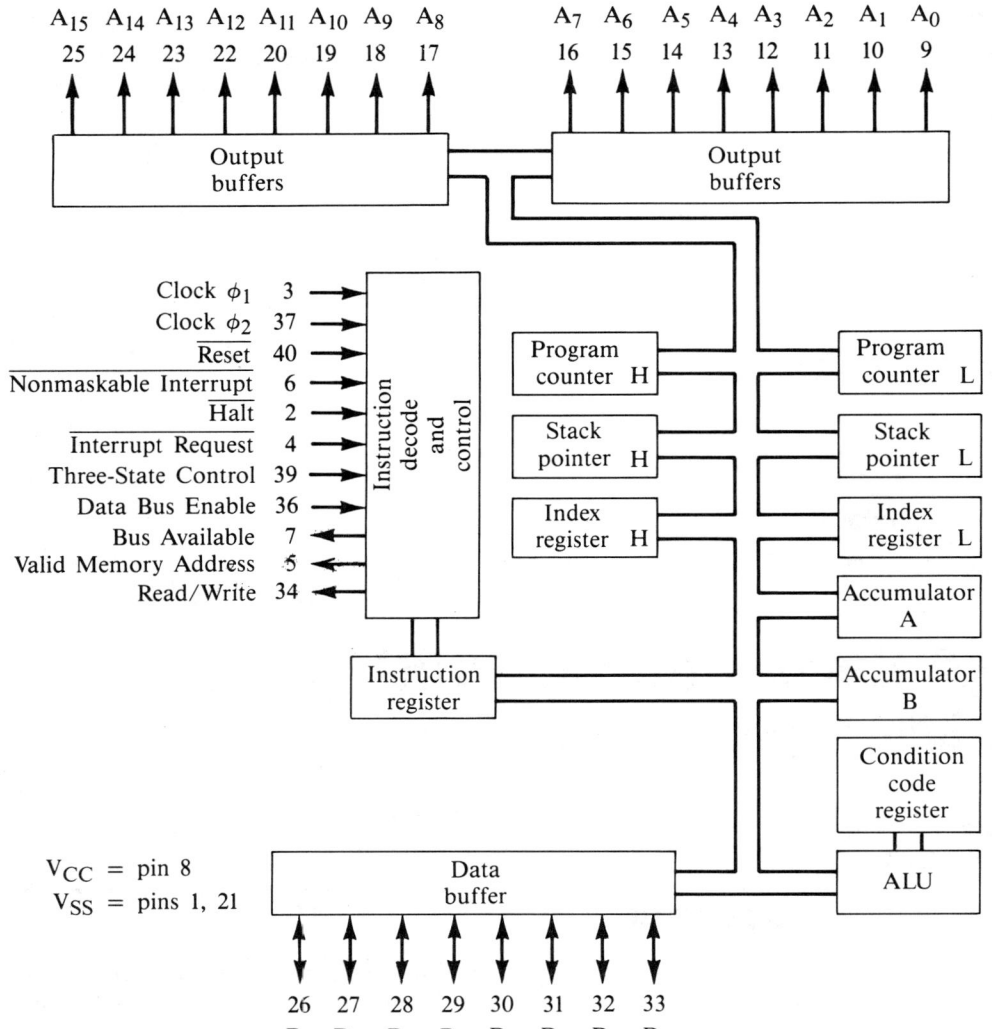

FIGURE 15-1. Architecture of the 6800 MPU. (Courtesy of Motorola, Inc.)

8080's architecture, discussed in Chapter 3. These differences are in the interrupt structure, the control signals, and the internal arrangement of registers.

Interrupt Structure. The 6800 microprocessing unit (MPU) has two interrupt inputs, which allow for multilevel interrupts. Each interrupt line to the MPU is capable of vectoring the MPU to a specified location in memory (to be seen later). However, the difference between the two interrupts is that the state of the $\overline{\text{IRQ}}$ (interrupt request) line can be enabled or disabled via a 6800 instruction. The $\overline{\text{NMI}}$ (nonmaskable interrupt) line is "nonmaskable," and therefore no instruction can be used to control the state of this interrupt line. The $\overline{\text{NMI}}$ line is therefore very similar to the TRAP line of the 8085. The $\overline{\text{IRQ}}$ line is very similar to the INT line of the 8080 except that there is no equivalent RST

N instruction to vector the MPU to different areas in memory; the 6800 uses another technique (described later) to accomplish this task.

Control Signals. The 6800 MPU has only two control signals to control the operation of external devices: VMA (valid memory address) and R/W (read/write). These two signals, together with the MPU's address lines, are used to select memory and I/O devices connected to the MPU. As the name suggests, the VMA control line is active whenever the MPU's address bus contains a valid memory address during a read or write operation to a memory or I/O device. The R/W line is used to distinguish between a read or write operation being performed on a memory or I/O device. If these are the only two control lines provided by the MPU, how does the MPU know whether it is accessing a memory or an I/O device? The answer to this question is: It does not distinguish a memory device from an I/O device; the 6800 MPU is designed for memory-mapped I/O, and unlike the 8080, does not provide a separate addressing scheme for memory and I/O devices (isolated I/O). Thus an I/O device is addressed in the same way as a location in memory, and the system's memory map will dictate the locations in memory that are assigned to I/O devices.

Internal Registers. The 6800 MPU contains six (user-accessible) general-purpose registers, compared to the 10 registers of the 8080. Table 15-1 lists the 6800 registers together with the equivalent 8080 register.

The stack pointer (SP) and program counter (PC) are 16-bit registers that are similar in function to the 8080's SP and PC. The index register (IX) is a 16-bit register that is used as a data counter and functions in a manner similar to the 8080's register pair H&L. The condition code register (CCR) is an 8-bit register containing six condition flags and provides the same function as the 8080's PSW. The 6800 MPU has two 8-bit accumulators: accumulator A and accumulator B. Both of these accumulators are capable of holding the results of arithmetic and logic operations; note that in the 8080 only register A was used to hold the result of an arithmetic or logic operation. Even though the 6800 MPU seems to be limited in the number of internal registers (when compared to the 8080), the instruction set of the 6800 contains various memory instructions that compensate for this shortage. These instructions can be used to treat memory

TABLE 15-1. Comparison of 8080/8085 and 6800 Register Set

6800 Registers		8080 Registers	
Size	Function	Size	Function
8	A—accumulator A	8	A—accumulator
8	B—accumulator B		None
8	CCR—condition code register	8	PSW—flags
16	IX—index register	16	Register pair H&L
16	PC—program counter	16	Program counter
16	SP—stack pointer	16	Stack pointer

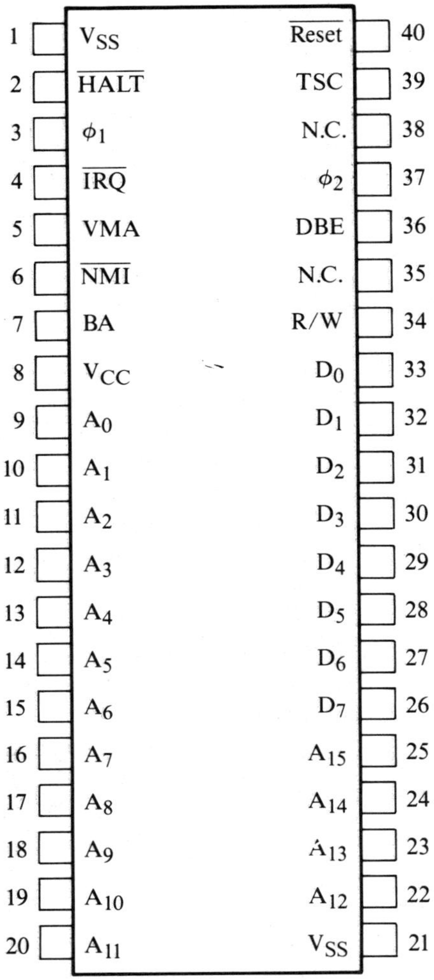

```
 1 — Vss        Reset — 40
 2 — HALT       TSC   — 39
 3 — Φ1         N.C.  — 38
 4 — IRQ        Φ2    — 37
 5 — VMA        DBE   — 36
 6 — NMI        N.C.  — 35
 7 — BA         R/W   — 34
 8 — Vcc        D0    — 33
 9 — A0         D1    — 32
10 — A1         D2    — 31
11 — A2         D3    — 30
12 — A3         D4    — 29
13 — A4         D5    — 28
14 — A5         D6    — 27
15 — A6         D7    — 26
16 — A7         A15   — 25
17 — A8         A14   — 24
18 — A9         A13   — 23
19 — A10        A12   — 22
20 — A11        Vss   — 21
```

FIGURE 15-2. Pin configuration of the 6800 MPU. (Courtesy of Motorola, Inc.)

locations as temporary storage registers, thus using external memory for "scratchpad" operations.

Besides the previously discussed differences, the 6800 has many similarities with the 8080 microprocessor. These similarities are best understood by an examination of the pin configuration of the 6800, shown in Figure 15-2.

Φ_1 *and* Φ_2: These inputs to the 6800 chip are the phase 1 and phase 2 clock pulses that are nonoverlapping and must be provided by an external clock generator. The logic levels required for these clocks are TTL (MOS levels for 8080) and the maximum clock rate is 1 MHz (2 MHz for 8080).

A_0–A_{15}: These 16 outputs are the address lines of the 6800 that form the address bus, and are similar in operation to the 8080's address lines. These address lines allow for accessing a combination of up to 65,536 memory locations and I/O devices. Since the 6800 uses memory-mapped I/O, the total number of memory locations and I/O devices cannot exceed 65,536. The address lines can be tri-stated for DMA operations.

D_0–D_7: The eight bidirectional data lines of the 6800 are similar to the 8080's data lines, and are used to transfer 8-bit data to and from memory or I/O devices. These lines form the data bus and can be tri-stated for DMA.

$\overline{HALT}$: This line can be used to put the MPU into a HALT state. When the $\overline{HALT}$ line is set low, the MPU enters an idle mode after completion of the current instruction. In the HALT state, all activity is stopped while the data and address lines are tristated. Note that the 8080 does not have the facility to put the CPU into a HALT state via a hardware line but can do so only through the execution of a HLT instruction.

TSC: The TSC (tri-state control) input to the MPU is similar to the HOLD input of the 8080 and is used for DMA operations. When the TSC input is in the high state, the MPU sets the address bus and R/W line to a high-impedance state, allowing for an external device to gain control of memory. The data bus is not affected by the TSC control but has a separate control (DBE).

DBE: The data bus enable line (DBE) is used to control the state of the data bus during DMA operations. The data bus drivers are enabled when DBE is high, and tri-stated (disabled) when DBE is low. The DBE line is very similar in operation to the $\overline{BUSEN}$ line of the 8228 controller chip.

R/W: The read/write (R/W) line is an output from the MPU used to signal a memory or I/O device whether the MPU is in a read (R/W = high) or write (R/W = low) state. In the read state, the MPU's data bus is in the input mode, and in an output mode during the write state. Since the 6800 uses memory-mapped I/O, this line *cannot* be used to distinguish between a memory or I/O device.

VMA: This output (when high) indicates to memory and I/O devices that there is a valid memory address on the MPU's address bus. This output, used in conjunction with selected address lines and the R/W line, can be used to select a memory or I/O device for read or write operations.

BA: The bus available (BA) output, when high, indicates that the MPU is in a HALT state and that the address bus is available. This line is similar in function to the HLDA line of the 8080, except that it is also active when the MPU is in a WAIT state.

$\overline{IRQ}$: The interrupt request ($\overline{IRQ}$) input to the MPU is a level-sensitive signal that causes an interrupt sequence to be generated within the machine. Interrupts on this line can be masked by means of a 6800 instruction. More will be said about interrupts in a later section.

$\overline{NMI}$: The nonmaskable interrupt ($\overline{NMI}$) causes a similar interrupt (as for $\overline{IRQ}$) sequence to be generated by the MPU except that interrupts arriving at the $\overline{NMI}$ line cannot be masked by the MPU.

RESET: This input is used to reset the MPU for initial startup. The function of the RESET input is similar to the 8080's reset line, as far as initial startup is concerned. However, the reset sequence generated by the MPU is very different from the 8080's reset sequence. Recall that on receiving a reset, the 8080 sets its program counter to 0000H; the CPU then accesses memory location 0, where it expects to find the first program instruction. On receiving a reset, the 6800 MPU automatically accesses the last two memory locations (FFFE, FFFF) to obtain the address at which the MPU will begin program execution. These two memory locations *must* contain the starting address of the program. This scheme is much more flexible, since it allows the MPU to begin execution at any address, rather than being limited to one address (as in the 8080). For example, if memory locations FFFE and FFFF contain the bytes 85 and 40, respectively, on receiving a reset, the MPU would start program execution at location 8540. Like the 8080, the 6800 disables interrupts (on the IRQ line only) upon being reset.

Notice in Figure 15-2 that the 6800 chip requires only a single 5-V power supply, which is provided to the V_{CC} and V_{SS} pins. This is an advantage over the 8080's three-power-supply requirement.

A study of the pin-outs of the 6800 MPU illustrates some interesting similarities and differences with the 8080 CPU. Since it would be redundant to investigate the similarities, the remainder of the chapter will deal with the three major differences between the 8080 and 6800 that were mentioned in this section.

15-3

6800 INTERRUPT STRUCTURE

The 6800 MPU can be viewed as a microprocessor that has four levels of interrupts: a restart interrupt, a nonmaskable interrupt, a software interrupt, and an interrupt request. On receiving any one of these interrupts, the MPU fetches a vector address from a predetermined memory location and transfers control to that location. The memory map for interrupt vectors is shown in Table 15-2. Each one of these interrupt levels will be discussed in this section, since it is this interrupt structure that makes the 6800 MPU unique.

Restart Interrupt

A restart interrupt is initiated when the MPU's RESET line is activated. In a 6800 system a reset is considered to be an interrupt since it stops execution of the MPU and transfers control to the address stored in memory locations FFFE and FFFF. It is not a true interrupt since control can never transfer back to the point of interruption (no return address is stored on the stack). The restart interrupt sequence for the 6800 MPU is shown in Figure 15-3.

As mentioned in Section 15-2, on receiving a reset, the MPU disables interrupts (on the IRQ line) by setting an internal interrupt mask (I_m). The program counter is then loaded with the contents of memory locations FFFE (high byte of PC) and FFFF (low byte of PC) and control transfers to that address. Notice

TABLE 15-2. Memory Map for Interrupt Vectors (Courtesy of Motorola, Inc.)

Vector MS	LS	Description
FFFE	FFFF	Restart
FFFC	FFFD	Nonmaskable interrupt
FFFA	FFFB	Software interrupt
FFF8	FFF9	Interrupt request

Contents	Address
$\overline{RES}$ (Low Byte)	FFFF
$\overline{RES}$ (High Byte)	FFFE
$\overline{NMI}$ (Low Byte)	FFFD
$\overline{NMI}$ (High Byte)	FFFC
SWI (Low Byte)	FFFB
SWI (High Byte)	FFFA
$\overline{IRQ}$ (Low Byte)	FFF9
$\overline{IRQ}$ (High Byte)	FFF8

that no return address is stored on the stack when the $\overline{RESET}$ line is activated. The MPU can therefore never return to the point of interruption before it was reset (received a restart interrupt).

Nonmaskable Interrupt

The $\overline{NMI}$ line to the MPU is used to generate a "high-priority" interrupt that cannot be disabled by means of software. The NMI interrupt sequence is shown

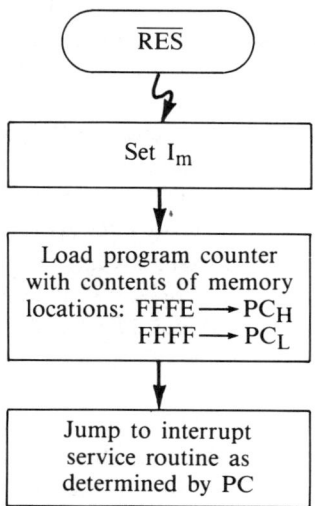

FIGURE 15-3. Restart interrupt sequence. (Courtesy of Motorola, Inc.)

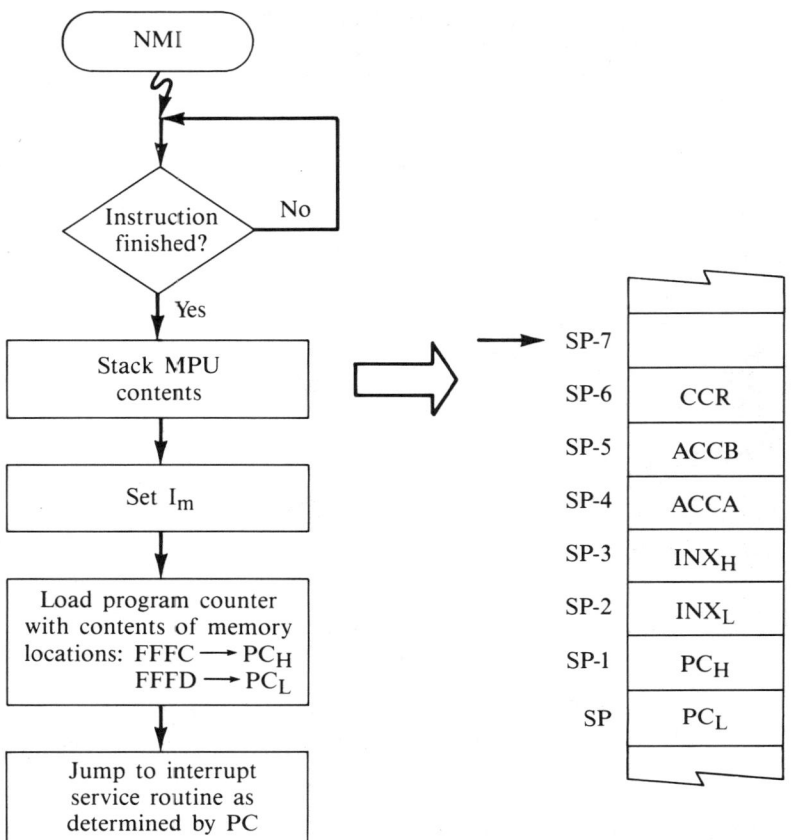

FIGURE 15-4. Nonmaskable interrupt sequence. (Courtesy of Motorola, Inc.)

in Figure 15-4. With reference to Figure 15-4, notice that when the $\overline{\text{NMI}}$ line of the MPU is activated, the MPU completes execution of the current instruction and then services the interrupt. The first interrupt operation is to store the contents of the MPU registers on the stack. Unlike the 8080 interrupt sequence, where a series of PUSH instructions has to be used to stack the CPU registers, the 6800 MPU does this automatically. First, the contents of the PC are stored on the stack, then the IX, the accumulators, and the CCR in the order shown. The interrupt mask is then automatically set to prevent any interrupts from being acknowledged over the IRQ line. The MPU then examines memory locations FFFC and FFFD (refer to Table 15-2) and obtains the vector address for the interrupt service routine. The data at memory locations FFFC and FFFD are stored in the high and low (respectively) bytes of the PC and control is transferred to that memory location.

On completion of the NMI interrupt sequence, the MPU must execute the RTI (return from interrupt) instruction. The RTI instruction restores the contents of the MPU registers in the order in which they were saved, resets the interrupt mask to allow for following interrupts, and returns control to the point of interruption.

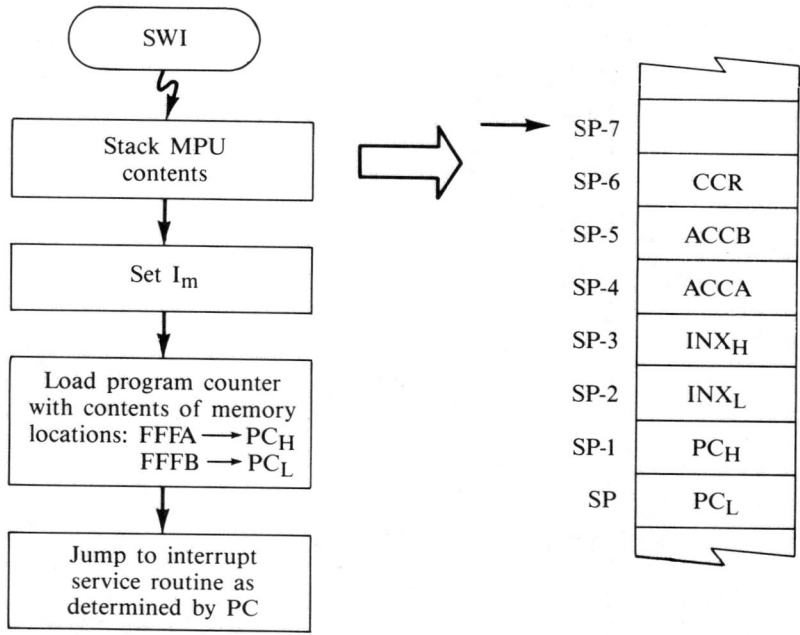

FIGURE 15-5. Software interrupt sequence. (Courtesy of Motorola, Inc.)

Software Interrupt

The 6800 MPU has the facility to generate a software interrupt by means of a special instruction, the SWI instruction. On execution of the SWI instruction, an interrupt sequence is "simulated" by the MPU. The software interrupt sequence conducted by the MPU is shown in Figure 15-5.

The sequence of events that occurs for a software interrupt as shown in Figure 15-5 is very similar to that of the NMI interrupt. On execution of the SWI instruction, the contents of the MPU registers is saved on the stack in the same way as was done for an NMI interrupt. The interrupt mask is set to block any other interrupts (excluding NMI). This time, however, the vector address for the SWI service routine (refer to Table 15-2) is taken from memory locations FFFA and FFFB and loaded into the high and low bytes of the PC, respectively. Control then transfers to the address stored in the PC. Return from a SWI service routine is also accomplished by the RTI instruction, since the contents of the MPU registers must be restored, the interrupt mask must be reset, and control must be returned in the instruction following the SWI.

The SWI interrupt is therefore very similar to the NMI hardware interrupt and is extremely useful as a breakpoint during the debugging of 6800 programs. Note that the RST N instruction of the 8080 can also be used to generate a somewhat similar software interrupt to the 8080 CPU.

Interrupt Request

The $\overline{IRQ}$ line to the 6800 MPU causes the interrupt sequence shown in Figure 15-6 to be conducted by the MPU. The sequence of events that occurs during

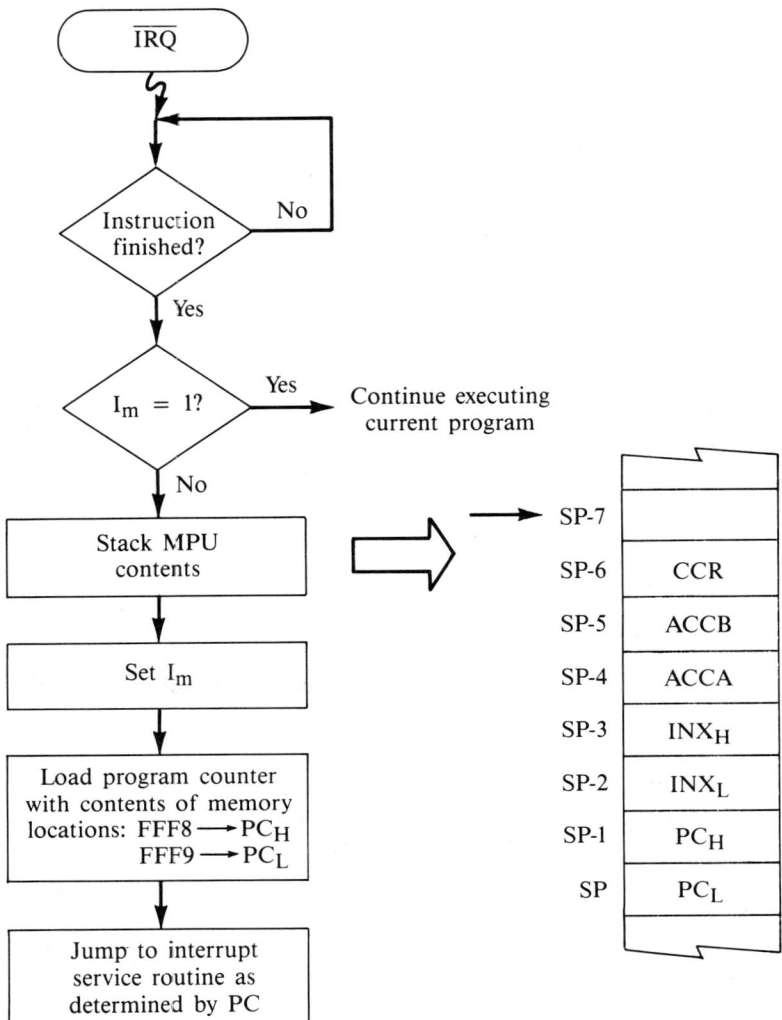

FIGURE 15-6. Interrupt request sequence. (Courtesy of Motorola, Inc.)

the IRQ interrupt request is similar to the NMI and SWI sequence except that on completion of the current instruction, the interrupt mask (I_m) is tested for a set or reset condition. If I_m is set by means of a SEI (set interrupt mask) instruction (or a previous interrupt), the interrupt is not acknowledged and the MPU continues with the execution of the current program. If I_m is reset, the MPU acknowledges the interrupt by stacking the contents of the MPU registers (as before), and blocking further interrupts over the IRQ line by setting I_m. The MPU then accesses memory locations FFF8 and FFF9 (refer to Table 15-2) to obtain the vector address of the service routine. Control then transfers to the address referenced by the PC. As before, the last instruction in the IRQ service routine should be an RTI instruction.

To summarize the interrupt structure of the 6800 MPU, one can think of the MPU as having four level of interrupts, two of them (IRQ and NMI) being true hardware interrupts. Each type of interrupt causes the MPU to load the contents of predetermined memory addresses into its PC, as shown in Table 15-2. Control is then transferred to the memory location whose address is stored in the PC. Since memory locations FFF8 through FFFF (inclusive) are always used to store these vector address, most 6800-based systems usually have ROM located in this area.

15-4

6800 MICROPROCESSOR SYSTEM

As with any type of microprocessor, the control signals and the address bus often dictate the design of a microprocessor system that encompasses the microprocessor and other memory and I/O chips. This section deals with the 6800 MPU's control signals and their application in a microprocessor system. Emphasis will be placed on the interface between the MPU and various memory and I/O support chips, rather than on the operation of these chips.

Figure 15-7 shows the design scheme of a simple 6800-based microprocessor system. The system includes 128 bytes of RAM (6810 chip), 1024 bytes of ROM (6830 chip), two parallel ports (6820 chip), and one serial port (6850 chip). System timing is provided by the 6871 clock generator.

6810 RAM Interface

With reference to Figure 15-7 notice that the 6810 RAM has six chip select inputs; CS3 and CS0 are active high, while the others are active low. Seven address inputs (A_0–A_6) are connected to the MPU's address bus to allow for 128 bytes of storage. The data I/O pins of the 6810 (D_0–D_7) are connected to the MPU's data bus to allow storage and retrieval of data. The R/W pin of the 6810 establishes the direction of data flow within the chip and is therefore connected to the R/W line of the MPU. CS0 is connected to the MPU's VMA line so that the chip is selected when a valid memory address appears on the address bus. The 6810 is addressed by using the high-order address lines of the MPU—A_{15}, A_{14}, A_{13}, A_{12}—to select the chip. The addressing scheme is shown in Table 15-3.

The six chip select lines provided by the 6810 RAM make the interface with the MPU ideal for linear addressing, as can be seen in Table 15-3. In Table 15-3, assuming that the "x" (unconnected) bits are zeros, the addressing scheme locates the 6810 at hexadecimal addresses 0000–007F. This is done by connecting address lines A_{15}–A_{12} to the active-low chip select lines shown. Since these address lines will be in the low state for addresses 0000–007F, the 6810 will be selected by the MPU when these addresses appear on the address bus and when the VMA line is active.

Notice in Table 15-3 that since address lines $\bar{A}_7$–A_{11} are not used in the addressing scheme, the same memory locations in the 6810 RAM chip could also be selected when addresses 0080 through 0FFF appear on the address bus. Recall from previous chapters that this area in memory (0080–0FFF) where the RAM chip could be accessed again is called the foldback area and serves no practical purpose. Observe that the 6810 addressed in this manner would never be selected if an address greater than 0FFF appears on the address bus.

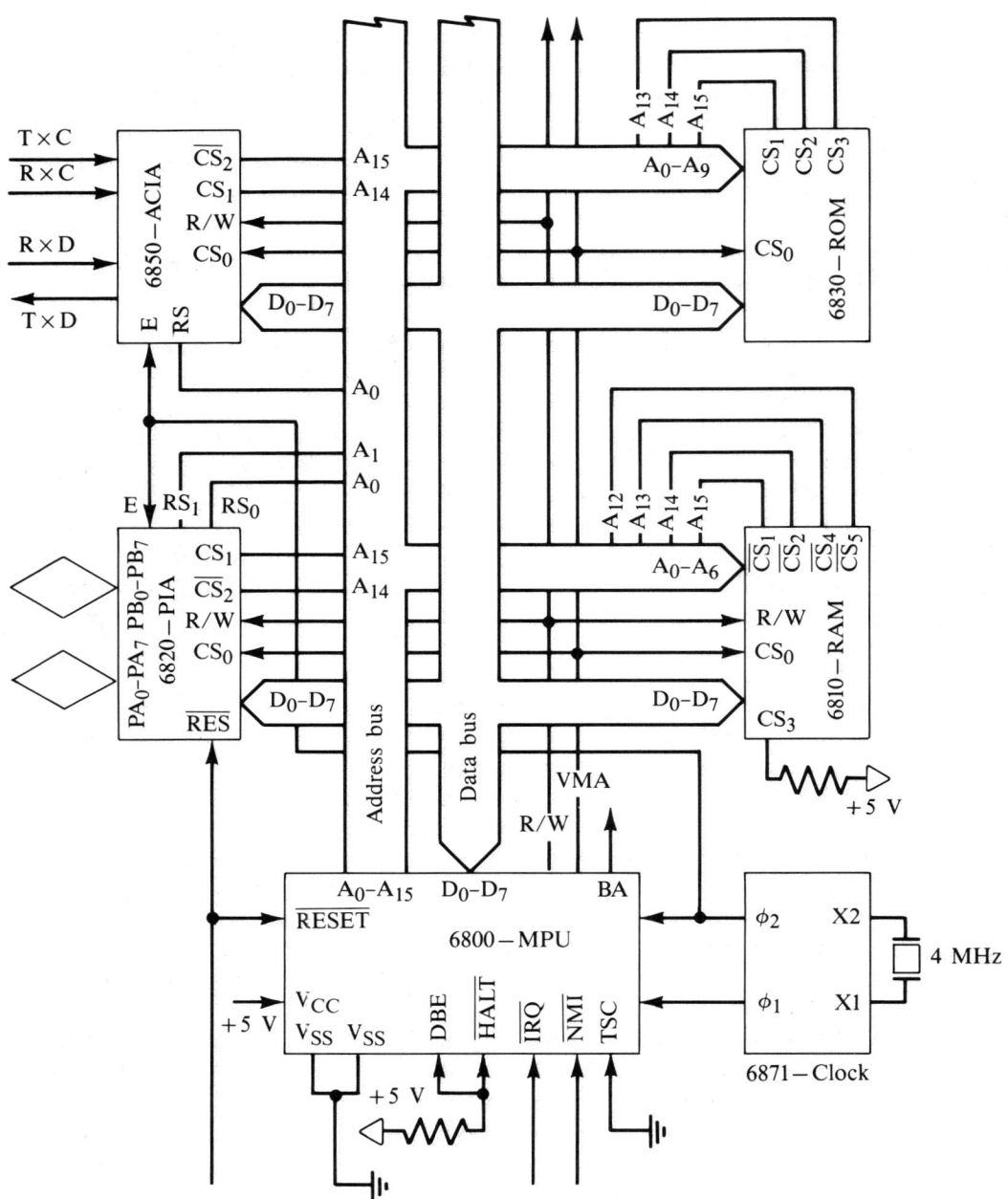

FIGURE 15-7. 6800-based microprocessor system.

6830 ROM Interface

The 6830 ROM chip is connected to the MPU (in Figure 15-7) in a manner similar to the 6810 RAM. The 10 address inputs (A_0–A_9) to the 6830 are connected to the MPU's address bus to allow 1024 bytes of memory to be accessed. Since the 6830 ROM can only have data read from it, no R/W input

TABLE 15-3. RAM Addressing Scheme

$\overline{CS_1}$	$\overline{CS_2}$	$\overline{CS_4}$	$\overline{CS_5}$						Connected to A_0–A_6						
↓	↓	↓	↓												
A_{15}	A_{14}	A_{13}	A_{12}	A_{11}	A_{10}	A_9	A_8	A_7	A_6	A_5	A_4	A_3	A_2	A_1	A_0	Location
0	0	0	0	x	x	x	x	x	0	0	0	0	0	0	0	0000
0	0	0	0	x	x	x	x	x	1	1	1	1	1	1	1	007F

is provided. As before, the MPU's VMA line is connected to the active high chip select input (CS0) to select the chip only when a valid memory address appears on the address bus. The 6830 ROM is addressed at hexadecimal locations FC00–FFFF as shown in Table 15-4.

Notice in Table 15-4 that the high-order address lines of the MPU—A_{15}, A_{14}, and A_{13}—are connected to the active-high chip select inputs CS1, CS2, and CS3, respectively. Thus whenever these three address lines are at the logic-high state (and VMA is active), the 6830 ROM will be selected. Then assuming that the unconnected address lines (A_{12}–A_{10}) are at the logic-low state, the 6830 ROM will be selected when the addresses FC00–FFFF appear on the address bus. As before, since address lines A_{12}, A_{11}, and A_{10} are not included in the addressing, foldback will appear at addresses E000–FBFF.

6820 PIA Interface

The 6820 peripheral interface adapter (PIA) is a programmable chip that provides the means of interfacing parallel-communicating external I/O devices to the MPU. The 6820 is very similar in function to the 8255 PPI discussed in Chapter 7. Like the 8255 (with reference to Figure 15-7), the 6820 PIA can be addressed as four ports via the register select, RS0, and RS1 inputs (similar to the A_0 and A_1 inputs to the 8255). Each of the four logic combinations of RS_0 and RS_1 will select an internal register or I/O port of the PIA. Since the PIA is capable of input and output, the R/W pin is connected to the R/W signal of the MPU to establish the direction of data flow. The reset signal to the MPU is also connected to the $\overline{RES}$ line of the PIA to initialize the internal registers during startup. The enable pulse (E) input to the PIA is used to maintain internal timing and synchronization and is provided by the Φ_2 clock pulse of the clock generator.

The addressing scheme used to interface the 6820 PIA to the MPU is done by connecting the chip select lines and the register select lines to the MPU's

TABLE 15-4. ROM Addressing Scheme

CS_1	CS_2	CS_3							Connected to A_0–A_9						
↓	↓	↓													
A_{15}	A_{14}	A_{13}	A_{12}	A_{11}	A_{10}	A_9	A_8	A_7	A_6	A_5	A_4	A_3	A_2	A_1	A_0	Location
1	1	1	x	x	x	0	0	0	0	0	0	0	0	0	0	FC00
1	1	1	x	x	x	1	1	1	1	1	1	1	1	1	1	FFFF

TABLE 15-5. PIA Addressing Scheme

CS$_1$ ↓ A$_{15}$	$\overline{CS_2}$ ↓ A$_{14}$	A$_{13}$	A$_{12}$	A$_{11}$	A$_{10}$	A$_9$	A$_8$	A$_7$	A$_6$	A$_5$	A$_4$	A$_3$	A$_2$	RS$_1$ ↓ A$_1$	RS$_0$ ↓ A$_0$	Location
1	0	x	x	x	x	x	x	x	x	x	x	x	x	0	0	8000
1	0	x	x	x	x	x	x	x	x	x	x	x	x	0	1	8001
1	0	x	x	x	x	x	x	x	x	x	x	x	x	1	0	8002
1	0	x	x	x	x	x	x	x	x	x	x	x	x	1	1	8003

address bus, as shown in Table 15-5. Observe in Figure 15-7 that the VMA line of the MPU is connected to the active-high chip select line CS$_0$, so that the PIA is selected only when there is a valid memory address on the address bus.

Referring to Table 15-5, notice that the 6820 PIA will be selected only when the MPU's address line A$_{15}$ is at a logic-high state and address line A$_{14}$ is at a logic-low state (and VMA is active). Since the register select bits RS$_0$ and RS$_1$ are connected to A$_0$ and A$_1$, respectively (assuming that the unconnected address lines are low), the PIA will occupy four locations in memory, 8000–8003. As in the previous memory interface, since linear addressing is used, and address lines A$_{13}$–A$_2$ are not included in the addressing scheme, foldback will exist from memory locations 8004–BFFF.

6850 ACIA Interface

The 6850 asynchronous communications interface adapter (ACIA) is an I/O chip that allows the 6800 MPU to communicate with external serial I/O devices. The operation of the 6850 ACIA is very similar to the 8251 USART discussed in Chapter 7. Like the 8251, the 6850 ACIA is a two-port device and will thus occupy two locations in memory. Referring to Figure 15-7, observe that the register select (RS) input to the ACIA allows the MPU to select the ACIA for data or control information (similar to the C/D line of the 8251). As in the 6820 PIA, the R/W and E inputs to the 6850 ACIA are connected to the R/W and Φ_2 (respectively) lines of the MPU. The VMA line of the MPU is tied to the active high chip select line (CS0) to select the ACIA only when a valid address appears on the address bus. The high-order address lines of the MPU (A$_{15}$ and A$_{14}$) are tied to the remaining chip select lines of the ACIA ($\overline{CS_2}$ and CS$_1$) to provide the addressing scheme shown in Table 15-6.

TABLE 15-6. ACIA Addressing Scheme

$\overline{CS_2}$ ↓ A$_{15}$	CS$_1$ ↓ A$_{14}$	A$_{13}$	A$_{12}$	A$_{11}$	A$_{10}$	A$_9$	A$_8$	A$_7$	A$_6$	A$_5$	A$_4$	A$_3$	A$_2$	A$_1$	RS ↓ A$_0$	Location
0	1	x	x	x	x	x	x	x	x	x	x	x	x	x	0	4000
0	1	x	x	x	x	x	x	x	x	x	x	x	x	x	1	4001

Notice in Table 15-6 that the ACIA will be selected only when the MPU's address line A_{15} is at a logic-low state and address line A_{14} is at a logic-high state. Since address line A_0 is used to select one of the two ACIA's internal registers, the ACIA will occupy memory locations 4000 and 4001 (assuming that the unconnected address lines A_{13}–A_1 are at the logic-low state). Again, since the unconnected address lines are not used in the addressing scheme, foldback will occur from memory locations 4002–7FFF.

The memory map for the basic 6800-based system is shown in Figure 15-8. Even though the term "memory map" is used, the map includes the addresses for memory as well as for I/O, since the 6800 can only have memory-mapped I/O.

The 6800-based microprocessor system shown in Figure 15-7 is a minimum system designed with the basic support chips in the 6800 family. The design incorporates only the simple concepts of interfacing memory and I/O devices to the MPU. As a result, it can be seen in Figure 15-8 that a considerable amount of memory space is wasted in foldback areas. No other memory or I/O device can be addressed in these foldback areas unless the addressing schemes are altered to prevent an addressing conflict. The linear addressing used to interface the support chips to the MPU led to the generation of foldback areas, but it did save a considerable amount of hardware in the form of logic gates and address decoders. Foldback does not provide any disadvantages in a simple design such as this if it is anticipated that the system will never be expanded. If expansion is desired, the same concepts of address decoding used for the 8080 system design can be applied to the 6800 to reduce the foldback areas.

Hexadecimal locations	
0000–007F	6810 RAM
0080–0FFF	6810 Foldback
4000–4001	6850 ACIA
4002–7FFF	6850 Foldback
8000–8003	6820 PIA
8004–BFFF	6820 Foldback
E000–FBFF	6830 Foldback
FC00–FFFF	6830 ROM

FIGURE 15-8. System memory map.

15-5

6800 INSTRUCTION SET

Since the 6800 microprocessor is designed for memory-mapped I/O, and since the internal registers of the MPU are limited in number, the instruction set of the 6800 is made up of extensive memory manipulation instructions. Recall that the 8080 microprocessor has only two I/O instructions that can be used in an isolated I/O hardware scheme—IN and OUT. However, in a 6800 system, all the memory reference instructions can be used for I/O devices since all I/O devices are mapped to memory locations.

Programming Model

Before examining the instruction set of the 6800 MPU, it is important to investigate the internal architecture of the MPU from a software point of view. Recall from Section 15-2 that the 6800 MPU has six internal registers that can be accessed by the instruction set. A knowledge of the functions of each of these registers is required in order to understand the instruction set of the 6800. Since the 6800 can be viewed, from a programming standpoint, as a set of registers, we can develop the programming model of the 6800 MPU shown in Figure 15-9.

Figure 15-9 illustrates the "programming model" of the 6800 MPU; that is, the 6800 microprocessor as seen from a software point of view. The 6800 has two 8-bit accumulators, ACCA and ACCB, either or both of which can be used in arithmetic and logic operations. The MPU has a 16-bit index register (IX) that is used in the indexed mode of addressing (discussed later). Basically, the index register provides the function of a data counter similar to the H&L register pair of the 8080 microprocessor. The 6800 MPU also has a 16-bit program counter (PC) and a 16-bit stack pointer (SP) whose function is exactly the same as the PC and SP of the 8080. An 8-bit condition code register (CCR) with six flags is used to signal the result of arithmetic and logic operations as well as to provide status on the interrupt system of the 6800. The CCR is similar to the 8080's five condition flags (PSW), with a few differences. Figure 15-10 shows the definitions of each bit in the CCR.

With reference to Figure 15-10, notice that the CCR has the six status flags located at bit positions 0–5. The two most significant bit positions of the CCR are always set to the logic high state and therefore serve no practical purpose.

- The half-carry bit (H) of the CCR is similar to the auxiliary carry flag of the 8080 and is used to signal a carryover from the third to the fourth bit position of ACCA or ACCB.
- The interrupt mask bit (I) signals the status of the 6800 MPU's interrupt system. If this bit is set, interrupts are disabled and the MPU will not acknowledge interrupts over the $\overline{\text{IRQ}}$ line. Note that interrupts will be accepted on the $\overline{\text{NMI}}$ line and the SWI instruction will be executed regardless of the state of I.
- The negative (N) bit is similar to the sign flag of the 8080 and is set if the most significant bit of the result of an operation is high (indicating a nega-

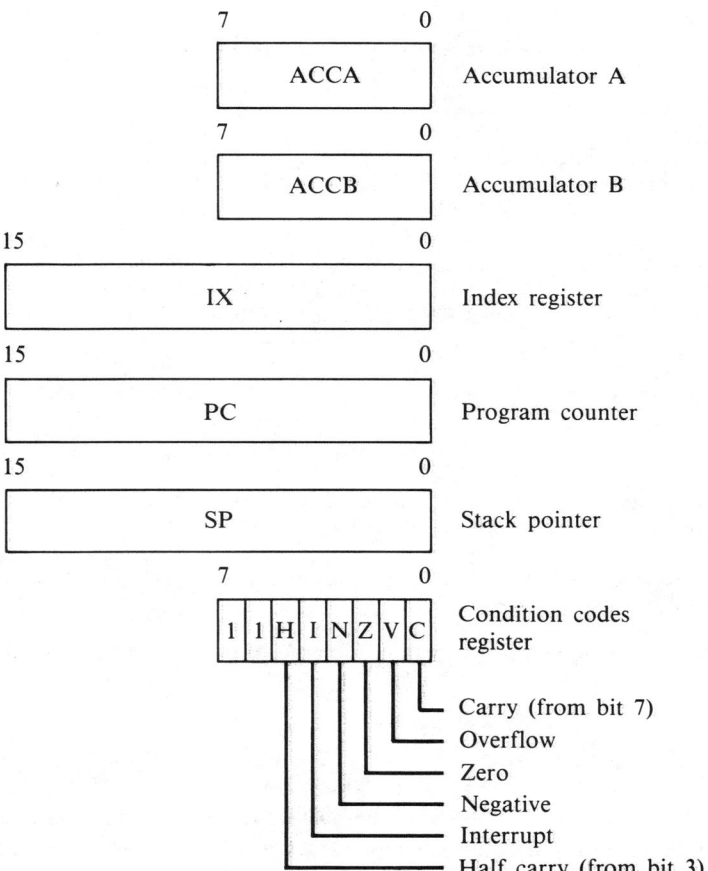

FIGURE 15-9. Programming model of the 6800 MPU. (Courtesy of Motorola, Inc.)

tive result). The N bit is reset if the most significant bit of the result is low (indicating a positive result).

The zero bit (Z) is similar to the zero flag of the 8080 and is set if the result of an operation yields a zero result. The Z bit is reset if the result yields a nonzero result.

The overflow bit (V) has no equivalent flag in the 8080 microprocessor. The V bit is used to signal a two's-complement overflow condition as the result of an arithmetic operation.

The carry bit (C) is similar to the carry flag of the 8080 and is set when there is a carry generated (from the seventh bit position) in the result of an arithmetic operation.

Notice that the 6800 does not have a parity bit, as did the 8080.

The 6800 MPU has 72 basic instructions, which include accumulator and memory instructions, index register and stack manipulation instructions, and jump and branch instructions. Tables 15-7 through 15-9 show the instruction set of the 6800 MPU organized into the previously mentioned categories.

15-5 6800 INSTRUCTION SET

b_5	b_4	b_3	b_2	b_1	b_0
H	I	N	Z	V	C

H = Half-carry; set whenever a carry from b_3 to b_4 of the result is generated by ADD, ABA, ADC; cleared if no b_3 to b_4 carry; not affected by other instructions.

I = Interrupt mask; set by hardware or software interrupt or SEI instruction; cleared by CLI instruction. (Normally not used in arithmetic operations.) Restored to a zero as a result of an RT1 instruction if I_m stored on the stack is low.

N = Negative; set if high-order bit (b_7) of result is set; cleared otherwise.

Z = Zero; set if result = 0; cleared otherwise.

V = Overlow; set if there was arithmetic overflow as a result of the operation; cleared otherwise.

C = Carry; set if there was a carry from the most significant bit (b_7) of the result; cleared otherwise.

FIGURE 15-10. Condition code register bit definitions. (Courtesy of Motorola, Inc.)

Addressing Modes

By briefly scanning through the operations shown in Tables 15-7 through 15-9, one can see many similarities with the 8080's instruction set. Notice, however, that in some operations, the mnemonics and machine codes are very different from the 8080 instruction set, even though the operation may be similar. Also notice that many instructions have four or fewer addressing modes.

An addressing mode is simply a different means by which the MPU obtains the data for an instruction. Thus even though a particular instruction may have up to four addressing modes, the end result of the instruction would be the same. For example, in Table 15-7, the ADDA instruction has four addressing modes: immediate, direct, indexed, and extended. These four modes of addressing will be discussed using the ADDA instruction as an example.

Immediate Addresssing Mode. In the immediate addressing mode the data for an instruction is fetched from the memory location(s) "immediately" following the operation code for the instruction. Instructions in the immediate mode of addressing will therefore always be two- or three-byte instructions. An example of immediate addressing in the 8080 would be the MVI A (move immediate to A) instruction.

Thus the ADDA instruction of the 6800 would be a two-byte instruction. For example, if it were required to add the hexadecimal byte "45" to the contents of ACCA using the immediate mode of addressing (referring to Table 15-7), the machine instruction code would be 8B45 (hexadecimal).

The same instruction would be written in 6800 assembler format as

ADDA #$45

TABLE 15-7. Accumulator and Memory Instructions. (Courtesy of Motorola, Inc.)

OPERATIONS	MNEMONIC	IMMED		DIRECT		INDEX		EXTND		IMPLIED		BOOLEAN/ARITHMETIC OPERATION (All register labels refer to contents)	COND. CODE REG.					
													5	4	3	2	1	0
		OP	~	#	OP	~	#	OP	~	#	OP	~	#	OP	~	#		H	I	N	Z	V	C
		OP	~	#	OP	~	#	OP	~	#	OP	~	#	OP	~	#							

OPERATIONS	MNEMONIC	IMMED OP	~	#	DIRECT OP	~	#	INDEX OP	~	#	EXTND OP	~	#	IMPLIED OP	~	#	BOOLEAN/ARITHMETIC OPERATION	H	I	N	Z	V	C
Add	ADDA	8B	2	2	9B	3	2	AB	5	2	BB	4	3				A + M → A	↕	•	↕	↕	↕	↕
	ADDB	CB	2	2	DB	3	2	EB	5	2	FB	4	3				B + M → B	↕	•	↕	↕	↕	↕
Add Acmltrs	ABA													1B	2	1	A + B → A	↕	•	↕	↕	↕	↕
Add with Carry	ADCA	89	2	2	99	3	2	A9	5	2	B9	4	3				A + M + C → A	↕	•	↕	↕	↕	↕
	ADCB	C9	2	2	D9	3	2	E9	5	2	F9	4	3				B + M + C → B	↕	•	↕	↕	↕	↕
And	ANDA	84	2	2	94	3	2	A4	5	2	B4	4	3				A · M → A	•	•	↕	↕	R	•
	ANDB	C4	2	2	D4	3	2	E4	5	2	F4	4	3				B · M → B	•	•	↕	↕	R	•
Bit Test	BITA	85	2	2	95	3	2	A5	5	2	B5	4	3				A · M	•	•	↕	↕	R	•
	BITB	C5	2	2	D5	3	2	E5	5	2	F5	4	3				B · M	•	•	↕	↕	R	•
Clear	CLR							6F	7	2	7F	6	3				00 → M	•	•	R	S	R	R
	CLRA													4F	2	1	00 → A	•	•	R	S	R	R
	CLRB													5F	2	1	00 → B	•	•	R	S	R	R
Compare	CMPA	81	2	2	91	3	2	A1	5	2	B1	4	3				A − M	•	•	↕	↕	↕	↕
	CMPB	C1	2	2	D1	3	2	E1	5	2	F1	4	3				B − M	•	•	↕	↕	↕	↕
Compare Acmltrs	CBA													11	2	1	A − B	•	•	↕	↕	↕	↕
Complement, 1's	COM							63	7	2	73	6	3				$\overline{M}$ → M	•	•	↕	↕	R	S
	COMA													43	2	1	$\overline{A}$ → A	•	•	↕	↕	R	S
	COMB													53	2	1	$\overline{B}$ → B	•	•	↕	↕	R	S
Complement, 2's (Negate)	NEG							60	7	2	70	6	3				00 − M → M	•	•	↕	↕	①	①
	NEGA													40	2	1	00 − A → A	•	•	↕	↕	①	①
	NEGB													50	2	1	00 − B → B	•	•	↕	↕	①	①
Decimal Adjust, A	DAA													19	2	1	Converts Binary Add. of BCD Characters into BCD Format	•	•	↕	↕	↕	③
Decrement	DEC							6A	7	2	7A	6	3				M − 1 → M	•	•	↕	↕	4	•
	DECA													4A	2	1	A − 1 → A	•	•	↕	↕	4	•
	DECB													5A	2	1	B − 1 → B	•	•	↕	↕	4	•

15-5 6800 INSTRUCTION SET

TABLE 15-7. (Continued)

OPERATIONS	MNEMONIC	IMMED OP	IMMED ~	IMMED #	DIRECT OP	DIRECT ~	DIRECT #	INDEX OP	INDEX ~	INDEX #	EXTND OP	EXTND ~	EXTND #	IMPLIED OP	IMPLIED ~	IMPLIED #	BOOLEAN/ARITHMETIC OPERATION (All register labels refer to contents)	H (5)	I (4)	N (3)	Z (2)	V (1)	C (0)
Exclusive OR	EORA	88	2	2	98	3	2	A8	5	2	B8	4	3				$A \oplus M \to A$	•	•	↕	↕	R	•
	EORB	C8	2	2	D8	3	2	E8	5	2	F8	4	3				$B \oplus M \to B$	•	•	↕	↕	R	•
Increment	INC							6C	7	2	7C	6	3				$M + 1 \to M$	•	•	↕	↕	⑤	•
	INCA													4C	2	1	$A + 1 \to A$	•	•	↕	↕	⑤	•
	INCB													5C	2	1	$B + 1 \to B$	•	•	↕	↕	⑤	•
Load Acmltr	LDAA	86	2	2	96	3	2	A6	5	2	B6	4	3				$M \to A$	•	•	↕	↕	R	•
	LDAB	C6	2	2	D6	3	2	E6	5	2	F6	4	3				$M \to B$	•	•	↕	↕	R	•
Or, Inclusive	ORAA	8A	2	2	9A	3	2	AA	5	2	BA	4	3				$A + M \to A$	•	•	↕	↕	R	•
	ORAB	CA	2	2	DA	3	2	EA	5	2	FA	4	3				$B + M \to B$	•	•	↕	↕	R	•
Push Data	PSHA													36	4	1	$A \to M_{SP}, SP - 1 \to SP$	•	•	•	•	•	•
	PSHB													37	4	1	$B \to M_{SP}, SP - 1 \to SP$	•	•	•	•	•	•
Pull Data	PULA													32	4	1	$SP + 1 \to SP, M_{SP} \to A$	•	•	•	•	•	•
	PULB													33	4	1	$SP + 1 \to SP, M_{SP} \to B$	•	•	•	•	•	•
Rotate Left	ROL							69	7	2	79	6	3				M	•	•	↕	↕	⑥	↕
	ROLA													49	2	1	A ⟲ C ← b7...b0	•	•	↕	↕	⑥	↕
	ROLB													59	2	1	B	•	•	↕	↕	⑥	↕
Rotate Right	ROR							66	7	2	76	6	3				M	•	•	↕	↕	⑥	↕
	RORA													46	2	1	A ⟲ C → b7...b0	•	•	↕	↕	⑥	↕
	RORB													56	2	1	B	•	•	↕	↕	⑥	↕
Shift Left, Arithmetic	ASL							68	7	2	78	6	3				M	•	•	↕	↕	⑥	↕
	ASLA													48	2	1	A C ← b7...b0 ← 0	•	•	↕	↕	⑥	↕
	ASLB													58	2	1	B	•	•	↕	↕	⑥	↕
Shift Right, Arithmetic	ASR							67	7	2	77	6	3				M	•	•	↕	R	⑥	↕
	ASRA													47	2	1	A b7...b0 → C	•	•	↕	R	⑥	↕
	ASRB													57	2	1	B	•	•	↕	R	⑥	↕
Shift Right, Logic	LSR							64	7	2	74	6	3				M	•	•	R	↕	⑥	↕
	LSRA													44	2	1	A 0 → b7...b0 → C	•	•	R	↕	⑥	↕
	LSRB													54	2	1	B	•	•	R	↕	⑥	↕

TABLE 15-7. (Continued)

OPERATIONS	MNEMONIC	IMMED OP	IMMED ~	IMMED #	DIRECT OP	DIRECT ~	DIRECT #	INDEX OP	INDEX ~	INDEX #	EXTND OP	EXTND ~	EXTND #	IMPLIED OP	IMPLIED ~	IMPLIED #	BOOLEAN/ARITHMETIC OPERATION (All register labels refer to contents)	H (5)	I (4)	N (3)	Z (2)	V (1)	C (0)
Store Acmltr.	STAA				97	4	2	A7	6	2	B7	5	3				A → M	•	•	↕	↕	R	•
	STAB				D7	4	2	E7	6	2	F7	5	3				B → M	•	•	↕	↕	R	•
Subtract	SUBA	80	2	2	90	3	2	A0	5	2	B0	4	3				A – M → A	•	•	↕	↕	↕	↕
	SUBB	C0	2	2	D0	3	2	E0	5	2	F0	4	3				B – M → B	•	•	↕	↕	↕	↕
Subtract Acmltrs.	SBA													10	2	1	A – B → A	•	•	↕	↕	↕	↕
Subtr. with Carry	SBCA	82	2	2	92	3	2	A2	5	2	B2	4	3				A – M – C → A	•	•	↕	↕	↕	↕
	SBCB	C2	2	2	D2	3	2	E2	5	2	F2	4	3				B – M – C → B	•	•	↕	↕	↕	↕
Transfer Acmltrs	TAB													16	2	1	A → B	•	•	↕	↕	R	•
	TBA													17	2	1	B → A	•	•	↕	↕	R	•
Test, Zero or Minus	TST							6D	7	2	7D	6	3				M – 00	•	•	↕	↕	R	R
	TSTA													4D	2	1	A – 00	•	•	↕	↕	R	R
	TSTB													5D	2	1	B – 00	•	•	↕	↕	R	R

LEGEND:
OP   Operation Code (Hexadecimal);
~   Number of MPU Cycles;
#   Number of Program Bytes;
+   Arithmetic Plus;
–   Arithmetic Minus;
•   Boolean AND;
M_{SP} Contents of memory location pointed to be Stack Pointer;
+   Boolean Inclusive OR;
⊕   Boolean Exclusive OR;
$\overline{M}$ Complement of M;
→   Transfer Into;
0   Bit = Zero;
00   Byte = Zero

Note — Accumulator addressing mode instructions are included in the column for IMPLIED addressing

CONDITION CODE SYMBOLS:
H   Half-carry from bit 3;
I   Interrupt mask
N   Negative (sign bit)
Z   Zero (byte)
V   Overflow, 2's complement
C   Carry from bit 7
R   Reset Always
S   Set Always
↕   Test and set if true, cleared otherwise
•   Not Affected

15-5 6800 INSTRUCTION SET

TABLE 15-8. Index Register and Stack Manipulation Instructions. (Courtesy of Motorola, Inc.)

POINTER OPERATIONS	MNEMONIC	IMMED			DIRECT			INDEX			EXTND			IMPLIED			BOOLEAN/ARITHMETIC OPERATION	COND. CODE REG.					
		OP	~	#	OP	~	#	OP	~	#	OP	~	#	OP	~	#		5 H	4 I	3 N	2 Z	1 V	0 C
Compare Index Reg	CPX	8C	3	3	9C	4	2	AC	6	2	BC	5	3				$X_H - M, X_L - (M+1)$	•	•	⑦	↕	⑦	•
Decrement Index Reg	DEX													09	4	1	$X - 1 \rightarrow X$	•	•	•	↕	•	•
Decrement Stack Pntr	DES													34	4	1	$SP - 1 \rightarrow SP$	•	•	•	•	•	•
Increment Index Reg	INX													08	4	1	$X + 1 \rightarrow X$	•	•	•	↕	•	•
Increment Stack Pntr	INS													31	4	1	$SP + 1 \rightarrow SP$	•	•	•	•	•	•
Load Index Reg	LDX	CE	3	3	DE	4	2	EE	6	2	FE	5	3				$M \rightarrow X_H, (M+1) \rightarrow X_L$	•	•	⑨	↕	R	•
Load Stack Pntr	LDS	8E	3	3	9E	4	2	AE	6	2	BE	5	3				$M \rightarrow SP_H, (M+1) \rightarrow SP_L$	•	•	⑨	↕	R	•
Store Index Reg	STX				DF	5	2	EF	7	2	FF	6	3				$X_H \rightarrow M, X_L \rightarrow (M+1)$	•	•	⑨	↕	R	•
Store Stack Pntr	STS				9F	5	2	AF	7	2	BF	6	3				$SP_H \rightarrow M, SP_L \rightarrow (M+1)$	•	•	⑨	↕	R	•
Indx Reg → Stack Pntr	TXS													35	4	1	$X - 1 \rightarrow SP$	•	•	•	•	•	•
Stack Pntr → Indx Reg	TSX													30	4	1	$SP + 1 \rightarrow X$	•	•	•	•	•	•

TABLE 15-9. Jump and Branch Instructions. (Courtesy of Motorola, Inc.)

OPERATIONS	MNEMONIC	RELATIVE OP	~	#	INDEX OP	~	#	EXTND OP	~	#	IMPLIED OP	~	#	BRANCH TEST	H	I	N	Z	V	C
Branch Always	BRA	20	4	2										None	•	•	•	•	•	•
Branch If Carry Clear	BCC	24	4	2										C = 0	•	•	•	•	•	•
Branch If Carry Set	BCS	25	4	2										C = 1	•	•	•	•	•	•
Branch If = Zero	BEQ	27	4	2										Z = 1	•	•	•	•	•	•
Branch If ≥ Zero	BGE	2C	4	2										N ⊕ V = 0	•	•	•	•	•	•
Branch If > Zero	BGT	2E	4	2										Z + (N ⊕ V) = 0	•	•	•	•	•	•
Branch If Higher	BHI	22	4	2										C + Z = 0	•	•	•	•	•	•
Branch If ≤ Zero	BLE	2F	4	2										Z + (N ⊕ V) = 1	•	•	•	•	•	•
Branch If Lower Or Same	BLS	23	4	2										C + Z = 1	•	•	•	•	•	•
Branch If < Zero	BLT	2D	4	2										N ⊕ V = 1	•	•	•	•	•	•
Branch If Minus	BMI	2B	4	2										N = 1	•	•	•	•	•	•
Branch If Not Equal Zero	BNE	26	4	2										Z = 0	•	•	•	•	•	•
Branch If Overflow Clear	BVC	28	4	2										V = 0	•	•	•	•	•	•
Branch If Overflow Set	BVS	29	4	2										V = 1	•	•	•	•	•	•
Branch If Plus	BPL	2A	4	2										N = 0	•	•	•	•	•	•
Branch To Subroutine	BSR	8D	8	2											•	•	•	•	•	•
Jump	JMP				6E	4	2	7E	3	3				See Special Operations	•	•	•	•	•	•
Jump To Subroutine	JSR				AD	8	2	BD	9	3					•	•	•	•	•	•
No Operation	NOP										02	2	1	Advances Prog. Cntr. Only	•	•	•	•	•	•
Return From Interrupt	RTI										3B	10	1		⑩					
Return From Subroutine	RTS										39	5	1		•	•	•	•	•	•
Software Interrupt	SWI										3F	12	1	See Special Operations	•	⑪	•	•	•	•
Wait for Interrupt	WAI										3E	9	1		•	•	•	•	•	•

COND. CODE REG.: 5 H, 4 I, 3 N, 2 Z, 1 V, 0 C

15-5 6800 INSTRUCTION SET

where the "#" symbol instructs the assembler that the operation code for the ADDA instruction in the immediate addressing mode (8B) is to be assembled. The "$" identifies the constant "45" to be hexadecimal; recall that the prefix "H" was used in 8080 assembly language to identify a hexadecimal constant.

Direct Addressing Mode. In the direct addressing mode, the instruction causes the MPU to fetch the data for the instruction from a memory location in the range 0000–00FF (page 0). An instruction in the direct addressing mode is a two-byte instruction—the first byte is the op code of the instruction (in the direct mode) and the second byte is the low-order address of the memory location where the data is to be found.

For example, if it were required to add the contents of memory location 0087 to ACCA, and assuming that the hexadecimal byte "45" was stored in this memory location (referring to Table 15-7), the machine instruction would be 9B87 (hexadecimal). "9B" is the operation code for the ADDA instruction in the direct mode and 87 is the low-order address of the memory location where the data (45) is to be found. The high-order address is always zero, and thus direct addressing is limited to page zero of the system's memory map.

The ADDA instruction would be written in 6800 assembler format as follows:

ADDA $87

Since the "#" symbol is left out, and since only a byte is specified for an address, the assembler will assume that the instruction is to be assembled in the direct mode.

Extended Addressing Mode. Notice that in the direct addressing mode, the data for an instruction could only be stored and accessed in page 0 of the memory map (locations 0000–00FF). The extended addressing mode allows the instruction to access data from any memory location (including page 0) in the memory map. An example of a similar 8080 instruction would be the LDA (load accumulator) instruction.

For example, if the byte "45" were to be added to ACCA and the byte was stored at memory location 5065, the ADDA instruction would have to be used in the extended mode to accomplish this task (since location 5065 is beyond page 0 and direct addressing cannot be used). Since a 16-bit address now has to be specified, instructions in the extended mode of addressing are always three byte instructions. Referring to Table 15-7, the machine code for the ADDA instruction would be BB5065 in the extended mode. The byte "BB" is the operation code for the ADDA (extended) instruction, and the following two bytes, 5065, is the address from which the data (45) is to be accessed. Notice that unlike the 8080, 16-bit addresses are stored with the most significant byte first.

The same ADDA instruction would be written in 6800 assembler format as

ADDA $5065

Since in this case a 16-bit address is specified, the assembler assumes that the instruction is to be assembled in the extended mode of addressing.

At this point it may seem that having the direct and extended modes of addressing would be wasteful, espeically since the extended mode can be used in placc of the direct mode. However, since most 6800 systems have RAM located in page 0 of the memory map, the direct mode can be used to access these memory locations. Since the direct mode requires only two bytes for an instruction (three bytes for extended), using the direct mode where applicable can result in a smaller program.

Indexed Addressing Mode. In the indexed addressing mode, the MPU uses the index register (IX) to point to the memory location where the data for the instruction is stored. This mode of addressing is similar to instructions of the 8080 that use register pair H&L as a data counter, for example, MOV A,M.

For example, if memory location 5065 contained the data "45" and the index register were set to 5065, the ADDA instruction could be used in the indexed mode to add "45" to the contents of ACCA. Referring to Table 15-7, the ADDA instruction (indexed mode) would be stored as AB00.

Notice that a "00" follows the operation code for the ADDA instruction (AB) in the indexed mode. Instructions in the indexed mode are always two-byte instructions. The second byte is the offset that is added to the value of the index register before the data is fetched. If the offset is zero, the data is fetched from the address contained in IX. For example, if it were required to add the contents of memory location 5067 to ACCA using indexed addressing and without changing the contents of IX, the offset would be 02 (5065 + 2 = 5067). Similarly, if it were required to add the contents of memory location 5063 to ACCA using indexed addressing and without changing the contents of IX, the offset would be FE (-2, in two's-complement form).

The same ADDA instructions discussed above would be written in 6800 assembler format as follows:

```
CODE      INSTRUCTION

AB00      ADDA   0,X      NO OFFSET
AB02      ADDA   2,X      TWO BYTES FORWARD
ABFE      ADDA  -2,X      TWO BYTES BACK
```

In the three examples shown above, the "X" symbol instructs the assembler to assemble the ADDA instruction in the indexed mode. In the first instruction, no offset is specified, while in the next two instructions, offsets of + and -2 are specified, respectively.

The previous example illustrated the use of four of the 6800 MPU addressing modes. Table 15-7 identifies another mode of addressing, called the implied or inherent addressing mode (sometimes known as the fifth addressing mode). This term is used to describe single-byte instructions that have no operands. Referring to Table 15-7, examples of such instructions are ABA (add ACCB to ACCA), CLRA (clear contents of ACCA), INX (increment contents of IX), and so on. Instructions in the implied mode are similar to the single-byte 8080 instructions.

Perhaps the most important differences between the instructions of the 6800 MPU and the 8080 lie in the jump and branch instructions. Referring to Table 15-7, notice that the 6800 MPU has only two jump instructions, an unconditional JMP and a jump to subroutine JSR (similar to the 8080's call instruction). Both jump instructions are three-byte instructions. The remaining program transfer instructions in the instruction set are branch instructions, which are two-byte instructions that use a scheme known as relative addressing.

Relative Addressing

Branch instructions use a technique known as *relative addressing* to cause control of the MPU to transfer to another address (conditionally or unconditionally). The memory location to which control is transferred is relative to the current value of the program counter. The first byte of a particular branch instruction is the operation code, while the second byte is a positive or negative offset that is added to the program counter to transfer MPU control to a forward or backward address. To illustrate the manner in which this is done, consider the following example.

Assume that a branch instruction is stored at locations 2000 and 2001. If the branch instruction is one that transfers control unconditionally to memory location 2010, the offset (second byte) of the branch instruction would be 0E. The value of the PC after the second byte of the branch instruction is fetched is 2002; the second byte (offset) is added to the PC (2002), which results in the PC containing 2010 (2002 + 0E); control then transfers to memory location 2010. This type of branching is known as branch ahead and the offset is always a positive number in the range 0 to 127 (decimal).

Now assume that the same branch instruction stored at locations 2000 and 2001 is to transfer control to memory location 1FF0. The offset for the branch instruction would be EE. Since after the offset (second byte of branch instruction) is fetched by the MPU, the value of the PC is 2002, 12 must be subtracted from 2002 to obtain a value of 1FF0. Since the offset is always added to the PC, it must be represented in two's-complement form, and therefore -12 in two's-complement form is EE. This type of branching is known as branch behind and the offset is always a negative number in the range 0 to -127 (decimal).

As a general rule, to calculate the offset for branch ahead or branch behind:

offset = location to be transferred − (location of branch instruction + 2)

There are two main advantages of having branch instructions in a microprocessor instruction set. The first advantage is that branch instructions are only two bytes in size and thus occupy less memory space than jump instructions. Second, a program constructed with branch instructions is naturally relocatable since the operands of branch instructions are not absolute addresses but are relative to the current value of the PC.

A major disadvantage of branch instructions in the 6800 instruction set is that control can only be transferred + or − 127 bytes ahead or behind. If it is desired to transfer control to a memory location greater than 127 bytes plus or minus the current value of the program counter, the branch must occur to the (absolute) unconditional JMP instruction and control must be transferred from there. This technique can also be used to simulate conditional call instructions by branching to the JSR instruction instead.

At this stage only some of the more outstanding 6800 instructions have been discussed. The addressing modes and the examples used were to illustrate the differences between the 6800 and the 8080 microprocessors. To deal with an in-depth study of the 6800 instruction set is beyond the scope of this chapter. However, to illustrate the difference between assembly language programs written for the 8080 and programs written for the 6800, we shall use the block-move algorithm from Chapter 8 to construct a 6800 program. A comparison of the 8080 implementation of the block-move program (from Chapter 8) and the 6800 implementation shown in Figure 15-11 should reinforce the concepts studied in this section.

The program shown in Figure 15-11 is similar to the 8080 implementation of the block-move algorithm discussed in Chapter 8. Before this program is executed, it is assumed that the starting address of the source block is stored at locations 2000 and 2001, and the starting address of the destination block is stored at locations 5000 and 5001. The number of bytes to be moved is 53 (35 hexadecimal).

The first instruction (LDAB) loads ACCB with the count of the number of bytes to be moved. This instruction uses immediate addressing to load the following byte into ACCB. Next, the LDX instruction loads IX with the address of the source block (previously stored in location 5000). Notice that since location 5000 is not in page 0, the LDX instruction is automatically assembled in the extended mode. The LDAA instruction uses indexed addressing to obtain a byte of data from the source block. The data from the memory location pointed to by IX is loaded into ACCA. The INX instruction is used to increment the contents of IX (point to the next source location). The updated address is then stored in memory location source by means of the STX instruction. The next LDX instruction sets the IX to the address of the destination block by obtaining

```
0035              COUNT   EQU   $35
2000              SOURCE  EQU   $2000
5000              DEST    EQU   $5000

ADDR  CODE

0000  C635              LDAB  #COUNT  * Store count in ACCB
0002  FE2000   MOVE     LDX   SOURCE  * Load IX with source address
0005  A600              LDAA  0,X     * Get source byte
0007  08                INX           * SOURCE = SOURCE + 1
0008  FF2000            STX   SOURCE  * Save source address
000B  FE5000            LDX   DEST    * Load IX with destination address
000E  A700              STAA  0,X     * Store source byte in dest
0010  08                INX           * DEST = DEST + 1
0011  FF5000            STX   DEST    * Save destination address
0014  5A                DECB          * COUNT = COUNT - 1
0015  26EB              BNE   MOVE    * Continue until done
0017  20FE     STOP     BRA   STOP    * Else stop
```

FIGURE 15-11. Block-move program for the 6800.

this value from location DEST. The STAA instruction in the indexed mode stores the previously received source byte in the memory location referenced by IX (destination address). The next two instructions update and store the destination address as was done for the source address. Next, the contents of ACCB is decremented to count down the number of bytes moved. Control transfers to location MOVE if the count is not zero; if the count is zero, the program terminates.

15-6

SUMMARY

As one can clearly see from this chapter, the major differences between the 8080 microprocessor and the 6800 MPU lie in three areas: the interrupt structure, the control signals, and the instruction set. Even though the operation of the 6800 MPU was quite different from that of the 8080, the concepts of operation of both microprocessors remained the same. This can be said of any microprocessor currently available.

It can also be seen that microprocessors are designed with specific applications in mind. The "memory-oriented" instruction set of the 6800, together with the memory-mapped I/O scheme, makes it an ideal processor for applications that require extensive I/O control and minimum memory requirements.

This chapter and the preceding chapter have examined two microprocessors, one similar (8085) and one quite different (6800) from the 8080 microprocessor studied in this book. The concepts of microprocessor operation and interfacing can easily be applied to almost any type of microprocessor. It is always important to remember that for a given application a microprocessor must be selected that best suits the application; conversely, the application should never be designed to fit the characteristics of the microprocessor.

REVIEW QUESTIONS AND PROBLEMS

1. Compare the differences between the 6800 MPU and the 8080/8085 microprocessor in terms of
   (a) The interrupt structure.
   (b) The control signals.
   (c) The internal arrangement of registers.

2. Describe the sequence of events that occurs when
   (a) The 6800 MPU is reset.
   (b) The 6800 MPU receives an interrupt over the $\overline{\text{NMI}}$ line.
   (c) The 6800 MPU executes a SWI instruction.
   (d) The 6800 MPU receives an interrupt over the $\overline{\text{IRQ}}$ line.

3. Which of the following interrupts will be acknowledged if the I_M bit is SET?
   (a) RESET (b) NMI (c) SWI (d) IRQ

4. Expand the 6800 microprocessor system shown in Figure 15-7 to include an additional 6820 PIA, 6850 ACIA, 6810 RAM, and 6830 ROM. Explain the addressing scheme used and draw a memory map of the expanded system.

5. Compare each bit of the 6800 CCR with each flag in the 8080 PSW. Discuss similarities and differences.

6. What is the purpose of the index register (IX)? Give a few examples of instructions that use the IX.

7. What is an addressing mode? How many modes of addressing does the 6800 have?

8. Assemble the instruction ORAA in each mode of addressing. Explain the operation of the ORAA instruction in each mode.

9. How is the offset used in the indexed mode of addressing? Give examples.

10. What is relative addressing? How does it compare to absolute addressing?

11. Hand-assemble the following 6800 program.

```
            ACIAC   EQU     $4000
            ACIAD   EQU     $4001
            TEMP    EQU     $0005

                    ORG     $2000

    START           LDAA    #$03
                    STAA    ACIAC
                    LDX     TEMP
    LOOP            LDAA    ACIAC
                    RORA
                    BCC     LOOP
                    LDAB    ACIAD
                    STAB    5,X
                    DECB
                    BNE     STOP
                    BRA     LOOP
                    STAA    TEMP
    STOP            BRA     STOP
```

12. Write a program (using the 6800 instruction set) to fill memory locations $E000–$F000 with the byte $55. Begin the program at location $1000.

APPENDIX A

Summary of the 8080/ 8085 Instruction Set

8080/85 CPU INSTRUCTIONS IN OPERATION CODE SEQUENCE

OP CODE	MNEMONIC	OP CODE	MNEMONIC	OP CODE	MNEMONIC	OP CODE	MNEMONIC	OP CODE	MNEMONIC	OP CODE	MNEMONIC
00	NOP	2B	DCX H	56	MOV D,M	81	ADD C	AC	XRA H	D7	RST 2
01	LXI B,D16	2C	INR L	57	MOV D,A	82	ADD D	AD	XRA L	D8	RC
02	STAX B	2D	DCR L	58	MOV E,B	83	ADD E	AE	XRA M	D9	—
03	INX B	2E	MVI L,D8	59	MOV E,C	84	ADD H	AF	XRA A	DA	JC Adr
04	INR B	2F	CMA	5A	MOV E,D	85	ADD L	B0	ORA B	DB	IN D8
05	DCR B	30	SIM	5B	MOV E,E	86	ADD M	B1	ORA C	DC	CC Adr
06	MVI B,D8	31	LXI SP,D16	5C	MOV E,H	87	ADD A	B2	ORA D	DD	—
07	RLC	32	STA Adr	5D	MOV E,L	88	ADC B	B3	ORA E	DE	SBI D8
08	—	33	INX SP	5E	MOV E,M	89	ADC C	B4	ORA H	DF	RST 3
09	DAD B	34	INR M	5F	MOV E,A	8A	ADC D	B5	ORA L	E0	RPO
0A	LDAX B	35	DCR M	60	MOV H,B	8B	ADC E	B6	ORA M	E1	POP H
0B	DCX B	36	MVI M,D8	61	MOV H,C	8C	ADC H	B7	ORA A	E2	JPO Adr
0C	INR C	37	STC	62	MOV H,D	8D	ADC L	B8	CMP B	E3	XTHL
0D	DCR C	38	—	63	MOV H,E	8E	ADC M	B9	CMP C	E4	CPO Adr
0E	MVI C,D8	39	DAD SP	64	MOV H,H	8F	ADC A	BA	CMP D	E5	PUSH H
0F	RRC	3A	LDA Adr	65	MOV H,L	8G	SUB B	BB	CMP E	E6	ANI D8
10	—	3B	DCX SP	66	MOV H,M	91	SUB C	BC	CMP H	E7	RST 4
11	LXI D,D16	3C	INR A	67	MOV H,A	92	SUB D	BD	CMP L	E8	RPE
12	STAX D	3D	DCR A	68	MOV L,B	93	SUB E	BE	CMP M	E9	PCHL
13	INX D	3E	MVI A,D8	69	MOV L,C	94	SUB H	BF	CMP A	EA	JPE Adr
14	INR D	3F	CMC	6A	MOV L,D	95	SUB L	C0	RNZ	EB	XCHG
15	DCR D	40	MOV B,B	6B	MOV L,E	96	SUB M	C1	POP B	EC	CPE Adr
16	MVI D,D8	41	MOV B,C	6C	MOV L,H	97	SUB A	C2	JNZ Adr	ED	—
17	RAL	42	MOV B,D	6D	MOV L,L	98	SBB B	C3	JMP Adr	EE	XRI D8
18	—	43	MOV B,E	6E	MOV L,M	99	SBB C	C4	CNZ Adr	EF	RST 5
19	DAD D	44	MOV B,H	6F	MOV L,A	9A	SBB D	C5	PUSH B	F0	RP
1A	LDAX D	45	MOV B,L	70	MOV M,B	9B	SBB E	C6	ADI D8	F1	POP PSW
1B	DCX D	46	MOV B,M	71	MOV M,C	9C	SBB H	C7	RST 0	F2	JP Adr
1C	INR E	47	MOV B,A	72	MOV M,D	9D	SBB L	C8	RZ	F3	DI
1D	DRC E	48	MOV C,B	73	MOV M,E	9E	SBB M	C9	RET Adr	F4	CP Adr
1E	MVI E,D8	49	MOV C,C	74	MOV M,H	9F	SBB A	CA	JZ	F5	PUSH PSW
1F	RAR	4A	MOV C,D	75	MOV M,L	A0	ANA B	CB	—	F6	ORI D8
20	RIM	4B	MOV C,E	76	HLT	A1	ANA C	CC	CZ Adr	F7	RST 6
21	LXI H,D16	4C	MOV C,H	77	MOV M,A	A2	ANA D	CD	CALL Adr	F8	RM
22	SHLD Adr	4D	MOV C,L	78	MOV A,B	A3	ANA E	CE	ACI D8	F9	SPHL
23	INX H	4E	MOV C,M	79	MOV A,C	A4	ANA H	CF	RST 1	FA	JM Adr
24	INR H	4F	MOV C,A	7A	MOV A,D	A5	ANA L	D0	RNC	FB	EI
25	DCR H	50	MOV D,B	7B	MOV A,E	A6	ANA M	D1	POP D	FC	CM Adr
26	MVI H,D8	51	MOV D,C	7C	MOV A,H	A7	ANA A	D2	JNC Adr	FD	—
27	DAA	52	MOV D,D	7D	MOV A,L	A8	XRA B	D3	OUT D8	FE	CPI D8
28	—	53	MOV D,E	7E	MOV A,M	A9	XRA C	D4	CNC Adr	FF	RST 7
29	DAD H	54	MOV D,H	7F	MOV A,A	AA	XRA D	D5	PUSH D		
2A	LHLD Adr	55	MOV D,L	80	ADD B	AB	XRA E	D6	SUI D8		

D8 = constant, or logical/arithmetic expression that evaluates to an 8 bit data quantity.

D16 = constant, or logical/arithmetic expression that evaluates to a 16 bit data quantity.

Adr = 16-bit address

All mnemonics © 1974, 1975, 1976, 1977 Intel Corporation.
Courtesy of Intel Corp.

APPENDIX B

The ASCII Codes

The 8080 and 8085 use the seven-bit ASCII code, with the high-order eighth bit (parity bit) always reset.

GRAPHIC OR CONTROL	ASCII (HEXADECIMAL)	GRAPHIC OR CONTROL	ASCII (HEXADECIMAL)	GRAPHIC OR CONTROL	ASCII (HEXADECIMAL)
NUL	00	+	2B	V	56
SOH	01	,	2C	W	57
STX	02	—	2D	X	58
ETX	03	.	2E	Y	59
EOT	04	/	2F	Z	5A
ENQ	05	0	30	[	5B
ACK	06	1	31	\	5C
BEL	07	2	32	]	5D
BS	08	3	33	∧ (↑)	5E
HT	09	4	34	— (←)	5F
LF	0A	5	35	`	60
VT	0B	6	36	a	61
FF	0C	7	37	b	62
CR	0D	8	38	c	63
SO	0E	9	39	d	64
SI	0F	:	3A	e	65
DLE	10	;	3B	f	66
DC1 (X-ON)	11	<	3C	g	67
DC2 (TAPE)	12	=	3D	h	68
DC3 (X-OFF)	13	>	3E	i	69
DC4 (~~TAPE~~)	14	?	3F	j	6A
NAK	15	@	40	k	6B
SYN	16	A	41	l	6C
ETB	17	B	42	m	6D
CAN	18	C	43	n	6E
EM	19	D	44	o	6F
SUB	1A	E	45	p	70
ESC	1B	F	46	q	71
FS	1C	G	47	r	72
GS	1D	H	48	s	73
RS	1E	I	49	t	74
US	1F	J	4A	u	75
SP	20	K	4B	v	76
!	21	L	4C	w	77
"	22	M	4D	x	78
#	23	N	4E	y	79
$	24	O	4F	z	7A
%	25	P	50	{	7B
&	26	Q	51			7C
'	27	R	52	} (ALT MODE)	7D
(	28	S	53	~	7E
)	29	T	54	DEL (RUB OUT)	7F
*	2A	U	55		

Courtesy of Intel Corp.

APPENDIX C

Standard Flowchart Symbols

Operation	Symbol	Description
Interrupt	(stadium shape)	Indicates a change in a program, such as start or stop
Process	(rectangle)	Indicates a processing operation in progress
Input/output	(parallelogram)	Indicates an I/O operation in progress. Process may also be used
Manual	(trapezoid)	Indicates a manual operation (no CPU intervention) in progress
Decision	(diamond)	Indicates a test, decision, and transfer operation
Connector	(circle)	Indicates a connection of two or more portions of a flowchart

APPENDIX D

Binary—Decimal— Hexadecimal Conversion Tables

POWERS OF TWO

2^n	n	2^{-n}
1	0	1.0
2	1	0.5
4	2	0.25
8	3	0.125
16	4	0.062 5
32	5	0.031 25
64	6	0.015 625
128	7	0.007 812 5
256	8	0.003 906 25
512	9	0.001 953 125
1 024	10	0.000 976 562 5
2 048	11	0.000 488 281 25
4 096	12	0.000 244 140 625
8 192	13	0.000 122 070 312 5
16 384	14	0.000 061 035 156 25
32 768	15	0.000 030 517 578 125
65 536	16	0.000 015 258 789 062 5
131 072	17	0.000 007 629 394 531 25
262 144	18	0.000 003 814 697 265 625
524 288	19	0.000 001 907 348 632 812 5
1 048 576	20	0.000 000 953 674 316 406 25
2 097 152	21	0.000 000 476 837 158 203 125
4 194 304	22	0.000 000 238 418 579 101 562 5
8 388 608	23	0.000 000 119 209 289 550 781 25
16 777 216	24	0.000 000 059 604 644 775 390 625
33 554 432	25	0.000 000 029 802 322 387 695 312 5
67 108 864	26	0.000 000 014 901 161 193 847 656 25
134 217 728	27	0.000 000 007 450 580 596 923 828 125
268 435 456	28	0.000 000 003 725 290 298 461 914 062 5
536 870 912	29	0.000 000 001 862 645 149 230 957 031 25
1 073 741 824	30	0.000 000 000 931 322 574 615 478 515 625
2 147 483 648	31	0.000 000 000 465 661 287 307 739 257 812 5
4 294 967 296	32	0.000 000 000 232 830 643 653 869 628 906 25
8 589 934 592	33	0.000 000 000 116 415 321 826 934 814 453 125
17 179 869 184	34	0.000 000 000 058 207 660 913 467 407 226 562 5
34 359 738 368	35	0.000 000 000 029 103 830 456 733 703 613 281 25
68 719 476 736	36	0.000 000 000 014 551 915 228 366 851 806 640 625
137 438 953 472	37	0.000 000 000 007 275 957 614 183 425 903 320 312 5
274 877 906 944	38	0.000 000 000 003 637 978 807 091 712 951 660 156 25
549 755 813 888	39	0.000 000 000 001 818 989 403 545 856 475 830 078 125
1 099 511 627 776	40	0.000 000 000 000 909 494 701 772 928 237 915 039 062 5
2 199 023 255 552	41	0.000 000 000 000 454 747 350 886 464 118 957 519 531 25
4 398 046 511 104	42	0.000 000 000 000 227 373 675 443 232 059 478 759 765 625
8 796 093 022 208	43	0.000 000 000 000 113 686 837 721 616 029 739 379 882 812 5
17 592 186 044 416	44	0.000 000 000 000 056 843 418 860 808 014 869 689 941 406 25
35 184 372 088 832	45	0.000 000 000 000 028 421 709 430 404 007 434 844 970 703 125
70 368 744 177 664	46	0.000 000 000 000 014 210 854 715 202 003 717 422 485 351 562 5
140 737 488 355 328	47	0.000 000 000 000 007 105 427 357 601 001 858 711 242 675 781 25
281 474 976 710 656	48	0.000 000 000 000 003 552 713 678 800 500 929 355 621 337 890 625
562 949 953 421 312	49	0.000 000 000 000 001 776 356 839 400 250 464 677 810 668 945 312 5
1 125 899 906 842 624	50	0.000 000 000 000 000 888 178 419 700 125 232 338 905 334 472 656 25
2 251 799 813 685 248	51	0.000 000 000 000 000 444 089 209 850 062 616 169 452 667 236 328 125
4 503 599 627 370 496	52	0.000 000 000 000 000 222 044 604 925 031 308 084 726 333 618 164 062 5
9 007 199 254 740 992	53	0.000 000 000 000 000 111 022 302 462 515 654 042 363 166 809 082 031 25
18 014 398 509 481 984	54	0.000 000 000 000 000 055 511 151 231 257 827 021 181 583 404 541 015 625
36 028 797 018 963 968	55	0.000 000 000 000 000 027 755 575 615 628 913 510 590 791 702 270 507 812 5
72 057 594 037 927 936	56	0.000 000 000 000 000 013 877 787 807 814 456 755 295 395 851 135 253 906 25
144 115 188 075 855 872	57	0.000 000 000 000 000 006 938 893 903 907 228 377 647 697 925 567 676 950 125
288 230 376 151 711 744	58	0.000 000 000 000 000 003 469 446 951 953 614 188 823 848 962 783 813 476 562 5
576 460 752 303 423 488	59	0.000 000 000 000 000 001 734 723 475 976 807 094 411 924 481 391 906 738 281 25
1 152 921 504 606 846 976	60	0.000 000 000 000 000 000 867 361 737 988 403 547 205 962 240 695 953 369 140 625
2 305 843 009 213 693 952	61	0.000 000 000 000 000 000 433 680 868 994 201 773 602 981 120 347 976 684 570 312
4 611 686 018 427 387 904	62	0.000 000 000 000 000 000 216 840 434 497 100 886 801 490 560 173 988 342 285 156
9 223 372 036 854 775 808	63	0.000 000 000 000 000 000 108 420 217 248 550 443 400 745 280 086 994 171 142 578

Courtesy of Intel Corp.

POWERS OF 16 (IN BASE 10)

16^n	n	16^{-n}
1	0	0.10000 00000 00000 00000 × 10
16	1	0.62500 00000 00000 00000 × 10^{-1}
256	2	0.39062 50000 00000 00000 × 10^{-2}
4 096	3	0.24414 06250 00000 00000 × 10^{-3}
65 536	4	0.15258 78906 25000 00000 × 10^{-4}
1 048 576	5	0.95367 43164 06250 00000 × 10^{-6}
16 777 216	6	0.59604 64477 53906 25000 × 10^{-7}
268 435 456	7	0.37252 90298 46191 40625 × 10^{-8}
4 294 967 296	8	0.23283 06436 53869 62891 × 10^{-9}
68 719 476 736	9	0.14551 91522 83668 51807 × 10^{-10}
1 099 511 627 776	10	0.90949 47017 72928 23792 × 10^{-12}
17 592 186 044 416	11	0.56843 41886 08080 14870 × 10^{-13}
281 474 976 710 656	12	0.35527 13678 80050 09294 × 10^{-14}
4 503 599 627 370 496	13	0.22204 46049 25031 30808 × 10^{-15}
72 057 594 037 927 936	14	0.13877 78780 78144 56755 × 10^{-16}
1 152 921 504 606 846 976	15	0.86736 17379 88403 54721 × 10^{-18}

POWERS OF 10 (IN BASE 16)

10^n	n	10^{-n}
1	0	1.0000 0000 0000 0000
A	1	0.1999 9999 9999 999A
64	2	0.28F5 C28F 5C28 F5C3 × 16^{-1}
3E8	3	0.4189 374B C6A7 EF9E × 16^{-2}
2710	4	0.68DB 8BAC 710C B296 × 16^{-3}
1 86A0	5	0.A7C5 AC47 1B47 8423 × 16^{-4}
F 4240	6	0.10C6 F7A0 B5ED 8D37 × 16^{-4}
98 9680	7	0.1AD7 F29A BCAF 4858 × 16^{-5}
5F5 E100	8	0.2AF3 1DC4 6118 73BF × 16^{-6}
3B9A CA00	9	0.44B8 2FA0 9B5A 52CC × 16^{-7}
2 540B E400	10	0.6DF3 7F67 5EF6 EADF × 16^{-8}
17 4876 E800	11	0.AFEB FF0B CB24 AAFF × 16^{-9}
E8 D4A5 1000	12	0.1197 9981 2DEA 1119 × 16^{-9}
918 4E72 A000	13	0.1C25 C268 4976 81C2 × 16^{-10}
5AF3 107A 4000	14	0.2D09 370D 4257 3604 × 16^{-11}
3 8D7E A4C6 8000	15	0.480E BE7B 9D58 566D × 16^{-12}
23 8652 6FC1 0000	16	0.734A CA5F 6226 F0AE × 16^{-13}
163 4578 5D8A 0000	17	0.B877 AA32 36A4 B449 × 16^{-14}
DE0 B6B3 A764 0000	18	0.1272 5DD1 D243 ABA1 × 16^{-14}
8AC7 2304 89E8 0000	19	0.1D83 C94F B6D2 AC35 × 16^{-15}

HEXADECIMAL-DECIMAL INTEGER CONVERSION

The table below provides for direct conversions between hexadecimal integers in the range 0-FFF and decimal integers in the range 0-4095. For conversion of larger integers, the table values may be added to the following figures:

Hexadecimal	Decimal	Hexadecimal	Decimal
01 000	4 096	20 000	131 072
02 000	8 192	30 000	196 608
03 000	12 288	40 000	262 144
04 000	16 384	50 000	327 680
05 000	20 480	60 000	393 216
06 000	24 576	70 000	458 752
07 000	28 672	80 000	524 288
08 000	32 768	90 000	589 824
09 000	36 864	A0 000	655 360
0A 000	40 960	B0 000	720 896
0B 000	45 056	C0 000	786 432
0C 000	49 152	D0 000	851 968
0D 000	53 248	E0 000	917 504
0E 000	57 344	F0 000	983 040
0F 000	61 440	100 000	1 048 576
10 000	65 536	200 000	2 097 152
11 000	69 632	300 000	3 145 728
12 000	73 728	400 000	4 194 304
13 000	77 824	500 000	5 242 880
14 000	81 920	600 000	6 291 456
15 000	86 016	700 000	7 340 032
16 000	90 112	800 000	8 388 608
17 000	94 208	900 000	9 437 184
18 000	98 304	A00 000	10 485 760
19 000	102 400	B00 000	11 534 336
1A 000	106 496	C00 000	12 582 912
1B 000	110 592	D00 000	13 631 488
1C 000	114 688	E00 000	14 680 064
1D 000	118 784	F00 000	15 728 640
1E 000	122 880	1 000 000	16 777 216
1F 000	126 976	2 000 000	33 554 432

	0	1	2	3	4	5	6	7	8	9	A	B	C	D	E	F
000	0000	0001	0002	0003	0004	0005	0006	0007	0008	0009	0010	0011	0012	0013	0014	0015
010	0016	0017	0018	0019	0020	0021	0022	0023	0024	0025	0026	0027	0028	0029	0030	0031
020	0032	0033	0034	0035	0036	0037	0038	0039	0040	0041	0042	0043	0044	0045	0046	0047
030	0048	0049	0050	0051	0052	0053	0054	0055	0056	0057	0058	0059	0060	0061	0062	0063
040	0064	0065	0066	0067	0068	0069	0070	0071	0072	0073	0074	0075	0076	0077	0078	0079
050	0080	0081	0082	0083	0084	0085	0086	0087	0088	0089	0090	0091	0092	0093	0094	0095
060	0096	0097	0098	0099	0100	0101	0102	0103	0104	0105	0106	0107	0108	0109	0110	0111
070	0112	0113	0114	0115	0116	0117	0118	0119	0120	0121	0122	0123	0124	0125	0126	0127
080	0128	0129	0130	0131	0132	0133	0134	0135	0136	0137	0138	0139	0140	0141	0142	0143
090	0144	0145	0146	0147	0148	0149	0150	0151	0152	0153	0154	0155	0156	0157	0158	0159
0A0	0160	0161	0162	0163	0164	0165	0166	0167	0168	0169	0170	0171	0172	0173	0174	0175
0B0	0176	0177	0178	0179	0180	0181	0182	0183	0184	0185	0186	0187	0188	0189	0190	0191
0C0	0192	0193	0194	0195	0196	0197	0198	0199	0200	0201	0202	0203	0204	0205	0206	0207
0D0	0208	0209	0210	0211	0212	0213	0214	0215	0216	0217	0218	0219	0220	0221	0222	0223
0E0	0224	0225	0226	0227	0228	0229	0230	0231	0232	0233	0234	0235	0236	0237	0238	0239
0F0	0240	0241	0242	0243	0244	0245	0246	0247	0248	0249	0250	0251	0252	0253	0254	0255

HEXADECIMAL-DECIMAL INTEGER CONVERSION (Cont'd)

	0	1	2	3	4	5	6	7	8	9	A	B	C	D	E	F
100	0256	0257	0258	0259	0260	0261	0262	0263	0264	0265	0266	0267	0268	0269	0270	0271
110	0272	0273	0274	0275	0276	0277	0278	0279	0280	0281	0282	0283	0284	0285	0286	0287
120	0288	0289	0290	0291	0292	0293	0294	0295	0296	0297	0298	0299	0300	0301	0302	0303
130	0304	0305	0306	0307	0308	0309	0310	0311	0312	0313	0314	0315	0316	0317	0318	0319
140	0320	0321	0322	0323	0324	0325	0326	0327	0328	0329	0330	0331	0331	0333	0334	0335
150	0336	0337	0338	0339	0340	0341	0342	0343	0344	0345	0346	0347	0348	0349	0350	0351
160	0352	0353	0354	0355	0356	0357	0358	0359	0360	0361	0362	0363	0364	0365	0366	0367
170	0368	0369	0370	0371	0372	0373	0374	0375	0376	0377	0378	0379	0380	0381	0382	0383
180	0384	0385	0386	0387	0388	0389	0390	0391	0392	0393	0394	0395	0396	0397	0398	0399
190	0400	0401	0402	0403	0404	0405	0406	0407	0408	0409	0410	0411	0412	0413	0414	0415
1A0	0416	0417	0418	0419	0420	0421	0422	0423	0424	0425	0426	0427	0428	0429	0430	0431
1B0	0432	0433	0434	0435	0436	0437	0438	0439	0440	0441	0442	0443	0444	0445	0446	0447
1C0	0448	0449	0450	0451	0452	0453	0454	0455	0456	0457	0458	0459	0460	0461	0462	0463
1D0	0464	0465	0466	0467	0468	0469	0470	0471	0472	0473	0474	0475	0476	0477	0478	0479
1E0	0480	0481	0482	0483	0484	0485	0486	0487	0488	0489	0490	0491	0492	0493	0494	0495
1F0	0496	0497	0498	0499	0500	0501	0502	0503	0504	0505	0506	0507	0508	0509	0510	0511
200	0512	0513	0514	0515	0516	0517	0518	0519	0520	0521	0522	0523	0524	0525	0526	0527
210	0528	0529	0530	0531	0532	0533	0534	0535	0536	0537	0538	0539	0540	0541	0542	0543
220	0544	0545	0546	0547	0548	0549	0550	0551	0552	0553	0554	0555	0556	0557	0558	0559
230	0560	0561	0562	0563	0564	0565	0566	0567	0568	0569	0570	0571	0572	0573	0574	0575
240	0576	0577	0578	0579	0580	0581	0582	0583	0584	0585	0586	0587	0588	0589	0590	0591
250	0592	0593	0594	0595	0596	0597	0598	0599	0600	0601	0602	0603	0604	0605	0606	0607
260	0608	0609	0610	0611	0612	0613	0614	0615	0616	0617	0618	0619	0620	0621	0622	0623
270	0624	0625	0626	0627	0628	0629	0630	0631	0632	0633	0634	0635	0636	0637	0638	0639
280	0640	0641	0642	0643	0644	0645	0646	0647	0648	0649	0650	0651	0652	0653	0654	0655
290	0656	0657	0658	0659	0660	0661	0662	0663	0664	0665	0666	0667	0668	0669	0670	0671
2A0	0672	0673	0674	0675	0676	0677	0678	0679	0680	0681	0682	0683	0684	0685	0686	0687
2B0	0688	0689	0690	0691	0692	0693	0694	0695	0696	0697	0698	0699	0700	0701	0702	0703
2C0	0704	0705	0706	0707	0708	0709	0710	0711	0712	0713	0714	0715	0716	0717	0718	0719
2D0	0720	0721	0722	0723	0724	0725	0726	0727	0728	0729	0730	0731	0732	0733	0734	0735
2E0	0736	0737	0738	0739	0740	0741	0742	0743	0744	0745	0746	0747	0748	0749	0750	0751
2F0	0752	0753	0754	0755	0756	0757	0758	0759	0760	0761	0762	0763	0764	0765	0766	0767
300	0768	0769	0770	0771	0772	0773	0774	0775	0776	0777	0778	0779	0780	0781	0782	0783
310	0784	0785	0786	0787	0788	0789	0790	0791	0792	0793	0794	0795	0796	0797	0798	0799
320	0800	0301	0802	0803	0804	0805	0806	0807	0808	0809	0810	0811	0812	0813	0814	0815
330	0816	0817	0818	0819	0820	0821	0822	0823	0824	0825	0826	0827	0828	0829	0830	0831
340	0832	0833	0834	0835	0836	0837	0838	0839	0840	0841	0842	0843	0844	0845	0846	0847
350	0848	0849	0850	0851	0852	0853	0854	0855	0856	0857	0858	0859	0860	0861	0862	0863
360	0864	0865	0866	0867	0868	0869	0870	0871	0872	0873	0874	0875	0876	0877	0878	0879
370	0880	0881	0882	0883	0884	0885	0886	0887	0888	0889	0890	0891	0892	0893	0894	0895
380	0896	0897	0898	0899	0900	0901	0902	0903	0904	0905	0906	0907	0908	0909	0910	0911
390	0212	0913	0914	0915	0916	0917	0918	0919	0920	0921	0922	0923	0924	0925	0926	0927
3A0	0928	0929	0930	0931	0932	0933	0934	0935	0936	0937	0938	0939	0940	0941	0942	0943
3B0	0944	0945	0946	0947	0948	0949	0950	0951	0952	0953	0954	0955	0956	0957	0958	0959
3C0	0960	0961	0962	0963	0964	0965	0966	0967	0968	0969	0970	0971	0972	0973	0974	0975
3D0	0976	0977	0978	0979	0980	0981	0982	0983	0984	0985	0986	0987	0988	0989	0990	0991
3E0	0992	0993	0994	0995	0996	0997	0998	0999	1000	1001	1002	1003	1004	1005	1006	1007
3F0	1008	1009	1010	1011	1012	1013	1014	1015	1016	1017	1018	1019	1020	1021	1022	1023

BINARY—DECIMAL—HEXADECIMAL CONVERSION TABLES

HEXADECIMAL-DECIMAL INTEGER CONVERSION (Cont'd)

	0	1	2	3	4	5	6	7	8	9	A	B	C	D	E	F
400	1024	1025	1026	1027	1028	1029	1030	1031	1032	1033	1034	1035	1036	1037	1038	1039
410	1040	1041	1042	1043	1044	1045	1046	1047	1048	1049	1050	1051	1052	1053	1054	1055
420	1056	1057	1058	1059	1060	1061	1062	1063	1064	1065	1066	1067	1068	1069	1070	1071
430	1072	1073	1074	1075	1076	1077	1078	1079	1080	1081	1082	1083	1084	1085	1086	1087
440	1088	1089	1090	1091	1092	1093	1094	1095	1096	1097	1098	1099	1100	1101	1102	1103
450	1104	1105	1106	1107	1108	1109	1110	1111	1112	1113	1114	1115	1116	1117	1118	1119
460	1120	1121	1122	1123	1124	1125	1126	1127	1128	1129	1130	1131	1132	1133	1134	1135
470	1136	1137	1138	1139	1140	1141	1142	1143	1144	1145	1146	1147	1148	1149	1150	1151
480	1152	1153	1154	1155	1156	1157	1158	1159	1160	1161	1162	1163	1164	1165	1166	1167
490	1168	1169	1170	1171	1172	1173	1174	1175	1176	1177	1178	1179	1180	1181	1182	1183
4A0	1184	1185	1186	1187	1188	1189	1190	1191	1192	1193	1194	1195	1196	1197	1198	1199
4B0	1200	1201	1202	1203	1204	1205	1206	1207	1208	1209	1210	1211	1212	1213	1214	1215
4C0	1216	1217	1218	1219	1220	1221	1222	1223	1224	1225	1226	1227	1228	1229	1230	1231
4D0	1232	1233	1234	1235	1236	1237	1238	1239	1240	1241	1242	1243	1244	1245	1246	1247
4E0	1248	1249	1250	1251	1252	1253	1254	1255	1256	1257	1258	1259	1260	1261	1262	1263
4F0	1264	1265	1266	1267	1268	1269	1270	1271	1272	1273	1274	1275	1276	1277	1278	1279
500	1280	1281	1282	1283	1284	1285	1286	1287	1288	1289	1290	1291	1292	1293	1294	1295
510	1296	1297	1298	1299	1300	1301	1302	1303	1304	1305	1306	1307	1308	1309	1310	1311
520	1312	1313	1314	1315	1316	1317	1318	1319	1320	1321	1322	1323	1324	1325	1326	1327
530	1328	1329	1330	1331	1332	1333	1334	1335	1336	1337	1338	1339	1340	1341	1342	1343
540	1344	1345	1346	1347	1348	1349	1350	1351	1352	1353	1354	1355	1356	1357	1358	1359
550	1360	1361	1362	1363	1364	1365	1366	1367	1368	1369	1370	1371	1372	1373	1374	1375
560	1376	1377	1378	1379	1380	1381	1382	1383	1384	1385	1386	1387	1388	1389	1390	1391
570	1392	1393	1394	1395	1396	1397	1398	1399	1400	1401	1402	1403	1404	1405	1406	1407
580	1408	1409	1410	1411	1412	1413	1414	1415	1416	1417	1418	1419	1420	1421	1422	1423
590	1424	1425	1426	1427	1428	1429	1430	1431	1432	1433	1434	1435	1436	1437	1438	1439
5A0	1440	1441	1442	1443	1444	1445	1446	1447	1448	1449	1450	1451	1452	1453	1454	1455
5B0	1456	1457	1458	1459	1460	1461	1462	1463	1464	1465	1466	1467	1468	1469	1470	1471
5C0	1472	1473	1474	1475	1476	1477	1478	1479	1480	1481	1482	1483	1484	1485	1486	1487
5D0	1488	1489	1490	1491	1492	1493	1494	1495	1496	1497	1498	1499	1500	1501	1502	1503
5E0	1504	1505	1506	1507	1508	1509	1510	1511	1512	1513	1514	1515	1516	1517	1518	1519
5F0	1520	1521	1522	1523	1524	1525	1526	1527	1528	1529	1530	1531	1532	1533	1534	1535
600	1536	1537	1538	1539	1540	1541	1542	1543	1544	1545	1546	1547	1548	1549	1550	1551
610	1552	1553	1554	1555	1556	1557	1558	1559	1560	1561	1562	1563	1564	1565	1566	1567
620	1568	1569	1570	1571	1572	1573	1574	1575	1576	1577	1578	1579	1580	1581	1582	1583
630	1584	1585	1586	1587	1588	1589	1590	1591	1592	1593	1594	1595	1596	1597	1598	1599
640	1600	1601	1602	1603	1604	1605	1606	1607	1608	1609	1610	1611	1612	1613	1614	1615
650	1616	1617	1618	1619	1620	1621	1622	1623	1624	1625	1626	1627	1628	1629	1630	1631
660	1632	1633	1634	1635	1636	1637	1638	1639	1640	1641	1642	1643	1644	1645	1646	1647
670	1648	1649	1650	1651	1652	1653	1654	1655	1656	1657	1658	1659	1660	1661	1662	1663
680	1664	1665	1666	1667	1668	1669	1670	1671	1672	1673	1674	1675	1676	1677	1678	1679
690	1680	1681	1682	1683	1684	1685	1686	1687	1688	1689	1690	1691	1692	1693	1694	1695
6A0	1696	1697	1698	1699	1700	1701	1702	1703	1704	1705	1706	1707	1708	1709	1710	1711
6B0	1712	1713	1714	1715	1716	1717	1718	1719	1720	1721	1722	1723	1724	1725	1726	1727
6C0	1728	1729	1730	1731	1732	1733	1734	1735	1736	1737	1738	1739	1740	1741	1742	1743
6D0	1744	1745	1746	1747	1748	1749	1750	1751	1752	1753	1754	1755	1756	1757	1758	1759
6E0	1760	1761	1762	1763	1764	1765	1766	1767	1768	1769	1770	1771	1772	1773	1774	1775
6F0	1776	1777	1778	1779	1780	1781	1782	1783	1784	1785	1786	1787	1788	1789	1790	1791

HEXADECIMAL-DECIMAL INTEGER CONVERSION (Cont'd)

	0	1	2	3	4	5	6	7	8	9	A	B	C	D	E	F
700	1792	1793	1794	1795	1796	1797	1798	1799	1800	1801	1802	1803	1804	1805	1806	1807
710	1808	1809	1810	1811	1812	1813	1814	1815	1816	1817	1818	1819	1820	1821	1822	1823
720	1824	1825	1826	1827	1828	1829	1830	1831	1832	1833	1834	1835	1836	1837	1838	1839
730	1840	1841	1842	1843	1844	1845	1846	1847	1848	1849	1850	1851	1852	1853	1854	1855
740	1856	1857	1858	1859	1860	1861	1862	1863	1864	1865	1866	1867	1868	1869	1870	1871
750	1872	1873	1874	1875	1876	1877	1878	1879	1880	1881	1882	1883	1884	1885	1886	1887
760	1888	1889	1890	1891	1892	1893	1894	1895	1896	1897	1898	1899	1900	1901	1902	1903
770	1904	1905	1906	1907	1908	1909	1910	1911	1912	1913	1914	1915	1916	1917	1918	1919
780	1920	1921	1922	1923	1924	1925	1926	1927	1928	1929	1930	1931	1932	1933	1934	1935
790	1936	1937	1938	1939	1940	1941	1942	1943	1944	1945	1946	1947	1948	1949	1950	1951
7A0	1952	1953	1954	1955	1956	1957	1958	1959	1960	1961	1962	1963	1964	1965	1966	1967
7B0	1968	1969	1970	1971	1972	1973	1974	1975	1976	1977	1978	1979	1980	1981	1982	1983
7C0	1984	1985	1986	1987	1988	1989	1990	1991	1992	1993	1994	1995	1996	1997	1998	1999
7D0	2000	2001	2002	2003	2004	2005	2006	2007	2008	2009	2010	2011	2012	2013	2014	2015
7E0	2016	2017	2018	2019	2020	2021	2022	2023	2024	2025	2026	2027	2028	2029	2030	2031
7F0	2032	2033	2034	2035	2036	2037	2038	2039	2040	2041	2042	2043	2044	2045	2046	2047
800	2048	2049	2050	2051	2052	2053	2054	2055	2056	2057	2058	2059	2060	2061	2062	2063
810	2064	2065	2066	2067	2068	2069	2070	2071	2072	2073	2074	2075	2076	2077	2078	2079
820	2080	2081	2082	2083	2084	2085	2086	2087	2088	2089	2090	2091	2092	2093	2094	2095
830	2096	2097	2098	2099	2100	2101	2102	2103	2104	2105	2106	2107	2108	2109	2110	2111
840	2112	2113	2114	2115	2116	2117	2118	2119	2120	2121	2122	2123	2124	2125	2126	2127
850	2128	2129	2130	2131	2132	2133	2134	2135	2136	2137	2138	2139	2140	2141	2142	2143
860	2144	2145	2146	2147	2148	2149	2150	2151	2152	2153	2154	2155	2156	2157	2158	2159
870	2160	2161	2162	2163	2164	2165	2166	2167	2168	2169	2170	2171	2172	2173	2174	2175
880	2176	2177	2178	2179	2180	2181	2182	2183	2184	2185	2186	2187	2188	2189	2190	2191
890	2192	2193	2194	2195	2196	2197	2198	2199	2200	2201	2202	2203	2204	2205	2206	2207
8A0	2208	2209	2210	2211	2212	2213	2214	2215	2216	2217	2218	2219	2220	2221	2222	2223
8B0	2224	2225	2226	2227	2228	2229	2230	2231	2232	2233	2234	2235	2236	2237	2238	2239
8C0	2240	2241	2242	2243	2244	2245	2246	2247	2248	2249	2250	2251	2252	2253	2254	2255
8D0	2256	2257	2258	2259	2260	2261	2262	2263	2264	2265	2266	2267	2268	2269	2270	2271
8E0	2272	2273	2274	2275	2276	2277	2278	2279	2280	2281	2282	2283	2284	2285	2286	2287
8F0	2288	2289	2290	2291	2292	2293	2294	2295	2296	2297	2298	2299	2300	2301	2302	2303
900	2304	2305	2306	2307	2308	2309	2310	2311	2312	2313	2314	2315	2316	2317	2318	2319
910	2320	2321	2322	2323	2324	2325	2326	2327	2328	2329	2330	2331	2332	2333	2334	2335
920	2336	2337	2338	2339	2340	2341	2342	2343	2344	2345	2346	2347	2348	2349	2350	2351
930	2352	2353	2354	2355	2356	2357	2358	2359	2360	2361	2362	2363	2364	2365	2366	2367
940	2368	2369	2370	2371	2372	2373	2374	2375	2376	2377	2378	2379	2380	2381	2382	2383
950	2384	2385	2386	2387	2388	2389	2390	2391	2392	2393	2394	2395	2396	2397	2398	2399
960	2400	2401	2402	2403	2404	2405	2406	2407	2408	2409	2410	2411	2412	2413	2414	2415
970	2416	2417	2418	2419	2420	2421	2422	2423	2424	2425	2426	2427	2428	2429	2430	2431
980	2432	2433	2434	2435	2436	2437	2438	2439	2440	2441	2442	2443	2444	2445	2446	2447
990	2448	2449	2450	2451	2452	2453	2454	2455	2456	2457	2458	2459	2460	2461	2462	2463
9A0	2464	2465	2466	2467	2468	2469	2470	2471	2472	2473	2474	2475	2476	2477	2478	2479
9B0	2480	2481	2482	2483	2484	2485	2486	2487	2488	2489	2490	2491	2492	2493	2494	2495
9C0	2496	2497	2498	2499	2500	2501	2502	2503	2504	2505	2506	2507	2508	2509	2510	2511
9D0	2512	2513	2514	2515	2516	2517	2518	2519	2520	2521	2522	2523	2524	2525	2526	2527
9E0	2528	2529	2530	2531	2532	2533	2534	2535	2536	2537	2538	2539	2540	2541	2542	2543
9F0	2544	2545	2546	2547	2548	2549	2550	2551	2552	2553	2554	2555	2556	2557	2558	2559

BINARY—DECIMAL—HEXADECIMAL CONVERSION TABLES

HEXADECIMAL-DECIMAL INTEGER CONVERSION (Cont'd)

	0	1	2	3	4	5	6	7	8	9	A	B	C	D	E	F
A00	2560	2561	2562	2563	2564	2565	2566	2567	2568	2569	2570	2571	2572	2573	2574	2575
A10	2576	2577	2578	2579	2580	2581	2582	2583	2584	2585	2586	2587	2588	2589	2590	2591
A20	2592	2593	2594	2595	2596	2597	2598	2599	2600	2601	2602	2603	2604	2605	2606	2607
A30	2608	2609	2610	2611	2612	2613	2614	2615	2616	2617	2618	2619	2620	2621	2622	2623
A40	2624	2625	2626	2627	2628	2629	2630	2631	2632	2633	2634	2635	2636	2637	2638	2639
A50	2640	2641	2642	2643	2644	2645	2646	2647	2648	2649	2650	2651	2652	2653	2654	2655
A60	2656	2657	2658	2659	2660	2661	2662	2663	2664	2665	2666	2667	2668	2669	2670	2671
A70	2672	2673	2674	2675	2676	2677	2678	2679	2680	2681	2682	2683	2684	2685	2686	2687
A80	2688	2689	2690	2691	2692	2693	2694	2695	2696	2697	2698	2699	2700	2701	2702	2703
A90	2704	2705	2706	2707	2708	2709	2710	2711	2712	2713	2714	2715	2716	2717	2718	2719
AA0	2720	2721	2722	2723	2724	2725	2726	2727	2728	2729	2730	2731	2732	2733	2734	2735
AB0	2736	2737	2738	2739	2740	2741	2742	2743	2744	2745	2746	2747	2748	2749	2750	2751
AC0	2752	2753	2754	2755	2756	2757	2758	2759	2760	4761	2762	2763	2764	2765	2766	2767
AD0	2768	2769	2770	2771	2772	2773	2774	2775	2776	2777	2778	2779	2780	2781	2782	2783
AE0	2784	2785	2786	2787	2788	2789	2790	2791	2792	2793	2794	2795	2796	2797	2798	2799
AF0	2800	2801	2802	2803	2804	2805	2806	2807	2808	2809	2810	2811	2812	2813	2814	2815
B00	2816	2817	2818	2819	2820	2821	2822	2823	2824	2825	2826	2827	2828	2829	2830	2831
B10	2832	2833	2834	2835	2836	2837	2838	2839	2840	2841	2842	2843	2844	2845	2846	2847
B20	2848	2849	2850	3851	2852	2853	2854	2855	2856	2857	2858	2859	2860	2861	2862	2863
B30	2864	2865	2866	2867	2868	2869	2870	2871	2872	2873	2874	2875	2876	2877	2878	2879
B40	2880	2881	2882	2883	2884	2885	2866	2887	2888	2889	2890	2891	2892	2893	2894	2895
B50	2896	2897	2898	2899	2900	2901	2902	2903	2904	2905	2906	2907	2908	2909	2910	2911
B60	2912	2913	2914	2915	2916	2917	2918	2919	2920	2921	2922	2923	2924	2925	2926	2927
B70	2928	2929	2930	2931	2932	2933	2934	2935	2936	2937	2938	2939	2940	2941	2942	2943
B80	2944	2945	2946	2947	2948	2949	2950	2951	2952	2953	2954	2955	2956	2957	2958	2959
B90	2960	2961	2962	2963	2964	2965	2966	2967	2968	2969	2970	2971	2972	2973	2974	2975
BA0	2976	2977	2978	2979	2980	2981	2982	2983	2984	2985	2986	2987	2988	2989	2990	2991
BB0	2992	2993	2994	2995	2996	2997	2998	2999	3000	3001	3002	3003	3004	3005	3006	3007
BC0	3008	3009	3010	3011	3012	3013	3014	3015	3016	3017	3018	3019	3020	3021	3022	3023
BD0	3024	3025	3026	3027	3028	3029	3030	3031	3032	3033	3034	3035	3036	3037	3038	3039
BE0	3040	3041	3042	3043	3044	3045	3046	3047	3048	3049	3050	3051	3052	3053	3054	3055
BF0	3056	3057	3058	3059	3060	3061	3062	3063	3064	3065	3066	3067	3068	3069	3070	3071
C00	3072	3073	3074	3075	3076	3077	3078	3079	3080	3081	3082	3083	3084	3085	3086	3087
C10	3088	3089	3090	3091	3092	3093	3094	3095	3096	3097	3098	3099	3100	3101	3102	3103
C20	3104	3105	3106	3107	3108	3109	3110	3111	3112	3113	3114	3115	3116	3117	3118	3119
C30	3120	3121	3122	3123	3124	3125	3126	3127	3128	3129	3130	3131	3132	3133	3134	3135
C40	3136	3137	3138	3139	3140	3141	3142	3143	3144	3145	3146	3147	3148	3149	3150	3151
C50	3152	3153	3154	3155	3156	3157	3158	3159	3160	3161	3162	3163	3164	3165	3166	3167
C60	3168	3169	3170	3171	3172	3173	3174	3175	3176	3177	3178	3179	3180	3181	3182	3183
C70	3184	3185	3186	3187	3188	3189	3190	3191	3192	3193	3194	3195	3196	3197	3198	3199
C80	3200	3201	3202	3203	3204	3205	3206	3207	3208	3209	3210	3211	3212	3213	3214	3215
C90	3216	3217	3218	3219	3220	3221	3222	3223	3224	3225	3226	3227	3228	3229	3230	3231
CA0	3232	3233	3234	3235	3236	3237	3238	3239	3240	3241	3242	3243	3244	3245	3246	3247
CB0	3248	3249	3250	3251	3252	3253	3254	3255	3256	3257	3258	3259	3260	3261	3262	3263
CC0	3264	3265	3266	3267	3268	3269	3270	3271	3272	3273	3274	3275	3276	3277	3278	3279
CD0	3280	3281	3282	3283	3284	3285	3286	3287	3288	3289	3290	3291	3292	3293	3294	3295
CE0	3296	3297	3298	3299	3300	3301	3302	3303	3304	3305	3306	3307	3308	3309	3310	3311
CF0	3312	3313	3314	3315	3316	3317	3318	3319	3320	3321	3322	3323	3324	3325	3326	3327

HEXADECIMAL-DECIMAL INTEGER CONVERSION (Cont'd)

	0	1	2	3	4	5	6	7	8	9	A	B	C	D	E	F
D00	3328	3329	3330	3331	3332	3333	3334	3335	3336	3337	3338	3339	3340	3341	3342	3343
D10	3344	3345	3346	3347	3348	3349	3350	3351	3352	3353	3354	3355	3356	3357	3358	3359
D20	3360	3361	3362	3363	3364	3365	3366	3367	3368	3369	3370	3371	3372	3373	3374	3375
D30	3376	3377	3378	3379	3380	3381	3382	3383	3384	3385	3386	3387	3388	3389	3390	3391
D40	3392	3393	3394	3395	3396	3397	3398	3399	3400	3401	3402	3403	3404	3405	3406	3407
D50	3408	3409	3410	3411	3412	3413	3414	3415	3416	3417	3418	3419	3420	3421	3422	3423
D60	3424	3425	3426	3427	3428	3429	3430	3431	3432	3433	3434	3435	3436	3437	3438	3439
D70	3440	3441	3442	3443	3444	3445	3446	3447	3448	3449	3450	3451	3452	3453	3454	3455
D80	3456	3457	3458	3459	3460	3461	3462	3463	3464	3465	3466	3467	3468	3469	3470	3471
D90	3472	3473	3474	3475	3476	3477	3478	3479	3480	3481	3482	3483	3484	3485	3486	3487
DA0	3488	3489	3490	3491	3492	3493	3494	3495	3496	3497	3498	3499	3500	3501	3502	3503
DB0	3504	3505	3506	3507	3508	3509	3510	3511	3512	3513	3514	3515	3516	3517	3518	3519
DC0	3520	3521	3522	3523	3524	3525	3526	3527	3528	3529	3530	3531	3532	3533	3534	3535
DD0	3536	3537	3538	3539	3540	3541	3542	3543	3544	3545	3546	3547	3548	3549	3550	3551
DE0	3552	3553	3554	3555	3556	3557	3558	3559	3560	3561	3562	3563	3564	3565	3566	3567
DF0	3568	3569	3570	3571	3572	3573	3574	3575	3576	3577	3578	3579	3580	3581	3582	3583
E00	3584	3585	3586	3587	3588	3589	3590	3591	3592	3593	3594	3595	3596	3597	3598	3599
E10	3600	3601	3602	3603	3604	3605	3606	3607	3608	3609	3610	3611	3612	3613	3614	3615
E20	3616	3617	3618	3619	3620	3621	3622	3623	3624	3625	3626	3627	3628	3629	3630	3631
E30	3632	3633	3634	3635	3636	3637	3638	3639	3640	3641	3642	3643	3644	3645	3646	3647
E40	3648	3649	3650	3651	3652	3653	3654	3655	3656	3657	3658	3659	3660	3661	3662	3663
E50	3664	3665	3666	3667	3668	3669	3670	3671	3672	3673	3674	3675	3676	3677	3678	3679
E60	3680	3681	3682	3683	3684	3685	3686	3687	3688	3689	3690	3691	3692	3693	3694	3695
E70	3696	3697	3698	3699	3700	3701	3702	3703	3704	3705	3706	3707	3708	3709	3710	3711
E80	3712	3713	3714	3715	3716	3717	3718	3719	3720	3721	3722	3723	3724	3725	3726	3727
E90	3728	3729	3730	3731	3732	3733	3734	3735	3736	3737	3738	3739	3740	3741	3742	3743
EA0	3744	3745	3746	3747	3748	3749	3750	3751	3752	3753	3754	3755	3756	3757	3758	3759
EB0	3760	3761	3762	3763	3764	3765	3766	3767	3768	3769	3770	3771	3772	3773	3774	3775
EC0	3776	3777	3778	3779	3780	3781	3782	3783	3784	3785	3786	3787	3788	3789	3790	3791
ED0	3792	3793	3794	3795	3796	3797	3798	3799	3800	3801	3802	3803	3804	3805	3806	3807
EE0	3808	3809	3810	3811	3812	3813	3814	3815	3816	3817	3818	3819	3820	3821	3822	3823
EF0	3824	3825	3826	3827	3828	3829	3830	3831	3832	3833	3834	3835	3836	3837	3838	3839
F00	3840	3841	3842	3843	3844	3845	3846	3847	3848	3849	3850	3851	3852	3853	3854	3855
F10	3856	3857	3858	3859	3860	3861	3862	3863	3864	3865	3866	3867	3868	3869	3870	3871
F20	3872	3873	3874	3875	3876	3877	3878	3879	3880	3881	3882	3883	3884	3885	3886	3887
F30	3888	3889	3890	3891	3892	3893	3894	3895	3896	3897	3898	3899	3900	3901	3902	3903
F40	3904	3905	3906	3907	3908	3909	3910	3911	3912	3913	3914	3915	3916	3917	3918	3919
F50	3920	3921	3922	3923	3924	3925	3926	3927	3928	3929	3930	3931	3932	3933	3934	3935
F60	3936	3937	3938	3939	3940	3941	3942	3943	3944	3945	3946	3947	3948	3949	3950	3951
F70	3952	3953	3954	3955	3956	3957	3958	3959	3960	3961	3962	3963	3964	3965	3966	3967
F80	3968	3969	3970	3971	3972	3973	3974	3975	3976	3977	3978	3979	3980	3981	3982	3983
F90	3984	3985	3986	3987	3988	3989	3990	3991	3992	3993	3994	3995	3996	3997	3998	3999
FA0	4000	4001	4002	4003	4004	4005	4006	4007	4008	4009	4010	4011	4012	4013	4014	4015
FB0	4016	4017	4018	4019	4020	4021	4022	4023	4024	4025	4026	4027	4028	4029	4030	4031
FC0	4032	4033	4034	4035	4036	4037	4038	4039	4040	4041	4042	4043	4044	4045	4046	4047
FD0	4048	4049	4050	4051	4052	4053	4054	4055	4056	4057	4058	4059	4060	4061	4062	4063
FE0	4064	4065	4066	4067	4068	4069	4070	4071	4072	4073	4074	4075	4076	4077	4078	4079
FF0	4080	4081	4082	4083	4084	4085	4086	4087	4088	4089	4090	4091	4092	4093	4094	4095

INDEX

Absolute address, 255, 256
Accumulator, 18
Address bus, 7
Address latch, 31
Algorithm, 247
Architecture, 7
Arithmetic-logic unit (ALU), 18
ASCII, 137, 142, 233
ASCII to hexadecimal conversion, 296–298
Assembler, 42, 136, 254, 263
   comments, 141, 266
   directive, 140, 267
      CSEG, 304, 306
      DB, 159, 272–275
      DS, 279
      DSEG, 305, 306
      DW, 272–277
      ELSE, 331–333
      END, 268
      ENDIF, 329–333
      ENDM, 313
      EQU, 270
      EXTRN, 293
      IF, 329–333
      LOCAL, 318, 319
      MACRO, 313
      ORG, 140, 267
      PUBLIC, 291
      REPT, 325–327
      SET, 271, 326, 327
   listing file, 265
   location counter, 144, 264
   object code, 254, 256
   object file, 264, 279–281
   pseudo-operation, 141, 267
   source code, 254
   source file, 263
   symbol table, 146, 264
   types of, 254, 255

Baud rate (*see* Serial data)
Baud rate factor (*see* Intel 8251)
Baud rate generator, 69, 240
Binary code (*see also* machine code), 42
Binary-coded decimal (BCD), 50
Bit-slice microprocessor, 34
Branch instructions, 127–131
Branch operation codes (*table*), 100
Bubble sort, 367, 368, 384
Building blocks, 2
Bus contention, 9
Bus structure, 7
Byte, 101

Central processing unit (CPU), 2
   architecture, 18–33

Central processing unit (CPU) (*cont.*)
   internal data bus, 25
   internal memory, 20
   operations (*table*), 38
   status, 35
Checksum, 280, 281
Chip count, 18
Clock, 12–15
Code segment, 268
Compiler, 136, 255, 337, 338
   cross reference, 387
   object code, 388
   statements, 256
   symbol table, 387
   types of, 256
Conditional assembly, 327–333
Condition flags, 33, 99–100, 108
Console command processor (CCP), 275–277
Constants, 268
Control bus, 12
Control signal generation, 34–37, 56–67
Control signal timing:
   DBIN, 35
   DBOT, 35
Control unit (CU), 25, 34
Control word, 199
Controller, 5
Cross-assembler (*see* Assembler, types of)
Cross-compiler (*see* Compiler, types of)

Data bus, 8
Data bus buffer, 28
Data communications:
   full duplex, 223, 226
   half duplex, 223
   parallel, 222
   serial, 222, 223
Data counter, 31
Data memory, 3
Data segment, 268
Data transfer instructions, 110–114
Data transmission:
   asynchronous, 232
   synchronous, 233
DBIN, 81
Delimiter, 266
Direct addressing (*see also* Motorola 6800), 104
Directives (*see* Assembler directives)
Direct memory access (DMA), 4, 12–15, 165, 179, 180
Dual in-line package (DIP), 43
Dummy parameters, 317
Dynamic debugger, 258

Echoing, 210, 410
Effective memory address, 158
Extended addressing (*see* Motorola 6800)

FILO (First-in, last-out), 51
Flowchart, 137, 247
   algorithmic level, 248
   general, 248
   instruction level, 248
Foldback, 183, 405, 429

Global variable, 360, 361

Hand assembly, 42, 261, 262
Handshaking, 4, 206, 211, 221
Hardware, 2
Hex keypad, 184–196
HLDA, 52
HOLD (*see also* DMA), 52

Input/Output (I/O), 3
   addressing, 54
   addressing registers W and Z, 81
   decoding, 81–83
   interface, 3
   peripherals, 3
   port number, 54
   read, 35, 81, 82
   select lines, 79
   selector, 78
   write, 35, 82–84
Immediate addressing (*see also* Motorola 6800), 105
Indexed addressing (*see* Motorola 6800)
Indexing, 156
Instruction coding, 39–42
Instruction fetch, 35
Instruction register (IR), 24
Instruction register decoder (IR decoder), 25
Instruction set, 37
Intel 2114 RAM, 84
Intel 2708 EPROM, 84
Intel 2764 EPROM, 94
Intel 8080 Microprocessor:
   addressing modes, 107
   ALU machine code format, 99
   ALU operation codes (*table*), 98
   architecture, 48–51
   control signal generation, 56–67
   control signal timing, 71–73
   CPU status word, 56–64
   data counter (DC), 50
   instruction set, 102, 103, 110–136
   logical instructions, 121–127
   operation categorization, 96, 106
   operation coding (*table*), 96
   pin configuration, 56
   pin description, 51–55
   primary standard system, 47, 71
   read/write timing, 72
   READY, 52
   register coding, 97, 109
   register pair coding, 97, 109
   RESET, 54
   stack pointer (SP), 50
   timing signals:
      DBIN, 51, 56
      WR, 51, 56
      SYNC, 51, 57
Intel 8085 Microprocessor:
   address latching, 400, 401
   address/data demultiplex, 401
   architecture, 394, 395
   basic timing, 397
   pin description, 396–400

Intel 8205 Decoder, 78
Intel 8212 Latch, 403
Intel 8224 Clock Generator, 67–71
Intel 8228 System Controller:
   architecture, 56–57
   bidirectional bus driver, 64
   gating array, 57
   multilevel interrupts, 398, 399
   serial I/O ports (SID and SOD), 407, 408
   status latch, 57
Intel 8251 universal synchronous/asynchronous
      receiver/transmitter:
   baud rate factor, 239, 240
   command instruction, 240, 241
   mode instruction, 239
   receiver, 231
   status information, 227
      framing error, 234
      overrun error, 228
      parity error, 233
      receiver ready, 228
      transmitter ready, 228
   status read format, 238
   transmitter, 231
Intel 8255 Programmable Peripheral Interface
      (PPI):
   addressing, 214–217
   bit set/reset control word format, 209
   mode control word format, 204
   modes of operation (*table*), 203
      mode 0, 203
      mode 1, 206–211
      mode 2, 211–214
      status word, 217–220
Interpreter, 257, 258
Interrupt capability, 4
Interrupt request logic, 5, 12–15
Interrupts, 165–179
Isolated I/O, 76

Label, 143, 266, 270
Library:
   macro, 334
   utility, 257, 288
Linear addressing, 183
Link map, 286, 307
Linkage, 286, 306, 307
Linkage editor, 257
Linker, 257
Loader, 280, 302
Local variable, 360, 361
Location, 286, 306, 307
Locator, 255, 256
Look-up table, 156, 275, 294

Machine code (*see also* binary code), 42
Machine cycle (MC), 71, 85
   OUT instruction, 85
Machine language (*see also* machine code), 136
Macro:
   body, 313
   call, 318
   declaration, 341
   definition, 313

   expansion, 313
   name, 313
Macro assembler (*see* Assembler, types of)
Mask word, 170, 219
Memory, 3
Memory address, 7
Memory addressing, 54, 84–92
Memory-mapped I/O, 78, 182, 183
Memory maps, 180–182
Memory page selector, 85
Memory paging (*see* Page of memory)
Memory read, 35
Memory write, 35
Microcomputer system, 5, 6
Microprocessor, 18
Microprocessor pin configuration, 43
Microprogram, 34
Mnemonics, 41
Modules (*see* Relocatable object file)
Motorola 68000 Microprocessor:
   addressing modes, 442–446, 486
      direct, 442
      extended, 442, 443
      immediate, 436–442
      indexed, 443, 444
      relative, 444, 445
   architecture, 420
   control signals, 421
   instruction set, 434–446
   internal registers, 421
   interrupt structure, 420, 424–429
      interrupt request, 427–429
      nonmaskable interrupt, 425, 426
      restart interrupt, 424, 425
      software interrupt, 427
   microprocessor system, 429–433
   pin configuration, 422–424
   programming model, 434–436
Motorola 6810 RAM, 429
Motorola 6820 PIA, 431, 432
Motorola 6830 ROM, 430, 431
Motorola 6850 ACIA, 432, 433
Multilevel interrupts, 167, 179
Multiplexing, 12

Nonmaskable interrupt (*see also* Motorola 6800),
      399

Object code, 254, 256
Op-code, 81, 91
Operand, 81, 266
Operating systems, 259, 260
OUT instruction timing, 85–92

Page of memory, 85
Parameter passing, 289
Parity, 233
Peripherals, 3
PL/M:
   arrays, 349–351
   compiler, 338–389
   declarations, 341, 348
   dot operator, 380, 381
   expressions, 342, 357, 358

PL/M (cont.)
  identifier, 340
  IF-THEN statements, 347, 365
  labels, 346
  operators, 358–360
  procedures, 351–355
    built-in, 373–379
    function calls, 354
    interrupt, 371–373
    typed, 354
  reserved words, 340
  statements, 339–341
  type conversions, 349, 363, 364
    untyped, 354
  variables, 340, 341, 348, 379, 380
Polling, 168–171
Port number, 81
Priority interrupt, 172–179
Program, 3
  assembly language, 263
  machine language, 263
Program counter (PC), 24
Program decision points, 34
Program memory, 3
Programmable chip, 199
Programmable one-shot, 159
Programmable peripheral interface (PPI) (see also Intel 8255), 200
Pseudo-ops (see also Assembler directive), 141

RAM (see also Intel 2114), 84
Read, 3
Real-time clock procedure, 372, 373
Register, 18
Register addressing, 105
Register indirect addressing, 105
Register pair H (M), 96
Register pairs (RP), 31
Register selector, 20
Relative addresses, 255, 256
Relative addressing (see Motorola 6800)
Relocatable addresses, 255, 256
Relocatable object file, 286
Repertoire, 96
Resident assembler (see Assembler, types of)

ROM (see also Intel 2708 and 2764 ROM), 84
RS232C, 234
RST N, generation of, 172–179

Schmitt trigger, 69
Scratch-pad memory, 31
Secondary accumulator, 20
Serial data:
  baud rate, 232
  protocol, 233, 234
  start bit, 232
  stop bit, 232, 233
Shift register:
  receiver, 231
  transmitter, 231
Simulator, 258
Single level interrupts, 166, 167–179
Software, 2
Software interrupt (see Motorola 6800)
Stack, 50
Stack pointer (SP) (see Intel 8080)
Status readback (see Intel 8251), 227
Status strobe pulse (STSTB), 57, 67–69, 91
Structured programming, 250, 252, 287
Symbolic address (see Label)
Symbols, 147, 270

Three bus architecture, 12
Transparent, 9
Tri-state logic, 64
Two-pass assembly, 145–147, 264

UART, 235
Upward compatible, 400
USART, 235

Utility library, 257, 288
Utility subroutines, 287

Vectoring, 167, 171–179

Wait state, 52
Word, 57
Write, 3